823.8   £19.50

THOMAS HARDY: THE CRITICAL HERITAGE

THE CRITICAL HERITAGE SERIES

GENERAL EDITOR. B. C. SOUTHAM, M.A., B.LITT.(OXON.)
Formerly Department of English, Westfield College, University of London

Volumes in the series include

JANE AUSTEN	B. C. Southam
BROWNING	Boyd Litzinger *St. Bonaventure University* and Donald Smalley *University of Illinois*
BYRON	Andrew Rutherford *University of Aberdeen*
COLERIDGE	J. R. de J. Jackson *Victoria College, Toronto*
DICKENS	Philip Collins *University of Leicester*
HENRY JAMES	Roger Gard *Queen Mary College, London*
JAMES JOYCE (2 vols.)	Robert H. Deming *University of Miami*
D. H. LAWRENCE	R. P. Draper *University of Leicester*
MILTON	John T. Shawcross *University of Wisconsin*
SCOTT	John O. Hayden *University of California, Davis*
SWINBURNE	Clyde K. Hyder
TENNYSON	J. D. Jump *University of Manchester*
THACKERAY	Geoffrey Tillotson and Donald Hawes *Birkbeck College, London*
TROLLOPE	Donald Smalley *University of Illinois*

THOMAS HARDY

THE CRITICAL HERITAGE

Edited by

R. G. COX

Senior Lecturer in English Literature
University of Manchester

ROUTLEDGE & KEGAN PAUL: LONDON, HENLEY AND BOSTON

First published in 1970
by Routledge & Kegan Paul Ltd
39 Store Street,
London WC1E 7DD
Broadway House,
Newtown Road,
Henley-on-Thames,
Oxon RG9 1EN and
9 Park Street,
Boston, Mass. 02108, USA
Reprinted 1978
Printed in Great Britain by
Weatherby Woolnough, Wellingborough, Northants

ISBN 0 7100 6590 6

General Editor's Preface

The reception given to a writer by his contemporaries and near-contemporaries is evidence of considerable value to the student of literature. On one side we learn a great deal about the state of criticism at large and in particular about the development of critical attitudes towards a single writer; at the same time, through private comments in letters, journals or marginalia, we gain an insight upon the tastes and literary thought of individual readers of the period. Evidence of this kind helps us to understand the writer's historical situation, the nature of his immediate reading-public, and his response to these pressures.

The separate volumes in the *Critical Heritage Series* present a record of this early criticism. Clearly, for many of the highly productive and lengthily reviewed nineteenth- and twentieth-century writers there exists an enormous body of material; and in these cases the volume editors have made a selection of the most important views, significant for their intrinsic critical worth or for their representative quality—perhaps even registering incomprehension!

For earlier writers, notably pre-eighteenth century, the materials are much scarcer and the historical period has been extended, sometimes far beyond the writer's lifetime, in order to show the inception and growth of critical views which were initially slow to appear.

In each volume the documents are headed by an Introduction, discussing the material assembled and relating the early stages of the author's reception to what we have come to identify as the critical tradition. The volumes will make available much material which would otherwise be difficult of access and it is hoped that the modern reader will be thereby helped towards an informed understanding of the ways in which literature has been read and judged.

B.C.S.

Contents

CONTENTS

CONTENTS

CONTENTS

ACKNOWLEDGMENTS

Anyone investigating the reception of Hardy's work must be conscious of how much has been done for him by earlier scholars. I am aware of a particular indebtedness to Dr. W. R. Rutland's *Thomas Hardy, a Study of his Writings and their Background* (Oxford, 1938) and to Professor Edmund Blunden's *English Men of Letters* volume, *Thomas Hardy* (Macmillan, 1942), both of which give very full accounts of contemporary criticism. References to the indispensable biography by Florence Emily Hardy are to the one-volume edition of 1962. I should like to thank the editors of the *Spectator* and *The Times Literary Supplement* for information about the authorship of reviews in their columns, and the editor of the *New Statesman* for similar information concerning the *Athenaeum*. I have been indebted throughout to my colleagues Professor J. D. Jump and Mr. F. N. Lees of the University of Manchester for general advice and suggestions of items I might otherwise have missed.

I should also like to thank the following for permission to quote from previously published material:

The Society of Authors, literary representative of the authors, for Havelock Ellis's reviews in the *Westminster Review*, and the *Savoy Magazine*, for Sir William Watson's review in the *Academy*, and Laurence Binyon's review in *The Bookman*: the Trustees of Max Beerbohm's estate for his article in the *Saturday Review*: Peter Newbolt for Sir Henry Newbolt's article in the *Quarterly Review*: Eleanor Manning and W. O. Manning for Frederic Manning's review in the *Spectator*: the Trustees of the Hardy Estate and Macmillan and Co. for the extract from Harold Orel's *Hardy's Personal Writings*: Oxford University Press for the extract from *Letters from G. M. Hopkins to Robert Bridges*: Tweedsmuir Trustees for John Buchan's review in the *Spectator*: Jennifer Gosse for E. Gosse's reviews in the *Speaker*, *Cosmopolis* and *Edinburgh Review*: William Blackwood and Sons Ltd. for Charles Whibley's article in *Blackwood's Magazine*: Mrs. A. S. Strachey, Chatto and Windus Ltd. and Harcourt Brace & World, Inc. for the extract from Lytton Strachey's *Characters and Commentaries*, copyright, 1933, 1961, by James Strachey: John Farquharson Ltd. for the extract from *The Letters of Henry James*, Vol. I.

NOTE ON THE TEXT

Most of the extracts given here are reprinted from the original periodicals. Nos. 9, 30, 50, 72 and 76 are taken from the reprints in volume form. All omissions are clearly indicated: these consist mostly of lengthy quotations and passages merely summarizing the narrative. Obvious misprints in the text have been corrected.

Introduction

From the point of view of publication and chronology Hardy may be said to have had two careers, each lasting about a generation. He appears as a late Victorian novelist and an early twentieth-century poet. Of course, this simple division will not do either for criticism or biography: we know that much of the verse which was published from 1898 onwards had actually been written earlier. But as far as the reception and influence of his poetry is concerned it is simple fact that two volumes appeared later than *The Waste Land* and that we have to deal with it as an Edwardian and Georgian phenomenon. All this raises special problems for any attempt to trace the growth of Hardy's reputation, or, as in this volume, to give a representative selection of the main documents illustrating the impact of his work upon contemporaries. In particular it makes especially difficult the choice of a terminal point. After a good deal of hesitation I have taken 1914 as a convenient landmark which allows the inclusion of some of the general surveys of the novels made at the time of the first collected editions, and which takes in reviews of the poems up to and including *Satires of Circumstance*. One exception from beyond this date seemed permissible—Edmund Gosse's essay of 1918 discussing the poems up to and including *Moments of Vision* and the Golden Treasury series selection. This is the first notable attempt to sum up Hardy's work as a poet, and it is by a fellow-Victorian and not much younger contemporary.

The forty-odd years from the appearance of Hardy's first novel in 1871 to 1914 saw a steady flow of reviews in the principal periodicals, increasing both in number and individual length until the nineties, when the special problems of *Tess of the D'Urbervilles* and *Jude the Obscure* roused controversy on a much larger scale. After the seventies the immediate reviewing of each new volume in turn was increasingly supplemented by general critical surveys and essays, and in the nineties the first book-length studies began to appear. All this material adds up to a formidable bulk and any selection must involve compromises. I have tried to give representative reviews of each of the major works, and to reproduce, virtually in full, the more important of the critical surveys. Since Hardy published some twenty-five volumes during the period up to 1914 the number of items is necessarily large, and they vary in length from a portion of an omnibus novel review of a few hundred words to a formal essay occupying thirty pages of a solid quarterly. It has been possible to abbreviate to some extent (and to avoid duplication) by omitting all but the shortest illustrative extracts from the works discussed, replacing them by appropriate references. Accounts of the plot of a novel have been cut where they seemed to have no other purpose than mere information, but these and other omissions have been clearly indicated in the text. Otherwise the aim has been to present the critic's discussion as fully as possible, developed in his own way and at his own pace.

It is not easy to discern any very clear pattern in the reception of Hardy's work for the first twenty years of his literary career. It did not take him an unduly long time to establish a reputation: with *Far from the Madding Crowd* (1874) he can be said to have arrived. It is possible to find a fair variety of opinion for each of his books: there are no outstanding rejections and no notable reversals of opinion. General surveys of his work began in the late seventies and were becoming fairly frequent by 1890. With the publication of *Tess of the D'Urbervilles* in 1891, and even more with *Jude the Obscure* (1895), critical discussion became obscured by questions of morality and general philosophy of life. To many readers Hardy seemed at this point to be striking at the roots of conventional sexual morality and conventional religion, and in deploring his iconoclasm or welcoming him as a pioneer of enlightenment critics often allowed their literary judgments to become distorted. On Hardy himself the effect was to bewilder and to some extent to embitter him, and the lack of understanding with which he felt these books were received undoubtedly contributed something to his abandonment of novel-writing in favour of poetry.

EARLY NOVELS TO *Far from the Madding Crowd* (1874)

The story of Hardy's literary reputation begins in 1868 when he sent to Macmillan the manuscript of a novel, entitled *The Poor Man and the Lady*. As a whole this has not survived, but it may have been partly drawn on for the short story 'An Indiscretion in the Life of an Heiress'. In his reply,[1] Alexander Macmillan said he had shown the manuscript to a friend, whose comments he enclosed. This was in fact John Morley, who spoke of 'a very curious and original performance', and concluded

'If the man is young he has stuff and purpose in him.' In the end Macmillan did not publish the story and Hardy took it to Chapman & Hall, who put him in touch with their reader, George Meredith. In a personal interview Meredith recommended Hardy not to publish this work, as injudiciously provocative and full of indiscriminate satire: he suggested either rewriting it and softening it down considerably, or attempting a different kind of novel with a more complicated plot. The second part of this advice led to the writing of *Desperate Remedies*, which was published anonymously in March 1871 by Tinsley at the standard three-volume price of 31s 6d. (The publisher's acceptance had been conditional on the author's depositing £75.) Of the edition of 500 only 209 seem to have been sold at the full rate: by June copies were being offered at a reduced price. The first reviews, in the *Athenaeum* (No. 1) and *Morning Post* (13 April 1871), were comparatively favourable, the latter noting the obvious imitation of Wilkie Collins, but judging the book 'eminently a success' of its kind. The *Spectator* (No. 2), however, took a severe view of the novel's morality and thought that in the future the author might well be glad to have published it anonymously. The reviewer did nevertheless quote several long passages to illustrate the author's descriptive power. Hardy appears to have reacted to this attack with a sensitiveness which seems somewhat excessive: the *Life* (p. 84) records his memory of reading the review 'as he sat on a stile leading to the eweleaze he had to cross on his way home to Bockhampton. The bitterness of that moment was never forgotten: at the time he wished that he were dead.' His friend Horace Moule, who wrote 'bidding him not to mind the slating', may himself have been responsible for a more favourable notice later in the year in the *Saturday Review* (No. 3) which, while not uncritical, concluded, 'We sincerely hope to hear of him again, for his deserts are of no ordinary kind.' All the reviews agree in selecting for praise those parts of the novel which point forward to Hardy's most characteristic later work; their censure is directed against sensationalism and an over-complicated plot.

Under the Greenwood Tree seems to have had its origin partly in John Morley's praise of the 'opening pictures of the Christmas-eve in the tranter's house' in *The Poor Man and the Lady*. The story was offered to Macmillan, who replied with a somewhat ambiguously-worded acceptance which Hardy in his over-sensitivity mistook for a refusal. He laid the manuscript aside for some months, but in May 1872 *Under the Greenwood Tree* was published, once more anonymously, by

Tinsley, who had paid £30 for the copyright. (He later made a further voluntary payment of £10.) Some two years later he was to refuse to sell the copyright for less than £300. Though Tinsley said the book did not sell well, it is worth noting that a 2s edition appeared in 1873 and an illustrated edition for Christmas 1875. The reviews were generally favourable. The *Athenaeum* (No. 4) commended the author of *Desperate Remedies* for working 'that vein of his genius which yields the best produce' and the *Pall Mall Gazette* (5 July 1872) praised his humour. In the *Saturday Review* (No. 5) Horace Moule spoke of 'the best prose idyll that we have seen for a long while past' and was reminded of Goethe's *Hermann and Dorothea*. The *Spectator* also praised the book, though somewhat belatedly (2 November 1872), and then only in a brief mention under 'Current Literature'. But perhaps the most significant fact for the development of Hardy's reputation was that *Under the Greenwood Tree* attracted the notice of Leslie Stephen (or perhaps was brought to his notice by Frederick Greenwood, as the latter claimed in an article on Hardy in the *Illustrated London News* for 1 October 1892). This led to Stephen's asking Hardy to contribute a serial novel to the *Cornhill*, and so to the appearance of *Far from the Madding Crowd* throughout 1874. In 1871, when Stephen became editor, the *Cornhill's* circulation was about 20,000: Hardy's work was therefore being introduced to a much wider public.

Meanwhile *Tinsley's Magazine* had been carrying the serial instalments of *A Pair of Blue Eyes*, which was published in book form in May 1873 and in America the same year. (It was reprinted in England in 1873 and 1877.) This time Hardy had negotiated better terms for himself, partly as a result of reading up *Copinger on Copyright*. The book was well received, and attracted more critical notice than the earlier works. The *Athenaeum* (28 June 1873) saw Elfride's adventures as rather farcical, but the *Graphic* (12 July 1873) said, 'Mr. Hardy seems to us to excel everyone but George Eliot', and the *Pall Mall Gazette* (25 October 1873) declared him 'distinctly a man of genius', adding 'there are chapters in *Under the Greenwood Tree* which rival the most admirable rustic pieces of George Eliot herself'. The *Saturday Review* (No. 6) thought the author had much to learn, but spoke of his 'great powers of imagination'. The *Spectator* (28 June 1873) praised especially the analysis of Knight's feelings while hanging over the cliff, and the rendering of rustic conversation. Coventry Patmore wrote to Hardy regretting that 'such unequalled beauty and power should not have assured themselves the immortality which would have been impressed

upon them by the form of verse' (*Life*, p. 105), and at a later date
Tennyson was to tell him that he liked *A Pair of Blue Eyes* the best of
his novels (*Life*, p. 137). It continued to be surprisingly popular up to
about the end of the century. In 1878 W. E. Henley was to commit
himself in print to the view that *A Pair of Blue Eyes* was better than
The Return of the Native (see No. 14).

When the first instalment of *Far from the Madding Crowd* appeared in
the *Cornhill* for January 1874, it attracted immediate attention, and the
Spectator wondered whether it might not in fact be by George Eliot.
(Stephen, writing to congratulate Hardy, spoke of 'the gentle *Spectator*,
which thinks that you must be George Eliot because you know the
names of the stars'.) The two-volume publication by Smith, Elder &
Co. in November 1874 soon sold 1,000 copies, and a further 500 were
printed in 1875. The book was greeted with a large number of reviews,
mostly respectful or enthusiastic, though not always uncritical. The
Echo (28 November 1874) thought the book in many respects superior
to the earlier work, and concentrated particularly on the scenes of
rustic conversation. *The Times* (25 January 1875), in a very full account,
said the only fault worth mentioning was that the reader suspected
conscious or unconscious imitation of George Eliot, and thought Hardy
would do well to avoid the implied comparison. The *Westminster
Review* (No. 10) was not surprised that the novel had been mistaken
for one by George Eliot, and made some detailed comparisons; but it
thought the influence not wholly beneficial. It also found faults of
sensationalism in many of the incidents of the story, such as Troy's
sword-play, the rick-fire and the Gadarene plunge of Oak's sheep.

The *Athenaeum* (No. 7), however, could not conceive how anyone
could ever have supposed this book to be by George Eliot; it suggested
a greater likeness in some of the incidents to Charles Reade. The
reviewer, one Britten, was puzzled by Hardy's inequalities of style, and
especially by his alternating between shrewd observation of the talk of
rustics and the putting into their mouths of unconvincingly sophisticated expressions. This point had been raised before by the *Athenaeum*:
it was to be taken up by others and to become a recurrent theme in the
criticism of Hardy. Andrew Lang in the *Academy* (No. 11) had reservations about the chorus of labourers—'all humourists in their way,
which is a very dreary and depressing way'. He found some dis-
crepancy between manner and matter in the philosophical account of
rural life and thought, and he considered the descriptions of nature and
the rural setting much more effective than the main characters and

their adventures. The *Saturday Review* (No. 12) praised the graphic descriptions of farming life, but the reviewer found his confidence in their truthfulness somewhat shaken by what he felt to be an idealized rendering of rustic wit and conversation. He also had some strong criticisms of the general style. The working-out of the plot, however, and the power and taste shown in the Fanny Robin episodes and other tragic scenes seemed to justify the belief that if the author would 'throw aside his mannerism and eccentricity' and cultivate his art, he might 'rise to a high position among English novelists'. R. H. Hutton in the *Spectator* (No. 8) echoed the general praise of the novel's freshness and imaginative power, but he found the farm labourers incredible in their biblical wit and 'intellectual banter'. He, too, notes the influence of George Eliot, adding, however, 'But George Eliot never confuses her own ideas with those of her dramatic figures, as Mr. Hardy seems to us so often to do.' Of the descriptive passages, Hutton singles out that evocation of the dawn after Bathsheba's night in the wood which has been so effectively analysed in our time by the late Douglas Brown (*Thomas Hardy*, 1961, pp. 135–7).

Far from the Madding Crowd is the first of Hardy's novels where it becomes important to consider a public outside this country. The *Life* (p. 103) records a request for a German translation, without saying whether this came to anything.[2] In France, however, readers of the *Revue des deux Mondes* (1875, XII, p. 838) were introduced to Hardy in a substantial article by Léon Boucher called 'Le Roman Pastoral en Angleterre'. This dealt with all Hardy's work to date, though *Desperate Remedies* received only a brief mention. Boucher found *Under the Greenwood Tree* 'as welcome as it was picturesque' and praised *A Pair of Blue Eyes* for 'a powerful study of feminine character, a subtle analysis of delicate feelings'. About twenty-three of the article's twenty-nine pages were given to *Far from the Madding Crowd*, from which Boucher quoted and translated numerous long extracts. He recounts the story at some length, commenting critically on the way its more pathetic parts approach melodrama. He praises the presentation of rural life, the rustic chorus, and the reality of the descriptions of nature, and predicts that Hardy will continue to command the respect of serious readers.

The progress of Hardy's reputation in the U.S.A. has been traced in detail by Carl J. Weber in his book *Hardy in America* (1946). The first review he records is of *Under the Greenwood Tree*, in the *Baltimore Southern Magazine*. From then on an increasing volume of comment accompanied each work. Publication in America was usually not much later than in this country; some of the novels were in fact serialized first in American periodicals (e.g. *Two on a Tower* in the *Atlantic Monthly*, and *Jude the Obscure* as *Hearts Insurgent* in *Harper's New Monthly Magazine*[3]). *Harper's Magazine* for March 1875 (L, p. 598) carried a short notice in the 'Editor's Literary Record' by W. D. Howells on *Far from the Madding Crowd*. He found 'considerable artistic power', but thought that the disciple of George Eliot fell short of his master. (It is of some interest that the next item in the chronicle is Blackmore's *Lorna Doone*.) The reviewer in *Scribner's Monthly Magazine* (March 1875, IX, p. 637), who may have been the editor, J. G. Holland, called Hardy 'the most original and impressive figure among young English fictionists'. But of all the transatlantic reviews of *Far from the Madding Crowd* the most interesting was undoubtedly that in the New York *Nation* by Henry James (No. 9). He takes up the relationship to George Eliot mainly to insist on the difference between original genius and clever imitation. He finds the book diffuse, with 'an ingeniously verbose and redundant style', and attributes this partly to the three-volume convention. James praises the descriptions of nature and the rural atmosphere, but Bathsheba, though put 'through the Charles Reade paces', seems to him always artificial, and the human element in general 'factitious and insubstantial'. But Hardy 'has gone astray very cleverly' and the book is 'a really curious imitation of something better'.

FROM *The Hand of Ethelberta* TO *Two on a Tower* (1876–82)

By 1875 Hardy was an established novelist, and he proceeded to disappoint expectations by turning away from country life for his next theme. *The Hand of Ethelberta* was serialized in the *Cornhill* and published in two volumes by Smith, Elder & Co. in 1876. Of this edition of 1,000 only 61 copies were remaindered two years later, but the one-volume edition of 1877 seems to have sold less well. Reviews tended to be rather lukewarm and lacking in enthusiasm. In the *Academy* (13 May 1876, IX, p. 453) George Saintsbury thought there was less laboured eccentricity in this novel than in earlier works, but found it scrappy. He complained that he could get no clear idea of the heroine, but liked Picotee. Britten in the *Athenaeum* (15 April 1876, p. 523) said that Hardy was here attempting the 'modern-romantic', which belonged to the second order of fiction. The *Saturday Review* (6 May 1876, XLI, p. 592) saw original force in the book, but misapplied to an unworthy theme. In the *Spectator* (22 April 1876, p. 530) R. H. Hutton allowed that it was entertaining, but thought the characters not very convincing and found 'some inadequacy in filling in the background of characters on which the dialogue is grounded'. The editor of *Harper's Magazine* was less polite in his 'Literary Record' (August 1876, LIII, p. 468): he said the book could be read 'with no intellectual effort and very little emotional excitement' and that the heroine was 'not intriguing enough to disgust nor unselfish enough to attract'. Hardy's own view, as expressed in his contribution to the *Life of Leslie Stephen* (Ch. XIII) was a claim to be in advance of his readers: he thought that the novel was published thirty years too soon. A bizarre fact noted by Professor Blunden is that *Ethelberta* was practically the only contemporary novel on Arnold's reading list for 1888.

Hardy's next novel, *The Return of the Native*, ran as a serial in *Belgravia* during 1878. It had been offered to Leslie Stephen for the *Cornhill*, but in his note contributed to Maitland's life of Stephen Hardy records that 'though he liked the opening, he feared that the relations between Eustacia, Wildeve and Thomasin might develop into something "dangerous" for a family magazine, and he refused to have anything to do with it unless he could see the whole'. Stephen was very conscious that the *Cornhill* was a 'family magazine', and he had found it necessary to warn Hardy to treat the seduction of Fanny Robin (in *Far from the Madding Crowd*) in a 'gingerly fashion', out of deference to his more prudish readers (*Life*, p. 130). These problems of serial publication were to recur frequently. The fact that a Victorian magazine was likely to be read aloud in the home played an important part in determining its editor's choice of fiction. Novels, too, were likely to be read *en famille*, and indeed the general nature of the novel-reading public in the Victorian age needs constantly to be borne in mind when considering the reception of Hardy's work. In the seventies this public was still relatively unstratified and unspecialized, though changes in these respects were taking place and the situation was different by the nineties. The readers of Wilkie Collins and Charles Reade were probably also readers of Dickens and Trollope and even George Eliot, whereas at the end of the century the readers of Ouïda and Marie Corelli were unlikely to be also reading James and Meredith. It seems safe to assume that many of the readers of Hardy's earlier books were looking for conventional and undisturbing entertainment, melodramatic in its turns of plot and liberally seasoned with the pathetic, but uplifting in tone and observing a strict moral propriety. Something can be gathered from the forgotten titles with which his first stories were grouped for review in batches. It was only as his work progressed that it became clear that he was aiming at a more intellectually advanced public, though in some respects, such as sensationalism of incident and plot development, he appeared to be influenced by popular expectations up to a late stage.

In three-volume form *The Return of the Native* was published by Smith, Elder & Co. in 1878. Of the first edition of 1,000 copies, 122 seem to have been remaindered. It was widely reviewed, but had rather a mixed reception. Britten in the *Athenaeum* (No. 13) judged it inferior to the earlier work: not ill-conceived, but clumsily expressed, with impossibly Elizabethan peasants. He saw Eustacia Vye as a kind of imitation Madame Bovary, distorted by being made to conform with English literary conventions. W. E. Henley in the *Academy* (No. 14) noted in Hardy 'a certain Hugoesque quality of insincerity', though admitting that he usually had a genuine motive even when he appeared artificial: something, however, seemed to be wanting in his personality. In general Henley's reaction appears somewhat mixed and inconclusive. The *Saturday Review* (No. 15) thought the book less entertaining than its predecessors and found even the vivid descriptions weakened by eccentric expressions and strained metaphors. Hardy's 'invention of characters' was said to be injudicious and their treatment unrealistic. On the other hand there was praise for the atmosphere of the setting, the vividness of individual scenes like the gambling by the light of glow-worms, and the humour of the rustics. The *Spectator* (No. 16) also had reservations. It found the peasants never quite acceptable as true pictures of rustic life, and noted a tendency for them to lapse into educated speech, while admitting that at times their language could be convincing. Once more the descriptions drew praise, and suggested to the reviewer that Hardy was 'not only a striking novelist, but in essence at least, a fine poet'. *The Times* (5 December 1878) found the world of Egdon remote and alien, and could 'scarcely get up a satis-factory interest in a people whose history and habits are so entirely foreign to our own. Yet the story is a striking one and well worth reading, were it only for those graphic scenes and descriptions with which the clever author has enriched his pages.' The *Illustrated London News* (14 December 1878, p. 562) thought the descriptions good, the movement slow, the personages uninteresting, the action poor and the conclusion flat. This reviewer, too, dwelt on the gambling scene, but warned Hardy against relying 'more upon the mere fringe of his story than upon his story itself for the exhibition of his powers'. In the *Contemporary Review* (1878, XXXIV, p. 205) the literary chronicle directed by Matthew Browne had a brief paragraph making the interesting comment that Hardy was 'one of that rare class whose faults cannot be spared from their work. Where else are we to look for anything like the same amount of rugged and fantastic power; the same naturalness mingled with the same quaintness?' He praised the descriptions of Nature, noting 'the author's trick of first painting a scene with the broadest colours and then bringing in his human figures as if they were an afterthought'. *Blackwood's* (March 1879, CXXV, p. 338), in a similar short paragraph, was cool and rather patronizing, speaking of 'irksome mannerisms' and saying that this might have been a clever parody of the earlier books. 'He never serves himself with a plain phrase, if he can find anything more far-fetched; and even those humorous peasants who used sometimes to remind us of Shakespeare's gravediggers and Dogberrys begin to talk like books—that is to say, like Mr. Hardy's books.'

In America, the 'Editor's Literary Record' of *Harper's* (March 1879, LVIII, p. 627) spoke of 'a descriptive and emotional novel of more than average artistic merit', but found the story 'powerfully scenic rather than regularly and continuously dramatic'. In *Scribner's Monthly* (April 1879, XVII, p. 910) the reviewer, possibly J. G. Holland, thought the book prolix. He praised the Shakespearian rustics, the character of Eustacia Vye, and the descriptions, but felt that the author had wasted great gifts in filling out the regulation three volumes.

In view of the repeated criticisms of the speech of Hardy 'speasants, it is interesting to find him attempting to defend himself on this score in a letter to the *Athenaeum* (30 November 1878, p. 688, repnrited in *Thomas Hardy's Personal Writings*, ed. Harold Orel, 1967):

An author may be said to fairly convey the spirit of intelligent peasant talk if he retains the idiom, compass and characteristic expressions, although he may not encumber the page with obsolete pronunciations of the purely English words, and with mispronunciations of those derived from Latin and Greek. In the printing of standard speech hardly any phonetic principle at all is observed, and if a writer attempts to exhibit on paper the precise accents of a rustic speaker he disturbs the proper balance of a true representation by unduly insisting upon the grotesque element; thus directing attention to a point of inferior interest, and diverting it from the speaker's meaning, which is by far the chief concern where the aim is to depict the men and their natures rather than their dialect forms.

It will be seen that this answers only one of the objections: most reviewers were concerned less with accurate representation of dialect than the ascription to the rustics of inappropriately sophisticated or literary expressions. Hardy's sensitivity to adverse criticism did not generally imply deference to the critics' advice: for the most part he pursued his own way with a certain dogged obstinacy.

The accusation of putting improbable language into the mouth of peasants was repeated by Britten in his *Athenaeum* review (No. 18) of *The Trumpet Major*, which came out in 1880 after running as a serial in *Good Words*, but his general tone was more favourable: 'Mr. Hardy seems to be in the way to do for rural life what Dickens did for that of the town.' Julian Hawthorne in the *Spectator* (No. 19) was more ready than earlier critics to accept Hardy on his own terms but he thought it unlikely that he would produce 'anything wholly unlike or superior to what he has already given us'. Hawthorne thought him not capable of deep tragedy and advised him to keep to pathos. *The Times* (1 February 1881) liked *The Trumpet Major* 'better than *The Return of the Native* and nearly as much as *Far from the Madding Crowd*'. The *Westminster's* brief notice (January 1881, CXV, p. 327) called it 'decidedly the best story which Mr. Hardy has yet written'. George Saintsbury in the *Academy* also thought the book better than some of the preceding work and spoke of its 'delicate composition and carefully elaborated grace'. The *Saturday Review* (6 November, 1880, L, p. 588) gave a full account of the story, with extracts, and over in Boston the *Literary World* (15 January 1881, XII, p. 25) said 'There is as much original flavour in this book as in *The Return of the Native* and it is to our taste a more pleasing story.' In spite of the reviews *The Trumpet Major* appears to have sold only about 750 of its edition of 1,000 in two years.

Most of Hardy's next novel, *A Laodicean*, which was serialized in *Harper's Magazine* (now published in England as well as America) was written, or rather dictated, during a protracted serious illness. Published in 1881, it seemed to many a new departure, though the *Saturday Review* (14 January 1882, LIII, p. 53) and the *Athenaeum* (No. 21) both referred back to *Desperate Remedies*. The former found the characters not sufficiently explained: the latter (Britten again) was mildly favourable, with one or two objections, for example: 'Without being in the least degree a "fleshly" writer, Mr. Hardy has a way of insisting on the physical attractions of a woman which, if imitated by weaker writers, may prove offensive.' In the *Academy* (7 January, 1882, XXI, p. 5) Arthur Barker protested against his 'most realistic

presentment of the conversation to be heard at a farmers' ordinary . . .
It is very likely that coarse and vulgar natures would discuss the
matrimonial and domestic arrangements of a great heiress in the
language reproduced by the author, but it is surely no part of the
functions of art to make use of such dialogue.' The *Spectator* (4 March
1882, p. 296) was mainly content to summarize the story, noting that
there was little of Hardy's usual humour and rather too much of architectural technicality.

Two on a Tower ran during 1882 in the *Atlantic Monthly* and was
published in three volumes late in the year. The first edition of 1,000
was sold in a few months and a new impression came out early in 1883.
In April 1883 the book was published in one volume. With the critics
it was hardly more popular than *A Laodicean*. Britten in the *Athenaeum*
(18 November 1882, p. 658) said Hardy had added to the novelist's
stock of properties and business, but he returned to the criticism of the
Shakespearian rustics: 'we must still take leave to doubt whether one
Dorsetshire village ever produced quite so many Touchstones at one
and the same time'. The *Saturday Review* (No. 22) thought the book
no improvement on *A Laodicean* and gave an ironical account of the
plot, while in the *Spectator* (No. 23) Harry Quilter found the story 'as
unpleasant as it is practically impossible . . . melodramatic without
strength, extravagant without object, and objectionable without
truth'.

The Mayor of Casterbridge AND *The Woodlanders* (1886–7)

Up to the mid-eighties the reviewers' chief points against Hardy had
been on grounds of style, and of melodramatic improbabilities in plot
and character, with occasional minor uneasiness about his handling of
sexual relations. With the next two works there is some tendency to add
to these the issue of 'pessimism'. Hardy's next novel, *The Mayor of
Casterbridge*, appeared in serial form on both sides of the Atlantic, in
Harper's Weekly and the *Graphic*, before publication in two volumes
in May 1886. Of the first edition of 758, about 600 copies were sold.
There was considerable revision and re-writing between the serial and
the book versions, but this was not simply a matter of bowdlerization
for the magazine public and subsequent restoration of a full text, as
happened with some later novels. Much of Chapter XLIV was omitted
by Hardy because he felt that to make Henchard leave Casterbridge
twice weakened the climax. It was an American admirer, a Miss Owen,

who persuaded him that the return to Elizabeth-Jane's wedding, with the incident of the caged goldfinch, should be restored, and this was done in the 1895 edition. Hardy was afraid that he had damaged the story by observing the need for a striking incident in every serial part, but this does not seem to have worried many readers of the complete novel.

For the most part, reviewers of *The Mayor of Casterbridge* were less appreciative than might have been expected. A short notice in the *Athenaeum* (No. 25) found Hardy not quite fulfilling expectations. It summed up his general merits, culminating in the imaginative power with which he could impress the world of his stories on the reader's imagination and the 'almost Olympian ruthlessness' towards his own creations which might have made him a great dramatist. At the same time it found his old faults of style as prominent as ever, particularly the unconvincing compromise of the diction of his peasants. The *Saturday Review* (No. 26) was disappointed, describing the story as slight and improbable and 'not thrilling'. Hardy's descriptive powers, says the critic, are as great as ever, but the book 'does not contain a single character capable of arousing a passing interest in his or her welfare'. In the *Spectator* (No. 27) R. H. Hutton thought the description 'a man of character' misleading, and objected to the 'fashionable pessimism' colouring the work, but he paid tribute to the 'grandeur of conception' of Henchard's portrayal. The *Westminster*, too (July 1886, CXXVI, p. 300), in its brief notice, declared the character of Henchard 'a grand study which has not, so far as we recollect, its prototype in fiction', and said it was 'drawn with infinite skill'. The book as a whole was said to be a worthy successor of *Far from the Madding Crowd*. In the Boston *Literary World* (12 June 1886, XVII, p. 198) a short paragraph in a chronicle of 'Minor Fiction' (which also included James's *The Bostonians*) spoke of the hand of a master in contrast to 'the pale average fiction of every day'. The editor of *Harper's Magazine* (November 1886, LXXXIII, p. 961) thought that Hardy had started with the intention of a merely adventurous tale and that the work had grown under his hand. Making comparisons with Tolstoy and Turgenev, he set the novel squarely in a European context: 'We suppose it is a condition of a novelist's acceptance by the criticism of a country now so notably behind the rest of Europe in fiction as England that he must seize the attention in an old-fashioned way, and we simply concede to Mr. Hardy the use of the wife-sale for this purpose. . . .'

Private comment by individuals was often more enthusiastic. The incident of the wife-sale was singled out for praise by Gerard Manley Hopkins in a brief reference to Hardy which appears in a letter of October 1886 (Letter CXXXVIII, *Letters of Gerard Manley Hopkins to Robert Bridges*, 1935, p. 238).

In my judgment the amount of gift and genius which goes into novels in the English Literature of this generation is perhaps not so much inferior to what made the Elizabethan drama, and unhappily it is in great part wasted. How admirable are Blackmore and Hardy! Their merits are much eclipsed by the overdone reputation of the Evans-Eliot-Lewis [sic]-Cross woman (poor creature! one ought not to speak slightingly, I know), half real power, half imposition. Do you know the bonfire scene in the *Return of the Native* and still better the sword-exercise scene in the *Madding Crowd*, breathing epic? or the wife-sale in the *Mayor of Casterbridge* (read by chance)? But these writers only rise to their great strokes, they do not write continuously well: now Stevenson is master of a consummate style and each phrase is finished as in poetry.

Stevenson himself wrote to Hardy in praise of *The Mayor* (*Life*, p. 179): 'Henchard is a great fellow, and Dorchester is touched in with the hand of a master. Do you think you would let me try to dramatize it?' Nothing seems to have come of this suggestion. In the same year, though without explicit reference to *The Mayor of Casterbridge*, we find George Gissing sending Hardy a respectful letter with the gift of one of his own novels: 'I have not been the least careful of your readers and in your books I have constantly found refreshment and onward help' (*Life*, p. 182).

The Woodlanders came out in *Macmillan's Magazine* from May 1886 to April 1887. While not so successful as the *Cornhill*, *Macmillan's* had a considerable circulation: its first number sold out an edition of 10,000 and had to be reprinted. The three-volume edition of the novel was published in March 1887. By the end of June only 170 copies out of the original 1,000 were left to be remaindered. Of the one-volume re-issue there were two impressions, each of 2,000 copies. Britten in the *Athenaeum* (No. 28) praised *The Woodlanders* as an example of Hardy's 'second manner'—less sensational, less broadly comic. 'The novel', he concluded, 'is distinctly not one for the "young person" of whom we have lately heard, but should be read by all who can tell masterly work in fiction when they see it.' The *Saturday Review* (No. 31) admired the atmosphere and description, but found some stiffness and artificiality in the incidents, especially in the earlier part. It also noted some inconsistency in the standard of conversation given to the villagers. Concluding with praise for the portrait of Giles Winterborne, the reviewer warns Hardy not to be led astray by the desire to idealize. R. H. Hutton in the *Spectator* (No. 29) thought the book at once 'powerful' and 'disagreeable'. He considered the author too tolerant to Fitzpiers and found the general moral effect blurred in consequence. The strongest part of the book, he said, lay in the pictures of genuine rural life, the weakest in the part dealing with Mrs. Charmond; and finally he lamented the general absence of faith and hope. In the *Academy* (No. 32) William Wallace the philosopher also thought that the novel would be found disagreeable, though decidedly the most powerful of Hardy's works since *Far from the Madding Crowd*. Fitzpiers is an 'exasperating scoundrel', and Mrs. Charmond 'too much of a third-rate French actress', but Marty South rises to the sublime. The *Westminster's* brief notice (April 1887, CXXVIII, p. 384) spoke of 'a treat for all lovers of imaginative literature of a high order'. In the *St. James's Gazette* (No. 30) Coventry Patmore made *The Woodlanders* the occasion for a general discussion of Hardy as a representative nineteenth-century novelist, praising his rendering of 'rustic manners and passions' and especially his heroines. In this latest novel he found the author at his least happy, but praised the pathos of Winterborne and Marty South. Over in Boston the *Literary World* (14 May 1887, XVIII, p. 149) spoke of the 'touch of a master's hand', but deplored the pessimism of the novel which leaves the reader 'baffled, stupified [sic], cast down'.

THE LAST NOVELS (1891–1897), AND THE SHORT STORIES

Hardy's last three novels (more especially *Tess of the D'Urbervilles* and *Jude the Obscure*) received an amount of comment and discussion much greater than any of his earlier works. This was largely due to the widespread controversy over their morality and their general attitude to life. With both *Tess* and *Jude* the trouble began at the stage of serial publication and led to the first appearance of each story in a bowdlerized version considered to be suitable for the magazine public. When the full text of each appeared in volume form it provoked a storm of critical argument involving prejudices and passions well outside the purely literary sphere. The sales of both *Tess* and *Jude* were far higher than those of earlier works. Of the three-volume edition of *Tess* two further impressions of 500 each had succeeded the first 1,000 within four months. The one-volume reprint at 6s ran to five impressions totalling 17,000 between September 1892 and the end of the year. *Jude* was published in one volume from the start, at 6s, and within three months it was in its twentieth thousand—something, it would appear, of a *succès de scandale*.

Tess of the D'Urbervilles was first intended for publication in serial form by the newspaper syndicate of Tillotson & Son of Bolton, but on seeing a substantial portion of the manuscript, including the seduction and the baptism scene, they rejected it.[4] It was offered in turn to *Murray's Magazine* and *Macmillan's Magazine*, but rejected by both, on similar moral grounds. Finally it was accepted by the *Graphic* in a severely modified form which omits the seduction and the illegitimate child, replacing them by a mock-marriage ceremony, and makes Angel Clare convey the dairymaids across the stream not in his arms, but in a wheelbarrow. The baptism scene was published in full by itself in the *Fortnightly Review* (May 1891) and the seduction episode in the Edinburgh *National Observer* (14 November 1891). From the *Life* it is not quite clear whether the bowdlerization was all performed in cynical anticipation of objections from the *Graphic's* editor or whether some at least of it was at his request. Hardy's feelings on the necessity for these subterfuges may be gathered from his article 'Candour in English Fiction' which was published in the *New Review* in January 1890 (See Orel, *Thomas Hardy's Personal Writings*, p. 125). He speaks there of the 'fearful price' that the artist 'has to pay for the privilege of writing in the English language—no less a price than the complete extinction, in the mind of every mature and penetrating reader, of sympathetic belief in his personages', and complains that 'a question which should be wholly a question of treatment is confusedly regarded as a question of subject'. When the full version appeared in volume form this confusion was certainly apparent in some of the reviews, which in general showed a very wide range of approval and disapproval.

In the *New Review* (No. 42) Andrew Lang, while acknowledging passages of power and beauty, made some criticisms of pedantry and abstractions in the style, and was generally uneasy about the bitterness of Hardy's mood. He took particular exception to the final phrase about the President of the Immortals as either blasphemous or meaningless. Hardy referred tartly to this review in his preface to the novel's second edition, and Lang answered at length in *Longman's Magazine* for November 1892 (No. 47), explaining that while he found *Tess*, like *Clarissa*, or *Le Père Goriot*, or *Madame Bovary*, 'forbidding in conception', his objection was that it was not like them credible and real, and that to this unreality the defects of style contributed. In the *Westminster* (No. 48) D. F. Hannigan supported Hardy against Lang's criticisms and went on to hail *Tess* as marking a distinct epoch in English fiction and as the greatest novel since George Eliot died. In the *Illustrated London News* (No. 39) Clementina Black praised the book's moral earnestness: its essence lay in 'the perception that a woman's moral worth is measurable not by any one deed, but by the whole aim and tendency of her life and nature'. The daily papers were in the main favourable. H. W. Massingham in the *Daily Chronicle* for 28 December 1891 declared the novel 'as pitiless and tragic in its intensity as the old Greek dramas'. He found the story painful, but treated in a masterly manner, though he saw no overwhelming necessity for the ease with which Tess was seduced. *The Times* reviewer (13 January 1892) began forthrightly, 'Mr. Hardy's latest novel is his greatest', praised the book's tragic power, and asserted, 'It is well that an idealist like Mr. Hardy should every now and then remind us how terribly defective are our means of judging others'. In the *Star* (No. 36) Richard le Gallienne described *Tess* as 'perhaps the very best' of Hardy's novels, though he criticized the style for its occasional self-consciousness and 'imperfect digestion' of scientific and philosophical ideas. The *Pall Mall Gazette* (No. 37) thought this 'a grim Christmas gift' but said Hardy had never exercised his art more powerfully. It found Angel Clare unconvincing, especially in comparison with the warm naturalness of Tess herself. Even *Punch* (27 February 1892) had a not unfavourable one-column notice, though it ridiculed Alec d'Urberville as stagey and melodramatic.

Of the more substantial periodicals, the *National Review* gave two pages to *Tess* in 'Among the Books' (February 1892, XVIII p. 849) calling the heroine a 'great creation' and praising the general atmosphere of pathos: 'Even Tess's heartrending letter to her husband does not move one much more than the landscape, which is always painted in tones that accord with the temper of the figures in it.' In April 1892 (XIX, p. 191), however, there appeared a semi-serious dialogue by W. Earl Hodgson called 'A Prig in the Elysian Fields', presenting a posthumous conversation between Tess, Alec and Angel, about their life. The prig is of course Angel (and not, as some accounts have implied, Tess herself) and he defends his position in the modern novel as a way of avoiding simple melodrama and giving adequate complexity: he represents 'the villainy of moral and intellectual posturing'. In *Blackwood's* for March 1892, Mrs. Oliphant gave *Tess* a very full consideration (No. 44) praising its life and reality and judging the story, in its force and passion, 'far finer in our opinion than anything Mr. Hardy has ever done before'. At the same time she objected strongly to the element of indignant didacticism and found Tess's return to Alec and all the last part of the story unconvincing. It was probably to be expected that the orthodox and conservative *Quarterly* should come out strongly against *Tess* on moral grounds. Here the reviewer was Mowbray Morris, who as editor of *Macmillan's Magazine* had already rejected *Tess* as a serial. His *Quarterly* article, entitled *Culture and Anarchy* (No. 45) discussed three novels by different authors, but consisted mostly of an ironical summary of *Tess* ending in a condemnation of it as unconvincing and morally unsound—'Mr. Hardy has told an extremely disagreeable story in an extremely disagreeable manner'. Hardy commented that the article was smart and amusing, 'but it is easy to be smart and amusing if a man will forgo veracity and sincerity . . . Well, if this sort of thing continues, no more novel-writing for me. A man must be a fool to deliberately stand up to be shot at' (*Life* p. 246).

Of the weeklies, the *Saturday Review* (No. 40) took an ironical line somewhat similar to the *Quarterly*, though praising the dairy-farm scenes and the account of the hardships of Flintcomb Ash. 'Few people will deny the terrible dreariness of this tale,' said the reviewer, 'which, except during the few hours spent with cows, has not a gleam of sunshine anywhere.' He found Tess's return to Alec thoroughly unconvincing, and objected to the detailed insistence upon her physical attractions: in general the characters seemed to him stagey. R. L. Purdy records that Hardy felt this attack 'so keenly that he considered resigning from the Savile Club to avoid encountering the magazine's reviewers': he wrote to Edward Clodd that the review 'has quickened the sale—I suppose the *animus* was too apparent'.

The *Athenaeum*, however (No. 38), thought the novel 'not only good, but great', and Tess 'in the very forefront of his women'. It regretted that Hardy should not have been content to present tragedy impartially without (chiefly in his preface and sub-title) descending to argumentation and moral controversy, and it made some incidental criticisms of style. R. H. Hutton's position in the *Spectator* (No. 41) was somewhat similar: he dwells more upon the claim of Tess to be called 'pure' and allows it only with qualifications, but he shows a full and sensitive appreciation of the tragic and dramatic power of the novel while admitting that his mind 'rebels against the steady assumptions of the author'. In the *Academy* (No. 43) William Watson began by calling the book Hardy's 'greatest work' and 'a tragic masterpiece'. It is, he admits, not flawless, and he objects particularly to 'over-academic phraseology' in the style. He has some interesting comments on the treatment of Clare's 'consistently inconsistent' behaviour, and on the relation of material and natural settings to the feelings of the characters.

The American reception of *Tess* was as mixed as the British. The *Atlantic Monthly's* ten columns (May 1892, lxix, p. 697) praise the book as Hardy's masterpiece and note particularly its effect of enlarging human sympathy: 'it has left at least one reader believing that many of the crimes served up morning and evening in the newspapers would seem less barbarous, less unintelligible, if there were at hand to explain the motives of them some seer of human nature, some Thomas Hardy'. The reviewer urges that future editions should restore the scene of the baptism of Tess's baby, which had been omitted in the American book form. The New York *Critic* (9 July 1892, n.8. xxi, p. 13) regretted the argumentative insistence on 'A Pure Woman' and found no excuse for Tess's first error, but it thought the book's strength and human interest undeniable. The Boston *Literary World* (13 February 1892, xxiii, p. 58) dismissed it in a short paragraph lamenting its 'unpleasantness': Tess's career ignores 'the plain unwritten instincts of morality'.

Tess was translated into a large number of European languages. The *Life* (pp. 246 and 274) mentions German, French, Russian, Dutch and Italian, and records that 'the Russian translation appears to have been read and approved by Tolstoi during its twelve months' career in a Moscow monthly periodical'. The novel was much discussed in society, and there is a story of the Duchess of Abercorn arranging her guests in groups according to their opinion of the heroine. Lord Salisbury was one of those who spoke up for the book. Henry James, in a letter to R. L. Stevenson (19 March 1892, *Letters*, I, 194) reported:

The good little Thomas Hardy has scored a great success with *Tess of the d'Urbervilles*, which is chock-full of faults and falsity and yet has a singular beauty and charm.

To this Stevenson seems to have replied with disagreement, for we find James writing on 17 February 1893 (*Letters*, I, p. 204):

I grant you Hardy with all my heart . . . I am meek and ashamed where the public clatter is deafening—so I bowed my head and let 'Tess of the D.'s' pass.

But oh yes, dear Louis, she is vile. The pretence of 'sexuality' is only equalled
by the absence of it, and the abomination of the language by the author's
reputation for style. There are indeed some pretty smells and sights and sounds.
But you have better ones in Polynesia.

(Hardy was later to call James and Stevenson the Polonius and the
Osric of novelists.) Meredith, writing to Frederick Greenwood on
11 January 1892, asks for the loan of *Tess*, since 'Hardy is one of the
few men whose work I can read. I had always great hopes of him.'
(*Letters*, II, p. 445). Returning the book on 23 February he reports
(*Letters*, II, p. 448):

The work is open to criticism, but excellent and very interesting. All of the
Dairy Farm held me fast. But from the moment of the meeting again of Tess
and Alec, I grew cold, and should say that there is a depression of power, up to
the end, save for the short scene on the plain of Stonehenge. If the author's
minute method had been sustained, we should have had a finer book. it is
marred by the sudden hurry to round the story. And Tess, out of the arms of
Alec, into (I suppose) those of the lily-necked Clare, and on to the Black Flag
waving over her poor body, is a smudge in vapour—she at one time so real
to me.

There is no doubt that, both from its intrinsic qualities and from the stir
roused by its subject, *Tess* did more than any other novel to widen
Hardy's reputation. W. R. Rutland records that between 1900 and 1930
it was reprinted some forty times in England alone.

Like *Tess*, *Jude the Obscure* appeared first in an emasculated serial
form. Hardy had found as the writing progressed that 'the development
of the story was carrying him into unexpected fields' and he asked to
cancel his agreement with *Harper's Magazine*, which had been for a
novel 'in every respect suitable for a family magazine'. The agreement
was not cancelled but the editor asked for bowdlerization, not on his
own account, but because 'our rule is that the Magazine must contain
nothing which could not be read aloud in any family circle'. The serial
form therefore was modified to an extent that completely altered Jude's
relations with Sue and Arabella and made nonsense of parts of the plot
(a detailed account is given in *Thomas Hardy: From Serial to Novel* by
Mary Ellen Chase, 1927). The title of the serial was *Hearts Insurgent*
(changed from *The Simpletons* after the first instalment): the full novel
was published by Osgood, McIlvaine & Co. in November 1895 as
Jude the Obscure.

It was received with a variety of opinions and a storm of controversy that put the discussion of all Hardy's earlier books in the shade—even that of *Tess*. In the *Athenaeum* (No. 49) B. Williams spoke of the bad work of great artists as like a Titan's overthrow, and declared that here was 'a titanically bad book by Mr. Hardy'. He objected to the bitter scolding tone of his attitude to Destiny and to Society, which had eclipsed both his sense of probability and his sense of humour. In the *Academy* (15 February 1896, xlix, p. 134) J. B. Allen wrote that it would be 'utterly superfluous to say of any new book from the pen of Mr. Thomas Hardy that it was powerful or dramatic' and 'unnecessary to state that the author is throughout true to nature'. Was there not, however, some desirable limit to such realism? Paintings from the nude did not give a photographic representation; and why should a novelist introduce subjects normally avoided in conversation? The *Illustrated London News* (No. 54) thought the death of the children, with the doctor's comment, a strain on the reader's credulity: 'we all know perfectly well that baby Schopenhauers are not coming into the world in shoals', and it found 'the perpetual shuffling of partners' 'dangerously near the ridiculous'. 'But', the reviewer concluded, 'read the story how you will, it is manifestly a work of genius . . . most of our fiction is to *Jude the Obscure* as a hamlet to a hemisphere.'

The tone of the reviewers varied as much as their opinions. A. J. Butler wrote in a fairly temperate and judicious way in the *National Review* (No. 57) on 'Mr. Hardy as a Decadent', beginning with a general survey of his powers and with particular praise for *The Woodlanders*. *Jude*, he objected, ignored the existence of genuine reformers and people of any elevated or generous feeling. He did not want the artist to ignore sex or to limit his subject matter unduly, but he thought Hardy at times showed signs of simply wanting to defy Mrs. Grundy. R. Y. Tyrrell in the *Fortnightly Review* (No. 58) took a rather heavier tone. Hardy being 'at the summit of British novelists', the public would 'endure anything from him', but this was 'a deplorable falling-off', 'a treatise on sexual pathology in which the data are drawn from the imagination, and are, therefore, scientifically invalid, and in which his dramatic faculty has largely deserted him'. Tyrrell also objected to faults of style, especially scientific pedantry and dramatic inappropriateness. Jude 'sometimes talks like Gibbon or Johnson, but oftener like Herbert Spencer'. The *Pall Mall Gazette* (12 November 1895) referred to the novel as 'Jude the Obscene', gave a facetious summary of the story (infants 'hanging each other with box-cord on little pegs all round the room'—'and they all lived unhappily ever after, except

Jude . . .') and adjured the author, 'Give us quickly another and cleaner book to take the bad taste out of our mouths'. In *Blackwood's Magazine* (No. 51) the elderly Mrs. Oliphant bracketed Hardy with Grant Allen for an article on 'The Anti-Marriage League'. This was perhaps the most thorough-going condemnation that *Jude* received: 'nothing so coarsely indecent as the whole history of Jude in his relations with his wife Arabella has ever been put in English print—that is to say, from the hands of a Master'. Hardy's main motive in writing such a story must be an attack on the institution of marriage—but how would the abolition of marriage have helped Jude? 'When Susan changed her mind would he have been less unhappy? when Arabella claimed him again would he have been less weak?' And what is to be the fate of the children? The only solution offered here is little Father Time's murder and suicide. After this it is perhaps not surprising that the *Spectator* did not review the novel at all: a note on 'Hill-Top Novels and the Morality of Art' in the number for 23 November 1895 couples Hardy with Grant Allen as a propagandist for the new morality, saying '*Jude the Obscure* is too deplorable a falling-off from Mr. Hardy's former achievements to be reckoned with at all.'

The *Saturday Review*, however, (No. 56) led the more favourable accounts, speaking of *Jude*, as the 'last and most splendid' of Hardy's works, and likening its 'foolish reception' to 'the New England Witch Mania'. It maintained that the sexual problems in the book were secondary, and stressed rather the new voice that Hardy had given to the educated proletarian. Periodicals of a radical and consciously advanced type came out strongly in the novel's favour, as might be expected: the enthusiasm seems sometimes tinged with propaganda motives. The *Westminster* for January 1896 carried D. F. Hannigan's review (No. 53) which hits out emotionally at the misrepresentations of 'smug journalistic critics', while classing Hardy with Fielding, Balzac, Flaubert, Turgenev, George Eliot and Dostoievsky. In the significantly named *Free Review* (January 1896, V. 387) Geoffrey Mortimer spoke of 'the supreme achievement of a great artist in the broad and splendid maturity of a notable career'. He found the scene of the child-murders 'one of the most heart-rending in fiction' and the general philosophy saner and more moral than any complacent glossing-over of unpleasant facts. Magazines associated with the Aesthetic movement also tended to give *Jude* a favourable reception. In Jerome K. Jerome's *Idler* (No. 55) Richard le Gallienne deplored Mrs. Oliphant's attack as both unjust and pointless, and declared the novel, in spite of some improbabilities, 'perhaps the most powerful and moving picture of human life which Mr. Hardy has given us'. The most substantial discussion of all was Havelock Ellis's article 'Concerning *Jude the Obscure*' in the *Savoy Magazine* (No. 59). Returning to Hardy thirteen years after his survey of the earlier novels in the *Westminster*, Ellis is chiefly interested in his feminine psychology, and considers *Jude* the greatest novel written in England for many years. Though 'intellectually Hardy is a mere child compared to Meredith', he finds him the truer artist. The one serious lapse in *Jude*, he thinks, is the melodrama of the child-murders. As for the accusation of immorality, Ellis sees this as resulting from the artist's faithful portrayal of the conflict between natural instincts and secondary social expedients. The whole article carries a marked air of wide literary experience and sophistication.

In the *Bookman* (January 1896, p. 120) Sir George Douglas dealt with some of the more extreme hostile reviews in an article 'On Some Critics of *Jude the Obscure*'. Why, he asked, should newspapers which vie with each other in praising Maupassant object to Hardy? A writer of proved greatness should have had his experiments treated with more reverent seriousness. A temperate summing up of the controversy may be seen in Gosse's article in the first number of the new review, *Cosmopolis* (No. 52). This starts by assuming that Hardy has achieved a rank which deserves criticism by the strictest standards. The thwarting of Jude's aspirations is admirably portrayed, but there is no excuse for the rhetorical diatribes against Oxford or at least for the author's apparent endorsement of them. The story is ghastly, squalid and abnormal, but it is so told as to hold our interest to the close, and we have no business to call in question the right of an author of Hardy's distinction to treat what themes he will. Hardy ought, however, to restrain 'the jarring note of rebellion which seems growing upon him', and 'as to the conversations of his semi-educated characters, they are really terrible. Sue and Jude talk a sort of University Extension jargon that breaks the heart.' The *Life* prints letters in which Hardy thanks Gosse for this review and discusses some of its points (pp. 271–3).

Of American reviews of *Jude* the most notable is probably W. D. Howells's in *Harper's Weekly* (7 December 1895) (No. 50). He sees the book as a tragedy of the Greek kind: it carries conviction although we know that in ordinary life compromises would prevent the various catastrophes from happening. The unpleasant incidents are not untrue to the human condition, and the questionings of convention and morality are such as to make us ask the reasons of things. Howells also notes in this book a 'unity very uncommon in the novel and especially the English novel'. Other American reviews show the same range of opinion as the English ones. Howells's praise appeared just one day before a thoroughgoing attack by Jeannette L. Gilder in the New York *World* (8 December 1895)—'When I finished the story I opened the windows and let in the fresh air and I turned to my bookshelves and I said: ' "Thank God for Kipling and Stevenson, Barrie and Mrs. Humphry Ward. Here are four great writers who have never trailed their talents in the dirt." ' The New York *Critic* (28 December 1895), after outlining the story, concluded: 'There is an undercurrent of morbid animality running through the book which is sickening to an ordinarily decent mind, and if these men and women and their companions in kindred fiction are to be taken as true to modern life, we may as well accept a cage full of monkeys as a microcosm of humanity'.

Reactions to the novel went to ridiculous extremes among ordinary readers as well as critics: Hardy received a packet of ashes from Australia purporting to be the remains of a copy that had been burnt. The Bishop of Wakefield (W. Walsham How, the hymn-writer) also claimed to have thrown *Jude* on the fire: more important, he secured its banning by W. H. Smith's library. Swinburne sent an enthusiastic letter—'The beauty, the terror, and the truth are all yours and yours alone. But (if I may say so) how cruel you are! Only the great and awful father of "Pierrette" and "L'Enfant Maudit" was ever so merciless to his children' (*Life*, p. 270).

Hardy's last full-length novel, *The Well-Beloved*, appeared in serial form simultaneously in the *Illustrated London News* and *Harper's Bazaar* during 1892, but was considerably revised for book publication in 1897. It is therefore not really a later work than *Jude*, and it had apparently been sketched much earlier. In the heated atmosphere left by the *Jude* scandal some reviewers managed to find it immoral: Hardy refused to answer such attacks, commenting to an editor who had raised the question: 'There is more fleshliness in *The Loves of the Triangles* than in this story—at least to me' (*Life*, p. 286). Britten in the *Athenaeum* (No. 60) reviewed it fairly favourably, and hoped that its publication indicated 'a desire to renew those pleasant relations with his readers that should never have been interrupted'. In fact it marks the end of Hardy's career as a novelist.

Not much need be said about Hardy's short stories: they appear to have been not widely or fully reviewed. *The Romantic Adventures of a*

Milkmaid, which came out in America in 1883, was severely dealt with by the Boston *Literary World* (28 July 1883) and the Philadelphia *Lippincott's Magazine*. *Wessex Tales* was praised by the *Westminster* in a short notice for its vivid pictures of rustic life (July 1888, CXXX, p. 115). *A Group of Noble Dames* drew from William Wallace in the *Academy* the comment that it was very characteristic in tragedy and in fantastic humour (22 August 1891, XL, p. 153) but the short notice in the *National Review* (August 1891, XVII, p. 845) said that the author of the novels was hardly to be recognized here except by 'ingenuity of invention' and the 'art of terse and pointed narrative'. Both Gosse and Minto include comments on Hardy as a short-story writer in their general articles of 1890 and 1891 (Nos. 34 and 35); so also does Trent in his essay of 1892 (No. 46). An account in the *Athenaeum* (1 November 1913, p. 488) of the last collection, *A Changed Man . . . and other Tales*, confined itself mainly to description and to relating the mood of the tales to the late prose period of *Tess* and *Jude*.

POEMS AND *The Dynasts* (1898–1918)

Hardy's abandonment of prose fiction in favour of poetry has often been seen as a direct consequence of the reception of *Tess* and *Jude*, and no doubt this played a considerable part. But his poetic ambitions were deeply rooted and went back to the beginning of his literary career. Further, it has been recently suggested (notably by Mr. Alvarez) that with *Jude* he had in fact completed what he had to say in the novel. The change from prose fiction to verse was marked by the appearance in 1898 of *Wessex Poems*, and reviewers were at first inclined to treat these as the usual sort of indulgence by an established prose writer, not to be taken very seriously. Their chief objections were that the poems were prosaic, awkward in style and form, and unrelieved in their pessimism. The *Academy* (No. 62) remarked that a novelist's whole training was necessarily anti-lyrical, and found Hardy best in his ballads, though it praised 'Neutral Tones' and said that he had the stuff of the poet in him. In the *Athenaeum* E. K. Chambers noted the use of neologisms and provincialisms, but suggested that these might help to revivify the poetic vocabulary. The *Westminster* (August 1899, CLII, p. 180) had a mild and somewhat superficial appreciation by W. B. Columbine: the verse does not detract from Hardy's reputation and may even extend the circle of his readers. A very laudatory account by Annie Macdonnell in the *Bookman* (February 1899, XV, p. 139) spoke of a Shakespearian intensity and concentration, but the reviewer in *Literature* (31 December 1898, III, p. 615) said that many of the narratives might as well have been in prose, and objected to the cloud of dreary pessimism over the whole collection. In the *London Quarterly Review* (1899, XCI, p. 223) this aspect was stressed by May Kendall who found the poems a 'grim and weighty challenge to Christendom' and wrote an eleven-page article mainly in rebuttal of Hardy's moral and religious views. The *Saturday Review* (No. 61) spoke of 'this curious and wearisome volume'; but it made some significant selections of individual poems for praise. In America the Chicago *Dial* (16 April 1899, XXVI, p. 274) included in an omnibus review by W. Morton Payne a one-column comment which treated the poems as 'the literary diversions' of a novelist, but noted some haunting poetic phrases such as 'mothy curfew-tide'. Payne thought the Wessex poems proper the least interesting part of the collection. Altogether the reception of this volume was mixed and uncertain, though the power of one or two individual poems did not pass unnoticed.

When *Poems of the past and present* appeared late in 1901, it became more necessary to treat Hardy as a poet in his own right. *The Times* (26 December 1901) found it 'strange that Mr. Thomas Hardy, whose style in prose is flowing, architectural, easy with the ease of a natural gift for construction perfected by art, should write crabbed, stiff verse' and thought he overdid the tendency to pack short poems too closely with thought. The *Saturday Review* (No. 64) made similar comments and described the best poems as 'brooding, obscure, tremulous, half-inarticulate meditations over man, nature and destiny'. It noted the link with Browning and praised especially 'An August Midnight' and 'De Profundis'. In the *Spectator* (No. 65) T. H. Warren, the President of Magdalen, said that Hardy was 'a master of fiction, but not a master of music'. His review is somewhat inconclusive, and he finds nothing in this volume as good as 'Friends Beyond' in the earlier one. In the Chicago *Dial* (1 May 1902, XXXII, p. 314) W. Morton Payne thought this second volume similar to *Wessex Poems* in its roughness of technique; for its ideas, however, it made 'an important contribution to our literature'.

Hardly had the critics accustomed themselves to thinking of Hardy as a poet before they had to cope with the gigantic dramatic experiment of *The Dynasts*, whose three parts appeared in 1904, 1906 and 1908. Their reactions to Part I tended to be unfavourable. The *Academy* (23 January 1904, LXVI, p. 95) held that such a 'vast venture' would

demand 'a poet of the largest power, the most uncompromising individuality, with the most practised and triumphant executive gift.
Here it is Mr. Hardy fails.' The reviewer thought that the personifications did not blend with the realistic characters and that much of the
dialogue was only 'the prose of the novelist cut into lengths'. He concluded: 'we would give many such dramas for one *Return of the Native*'.
Max Beerbohm in the *Saturday Review* (No. 66) wished that Hardy had
written in prose. He too thought that the conception made impossible
demands: it would really need 'a syndicate of much greater poets than
ever were born'. The *Spectator's* reviewer, John Buchan (No. 67),
described *The Dynasts* as 'the work of a poet, but rarely poetry', discerning what seemed to him the outlines of a great conception behind
the 'misty philosophy and awkward rhythms'. Harold Child in *The
Times Literary Supplement* (15 January 1904, p. 11) objected to the
whole idea of a play intended only for reading, and complained of a
lack of human characters: the historical figures were seen only in their
public aspect, and the use of the spirits of the over-world tended to
reduce humanity to puppets. As for the blank verse, 'it sometimes
reaches dignity but never achieves distinction'. An opinion from Meredith is recorded in a letter to Gosse of 2 July 1905 (*Letters II*, 567): 'He
[Hardy] questioned me as to *The Dynasts*. I spoke (needlessly) in
favour of his continuing it now that it had a commencement. It was
useless to say, as I think, that he would have made it more effective in
prose, where he is more at home than in verse, though here and there
he produces good stuff. Of much of Browning I could say the same.'
The *Atlantic Monthly* (May 1904, XCIII, p. 713) found *The Dynasts* 'the
work of a master of realistic fiction in a field altogether alien to his
powers', and the verse 'for the most part an achievement of elaborate
mischance', while the New York *Tribune* (23 January 1904) called the
work 'a fearsome hybrid, lacking all unity and charm', a 'formless
cloudy play, reminding us of nothing so much as one of William Blake's
amorphous productions'.

Reviews of Part II were somewhat less critical: for example, *The
Times Literary Supplement* reviewer, a certain Miss Fletcher, spoke of
the work as a 'great, modern Epic of the Intelligence' (16 February
1906). Part III drew fuller discussions, often looking back over the
whole work, and these were generally more favourable still. *The Times
Literary Supplement* for 27 February 1908 gave a front-page article to
the complete drama (No. 69) praising both the total vision and the
individual characterization. *The Dynasts*, says the reviewer (Harold

Child again), is a great work of art, though by all the rules it should have been a colossal failure: for a like achievement we can only go back to the historical plays of Shakespeare. The *Academy* reviewer (14 March 1908, LXXIV, p. 555), in a rather mannered eulogy, praised the philosophical unity of the work and the 'hundred fine things in it': 'outweighing every defect . . . there is a singular comprehensive power and clarity of imagination in the vast views which the author commands by a single phrase'. He laid a good deal of stress on the final chorus: 'The illumination of the Will itself is indicated, and the consequent redemption of the illimitable failure of the world'. The *Edinburgh Review*, in an eighteen-page essay (No. 70) gave a very full and respectful account of the whole enterprise, praising Hardy's breadth of vision and skill in shifting his point of view. At the same time the critic notes the large amount of inferior verse, while he praises the poetic imagination of much of the prose description. Almost as full a discussion appeared in the *Quarterly* by Sir Henry Newbolt, under the title 'A New Departure in Modern Poetry' (No. 71). Newbolt has been suggesting that perhaps what modern poetry needs is a new form: Hardy has produced a new development which may possibly indicate the line of future growth, especially in the long poem, by combining the epic and the closet-drama. There are blemishes of style, and inconsistencies in the philosophy, he says, but 'I do not care to imagine a time when Englishmen will not read this poem with delight'.

In reviewing *Time's Laughingstocks* (8 January 1910, p. 34) the *Athenaeum* noted the effect of sensitiveness or idealism pushed to excess, and spoke of the 'vibrating precision' of Hardy's execution. Dealing with *Satires of Circumstance* (28 November 1914, p. 552) the same journal found some degree of 'embittered sentimentalism', but made particular mention of the *Veteris Vestigia Flammae* group. Two notable reviews of this volume were Lytton Strachey's in the *New Statesman* (No. 76), with its analysis of Hardy's conversational tone and rhythms; and Laurence Binyon's in the *Bookman* (No. 77) with its remarks on the incongruity 'between the prosaic plainness of the speech and the tight structure of rather elaborate lyric to which it is trimmed', and on 'the tenderness that is very deep in the texture of his art'. The last article reprinted in this selection (No. 78) is Gosse's 1918 essay in the *Edinburgh Review* on Hardy's lyrical poetry up to and including *Moments of Vision*, a very fair and perceptive account, if sometimes over-indulgent to defects. Gosse has some good comments on Hardy's consistency ('During the whole of his long career Mr. Hardy has not budged an inch from his original line of direction'), on his 'habitual serenity in negation', on the parallel with Crabbe, and on his power of rendering the momentary and apparently trivial experience.

GENERAL CRITICAL SURVEYS TO 1914

Critics began to write essays summing up Hardy's achievement when his work had been less than ten years before the public. Apart from Boucher's article, mentioned earlier, the first seems to have been that in the *New Quarterly Magazine* for October 1879 (No. 17), a fairly perceptive survey suggesting that *The Return of the Native* might mark a new departure, with perhaps more conscious purpose and less unconscious inspiration. In 1881 the Nonconformist *British Quarterly Review* had a full account of the main works up to and including *The Trumpet Major* (No. 20), finding the highest achievement in *The Return of the Native*. The article devotes a good deal of attention to Hardy's women characters, and is quoted on the subject by Havelock Ellis in his very substantial essay in the *Westminster* for April 1883 (No. 24). This runs to thirty pages and goes into considerable detail, especially on the psychology of the heroines. Ellis notes an affinity with Schopenhauer—probably the first time this connection was made. He thinks that Hardy will scarcely write another novel of the peculiar power (and weakness) of *Far from the Madding Crowd*: he is more likely to continue in the comedy vein of *A Laodicean* and *Two on a Tower*. When John Gawsworth reprinted this article (and that on *Jude*) in *From Marlowe to Shaw: the Studies,1876–1936, in English Literature of Havelock Ellis* (1950) he printed as prefatory to the collection Hardy's letter to Ellis expressing his appreciation of 'your generous treatment of the subject. I consider the essay a remarkable paper in many ways, and can truly say that the writing itself, with its charm of style, and the variety of allusion, occupied my mind when first reading it far more than the fact that my own unmethodical books were its subject-matter.' Apart from Coventry Patmore's tendency to range more widely while nominally reviewing *The Woodlanders* (No. 30) the next general account is J. M. Barrie's in the *Contemporary Review* in 1889 (No. 33). Here the emphasis is largely on the picture of rural life caught at the point of change, and there are comparisons with George Eliot and Richard Jefferies.

Round about 1890, when Hardy had been writing for almost twenty years, the general discussions begin to multiply. Gosse's sketch in the

Speaker for 13 September 1890 (No. 34) considered the frequent comparison with Meredith, the unpopularity of Hardy with women readers, his power of landscape, and his humour. Professor W. Minto, writing in the *Bookman* in December 1891, was able to include *Tess* in his account (No. 35), and rated Hardy higher than George Eliot, while suggesting that his predilection for scientific language and psychological analysis might have cost him some popularity. In the *Westminster* for February 1892 (CXXXVII, p. 153) Janetta Newton Robinson gave an eleven-page general summary of Hardy's career, sensible and straightforward but otherwise undistinguished, and to the *Illustrated London News* for 1 October 1892 (p. 431) Frederick Greenwood contributed a popular appreciation of 'The Genius of Thomas Hardy'. In America John A. Steuart had included Hardy in his *Letters to Living Authors* of 1890, and in January 1892 William Sharp published an essay on 'Thomas Hardy and his Novels' in the New York *Forum* (subsequently reprinted in his *Papers Critical and Reminiscent*, 1912). This stressed Hardy's realism and masculinity, his Englishness and his unsentimental pathos, and spoke of him as an incomparably finer artist than Zola. Sharp put the *Native*, *The Woodlanders* and *Tess* at the head of the list. In 1892, the first article of the first number of the *Sewanee Review* was W. P. Trent's essay on Hardy (No. 46), a full and judicious critical survey of his career and achievement which ranked *Tess* first, then *Far from the Madding Crowd* and *The Return of the Native*. Trent's one eccentric judgment is that in *The Mayor of Casterbridge* 'the sun of Mr. Hardy's genius seems almost sunk from sight'.

In the early years of the twentieth century there were published several articles surveying Hardy's work as a whole. In the *Quarterly* for April 1904 Edward Wright used the occasion of Macmillan's uniform edition for a twenty-four page essay (No. 68). This is chiefly concerned with Hardy's insight into country life and peasant character: it concludes with a comparison of Hardy to Euripides, and the judgment that in certain of his later works he is, as a 'sentimental materialist'. a 'misdirected force'. In April 1908 a writer in the *Edinburgh Review* (CCVII, p. 448) on 'Ugliness in Fiction' used *Tess* and some of the short stories among his examples. (Others included *The Secret Agent* and *The Man of Property*.) A more substantial *Edinburgh Review* article was occasioned by F. Hedgcock's study of Hardy, in French (1911), and the Macmillan Pocket Edition of 1909, under the title 'The Wessex Drama' (January 1912, CCXV, p. 93). The 1912 collected edition was the occasion of an interesting article in the *Spectator* 'Novels of Character and Environment' (No. 73) by F. Manning. Hardy's didacticism is seen as a flaw in his work: considered purely as works of art, *Tess* and *Jude* are not the height of his achievement, for all their peculiar merits: in some ways *The Return of the Native* is more complete as a representation of life. *Blackwood's* also noticed this edition in a general essay by Charles Whibley (No. 74) which gives a fair idea of Hardy's critical reputation at this time. It touches on his 'intense feeling of locality', both in its human associations and its natural atmosphere and his profound awareness of rural life: 'never since the Georgics have the industries of the countryside been turned to literary account with so fine a sense of their enduring importance'. Against this background he sets dramas 'tense and simple, like the dramas of Sophocles'. His blemishes of style are superficial, and he will certainly survive more as a novelist than as a poet.

American periodicals from 1900 onwards show a similar increase in the number of general surveys of Hardy's work. In 1901 W. D. Howells's *Heroines of Fiction* had included two chapters dealing with Hardy, and P. H. Frye's *Literary Reviews and Criticisms* (1908) contains an essay on 'Nature and Thomas Hardy' which is largely a discussion of his tragic pessimism and 'cosmic irony'. The Boston *Atlantic Monthly* in 1906 (XCVIII, 354) had thirteen double-columned pages by Mary Moss commenting on all the novels in turn. She sums up Hardy's achievement as like Tennyson's in that 'he bridges the gulf between poetry and science. He holds fast to romance without slurring or ignoring the facts of actual life.' His intellectual irony would finally grow unbearable if it were not that 'the discouragement wrought by his pitiless logic is forever cancelled by his indestructible human sympathy'. Also from the *Atlantic Monthly* was W. L. Phelps's article, reprinted in his *Essays on Modern Novelists* in 1910 (No. 72). Phelps gives a brief life and summary chronological survey. He distinguishes between the pessimism of the earlier novels, which had been 'a noble ground quality', and 'the merely hysterical and wholly unconvincing' didactic pessimism of *Jude the Obscure*; and he praises especially Hardy's uncanny intimacy with nature. Finally there is the article contributed by Harold Williams to the *North American Review* for January 1914 (No. 75). This puts the stress on the more specifically Wessex novels, not simply as pictures of village manners, but as tragedy conveying a realization of the unity of the individual with universal life. The typical achievement is *The Woodlanders*, but the five tragedies culminate in *Tess*, the other three being *Far from the Madding Crowd*, *The Return of the*

Native, and *The Mayor of Casterbridge*. These are the same five that Douglas Brown was to select as central in his study some forty years later.

The volume of other material has made it impossible to include here any selections from full-length books on Hardy, but it should be noted that these had begun to appear as early as 1894. Lionel Johnson's *The Art of Thomas Hardy* devoted chapters to (among other topics) his choruses of country folk, his principal characters of men and women, and his idea of tragedy, especially as embodied in *Tess*. Though by modern standards excessively verbose and obtrusive of the critic's own personality, it raises a number of basic critical points and was for many years the best work on its subject. It was re-issued nearly thirty years later, in 1923, with a supplementary chapter on the poems. Also in 1894 there was published Annie Macdonell's less ambitious descriptive survey, which performed a useful function in its time. In the early 1900s books began to appear on Hardy's Wessex, and F. O. Saxelby brought out *A Thomas Hardy Dictionary*. By 1911 academic studies were getting into their stride with Helen Garwood's *Thomas Hardy: an Illustration of the Philosophy of Schopenhauer* and F. A. Hedgcock's *Essaie de Critique: Thomas Hardy penseur et artiste*. Lascelles Abercrombie's *Thomas Hardy: a Critical Study* (1912) typifies the critical attitude of the end of our period: Hardy is now the established man of letters and great tragic artist to be compared with Sophocles and Aeschylus: the acceptance is complete and the respect tends to be rather over-solemn.

The stages by which this position had been reached may be briefly summarized. At first the critics received rather coolly what they saw as the first experiments of a young writer under the influence now of Wilkie Collins, now of George Eliot. As Hardy developed his characteristic rural themes, George Eliot increasingly appeared the obvious comparison, and for the more discerning, a standard by which to judge him. Points about which the critics had misgivings were sensationalism in the development of plot, clumsiness and pedantry in the style where the author was speaking in his own person, and an unreal heightening of the wit and humour, as well as the general level of speech, of the rustic chorus. As George Eliot's reputation declined in the reaction soon after her death, she was less often invoked as a standard of comparison, and critics even began to blame her influence for the pedantic element in Hardy's style. Meanwhile appreciation was growing of his feeling for the rural tradition, his descriptions of nature, and his creation of atmosphere. Havelock Ellis's 1883 appraisal marks a further stage with its claims for psychological insight in the portrayal of women. Generally Hardy's urban and upper-class characters were felt to be unconvincing, and his strength was seen in rural tragedy. Occasionally the critics of the eighties would touch on his pessimism, or object, as with *The Woodlanders*, to a 'disagreeable' handling of sexual morality, but it was not until the nineties, with *Tess* and *Jude*, that critical discussion tended to be seriously distorted by outraged conventionality and the concentration upon moral and philosophical issues. The blunting of critical sensitiveness appears in the more extreme views of both sides in the debate: Hardy's most perceptive critics were not always those who spoke most loudly in defence of him as progressive and advanced. By the time the storm had died down, his work as a novelist was finished and could be surveyed as a whole in an increasingly distanced perspective. His thought was analysed and his tragic fictions classified and fitted into academic categories. The tendency to work out parallels with the classical tragedians was increased by the vast epic scale of *The Dynasts*: W. L. Courtney contributed a significant two-part essay to the *Fortnightly* on 'Mr. Hardy and Aeschylus'. But now the qualities of style and narrative technique which had provoked criticism earlier were less often remarked on, or tended to be played down.

CRITICISM SINCE 1914

The development of critical writing on Hardy since 1914 has been, first, a reaction against solemn academic adulation, with some tendency to turn to the poems rather than the novels,[5] and then the beginning of an attempt to make a new approach with a frank admission of faults, awkwardnesses of style and dated elements generally. Modern criticism is marked by a strong sense that Hardy's work is very mixed in quality and that its positive merits require careful disentangling: as yet the process can hardly be said to be complete. After the upheaval of the 1914–18 war, Hardy's work was bound to seem less subversive and startling than in the nineties: his essential Victorianism became more obvious, his assumptions of a solid background and a stable world that had now gone. An age that was learning to accept Lawrence and Joyce, an age re-discovering Conrad and James, tended rather to neglect the world of Wessex, though the older type of thorough exposition continued to be made (e.g. H. C. Duffin's *Thomas Hardy*, first published in 1916 and revised in 1937). The early criticisms of style were taken further in an influential piece of analysis of a passage from *Tess* by Vernon Lee (herself of course a Victorian) in *The Handling of Words* (1923). T. S. Eliot in his heresy-hunting phase in *After Strange Gods* (1934) reverted to something of the manner of Mowbray Morris or Mrs. Oliphant, though characteristically not without the occasional sharp perception embedded in a generally perverse judgment.[6] D. H. Lawrence's highly personal and idiosyncratic study was actually begun in 1914, though not published until after his death (in *Phoenix*, 1936). Middleton Murry had set the tone for a high valuation of Hardy's poetry in his *Athenaeum* essay, reprinted in *Aspects of Literature* (1920), and F. R. Leavis in *New Bearings in English Poetry* (1932) and later in *Scrutiny* (1952) gave penetrating analytical appreciations of the few poems that he held to achieve greatness. The modern sifting process referred to above may be most conveniently dated from the essays in the *Southern Review* Hardy Centennial Issue of summer 1940, certainly a landmark in Hardy criticism, though it is fair to note an anticipation of it in Frank Chapman's essay of 1934 in *Scrutiny*. Several of the *Southern Review* essays have been recently republished in the 'Twentieth Century Views' collection of essays on Hardy edited by Albert Guerard, whose own book on the novels appeared in 1949. Since then the most notable study, and possibly in its quiet way the most influential, has been Douglas Brown's *Thomas Hardy* of 1954, revised in 1961. Besides its sustained attempt to discriminate, through particular analysis of style and treatment, this embodies a further typical element in modern Hardy criticism, a strong sense of the relation between his work and the social and economic history of Victorian rural England.

NOTES

1. The main paragraphs of the letter are reprinted as an appendix to W. R. Rutland's *Thomas Hardy: A Study of his Writings and their Background* (1938), and the full text appears in Macmillan's collected *Letters* (1908).
2. According to Rutland, Hardy was never popular in Germany: he quotes a statement of 1928 that several attempts to get the novels taken up by a German publisher had failed. He notes, however, that *Tess* was translated and that *Jude* ran successfully as a serial in Germany (Rutland, p. 172 n.).
3. It is worth noting, however, that at this time *Harper's Magazine* was published simultaneously on both sides of the Atlantic.
4. R. L. Purdy, *Thomas Hardy, a Bibliographical Study* (pp. 71-3) records the negotiations in detail, and points out that Trollope in his *Autobiography* describes a similar experience with *Rachel Ray* and the editor of *Good Words*.

5. Cf. Ezra Pound's remark, in a letter of 1937, on Hardy's *Collected Poems:* 'Now *there* is clarity. There *is* the harvest of having written 20 novels first' (*Letters*, 1954).
6. It should be recorded that Eliot was dissatisfied with this book and allowed it to go out of print.

DESPERATE REMEDIES

March 1871

1. From an unsigned review, *Athenaeum*

1 April 1871, 398–9

In the editorial file this review is marked 'Callzer'. It is an extract from an article reviewing three novels by different authors.

Desperate Remedies, though in some respects an unpleasant story, is undoubtedly a very powerful one. We cannot decide, satisfactorily to our own mind, on the sex of the author; for while certain evidence, such as the close acquaintance which he or she appears (and, as far as we can judge, with reason) to possess with the mysteries of the female toilette, would appear to point to its being the work of one of that sex, on the other hand there are certain expressions to be met with in the book so remarkably coarse as to render it almost impossible that it should have come from the pen of an English lady. Yet, again, all the best anonymous novels of the last twenty years—a dozen instances will at once suggest themselves to the novel-reader—have been the work of female writers. In this conflict of evidence, we will confine ourselves to the inexpressive 'he' in speaking of our present author, if we chance to need a pronoun.

As to the story itself, it is, as we have said, disagreeable, inasmuch as it is full of crimes, in the discovery of which lies the main interest of the tale. We will not particularize them, as to do so would be to reveal the whole plot; but we may say that they are never purposeless, and that their revelation comes upon us step by step, and is worked out with considerable artistic power. The construction of the story is very curious. The various periods are accurately marked out in the headings of the chapters, and the sections into which they are divided. We have, for instance, 'Chapter III. The events of five days', and this will be subdivided into '1. November the twenty-ninth', '2. From November the twenty-ninth to December the second', and so throughout. If carefully carried out, as it is in the present book, this gives an air of reality which is far more satisfactory than the popular mottoes from some book of quotation which form the headings of chapters in nine-tenths of novels, though at the same time it may easily become an affectation.

The characters are often exceedingly good. The parish clerk, 'a sort of Bowdlerized rake', who refers to the time 'before he took orders', is really almost worthy of George Eliot, and so is the whole cider-making scene at the end of the first volume. The west-country dialect is also very well managed, without being a caricature. Occasionally, too, we come across a very happy hit—as, for instance, the allusion to 'the latent feeling which is rather common in these days among the unappreciated that, because some markedly successful men are fools, all markedly unsuccessful men are geniuses'; and the like.

There are a few faults of style and grammar, but very few. 'Whomsoever's' is an odd formation, and 'factitiously pervasive' is a clumsy expression. A lawyer, too, might find fault with a deed full of stops, and containing the phrase 'on the determination of this demise', and a surgeon with '*os femoris*', but these technical errors are few. On the whole, the chief blemish of the book will be found in the occasional coarseness to which we have alluded, and which we can hardly further particularize, but which, startling as it once or twice is, is confined wholly to expressions, and does not affect the main character of the story. If the author will purge himself of this, though even this is better than the prurient sentimentality with which we are so often nauseated, we see no reason why he should not write novels only a little, if at all, inferior to the best of the present generation.

2. Unsigned review, *Spectator*

22 April 1871, 481–3

See Introduction, p. xv.

This is an absolutely anonymous story; no falling back on previous works which might give a clue to the authorship, and no assumption of a *nom de plume* which might, at some future time, disgrace the family name, and still more, the Christian name of a repentant and remorseful novelist—and very right too. By all means let him bury the secret in the profoundest depths of his own heart, out of reach, if possible, of his own consciousness. The law is hardly just which prevents Tinsley Brothers from concealing their participation also.

There are things which men do voluntarily, against their own better judgment, but for which they have, at least, this excuse, that it is expected of them, and non-fulfilment of this expectation would lead to difficulty and complication; as when a clergyman professes belief in all that the Church teaches, and when a Chancellor of the Exchequer removes a tax which the people have decided is obnoxious. But we never heard of the man who got himself into difficulties by refusing to write a novel which no one but himself has had any thought of his writing. So that it seems to follow that our unknown author thinks either that his story is justifiable, or that he cannot do a better description of work, and must do something. On the first hypothesis, however, professing—as all novelists do, who do not wish to see their works scouted—and probably feeling sympathy with goodness and purity, he can scarcely uphold deliberately the propriety of encouraging, as far as in him lies, low curiosity about the detail of crime. Here are no fine characters, no original ones to extend one's knowledge of human nature, no display of passion except of the brute kind, no pictures of Christian virtue, unless the perfections of a stock-heroine are such; even the intricacies of the plot show no transcendent talent for arrangement of complicated, apparently irreconcilable, but really nicely-fitting facts. But there is—and therefore the second hypothesis notably fails also—an unusual and very happy facility in catching and fixing phases of peasant

3

life, in producing for us not the manners and language only, but the tone of thought—if it can be dignified by the name of thought—and the simple humour of consequential village worthies and gaping village rustics. So that we are irresistibly reminded of the paintings of Wilkie, and still more, perhaps, of those of Teniers with their lower moral tone and more unmistakable, though coarser humour. The scenes allotted to these humble actors are few and slight, but they indicate powers that might and ought to be extended largely in this direction, instead of being prostituted to the purposes of idle prying into the way of wickedness. If we dwell on the one or two redeeming features, and step in silence over the corrupt body of the tale, it is because, should our notice come under the eye of the author, we hope to spur him to better things in the future than these 'desperate remedies' which he has adopted for ennui or an emaciated purse. Here is a group round a cidermill, under a tree in front of the village inn:

[quotes ch. VIII, 3 from ' "And have you seen the steward . . ." ' to ' "God bless her!" ']

And here is another of wedding-bell ringers inside the old church tower in the moonlight. We wish we had space for the scene-painting as well as for the gossip:

[quotes ch. VIII, final section, from 'The triple-bob-major' to ' "There's more in Teddy." ']

This nameless author has, too, one other talent of a remarkable kind—sensitiveness to scenic and atmospheric effects, and to their influence on the mind, and the power of rousing similar sensitiveness in his readers. Take, for instance, this description of what the heroine sees through a window during the progress of a mid-day entertainment in a cool town-hall. The contrast between what is going on around her and what is going on at the spot that has absorbed her attention strikes us vividly, without being even alluded to; and her helplessness to prevent what we foresee is going to happen adds an awe to the dreaminess of a scene, commonplace enough, but for its height and distance and silence:

[quotes ch. I, from 'The town hall' to 'a new stone they were lifting.']

And the following brief description of a midsummer mid-day is a further illustration of the power, with a few effective strokes, not only

4

of giving the physical aspect of the scene, but of suggesting vividly the languor and aridity of the corresponding mental condition:

The day of their departure was one of the most glowing that the climax of a long series of summer heats could evolve. The wide expanse of landscape quivered up and down like the flame of a taper, as they steamed along through the midst of it. Placid flocks of sheep reclining under trees a little way off appeared of a pale blue colour. Clover fields were livid with the brightness of the sun upon their deep red flowers. All waggons and carts were moved to the shade by their careful owners; rain-water butts fell to pieces; well-buckets were lowered inside the covers of the well-hole, to preserve them from the fate of the butts, and generally, water seemed scarcer in the country than the beer and cider of the peasantry who toiled or idled there.

We wish we had space for the description of a village fire, and of its silent and stealthy growth in the autumn night, till 'the bewildered chimes' (of midnight), 'scarcely heard amid the crackling of the flames, wandered through the wayward air of the Old Hundred-and-Thirteenth Psalm'.

The story is disagreeable, and not striking in any way, and with the exception of the use made of a word in a sonnet which is certainly clever, is worked out by machinery always common-place, and some-times clumsy. A murder is at the root of it, of course; but though suspected, it is only brought home at last by the very dull expedient of a detective *seeing* the murderer remove the body from the oven of an unused building to a hole in a wood. With a vast superfluity of not remarkably clever invention, two other people, and all three unknown to each other, watch the same proceeding. The merest sensuality is the murderer's only motive—he has a wife, and wants another, and he even fills the interregnum with a mistress. His mother, an *un*married lady of position and fortune, is a miserable creation—uninteresting, unnatural, and nasty. But we have said enough to warn our readers against this book, and, we hope, to urge the author to write far better ones.

3. Unsigned review, *Saturday Review*

30 September 1871, xxxii, 441–2

This review may have been by Hardy's friend Horace Moule (see headnote to No. 5).

Under the rather sensational title of *Desperate Remedies*, a remarkable story has been written by a nameless author. Whole batches of novels come to the light of which little else can be said than that, in spite of general weakness, they have some element or other of attractiveness about them. There are plenty of novels of sensation, constructed with the object of taking one's breath away by bursting surprise or chronic suspense; novels of sentiment, of fashion, of sporting life—of all the highways of existence, in short, as well as of what are called the byways, clean or dirty. In many or most of these everything is sacrificed to the single specialty of the book, and art is but little thought of, or very feeble work indeed is done in its name. The consequence is that, though novels abound of which some individual good thing may be said, there are fewer than ever of which one would like to risk the downright opinion that they are worth reading. About *Desperate Remedies*, however, we should be willing to say as much as that cordially and without hesitation. The plot is worked out with abundant skill. Incidentally there are situations well fitted to enchain the fancy of the sincerest lover of melodrama; but not one of these is a *purpureus pannus* stitched into a circumjacent groundwork of dullness; nor, when all are taken together, can it be said that of these is the essence of the book. The essence of the book is precisely what it ought to be—namely, the evolution of character; and Cytherea Graye, the young beauty, with Miss Aldclyffe, the haughty but affectionate patroness who has a skeleton in the closet, are studies of very unusual merit.

None of the male characters come quite up to these protagonists among the women; but there is plenty of distinctive design and colouring all through the book, in men and women alike. The parish clerk, one Crickett, a 'Bowdlerized rake' with the rheumatism in his left hand and a great idea of his clerical position, is drawn something after the idea of Mr. Macey in *Silas Marner*; and, though he is far from equalling that admirable sketch, yet neither is he a copy, nor does he want life and movement of his own. Old Springrove, host of the Three Tranters Inn (tranters are irregular carriers), is the type of a class fast disappearing except in remote country districts. He is landlord of the inn, but more farmer than landlord; and for two months in the year more cider-maker than farmer. He is not provident, yet not imprudent; an employer of labour of the old school, who works himself among his men; and the sketch of him, like many other touches in this original and careful narrative, reminds us of the close and truthful drawing in Mr. Barnes's delightful *Dorset Poems* and *Hwomely Rhymes*. Edward Springrove, nephew of the landlord and the winner of Cytherea after a cruelly rugged series of love-passages, is not a particularly interesting character. Owen Graye, the beauty's brother, stands towards her very much as a more refined and sympathetic Tom Tulliver might have stood towards Maggie. Æneas Manston is the villain of the story; he is 'a voluptuary with activity, a very bad form of man, as bad as it is rare'; and withal he is the natural son of Miss Aldclyffe, born in the distant days of her youth (she is now between forty and fifty), long before she had the remotest idea of becoming mistress of Knapwater Hall. With the exception of a rather common fault in able sketches of villains, Manston is well done. The fault we mean is a cumulation of gifts and excellences, bodily and mental, on the undesirable person, until he becomes an Alcibiades in form and brain, and a Crichton in accomplishments. Even this fault, however, runs to no wild excess in the volumes before us; the author of *Desperate Remedies* has from first to last kept himself well in hand, and he has much too clear an eye for art to indulge himself, as some writers do, in drawing what is hideous or monstrous for mere monstrosity's sake.

[here follows a full summary of the story with extracts.]

We will conclude with one or two general remarks on the style and structure of the book. Like George Eliot the author delights in running off to *sententiæ*, in generalizing abstractions out of the special point in hand. He inclines to this intellectual pastime a little too often, and with a little too much of laboured epigram. For example:

A great statesman thinks several times, and acts; a young lady acts, and thinks several times.

Some women kindle emotion so rapidly in a man's heart, that the judgment cannot keep pace with its rise, and finds, on comprehending the situation, that faithfulness to the old love is already treachery to the new. Such women are not necessarily the greatest of their sex, but there are very few of them.

Nyttleton was a man who surveyed everybody's character in a sunless and shadowless northern light. A culpable slyness, which marked him as a boy, had been moulded by Time, the Improver, into honourable circumspection.

We frequently find that the quality which, conjoined with the simplicity of the child, is vice, is virtue when it pervades the knowledge of the man.

This is all good in its way, but a book may be easily overloaded with it. We may add that a familiarity with several kinds of manual work adds great point to the author's natural power of vivid description. The cider-making scene is too long to quote, but it is excellent reading; it is the same sort of thing in written sentences that a clear fresh country piece of Hobbema's is in art. We might mention other passages of rare merit; the long talk of Cytherea with her brother on the wedding-day contains, for example, a very remarkable analysis of thought and feeling. But we have said enough to indicate our opinion of the author. We sincerely hope to hear of him again, for his deserts are of no ordinary kind.

UNDER THE GREENWOOD TREE

May 1872

---

4. From an unsigned review, *Athenaeum*

15 June 1872, 748-9

In the editorial file this review is marked 'Callzer'. It deals with three other novels besides Hardy's.

We quite agree with the opinion expressed the other day by a contemporary, that every author who does not wish to publish his or her name, should be compelled to adopt and adhere to a *nom de plume*. One of the letters of the alphabet would do, and when these were exhausted, we might have all their possible permutations taken two or three together. Anything would be better than the nuisance of having to write, 'The author of this, that, or the other', every time that we wish to indicate the person whose work we are considering. In spite of this objection, however, we are glad to meet again with the author of *Desperate Remedies*, and to find that in his new novel he has worked principally that vein of his genius which yields the best produce, and wherein his labours result in more satisfaction to his readers than did his explorations into the dark ways of human crime and folly. Our readers may possibly remember, that while praising *Desperate Remedies* for many marks of ability, we especially commended it for its graphic pictures of rustic life somewhere in the West Country. Here the author is clearly on his own ground, and to this he has confined himself in the book before us. *Under the Greenwood Tree* is simply the history of a young man's courtship of a young woman, the young man being the son of the local 'tranter', or occasional carrier, and the young woman the certificated schoolmistress of the village. It is an old commonplace to say that there is just as much romance, together with just as keen an interest in the loves of two young persons of this humble station, as in

9

any courtship which ends at St. George's. But it is not every one who can make as good a novel out of the one as out of the other, or produce out of such simple materials a story that shall induce us to give up valuable time in order to see the marriage fairly accomplished. Nor is our author destitute of humour, whether he is relating the peregrinations of the village choir at Christmas, or the incidents which accompany the process of taking honey from the hive. We must give our readers a fragment of this last episode. Geoffrey Day, gamekeeper and bee-master, is the hero of it:

'Have the craters stung ye?' said Enoch to Geoffrey.—'No, not much—only a little here and there,' he said with leisurely solemnity, shaking one bee out of his shirt-sleeve, pulling another from among his hair, and two or three more from his neck. The others looked on during this proceeding with a complacent sense of being out of it—much as a European nation in a state of internal commotion is watched by its neighbours. 'Are those all of them, father?' said Fancy, when Geoffrey had pulled away five.—'Almost all, though I feel a few more sticking into my shoulder and side. Ah! there's another just begun again upon my backbone. You lively young martels, how did you get inside there? However, they can't sting me many times more, poor things, for they must be getting weak. They may as well stay in me till bedtime now, I suppose.' As he himself was the only person affected by this arrangement, it seemed satisfactory enough.

We have seldom met with anything much better than the calm superiority which regards the angry bees as 'poor things'.

As to the faults of the book. First of all, there is the tendency of the author to forget his part, as one may call it, and to make his characters now and then drop their personality, and speak too much like educated people. We cannot conceive such a dialogue as this between a small farmer and a gamekeeper's daughter, certificated though she be:

'You don't accept attentions very freely.'—'It depends upon who offers them.' —'A fellow like me, for instance.'—'It then depends upon how they are offered.' —'Not wildly, and yet not indifferently; not intentionally, and yet not by chance; not actively nor idly; quickly nor slowly.'—'How then?' said Fancy.— 'Coolly and practically,' he said. 'How would that kind of love be taken?'— 'Not anxiously, and yet not carelessly; neither quickly nor slowly; neither redly nor palely; not religiously nor quite wickedly.'—'How then?'—'Not at all.'

This would have drawn down the house in a comedy by the late Mr. Robertson, but it is not the talk of rustics. A little more observation, or rather cultivation of that gift (which the author possesses in abundance), would show him this, and he would then give us what this book, in spite of its second title, falls short of being, a 'Rural Painting of the Dutch School'. His present work is rather a number of studies for such a painting. The ability to paint is there, but practice only can give the power of composition.

5. Horace Moule, *Saturday Review*

28 September 1872, xxxiv, 417

Horace Moule was a classical scholar, critic and leader-writer, and an early friend of Hardy. He committed suicide in 1873.

This novel is the best prose idyl that we have seen for a long while past. Deserting the more conventional, and far less agreeable, field of imaginative creation which he worked in his earlier book, called *Desperate Remedies*, the author has produced a series of rural pictures full of life and genuine colouring, and drawn with a distinct minuteness reminding one at times of some of the scenes in *Hermann und Dorothea*. Anyone who knows tolerably well the remoter parts of the South-Western counties of England will be able to judge for himself of the power and truthfulness shown in these studies of the better class of rustics, men whose isolated lives have not impaired a shrewd common sense and insight, together with a complete independence, set off by native humour, which is excellently represented in these two volumes.

Reuben Dewy, the 'tranter' or irregular carrier, is the principal character in the book, and is the most fully worked-out type of the class we have been mentioning. At the very outset of events, during the rounds made by the Christmas 'waits' of Mellstock parish church, Dick Dewy, the son and partner of Reuben, falls in love with Fancy Day, daughter of a neighbouring keeper well to do in the world, and newly appointed schoolmistress of the parish. The 'course of true love' in this simple village couple, interrupted only by the gawky attentions of Mr. Shinar, a wealthy farmer and churchwarden, and by a curious episode with the vicar towards the end, forms the unpretending thread of the story. But the subsidiary scenes, such as the description of the carol-singers' rounds, the village-party at the tranter's, the interview of the choir with the vicar, and the bee-taking at the keeper Geoffrey Day's, are worked in with as much care as if the writer had been constructing a sensation plot of the received model; and each one of these scenes contributes its share to a really pleasant and entertaining whole.

Under the Greenwood Tree is filled with touches showing the close sympathy with which the writer has watched the life, not only of his fellow-men in the country hamlets, but of woods and fields and all the outward forms of nature. But the staple of the book is made up of personal sketches, the foremost figure, as we have said, being that of the 'tranter' Dewy, a man 'full of human nature', fond of broaching his cider with his village friends about him, straightforward and outspoken, yet inclined from good nature towards compromise, not however to the excessive degree that his duties as publican imposed upon Mr. Snell in *Silas Marner*. Grouped around the tranter are several figures, all distinctive and good in their way, the chief of whom are old William Dewy, the grandfather, and the leader in all things musical, Mr. Penny the bootmaker, and Thomas Leaf, who sang treble in the choir at a preternaturally late date, and whose upper G could not be dispensed with, though he was otherwise 'deficient', and awkward in his movements, 'apparently on account of having grown so fast that before he had had time to grow used to his height he was higher'. The description of the old choir-leader is too good to be passed over:

His was a humorous and gentle nature, not unmixed with a frequent melancholy; and he had a firm religious faith. But to his neighbours he had no character in particular. If they saw him pass by their windows when they had been bottling off old mead, or when they had just been called long-headed men who might do anything in the world if they chose, they thought concerning him, 'Ah, there's that good-hearted man—open as a child!' If they saw him just after losing a shilling or half-a-crown, or accidentally letting fall a piece of crockery, they thought, 'There's that poor weak-minded man Dewy again! Ah, he'll never do much in the world either!' If he passed when fortune neither smiled nor frowned on them, they merely thought him old William Dewy.

We doubt whether the night's doings of a party of carol-singers have ever been half so well told as in this novel.

[here follows a descriptive account, with quotations.]

It is strong praise of any book to say that, besides being a novel of great humour and general merit, it would make no bad manual for any one who, from duty or from choice, is desirous to learn something of the inner life of a rural parish. Yet *Under the Greenwood Tree* fairly deserves the amount of praise. It is a book that might well lie on the table of any well-ordered country house, and that might also be borne in mind by the readers during kindly rounds undertaken among the cottages. There are, to be sure, weak points in the writing. The love passages of Dick and Fancy incline here and there to be unnecessarily prolonged, and it is needful throughout to recollect that they are being faithfully drawn as *rustic* lovers. There is also one definite fault in the dialogues, though it makes its appearance only at wide intervals. We mean an occasional tendency of the country folk, not so much to think with something of subtle distinction (for cottagers can do that much more completely than the well-dressed world are apt to suppose), but to express themselves in the language of the author's manner of thought, rather than in their own. The tranter, for example, should not be allowed to call the widow Leaf (in an otherwise very amusing passage) an 'imaginative woman on the subject of children'; nor should old William speak of barrel-organs and harmoniums, even though he has wound himself up for a great effort, as 'miserable machines for such a divine thing as music'.

There is nothing better in the whole book than the pictures of Geoffrey Day and his house in the greenwood. Geoffrey was a man of few words. His neighbours were fully alive to this 'Silent', they would say: 'ah, he is silent! That man's silence is wonderful to listen to. Every moment of it is brimming over with sound understanding.' His trapper Enoch was almost as silent as himself. This man was admitted to take his dinner at the keeper's table, and would come in behind his master, at the carefully considered interval of three minutes. 'Four minutes had been found to express indifference to indoor arrangements, and simultaneousness had implied too great an anxiety about meals.' The keeper's description of his second wife, 'your stap-mother, Fancy', is very amusingly done:

'Yes: you see her first husband was a young man, who let her go too far; in fact, she used to kick up Bob's-a-dying at the least thing in the world. And when I'd married her and found it out, I thought, thinks I, " 'Tis too late now to begin to cure ye;" and so I let her bide. But she's quare,—very quare, at times!'

'I'm sorry to hear that.'

'Yes: there; wives be such a provoking class of society, because though they be never right, they be never more than half wrong.'

The double sets of furniture, one being destined for Fancy whenever she should marry, and the two eight-day clocks, 'which were severally two and a half minutes and three minutes striking the hour of twelve', and which bore respectively the names of two rival clockmakers, long since departed, Thomas Wood and Ezekiel Sparrowgrass—these and innumerable other touches combine to make up the picture of an interior entirely justifying the author's mention of the Dutch school upon his title-page. The bee-taking we must leave alone, though it is a thoroughly amusing and well-drawn scene; and the same may be said of the passage about Elizabeth Endorfield, the witch, or, in more modified terms, the 'deep body, who was as long-headed as she was high'. We will take leave of Geoffrey with one brief and characteristic touch, which will come home to any one who has observed the ways of dogs. Having been out with his trapper, he had been made unusually pensive by that person's account of the pining state into which Fancy had been thrown by her father's temporary refusal of Dick's offer, and his preference for Mr. Shinar. Upon this 'the keeper resumed his gun, tucked it under his arm, and went on without whistling to the dogs, who however followed, with a bearing meant to convey that they did not expect any such attentions when their master was reflecting'. It is needless to say that their master soon relented, and that all ends happily. The portraiture of Fancy herself conveys a kind of satire on the average character of a girl with good looks, capable of sound and honest affection, but inordinately moved by admiration. Serious mischief threatens for a moment, just towards the close, on the side of the Vicar; but this episode, whether wisely introduced or not, is too brief to signify much in the working out of the story.

Regarded as a whole, we repeat our opinion that the book is one of unusual merit in its own special line, full of humour and keen observation, and with the genuine air of the country breathing throughout it.

A PAIR OF BLUE EYES

May 1873

6. Unsigned review, *Saturday Review*

2 August 1873, xxxvi, 158-9

Many readers of the fresher and truer sorts of fiction will be glad to welcome another story from the author of *Under the Greenwood Tree*, who now for the first time assumes his real name. Mr. Hardy produces rapidly, but the novel now before us is a thoroughly matured work of its kind, and bears none of the traces of viciously stimulated workmanship. He still has a sprinkling of small oddities in style, and of minor errors of taste. He occasionally uses cumbrous words, like 'synthetized' and 'filamentous', where simpler ones would have served the purpose; and the word 'empirically' occurs in a passage where it cannot be said accurately to retain its own meaning or to convey the author's. He puts the phrase 'sweetheart' into a position which it does not really hold among the social class which he is describing, although it is hard to assign any good reason on their part for discarding a word of Elizabethan use, before finding a worthy equivalent. He also designs the mode of life led by the heroine and her lovers with a kind of defiance of conventionality, though in each case the circumstances go far to justify what is done. Yet, when all drawbacks have been enumerated, few readers would charge *A Pair of Blue Eyes* with having been produced before its time. It is one of the most artistically constructed among recent novels. And, from considerations affecting higher matters than mere construction, we would assign it a very high place among works of its class.

The distinctive feature of this novel is that out of simple materials there has been evolved a result of really tragic power. The whole centres round the figure of Elfride, bred in the solitudes of the West country, the motherless and only daughter of a Cornish vicar; and the tragedy consists in the operation of quite ordinary events upon her sensitive and conscious, but perfectly simple, nature. By some of his former critics Mr. Hardy has been unwisely compared with George Eliot. In reality, no two writers could be more unlike in their general methods. But in one respect there is a decided resemblance—namely, that Mr. Hardy has in the book before us developed, with something of the ruthlessness of George Eliot, what may be called the tragedy of circumstance, the power of mere events on certain kinds of character. By mere events we mean a sequence in the evolution of which no moral obliquity, no deliberate viciousness of choice, can be said to have had a share. For this is another point of merit in Mr. Hardy's book, that he has kept up interest throughout it at an unusually high degree, not only without a single crime or a single villain, but with men of honest hearts and high aims for the pillars of his story, and literally without resorting, on any one's part, to a single action which when weighed and sifted, can be condemned outright.

Mr. Swancourt, Elfride's father, is well drawn as a relief and a background to the delicate and tremulous figure of his daughter. He is a worldly, gentlemanlike, commonplace parson of the old school. Belonging to an ancient but impoverished stock, he is prouder of that than of an indirect connection, through Elfride's dead mother, with the neighbouring peer, Lord Luxellian. While still regarding Stephen Smith, Elfride's first lover, in his actual and personal position of a promising young London architect, he recklessly favours the attachment between the two; but when it turns out that the same Stephen Smith is by parentage son to John Smith, Lord Luxellian's master mason, he as promptly turns his back, and pronounces a characteristic condemnation:

'I was inclined to suspect him, because he didn't care about sauces of any kind. I always did doubt a man's being a gentleman if his palate had no acquired tastes. An unedified palate is the irrepressible cloven foot of the upstart. The idea of my bringing out a bottle of my '40 Martinez—only eleven of them left now —to a man who didn't know it from eighteen-penny!'

With this discovery about Stephen Smith the weaving of the tragic web begins. He has gained a favourable footing in the Vicarage, as the responsible emissary of a London house charged with the restoration of the church; and he weakly but pardonably puts off disclosing his real birth to the Vicar until an accident that befalls his father lays everything open. It need hardly be said that this family connection of

Stephen's enables Mr. Hardy to throw in many of those sketches of genuine country life in drawing which he has already shown a master's hand. The rustic circle makes a little gallery of portraiture as distinct as it is lifelike.

[here follows a passage of descriptive summary and illustrative quotation.]

But the peculiar position of Stephen Smith serves for much more than the mere canvas on which to lay these scenes from the remote country. In place of an unreal and nonsensical picture of passion defying the social barriers of actual life, the novel conveys (without the appearance of intending it) a powerful representation of what those barriers are in fact, and of what, though perhaps in a modified degree, they are likely to remain. In the case of Elfride herself, though she is as superior to social differences as any finehearted girl could be expected to be, yet after the arrival of the second lover these differences work their sure part in the cumulation of her sorrows. To the principal tragic thread of the book we must now recur. We have abstained from any definite analysis of the story, because, where sequence and connection are so delicately worked as they are here, that is hardly fair to either writer or reader; but we hasten on to the points which are essential.

After the *dénouement* brought about by his father's accident, Stephen takes his departure, and by and by goes to fulfil some commissions in India, which lead to his rapid advance. But before he finally leaves, the young pair plan a sort of escapade, which need not here be further explained, entirely innocent in its design as well as in its imperfect execution, but painfully liable to misconception, and unhappily discovered by a single pair of hostile eyes. In due course the new lover appears. He has the advantage of being several years older than his predecessor, a matured man of experience, a writer in reviews, and withal a relative of the rich widow whom Mr. Swancourt opportunely marries. He is the least natural character in the book, and he inclines here and there unmistakably to priggishness. Yet prigs are, as a matter of fact, to be met with in society; and it was essential that he should be a little stilted, and something of a purist in his notions about women. Little by little, and without a trace of conscious effort, he acquired a complete ascendency over Elfride. He 'swayed her as the tree sways the nest'. All the most refined and most thoroughly womanly elements in her nature contend on the side of the new comer. She longs not to be a queen, but to lean and to be governed; to be a necessity indeed, but rather to worship than be worshipped. It must be added that this new man, Henry Knight, has been the benefactor of Stephen, has helped him forward in the world, and has been in earlier days belauded to her by his *protégé*, until she would grow jealous of the clever friend who now dominates her. Yet, even so, she would have remained faithful to her first lover but for an adventure on the cliffs, when the imminent presence of death forces Knight and herself into an unconscious and inevitable avowal. Of the two chapters which record the ten minutes spent by Knight while he hangs between life and death on the edge of the seacrag, and his final rescue by the despairing wit and devotion of Elfride, we will only say that they are worked out with extraordinary force, and that they recall the intense minuteness and vivid concentration of the most powerful among French writers of fiction.

[summary of the latter part of the story follows.]

The author of *A Pair of Blue Eyes* has much to learn, and many faults yet to avoid. But he is a writer who to a singular purity of thought and intention unites great power of imagination, strong enough to sustain interest at a very high point of vitality, without resorting to mere surprises or descending to what is ignoble.

FAR FROM THE MADDING CROWD
November 1874

7. From an unsigned review, *Athenaeum*
5 December 1874, 747–8

In the editorial file this review is marked 'Britten'. It deals with
five other novels besides Hardy's.

Mr. Hardy, who has now, we think, for the first time allowed his
name to appear on a title-page, is at once an interesting and a disappointing writer. He is, perhaps, the most vigorous of all the novelists
who have appeared within the last few years; his powers of description,
his skill in devising 'situations', his quaint humour, secure him a high
place among novelists of any age; while, on the other hand, a sort of
recklessness seems at times to overcome and neutralize all these qualities, and the coarseness upon which we remarked in reviewing his
Desperate Remedies, some four years ago, still disfigures his work and
repels the reader. He is evidently a shrewd observer of the talk and
habits of the Somersetshire rustics; and yet he puts such expressions
into their mouths as 'Passably well put', 'Every looker-on's inside
shook with the blows of the great drum to his deepest vitals, and there
was not a dry eye throughout the town', and so on—expressions which
we simply cannot believe possible from the illiterate clods whom he
describes. Then, though his style is often admirable, he gives us such
monstrous periphrases as 'a fair product of Nature in a feminine direction', and other specimens of the worst 'penny-a-liner's' language, till
we almost despair of him; and then, a little further on, we come to
such an admirable variation of an old aphorism as 'Men take wives
because possession is not possible without marriage, and women accept
husbands because marriage is not possible without possession.' And so
on throughout the book, 'nil fuit unquam sic impar sibi'; and we are

19

alternately attracted and repelled by admirable delineations of man and nature on the one hand, and gross improbabilities on the other, till we lay it down, unable to say whether the author is an ill-regulated genius or a charlatan with some touches of cleverness. How his present story could ever have even been supposed to be written by George Eliot we cannot conceive, though her influence has been plainly visible in some of his former books; we should say, on the contrary, that some of the scenes, notably that where Sergeant Troy goes through the sword exercise before Bathsheba, are worthy, in their extravagance, of Mr. Reade, and of him only; while the stronger parts are Mr. Hardy's own. At least we know of no other living author who could so have described the burning rick-yard, or the approaching thunderstorm, or given us the wonderful comicalities of the supper at the malthouse. The contrasted characters of the three chief men of the story are also well worked out; the man of single eye, who waits and works patiently, scarcely hoping even for recognition, but ready to help the woman he loves, literally through fire and water; the profligate soldier, who comes, sees, and, for a time, conquers; and the reserved, middle-aged farmer, falling in love for the first time at forty, and then driven almost, if not quite, to insanity by disappointment—all play their parts well, and take their due shares in the development of the story. On the whole, we leave Mr. Hardy with some hope. He ought to hold his peace for at least two years, revise with extreme care, and refrain from publishing in magazines; then, though he has not done it yet, he may possibly write a nearly, if not quite, first-rate novel.

8. R. H. Hutton, *Spectator*

19 December 1874, 1597-9

R. H. Hutton (1826–97), theologian, journalist, and man of letters, was at first a Unitarian, but later accepted the principles of the Church of England. He edited several periodicals during the fifties, and from 1861 to 1897 was joint editor and part-proprietor of the *Spectator*.

No one who reads this very original and amusing story will doubt for a moment that it is the production of a very high order of ability and humour. Everything in the book is fresh, and almost everything in the book is striking. The life of the agricultural districts in the South-Western counties—Dorsetshire probably—is a new field for the novelist, and at least so far as the physical forms of nature and the external features of the farm-work are concerned, it has been mastered by the author of this tale. The details of the farming and the sheep-keeping, of the labouring, the feasting, and the mourning, are painted with all the vividness of a powerful imagination, painting from the stores of a sharply-outlined memory. The reader sees in turn the life of the shepherd in lambing-time, of the bailiff and his out-door labourers at the homestead, of the mistress on her pay-day, the interior of the malt-house and its gossip, the corn-market at the county town, the thunder-storm which breaks up the fine harvest weather, the rural inn and its company, the sheep-fair on the downs, the tenant-farmer's Christmas merry-making or effort at merry-making, and the village group which watches the entrance of the Judge into the Assize town; and from everything he reads he carries away new images, and as it were, new experience, taken from the life of a region before almost unknown. A book like this is, in relation to many of the scenes it describes, the nearest equivalent to actual experience which a great many of us are ever likely to boast of. But the very certainty we feel that this is the case—that we have no adequate means of checking a good deal of the very fresh and evidently closely-observed detail which we find in this book—puts us upon asking all the more anxiously whether all the vivacious description we have here is quite trustworthy, not only in its picture of the scenery and ways of life, but in its picture of the human beings who give the chief interest to that scenery and those ways of life. And here the reader who has any general acquaintance with the civilization of the Wiltshire or Dorsetshire labourer, with his average wages, and his average intelligence, will be disposed to say at once that a more incredible picture than that of the group of farm labourers as a whole which Mr. Hardy has given us can hardly be conceived—that he has filled his canvas with an assemblage of all the exceptional figures which a quick-witted humorist might discover here and there and sift with much pains out of a whole county; that if any one society of agricultural labourers were at all like that which we find here, that class, as a whole, must be a treasure-house of such eccentric shrewdness and profane-minded familiarity with the Bible, as would cancel at once the reputation rural England has got for a heavy, bovine character, and would justify us in believing it to be a rich mine of quaintnesses and oddities, all dashed with a curious flavour of mystical and Biblical transcendentalism. Even in the delineations of the less humble characters there is plenty of reason to suspect that Mr. Hardy has from time to time embodied in the objects of his studies some of the subtler thoughts which they have suggested to his own mind, or some of the more cultivated metaphors to which he would himself have given utterance had he been in their place, but which come most unnaturally from the mouths from which they actually proceed. Thus when the farm-labourers are coming up to be paid, the maltster's great grand-daughter, Liddy Smallbury, who is the farming heroine's humble companion—half-friend, half-servant—announces this event to her mistress in the words, 'The Philistines are upon us!' just as an art critic might say when the general public swarm in on the day of a private view; and again, the old maltster, who can't either count or speak English, is made to say, when moralizing on the uprooting of an apple-tree and the transformation of a pump, with an extravagance that must be intended for broad humour, 'How the face of nations alter, and what great revolutions we live to see now-a-days!' Nay, even the poorest creatures in the story break out into the same kind of intellectual banter, not only at times, but almost habitually. For instance, Jan Coggan, a rural labourer, who, on his first introduction, is delineated as the joker of his class, though an elderly member of it, is described as bantering a poor fellow named Laban Tall (who is under the strict dominion of a wife he has just married), on his early retreat from their social gathering, in the following words, 'New lords, new laws, as the saying is!'—a remark, as it seems to us, of quite another moral latitude and longitude, just as the repeater-watch which, it appears, on the occasion of a drunken revel in the barn—in celebration of the harvest and of the mistress's marriage—that the same Jan Coggan carries in his waistcoat-pocket, seems to suggest a totally different world of physical belongings. But the peculiarity, as we have already hinted, of this tale is, that not merely one or two, but almost all the labourers introduced in it talk in a peculiar style, deeply infiltrated with the suggestions of a kind of moral irony mostly borrowed, no doubt, from the study of the Bible, but still applied in a manner in which neither uneducated Churchmen nor uneducated Dissenters (and these people are all of the Church) would dream of applying it. When Mause Headrigg, in *Old Mortality*, says, 'By the aid of my God I have leaped over a wall', the humour is in the novelist, not in her who applies the text in grim puritanic seriousness. But when Bathsheba Everdene reproaches her servant, Maryann Money, 'a person who for a face had a circular disc, furrowed less by age than by long gazes of perplexity at distant objects', with not being married and off her hands, and that individual replies, 'What between the poor men I won't have, and the rich men who won't have me, I stand forlorn as a pelican in the wilderness—ah poor soul of me!' we recognize at once the introduction of a satiric vein belonging to the author's own mental plane into the language of a class very far removed from it. The same traces of an intellectual graft on coarse and vulgar thoughts are visible in every one of the many amusing and often most humorous conversations recorded in this book. The whole class of hoers, sowers, ploughmen, reapers, &c., are—if Mr. Hardy's pictures may be trusted —the most incredibly amusing and humorous persons you ever came across, full of the quaintest irony and the most comical speculative intelligence. Mrs. Gamp is an impossible though most amusing impersonation of the monthly nurse. But Mrs. Gamp makes no claim to any shrewdness beyond the shrewdness of the most profound selfishness; for the rest, she is only a delightful and impossible concentration of the essence of all conceivable monthly-nurse experiences. But these poor men are quizzical critics, inaccurate divines, keen-eyed men of the world, who talk a semi-profane, semi-Biblical dialect full of veins of humour which have passed into it from a different sphere.

Mr. Hardy himself has adopted a style of remark on his own imaginative creations which is an exaggeration of George Eliot's, but he has made the mistake which George Eliot never makes, of blending a good deal of this same style of thought with the substance of his drawings. The following passage strikes us as a study almost in the nature of a careful caricature of George Eliot:

The phases of Boldwood's life were ordinary enough, but his was not an ordinary nature. Spiritually and mentally, no less than socially, a commonplace general condition is no conclusive proof that a man has not potentialities above that level. In all cases this state may be either the mediocrity of inadequacy, as was Oak's, or what we will venture to call the mediocrity of counterpoise, as was Boldwood's. The quiet mean to which we originally found him adhering, and in which, with few exceptions, he had continually moved, was that of neutralization: it was not structural at all. That dullness, which struck casual observers more than anything else in his character and habit, and seemed so precisely like the rest of inanition, may have been the perfect balance of enormous antagonistic forces—positives and negatives in fine adjustment. His equilibrium disturbed, he was in extremity at once.

Again, the words we have italicized in the following short description of the labourer Joseph Poorgrass, when he is in a state of alarm at Shepherd Oak's burst of wrath, are still more close to George Eliot's ordinary style of criticism on her characters, and might easily have betrayed a casual reader into a belief that it was her work he had taken up:

'We hear that ye be an extraordinary good and clever man, shepherd,' said Joseph Poorgrass, with considerable anxiety from behind the maltster's bedstead, whither he had retired for safety. ' 'Tis a great thing to be clever, I'm sure,' he added, *making small movements associated with states of mind rather than body;* 'we wish we were, don't we, neighbours?'

But George Eliot never confuses her own ideas with those of her dramatic figures, as Mr. Hardy seems to us so often to do. For instance, the exceedingly amusing but rather impossible person just referred to in the previous extract, Joseph Poorgrass, is made to say, in the course of a speech intended to prove that he must leave his drinking companions and get to his work, 'I've been drinky once this month already, and I did not go to church a-Sunday, and I dropped a curse or two yesterday; so I don't want to go too far from my safety. *Your next world is your next world, and not to be squandered lightly*'—where we maintain that the last sentence is quite out of the plane of the rest of the speech, and much more in the style of half-cynical culture. Again, in the same conversation, Jan Coggan remarks, 'Joseph Poorgrass, don't be so miserable. Parson Thirdly won't mind. He's a generous man; he's found me in tracts for years, and *I've consumed a good many in the course of a long and rather shady life*; but he's never been the man to complain of the expense, sit down',—where, again, we maintain that the tone of the words we have italicized is not the tone of such a labourer at all, but the tone of a man of some culture girding at himself. Indeed, throughout his most amusing and humorous pictures of the rural labourer's talk, Mr. Hardy seems to us, while using first-rate materials derived from real observation, constantly to be shuffling his own words or tone of thought with those of the people he is describing. It is the main fault of drawing in a most amusing book. But it is a great one.

As to the main characters of the story, it seems to us that two, namely, Sergeant Troy and Farmer Boldwood, are both of them conceived and executed with very great power, while Shepherd Oak and Bathsheba remain from the beginning to the end only half-conceived and half-drawn figures. The stiffness, the awkward reserve, the seeming stolidity, the latent heat, and the smouldering passion which when once kindled eats up Farmer Boldwood's whole nature, are painted with the pen of a considerable artist, nor does the vigour of the picture ever flag for a moment; and the tragical *dénouement* is in the strictest keeping with the first description of Boldwood's mode of receiving Bathsheba's careless Valentine; Again, Sergeant Troy's bold and unprincipled gallantry, his reckless selfishness, and his bursts of at once cruel and remorseful passion when he finds he has killed the only woman he ever loved, without casting a thought on the fact that he has also ruined the happiness of the woman he married, but did not love, are equally strongly painted, and the scene in which he exhibits to Bathsheba his dexterity with his sword is one of quite exceptional power and skill. Among the minor characters, the common-place, but good-natured Liddy Smallbury, Bathsheba's servant-companion, and Fanny Robin, the victim of Sergeant Troy, seem to us much the most complete and consistent. There are delicacy and finish in both these common-place studies, and barring the one exclamation we have quoted from Liddy, 'The Philistines are on us', there is nothing whatever out of drawing. Liddy's language of familiar praise and remonstrance to her mistress is always admirably conceived, and even in the smallest details her bearing is perfectly imagined, as, for instance, in the scene where her mistress summons the labourers on the farm to make it known that she will employ no bailiff for the future, but at the same time inaugurates her own reign by the generous present of half-a-sovereign each. When Bathsheba poured out her small heap of coin on the table, 'Liddy took up a position at her elbow, and began to sew, sometimes pausing and looking round, or, with the air of a privileged person, taking up one of the half-sovereigns lying before her, and admiringly surveying it as a work of art merely, strictly preventing her countenance from expressing any wish to possess it as money'. That is but a touch. But everything seems to us to be in keeping with that touch. And the few scenes in which Fanny Robin is sketched are equally skilful.

It is a disappointment to us not to speak equally well of the hero and heroine, as they may be called, Oak and Bathsheba. But they appear to us to have shared the fate of so many heroes and heroines in more cultivated classes, of being liable to the charge of a certain want of intellectual meaning. Oak is from the first a paragon of a shepherd and manager, and though he can speak his mind plainly enough to the mistress to whom he is so much devoted, there is always a sense on the reader's part of not really knowing the background of his character. Bathsheba is at first much more strongly outlined, and during the scenes in which she falls in love with Troy we begin to think Mr. Hardy is likely to make something great of her. But, on the whole, she falls back into an uninterestingness of which we cannot exactly define the reason, unless it is her disposition to shilly-shally with Farmer Boldwood after her loss of Troy, which seems unnatural in a young woman of so very strong a character, who had already had so much experience of the consequences of a false step.

It would be a very defective criticism of this striking tale which said nothing of the beauty of its descriptive sketches. Many of them are pictures of the most delicate and vivid beauty—watercolours in words, and very fine ones too. Take this, for instance, of a summer dawn:

[quotes ch. XLIV 'A coarse-throated chatter' to 'as Bathsheba had anticipated.']

On the whole, the book is amusing and exceedingly clever even in its mistakes and faults—and so that whether we admire its delineations of life, or think them impossible, we are always interested, and always inclined to admire the author, though not *for* his mistakes. This is a very rare characteristic of modern novelists. Most of them are conventional when they go wrong; Mr. Hardy goes wrong by being too clever—preposterously clever where the world is stupid—too original where he ought to be accommodating himself to the monotonous habits of a world which is built on usage. It is a rare kind of mistake.

9. Henry James, *Nation*

24 December 1874

The *Nation* was a New York paper. This article was reprinted in *Literary Reviews and Essays by Henry James*, edited by A. Mordell, 1957.

Mr. Hardy's novel came into the world under brilliant auspices—such as the declaration by the London *Spectator* that either George Eliot had written it or George Eliot had found her match. One could make out in a manner what the *Spectator* meant. To guess, one has only to open *Far from the Madding Crowd* at random: 'Mr. Jan Coggan, who had passed the cup to Henery, was a crimson man with a spacious countenance and a private glimmer in his eye, whose name had appeared on the marriage register of Weatherbury and neighbouring parishes as best-man and chief witness in countless unions of the previous twenty years; he also very frequently filled the post of head godfather in baptisms of the subtly-jovial kind.' That is a very fair imitation of George Eliot's humorous manner. Here is a specimen of her serious one: 'He fancied he had felt himself in the penumbra of a very deep sadness when touching that slight and fragile creature. But wisdom lies in moderating mere impressions, and Gabriel endeavoured to think little of this.' But the *Spectator's* theory had an even broader base, and we may profitably quote a passage which perhaps constituted one of its solidest blocks. The author of *Silas Marner* has won no small part of her fame by her remarkable faculty as a reporter of ale-house and kitchen-fire conversations among simple-minded rustics.

Mr. Hardy has also made a great effort in this direction, and here is a specimen—a particularly favourable specimen—of his success:

[quotes ch. viii '"Why, Joseph Poorgrass,"' to '"my few poor gratitudes."']

This is extremely clever, and the author has evidently read to good purpose the low-life chapters in George Eliot's novels; he has caught very happily her trick of seeming to humour benignantly her queer people and look down at them from the heights of analytic omniscience. But we have quoted the episode because it seems to us an excellent example of the cleverness which is only cleverness, of the difference between original and imitative talent—the disparity, which it is almost unpardonable not to perceive, between first-rate talent and those inferior grades which range from second-rate downward, and as to which confusion is a more venial offence. Mr. Hardy puts his figures through a variety of comical movements; he fills their mouths with quaint turns of speech; he baptizes them with odd names ('Joseph Poorgrass' for a bashful, easily-snubbed Dissenter is excellent); he pulls the wires, in short, and produces a vast deal of sound and commotion; and his novel, at a cursory glance, has a rather promising air of life and warmth. But by critics who prefer a grain of substance to a pound of shadow it will, we think, be pronounced a decidedly delusive performance; it has a fatal lack of magic. We have found it hard to read, but its shortcomings are easier to summarize than to encounter in order. Mr. Hardy's novel is very long, but his subject is very short and simple, and the work has been distended to its rather formidable dimensions by the infusion of a large amount of conversational and descriptive padding and the use of an ingeniously verbose and redundant style. It is inordinately diffuse, and, as a piece of narrative, singularly inartistic. The author has little sense of proportion, and almost none of composition. We learn about Bathsheba and Gabriel, Farmer Boldwood and Sergeant Troy, what we can rather than what we should; for Mr. Hardy's inexhaustible faculty for spinning smart dialogue makes him forget that dialogue in a story is after all but episode, and that a novelist is after all but a historian, thoroughly possessed of certain facts, and bound in some way or other to impart them. To tell a story almost exclusively by reporting people's talks is the most difficult art in the world, and really leads, logically, to a severe economy in the use of rejoinder and repartee, and not to a lavish expenditure of them. *Far from the Madding Crowd* gives us an uncomfortable sense of being a simple 'tale', pulled and stretched to make the conventional three volumes; and the author, in his long-sustained appeal to one's attention, reminds us of a person fishing with an enormous net, of which the meshes should be thrice too wide.

We are happily not subject, in this (as to minor matters) much-emancipated land, to the tyranny of the three volumes; but we confess that we are nevertheless being rapidly urged to a conviction that (since it is in the nature of fashions to revolve and recur) the day has come round again for some of the antique restrictions as to literary form. The three unities, in Aristotle's day, were inexorably imposed on Greek tragedy: why shouldn't we have something of the same sort for English fiction in the day of Mr. Hardy? Almost all novels are greatly too long, and the being too long becomes with each elapsing year a more serious offence. Mr. Hardy begins with a detailed description of his hero's smile, and proceeds thence to give a voluminous account of his large silver watch. Gabriel Oak's smile and his watch were doubtless respectable and important phenomena; but everything is relative, and daily becoming more so; and we confess that, as a hint of the pace at which the author proposed to proceed, his treatment of these facts produced upon us a deterring and depressing effect. If novels were the only books written, novels written on this scale would be all very well; but as they compete, in the esteem of sensible people, with a great many other books, and a great many other objects of interest of all kinds, we are inclined to think that, in the long run, they will be defeated in the struggle for existence unless they lighten their baggage very considerably and do battle in a more scientific equipment. Therefore, we really imagine that a few arbitrary rules—a kind of depleting process—might have a wholesome effect. It might be enjoined, for instance, that no 'tale' should exceed fifty pages and no novel two hundred; that a plot should have but such and such a number of ramifications; that no ramification should have more than a certain number of persons; that no person should utter more than a given number of words; and that no description of an inanimate object, should consist of more than a fixed number of lines. We should not incline to advocate this oppressive legislation as a comfortable or ideal finality for the romancer's art, but we think it might be excellent as a transitory discipline or drill. Necessity is the mother of invention, and writers with a powerful tendency to expatiation might in this temporary strait-jacket be induced to transfer their attention rather more severely from quantity to quality. The use of the strait-jacket would have cut down Mr. Hardy's novel to half its actual length and, as he is a clever man, have made the abbreviated work very ingeniously pregnant. We should have had a more occasional taste of all the barn-yard worthies—Joseph Poorgrass, Laban Tall, Matthew Moon, and the rest—and the vagaries of Miss Bathsheba would have had a more sensible consistency. Our restrictions would have been generous, however, and we should not have proscribed such a fine passage as this:

Then there came a third flash. Manoeuvres of the most extraordinary kind were going on in the vast firmamental hollows overhead. The lightning now was the colour of silver, and gleamed in the heavens like a mailed army. Rumbles became rattles. Gabriel, from his elevated position, could see over the landscape for at least half a dozen miles in front. Every hedge, bush, and tree was distinct as in a line engraving. In a paddock in the same direction was a herd of heifers, and the forms of these were visible at this moment in the act of galloping about in the wildest and maddest confusion, flinging their heels and tails high into the air, their heads to earth. A poplar in the immediate foreground was like an ink-stroke on burnished tin. Then the picture vanished, leaving a darkness so intense that Gabriel worked entirely by feeling with his hands.

Mr. Hardy describes nature with a great deal of felicity, and is evidently very much at home among rural phenomena. The most genuine thing in his book, to our sense, is a certain aroma of the meadows and lanes—a natural relish for harvesting and sheep-washings. He has laid his scene in an agricultural county, and his characters are children of the soil—unsophisticated country-folk. Bathsheba Everdene is a rural heiress, left alone in the world, in possession of a substantial farm. Gabriel Oak is her shepherd, Farmer Boldwood is her neighbour, and Sergeant Troy is a loose young soldier who comes a-courting her. They are all in love with her, and the young lady is a flirt, and encourages them all. Finally she marries the Sergeant, who has just seduced her maid-servant. The maid-servant dies in the workhouse, the Sergeant repents, leaves his wife, and is given up for drowned. But he reappears and is shot by Farmer Boldwood, who delivers himself up to justice. Bathsheba then marries Gabriel Oak, who has loved and waited in silence, and is, in our opinion, much too good for her. The chief purpose of the book is, we suppose, to represent Gabriel's dumb, devoted passion, his biding his time, his rendering unsuspected services to the woman who has scorned him, his integrity and simplicity and sturdy patience. In all this the tale is very fairly successful, and Gabriel has a certain vividness of expression. But we cannot say that we either understand or like Bathsheba. She is a young lady of the inconsequential, wilful, mettlesome type which has lately become so much the fashion for heroines, and of which Mr. Charles Reade is in a manner the inventor—the type which aims at giving one a very intimate sense of a young lady's *womanishness*. But Mr. Hardy's embodiment of it seems to us to lack reality; he puts her through the Charles Reade paces, but she remains alternately vague and coarse, and seems always artificial. This is Mr. Hardy's trouble; he rarely gets beyond ambitious artifice—the mechanical simulation of heat and depth and wisdom that are absent. Farmer Boldwood is a shadow, and Sergeant Troy an elaborate stage-figure. Everything human in the book strikes us as factitious and insubstantial; the only things we believe in are the sheep and the dogs. But, as we say, Mr. Hardy has gone astray very cleverly, and his superficial novel is a really curious imitation of something better.

10. Unsigned Review, *Westminster Review*

January 1875, ciii, n.s. xlvii, 265

The extract represents three pages of the section on Belles Lettres.

'Not profitable for doctrine, for reproof, for edification, for building up or elevating in any shape! The sick heart will find no healing here, the darkly struggling heart no guidance, the heroic that is in all men, no divine awakenment.' Thus wrote Carlyle of the Waverley Novels. What Carlyle would say to our present novels we will not undertake to say. To even review them is a difficult matter, for as the ancient philosopher observed, it is no easy thing to stick soft cheese on a hook. Their dulness is their security. One novel, however, has at all events marked the past year. *Far from the Madding Crowd* stands to all contemporary novels precisely as *Adam Bede* did to all other novels some sixteen years ago. In fact, when the first chapters of Mr. Hardy's story appeared in the *Cornhill Magazine* many good judges pronounced it to be a work of George Eliot's. Nor was their critical sagacity so very far wide of the mark. Mr. Hardy has not reached the splendid heights which George Eliot has attained, nor sounded her spiritual depths, but his new work will certainly in many other respects bear favourable comparison with *Adam Bede*. And there are many obvious points of comparison. George Eliot in that story dealt with the farming class in the North Midlandshire Counties. Mr. Hardy has taken his characters from the same class in the Western Counties. There is no imitation on Mr. Hardy's part, but if we may use the word in no invidious sense, a challenge. George Eliot has introduced into her story a number of rustic scenes, notably a harvest home. Mr. Hardy has replied also with a number of rustic scenes, but most prominently with a sheep-shearing supper. George Eliot has made one of her chief characters a young squire, an officer in the militia. Mr. Hardy also has introduced a soldier, but he has in this instance avoided George Eliot's failure. George Eliot's Arthur Donnithorne is a simple impossibility. No man in his position could have acted in the way in which he behaved to Hetty after seducing her. Sergeant Troy's conduct to Fanny Robin is at least consistent with his character and bearing. Arthur Donnithorne, on the other hand, is represented as not only a man of high social position in his county, but a gentleman in feeling, yet he acts like a cur. Men in the army are not very squeamish about seduction, but Arthur Donnithorne would have been scouted by his brother officers for his base desertion of Hetty. Mr. Hardy at least has steered clear of this mistake. Sergeant Troy is simply what he is represented. He has no higher morals than most privates in the army. His character is fairly revealed to us on his first introduction in the fir wood with Bathsheba. We are more fully introduced to him afterwards, especially in the drunken orgy in the barn. His subsequent behaviour is all in keeping. In one other respect, too, Mr. Hardy has shown better judgment than George Eliot. In both stories there is a reprieve-scene. Every one will remember the melodramatic scene in *Adam Bede* of Arthur Donnithorne arriving at the last moment waving a reprieve in his hand. Mr. Hardy has not fallen into this absurdity. But the fault of *Far from the Madding Crowd* is undoubtedly its sensationalism. We are not so well acquainted with Mr. Hardy's previous writings as to entitle us to speak with perfect confidence, but as far as we can remember they were distinguished for their pastoral tone and idyllic simplicity rather than for violent sensationalism. At all events sensationalism was a secondary element.

But in *Far from the Madding Crowd* sensationalism is all in all. If we analyse the story we shall find that it is nothing else but sensationalism, which, in the hands of a less skilful writer than Mr. Hardy, would simply sink the story to the level of one of Miss Braddon's earlier performances. Take the career of Gabriel Oak, who is the least sensational of the chief characters. He loses the whole of his property in a sensation scene of two or three hundred sheep being driven by a dog over a precipice. He finds his mistress in a sensation scene of blazing ricks. He regains her estimation in another sensation scene of thunder and lightning in the same rick-yard. So the story progresses in a succession of sensation scenes. But sensation scenes are no more Mr. Hardy's strong point than they are George Eliot's. The scene in which Troy woos Bathsheba with his sword is a piece of mad extravagance, fit only for the boards of some transpontine theatre. The whole chapter is simply a burlesque upon the cavalier poet's lines, 'I'll make thee famous by my pen, and glorious by my sword.' Mr. Hardy has not done this, but only made the one step from the sublime to the ridiculous. Of course Mr. Hardy has had good reasons for dealing us such a dose of sensation. He knows what true art is, but he prefers in this story at least to give his readers a bastard substitute. As we have already hinted, many comparisons may be found between *Far from the Madding Crowd* and *Adam Bede*. We have already touched upon the question of seduction and the conduct of the two seducers. Sergeant Troy, we must say, is far more true to life than Arthur Donnithorne, who is one of George Eliot's failures. Again a comparison might be made between Adam Bede and Gabriel Oak. Here, again, we think that Mr. Hardy's character, making allowance for the sensation scenes, is truer to nature. Adam Bede is, if we may use the expression, too much infected with selfconsciousness. George Eliot has, by the wealth of her language, and a certain pomp of diction, rather overdone him. We are inclined to say, was there really ever a working-man like Adam Bede? This we never ask about Gabriel Oak. We thoroughly sympathize with him and pity him, and we must say that he deserved a far better woman for a wife than such a vain and selfish creature as Bathsheba Everdene. And this brings us to the heroine of Mr. Hardy's story. Upon her he has lavished all his skill. She may for a moment be compared, not from any resemblance, but by way of contrast, with Hetty Sorrel. The famous incident of the looking-glass by-the-bye is repeated with a slight variation by Mr. Hardy. There is, however, not the least ground for accusing Mr. Hardy of plagiarism. The incident is common enough. We have seen not only precisely the same scene which Mr. Hardy describes, but have known farm servant-girls take bits of glass out of their pockets and admire themselves in the market-place. Human nature is the same in every rank of life. Ladies have looking-glasses let into their fans and prayer-books, and poor girls carry broken bits in their pockets. The looking-glass is still *civilis sarcina belli*. But to return. Both Hetty and Bathsheba are represented as pretty and vain. But their prettiness and vanity are of two very different kinds. And in her description of the charms of Hetty's prettiness, George Eliot shows herself far more of a poet than Mr. Hardy. Mr. Hardy tells us that Bathsheba was beautiful, and gives us an idea of what her beauty was, but he does not paint it with the same feeling with which George Eliot paints Hetty's face. But neither beauty nor vanity are the key to Bathsheba's character. Whatever Mr. Hardy may wish us to think of his heroine, the one leading trait of her character, and of all such characters, is at the bottom—selfishness. She plays fast and loose with poor Gabriel Oak. She blows hot and cold upon Farmer Boldwood. She flirts with Oak in the most heartless manner. She sends Boldwood a valentine with the words 'Marry Me' on the seal. Her very selfishness makes her wayward and inconstant. When she is entrapped by Sergeant Troy with his scarlet coat and his vulgar love-making we feel no pity for her. She never really cared a straw for Troy. She was fascinated by his swagger and his flattery. Her behaviour, however, at his death seems to us most inexplicable, and is the only part of her history which is out of drawing. It is open to grave objections. In all other respects she is described with great skill. She is hard and mercenary. When she at last marries Gabriel Oak we feel, whatever Mr. Hardy may intend to the contrary, that she marries him not from any admiration of his nobility of character, but simply because he will manage her farm and keep her money together. Bathsheba is the character of the book, and Mr. Hardy may be proud of having drawn such a character. But she is a character not to be admired, as he would seem to intimate. We have left ourselves no space to dwell upon the individual merits of *Far from the Madding Crowd*. We must briefly repeat that it will bear favourable comparison with *Adam Bede* for its humour, its power of description, and character-drawing. This is high praise, but we give it not without due deliberation. Some of the faults, especially the sensationalism, we have mentioned. There are others which seem to be due to George Eliot's influence—a use of a semi-scientific phraseology and a striving after profundity of meaning. As Mr. Hardy has followed George Eliot in her defects, we hope he will imitate her in another direction—not write too fast.

11. Andrew Lang, *Academy*

2 January 1875, vii, 9

Andrew Lang (1844–1912) was a scholar, folk-lorist, poet and man of letters. With Butcher, Leaf and Myers he produced prose translations of the *Odyssey* and the *Iliad* which had a wide currency.

Far from the Madding Crowd is so clever a novel, so original in atmosphere and in character, that its brilliant qualities are likely to neutralize the glare of its equally prominent faults. The writer has the advantage of dealing with an almost untouched side of English life. His scene is laid somewhere in the country of Mr. Freeman's favourite Seaxsaetas, in a remote agricultural and pastoral district of southwestern England. Among peasants who look on Bath as a distant and splendid metropolis, it is likely that much of the old country existence lives on undisturbed. The country folk in the story have not heard of strikes, or of Mr. Arch; they have, to all appearance, plenty to eat, and warm clothes to wear, and when the sheep are shown in the ancient barn of Weatherbury, the scene is one that Shakespeare or that Chaucer might have watched. This immobile rural existence is what the novelist has to paint. 'In comparison with cities,' he says,

Weatherbury was immutable. The citizen's *then*, is the rustic's *now*. In London, twenty or thirty years ago are old times; in Paris, ten years or five; in Weatherbury, three or four score years were included in the mere present, and nothing less than a century set a mark on its face or tone. Five decades hardly modified the cut of a gaiter, the embroidery of a smock-frock, by the breadth of a hair.

Ten generations failed to alter the turn of a single phrase. In these nooks the busy outsider's ancient times are only old, his old times are still new, his present is futurity.

No condition of society could supply the writer who knows it well with a more promising ground for his story. The old and the new must meet here and there, with curious surprises, and our world may find itself face to face with the quaint conceited rustics of Shakespeare's plays. Such a story might be written as George Sand has often told of the *vallée noire*, sober characters and simple might appear in the foreground of scenes exquisitely quiet and harmonious. In our opinion the writer of *Far from the Madding Crowd* has only partially succeeded in making the best of his theme, and though his failure is more valuable than many successes, he has been misled by attempting too much. In his way of looking at his subject he rather resembles George Eliot than George Sand. He contemplates his shepherds and rural people with the eye of a philosopher who understands all about them, though he is not of them, and who can express their dim efforts at rendering what they think and feel in language like that of Mr. Herbert Spencer. It is this way of writing and thinking that gives the book its peculiar tone. The author is telling clever people about unlettered people, and he adopts a sort of patronizing voice, in which there are echoes, now of George Eliot, and now of George Meredith. Thus there are passages where the manner and the matter jar, and are out of keeping.

There are three circles of interest in this story—first, the rural surroundings, the effects of weather and atmosphere, the labours of beasts and men, as the lambing of sheep, and such mild struggles with Nature's storms and rains as M. Victor Hugo would scarcely find dramatic enough for his tremendous canvas. Next, there are the minor characters—a sort of chorus of agricultural labourers, very ready with advice, very helpless, and very much taken up with themselves, as was the way with the ancient chorus. Last, there are the main persons of the drama—the people in whose passions and adventures the interest ought to centre. Of these three component parts of the tale, the first may be pronounced nearly perfect, and worthy of all praise. We might instance the description of Norcombe Hill by starlight, in the beginning of the second chapter, as an original and admirable treatment of nature—of nature which is more and more tending to become a main interest in our modern fiction. We prefer to quote the enumeration of the signs by which the hero detected the approach of a storm, because the quotation includes the sheep, whose birth and death, in this tale, are narrated with great minuteness.

[quotes ch. XXXVI from 'They were crowded close together' to 'nothing of the later rain.']

When the thunder-storm bursts, it is described with much pictorial effect; and is a quite disagreeable enough trial to Oak, the English Gilliat, and contender with Nature.

Coming from the scenery to the chorus, we are a good deal puzzled. Few men know the agricultural labourer at home, and it is possible that he is what Mr. Hardy describes him. The labourers are all humorists in their way, which is a very dreary and depressing way. Odd scraps of a kind of rural euphuism, misapplications of scripture, and fragments of modern mechanical wit, are stirred up into a queer mixture, which makes the talk of Henery Fray, Cainy Ball, Jan Coggan and especially of that pre-eminent bore, Joseph Poorgrass. Do labourers really converse like this—

'I look round upon life quite promiscous. Do you conceive me, neighbours? My words, though made as simple as I can, may be rather deep for some heads.'

'Oh yes, Henèry, we quite conceive ye.'

'A strange old piece, goodmen—whirled about from here to yonder, as if I were nothing worth. A little warped too. But I have my depths; ha, and even my great depths! I might close with a certain shepherd, brain to brain. But no; oh, no!'

Here is another specimen of rural speech.

'For a drunk of really a noble class, and on the highest principles, that brought you no nearer to the dark man than you were afore you began, there was none like these in Farmer Everdene's kitchen. Not a single damn allowed, no, not a bare poor one, even at the most cheerful moment when all were blindest, though the good old word of sin thrown in here and there would have been a great relief to a merry soul.'

'True,' said the maltster, 'nature requires her swearing at the regular times, or she's not herself; and unholy exclamations is a necessity of life.'

And so on. Shepherds may talk in this way: we hope not; but if they do, it is a revelation; and if they don't, it is nonsense, and not very amusing nonsense.

Leaving the servants, and coming to their master and mistress, we cannot say that we are greatly fascinated with the persons, or much concerned in their fortunes. Nothing could be more true or more careful than the study of Troy, the handsome sergeant, with his half education, his selfishness, his love, which he only finds out to be something like true love under the influence of remorse. When the soldier erects a costly tomb to the woman whose heart he has broken, and plants flowers on her grave, in such a way as to wound to the quick the woman he has married, we recognize an insight, and a touch, like that of Flaubert. But we cannot easily pardon Bathsheba, the heroine, for losing her heart to Troy's flattery, and to the glitter of his brass and scarlet. Indeed we have some difficulty in being much moved by Bathsheba's character and mischances. When we first see her, she is stealing a look at herself in a mirror, unconscious of the presence of young Farmer Oak. When she hears that Oak has asked her aunt for leave to court her, and has been discouraged, she runs after the exemplary man, and explains that she is heart free. Then she sends a valentine, with a seal *marry me*, to Farmer Boldwood, and so fascinates that apparently calm, but really passionate rustic. Meanwhile, Oak fails as a farmer, and Bathsheba, having become a farmer in her own right, takes him on as shepherd, and has 'curiously confidential' passages with him. At last, the gay sergeant fixes her fancy with a display of swordsmanship, and she drives alone at night to Bath, and is married to him. We feel inclined to say to her, as Mr. Buckstone does to Galatea in the play, ' You're *sure* it's innocence?' The young lady's misfortunes deepen, as Troy spends her money, and takes to drinking. There is a very powerful and strange scene between them when she opens the coffin of her dead rival, Fanny Robin, and her husband kisses the lips of the corpse, and tells his wife that he only loved the dead. It is a situation worthy of the drama of Webster or of Ford, and wild as it is, is led up to in a perfectly natural way. This part of the tale, including Fanny Robin's terrible walk, to her rest in the workhouse, is eminently tragic, and is not improved by the commonplace tragedy of the *dénouement*. We leave Bathsheba wedded to the worthy Oak, a capital overseer, and a husband who may be trusted. We hope the babies were 'put in the papers, every man jack of them', as Mr. Oak promised when he wooed. Bathsheba is so seldom on the level that her troubles with her husband raise her to, that we feel she does not decline on Oak, and have no sense of her as wasting her sweetness. It is unlikely that even her remorse for having tempted Boldwood would lead her into her foolish latter relations with such a man, and, on the whole, we cannot look on Bathsheba as a firmly designed character. In spite of this want of success, and of incongruities of tone, *Far from the Madding*

Crowd displays undeniable talent, which has scarcely as yet found its best and easiest and most natural expression. In taking leave of an interesting, provoking, and clever story, we must say a word in praise of the graceful illustrations.

12. Unsigned review, *Saturday Review*

9 January 1875, xxxix, 57–8

Mr. Hardy still lingers in the pleasant byways of pastoral and agricultural life which he made familiar to his readers in his former novels, *Under the Greenwood Tree* and *A Pair of Blue Eyes*. Indeed the first of these can hardly be called a novel. It was rather a series of rustic sketches —Dutch paintings of English country scenes after the manner of *Silas Marner*. But, like its successor, *A Pair of Blue Eyes*, it brought with it a genuine fresh flavour of the country, and of a part of the country that has not yet become hackneyed. There was promise, too, in both these books of something really good being produced in future works. And that promise, though not quite fulfilled, is given again in *Far from the Madding Crowd*. It is nearer fulfilment than it was, though much nearer in the first half of the first volume than in the remainder of the book, where the characters both of the heroine and of the hero fall off. But there is still a good deal wanting, and Mr. Hardy has much to learn, or perhaps we ought to say, to unlearn, before he can be placed in the first order of modern English novelists. He takes trouble, and is not in a hurry to work off his sketches. They are imaginative, drawn from the inside, and highly finished. They show power also of probing and analysing the deeper shades of character, and showing how characters are affected, and how destinies are influenced for good or evil, by the circumstances which act upon them. But Mr. Hardy disfigures his pages by bad writing, by clumsy and inelegant metaphors, and by mannerism and affectation. What, for instance, could be worse as a piece of composition than the following?

His tone was so utterly removed from all she had expected as a beginning. It was lowness and quiet accented: an emphasis of deep meanings, their form, at the same time, being scarcely expressed. Silence has sometimes a remarkable power of showing itself as the disembodied soul of feeling wandering without its carcase, and it is then more impressive than speech.

The grammar in this passage is faulty, the metaphor is far-fetched and awkward, the thought poor, and the expression of it affected. Again, how could a man of good taste—and good taste Mr. Hardy certainly has—permit this hideous metaphor to appear?—'It' ('the element of folly') 'was introduced as lymph on the dart of Eros, and eventually permeated and coloured her whole constitution'. A quack doctor before the days of Public Vaccinators might have written such a sentence as a taking advertisement. But a man of refinement, and not without a sense of humour, might surely have put the not unprecedented fact that a girl fell in love with a soldier in simpler and less professional language. Why, again, should he talk of Bathsheba's beauty 'belonging rather to the redeemed-demonian than to the blemished-angelic school', or of 'a little slip of humanity for alarming potentialities of exploit', or of 'the spherical completeness of his existence heretofore slowly spreading into an abnormal distortion in the particular direction of an ideal passion'? Eccentricities of style are not characteristic of genius, nor of original thinking. If Mr. Hardy is not possessed of genius, he is possessed of something quite good enough for the ordinary purposes of novel-writing to make him independent of anything like counterfeit originality or far-fetched modes of thought. If he has the self-control to throw aside his tendency to strain after metaphorical effects, and if he will cultivate simplicity of diction as effectually as he selects simple and natural subjects to write about, he may mellow into a considerable novelist. But if he suffers this tendency to grow into a habit—and there is quite as much of it in this as in his previous novels—he will very speedily lose the not inconsiderable reputation which he has justly gained.

Mr. Hardy, whether by force of circumstances or by fortunate selection, has in this story hit upon a new vein of rich metal for his fictitious scenes. The English Bœotian has never been so idealized before. Ordinary men's notions of the farm-labourer of the Southern counties have all been blurred and confused. It has been the habit of an ignorant and unwisely philanthropic age to look upon him as an untaught, unreflecting, badly paid, and badly fed animal, ground down by hard and avaricious farmers, and very little, if at all, raised by intelligence above the brutes and beasts to whom he ministers. These notions are ruthlessly overturned by Mr. Hardy's novel. Under his hand Bœotians became Athenians in acuteness, Germans in capacity for philosophic speculation, and Parisians in polish. Walter Scott has left many sketches and some highly finished portraits of the humbler class of Scotch peasants, and has brought out the national shrewdness and humour, and the moral and intellectual 'pawkiness' for which that class of Scotch society is justly celebrated. But he had good material to work on and two out of every three of his characters were in all probability drawn from life. George Eliot in her early books, and even in *Felix Holt*, has drawn specimens of the illiterate class who talk theology like the Bench of Bishops—except that they are all Dissenters—and politics like the young Radicals who sit, or used to sit, below the gangway. But the reader felt that the author had seen these rustic theologians and politicians and heard their conversations. Shakespeare also has his metaphysical clowns ready by force of mother-wit to discuss generalities on most subjects. But neither his clowns, nor George Eliot's rustics, nor Scott's peasants, rise to anything like the flights of abstract reasoning with which Mr. Hardy credits his cider-drinking boors. Humorous many of his descriptions of them certainly are; as, for instance, the following account of the various ways in which the news of Bathsheba's sheep breaking fence on Sunday and 'blasting' themselves with young clover affected the farm servants individually:

Joseph's countenance was drawn into lines and puckers by his concern. Fray's forehead was wrinkled both perpendicularly and crosswise, after the pattern of a portcullis, expressive of a double despair. Laban Tall's lips were thin, and his face was rigid. Matthew's jaws sank, and his eyes turned whichever way the strongest muscle happened to pull them.

'Yes,' said Joseph, 'and I was sitting at home, looking for Ephesians, and says I to myself, " 'Tis nothing but Corinthians and Thessalonians in this danged Testament," when who should come in but Henery there: "Joseph," he said, "the sheep have blasted themselves—" '.

No objection could be taken to the treatment of these choruses of agricultural labourers if it were confined to such descriptions. But when we find one of these labourers—'a cherry-faced' shepherd lad, 'with a small circular orifice by way of a mouth'—discourse on ecclesiastical politics in this style—

'There's two religions going on in the nation now, High Church and High Chapel. And thinks I, I'll play fair; so I went to High Church in the morning and High Chapel in the afternoon . . . Well at High Church they pray singing, and believe in all the colours of the rainbow; and at High Chapel they pray preaching, and believe in drab and whitewash only'—.

we feel either that we have misjudged the unenfranchised agricultural classes, or that Mr. Hardy has put his own thoughts and words into their mouths. And this suspicion necessarily shakes our confidence in the truthfulness of many of the idyllic incidents of rustic life which are so plentifully narrated throughout these volumes. The descriptions of the farming operations, for instance, the sheepshearing, and the hay-making, and the sheep-washing, with the tender episode attached to it, and the lambing in the cold winter months among the snow, are graphically given. There is a vivid reality about the description of the fire in the farmsteading, the terrible thunderstorm that ruined love-lorn Farmer Boldwood's stacks, though it failed to awaken the drunken revellers in Bathsheba's barn, and the midnight pursuit of Bathsheba when she stole away to Bath. Then there is that most unconventional picture in 'the hollow amid the ferns.' Here Sergeant Troy with startling dexterity performs a rape of a lock from the shoulder of his mistress with a cut of a heavy cavalry sabre—or, as Mr. Hardy more finely puts it, with 'a circumambient gleam accompanied by a keen sibillation that was almost a whistle'—and in the next moment trans-fixes with the same instrument a caterpillar on her breast, or, to use the gallant Sergeant's words, 'gave point to her bosom where the cater-pillar was, and instead of running her through, checked the extension a thousandth of an inch short of her surface'. Doubting the authenticity of the conversations, we are led to question the truthfulness of such scenes as these. Are they a faithful rendering of real events taking place from time to time in the South-Western counties, or are they not imag-inary creations with possibly some small groundwork of reality?

These are difficulties which suggest themselves to the most cursory reader. But perhaps it does not very much matter (except to the student of the political capabilities of the agricultural labourer) whether either the conversations or the descriptions are true or false. They are in keeping with the general character of the novel to this extent, that they are worked up with unusual skill and care. Each scene is a study in itself, and, within its own limits, effective. And they all fit into the story like pieces of an elaborate puzzle, making, when they are so fitted in, an effective whole. Mr. Hardy's art consists principally in the way in which he pieces his scenes one with the other. He determines, for instance, that the moral discipline through which his heroine has to pass to render her a fitting helpmate to Gabriel Oak shall culminate in the scene where she sees her husband weeping over the coffin of her rival and kissing her dead lips. But how is this crisis to be brought about in a natural and ordinary way? Fanny Robin dies in the workhouse, and Joseph Poorgrass is sent for her coffin so that she may have a decent burial in the parish churchyard by Bathsheba's house. Joseph arrives late on an autumn afternoon. Driving homewards, with his burden covered over with evergreens, a thick sea fog—the first of the autumn fogs— rolls up quite naturally, overshadowing the whole country, and wetting Joseph to the skin. By the roadside, not two miles from the churchyard where the parson is waiting for him, stands the 'Buck's Head Inn'. Wet and miserable, Joseph cannot pass the familiar door. Two of his boon companions—'owners of the two most appreciative throats in the neighbourhood'—are in the warm kitchen sitting face to face over a three-legged circular table like 'the setting sun and the full moon shining *vis-à-vis* across the globe'. They drink and talk as only Mr. Hardy's rustics can talk, especially with such a topic as death for a text, and Joseph joins them—his sense of duty urging him to leave, but the talk and the drink prevailing on him to stay. Oak comes in upon them, and, finding Joseph helpless, leaves him in the inn, and drives the cart to the churchyard. The parson is still there, though the night is closing in. It is not too late. But 'Have you the Registrar's certificate?' No, Joseph had omitted to give it, and Joseph was two miles off, at the 'Buck's Head', helplessly drunk. The funeral had to be put off, and the coffin is taken for the night to Bathsheba's house. Thus Bathsheba learned the secret of poor Fanny's death, and saw revealed to her Troy's selfish perfidy to Fanny, and felt the weight of his cruelty to herself. And this, the most dramatic incident in the book, is brought about by what? By Joseph Poorgrass's innocently and naturally going into the 'Buck's Head' to warm himself at the kitchen fire. In this careful fitting in of the pieces of his puzzle, and in the use of trifling circumstances either to work up to the *dénouement* or to prepare the mind for the incidents which are to follow, Mr. Hardy shows his skill. The book is prodigal of incidents apparently irreconcilable with each other. But by delicate contrivances of the kind indicated they are made to cohere, and to form a connected and not altogether incredible story.

It is impossible to give the roughest outline of the plot, nor can we even attempt to analyse the characters. 'Bathsheba and her Lovers' the novel might have been called (except that its own title is very much better), and the interest of the story consists in contrasting the three lovers in their respective attitudes towards the heroine. She is a rustic beauty fond of admiration, loving her independence, without much heart but with a brave spirit, a sharp hand at a bargain, an arrant flirt over-flowing with vanity, but modest withal. 'As a girl, had she been put into a low dress, she would have run and thrust her head into a bush; yet she was not a shy girl by any means. It was merely her instinct to draw the line dividing the seen from the unseen higher than they do in towns.' 'She has her faults', says Oak to the toll-keeper, after his first meeting with her, 'and the greatest of them is—well, what it is always—vanity.' 'I want somebody to tame me', she says herself; 'I'm too independent.' Oak is not the man to perform so difficult an achievement. He has too many Christian characteristics and too limited a power of utterance to succeed with Bathsheba. He finds difficulty in 'mapping out his mind upon his tongue'. He wishes she knew his impressions, but 'he would as soon have thought of carrying an odour in a net as attempting to convey the intangibilities of his feeling in the coarse meshes of language.' He serves her like a faithful dog for many weary years, suffering patiently more than the usual share of ill-treatment, until, after various vicissitudes in her existence and in that of her two more favoured lovers, he finally reaps the reward of his dumb devotion.

The main stream of the narrative, though sparkling with fun, and sunshine, and green fields, is deeply tragic, culminating in murder, madness, and something very like what Jan Coggan (one of the rustics) calls 'committing the seventh'. But inside the main stream and eddying, as it were, beneath it, there runs a sad episode, the episode of Fanny Robin. She appears only three times; once when she meets Oak on the night of the fire when she is running away from home; a second time, wandering all alone by the riverside in the dark winter night, and attempting to attract Troy's attention by feebly throwing little fragments of snow at his barrack-room window 'till the wall must have become pimpled with the adhering lumps of snow'; and a third time struggling faintly and with faltering steps to the workhouse, when her exhausted nature could scarce support the weight of the wretched burden it had to bear. The author has put out his whole force in the description of these last two incidents. The first is original. The second may have been suggested by the well-known chapter in *Adam Bede* entitled 'The Journey in Despair'. But, whether so suggested or not, it stands comparison not unfairly even with that most painful narrative of the shipwreck of a girl's life. And the power and taste which Mr.

Hardy shows in these scenes and in others, some of which we have noticed indirectly, justify the belief that, if he will only throw aside his mannerism and eccentricity, and devote himself zealously to the cultivation of his art, he may rise to a high position among English novelists.

THE RETURN OF THE NATIVE

November 1878

13. Unsigned review, *Athenaeum*

23 November 1878, 654

The editorial file marks this review 'Britten'. Hardy's is one of five 'Novels of the Week' under review.

Where are we to turn for a novelist? Mr. Black having commanded success, appears to be in some little danger of allowing his past performances to remain his chief title to deserving it; and now Mr. Hardy, who at one time seemed as promising as any of the younger generation of story-tellers, has published a book distinctly inferior to anything of his which we have yet read. It is not that the story is ill-conceived—on the contrary, there are the elements of a good novel in it; but there is just that fault which would appear in the pictures of a person who has a keen eye for the picturesque without having learnt to draw. One sees what he means, and is all the more disappointed at the clumsy way in which the meaning is expressed. People talk as no people ever talked before, or perhaps we should rather say as no people ever talk now. The language of his peasants may be Elizabethan, but it can hardly be Victorian. Such phrases as 'being a man of the mournfullest make, I was scared a little', or 'he always had his great indignation ready against anything underhand', are surprising in the mouth of the modern rustic. Indeed, the talk seems pitched throughout in too high a key to suit the talkers. A curious feature in the book is the low social position of the characters. The upper rank is represented by a young man who is assistant to a Paris jeweller, an innkeeper who has served his apprenticeship to a civil engineer, the daughter of a bandsman, and two or three of the small farmer class. These people all speak in a manner suggestive of high cultivation, and some of them intrigue almost like dwellers in Mayfair, while they live on nearly equal terms with the furze-cutting rustics who form a chorus reminding one of 'On ne badine pas avec l'amour.' All this is mingled with a great deal of description, showing a keen observation of natural things, though disfigured at times by forced allusions and images. The sound of reeds in a wind is likened to 'sounds as of a congregation praying humbly'. A girl's recollections 'stand like gilded uncials upon the dark tablet of her present surroundings'. The general plot of the story turns on the old theme of a man who is in love with two women, and a woman who is in love with two men; the man and the woman being both selfish and sensual. We use the last word in its more extended sense; for there is nothing in the book to provoke a comparison with the vagaries of some recent novelists, mostly of the gentler sex. But one cannot help seeing that the two persons in question know no other law than the gratification of their own passion, although this is not carried to a point which would place the book on the 'Index' of respectable households. At the same time it is clear that Eustacia Vye belongs essentially to the class of which Madame Bovary is the type; and it is impossible not to regret, since this is a type which English opinion will not allow a novelist to depict in its completeness, that Mr. Hardy should have wasted his powers in giving what after all is an imperfect and to some extent misleading view of it.

14. W. E. Henley, *Academy*

30 November 1878, xiv, 517

Hardy's novel is here dealt with as the first of a batch of five. W. E. Henley (1849–1903) was at this time only just becoming known. In 1875 Leslie Stephen had published some of his 'Hospital Verses' in the *Cornhill*, and had introduced him to R. L. Stevenson, of whom he became a friend and collaborator.

In Mr. Hardy's work there is a certain Hugoesque quality of insincerity; but there is withal so much to admire and be grateful for that it takes high rank among the good romantic work of the generation, and perhaps this quality of insincerity itself is rather apparent than real. Mr. Hardy is so much in earnest in all he does that, even when he is most artificial, he is not without his motive, and has in his own consciousness of well-doing and well-meaning a complete answer to any such charge that may be brought against him. For this reason one feels a great deal of deference in rendering account of him. His work may be, to an outsider, neither wholly satisfactory nor wholly right; but it has so much in it of intention and of execution that the outsider, compelled to strike a balance of opinion, finds that balance immensely in his author's favour. Mr. Hardy has such a right and masterful faculty of analysis; he perceives and apprehends his characters so completely; he has such a strong poetic and dramatic feeling for scenery; such a clear and vivid habit of description; he phrases so adequately and so lucidly, that, carried away by the consideration of these qualities, one fails to remember that his dialogue is only here and there dramatic in the highest sense; that there is much of what looks like affectation in his work; that his sympathy with his personages is rather intellectual than emotional; that he rarely makes you laugh and never makes you cry, and that his books are valuable and interesting rather as the outcome of a certain mind than as pictures of society or studies in human nature; that his tragedy is arbitrary and accidental rather than heroic and inevitable; and that, rare artist as he is, there is something wanting in his personality, and he is not quite a great man. In *The Return of the Native*

—which, it may be said in passing, is not by any means so good a book as *A Pair of Blue Eyes*—these defects and these merits are exampled pretty strongly, and the general impression it produces is the one I have tried to set down. The story is a sad one; but the sadness is unnecessary and uncalled for. A chapter of accidents makes the hero seem to cast off his mother, who thereupon dies; a second chapter of accidents sends the heroine to death by drowning. And the hero, burdened with a double remorse, is left to live on, and to take what is substantially the place in the world that he had desired ere destruction came upon him. It is all very mournful, and very cruel, and very French; and to those who have the weakness of liking to be pleasantly interested in a book it is also very disagreeable. Perhaps, too, it is false art; but of that, believing Mr. Hardy to have a very complete theory about his books, I will not speak. To me, however, nearly all that is best in the novel is analytic and descriptive. I know of nothing in later English so striking and on the whole so sound as the several pictures of Egdon Heath, or the introductory analysis of the character of Eustacia Vega. In these Mr. Hardy is seen at his best and strongest. Acute, prescient, imaginative, insatiably observant, and at the same time so rigidly and so finely artistic that there is scarce a point in the whole that can be fairly questioned, he seems to me to paint the woman and the place as no other living writer could have done. Whether he makes the best use of them afterwards need not be here discussed. Nearly all the characters are, it should be added, of value and of interest; Mrs. Yeobright, I think being particularly to be commended. But so far as its dramatics are concerned *The Return of the Native* appears to be rather well meant than happily done. Such a speech as this, for instance, is admirable: 'Well, then I spoke to her in my well-known merry way, and she said, "O that what's shaped so venerable should talk like a fool!"—that's what she said to me. I don't care for her, be jowned if I do, and so I told her. "Be jowned if I care for 'ee," I said. I had her there—hey?' So, too, is this other, a page or two further on:—'I han't been [to church] these three years,' said Humphrey, 'for I'm so dead sleepy of a Sunday; and 'tis so terrible fur to get there; and when you do get there 'tis such a mortal poor chance that you'll be chose for up above, when so many baint, that I bide at home and don't go at all.' And there are things as good as these of frequent occurrence; but they do not constitute the body of what may be called the comic dialogue, and the impression that it produces is, as a consequence, unsatisfactory. To turn to the tragic part is, I think, to have yet more room for sorrow; in one scene—the scene where Clym is informed of the way of his mother's death—Mr. Hardy rises to the situation, and does nobly; but elsewhere he is only excessively clever, and earnest, and disappointing. But, in spite of these shortcomings, the novel is so clever and so strong that it excites both interest and admiration, and takes a first place among the novels of the season. Mr. Hardy has, I ought to note, been at the pains of making a map of his locality, which should be consulted attentively, as it is of considerable use.

15. Unsigned review, *Saturday Review*

4 January 1879, xlvii, 23-4

The question is perpetually suggesting itself nowadays whether it is better for a novel-writer to be clever or entertaining. Personally we have no doubt on the matter, but then the feelings of even a professional critic are apt to get the better of his principles. Possibly, in the interests of the highest art, we ought to hold up to the discriminating admiration of our readers the talent which we are compelled to recognize, although it has impressed more than delighted us. But we fear that if we took that sublime view of our vocation we should fail to carry our readers along with us; and, on the whole, it may be more advisable to be absolutely frank and speak out all we have upon our minds. We may appreciate the depth and brilliancy of George Eliot's later writings; but somehow we cannot fall into the same kindly and familiar companionship with *Middlemarch* and *Daniel Deronda* as with *Adam Bede* or the *Mill on the Floss*; and there is a rising school of novelists, of which Mr. Hardy is one of the ablest members, who seem to construct their fictions for themselves rather than for other people. It would be scarcely fair to say that they are dull; and they give us the fullest persuasion of a latent power which would enable them, as our ideas go, to write infinitely more agreeably if it pleased them. In one respect they resemble those fashionable and self-opinionated artists who embody their personal conceptions of art in forms that scandalize traditional opinions. In another respect, as we are glad to think, they differ from them very widely. For, whatever may be our estimate of their manner in the main, there is no denying the care they bestow upon their workmanship, and this is a thing to be grateful for in these days of slovenly writing. After all, however, we are brought round again to the point we started from. We maintain that the primary object of a story is to amuse, and in the attempt to amuse us Mr. Hardy, in our opinion, breaks down. In his case it has not been always so; but he would seem to be steadily subordinating interest to the rules by which he regulates his art. His *Under the Greenwood Tree* and *Pair of Blue Eyes*, partly perhaps because of rather unpromising names, were books that received less attention than they deserved. But his *Far from the Madding Crowd* was launched under favourable circumstances in a leading magazine, and—with reason—it won him a host of admirers. There may have been too much of the recurrence of marked mannerisms in it, with a good deal of what was hardly to be distinguished from affectation. But its characters were made living and breathing realities; there was a powerful love tale ingeniously worked out; the author showed a most intimate knowledge of the rural scenes he sympathetically described; and, above all, as is almost invariably his habit, he was quaintly humorous in the talk which he put into the mouths of his rustics. In this *Return of the Native* he has been less happy. The faults of *Far from the Madding Crowd* are exaggerated, and in the rugged and studied simplicity of its subject the story strikes us as intensely artificial. We are in England all the time, but in a world of which we seem to be absolutely ignorant; even a vague uncertainty hangs over the chronology. Every one of the people we meet is worked in as more or less of 'a character'; and such coincidence of 'originals', under conditions more or less fantastic, must inevitably be repugnant to our sense of the probable. Originality may very easily be overdone, especially when it is often more apparent than genuine. We need not say that Mr. Hardy's descriptions are always vivid and often most picturesque. But he weakens rather than increases their force by going out of his way for eccentric forms of expression which are far less suggestive of his meanings than the everyday words he carefully avoids. His similes and metaphors are often strained and far-fetched; and his style gives one the idea of a literary gymnast who is always striving after sensation in the form of some *tour de force*. In his very names he is unreal and unlifelike; so much so that we doubt whether nine in ten of them are to be met with in the pages of the London Directory. It is true that they may possibly be local for all we know to the contrary; and, if so, we may praise them as being in happy harmony with the theatrically local colouring of his fiction.

At the same time, having decided to write a story which should be out of the common, Mr. Hardy has shown both discretion and self-knowledge in the choice of its scene. It gives him ample opportunity for the display of his peculiar gifts and for the gratification of his very pronounced inclinations. Egdon Heath is one of the wildest spots in all England, and is situated among some of the most sequestered of parishes. The people seem to know nothing of high-roads or stage-coaches; there is nothing of a market-town in the immediate vicinity where the men might brush up their bucolical brains by weekly gossip on a market day; there is not a good-sized village, and hardly even a hamlet. The inhabitants live chiefly in lonely dwellings, where the snow heaps itself round the doors in the dreary winter-time, and where they lie listening in their tempestuous weather to the melancholy howling of the winds. The very public-house stands by itself, and bears the quaint sign of 'The Quiet Woman', who is a lady carrying her head under her arm. So that naturally we have the unadorned simplicity of nature in every shape. There must have been landed proprietors, we presume, and yet we hear nothing of a squire; while there is only incidental notice of a parson when some of the natives are joined together in matrimony. The people above the class of labourers or paupers are still in very humble stations, and for the most part extremely eccentric in their habits. There is a veteran captain of the merchant service who has come to moorings in his old age in a solitary cottage in the middle of those desolate wastes, which give every convenient facility for assignations to his beautiful granddaughter, who is one of a pair of heroines. There is a Mrs. Yeobright, who is tolerably well-to-do and the mother of 'the Native' whose return is chronicled; and there is the innkeeper, Mr. Wildeve, who is comparatively rich, and who figures relatively as a man of the world and a gay and fascinating Lothario. It is of these somewhat unpromising materials that Mr. Hardy has undertaken to weave his romance, and he has so far overcome the initial difficulties by making his hero, 'the Native', with his leading heroine, superior by their natures to their situation and surroundings. It was their lot to be born into 'a wale', as Mrs. Gamp says, and they have to take the consequences. But we are given to understand that, had their circumstances been different, or if fortune and ambition had served them better, they might have played a very different part in the grand drama of the world:

Eustacia Vye was the raw material of a divinity. On Olympus she would have done well with a little preparation. She had the passions and instincts which make a model goddess—that is, those which make not quite a model woman. Had it been possible for the earth and mankind to be entirely in her grasp for a while, had she handled the distaff, the spindle, and the shears at her own free will, few in the world would have noticed the change of government.

Again, 'in Clym Yeobright's face could be dimly seen the typical countenance of the future. Should there be a divine period to art here-after, its Phidias may produce such faces'. Those natures of élite tend towards each other instinctively. And when the lovers have one of their meetings, after three short months of acquaintance, 'they remained long without a single utterance, for no language could reach the level of their condition. Words were as the rusty implements of a barbarous bygone epoch, and only to be occasionally tolerated'. The harmony of ill-tutored minds so highly pitched could hardly fail in a sensational novel to end in discord and tragedy. Clym prevails on Eustacia to marry him; he loses money and health, and sees his dreams of good fortune gradu-ally dissipated, while the brooding shadows of despondency fall thickly on his domestic horizon. For Eustacia is equally disenchanted of her expectations. She had given admiring devotion to her husband, con-trasting him with the boors about him; she had recognized the superi-ority of his manners, acquirements, and intellect; but she had looked, above all, to being introduced by him to some of the wonders of the world, and to the dazzling delights of Parisian society. For before Clym Yeobright is presented to us as 'the Native' returning to his native wilds he had been serving an apprenticeship as a shopman in Paris. But when Eustacia sees herself shut up with him in a lonely cottage on that Egdon Heath of which she has grown so heartily sick; when she sees him labouring to keep their bodies and souls together by cutting furze and sods like a common day labourer; when she sees him covering up his expressive eyes with spectacles; and, in short, when she is settling down to the monotony of penury, feeling at the same time that she might have done far better for herself, then she decides to take leave of the world. With 'her soul in an abyss of desolation seldom plumbed by one so young', she quits her home to strike across the moors, 'occasionally stumbling over twisted furze-roots, tufts of rushes, or oozing lumps of fleshy fungi, which at this season lay scattered about the heath like the rotting liver and lungs of some colossal animal', and seeks a refuge from her troubles in a deed of desperation. She and her husband, and her admirer, Damon Wildeve, all have a meeting at last in the gloomy waters; and the crowning horror of a succession of sombre descriptions is in the search for the senseless bodies in Shadwater Weir. Unfortunately, our sympathies have never been strongly enlisted in any of the three. Even the style of Eustacia's beauty is so vaguely and transcendentally described that it neither wins our heart nor takes our fancy. For the rest she is a wayward and impulsive woman, essentially commonplace in her feelings and wishes, who compromises herself by vulgar indiscretions. Thus she bribes a country lad to help her to carry out a whim of hers by permitting him to hold her hand for fifteen minutes, although she knows that he exacts those terms because he has fallen hopelessly in love with her. Damon Wildeve, the innkeeper, although in a measure idealized in a doubtful atmosphere of romance, is in reality an underbred country clodhopper who plumes himself on his substance and gentility, and an education superior to that of his neighbours; while Clym Yeobright is a moon-struck dreamer, who seems singularly out of place among the eminently practical population of Egdon.

Still we would not be misunderstood, nor would we wish to do Mr. Hardy injustice. We think he has been injudicious in his invention of characters, and that he has deliberately prepared disappointment for us in his method of treatment, if he aimed at making his story in any degree realistic. But, as usual, there are dialogues of true and quaint humour, which have never been rivalled by any writer of the present day, and which remind one of Dogberry and Verges; and there are many *tableaux* of wild and powerful picturesqueness. Take, for example, the opening scene, where the whole of the barren country on a dreary November night is kindling to the blaze of the roaring bonfires; when we are introduced to the old-fashioned parishioners of Egdon, crowding round the pyramid of furze, thirty feet in circumference, that crowns the summit of the tumulus of Blackbarrow; and there, in his description of the excited little mob, we have some of Mr. Hardy's most distinctive touches:

All was unstable: quivering as leaves, evanescent as lightning. Shadowy eye-sockets, deep as those of a death's head, suddenly turned into pits of lustre; a lantern jaw was cavernous, then it was shining; wrinkles were emphasized to ravines, or obliterated entirely by a changed ray. Nostrils were dark wells; sinews in old necks were gilt mouldings; things with no particular polish in them were glazed; bright objects—such as the tip of a furze-hook one of the men carried—were as glass; eye-balls glowed like little lanterns. Those whom Nature had depicted as merely quaint became grotesque, the grotesque became preternatural—for all was in extremity.

Or, again, when the fair and stately Eustacia Vye steals through the darkness of the night into the glowing reflection of the balefire to keep an appointment with Wildeve, who was then paying his court to her; or when Wildeve, in his wretchedness and recklessness, later in the story, sits down to gamble by lantern-light on the lonely moors with an enemy and rival, who has thrown himself into the game with all the rancour of inveterate hatred. They are scared by spectral shadows falling across the stone table and the dice, which turn out to come from a gang of moorland ponies. When the lantern is extinguished by a great death's-head moth, they replace it with the handful of glow-worms that they gather, and the wild game goes on, in its alternations of triumph and despair, till Wildeve loses his last sovereign. This scene has striking vividness and power. There can be no doubt that Mr. Hardy has no ordinary talent; and we regret the more that he should not condescend to human frivolity, and exert his unquestionable powers in trying to be more natural and entertaining. We dare say the effort would soon come easily to him, and then our gratitude might give him less stinted praise.

16. Unsigned review, *Spectator*

8 February 1879, 181-2

Possibly by R. H. Hutton (see headnote to No. 8), but there is no record.

The Return of the Native is a story of singular power and interest—very original, very gloomy, very great in some respects, though these respects are not the highest—and from beginning to end in the highest degree vivid. But there is one great defect in almost all Mr. Hardy's books, which reappears here, that the strange figures of his Wessex peasantry, though full of picturesque and humorous elements, are never so presented that the reader is able to accept them as true pictures of rustic life even on these wild moors; and in *The Return of the Native* there is one other great defect peculiar to itself, that the book, which is meant to be tragic in its gloom, and would assuredly be tragic but for a tendency, which we attribute to the sombre fatalism of the author, to lower appreciably below the truth the whole tone and significance of human destiny, treats tragedy itself as hardly more than a deeper tinge of the common leaden-colour of the human lot, and so makes it seem less than tragedy—dreariness, rather than tragedy—by making human passion in general commonplace and poor. These are the two leading defects of a book of brilliant talent, even of high genius here and there, especially in the touches which describe the life and spirit of the great heath; and also of very considerable power of plot.

We will try and make what we mean clear in relation to both points, and yet illustrate at the same time the great ability of the story. Mr. Hardy makes the talk of his Wessex peasants, as we have said, most amusing and original; but he constantly slips in touches that show him to be painting something compounded of his knowledge of the most original rustics of the class, and of the kind of reflections on them which he himself would probably indulge in. Take this very amusing picture of a conversation round a Fifth of November bonfire on Egdon Heath:

[quotes ch. III ' "Didst ever know a man" ' to ' "that's the cause o't." ']

It would not be easy to find any picture of rustic talk in our literature more effective than that, but for Timothy Fairway's comment on poor Christian Cantle's confession. 'Not encouraging, I own', 'Even that might be overcome by time and patience', is not the way in which one of these peasants would comment on such a speech of another's, but rather the way in which Mr. Hardy would himself comment on it. And this is the general fault in the rustic elements of his books. We almost always find ideas and words more or less belonging to the stratum of comparative culture, blending with the ideas and words of rough and superstitious ignorance; and the mingling of the two bewilders and confuses the reader of his books, till he finds it impossible to determine what odd *tertium quid* it is that Mr. Hardy has created in his imagination, which is neither rustic nor critic, but something half-

way between the two. It is the same with Christian Cantle's comment
on the dice with which he has won a prize at a raffle:

'Well, to be sure!' said Christian, half to himself. 'To think I should have been
born so lucky as this, and not have found it out until now! What curious
creatures these dice be,—powerful rulers of us all, and yet at my command.
I am sure I never need be afeard of anything after this.'

'Powerful rulers of us all, and yet at my command',—though it may
express well enough his idea, certainly is not the kind of language one
would expect from such a one as Christian Cantle. But in all Mr.
Hardy's books it is the same. We seem to see a constant intertwining
of two distinct phases of either thought or language, or both, with
grotesque and yet often amusing results. Sometimes, however, he gives
a bit of rustic description pure and simple. Nothing can be more
amusing than Timothy Fairway's account of the late Mr. Yeobright's
performance on the bass-viol:

[quotes ch. V, ' "And there were few in these parts" ' to 'performance
described?']

It is hardly possible, we suppose, to surpass the graphic vernacular of
that description.

To illustrate our second criticism, that Mr. Hardy's gloomy fatalism
lowers the effect of his tragedy, by lowering almost all the passion and
sentiment in his book to something rather near the same dead-level of
dreary light, or not much more dreary shade, it is necessary to quote
some few passages illustrative of Mr. Hardy's general creed:

In Clym Yeobright's face could be dimly seen the typical countenance of the
future. Should there be a classic period to art hereafter, its Phidias may produce
such faces. The view of life as a thing to be put up with, replacing that zest for
existence which was so intense in early civilizations, must ultimately enter so
thoroughly into the constitution of the advanced races, that its facial expression
will become accepted as a new artistic departure. People already feel that a man
who lives without disturbing a curve of feature, or setting a mark of mental
concern anywhere upon himself, is too far removed from modern perceptiveness to be a modern type. Physically beautiful men—the glory of the race when
it was young—are almost an anachronism now; and we may wonder whether,
at some time or other, physically beautiful women may not be an anachronism
likewise. The truth seems to be that a long line of disillusive centuries has
permanently displaced the Hellenic idea of life, or whatever it may be called.
What the Greeks only suspected we know well; what their Æschylus imagined
our nursery children feel. That old-fashioned revelling in the general situation

grows less and less possible as we uncover the defects of natural laws, and see the quandary that man is in by their operation.

And at the close he speaks thus apologetically of his hero's faith in the Power which guides the development of human life:

He did sometimes think he had been ill-used by fortune, so far as to say that to be born is a palpable dilemma, and that instead of men aiming to advance in life with glory, they should calculate how to retreat out of it without shame. But that he and his had been sarcastically and pitilessly handled in having such irons thrust into their souls he did not maintain long. It is usually so, except with the sternest of men. Human beings, in their generous endeavour to construct a hypothesis that shall not degrade a First Cause, have always hesitated to conceive a dominant power of lower moral quality than their own; and, even while they sit down and weep by the waters of Babylon, invent excuses for the oppression which prompts their tears.

All this pessimism, of which Mr. Hardy speaks with the calm confidence of one who has found Schopenhauer far superior to all the prophets and all the seers, tells upon his picture of human character and destiny. His coldly passionate heroine, Eustacia Vye, never reproaches herself for a moment with the inconstancy and poverty of her own affections. On the contrary, she has no feeling that anything which happens within her, has relation to right and wrong at all, or that such a thing as responsibility exists. This state of feeling lowers sensibly the glow of her love, when she is in love, and makes her even in its highest moment forecast clearly its rapid decay; and then again, when the decay comes, and she has lost the love which made her so happy, she is not remorseful, but only dull, in its loss. Hence, in her case, we never really reach the point of tragedy at all. Tragedy is almost impossible to people who feel and act as if they were puppets of a sort of fate. Tragedy gives us the measure of human greatness, and elevates us by giving it in the very moment when we sound the depth of human suffering. Mr. Hardy's tragedy seems carefully limited to gloom. It gives us the measure of human miserableness, rather than of human grief—of the incapacity of man to be great in suffering, or anything else, rather than of his greatness in suffering. The death of Mrs. Yeobright—the mother of the hero—is gloom in its deepest intensity; and even her son's excruciating self-reproaches, though they at least have plenty of remorse in them, are too little softened by religious feeling or anything else to express anything but misery. Mr. Hardy refuses to give us what, even without any higher world of feeling, would have raised this alienation of mother and son into tragedy—the mutual recognition of mother and son, and the recognition of their misunderstanding, before her death. The hero's agony is pure, unalloyed misery, not grief of the deepest and noblest type, which can see a hope in the future and repent the errors of the past. And so it is with the other features of the tale. Eustacia's inability to tell whether she really loves her husband or not, whether she really loves Wildeve or not, and Wildeve's inability to tell whether he really loves his wife or not—whether his passion for Eustacia is nothing but jealousy of another man—and the death which overtakes them both when on a doubtful errand, concerning which neither of them is quite certain whether it is to be innocent or not—all these are characteristics of a peculiar imaginative mood—a mood in which there seems to be no room for freedom, no great heights, no great depths in human life, only the ups and downs of a dark necessity, in which men play the parts of mere offsprings of the physical universe, and are governed by forces and tides no less inscrutable. To us, Mr. Hardy is at his best when analysing, as he does with a touch of rare genius, the natural life of such a solitude as Egdon Heath:

[quotes ch. VI 'It might reasonably have been supposed' to 'speaking through each in turn.']

That is a passage—and there are many others equally fine—which proves Mr. Hardy to be not only a striking novelist, but in essence at least, a fine poet.

This is the first article in English to make a general survey of Hardy's work to date. The extract omits a central section of seven pages and one other passage, containing all accounts of the narratives of the early novels, especially *A Pair of Blue Eyes*.

It may not be much to say that when, five years ago, *Far from the Madding Crowd* appeared, it brought a new sensation to the novel-reading world; for that world is one which appreciates slight novelties, and a new literary sensation is at best often ephemeral. A good first novel is often the product of a personal experience which does the work of invention till a second attempt betrays its insufficiency; and on these occasions a startling pleasure is followed by a proportionate disappointment. But Mr. Hardy's success has not been of this kind. It revealed itself from the first as the result of that sustained and genuine inspiration which draws its materials from without, and is original from the very fact of being impersonal; and even before the appearance of this, his most popular work, it was evident that a new genius had arisen amongst us. This genius was typically and completely manifested in *A Pair of Blue Eyes*, but from some unexplained circumstance many readers were first introduced to it in *Far from the Madding Crowd*; and since the common authorship of the two books could be overlooked, it is perhaps not surprising that a very different person was for a moment credited with the latter. Yet the fact is, that whatever superficial resemblances may connect Mr. Hardy with other writers of fiction, he is, in the main, as consistently unlike any other as he is consistently like himself; and that he not only cannot be compared with other writers, but cannot be classified under any known formula of literary art. With a single exception his novels are not sensational, though they contain highly dramatic situations. They are not purely psychological, though the element of character is prominent in them. They are minutely worked out; but their minuteness results not in a mosaic of detail, but in a strong cumulative impression of the things and persons described; and though the author's descriptive attitude is impartial almost to indifference, he is redeemed from the reproach of cynicism which impartial writers so often incur, by his obvious belief in a moral order to which human action is subject, if not responsible. It is only in his last work that we find any reference to a moral ideal; but the lives of all his personages bear witness to that principle of natural retribution or of natural consequences which is the practical form of the moral law. His pictures of life have, in short, a dramatic reality which we acknowledge even when we demur to his preference for certain aspects of the real, or to the conclusions conveyed in the selection, even when the characters by which he chooses to illustrate them appear in some degree arbitrary or improbable. His rustic personages are clearly drawn from nature, and if we were in a position to question their truth, we should have no desire to do so. The others we believe in for the moment because he himself believes in them. They are no more mathematical constructions to be made or unmade than they are shadowy forms to be filled in at the reader's pleasure. They are living creatures which we must learn to know.

It is difficult to do justice to this quality of Mr. Hardy's genius, and yet lay sufficient stress on the conditions which determine, and even limit, its exercise; but in failing to recognize them, we should even less over-rate its extent than under-rate its interest. We should ignore the distinctive character which pervades his most direct presentations of life, and which affects us as a pungent, intellectual perfume gathered from the atmosphere of his own western wilds. It is a mistake to identify him with his studies of the western heath country and its inhabitants, as it is a mistake to identify any truly productive genius with the objects which have nourished, or even consciously inspired it. If Mr. Hardy has described this order of associations with the vividness of long personal intimacy, they by no means always occupy the foreground of his pictures; from some, and not the least powerful, they are absent altogether; but they are closely allied to the constant bent of his imagination, and we cannot practically disconnect them from it. The minuteness of observation, the sense of natural truth, the combined unconventionalism and delicacy, impartiality and prejudice, so strongly typical of everything he writes, point directly to this contact with the deeper solitudes of life, and have been fostered if they were not created by it. The artistic bias thus confirmed is not likely to disappear; how far the corresponding mental bias will yield to later experiences is a still open question, and one which carries into our reading of each new work of his a critical curiosity distinct from all other kinds of interest.

For the time being, and with such superficial exceptions as prove the rule, Mr. Hardy's genius strikes us as gothic in expression, but largely pagan in spirit. It tends always to a primitive conception of human life and character. Man seems to impress him as a natural, rather than social, or at least, socialized being; capricious rather than complex; possessing the power of growth, and free from innate obligation to grow into any given form; and in this view society presents itself as an arrangement rather than an organism, and social tradition as a mechanical agent rather than a vital fact. Thus, though he distinguishes the ignorant from the instructed, the natural from the artificial, he ignores the endless combinations of ignorance and artificiality, the instructed ignorance and the artificialized nature which the presence of social ideals always tends to create; and while he fails to illustrate the highest refinements of human culture, he leaves the whole province of *vulgarity* unexplored. It has no existence for him. To whatever social category his personages belong, they are as free from it as if they were so many Grecian gods; and they are so, we are convinced, not only because he has not chosen to describe vulgarity, but because he would not know how to do it. His choice of subjects has hitherto favoured this turn of thought, and rendered the charm it gives to his conceptions compatible with truth; but it might seriously hamper him in any larger handling of the realities of social life.

Another and analogous feature of Mr. Hardy's judgment is his estimate of the nature of women; and if the simplicity of his point of view is generally synonymous with breadth, in this particular aspect it at least approaches narrowness. We might dismiss it by saying that his women are invariably men's women—a term which all female readers would understand; but the men's women of ordinary novels fill a secondary place, whereas Mr. Hardy's female characters are never secondary. His story is always the story of one woman in her relations to two or three men; and it is part of this scheme that, though the men do not lack individuality, they are chiefly introduced with reference to the women, and only fully developed at the points of contact with them. No writer has painted love more delicately than Mr. Hardy, or with more conviction of its being in its due season the grand business of life; but none has painted it as on the man's side more entirely distinct from esteem; and his idea of women is that of a pagan grace which does not require and often excludes the estimable. Though the vanity of his heroines is ever present and insatiable, they have none of the meanness which is imputed to feminine vanity by most male and by all female writers who take an exaggerated view of it. Their most universal desire for admiration will coexist with an honest passion for a particular man, and their utmost passion is never dissociated from a nymph-like and perfectly spontaneous purity. On the other hand, he represents the genuine, and, as such, successful woman, as necessarily weak, silly in spite of intelligence and knowledge, petulant, without conscience, and more easily led by force than kindness. His most lovable and most beloved female character, Elfride Swancourt, unites these weaknesses to the largest extent, petulance being the only one absent; and though he as little 'extenuates' as he 'sets down in malice', he has, to the mind of all female readers who believe in their own sex, added insult to injury by infusing into this compound a constant aroma of womanly pathos and tenderness. Bathsheba Everdene develops a con-science; it was therefore latent in her. Ethelberta Petherwin sacrifices her love to her sister's happiness; being, however, so constituted that the sacrifice is a small one. *The Return of the Native* contains three women of whom one is more individual, and two are more estimable, than the heroines of the preceding works; but the limitations which Mr. Hardy's theory has fastened upon them adhere equally to all. As the widening sphere of his female existences fails to introduce us to any touch of vulgar mental artificiality, so does its ascending scale fail to introduce us to any instance of mental discipline, or even practical mental culture. His women develop from the moral and the aesthetic side, but they never become thoroughly responsible creatures. There is doubtless something dramatic in the complete contrast which deprives one sex of all the mental qualities of the other. It may be a question if the finer differences which constitute the poetry, and, in some sense, the reality of their intercourse, can be dramatically reproduced; and those who believe, with the present writer, that the old antithesis of 'manly' and 'womanly' covers an essential natural truth, will not quarrel with Mr. Hardy for the exaggeration which is in the main a tribute to it. But he would have served its cause better by raising his idea of sexual difference, and hence of sexual magnetism, into a higher key; and there are passages even in his earliest novel through which the transposition might have taken place. In its heroine, Cytherea Graye, as in Elfride, in Bathsheba, in Eustacia, he constantly, so to speak, 'grazes' a more intellectual conception of feminine charm. Even when dwelling on personal details, and when describing the love inspired by them as entering entirely through the eye, he gives an expressiveness to their beauty which would excuse, even if it could not satisfy, a more idealizing attachment; nor would love be the power he represents it as being if it could not thus enlist the higher nature, and on occasion delude it; and if a half-delusion thus raised could not sometimes convert itself into truth. His women would often be better if they were better loved: that is to say, if their lovers expected better things of them. Elfride Swancourt deteriorates under the influence of a man to whom virginity of feeling is worth more than a tried devotion; and if Clym Yeobright suffers from his wife's deficient mental sympathies, he makes not the slightest effort to develop them. Whether Mr. Hardy thinks that no charming woman can be other than he describes her, or that no man desires her to be so, we have no means of inferring.

If his judgments are in this sense an artistic defect, and to some minds undoubtedly they are, they become so only by repetition. No one of his books condemns itself either by his choice of characters, or his mode of working them out. The statement requires qualifying with reference to his last work. Still, taken in itself, each character is possible, and in the given surroundings its experiences are not only possible but necessary. While his faults are cumulative, his merits strike us afresh in every new production. It has been said that men distinguish themselves from women by their power of telling a story; and if by 'telling' a story is meant also inventing it, we shall fairly define Mr. Hardy's genius by calling it masculine. His power of making a plot, of setting characters in motion, of arousing and sustaining interest is unsurpassed, perhaps unrivalled in modern fiction; and while it uses at pleasure exceptional incidents or the occurrences of everyday life, his success is proportioned in due dramatic manner to the absence of intention with which he appears to have set to work.

[seven pages are omitted here.]

Stephen Smith is so entirely to our mind the hero of this situation, that we grow rather angry with Mr. Hardy for the disparaging tone which he now adopts towards him, though we understand his reason for adopting it. He has clearly intended that Stephen's low birth should so imperceptibly leaven his character as not to condemn Elfride's love, and still help to justify her defection; and as it is not essential to the outward course of the story, however at first sight it may appear so, it could be artistically justified on no other grounds. But he has failed to carry out this intention; partly because he has put Stephen in a position which merges the gentleman in the man; and partly because the qualities or the failings of a half-gentlemanliness have no place in his imagination; and he is vaguely troubled by the idea that he will impress the reader too favourably. His genius nearly helps him out of this strait. He more than once 'burns' when feeling his way to a link between Stephen's defects and his antecedents; as for instance, when he gives him a keen sense of social distinctions, and a blunt perception of individual difference; but he always ends by characterizing him as simply immature; and the plasticity of mind to which his worldly success is imputed puts the rustic origin out of court. As a lover he is less refined than Knight, in so far that he is less reserved. He snatches a kiss whenever the occasion justifies it, whereas his rival is slow to claim such a privilege, and approaches his lady's face, when he does so, '*with the carefulness of a fruiterer touching a bunch of grapes so as not to disturb them*'; and this contrast between an awkwardness which is not diffident and a diffidence which is not awkward might have been worked out in the sense of a fundamental difference, but it is not so worked out. It simply shows that the one man was aesthetically refined, and the other morally healthy; and we cannot see that the comparisons which are instituted between them give any moral advantage to the former. Fortunately for the interest of the narrative, the author has shown himself too profound an artist to allow any personal preference to disturb it. He tickets Knight superior as he tickets Smith secondhand; but he does not colour the actions of either to justify the inscription; and he frankly admits that the success of the second lover in displacing the first lay in many things beside his actual superiority to him.

The same neutral criticism is subsequently applied to her want of frankness. Mr. Hardy is uncertain whether a young girl can justly be tried by the same standards of honesty as a man. '*Much*', he says, '*of a woman's charm lies in her subtlety in matters of love.*' But if Elfride's want of honesty was a fault, then was she so far inferior to Knight—'not good enough for him'.

[paragraph omitted.]

Bathsheba Everdene is as unlike Elfride Swancourt as a rustic version of what is essentially the same woman allows her to be. She has the same restless vanity, the same disposition to yield to tyranny and underrate devotion; at moments, the same tenderness; but nature and education have made her more hardy in mind as well as body, and she has a desire for independence which renders her lapses into subjection piquant and often pathetic. She is more shrewd than Elfride, but being braver is also more honest; less susceptible in feeling, and also more constant. There is an innocent savagery about her which displays itself alternately in a boyish boldness and a maidenly reserve.

Gabriel Oak represents one of the author's favourite types. He has worked it out carefully, and repeats it in *The Return of the Native* as Diggory Venn. It is a necessary complement to his conception of women; and it might be untrue to the capabilities of real life to say that it is too dramatic to be entirely living; but we find it difficult to reconcile in the abstract so much singleness of heart with so much power of dissimulation. Mr. Hardy has been more undeniably successful in the young soldier and adventurer whose appeal to Bathsheba's girlish fancy is so sudden and so overpowering. Artistically, this seems to us the most successful of his male characters. It is that which we can best see through. Henry Knight, Gabriel Oak, and even Farmer Boldwood are not less vividly drawn, and they are in themselves far more impressive; but they are drawn under the conditions of an absorbing attachment, and in a manner obscured by it. Troy has no such attachment. The elements of his nature play freely before us; and though he is more complex than they, he is also more transparent. Several paragraphs are devoted to a description of him; but this we think rather supplements his action than entirely explains it. He strikes us, briefly, as possessing just so much goodness, intelligence, and strength, as is consistent with the absence of all effective principle, a perfect slavery to the impulse of the moment, and a perfect blindness to everything beyond it. He marries Bathsheba with enough of love to excuse the deed as far as she is concerned; but to the sacrifice of a woman who is his wife in fact, and was on the point of becoming so in law. Bathsheba's disenchantment soon assists his fancy to drift back to her who has trusted him only too much; and when Fanny Robin again crosses his path, her destitution makes almost a virtue of the revulsion of feeling which would have set in without it. He collects all he can of his wife's money to take to her, and when he has returned from a fruitless tryst to find her coffin, which a train of simple circumstances has brought to Bathsheba's house, he sinks down before it with words and gestures of a reverential tenderness which would be exquisite, if the presence of his injured and for the moment broken-spirited wife did not render it brutal. Death overtakes him at the moment of a second reaction.

The small rustic personages who form the background of *Far from the Madding Crowd*, and those more important who enter into its action, are the first illustration on a large scale of the author's genius for that kind of portraiture; and in this sense they have met with abundant comment and abundant praise; but we cannot close even so scanty a notice without a tribute of admiration to the skill which has maintained the due balance between the individual and the type where it was so difficult not to develop the one at the expense of the other. Most of these Weatherbury men resolve themselves in the memory into a general impression of quaint thought and epigrammatic speech; but they become distinct again whenever we hold the picture nearer to the eye; and some few occupy a middle distance upon it at which they always remain. Cainy Ball's habit of running till he chokes keeps him only too vividly before us; and when once we have seen the word 'James', as printed by Joseph Poorgrass on Farmer Everdene's carts, with the inverted E which he can never remember to turn the right way, we scarcely need the remaining particulars to feel fully acquainted with him. This Joseph Poorgrass is a pious individual, but too much afflicted by what he calls 'a multiplying eye'; and an attack of this disorder incurred in a wayside public-house at a critical moment of the story exerts a decided influence on its events.

If *The Hand of Ethelberta* could be taken seriously, it would be the most vigorous disclaimer of social disabilities ever embodied in fiction; and we must so far take it seriously that the genuine ladyhood of the butler's daughter is the one fact which makes the fiction possible; but half the point of her adventures lies in their incongruity; and Mr. Hardy presents this in too laughable an aspect to permit any doubt of his intending us to laugh at it. The story has of course no thrilling interest, but it excites a lively curiosity which is sustained almost to the end; and as an instance of the author's constructive skill, it is inferior to nothing he has written. It is a fantastic interlude to his more serious work, and gives it the force of contrast without suffering from the comparison.

The Return of the Native presents a new phase, and perhaps a new departure in the development of Mr. Hardy's genius. It repeats the tragedy of *Far from the Madding Crowd* on a larger scale, with stronger intellectual elements, with a deeper perception of the contrast between human passion and natural repose, with a more subtle sense of their affinity. It has less of the irony of life, and more of its serious sadness. It is, in short, a more serious work than any of its predecessors. We believe it is generally considered to be in every sense 'stronger.' The present writer does not, however, share this opinion, and for the following reason. If *The Return of the Native* is more earnest than *A Pair of Blue Eyes* or *Far from the Madding Crowd*, it is also less spontaneous. It suggests a more definite intention on the author's part, but also, dramatically, though not otherwise, a less equal inspiration. In his earlier works character is developed by circumstance; we cannot predict what is coming, and when the end comes, we can imagine no other to have been possible. In the present work the characters are defined from the first, the action soon becomes transparent, and the catastrophe nevertheless brings a kind of shock in which there is a decided element of objection. Hitherto the tragedy has been rooted in the facts of the story. In the present instance it is more or less imported into them. This process has not been direct. Mr. Hardy is too profound an artist to place any event before us without first creating its conditions. But we see the creation taking place. Mrs. Yeobright's death is a case in point. It is brought about by a concurrence of circumstances, possible in itself, and more than adequate to the result—tropical heat, an exhausting walk, some latent heart-disease, the known impulsiveness which prompts her both to seize so unfitting a day for the visit to her son and to jump at a totally wrong conclusion from his wife's delay in admitting her, the subsequent sting of an adder; and if the event had only ordinary consequences, we should not wish to dispute its likelihood. But when we reflect that it converts its object into a martyr, to whom indirectly two other lives are sacrificed; that its one exciting cause is a short delay in opening a door, due more to accident than to ill-will; and that this cause depends for its effect on the coincidence of a hitherto unsuspected physical weakness with the other predisposing facts, the situation strikes us as morally strained, however well worked out from an artistic point of view.

Our objections to the tragic termination of Eustacia's life strike deeper down, assuming of course that she willed it. If it were otherwise, our argument would fall to the ground, but we should still less recognize Mr. Hardy's best manner in the presenting it as an accident. Here also, at first sight, we find the necessary conditions of the catastrophe. There is a subtle connection between her previous moods and this final act of despair. Hope has presented itself in the form of Wildeve's protection, but pride and prudence alike forbid her retaining it. There is much in her position to make life a burden to her; in her character, to make it intolerable. But on reviewing her later experiences, we discover something more than this. We discover a conscientious shrinking from renewed intimacy with her lover, which must oppose itself to her one chance of escape, and being once admitted into the situation must be accepted as a principal factor in it; and it appears to us that, at the moment in which a definite moral sense is introduced into her nature, it is transposed from its original key. Mr. Hardy concludes his first description of her, by saying that she had the making of a perfect goddess, but an indifferent woman; and this is precisely what he makes us feel. Gloomy, self-conscious, and self-tormenting, she is still pagan in spirit. She has as pure a passion for the beautiful in life as is consistent with a shallow heart and an uncultivated mind; and it is only through this passion that her heart and mind could have been enlarged—that the voice of duty could have been brought home to her. No such channel was employed. Her married life was made to disappoint her desires, and jar upon her sensibilities. Her husband followed his own ideas, and did not even attempt to reconcile her to them. While he loved and trusted her, his claims on her fidelity were such as even her nature might recognize; when he had driven her from him, unjustly and cruelly, they no longer were so. We are at all events unprepared for the tone of orthodox propriety which she and her former lover endeavour to maintain. Was she conventionally timid, though naturally the reverse? There are no traces of conventionality in her. Was she influenced by religious fears? We do not gather that she had any. If Eustacia Vye were more distinctly drawn she might prove less original, and she would certainly be less pathetic; but we cannot help feeling that her author has not had all the courage of his imagination, and that having conceived her for a larger stage, he has modified her to suit a small one. We have the same impression of an extemporized conscience in Wildeve's later proceedings, though we see that it is calculated to break down if temptation grows strong; but this character, which is on the pattern of Sergeant Troy's, is of the kind to which no transformation is impossible; and we may allow a good deal for the temporary dignity which the accession to fortune and the new power of usefulness might give it. We must object, however, even more in his case than in that of Eustacia, to the suggestion of a latent nobleness of soul, and a timely spiritual rescue which the dead face is intended to convey.

The 'Native' himself affords the fullest proof of the change which has come over the spirit of Mr. Hardy's dream, and apparently indicates its tendency. He is well-conceived and finely brought out, by the contact with his mother and wife; his relations to the former being a touching instance of the kind of estrangement which may arise between persons who deeply love each other, when natural sympathy is crossed by an acquired difference of views. But he is chiefly remarkable as being the first of Mr. Hardy's characters who is actuated by any large appreciation of human duty. Clym Yeobright is in fact a humanitarian, touched with the asceticism of a certain positivistic school; and though his life does not recommend his doctrine, or the course of the story depend materially upon it, its serious introduction must stand for what it is worth.

This, then, is our impression of the case. At the climax of his dramatic genius, Mr. Hardy has been overtaken by a motive, or by a moral self-consciousness which is equivalent to one. His fancy has, it is true, never shown itself more picturesque, or more varied than in the present work. Of its most important personages, three are new creations. He has added two types to his rustic repertoire, in the grandfather and grandson Cantle. In the description of Egdon Heath he has conjured up a very mystery of solitude, of brooding silences, and of unearthly sounds. The details of the bonfire on Blackbarrow, if somewhat laboured, are full of imaginative observation. The game of dice, played by the light of glow-worms, between Wildeve and Venn is a masterpiece of fantastic power. What we take for a motive may be merely an accident of dramatic inspiration involving greater difficulties than his earlier efforts, and therefore more unequal results; but we do not believe it to be so; and if it is not, the question stands thus; imagination and intellect are fighting for mastery in Mr. Hardy's work. Which will prevail? Will the unconscious inspiration assimilate the motive? or will the consciousness of the motive paralyse the inspiration? This question is distinct from that which has been suggested at an earlier stage of these remarks; though the one, to a certain extent, may include the other. No assumption that the answer will be favourable could be more respectful than the interest with which we await it.

THE TRUMPET MAJOR

October 1880

18. Unsigned review, *Athenaeum*

20 November 1880, 672

The editorial file marks this review 'Britten'. Hardy's is the first of four 'Novels of the Week' discussed in one article.

Mr. Hardy seems to be in the way to do for rural life what Dickens did for that of the town. Like the elder novelist, he finds his characters entirely in the middle or lower middle class. With the 'nobility and gentry' he has nothing to do. In one respect, indeed, he is more fortunate than Dickens. Readers who, like the old Scot, would rather hear the lark sing than the mouse squeak, are probably in these days the majority, and for them Overcombe Mill and the downs of Dorsetshire will have more attractions than the neighbourhood of Golden Square or Lant Street in the Borough. But setting aside invidious comparisons, it may be said that in the ten years or so which have elapsed since Mr. Hardy's first anonymous novel raised hopes that the yeoman class had found its *sacer vates*, his steady progress has fully justified these anticipations. No doubt he still retains one or two of his old mannerisms, notably his tendency to far-fetched similes—as when he compares the ruddy Festus Derriman's teeth to 'snow in a Dutch cabbage', and elsewhere to white chessmen hemmed in by the red—and his habit of putting into the mouths of illiterate rustics idioms which we can hardly believe to be theirs, and expressions which are surely not characteristic. His practice, which no doubt has much to justify it, of refusing (in his own words) 'to encumber the page with obsolete pronunciations of the purely English words, and with mispronunciations of those derived from Latin and Greek', adds to the unnatural effect of such sentences as these:

71

If Boney could only see ye now, sir, he'd know too well that there's nothing to be got from such a determined skilful officer but blows and musket balls . . . You would outshine 'em all, and be picked off at the very beginning as a too-dangerous brave man.

Mr. Hardy has in former books done worse than this, but this is bad enough. Not even his undoubted accuracy of observation in some matters can make us credit that such language as this, even if translated into the correct dialect, would have been within the compass (to use another word of Mr. Hardy's own) of the man-of-all-work in a small Dorsetshire farmhouse at the date when 'Boney' was an object of terror. So much for minute criticism. When we come to more substantial matters we have nothing but praise for *The Trumpet Major*. It will probably disappoint readers who crave for 'sensation', albeit there are plenty of sufficiently exciting incidents in it. The author has not that power of enthralling the reader's interest which is possessed, for instance, by Mr. Blackmore; or if he has it he does not care to exercise it. But he is second to no living writer in the art of making one see his scenes and know his characters. He called one of his earlier books 'a Dutch picture'. In *The Trumpet Major* there are a dozen such. The supper at Miller Loveday's, in the course of which several of the leading personages are introduced to the reader, is simply perfect of its kind; only the reader will wish Mr. Hardy had given a little more of Sergeant Stanner's song. Excellent, too, almost Rabelaisian in its profusion, is the account of the preparations for Bob Loveday's wedding feast; and full of spirit the description of the same Bob's flight from the press-gang. Nor have we ever in the present story to complain of the introduction without due cause of incidents beyond the bounds of reasonable probability. The personages, too, are admirably touched. It is true, no doubt, that the heroine is, not to put too fine a point upon it, a fool, and the gallant Bob Loveday another; and that the reader cannot help feeling more regard for Matilda of the doubtful reputation than for the correct and ladylike Anne. But Mr. Hardy has always inclined to the cynical rather than to the sentimental; and it should be said also that, like a true artist, he never attempts by any indication of his own preferences to bias his reader's judgment. Yet it can be hardly doubted that he likes his hero. John Loveday, the trumpet-major from whom the book takes its title, is the best character that Mr. Hardy has ever drawn. Indeed, there are few figures in all fiction more pathetic, and in a quiet way heroic, than this simple, loyal, affectionate soldier, who no more dreams of breaking a promise made in a hurry to a number of drunken roisterers than he objects to thrashing one of these very roisterers at a later period for impertinence to the girl he loves, or hesitates to receive on his own bare hands a stream of boiling water to save the same girl from a possible scalding. In all he does he is influenced by two motives: affection for his brother Bob, an easy-going sailor, who exercises to the full his sailor's privilege of being on with the new love before he is off with the old, and love for Anne Garland. Between these two poor John is sorely tried; yet, as Anne is obviously unworthy of him, the reader is hardly inclined either to sympathize fully with his trials or to regret the final result. Still, when the poor steadfast and unselfish man goes off 'to blow his trumpet till silenced for ever upon one of the bloody battle-fields of Spain', one feels that, to himself at least, his parting joke about 'a soldier's heart not being worth a week's purchase' is eminently inapplicable. In conclusion, we may say that *The Trumpet Major*, while it is not one of those books which once begun make the reader forget all his duties until he has reached the end, is distinctly one which, having finished, he will be inclined to keep on his table and look back into once and again.

19. Julian Hawthorne, *Spectator*

18 December 1880, 1627

The author of this review was a minor novelist.

There is a class of novels which we are compelled by critical canons to call good, and which, nevertheless, we read only with a certain effort, and from a sense of duty. There is another class, which a conscientious regard for literary integrity warns us to call bad, but which, notwithstanding, we cannot help finding extremely readable. And there is a third class, which are both readable and good; and it is to this class that *The Trumpet Major*, and the majority of the other novels which Mr.

Hardy has written, may be said to belong. He is not like any other novelist, and in no respect is he more unique than in this: that he is a novelist born, not made. His genius is observant, truthful, humorous, and at once masculine and shy. We have brought together the last two traits, as forming a somewhat unusual combination, though it is, perhaps, not so unusual as might naturally be expected. The feminine genius that concerns itself with modern fiction cannot be said to be uniformly shy. Be that as it may, Mr. Hardy is what we have said; it is one of his most distinctive and valuable qualities. He has a telling instinct for the value of sex; his heroines are profoundly feminine; his heroes thoroughly, and at times comically, masculine. His shyness, connected as it is with an almost morbid keenness of observation, imparts to his humour a peculiarly delicate and delightful aroma; he never misses the comic aspect of a situation or episode, and yet he never enforces it by a coarse or unsympathetic touch; the light falls gently and sweetly upon it, and passes on. A great many modern novelists would never be humorous, if there were not so great a demand for humour now-a-days—a demand which they feel in duty bound to supply, to the best of their ability; but Mr. Hardy is humorous, inevitably and inadvertently—and would be so, if humour in literature were a thing unheard of until he wrote. In view of his sensitiveness to impressions, it might be supposed that he would find it difficult to be original, that he would be prone to catch the tone and manner of other writers. Nor has he always been altogether free from this reproach; but never for long, and never when he is at his best. The reason is, that his fine literary organization finds itself clogged or hampered by the assumption of any method not spontaneous to itself; it cannot breathe in any other than its native atmosphere; and very soon it withdraws itself from foreign support and influence, and is almost surprised to find how excellently it can walk alone. In other words, the essential veracity of Mr. Hardy's insight is potent enough to correct his tendency to self-distrust; he discovers that he can be more accurate when he depends upon his own vision, than when he accepts the spectacles of minds stronger and more positive than his own.

This fineness of organization, however, carries the penalty of being open to certain faults, and from these faults Mr. Hardy's work is not free. A faculty of seeing more in things than ordinary eyes can discern, opens the way to making mountains out of molehills—to attaching more than their due importance to things really or comparatively insignificant. Thus it may sometimes happen that when Mr. Hardy has nothing very striking to relate, he too readily seeks compensation in magnifying and elaborating trifles. The result is an impression of thinness; the workmanship is as good as ever, but the subject is inadequate; and the best workmanship is apt, under these circumstances, to become fantastic and whimsical. On the other hand, genius of Mr. Hardy's order is not capable of the loftier and more powerful efforts of tragedy; its further range in this direction should be limited by the pathetic, and this involves never altogether losing sight of the humorous. Now, in true pathos Mr. Hardy has no living superior, but his attempts in the way of tragedy have not been satisfactory. His voice, so melodious within its proper compass, breaks when strained at more powerful notes. The episodes which occupy the closing chapters of *The Return of the Native*, for example, have not a true ring; they seem arbitrary, and the reader does not feel convinced that they really happened. When Shakespeare shows us a Lady Macbeth or an Othello, we at once perceive that tragedy is inherent in them; and when the tragic action comes, we feel it to be the irrepressible manifestation of even greater tragic possibilities within; there is no forcing on of the agony, if anything, it is rather repressed. But in Mr. Hardy's case, the tragic garb wherewith he drapes his characters is not suited to them, it 'fits them too much', as the Americans say. He conceives his tragic episode forcibly enough, but he does not give his actors the strength to carry it out; they seem to do the thing, but they are not themselves when they do it; they achieve it only at the cost of their own lives, so to speak. When Othello kills Desdemona, the act only makes him more Othello than he was before; but when Eustacia drowns herself on Egdon Heath, she leaves the Eustacia that we believe in safe on the bank. How much less effective is that elaborate scene than the simple sentence which concludes the story of *Under the Greenwood Tree*, where the heroine has become the wife of the worthy fellow she does not love, and thinks of 'the secret that she would never tell'. There is genuine heartbreak in those words, so gentle and so grievous.

The present story is not Mr. Hardy's best, but it has much of his best work in it, and the subject is one calculated to show the author in his happiest light. The heroine, Anne Garland, belongs to a class of women who are found nowhere else in literature than in Mr. Hardy's novels; whether they also exist in real life, we do not undertake to say, but after reading about them, we cannot help believing that they do. Anne is personally lovely and attractive; she is, moreover, amiable, innocent, generous, and tender-hearted, and yet she makes woeful

havoc of the heart of a worthy man. She is selfish, as Mr. Hardy's
heroines are selfish—not wilfully or intellectually, but by dint of her
inborn, involuntary, unconscious emotional organism. She recognizes
John Loveday's goodness, his self-abnegation, his lovableness, and she
can no more justify herself in not loving him than she can in loving his
scamp of a brother; nevertheless, and despite all the obstacles of self-
respect, gratitude and expediency, she marries Bob, and sends John to
die on a Spanish battle-field. It is Mr. Hardy's delight to show his
chosen woman doing these things; a hasty criticism might deem him
cynical, but to us this judgment seems uncalled for. The truth is,
such a character is not only picturesque in itself, but the cause of
picturesqueness in others, and is, therefore eminently suited for literary
purposes. Compare a woman like Anne Garland with a woman like—
to take an extreme case—*David Copperfield's* Agnes, or with any of
Scott's pattern heroines. When a woman is governed by reason, con-
forms to the canons of respectability, obeys the dictates of prudence
and strict propriety, and sacrifices herself on the altar of what she is
pleased to consider her womanhood, the less we hear of that woman
(in fiction), the better are we content. What we want, and what artistic
beauty demands, is colour, warmth, impulse, sweet perversity, pathetic
error; an inability to submit the heart to the guidance of the head, a
happiness under conditions against which a rational judgment protests;
and all this, and more, we get in Anne Garland and her kindred. Their
conduct is indefensible, but it is charming—we love them the better for
their tender naughtiness. We are appalled to see what harm these
gentle, compassionate, sweet-tempered creatures can do; to remark the
naïve cruelty and hardness that underlie it all; but we are fain to confess
that it is nature, and incorrigible—we must even admit that humanity
would be dry and frigid without it. For the selfishness is always
passionate, never calculating. Whatever pain Anne Garland inflicts
upon John, whom she esteems, she would herself suffer in tenfold
degree for Bob, whom she loves. And let the moralist be appeased,
since we may see with half a glance that the fault carries its full punishment with it.

Although the story has this thread of pathos running through it, it
is replete with true comedy, both in construction and in detail. Uncle
Benjy, with his precious tin box of deeds and documents, his ravening
anxiety concerning the same, his relations with his nephew Festus, all
are humorous in the extreme. Or what could be more finely comic than
to see Bob (at that time nominally in love with Matilda) kissing Anne's

hand, and then striving to appease her indignation by protesting that he only did it out of a general admiration for the sex, and not from any special tenderness for her? 'I do love Matilda best', he cries, 'and I don't love you at all!' a plea of somewhat doubtful value for poor Anne, who is all the time consumed with secret anguish at his loving Matilda instead of herself.

The story, from beginning to end, is conceived and put together with capital ingenuity. It was a happy thought to lay it in the year '14, or thereabout, and to make Bob a sailor and John a soldier. By this means an immense deal of colour and incident is introduced, which must otherwise have been lost; the setting is in no way essential to the plot, but it helps vastly in the telling of the tale. It was a picturesque idea to put the widow and her daughter under the same roof with the miller, on the genteel side of the house, instead of sending them off to occupy a separate dwelling of their own. It was wisely done to represent Bob as a fine fellow in all ways except his fickleness, and to make the character who comes nearest to being the villain of the piece also one of the most laughable. These touches preserve the 'tone' of the picture, and would not have suggested themselves to a less careful artist than Mr. Hardy. The work, as a whole, is better reading than a detailed analysis of it would indicate; indeed, it is better in the reading than in the recollection, insomuch that we are surprised, on a second perusal, to find how many minor and verbal felicities we had forgotten. At the same time, we are of opinion that, in the first place, John Loveday became, in real life, the husband of Anne Garland; and in the second place, we think that Mr. Hardy became a trifle impatient with his third volume, and was sorry that it was not permitted him to compress the novel into two volumes. At all events, the third volume, especially the latter part of it, bears evidence of haste and of a subsidence of interest on the author's part, although it is to be particularly noted that in the last three or four pages, and notably in the last one or two, he fully recovers his best standard. But all allowances made, if Mr. Hardy never writes a worse book than *The Trumpet Major*, he will maintain a literary level which any contemporary writer of English prose fiction might be glad to attain. We may not, perhaps, look to see him produce anything wholly unlike or superior to what he has already given us; but we shall listen to his variations more comfortably than to the novelties of most novelists.

20. Survey, *British Quarterly Review*

1881, lxxiii, 342–60

The British Quarterly Review was a serious and respected Non-conformist organ which flourished from 1845 to 1886. At this time the editor was the Congregationalist minister Henry Allon, and literary contributors included Mark Pattison, Walter Besant, Vernon Lee and R. H. Hutton. This article is unsigned, and there is no reference to it in Allon's correspondence as published in A. Peel, *Letters to a Victorian Editor*. For the Review generally, see the article by R. V. Osbourn in *The Review of English Studies*, April 1950, n.s.1, p. 147.

When George Eliot died it was not unnatural that men should at once ask themselves if she who had been confessedly the greatest living English novelist had left any successor in the true province of literature. The question, floating in so many minds, was answered promptly and decidedly by one journal, not without influence on opinion, which claimed the falling mantle for Mr. Thomas Hardy. It was a surprise to many who read the words that such a claim should have been made; the English public, greedy for amusement, careless about good, finished, and subtle literary work, is very slow to understand that of stories which have charmed a leisure hour some are destined to pass into complete forgetfulness, having merely served to waste a part of the season, while others become a part of the literature of the country, to be read and re-read, and to place their characters as living beings among the viewless companions of our thoughts.

The power of creating personages which live, and become even more real than many historic phantasms is rarer than we may think. Most people who make pretensions to the study of literature have read not only Shakspere, but Ben Jonson and Dryden, to say nothing of Marlowe, Beaumont and Fletcher, Wycherly, Congreve, Farquhar. Yet while the mere titles, the plot, and many isolated passages remain in the memory, how few there are who could name more than the title-character of any one play, who could be sure that they would not give to one author or to one play the *dramatis personæ* of another, while they no more confuse Shakspere's plays than they mentally assign the children or the wife of one friend to another, or travel into the Midland Counties to visit one who lives in Devonshire.

Now if we ask ourselves who in English fiction have made their brain children our familiar friends, whom not to know is to be wanting in acquaintance with letters, and with the thought of the past and present, we shall find they are but few, Shakspere, Fielding, Richardson, Miss Burney, perhaps—though her king, princes, and royal household are, for a wonder, more real than her fictitious characters—Sir Walter Scott, Miss Austen, Dickens, Thackeray, George Eliot, and for those who have once become imbued with the spirit of his works, Hardy.

We shall see the difference between any of these and their fellows by taking authors whose works ran side by side—Miss Ferrier with Sir Walter Scott, Mrs. Brunton with Miss Austen. In Miss Ferrier's work Miss Pratt stands out with exceeding vividness, but we believe that many would find it difficult to say in which novel she found her place; and who can recall a single character in Mrs. Brunton's very clever novels, *Self Controul* and *Discipline*? In the creation of living persons, not mere lay figures round whom dress, furniture, scenery are to be arranged, we believe that the author we are now to study is the successor of George Eliot. The test is one any reader can apply, and to those who do so we have every confidence that Fancy Day and Dick Dewy, Ethelberta Petherwin, Clym Yeobright and Eustacia Vye, Parson Swancourt, and all the host of minor persons, each with its own distinctive mark, will become to their minds and memories as real and indestructible, say, as Adam Bede or Romola, and even as those drawn by Shakspere's mighty hand, though they lack his perfect art.

Another test is one which is not so sure, since there is not, in spite of Mr. Matthew Arnold, any definite standard of literary excellence. There are those who imagine that Mrs. Henry Wood writes English, and that Ouida knows the value of the words she uses; they are wholly unable to distinguish between the faculty which is amused by an intricate if impossible plot, and that which tries and weighs style, plot, characters, the thought and learning involved in rather than displayed upon the book, against the masterpieces of fiction which the criticism of time has already tested and pronounced genuine. This test is that of literary style, wholly neglected by the majority of our novelists, whose

name is Legion. The most part aim at telling their story, and depend
on the story only for any value the book may possess. Some who are
agreeable narrators, and who give a picture of the time in which we
live fairly enough in its superficial aspects, write in a style which we feel
to be simply abominable the moment we pause to consider the words
in which the story is conveyed. Perhaps no writers of the non-enduring,
merely ephemeral, yet pleasant kind, have ever written more or been
more widely read than Mr. Trollope and Mrs. Oliphant. We doubt if
there is in all their writings one single passage on which any reader has
ever dwelt for its own sake, for the thought conveyed in the given
sentence, for the music of the words, or for the description of scenery
apart from the context. We should be surprised to find that any intelligent person who keeps a book of extracts, no mean test of the
beautiful in literature, has ever taken the trouble to copy into it a
passage from either of these writers. To hurry through the mere story
and see what is done with the puppets is the aim of the reader; none
dwell on the page as they dwell on the words of Scott, some of whose
prose chapters are little more difficult to learn by heart than is his
ordered verse, or on scenes like that at the Rainbow in *Silas Marner*,
or *Dinah's* preaching, or Hetty's dreadful pilgrimage in *Adam Bede*, or
as now and then they lingered leisurely over Kingsley in his rich word-
painting of a South American forest, or of the blazing solitude of the
African desert. A really great novelist has always chapters that are
quotable and readable apart from the context, for the pleasure which
they give of themselves, just as scenes of a dramatist, or a chapter in
the Bible can be read detached: it is in fact a note of true literature. The
abdication of Mary Stuart in *The Abbot*, the interview between Jeannie
Deans and Queen Caroline in *The Heart of Midlothian*, are types of
chapters to be found in the works of all really great writers; but who
ever cared to read a solitary chapter of more than two or three persons
within our own memory?

But more is wanted than the power of creating characters and a good
literary style. The first-rate workman rarely writes with set purpose
to draw a moral. It is inconceivable that Shakspere should have called
one play 'Jealousy or the Moor of Venice', or another, 'God's Revenge
against Murther'. He thinks of a man, Othello or Macbeth, and exhibits
his qualities, he does not think of qualities and the consequences of
qualities and invent men and incidents for them. Perhaps the only
exception to this among really great writers is Dickens. He, no doubt,
set himself in one book to demolish Yorkshire schools, in another to

reform sick nursing, and so on; but in so far as he is didactic he is tedious. Smike is a bore, and the case of Jarndyce *v.* Jarndyce could scarcely be more wearisome in the Court of Chancery itself than it is in *Bleak House.*

Again, a writer must strike some deep human interest which shall be quite independent of the circumstances of the time in which the scene is laid. Garrick probably moved men as much, or more, playing Hamlet or Macbeth in the wig of the period than a modern actor in a costume studiously archaeological, in conformity with some feigned but definite period in Denmark's history, or the most recognized Celtic traditions. It is by his intensely human sympathy that Scott triumphs, in spite of the fetters which he imposes on himself by his archaeological details; and Romola because she is so true a woman makes us forget the somewhat too elaborate though very clever 'cram' with which the story of her life is overladen. In her other works George Eliot has for the most part taken a society which changes little—homely people with homely lives. It has been remarked that a boundless sympathy was her characteristic, but on a somewhat low level. Mr. Hardy, in the same way, but even to a greater extent, takes life where it changes least, and considers it in its most simply human aspects.

It is because there is in another remarkable writer of our day little sympathy with humanity, as such, that we do not mention him as the literary successor of George Eliot. Mr. George Meredith has no feeling of toleration for a fool. He is an accomplished literary artist, limited by this, that the only men and women worth writing about at all are those who speak in epigrams as brilliant as his own writing which describes them. When he introduces a fool and a bore the things he makes him say are often excellent; it is difficult to tell by what stroke of genius it is that the man who says so good things is yet so intolerable. Mr. Meredith is a delightful study to the diligent reader, but he is a study; he is laboured and affected, difficult sometimes as the chorus of a Greek play, always, we fear, caviare to the general, whereas the true novelist should, like the true dramatist, appeal to the many. Men must be amused, and they come to the novel as the relaxation from work. The 'Lustige Person' and the Manager in the Prologue to Faust have reason on their side against the highflown arguments of the poet. The most broadly human is the truest artist after all.

All great writers are autobiographical; at least, have drawn largely from their own experiences; where we do not know that they are so, as in the case of Shakspere, it is probably because we know so little about them. The true artist must use up what has come to him, and the highest originality is the transmutation in the alembic of the brain of the material accumulated by the worker, or by others who have gone before. Originality which is not based in a large degree on personal experience is a making of bricks not only without straw, but with very little clay.

Few men have used their own experiences so much as Mr. Hardy, to whom we definitely turn after this somewhat long exordium, yet few have ever seemed so original to those who are in sympathy with the life which he describes. That he is less known than some far inferior people, arises from the fact that a certain country training, and somewhat of his own wide sympathy with nature, and with the simpler forms of country life, is needed before he is read and understood. In these days of overgrown towns men only take short rushes into country life, and know but little intimately of what they see; yet more than ever, and increasingly is it the case, that the readers of books are in towns and not in the country. We do not pretend to be wholly ignorant of some personal details of the author's life, but are sure that even one who was so would construct without difficulty a theory which would not fail widely when it came to be verified. That Mr. Hardy, like Mr. Barnes the Dorset poet, is sprung of a race of labouring men in a county where the real old families are attached to the soil, and the county aristocracy, except perhaps in Purbeck, are comparatively new comers; that he is not 'too proud to care from whence he came', that, on the contrary, he regards his stock as reason for exceeding pride on two grounds—one the dignity of labour, the other that the country working-man is of nearer kin to that nature which he idealizes and personifies, till it has all the characteristics of some great supra-natural human being;—that he is thus anthropomorphic, but not in a theological sense, is apparent on the face of what he writes.

A closer observer might go further, and find autobiographic hints in the account of a young architect's life in *A Pair of Blue Eyes*, and in *A Laodicean*, now publishing in *Harper's Magazine*; yet more in the minute touches whenever a building of any kind occurs in the course of his story; in the relations, apart from those of rivalry in love, existing between the same young architect and his friend Henry Knight; in other family revelations wherein it were impertinent to follow; especially as we must always remember that only the simplest basis of fact is used for the embroidery of fiction.

Mr. Hardy's first novel scarcely gave promise of the great merit of his later work. *Desperate Remedies* is in the wildest style of extravagant romance. The hint of the *dénoûment* is given, and the *dénoûment* itself hangs on, not a lock of hair, but a single hair, a thread so minute that in real life no one would see it, much less would it play the part it here plays. The only thing to be said for the story, considered as literature, is that it is better than the sensational fictions, as they are called, which the writer took for his model. We remember an argument many years ago, in which Charles Kingsley was one of the disputants, on the authorship of *Titus Andronicus*. Kingsley claimed the play for Shakspere, not basing the claim on the well-known lines, 'The hunt is up', &c., nor on Tamora's speech to Aaron in the same hunt, but simply on the bloody murders and mutilations which strew their horror over the dreary acts. He considered it Shakspere's first play, in which the young writer, imitative, as all such are, before he found his true style, simply outdid the raw-head-and-bloody-bones tragedies which he found all around him, and having beaten the purveyors of horrors on their own ground, turned to that which was his natural field.

The publication of *Under the Greenwood Tree* not only at once stamped its author as an original and excellent writer, but has since attained that fatal gift of popularity which makes the book inaccessible in a decent cover. It is apparently now to be procured only in a vile binding of red and yellow, with advertisements of patent medicines on the back. But the book itself is a most delightful idyll, in the true sense of that much-suffering word, though composed of the very simplest elements. The scene shifts only from a country village to a gamekeeper's lodge in a wood, with the merest hint of the externals of town life. The *dramatis personae* are the parson, churchwarden, schoolmistress, and ordinary villagers of a hamlet. The young people revolve round the pretty schoolmistress as moths round a candle, even the grave bachelor vicar singes his wings; and Fancy Day, the girl in question, makes a homely but suitable marriage with the carrier's son. But the book is delightful because all the sweet and liberal air of Dorset blows through it, because a county little known to the world beyond it, but loved well by those who are Dorset born, or have made it their home, is lovingly presented in all its pleasant aspects, its rough frank life, its genuine English language, the fair scenery of its woods and wolds.

In it Mr. Hardy has laid down the lines of his work, so to speak, and we may therefore examine some of his special excellences before proceeding further. First, Mr. Hardy has interpreted for us the village

83

life which is so difficult to understand. The dweller in towns thinks the country labourer a lout because his speech differs greatly from his own, the real fact being that the dialect is far less debased than the clipt and smooth language of educated people, which tends more and more to reduce all the vowels to one sound. The townsman thinks his country brother stupid because he often is unable to read and write, forgetting the compensating memory which is cultivated to its highest point because verbal memoranda are lacking; and finding that the country-man is ignorant of some terms of town use, jumps to the conclusion that the whole vocabulary of the labourer is extremely slender. But says Mr. Barnes—

If a man would walk with me through our village, I could show him many things of which we want to speak every day, and for which we have words of which Johnson knew nothing.[1]

And again—

There came out in print some time ago a statement wonderful to me, that it had been found that the poor land folk of one of our shires had only about two hundred words in their vocabulary, with a hint that Dorset rustics were not likely to be more fully worded. There can be shown to any writer two hundred thing-names known to every man and woman of our own village for things of the body and dress of a labourer, without any mark-words [adjectives], or time-words [verbs], and without leaving the man for his house, or garden, or the field, or his work.[2]

And the fact that the countryman has not the town speech in full measure, and uses words and accent which are strange to the town, leads to the mistake that the language is radically different, that the labourers never talk like their employers and chance visitors, and if shown at all in fiction should always employ few words and a quite unintelligible tongue. Shakspere should have taught us otherwise, though he only introduces his countrymen incidentally, and usually in his more comic scenes: he was bound to amuse his town audience, but he never did so at the expense of truth.

Now Mr. Hardy gives us always sufficient indication of dialect to produce the impression he wishes. One who knows the country of which he speaks catches the keynote and has the tune always in his ear; but the outsider is not puzzled by too much dialect and many strange words; the author has the true sense of what is needed for his art, and the strength of reserve.

[1] *English Speech-Craft*, p. v.   [2] Ibid., p. 89.

Here, for instance, is a scene at the village shoemaker's, when the choir are criticizing the parson, who will not stand by them, and wishes to introduce a harmonium to lead the services—

[quotes Part Second, ch. II 'His visitors' to 'well before the meeting.']

Mr. Hardy's books are full of such passages, some far better, such as the scene in the vault, in *A Pair of Blue Eyes*, the 'Sunday hair-cutting at Egdon', in *The Return of the Native*, the conversation in the barn, in *Far from the Madding Crowd*. But we have taken his earlier work because in it he first showed that here was a man who could put before us the life of English peasants, so wholly unknown to the great mass of English readers. And having lived among West country folk from childhood, the writer of these lines believes there is not in all Mr. Hardy's works one exaggerated or untrue word in his descriptions of those whom he knows so well.

And next he is an interpreter of the simpler aspects of nature to many who have no time to commune with her, and learn her secrets at first hand. Year by year masses of our people, and they our chief readers, see less and less of simple quiet country scenes. Brick and mortar swallow up our lives, and when we escape from them, it is to the sea or to the mountains, not to lose ourselves in English woods, or wander over the downs and in the green lanes which exist only here, and date from British days, older still than the great Roman roads still to be traced in the west in unexpected places, green across hill and dale. Only a few days since we spoke to a young clerk who had escaped from London on Sunday into one of the loveliest districts of Surrey, and we asked if he had walked through a certain yew-tree grove, the wonder of the neighbourhood. To one country-bred there was something pathetic in the avowal that he did not know a yew-tree nor indeed any one tree from another. To such a one it would be a revelation, to many another a sweet memory, to hear that—

To dwellers in a wood, almost every species of tree has its voice as well as its feature. At the passing of the breeze, the fir-trees sob and moan no less distinctly than they rock; the holly whistles as it battles with itself; the ash hisses amid its quiverings; the beech rustles while its flat boughs rise and fall; and winter, which modifies the note of such trees as shed their leaves, does not destroy its individuality.[1]

Or again, take and analyse this description of the wind blowing over a great heath.

[1] *Under the Greenwood Tree.*

[quotes *The Return of the Native*, ch. VI 'The wind, indeed' to 'as vast as a crater.']

That is admirable. Only those who do not know the country, or whose ears are somewhat hard of hearing, will think it overstrained, and they, perhaps, to a less degree if they remember how Keble, cradled among the Gloucestershire hills, where winds blow less strongly than in the wild west, spoke of a somewhat analogous sound—

> Lone Nature feels that she may freely breathe,
> And round us and beneath
> Are heard her sacred tones: the fitful sweep
> Of winds across the steep
> Through withered bents—romantic note and clear,
> Meet for a hermit's ear.

In all his books, without any effort, Mr. Hardy brings in nature as a personality, now aiding, now at war with man, now subdued, now triumphant, but always as living and in relation to human life. There is something of the relic of old paganism in his way of viewing her, as indeed there is so much of it in his own county. And he likes to take us where we see her moods—with the keeper into the heart of the wood; with Gabriel Oak the shepherd, to the wild hill-side and the chalk-pit; with the reddleman across lanes and commons known to but few even of the country folk; to the brow of the cliff beetling over the sea, where 'it rained upwards instead of down, the strong ascending current of air carried the raindrops with it in its race up the escarpment'. He has learned many of the multitudinous languages in which nature speaks, both with tongues and looks, as truly as the king in the *Arabian Nights* had learned the speech of beast and bird.

In his second novel—*A Pair of Blue Eyes*—Mr. Hardy showed that he had made a great advance in his power of drawing character and in the construction of a story. The first was a clever sketch; here was a finished and excellent study. It is needless to tell the story, and unfair to those who have not read it. But in it was given a hint of one of the writer's limitations. Elfride Swancourt, though in a higher station, is own spiritual sister to Fancy Day, and, with one exception, all Mr. Hardy's women have a family likeness. They are all charming; they are all flirts from their cradle; they are all in love with more than one man at once; they seldom, if they marry at all, marry the right man; and while well conducted for the most part, are somewhat lacking in moral sense, and have only rudimentary souls. Undines of the earth, the thought of death scarce occurs in connection with them, and the pathos is all the deeper when Elfride dies, like the Lady of Burleigh, 'with the burden of an honour unto which she was not born', and the blight of three men's lives as an added weight.

The funeral of Elfride, Lady Luxellian, is one of two scenes connected with death in *A Pair of Blue Eyes*, and in each of them there is a whimsicality of treatment which is strange, but neither jarring nor irreverent. Dealing as he does with life in its purely human and temporal aspect, leaving to the preacher all which may be asserted or conjectured about the great issues to which it leads, he has only to do with the terrible irony of the fact of the rigid and impenetrable veil which shuts suddenly like a portcullis behind the retreating figure. To deal with this in the great tragic style would be quite alien to Mr. Hardy's temperament and purpose; to deal with it as a theologian would be perhaps impossible, certainly incongruous; he softens the thought of it by those gleams of humour inseparable from what we have called the irony of death. 'I should have gone mad in my sorrow', said a believing Christian, who was for a time stunned, as it were, to all religious comfort, 'if I had not been sustained by my sense of humour.'

The labourers are enlarging the vault for the first Lady Luxellian, Elfride's predecessor. One says—

'She must know by this time whether she's to go up or down, poor woman!'
    'What was her age?'
'Not more than seven or eight and twenty by candlelight. But Lord! by day 'a was forty if 'a were an hour.'
'Ay, night time or day time makes a difference of twenty years to rich feyriees,' observed Martin.
'I seed her, poor soul,' said a labourer from behind some removed coffins, 'only but last Valentine's-day of all the world. 'A was arm in crook wi' my lord. I says to myself, You be ticketed Churchyard, my noble lady, although you don't dream on't.'
'I see a bundle of letters go off an hour after the death. Sich wonderful black rims as they letters had—half-an-inch wide, at the very least.'
'Too much,' observed Martin. 'In short, 'tis out of the question that a human being can be so sorrowful as black edges half-an-inch wide. I'm sure people don't feel more than a very narrow border when they feels most of all.'

So, again, in *Under the Greenwood Tree*, young Dick Dewy is coming home from a friend's funeral, and passes the house of the girl to whom he is engaged.

'O Dick, how wet you are!' she said. 'Why your coat shines as if it had been varnished, and your hat—my goodness, there's a streaming hat!'

'O, I don't mind, darling!' said Dick, cheerfully. 'Wet never hurts me, though I am rather sorry for my best clothes. However, it couldn't be helped; they lent all the umbrellas to the women.'

'And look, there's a nasty patch of something just on your shoulder.'

'Ah, that's japanning; it's rubbed off the clamps of poor Jack's coffin, when we lowered him from our shoulders upon the bier. I don't care for that, for 'twas the last deed I could do for him; and 'tis hard if you can't afford a coat to an old friend.'

What Mr. Hardy does in reference to death he does also in reference to the other ills attendant on life—disease, sorrow, superstition. He could not bear the tragedy, or help us to bear it, unless he showed the strand of comedy interwoven; he is ironical in the deepest sense.

In *Far from the Madding Crowd* he touched deeper notes, but we do not think the book so great a success as his earlier or his later work. The heroine, who as usual plays fast and loose with her lovers, a young farmeress and heiress in one, is a less womanly woman, with all her coquettish ways, than are his other fantastic creations. The tragedy of Bold's suicide, and of the death of the girl Bathsheba's husband has betrayed, is somewhat too deep for its surroundings. Not that such subjects are unfit for fiction; to assert they were so would be to be unleal to Shakspere and Scott; but in *Far from the Madding Crowd* the character of the piece, so to speak, is melodramatic rather than tragical, while the incidents, or some of them, require a more harmonious setting. Still there are great merits in the book, the same love of nature, the same subtle analysis of motive, unexpected yet true complications of plot, as in *A Pair of Blue Eyes*. What is especially *new* in the work is not of any very deep interest.

In *The Hand of Ethelberta* the writer has taken a fresh departure, and produced one of the most striking works of English fiction. It is throughout comedy, even approximating to farce, yet in it was put forth one side of the author's view of duty as the moving principle of life, to be worked out grandly and seriously in a yet maturer work. We have to admit, as in witnessing a comedy, unlikely though not wholly impossible premises. Ethelberta Petherwin has sprung of very refined parents, though in humble life—both domestic servants. She has passed, by the time she is eighteen, through the stages of pupil-teacher in a good school, nursery governess, a clandestine marriage to a rich youth, widowhood, and recognition by her husband's mother.

She is launched on society, clever, beautiful, brave, with unknown antecedents, and, by an accident, almost penniless. A less able artist with this conception in his brain would scarcely have avoided imitation of a great model; he would have drawn an adventuress of the Becky Sharpe type. Ethelberta is saved from this, and from all temptation to this, by her complete unselfishness. Her moving principle is love for her family, the desire to advance them in such ways as they, not she, consider best. It is a first step in the conception of a great unselfish love for mankind to be brought out hereafter. We rise to the thought of an abstract humanity to which each has his duties, to which each owes a true unselfish love, through the idea of a family. How this is worked out—through coquetries, of course, otherwise Ethelberta were none of Mr. Hardy's heroines; through difficulties which might well perplex a braver spirit, and seriously embarrass one with any real conscience or more than embryonic soul—we need not here tell. What we have said is enough to give the key to the work when read.

Though the scene is laid partly in London, the whole country portion of it is pure Dorset; but in his treatment of the scenery we could wish that Mr. Hardy had either been less minute or more accurate. To a non-native it does not matter, but to those who know it is perplexing to find Swanage made forty miles instead of twenty by road from Bournemouth, and that the trees of Lulworth can be seen in a gap of the hills from Corfe Castle. But the breeze of the Purbeck down, and the wash of the Purbeck sea are felt and heard through the book as though we rode with Ethelberta to Corfe, or waited for the steamer on Swanage pier.

In *The Return of the Native* Mr. Hardy has touched his highest level, and we doubt if he will ever surpass it. Not that he has not many years of good work in him—he is still a young man—but because there is in it a sustained philosophy, a grasp of the problems of life, a clear conception of human duty which a man rarely puts into words twice and under more than one form. The leading thought is man's duty to man under discouragement, under the loss of love and health, and of hope for self. We scarcely know where in the range of English fiction to look for a more noble, more pathetic figure than that of Clym Yeobright, the itinerant open-air lecturer, who, after his life was shattered, still 'went about doing good'.

He left alone set creeds and systems of philosophy, finding enough, and more than enough, to occupy his tongue in the opinions and actions common to all good men. Some believed him, and some believed him not; some said that his words were common-place, others complained of his want of spiritual doctrine; while others again remarked that it was well enough for a man to take to preaching who could not see to do anything else. But everywhere he was kindly received, for the story of his life had become generally known.

The scene of the story, the great Dorset heathland, is little known. We remember hearing Mr. Hardy say that, when he was writing it, he thought to himself that only Mr. —— among all his probable readers in London would know accurately the district of his story. But without effort it has all the charm of the revelation of a new land, the customs and thoughts of a very peculiar and conservative people are wonderfully brought before us, and we are made to feel that, with all their unusual surroundings, they are of the same land and race as we are, moved by the same passions, hopes and fears.

For *The Trumpet Major* we care less; the mere novel-reader will probably like it better. But to us it labours under the defect of dealing with a time rather different from our own; the author has had to cram or be crammed for it, and the effort to reproduce that which is not a part of his own life is apparent. We are aware it shares this disadvantage with some very great works—with *Romola*, with *Esmond*, with *The Fortunes of Nigel*,—and to say Mr. Hardy has not wholly failed where Scott has only partially succeeded, is to give high praise. The time is that of the alarm of a French invasion during the First Empire, and no doubt all is carefully studied from tradition, but the costumes of the day give somewhat the effect of a stage revival.

Of the story now publishing in the pages of *Harper's Magazine* it is obviously impossible to speak, nor have we space to do more than name two admirable stories contributed to the now defunct *New Quarterly Magazine*, 'The Distracted Young Preacher', and 'Fellow Townsmen'. In these there is no disguising of distances, no confusion of place. The village in the one, the town in the other are as much Ower Moyne and Bridport as St. Oggs in the *Mill on the Floss* is Gainsborough, and the incidents in the former tale are true, transfigured and in some degree softened by an able artist hand.

In reviewing the whole series of Mr. Hardy's works—not at all too great in quantity to be admirable in quality during a period of ten years—the first general fact that strikes us, assuming him to be an accurate observer, is the unchanging character of the country side and the country folk. The old features of the landscape remain more per-haps in Dorset than in any other county, the road for instance from Wareham to Corfe Castle is the same, and over the same unenclosed heath as it was when the murdered Edward was dragged by the stirrup along the wild four miles; the speech, the dress in many parts—smock and long leather greaves—is the same; the food the same as when Wamba and Gurth discovered that bacon was the only real English word for cooked meat. Twice only, as far as we remember, does Mr. Hardy speak of the flesh food of the peasantry, and in both cases it is pig's liver. We take from *Under the Greenwood Tree*—

'Once I was sitting in the little kitchen of the "Three Choughs" at Casterbridge, having a bit of dinner, and a brass band struck up in the street. Sich a beautiful band as that were! I was sitting eating fried liver and lights, I well can mind— ah I was! and to save my life I couldn't help chawing to the tune. Band played six-eight time; six-eight chaws I, willynilly. Band plays common; common time went my teeth among the fried liver and lights as true as a hair. Beautiful 'twere! Ah, I shall never forget that there band.'

And in *A Pair of Blue Eyes*—

'Owing to your coming a day sooner than we first expected,' said John, 'you'll find us in a turk of a mess, sir'—'sir' says I to my own son!—but ye've gone up so, Stephen—we've killed the pig this morning for ye, thinking ye'd be hungry, and glad of a morsel of fresh mate. And 'a won't be cut up till to-night. How-ever, we can make ye a good supper of fry, which will chaw up well wi' a dab o' mustard and a few nice new taters, and a drop of shilling ale to wash it down.'

Perhaps nothing is more surprising to those who have only known English country life from such novels as Miss Yonge's than to see the extraordinarily small part played by the clergy in Mr. Hardy's books. In truth, the ordinances of religion summed up in the parson have but scant influence on the life of the English labourer, and of the country folk generally. He is not the all-pervading spiritual presence which the religious spinster of the upper class supposes; he is a gentleman who touches their lives at sundry points, but is to keep within his own limits, and intrude on them no more than they intrude on him. Of dogmatic differences in the Church they are wholly ignorant. We have known a succession of clergymen in the same country parish within five years, varying from the extremest Calvinism, through a phase of High Churchism scarcely to be distinguished from Popery, to a liberalism differing in nothing but name from Unitarianism. All were accepted by the parishioners, the differences of doctrine were never distinguished except so far as they implied differences in practice, or interfered with any of the habits of an unchanging people.

The Church in Wessex has not eradicated superstition (how, indeed, should it do so?), has only affected morals to an unappreciable extent.

while even education has waited for the day of School Boards and modern Acts affecting labour. Were it to be objected to Mr. Hardy's books that there is about them here and there a kind of frank paganism, an acceptance, without moral blame, of superstition, no hasty scouting of the possibility of witchcraft, a forgetfulness of the triumphs of civilization; we should reply that these are some of the essential characteristics of the people and the country among which he has lived, that he gives life as he sees it, and not as it ought to be according to the ideas of certain outsiders.

With regard to one side of country life, on which he is as well informed as all others, it may be thought that he deliberately chooses only that which is fair and virtuous and pure for the sake of the picture he wishes to draw, and into the grace of which he will introduce no incongruous feature, that he has left out the most essential elements. This is not so. The English labourer is frank, but he is not coarse, save as Fielding's novels are coarse; that is, he introduces words which do not find their way into drawing-rooms, but he would recoil as from a snake in the grass at the thoughts and suggestions which are in many fashionable novels; his very vices have in them more of clumsiness and horse-play than of deliberate evil. He is purer than his town neighbours: if chastity consist in truth to one woman through life, so that the chaste man might adopt Arthur's words to Guinevere, 'For I was ever virgin save for thee', we assert that the agricultural labourer stands higher than any other class in the community; he is truthful, honest, and trustworthy, and if he exceed in liquor, he certainly in this has no monopoly of vice or of needless indulgence.

If Mr. Hardy has indeed drawn his characters on the whole favourably, in spite of their many shortcomings; if he has drawn true gentlemen in his village carpenter John Smith, the reddleman Diggory Venn, the tranter Dick Dewy, it is because these men and their prototypes are so in fact. 'Though', as Dickens said of the brothers Cheeryble, 'they eat with their knives and never went to school', we never expect to find in any rank or position truer or more high-minded gentlemen than some Dorset labourers we are proud to call friends. But those who associate with them—a difficult matter for whomsoever is not bred among them—must expect that plainness of speech so graphically described in the novels under consideration—

[quotes *Under the Greenwood Tree*, Part Second, ch. IV ' "O, sir, please here's tranter Dewy" ' to ' "excusen my uncivility, sir" '; and ch. VI

' "Why don't your stap-mother come down?" ' to ' "never more than half wrong." ']

Mr. Hardy not only reproduces the humours of the country for us; he is brimful of humour himself. One of the ways in which this manifests itself is in his similes and analogies. We find, quite at random, opening the pages of the 'Distracted Young Preacher'; the poor lad, fresh from college, and wholly ignorant of the country, trapped into association with smugglers whether he will or no—

Lizzy looked alarmed for the first time. 'Will you go and tell our folk?' she said. 'They ought to be let know.' Seeing his conscience *struggling within him like a boiling pot*, she added, 'No, never mind, I'll go myself.'

And the same sort of unexpectedness appears in the simplest narrative, where no deliberate simile is intended. In the *Hand of Ethelberta* the Honourable Edgar Mountclere and Soloman Chicherel, a carpenter, are unexpectedly benighted fellow-travellers, hoping to get shelter and food at a roadside public-house—

'Come, publican, you'd better let us in. You don't dare to keep nobility waiting like this.'
'Nobility!'
'My mate hev the title of Honourable, whether or no; so let's have none of your slack,' said Sol.
'Don't be a fool, young chopstick!' exclaimed Mountclere. 'Get the door opened.'
'I will—in my own way,' said Sol, testily. 'You mustn't mind my trading upon your quality, as 'tis a case of necessity. This is a woman nothing will bring to reason but an appeal to the higher powers. If every man of title was as useful as you are to-night, sir, I'd never call them lumber again as long as I live.'
'How singular!'
'There's never a bit of rubbish that won't come in use, if you keep it some years.'

And of a young Wesleyan minister climbing a church tower—

The young man ascended and presently found himself among consecrated bells for the first time in his life, Nonconformity having been in the Stockdale blood for some generations. He eyed them uneasily, and looked round for Lizzy.

In *The Trumpet Major* this imaginative power has perhaps played tricks with Mr. Hardy. He has carried the analogies he sees between the human face and a landscape too far; there are places in all his works in which he treads on the borders of what is strained. But it is seldom that he does so, and he rarely ever passes them. It is much to find even here a man who sees more than others, and does not rest for ever in the obvious and commonplace.

Our pleasant task is almost done. We think we have said enough to show that here is a novelist who—while he excites little short of wonder and enthusiasm in a certain section of the public, the comparatively few who know him—has not at all taken hold on the great popular mind, sometimes slow to discover when a new genius has arisen in the intellectual sky.

We have only to say more, that while Mr. Hardy is never didactic, never dogmatic, never definitely religious—the novelist who is so imperfectly apprehends the difference between a novel and a sermon, spoiling both—his whole influence is pure, ennobling, and gracious; there is no line from beginning to end of his works we could wish to blot, no book which does not leave the reader heartily amused and raised in moral tone.

That Mr. Hardy has taken his place in the true literature of England is to us beyond question. For his sake and for their own we trust the larger public will recognize the fact, and steep themselves in the fresh healthy air of Dorset, and come into contact with the kindly folk who dwell there, through these pages, and then test their truth, as they can, in summer visits to the wolds, hill-sides, and coasts, which their 'native' has described so well.

A LAODICEAN

December 1881

---

21. From an unsigned review, *Athenaeum*

31 December 1881, 899–900

In the editorial file this review is marked 'Britten'. It forms about the first third of an article on 'Novels of the Week'.

Mr. Hardy would seem to have set before himself the task of illustrating in every conceivable way the Virgilian dictum about the nature of women. His heroines have their stations in many ranks of life; they are diverse in character and in attraction; but all have the common fault of their sex, they cannot make up their minds. Paula Power, the 'Laodicean', earns her title by withdrawing at the last moment from the rite which she had undertaken to go through by way of testifying to her steadiness in the Baptist principles wherein she has been reared. The minister thereupon makes her the object of a discourse founded on a well-known verse in the Revelation. The same hesitation clings to her for a long time. She will not refuse her lover and will not accept him, though preferring him all the while; and it needs the double shock of an unmerited suspicion and the discovery of the unworthy means employed to produce it to bring Paula to a decision. When she has once decided she acts vigorously enough, and the reader is left to infer that her love of uncertainty will henceforth only take the form of what children call 'wishing backwards'. With all her faults it must be said that she is perhaps the most charming of Mr. Hardy's heroines; nor will any male reader wonder at the alacrity with which George Somerset passed from the *rôle* of architectural adviser to that of aspirant husband. They will be more likely to regret that, instead of this amiable but somewhat commonplace young man, she should not have been mated with one more like our friend of last year, John Loveday, the trumpet-major. But Mr. Hardy, even when he makes his stories 'end happily', takes a somewhat desponding view of things. Perhaps he is right; but as we know that he is not hindered by want of power, he might just for once let matters take the old-fashioned course, and bring together a man and a woman who both deserve to interest the reader in their fortunes by their own characters, and not merely by the positions which they occupy in the story. The reader will be reminded more than once when perusing *A Laodicean* of Mr. Hardy's earliest work. The architectural 'business', the introduction of two persons in somewhat mysterious relation to each other, the comparatively sparing use of the rustic element, all carry the mind back to *Desperate Remedies*. It is interesting in many ways to observe the improvement which ten years have brought. There are still, however, traces of the old crudity. The scenes in which Dare and Capt. de Stancy are concerned, at the beginning of the second volume, are gratuitously cynical; and the modern version of the story of Gyges will displease many readers. Without being in the least degree a 'fleshly' writer, Mr. Hardy has a way of insisting on the physical attractions of a woman which, if imitated by weaker writers, may prove offensive. It should be added that when the rustic chorus does appear, it is equal to any which the author has ever yet, in Greek phrase, instructed.

TWO ON A TOWER

October 1882

22. Unsigned review, *Saturday Review*

18 November 1882, liv, 674-5

Mr. Hardy's novel, *A Laodicean*, can hardly have been thought an improvement on the previous works by which he delighted so many readers and made for himself so just a fame as a novelist; and, unfortunately, it is not easy to think that *Two on a Tower* is much of an improvement on *A Laodicean*. Nor are the reasons, or at least some of them, for this far to seek. It is no doubt intelligible that Mr. Hardy should grow tired of relying almost exclusively upon scenes of rustic or semi-rustic life for his effects; but the mode of change which he has affected is perhaps less easy to understand. In *A Laodicean* the author showed us very queer people doing very queer things, which seemed the odder because the background against which the characters stood out was that of life in a country house, and the characters themselves were of such a kind that it was imprudent to assign to them precisely the oddities which the author did assign. Captain de Stancy, for instance, a man of position and a man of the world, tried our patience, to begin with, in various small matters, but at two points—the scene in the picture gallery and that of the gymnastics—he became completely incredible, and one had after that to accept him as a mere puppet which the author chose to manoeuvre in a remarkable fashion. In *Two on a Tower* Mr. Hardy has shown more skill, in that he has provided for some oddness in his characters' doings by peculiarities in their circumstances, and strange behaviour is less startling on the top of an astronomical tower than in an ordinary drawing-room. Yet even so there is too much incongruity in the treatment, too little explanation of motives and reconciling of seeming discrepancies. Nor can it be said that the wicked personage in *Two on a Tower* is much more probable or plausible than was the wicked person in *A Laodicean*, for whose extreme oddity some sort of excuse was forthcoming which is not found in the present work. Again, Mr. Hardy has fallen too much in this book into the trick of attempting analytical discussion of mental processes—a trick which is but too apt to lead the way to dulness. Here is a passage which may illustrate our meaning:

He hurriedly returned an obedient reply, and the circumstance was enough to lend great freshness to her manner next morning, instead of the leaden air which was too frequent with her before the sun reached the meridian, and sometimes after. The mental room taken up by an idea depends as largely on the available space for it as on its essential magnitude; in Lady Constantine's life of infestivity, in her domestic voids, and in her social discouragements, there was nothing to oust the lightest fancy. Swithin had, in fact, arisen as an attractive little interpolation between herself and despair.

'Paraphrase this briefly', one might say to an intelligent schoolboy, and on getting the answer, 'She was pleased to hear that he would come, as his visit would be a break in her dull and disappointed life,' one might go on to ask the author, 'Why all this bother and affectation of profundity to express so very simple and common-place a notion?' It must be also noted that the story has an extremely repulsive element, on which, to be sure, Mr. Hardy touches as lightly as possible—but he would have done better to exclude it altogether; and that the author should have taken care to save himself from so odd a blunder as making his heroine become Lady Helmsdale by marrying Bishop Helmsdale. So far as regards general construction, the story is far too full of minor incidents which really have nothing to do with its action, such as Swithin's confirmation after he is grown up and the Bishop's finding the bracelet in his room; while the one very important incident referred to above, Lady Constantine's marriage under very peculiar conditions to the Bishop, might, as we have suggested, have been avoided with great advantage. Besides, Mr. Hardy has apparently failed to see that, in such a country place as that to which he introduces us, ill-natured gossip would almost inevitably have been started by the circumstances he describes.

Mr. Hardy's heroine is Lady Constantine, wife of Sir Blount Constantine, who has, as she tells Mr. Torkingham, the clergyman of the parish, left her, in consequence of

a mania for African lion-hunting, which he dignified by calling it a scheme of geographical discovery; for he was inordinately anxious to make a name for himself in that field. It was the one passion that was stronger than his mistrust of me. Before going away he sat down with me in this room, and read me a lecture, which resulted in a very rash offer on my part. When I tell it to you, you will find that it provides a key to all that is unusual in my life here. He bade me consider what my position would be when he was gone; hoped that I should remember what was due to him, that I would not so behave towards other men as to bring the name of Constantine into suspicion; and charged me to avoid levity of conduct in attending any ball, rout, or dinner to which I might be invited. I, in some indignation at his low opinion of me, responded perhaps too spiritedly. I volunteered then and there to live like a cloistered nun during his absence; to go into no society whatever, not even to a neighbour's dinner-party; and demanded bitterly if that would satisfy him. He said yes, instantly held me to my word, and gave me no loophole for retracting it.

Oddly enough, we have been told all this story only a few pages before, and told it in a much more amusing way by means of one of the scraps of rustic conversation which one wishes were far more frequent in the book than they are:

'Ah, poor woman!' said granny. 'The state she finds herself in—neither maid, wife, nor widow, as you may say—is not the primest form of life for keeping in good spirits. How long it is since she has heard from Sir Blount, Tabitha?'

'Two years and more,' said the young woman. 'He went into one side of Africa, as it might be, three St. Martin's days back. I can mind it, because 'twas my birthday. And he meant to come out the other side. But he didn't. He has never come out at all.'

'For all the world like losing a rat in a barley-mow,' said Hezekiah, glancing round for corroboration. 'He's lost, though you know where he is.'

His comrades nodded.

'Ay, my lady is a walking weariness, that's plain. I seed her yawn just at the very moment when the fox was halloaed away by Harton Copse, and the hounds runned en all but past her carriage wheels. If I were she I'd see a little life; though there's no fair, club-walking, nor feast, to speak of, till Easter week,— that's true.'

'She dares not. She's under solemn oath and testament to do no such thing.'

'Be cust if I would keep any such oath and testament! But here's the pa'son, if my ears don't deceive me.'

There is certainly some compensation for the mingled dulness and eccentricity of the greater part of the book in the sayings of those delightful personages Sammy Blore, Nat Chapman, Hezekiah Biles, and Haymoss Fry:

'When a feller's young' (says Haymoss, in reference to his stiff joints), 'he's too small in the brain to see how soon a constitution can be squandered, worse luck!'

'True,' said Biles, to fill the time while the parson was engaged in finding the Psalms. 'A man's a fool till he's forty. Often have I thought, when hay-pitching, and the small of my back seeming no stouter than a hornet's. The devil send that I had but the making of labouring men for a twelvemonth! I'd gie every man jack two good backbones, even if the alteration was as wrong as forgery.'

Shortly afterwards he says that 'then next I'd move every man's wyndpipe a good span away from his glutchpipe, so that at harvest time he could fetch breath in 's drinking, without being choked and strangled as he is now'. However, such touches as these come, as we have said, in too infrequent episodes, while the main purpose of the book is devoted to the loves of Lady Constantine and Swithin St. Cleeve, the son of a well-born clergyman, who made a *mésalliance* in the ranks of the peasantry.

[a summary of the plot follows, up to the point where Lady Constantine marries Bishop Helmsdale to legitimize her unborn child.]

Surely we have not spoken one whit too harshly in calling this a most repellent incident, which the author was extremely ill advised to include in the scheme of his plot. What happens after the marriage and how the book comes to a conclusion readers may discover for themselves. We cannot but think that the work is extremely disappointing, and hope that the result of the author's next venture may be more in accordance with his former triumphs.

23. Harry Quilter, *Spectator*

3 February 1883, 154

Harry Quilter (1851–1907), an art critic and journalist, wrote mainly for the *Spectator* and *The Times*.

As a general rule, we hold a reviewer is scarcely justified in revealing the purport of any work of fiction upon which he writes. His opinion should be given in such a way as not to destroy the interest of the book for those who read it subsequently to his criticism; in fact, the author should be left to tell his story himself, and not have it compressed into half-a-dozen sentences. But there are exceptions to this, as to all other rules, and we intend to make an exception here. Mr. Hardy is an author who has given us, as he has given most of his readers, great pleasure in several of his books. His fiction is distinguished by an originality and a power which remove him from the ordinary herd of novel-writers, and in his best works he bestows an amount of attention upon the subordinate characters and the local surroundings of his tales such as we can scarcely parallel amongst living writers. Without entering into any description of his general merits, of which we have often spoken, and which are, by this time, quite familiar to most of our readers, we say at once that, in return for much pleasant reading at his hands, we consider the greatest kindness we can show him in the review of *Two on a Tower* is to tell its story in plain words. If that story so told should prevent any of Mr. Hardy's admirers from reading the book itself, we think the author will have every reason to be grateful to us.

[an ironical summary follows.]

We may, of course, be quite wrong, but, in our opinion, this is a story as unpleasant as it is practically impossible. There is not, from beginning to end, a single gleam of probability in the plot, and what good end can be served by violating all natural motives in order to produce such unpleasant results we are at a loss to see. But it is not alone in the unpleasant character of the plot, and its forced and unnatural situations, that we think this book so unworthy of Mr. Hardy's reputation. The manner of treatment is even more objectionable. Lady Viviette's passion for Swithin St. Cleeve, which is the main motive of the book, is a study which, in its mingling of passion, religion, and false self-sacrifice, appears to us to approach very near to the repulsive, and the more so, perhaps, for a certain peculiar reticence with which it is dwelt upon. Lady Viviette herself is meant to be very nice, but is so self-contradictory as to lack all reality; she is more of a shadow at the end of the book than she is in the first chapter. The rest of the characters are the merest lay figures; and the rustics, to whose appearance Mr. Hardy has accustomed us, are but the palest shadows of those in *Far from the Madding Crowd*, etc. That there are throughout the book many little touches delicately descriptive of Nature, and many flashes of quaint village wit, is only to say that it is by Mr. Hardy. He cannot help being impressive when he talks of natural scenery; and no writer has ever conveyed more subtly the silence of the country at night, and the weird suggestiveness of little natural sounds of wind, or beast, or bird, when heard in the absence of human voices. But the book, as a whole is bad—the worst the author has written. So much we may say confidently. It is melodramatic without strength, extravagant without object, and objectionable without truth.

We have spoken frankly our opinion of this book, for Mr. Hardy is one of those authors in whom it is not impossible that frank speaking may produce good results. Let us now, as some set-off to our unfavourable opinion of this latest work, quote the passage which describes the meeting of Swithin St. Cleeve with Lady Viviette, on his return to England. It must be remembered that in the interval his early love has been wedded and widowed, and that St. Cleeve's purpose in returning to England is to marry her. He finds Lady Helmsdale (such is now her name) sitting at the top of the old tower, with her (and his) child at her feet.

'Viviette!' he said. 'Swithin!—at last!' she cried. The words died upon her lips, and from very faintness she bent her head. For, instead of rushing forward to her, he had stood still; and there appeared upon his face a look which there was no mistaking. Yes; he was shocked at her worn and faded aspect. The image he had mentally carried out with him to the Cape he had brought home again as that of the woman he was now to rejoin. But another woman sat before him, and not the original Viviette. Her cheeks had lost for ever that firm contour which had been drawn by the vigorous hand of youth, and the masses of hair that were once darkness visible had become touched here and there by a faint grey haze, like the Via Lactea in a midnight sky. Yet to those who had eyes to understand as well as to see, the chastened pensiveness of her once handsome features revealed more promising material beneath than ever her youth had done. But Swithin was hopelessly her junior. Unhappily for her, he had now just arrived at an age whose canon of faith it is that the silly period of a woman's life is her only period of beauty. Viviette saw it all, and knew that time had at last brought about his revenge.

24. Havelock Ellis, 'Thomas Hardy's Novels', *Westminster Review*

April 1883, cxix n.s. lxiii, 334–64

H. Havelock Ellis (1859–1939), psychologist and man of letters, had returned to England in 1879 after five years in Australia, and at this time was studying medicine in London.

This was certainly the most important article on Hardy before the publication of *Tess of the D'Urbervilles*, and one of the most notable during his lifetime. It is reprinted in *From Marlowe to Shaw: The Studies, 1876–1936, in English Literature, of Havelock Ellis*, edited by John Gawsworth (1950).

The high position which the author of *Far from the Madding Crowd* holds among contemporary English novelists is now generally recognized. When, however, that novel appeared anonymously in the pages of *Cornhill*, now nine years ago, Mr. Hardy's name was almost unknown. At that time it happened that the writer who stood at the head of English novelists had been silent for some years, and it seemed obvious to one or two critics that *Far from the Madding Crowd* was written by George Eliot. It was soon manifest that this was a mistake. Not only was this new novel without the massive quality, and the serious sustained power of George Eliot's work, but it possessed a vivid freshness, a quaint, unconventional simplicity equally without correspondence in George Eliot. Even when this was seen, many people were still uncertain about the sex of the new writer, and reviewers of Thomas Hardy's works were occasionally doubtful whether to speak of 'him' or 'her'. The cause of this uncertainty is not hard to find. The minute observation, the delicate insight, the conception of love as the one business of life, and a singularly charming reticence in its delineation, are qualities which, if not universally characteristic of woman's work in fiction, are such as might with propriety be attributed to it—at all events from an *a priori* standpoint. And it must be remembered that it seems now to stand beyond question that the most serious work in modern English fiction (contrasting in this respect with French fiction) has been done by women. M. Taine has defined the novelist as nothing else nor more than a psychologist. Such a definition seems certainly defective; it fails to take into account the constructive element. Perhaps it would be more approximately correct to say that the novelist is a psychologist who is also an artist. It may certainly be asserted that no definition can be adequate which fails to give a foremost place to the elements of art and psychology, or that *art* of psychology which Mill called ethology. And, if that is so, it would be hard to find any English novelists whose names may legitimately precede those of Jane Austen, Charlotte Brontë and George Eliot; certainly not Dickens, who so signally failed in the adequate and accurate realization of character, or Thackeray, whose art-instincts (one must not forget *Esmond*, the splendid exception) only ruled at lucid intervals. It is not difficult to differentiate Mr. Hardy's art from that of the women novelists just mentioned, and indeed no woman could have created a series of heroines of so persistently narrow range and such consummate fascination within that range. But it is not too much to say that with them he may claim to rank. Notwithstanding, however, that this distinguished place is generally conceded to Mr. Hardy, very few attempts have been made to determine what are those new things in literature which entitle him to that position. The object of the present paper is to point out at least the most prominent of these, and it may be well to state them at the outset. He has created a group of peasants, for the like of whom, in strong and living individuality, in wealth of quaint humour, we must go back to Shakspere; he has given us a gallery of women—'Undines of the earth', they have been felicitously called—whose charm is unique; they have no like anywhere; he has added a fresh delight to certain aspects of Nature.

The English agricultural labourer is a figure which few novelists have succeeded in describing. Few, indeed, have had an opportunity of knowing him. George Eliot, who has represented so much of the lower strata of English rural life, has not reached him. At best he is only visible in the dim background. We look in vain through *Adam Bede* or *Silas Marner* for the counterpart of Jan Coggan or Grandfer Cantle. But we may find them in miniature in the clowns of *Hamlet* and *The Winter's Tale*. It is surprising, indeed, to see how close is the relationship between those clowns of Shakspere's and their modern representatives in Mr. Hardy's novels. The humour of them is often not to be distinguished. And, save when we go back to those light and sure sketches, it is difficult to find anywhere fit comrades for the quaint and worthy fellowship, so racy of the earth, who greet us from the pages of *Far from the Madding Crowd*, and *The Return of the Native*. They seem to be born of the earth in a more special sense than her other children. The forms which pass in procession along the ridge in the twilight at the beginning of *Under the Greenwood Tree*, who look, as they are silhouetted on the sky, like the processions on the walls of Egyptian chambers, have grown to have something of the contours of the things among which they live; their 'nature is subdued to what it works in, like the dyer's hand'. And Mr. Hardy reveals the same lines in the contours of their mental and emotional nature. Perhaps the most marked general characteristic of them is their limited range. They never soar very high, or, indeed, at all; but, on the other hand, they never sink very low. Timorous they often are without a cause. Mr. Hardy represents them as, on the whole, a rather feeble folk, but they are never besotted, never coarse; the only effect of an immoderate pull at the cider-can is to render the receiver's humour rather more *spirituel* than usual. And that humour, how delightful! It is the grand characteristic of these men, a delicate and involved humour, which carries itself solemnly, with a tone of gentle banter in it, which is instinctively tolerant without always seeing a reason for tolerance. There are many distinct individualities, but in this respect they are all alike—this humour is common to them all.

And then, secondly, we have to note Mr. Hardy's heroines, those instinct-led women, who form a series which, for subtle simplicity, for a certain fascinating and incalculable vivacity which is half ethereal and half homely, can hardly be matched. It is true that they are all sisters—the Viviette Constantine of Mr. Hardy's latest novel has features in which one may easily trace a resemblance to the Cytherea Graye of his earliest. But this is a fact which few probably of Mr. Hardy's readers have ever regretted. No one, who has once felt the charm of the dream-wrapt faces which Mr. Burne Jones loves to delineate, has cared that the artist should seek for fresh types of loveliness; and it is equally easy to be content with the type of womanhood which Mr. Hardy gives us in all its delicate variations. So great, however, is the general resemblance among the fresh and piquant figures in this gallery of fair women, that there is scarcely a dominant quality in one of them which is not shared by the whole group. Ethelberta's notions about love are not distinguishable from Fancy Day's; the same maxims of conduct which are explicit in Cytherea Graye are implicit in Paula Power. What we notice about them first, perhaps, is the mingling of simplicity and piquancy. It is true that simplicity, in the sense of direct candour—the truthful nature of a Shirley or a Dorothea Brooke—lies nowhere in them. Such strong simplicity is a force which breaks through circum-stance; and what we see here, rather, are young healthy creatures, chiefly instinct-led, in their reaction with circumstance, circumstance mostly against them, but which they are rarely wishful, very rarely able, to break through. So interesting are they thus, that they scarcely need the bright natural vivacity which never fails them. They are fascinating to us at once, and irresistibly, because they are so simple by nature, so involved by circumstance. What we see in them, then, is the individual and egoistic instincts in a reaction with circumstances which is only faintly coloured by an elementary altruistic consciousness. Morals, observe, do not come in. Not that these beings yield in a passive unlimited way to the stream of occurrences. Shakspere has given us in Mrs. Quickly, as Coleridge pointed out, this absolute submission to circumstance. But Mrs. Quickly is not instinctive. Mr. Hardy's heroines are characterized by a yielding to circumstance that is limited by the play of instinct. They are never quite bad. It seems, indeed, that this quality in them, which shuts them out from any high level of goodness, is precisely that which saves them from ever being very bad. They have an instinctive self-respect, an instinctive purity. When they err, it is by caprice, by imagination. Even Eustacia Vye has no impure taint about her. One feels compelled to insist on the instinc-tiveness of these women. There is, in truth, something elemental, something *demonic* about them. We see at once that they have no souls. And that is why the critic, who called them 'Undines of the earth', was striking the keynote of every one of them. In their ever-varying and delicate moods and caprices, which are never untouched by the elemental purity of nature, in their tenderness, in their unconscious selfishness, Fancy, Elfride, Eustacia, Lizzie, Anne, they are all Undines. And few, probably, will care to say that they are, for that, less women.

But even these untamed children of Nature are not quite without some principles of conduct, though generally their obedience to such rules is an involuntary and unreasoned obedience. The traces of these guides to conduct are slight, but they are distinct. And it is interesting to compare this morality with that of Charlotte Brontë and of George Eliot, both writers whose books are deeply impressed with ethical conceptions, although those conceptions were very different in each. With Charlotte Brontë morality is always a very simple thing. It is duty against passion, and for her passion has no rights. The wave of passion must always be broken against the rigidity of moral law. It never occurs to her even that the question admits of being put in any other way. Only there is a great pang of self-sacrifice. And Charlotte Brontë never underrates that pang. Right is simple to her, nowise easy. George Eliot, on the other hand, with that large and profound outlook which makes her words of such significance, sees that the problem is at the very outset far more complex and difficult of solution than Charlotte Brontë thought. Morality is not a mere dead formula to be obeyed blindly. If Maggie Tulliver had been in Jane Eyre's place, she would not have acted as Jane Eyre acted; it is probable that she would not have left Rochester. 'The great problem of the shifting relation between passion and duty is clear to no man who is capable of apprehending it.' But George Eliot will not sacrifice the desires of the individual because they are contrary to a general principle; she will seek to make those desires true to their relations, 'to *all* the motives that sanctify our lives', as Maggie Tulliver says. And George Eliot pronounces, not too severely, the condemnation of those whose ready-made method of attaining truth admits of no reference to the circumstances of the individual lot, and who cannot see that complex human lives may not be laced up in formulas that refuse the divine promptings of insight and sympathy. But with Mr. Hardy the individual self with its desires is neither *per se*, a devil to be resisted, nor a soul to receive its due heritage in the fellow-ship of souls. It is an untamed instinctive creature, eager and yet shy, which is compelled to satisfy its own moderate desires for happiness before it can reflect its joyousness on others. It is instinct only that saves so egoistic and primitive a moral conception—if it can be so termed—from becoming utterly evil. In so far as it is a guide to conduct, it stands at the opposite pole to Charlotte Brontë's. Mr. Hardy is not concerned, as George Eliot is, with the bearing of moral problems on human action, and his heroines do not talk the language of morals, but a very exquisite language of love. And it happens, therefore, that only one of them, and that the earliest, has expressed her thoughts on such questions. The passage in which she does so is worth quoting:

Though it may be right to care more for the benefit of the many than for the indulgence of your own single self, when you consider that the many, and duty to them, only exists to you through your own existence, what can be said? . . . And they will pause just for an instant, and give a sigh to me, and think, 'Poor girl,' believing they do great justice to my memory by this. But they will never, never realize that it was my single opportunity of existence, as well as of doing my duty, which they are regarding; they will not feel that what to them is but a thought, easily held in those two words of pity, 'Poor girl,' was a whole life to me; as full of hours, minutes, and peculiar minutes, of hopes and dreads, smiles, whisperings, tears as theirs; that it was my world, what is to them their world, and they in that life of mine, however much I cared for them, only as the thought I seem to them to be. Nobody can enter into another's nature truly, that's what is so grievous.

Cytherea is speaking for all her sisters, for Elfride, for Eustacia, for Viviette. And it is to the credit of these latter that they act thus for the most part unconsciously, and are rarely able to formulate their actions in any large or precise way.

We have been quoting from *Desperate Remedies*. As Mr. Hardy's first essay in fiction it need not long detain us. There is very considerable energy about it, a carefully constructed and rather complex plot; it is marred by those crude and unconnected attempts at emotional disintegration which are the characteristic of the sensational novel. An air of preternatural liveliness pervades, at all events, the earlier portions, and marks the young novelist. All the notes, however, by which we recognize Mr. Hardy's work, except, perhaps, the Nature-love which first appears in the next, are struck in this first story. Manston is a very melodramatic predecessor of Wildeve and Troy. Springrove is only differentiated by his sketchiness from Stephen Smith or George Somerset, all three architects. And Cytherea, too, is, though undeveloped, in all points one of Mr. Hardy's heroines; nowhere more so than at the last page. When we turn to *Under the Greenwood Tree*, we feel at once that we are far away from the murky atmosphere of *Desperate Remedies*. Mr. Hardy has found his vocation and exercises it already like a master. The interest which comes from plot is here, and, generally henceforth, in abeyance, and we have instead certain original

and clearly-seen aspects of Nature and character. It is a sketch, short
and slight, of rural life, but a sketch of the freshest and most delightful
order, only comparable, if at all, with the best of George Sand's rural
studies, with *La Mare au Diable. Under the Greenwood Tree* is the history
of the love affairs of Fancy Day, village schoolmistress, and daughter
of Geoffrey Day, gamekeeper. We first hear of Fancy Day—note the
sunny coquettishness of the name—at a meeting, one Christmas Eve,
of the village choir (who are about to go a traditional round of carol-
singing), which takes place at the cottage of Reuben Dewy, the tranter
or carrier. Mr. Penny, the cobbler, has just produced Miss Fancy's boot
which he had forgotten to take home.

There, between the cider-mug and the candle, stood this interesting receptacle
of the little unknown's foot; and a very pretty boot it was. A character, in
fact—the flexible bend at the instep, the rounded localities of the small nestling
toes, scratches from careless scampers now forgotten—all, as repeated in the
tell-tale leather, evidencing a nature and a bias. Dick surveyed it with a delicate
feeling that he had no right to do so without having first asked the owner of
the foot's permission.

Mr. Hardy, be it observed in passing, has, like Sir Frederick Leighton,
devoted special study to the foot, to what may be called the psychology
of it. In *The Hand of Ethelberta*, for instance, on one occasion 'Picotee
curled up her toes, fearing that her mother was going to moralize.' As
Mr. Spinks observes in the present chapter: 'I know little, 'tis true—I
say no more; but show *me* a man's foot, and I'll tell you that man's
heart.' In due time the choir arrive at the schoolhouse, and we eventually succeed in obtaining a momentary vision of a young girl with a
candle framed as a picture by the window architrave, with twining
profusion of hair falling down her shoulders, and 'bright eyes looking
into the grey world outside with an uncertain expression, oscillating
between courage and shyness'. Then, said lightly and warmly, comes:—
'Thank you, singers, thank you', and the vision has vanished. Some
time afterwards, however, Dick Dewy, the tranter's son, was found
still·gazing up at the lattice. We need not follow the successive stages
of Dick's lovemaking. He is a shy and awkward youth, and small
favours go far with him. Mr. Hardy's heroines are, on principle,
seldom more demonstrative than they can help; they think it advisable
that the man they incline to should not be too certain of their favour.
Of course, Dick is not without rivals. He is somewhat unnecessarily
jealous of a certain Mr. Shinar, farmer and churchwarden. But Mr.

Shinar is not the most formidable claimant for Fancy's hand. The vicar himself, Mr. Maybold, had been attracted by the fresh charm of that 'bright little bird', as Mr. Hardy calls her. Dick, however, has really gained Fancy's affections, as he succeeds at last in learning from her. She gives a still more decisive proof by thinking, quite unfoundedly, that Dick has been paying too much attention to somebody else, and tries to make him jealous by telling of Shinar's advances. Dick, for all his awkwardness and bluffness, has sense, and while she is superior in intellect and quickness of perception, Dick's moral strength always, unconsciously to himself, predominates. He discovers that she is trying to make him jealous and she is immediately reduced to submission:

'And I know what you've done it for,—just because of that gipsy-party!' He turned away from her and walked five paces decisively, as if he were alone in a strange country and had never known her.—'You did it to make me jealous and I won't stand it.' He flung the words to her over his shoulder and then stalked on, apparently very anxious to walk to the colonies that very minute.

'O, O, O, Dick—Dick!' she cried, trotting after him like a pet lamb, and really seriously alarmed at last, 'you'll kill me! my impulses are bad—miserably wicked,—and I can't help it; forgive me, Dick! And I love you always; and those times when you look silly and don't seem quite good enough for me,— just the same, I do, Dick!'

Soon a crisis arrives at which Fancy's love is brought to a test. Mr. Maybold has hitherto kept silence; he knew nothing of her relations to Dewy, and unexpectedly came and asked her to be his wife. Dick had just seen her for a few minutes, after attending the funeral of a friend in the rain, and this is her reflection as he goes away: 'I like Dick, and I love him; but how poor and mean a man looks in the rain, with no umbrella and wet through!' Then the vicar walks up, not without an umbrella, and, after a few preliminaries, brings out the object of his visit: 'Fancy, I have come to ask you if you will be my wife?'

She is startled, agitated; she almost pants. 'I cannot, I cannot, Mr. Maybold—I cannot. Don't ask me!'

But he grows eloquent, and at last:

'Will you, Fancy, marry me?'

Another pause ensued, varied only by the surging of the rain against the window-panes, and then Fancy spoke in a faint and broken voice:— 'Yes, I will.'

The next day the vicar learns accidentally from Dick himself that he is engaged to Fancy. He immediately writes to her, asking if she can honourably forsake Dick. But Fancy has already discovered her mistake, and has written asking if she may withdraw her too hasty answer. He sends these few words in reply: 'Tell him everything; it is best. He will forgive you.' She never does so, and that is the flaw in the sweet bird-nature of Fancy Day. With all her superiority of intellect and refinement, the generous and straightforward Dick, dull and awkward as he is, is easily master. We are reconciled to their union:

'O Dick!' she exclaimed, 'I am so glad you are come! I knew you would, of course, but I thought, Oh, if you shouldn't!'

'Not come, Fancy! Het or wet, blow or snow, here come I to-day! Why what's possessing your little soul? You never used to mind such things a bit!'

'Ah, Mr. Dick, I hadn't hoisted my colours and committed myself then! . . .'

Dick fanned himself with his hat. 'I can't think,' he said thoughtfully, 'whatever 'twas I did to offend Mr. Maybold,—a man I like so much too. He rather took to me when he came first, and used to say he should like to see me married, and that he'd marry me, whether the young woman I chose lived in his parish or no. I slightly reminded him of it when I put in the banns, but he didn't seem to take kindly to the notion now, and so I said no more. I wonder how it was!'

'I wonder!' said Fancy, looking into vacancy with those beautiful eyes of hers —too refined and beautiful for a tranter's wife; but, perhaps, not too good.

No, not too good. These Undines are not too good. Woman, in Mr. Hardy's world, is far from being 'the conscience of man'; it is with the men always that the moral strength lies. It is only necessary to think of Bathsheba Everdene and Gabriel Oak, of Eustacia Vye and Clym Yeobright, of Anne Garland and John Loveday. The women may be clever, practical, full of tact; they are always irresistibly fascinating; but veracity, simplicity, rectitude are with the men. Maggie Tulliver was strong; if once her moral sense was lulled, it was native to her, and she soon awoke to it. But when Elfride Swancourt consents to go to London with Stephen Smith, and, on getting there, immediately returns, it can scarcely be said that the mental process was in her case the same. She is throughout full of irresolutions, and that hesitation at the final leap which sends her home is only one of those irresolutions. The line of least resistance is only accidentally coincident with the line of right conduct.

Elfride Swancourt brings us to *A Pair of Blue Eyes*. In that story, the delicate power and fine insight of Mr. Hardy's work were first fully revealed. Elfride's character, in a last analysis, would probably be indistinguishable from Fancy Day's, but the elements are here united in a more complex, a more unstable, manner. There are finer possibilities about her; she is more refined, she is braver, she is more candid. She has, too, a sweet and clinging tenderness which is not hidden by the *grata protervitas* which characterizes all Mr. Hardy's heroines. In *Under the Greenwood Tree* we breathe throughout an atmosphere of pure comedy; Elfride is shrouded from us at last in a tragic gloom. And this tragedy is wrought with an art so like artlessness, so overwhelming in its simple and passionate pathos, as Mr. Hardy has never quite attained since. *A Pair of Blue Eyes* contains the first serious study of Mr. Hardy's favourite hero, who belongs to the class that enters modern literature as *Wilhelm Meister*, and finds its most prominent recent representative in *Daniel Deronda*. It is true that in Goethe's novel, and in George Eliot's, larger issues are involved than anywhere in Mr. Hardy's. 'You seem to me like Saul, the son of Kish, who went forth to seek his father's asses and found a kingdom.' That, as Goethe said, was the moral of *Wilhelm Meister*. With George Eliot the case was generally quite opposite. The ardent young soul started in search of kingdoms, and found at last a certain exquisite satisfaction in tending asses. If Daniel Deronda seems an exception, it must be acknowledged that the kingdom he attained is only dimly shadowed forth. Mr. Hardy, however, is mostly indifferent to these things; his hero passes through no such process of development one way or another. In general he is a sensitive being, gentle and pure as a woman, characterized by nothing so much as his receptivity. In fact, critics who cling to the Byronic ideal would probably extend to him the appellation they give to Wilhelm Meister and Daniel Deronda; they would call him a milksop. Nevertheless, he succeeds in escaping weakness; perhaps because, as George Eliot says, receptiveness itself, like fortitude, is a rare and massive power; perhaps because of a certain moral strength which we have seen in Dick Dewy and which is elsewhere brought out still more distinctly. There is a little piece of psychological analysis in this book which is worth quoting; it is one of the few passages in which Mr. Hardy attempts such analysis:

His constitution was made up of very simple particulars; one which, rare in the spring-time of civilizations, seems to grow abundant as a nation gets older, individuality fades, and education spreads—that is, his brain had extraordinary receptive powers, and no great creativeness. Quickly acquiring any kind of knowledge he saw around him, and having a plastic adaptability more common in woman than in man, he changed colour like a chameleon as the society he found himself in assumed a higher and more artificial tone. He had not many original ideas, and yet there was scarcely an idea to which, under proper training, he could not have added a respectable co-ordinate.

This is true, not only of Stephen Smith, but of Egbert Mayne, of George Somerset, even of Clym Yeobright. There is a remarkable passage in *Daniel Deronda* in which George Eliot has analysed a stage of Deronda's development, which may very well be compared with the passage just quoted, to illustrate both the points of contact between George Eliot's hero and Mr. Hardy's, and the respective analytical powers of the two writers.

With all its great and fascinating qualities, *A Pair of Blue Eyes* is by no means free from faults. Mr. Hardy was breaking new ground, reaching after higher things than those he had so perfectly expressed in *Under the Greenwood Tree*. This may be noticed especially in regard to a characteristic which appears first in *A Pair of Blue Eyes*, and to which the pathos of it is so largely owing, which constitutes, indeed, a new point of departure in Mr. Hardy's art. This is a quality which at its best should be called a kind of tragic irony, but which too often appears as a series of impossible coincidences and situations, connected sometimes with a pointless cynicism. These are the more irritating to the reader, as that by which Mr. Hardy's work is so fascinating, far from consisting in any tricks of cleverness, lies, rather, in the fresh and direct qualities of genius. In the book before us, the incident of the lost earring is so subtly indicative, it is so suggestive of pathos, that it becomes a touch of genius. In Elfride and her father, unknown to each other, leaving home at the same hour to be privately married, we have another coincidence, not perhaps much more absurd than the other, but, because it is unnecessary, because it is more than the situation requires, it becomes, not a touch of genius, but rather of farce. And in *A Pair of Blue Eyes* there are many such touches of farce. It is impossible, however, to leave it with a note of dispraise. Nowhere else are certain qualities of Mr. Hardy's work, its sensitiveness, its sincerity, so conspicuous. The pathetic figure of Elfride, with her eager and delicate instincts, her sweet hesitations, her clinging tenderness, has a charm for the memory, which no other of Mr. Hardy's heroines possesses in so great a degree.

We have noticed that in *A Pair of Blue Eyes* occurs the first development of Mr. Hardy's irony. A step in the development of his humour is also to be noted. William Worms, with his iterated conviction that 'life's a strange bubble', is a rather wearisome personage, but he represents the first important appearance of that vein of humour which henceforth marks Mr. Hardy's rustics. He is the prototype of Joseph Poorgrass. It is in the next of the series, *Far from the Madding Crowd*, that we find this humour at its richest and strongest. Jan Coggan, Mark

Clark, Cainy Bell, and above all, Joseph Poorgrass, with his saintly profile, his multiplying eye, his cheerful sigh, and his 'scriptural manner, which is my second nature', these, and the rest of that pleasant company which met at Warren's Malthouse, form a group of distinct and humorous individualities which one is not easily tired of contemplating. The pages in which they are delineated will be counted among the good things in our literature. It cannot be denied that many hard words have been said about these agricultural labourers, who are almost the most interesting personages in *Far from the Madding Crowd*, and who form a Greek chorus in nearly all Mr. Hardy's novels. It is said that they doubtless talk after a sufficiently clever and amusing fashion, but that no agricultural labourers ever did talk so, none ever could, that they are in short utterly unnatural. In defence of such a statement, it is permissible to quote Mr. Barnes, as loving an exponent of Dorsetshire as Mr. Hardy, and the ponderous and unapparent humour which he offers as the native brand. Mr. Blackmore's Devonshire humour, too, a pointless and good-natured *bonhomie*, hearty rather than refined, and redolent of roast-beef and plum-pudding, that traditional basis of the British constitution, has little in common with the *spirituel* qualities of Mr. Hardy's. On the other hand, a critic who claims to speak with full knowledge has stated emphatically that he 'believes there is not, in all Mr. Hardy's works, one exaggerated or untrue word in his descriptions of those whom he knows so well'. It must be remembered, too, that, as Mr. Hardy paints them, a large part of the humour of these rustics is bound up with their use of scriptural language. They have a very exact knowledge of the Bible. Grandfather William quotes Jeremiah; Maryanne compares herself, like the Psalmist, to a pelican in the wilderness. We know that Poorgrass studied the Bible, for he mentions once how he was 'sitting at home, looking for Ephesians, and says I to myself, "Tis nothing but Corinthians and Thessalonians in this danged Testament."' And nobody who knows how deeply the English Bible has been assimilated by our peasants, will be prepared to assert that Mr. Hardy has herein departed from the truth of Nature. The similarity these rustics bear to some of Shakspere's clowns has already been alluded to; and when the critics who deny them the right of existence have succeeded in dismissing the gravediggers in *Hamlet*, it will be time to lay hands on Joseph Poorgrass and Grandfer Cantle.

Far from the Madding Crowd is, on the whole, perhaps the finest, as it is certainly the most popular, among Mr. Hardy's novels. Not because it is faultless, but because it is more than any other distinguished by power. It is not deficient—Mr. Hardy's work never is—in subtlety; but here the subtlety is subordinate to the production of effects which are broad and strong rather than subtle. There is a certain sure and easy sense of mastery about it, which dominates the growing tendency towards extreme elaboration. From the first page, with its minutely realized portrait of Gabriel Oak, to the last, where Gabriel and Bathsheba are united, and the familiar group of rustics join in their chorus of delightful comment, there is nothing so distinct about *Far from the Madding Crowd* as this adequacy of power. It is here also that Mr. Hardy has lavished most freely his intimate knowledge of rural life. The description of the storm, with its elaborate details of Nature's hints of the coming catastrophe, given by the toad, the spider, the dog, the sheep, could not be surpassed for vivid intensity. And the same may be said of that last episode in the life of Fanny Robin, creeping painfully to Casterbridge Union, counting her weary progress along the road by the rails she had to pass, and helped on her way by a big dog. 'There is a dog outside,' murmured the overcome traveller, 'where is he gone? He helped me.' 'I stoned him away', said the man. The whole scene which ends with this simple touch of pathos, Mr. Hardy has never excelled for subdued dramatic power. The defect of *A Pair of Blue Eyes* lay in an abuse of its chief excellence, its irony. And the grave faults which disfigure *Far from the Madding Crowd* may, in the same manner, be described as an abuse of the splendid dramatic power shown in such scenes as this. Having tried to indicate the great qualities of this work, it is impossible to pass on without noting that this drama often degenerates into melodrama. The scenes just mentioned, the storm, and Fanny Robin's last journey, touch the extreme verge of dramatic vividness, if they rarely overpass it. Serjeant Troy, who belongs to the same class as Wildeve, is thoroughly successful. Boldwood, however, drawn on the whole in hard and unsympathetic outline, we are compelled to consider a failure. His mad passion for Bathsheba is marked by a crudity, a want of reality, an exaggeration which strikes a discordant note in the last volume of *Far from the Madding Crowd*.

In this novel that delicate and playful fancy, which no reader of Mr. Hardy's books can fail to notice, first attains a perfectly facile expression. There are traces of it in *A Pair of Blue Eyes*, where, on one occasion, 'the very stones of the road cast tapering dashes of darkness westward, as long as Jacob's tent-nail'. But here it is always springing up with a wantonness which is sometimes charming, sometimes simply extravagant. Gabriel, before going to ask Bathsheba to marry him, exhausts his supply of hair-oil, thus producing 'a splendidly novel colour, between that of guano and Roman cement, making it stick to his head like mace round a nutmeg, or wet seaweed round a boulder after the ebb'. And when on another occasion he found Clark, Coggan and Poorgrass enjoying a prolonged period of refreshment at a public-house, instead of conveying the coffin containing poor Fanny's body, 'the one lengthy and two round faces of the sitters confronted him with the expressions of a fiddle and a couple of warming-pans'. But this wild fancy, half elfin and half goblin, is connected with a strain of fine and detailed observation which, at its best, rises to insight, and in Mr. Hardy's hands often takes the place of direct psychological analysis.

Far from the Madding Crowd was immediately succeeded by *The Hand of Ethelberta*. Probably most readers who came to it fresh from the perusal of the former were disappointed. Like most of Mr. Hardy's books it represents a new point of departure and a new development; for he is a writer who moves within a limited range, but is yet capable of producing many variations within that range, variations in the defects as well as in the merits of his work. If *Under the Greenwood Tree* is a comedy, and *A Pair of Blue Eyes* a tragedy, if it is possible to find traces of melodrama in *Far from the Madding Crowd*, there is something of farce in *The Hand of Ethelberta*. Mr. Hardy begins by accepting what may be called an impossible situation, and then works it out *ad libitum*. It is necessary to recognize this before the story can be appreciated at all. There is much of the irony of *A Pair of Blue Eyes*, much of the dramatic power of the work which immediately preceded it, and the whole is worked out with a facile—a too facile—brilliance, which, since then, Mr. Hardy has wisely restrained. In method and style it may be said to occupy the same place among the author's works as *Maud* among Mr. Tennyson's. Ethelberta Chickerel (her mother had been a lady's-maid and was fond of grand names) was a butler's daughter who had formed a runaway match with a knight's son who immediately afterwards died. Upon this his mother became reconciled to Ethelberta, now Mrs. Petherwyn, educated her and brought her into society. The old lady subsequently died, leaving Ethelberta her town-house and nothing else, and *The Hand of Ethelberta* is an account of the after-history of this clever young adventuress. It is not difficult to find her relation to her sister heroines. Bathsheba was not like Elfride, in that she was placed in different circumstances. There was independence and strength about her. She was a child of the people; her instincts were fundamentally the same as Elfride's, only less delicate, less refined in the manifestation. The breezy strength and healthfulness of her native downs is in her, and, with all her capacity for suffering, she would be always saved from going to the tragic end of Elfride. In Ethelberta we see nothing else than Bathsheba taken out of her healthy natural environment and placed in another of superfine civilization with which she is out of harmony. Mr. Hardy calls the story a comedy, and the pure comedy of it lies in the reactions between Ethelberta and her new environment. There is much else of a professedly comic kind, but the Montcleres, the Neighs, the Ladywells and so on, are caricatures of so genuinely hard and unsympathetic a character that they almost succeed in driving the reader away altogether. They are, indeed, outside Mr. Hardy's *genre*. Ladywell cannot compare for a moment with Mr. Henry James's Rosier. Nor is Christopher Julian, who 'would receive quite a shock if a little dog barked at his heels, and be totally unmoved when in danger of his life', or the ever-blushing Picotee, with her 'abstracted ease of mind which people show who have their thinking done for them, and put out their troubles as they do their washing', at any time very interesting. The interest of the story lies throughout with Ethelberta, and Mr. Hardy seems to have devoted more elaboration to her than to any other of his heroines, except Eustacia Vye. Ethelberta, although she has really lost none of her native instincts, although she is at heart still a child of the people, is not by any means a lamb among wolves. She has succeeded in adapting herself to the maxims of the society into which she has been translated. These maxims ally themselves with that native insincerity from which Ethelberta, like most of her sisters, rarely emerges. Thus, when Christopher leaves off coming to see her, she is miserable; he calls when she is out, she is delighted:

'Now, won't I punish him for daring to stay away so long!' she exclaimed as soon as she got upstairs. 'It is as bad to show constancy in your manners as fickleness in your heart at such a time as this!'

'But I thought honesty was the best policy?' Picotee said.

'So it is for the man's purpose. But don't you go believing in sayings, Picotee; they are all made by men for their own advantages. Women who use public proverbs as a guide through events are those who have not ingenuity enough to make private ones as each event occurs.'

On another occasion she travels from Knollsea to Coomb Castle (which we may identify with Corfe) to a meeting of the Imperial Archaeological Association. To save expense she performs the journey on a rustic donkey, dismounting before she joins the party. When the donkey is found browsing among the ruins she disowns him:

'Many come and picnic here,' she said, serenely, 'and the animal may have been left till they return from some walk.'

'True,' said Lord Mountclere, without the slightest suspicion of the truth. The humble ass hung his head in his usual manner, and it demanded little fancy from Ethelberta to imagine that he despised her. And then her mind flew back to her history and extraction, to her father—perhaps at that moment inventing a private plate-powder in an underground pantry—and, with a groan at her inconsistency in being ashamed of the ass, she said in her heart, 'My God, what a thing am I!'

She is brilliant, she is ambitious, she has just enough heart to be very fascinating; she is very beautiful, this 'squirrel-haired Ethelberta'; but when we leave her at last with all her desires apparently satisfied, the wife of a rich nobleman, it is scarcely with much regret. 'Ethelberta's gradient had been regular: emotional poetry, light verse, romance as an object, romance as a means, thoughts of marriage as an aid to her pursuits, a vow to marry for the good of her family; in other words, from soft and playful romanticism to distorted Benthamism. Was the moral incline upward or down?' Mr. Hardy refrains from attempting to solve that problem; he is always more given to suggesting than to answering questions: and it may be well here to follow his example, and to pass on to *The Return of the Native*.

Here again we have, above all, the life-history of a woman in its relations; this time, as in the case of Elfride, ending in failure. Eustacia Vye seems at first to stand apart from Mr. Hardy's heroines. On closer examination, however, we may find that she has her natural place in the series. She follows Ethelberta, as Ethelberta followed Bathsheba. Ethelberta, thrown altogether under the wrong conditions—conditions with which she is unable to fight—undisciplined, and with little capacity for discipline; Ethelberta, not without the spice of devilry in her composition, would not have acted very differently from Eustacia Vye. For the great flaw in Eustacia's nature—the cause of that want of adaptation to her environment which we soon see will make life impossible to her—lies in this lack of discipline. Mr. Hardy characterizes her well as 'a rebellious woman'. She was 'the raw material of a divinity', her features suggested those of Marie Antoinette and Mrs. Siddons, and she lived on a heath with her grandfather, an old sea-captain, not altogether without a rough kindliness, but who was willing for the most part to leave her to herself. And with her passionate and abstract desire for love, her greedy egotism, her 'instincts towards social nonconformity', her outcries against destiny, we soon learn how ill able she must ever be to carry on adequately that complex and continuous adaptation of internal relations to external relations, which is life. Superficially she was timid; it was beneath that timidity that her stronger and more rebellious spirit dwelt. It is easy to see how hard it was for a woman thus morally featured to be sincere. And it is the cowardice of insincerity more than anything else which is the immediate cause of her failure in life. A worker in the fields of philosophy, whom we have but recently lost, has declared that, 'technically considered, sincerity is, in fact, the prime virtue, which nothing else can substitute'; and if it were possible to suspect Mr. Hardy of an ultimate moral aim, it would be the enforcement of this virtue. Somewhere, at some time or other, through some person or other, insincerity brings misunderstanding and misfortune among Mr. Hardy's men and women, and it is because Eustacia fails to hold fast that 'very staff of our life' that she eventually fails. She cannot act so as to avoid mistakes, and she cannot face the consequences of those mistakes. In spite of all this, she is never without womanliness, never quite without a little of our love. Clym Yeobright, who contributes to the tragedy of *The Return of the Native*, has many elements of nobility, though, it is true, of a formal and limited sort. His mother says of him that he can be as hard as steel, and, with a nature so unsympathetic and unyielding, only varied by hysterical outbursts, he could never understand or influence Eustacia. The elements of tragedy lie in his nature as clearly as in hers. There is one decisive point in his history when his own fortune as well as that of Eustacia was within his grasp. It is after that discovery of her weakness and insincerity which causes their separation. The rebellious spirit of his wife lay crushed before him; but he is blind and prejudiced, and the opportunity of reconciliation passed for ever. In that consisted his failure to live the life that was presented to him. When all that he valued was gone, he became an itinerant open-air preacher or lecturer. 'He stated that his discourses to people were to be sometimes secular, and sometimes religious, but never dogmatic, and that his texts would be taken from all kinds of books.' It was an excellent programme. Eustacia once said that Clym reminded her of the Apostle Paul. One fears, however, that the resemblance was a little superficial. We find that some people complained of his want of spiritual teaching; it is rather doubtful whether he had a 'vocation' at all. Mr. Hardy appears to have had a misgiving on this point. He takes the trouble to write out for us a long text of Yeobright's on one occasion, but of the discourse itself we have no hint.

In *The Return of the Native*, Mr. Hardy has found more adequate expression than elsewhere for the instincts of love and art which bind him to the familiar heath-land of Wessex. The book is full of passages which show with what fine appreciation he has entered into the meaning of that country whose general aspect is one of weird and silent gloom. To Mr. Hardy it is rich with all the complex possibilities of an organic life; he has discerned its varying moods of day and gloaming and night; he has heard and understood its mysterious voices, from the almost inaudible recitative of the dead heath-bells in autumn to the wind's chorale at midnight. All the harmonies that air makes with earth Mr. Hardy has learnt to discriminate and to love; and he writes of them with at once the accuracy of a specialist and the enthusiasm of an artist. One instinctively recalls Emily Brontë, and the passionate love of that ardent and austere spirit for the bleak moors around Keighley, those moors which were the deepest springs of her spiritual life. There is the same instinct of Nature-worship, the same quality of freshness; but Mr. Hardy's treatment, subtle rather than keen, has little in common with the direct glance of the wonderful Yorkshire girl. It has little in common, indeed, with that of any writer of the descriptive school. There is much excellent word-painting of Nature which very soon wearies. The reason partly is that it comes not so much from Nature's seers as from her showmen, and the continuous strain of admiration is hard to keep up. When Madame de Staël went to Germany, Heine tells us, she rushed like a hurricane through that peaceful country, eagerly inhaling beauty and purity and *naïveté*. 'How delightful you Germans are! How deliciously cool it is in your woods! What refreshing perfume of violets! You are a good people, and cannot conceive the corruption that reigns in the Rue du Bac.' That is the attitude which many, even of our best descriptive writers, take up towards Nature, Mr. Black for instance. For in life, as it exists in our modern England, it is hard for most of us to live near the heart of Nature; we are compelled to adopt a method not unlike that of Madame de Staël, and it is a method that soon becomes wearisome. But in Mr. Hardy's pages we breathe a different atmosphere; we are conscious of the voice of one who has worshipped at the temple's inner shrine. We feel in his work not subtlety only, but a certain freshness of vision in looking both at Nature and at life, which is at once intensely original, and at its highest point altogether impersonal. Blake had it in a supreme degree; Wordsworth now and then; Mr. Ruskin at his best; the Brontës had it; this freshness of insight as regards peasant life is one of the points in which

Mr. Hardy resembles Tourguéneff, although he can make no claim to the delicacy and precision of touch which marks the great Russian novelist. It is largely on account of this quality—this freshness of insight into certain aspects of Nature and human character—that Mr. Hardy's work is so interesting. In spite of what seems an exaggerated and almost microscopical minuteness of vision, he never wearies us; we may return again and again to his pages and the charm is still there. But it is a charm—at all events in Nature-painting—singularly hard to analyse. The following passage from *The Hand of Ethelberta* may not be the most characteristic that might be chosen; it is very distinctly Turneresque; but it illustrates this freshness of vision, and the truth of it may be witnessed by any one who knows the grand and delicate colour-harmonies which may be seen from the heights on the Dorset coast. Ethelberta is travelling from Knollsea to Coomb Castle on the donkey with whom we are already acquainted:

[quotes ch. XXI, 'Turning to the left' to 'both sides of her.']

Between *The Return of the Native* and Mr. Hardy's next important work, *The Trumpet Major*, three short sketches intervened which must not be passed without mention. They were all three published in the *New Quarterly Magazine* for 1879–80, a defunct and inaccessible periodical, and it is to be hoped they will be republished. *An Indiscretion in the Life of an Heiress*, is only another version in the old legend of young love. That story is always fresh and delicate in Mr. Hardy's hands. Egbert Mayne, the village schoolmaster, loves Geraldine Allenville, the rich squire's daughter, and she loves him. He is a man of the people, but Mr. Hardy attributes to him 'luminousness of nature', and he writes a book which makes him famous. The squire is still unyielding, and, on the eve of wedding a lord, Geraldine comes in the night to Egbert, and is married to him the next morning. All such Romeo and Juliet stories must end in tragedy; the artist has too deep a conception of life for it to be otherwise, and in a few days Juliet is dead. Geraldine Allenville, except in the one decisive action of her life, has little of the demonic element that slumbers in most of Mr. Hardy's heroines, but she is among the truest and gentlest of his creations of delicate girlhood, and takes her place not very far from Elfride Swancourt. *Fellow Townsmen* is interesting, chiefly because it contains sketches of characters which are not altogether like those Mr. Hardy has accustomed us to. They are not especially grand or fascinating, but they are sketched with a quiet and tender truth in which one might perhaps trace the influence of *Scenes of Clerical Life*. Downe is such a sketch; Barnet has elements of a nobility which is not generally present in Mr. Hardy's heroes. Lucy Savile may be briefly described as an Undine *manquée*. Her nature, not a large one, suffers from a persistent defect of direct impulse; she does not spoil her life by her ill-regulated desires like Eustacia, or her irresolutions, like Elfride. Her mistake may be rather described as a repeated and almost deliberate refusal to seize the forelock of opportunity. And this gives to her life a sense of failure. But the most delightful of these brief tales is *The Distracted Young Preacher*. The story of Lizzie Newberry, the young widow, who is one of the leaders of a band of smugglers, who goes out at night in her late husband's great-coat to pursue an occupation in which she can see nothing wrong, which her father and grandfather have followed before her, who falls in love with her lodger, the handsome young Methodist preacher, who struggles between love and the smuggling propensities which are part of her life, a struggle which ends temporally in the conquest of the latter—all this, said to be 'founded on fact', is told briefly and simply and vivaciously in Mr. Hardy's most delicate vein of comedy. Lizzie, sweet, practical, and womanly, not without a touch of the *grata protervitas*, full of healthy rustic nature, mingled with the inimitable grace which (with or without the rusticity) is part of the souls of Mr. Hardy's women, is a figure that lingers in the memory. The preacher is an honest and manly young fellow, and he comes back and marries her at last, but not before the band of smugglers had been broken up:

He took her away from her old haunts to the home that he had made for himself in his native county, where she studied her duties as a minister's wife with praiseworthy assiduity. It is said that in after years she wrote an excellent tract called "Render unto Cæsar; or, the Repentant Villagers", in which her own experience was anonymously used as the introductory story. Stockdale got it printed after making some corrections, and putting in a few powerful sentences of his own; and many hundreds of copies were distributed by the couple in the course of their married life.

In *The Trumpet Major*, forsaking for a while the carefully elaborated method of *The Return of the Native*, Mr. Hardy adopted a style which recalled *Far from the Madding Crowd*. It is slighter and less powerful, possesses less unity of effect, but the same fresh Dorset air blows through it, the same wanton fancy plays pleasant or mischievous tricks; it is marked by the same touch of melodrama. Uncle Bengy is clever, but he represents an element which is foreign to Mr. Hardy's genius, and which he fails to make interesting. On the other hand, how delightful a study is old Miller Loveday! All the bluff heartiness, the cheery hospitality of the traditional jolly miller, are there in full measure; he is what people of platonizing tendency call 'typical'. And his son Bob is an almost equally good representative of the traditional sailor; he, too, is a 'type', presenting some curious points of similarity to that of the miller. John Loveday, the miller's other son, is the one unquestionably noble figure which Mr. Hardy has given us in any detail, and the book is worthily called after him. He is the son of Colonel Newcome, who was the son of Uncle Toby. Like those grand and guileless heroes, he is a soldier, and he enjoys the advantage of being considerably younger and considerably less ludicrous. It may be presumed that Uncle Toby, before he went to the wars in Flanders, was not yet given to whistling Lillibullero at critical moments, to the construction of miniature sieges on the bowling-green at Shandy, or to the other peculiarities which have rendered him famous to posterity. From all these, therefore, John Loveday is free, and we may say of this book, as of no other of Mr. Hardy's, that the hero is almost more interesting than the heroine. His strong, gentle, straightforward nature is incapable of gauging the delicate deflections of less noble natures. It need scarcely be said that in the relations of a man like Loveday with one of Mr. Hardy's heroines, even when she is so vaguely sinuous as Anne Garland, lies irony and pathos. And the best parts of *The Trumpet Major*—and its best parts are of Mr. Hardy's best—are concerned with the relations of John Loveday to Anne Garland and the kindly but insensitive Bob. These parts of the book are worked out with fine power and insight, and Anne Garland, tender, womanly, coquette, with the 'row of round brown curls, like swallows' nests under eaves', peeping out between her forehead and the borders of her cap, is among Mr. Hardy's most perfect and delicate creations. We cannot quite forgive her for marrying Bob instead of John; but such failures of perception are customary with Mr. Hardy's heroines, and Anne's womanly instincts never forsake her. Observe with what subtle truth Mr. Hardy has rendered the sweet sharpness of her behaviour towards Bob, when she wishes to punish him for his adventure with Matilda. There is something homely in Anne's fresh and charming nature which separates her from the series which we found were formed by Bathsheba, Ethelberta and Eustacia. She comes nearer to Fancy Day; but the hand that drew Anne Garland and the Trumpet Major has gained a new mastery of art since *Under the Greenwood Tree* was written, exquisite as was the early effort. There is here a precision, a delicacy, an easy adaptation of means to end, which can only come late. *The Trumpet Major* is full of passages etched in, as it were, with slight workmanship, where the touches are few, but where every line tells. It cannot be claimed for *The Trumpet Major* that it equals several of its predecessors in colour and intensity; it is inferior also in architectonics, though it is impossible to· pass over without mention the beautifully wrought frame in which the story is set; the murmur of war which is never too obtrusive; Weymouth with the quaint Georgian flavour which is yet strong about it; Portland with its bold outlines and the wonderful atmospheric effects around. The 'measured flounce of the waves' sounds throughout. It is not, however, by any impression of power and unity in the whole that *The Trumpet Major* is chiefly remarkable; but rather by its *verve*, its fresh and careless vivacity, the proof it offers that Mr. Hardy's genius is yet far from being exhausted.

A Laodicean has scarcely a single point of resemblance to *The Trumpet Major*. All the characteristic features which go to make up the charm of the latter are here absent. Mr. Hardy had set himself to write a story which is perhaps more faultless, and certainly less mannered, than anything that he had yet produced. The fancy which ran wild in *The Trumpet Major* is here chastened to one or two delicate touches. The eager and animated narrative has given place to a single thread of love-story, and, for the rest, relies on the charm of exquisite workmanship. We have not, however, escaped the melodramatic element. Captain de Stancey's illegitimate son, Dare, a very choice villain, and Abner Power continue what has come to be a sort of tradition in Mr. Hardy's books. And, although they are perhaps especially objectionable in what claims to be 'a story of to-day', it may be acknowledged that they are cleverly enough contrived. George Somerset, the hero, is a superior version of a character we are already familiar with. He succeeds in obtaining the reader's sympathies, although it is difficult to conceive of him apart from his love for Paula. Paula Power herself, the Laodicean, is through the greater part of the story an enigma, but in the end she acts with decision worthy of a Philadelphian, and we find her to be a more capable, human and lovable woman than perhaps Mr. Hardy has ever given us. The *dénouement* is worked out in his finest manner. He has written·no other novel which succeeds so entirely in satisfying the reader's emotional sense. And the architectonics of the story, its admirable balance, the way in which any other conclusion is rendered impossible, although the reader is kept in suspense—all this witnesses to the perfect mastery of art which Mr. Hardy had attained. If *A Laodicean* can scarcely become one of its writer's most popular stories, it yet marks distinctly the continuous development and the versatility of his genius.

In *Two on a Tower*, Mr. Hardy has to a great extent proceeded on the lines laid down in the previous novel. It is less delightful, but even more finished. Here, at length, we are freed from the depressing element of melodramatic villainy. Louis Glanville, indeed, looks a promising villain, but on nearer view he grows less terrible, and 'roars you as gently as any sucking dove'. Viviette is a refined Eustacia with incoherent moral aspirations. She scarcely attracts us at first, but succeeds eventually in winning our sympathy. One characteristic which comes out here may be noted. Mr. Hardy has given to each of his later novels a distinct and dominating background. In *The Return of the Native* the Dorset heathland formed a landscape in the manner of Old Crome which was visible throughout. The bustle of military preparation is used with admirable skill and reticence in *The Trumpet Major*. *A Laodicean* is an architectural novel, and *Two on a Tower* is astronomical. This method adds to the charm of freshness and variety which distinguishes Mr. Hardy's work; but on the whole is progressively unsatisfactory. The astronomical enthusiasm is wanting in spontaneity. We prefer Mr. Proctor for popular astronomy. If, however, *Two on a Tower* may be said to lack inspiration, it is still the work of a writer who has a finer sense of his art than any living English novelist; and, notwithstanding the light and delicate touch that Mr. Hardy has attained, there is no sacrifice of breadth.

We have now passed with necessarily brief notice the whole series of Mr. Hardy's works. And, looking at them as a whole, what one observes about them first is that they are all love-stories. There is something very fresh and delightful, turning from the writers with whom love is only interesting from the moral problems it may involve, or is at most the history of a passion, to find a writer of such distinct genius who has little or nothing to say about either morals or passion, and yet thinks love is the chief business of life, and can devote himself so frankly to the rendering of its devious ways. From the first Mr. Hardy showed how well he could deal with so old a theme. This is how Dick makes love to Fancy in *Under the Greenwood Tree*:

[quotes Part Third, ch. II, from ' "Now, Fancy," ' to ' "here's someone coming," she exclaimed.']

That is a rustic love-passage of the most elementary kind, but rendered with what charming freshness, what delicate simplicity! The same qualities, with an added subtlety, are visible throughout *A Pair of Blue Eyes*. *The Hand of Ethelberta* contains some such little scenes, dashed in with a brilliance and *verve* which, on the whole, are not Mr. Hardy's most prominent characteristics. In *The Trumpet Major*, the scenes between Anne and Bob are among the finest of the kind in modern literature. The entire interest of *A Laodicean* lies in the love history of Paula. Independent, self-repressed, 'deep as the North star': that enigmatical lady is supposed to be a sort of representative of the modern spirit. This is the way she responds to Somerset's advances,

[quotes Book I, ch. XV, from ' "We cannot go in" ' to 'she answered, walking away.']

By-and-by the season comes, and the situation is to some extent reversed.

Mr. Hardy's way of regarding women is peculiar and difficult to define, not because it is not a perfectly defensible way, but because it is in a great degree new. It is, as we have already noted, far removed from a method, adopted by many distinguished novelists, in which women are considered as moral forces, centripetal tendencies providentially adapted to balance the centrifugal tendencies of men; being, indeed, almost the polar opposite to that view. It is perhaps unnecessary to say that it is equally removed from the method of those who are concerned to work out Tertullian's view of woman as *janua diaboli*. Mr. Hardy's women are creatures, always fascinating, made up of more or less untamed instincts for both love and admiration, who can never help some degree of response when the satisfaction of those instincts lies open to them. They are all ultimately that; but with what intelligence, what an innate grace, at once delicate and frank, these instincts are manifested, any one knows who has followed the history of Elfride Swancourt or Anne Garland. The charm of woman for Mr. Hardy is chiefly physical, but it is a charm which can only be interpreted by a subtle observation. Generally, he is only willing to recognize the psychical element in its physical correlative. This dislike to use the subjective method or to deal directly with mental phenomena is a feature in Mr. Hardy's psychology which has left a strong mark on his art. It is nowhere more remarkable than in *A Laodicean*. We are scarcely brought face to face even with Somerset. He moves before us, he draws out his plans, he makes love, but for the rest he is a shadow; we are only helped to reach the man himself by the fine suggestions of a keen observer. He is not so much a creation as an observation. And, if this is true of Somerset, it is true in a far greater degree of Paula Power. With the exception of a dawning glimpse towards the end, she is an enigma for us as she is for Somerset. This is throughout a distinct note of Mr. Hardy's art. He is not with the writers who are concerned above all with the interest that comes from plot, nor is he with those who, like Mr. Blackmore at his best, write stories of adventure. The interest here is an interest of drama certainly, but, above all, of character, of psychology. And Mr. Hardy seems to feel that the problems thus raised, fascinating as they are, much as the novelist has to do with them, are, after all, infinitely difficult of adequate presentation, that the utmost possible is by the exercise of a fine and suggestive observation to indicate them. For Mr. Hardy is not satisfied with a purely ideal arrangement of the elements of life; he aims at a realistic representation. *Under the Greenwood Tree* is described on the title-page as 'a rural painting of the Dutch school'. George Eliot claimed to be an artist of the Dutch school, and with justice; she was a disciple of Rembrandt. But Mr. Hardy is certainly not this. He has little in common with Rembrandt or Ostade or Douw. And, if he will have it that his work belongs to the Dutch school, while we may see in it, if we like, something of De Koninck, something of Teniers, the nature-life of the one, the peasant-life of the other, we should say that he is more especially the disciple of a great master who in his best moments stands alone. Only the vivacity, the grace, the fine catching of situations, the irony of Jan Steen among the Dutch painters is at all like Mr. Hardy's work. Such analogies are necessarily more or less fanciful, and Mr. Hardy is not a writer with many affinities. In his standpoint, as regards art and the treatment of women, there is occasionally what seems like an influence from Thackeray; but, if Thackeray has the more range, eloquence, style, Mr. Hardy possesses beyond question a more delicate insight, and a far finer sense of his art. He is not a Philistine, and he never proses. In spirit and psychological method, some of his later novels recall Beyle; this is especially the case with *Two on a Tower*. From George Eliot, although he was once mistaken for her, Mr. Hardy is far removed. And, to any one who has learnt to enjoy the massive style and method of George Eliot, the thorough analysis the intense emotional atmosphere, it is hard at first to catch the suggestive quality, the light irony, the piquant traits which abound in *The Hand of Ethelberta*.

There is an artist with whom Mr. Hardy is related on another side, and, indeed, no writer can deal much with Dorset scenes and Dorset folk, without having points of contact with Mr. Barnes. It is curious, however, seeing how few of them there are, in what strikingly different manner the two writers touch the same things. We have already seen the dissimilarity in their respective treatment of the Dorset humour. There is, too, an initial divergence in the use of the dialect itself. Mr. Barnes, with the accuracy of the philologist, has reproduced that dialect (except in his smaller and less successful volume, *Poems of Rural Life in Common English*) with a minute and loving exactness, and we are grateful to him for doing so. But Mr. Hardy has chosen a method which is much better adapted for the purposes of the artist, a method which he has explained in a letter to the *Spectator* (Oct. 15, 1881):

The rule of scrupulously preserving the local idiom, together with the words which have no synonym among those in general use, while printing in the ordinary way most of these local expressions which are but a modified articulation of words in use elsewhere, is the rule I usually follow; and it is, I believe, generally recognized as the best, where every such rule must of necessity be a compromise, more or less unsatisfactory to lovers of form.

They contrast also as regards the way in which they look at Nature, and it is generally Mr. Hardy who sees her with the poet's eye. This is the way Mr. Barnes writes of one of the most familiar and characteristic features of the Dorset downs:

> The zwellèn downs, wi' chalky tracks
> A-climmèn up their zunny backs,
> Do hide green meäds an' zedgy brooks,
> An' clumps o' trees wi' glossy rooks,
> An' hearty vo'k to laugh an' zing,
> An' parish-churches in a string,
> Wi' towers o' merry bells to ring,
>   An' white roads up athirt the hills.

We have seen, in a passage already quoted, how Mr Hardy refers to the same feature: 'The Silver sunbeams lighted up a many-armed inland sea, which stretched around an island with fir-trees and gorse, and amid brilliant crimson heaths, wherein white paths occasionally met the eye in dashes and zigzags like flashes of lightning'. There can be no question with whom the imaginative insight lies here. At the same time, in the tender and faithful delineation of commonplace things, Mr. Barnes is incomparable. Mr. Hardy has written nothing to compare with so exquisite an idyll, perfect every way, as 'Evenèn in the Village'.

> Now the light o' the west is a-turn'd to gloom,
>   An' the men be at hwome vrom ground;
> An' the bells be a-zendèn all down the coombe,
>   From tower, their mwoansome sound.
>   An' the wind is still,
>   An' the house-dogs do bark,
> An' the rooks be a-vled to the elems high an' dark,
>   An' the water do roar at mill.
>
> An' the flickerèn light drough the window-peäne
>   Vrom the candle's dull fleäme do shoot,
> An' young Jemmy the smith is a-gone done leäne,
>   A-playèn his shrill-voiced flute.
>   An' the miller's man
>   Do zit down at his ease
> On the seat that is under the cluster o' trees,
>   Wi' his pipe an' his cider can.

Little has been said hitherto of the limitations of Mr. Hardy's art. But having tried to show what are the great qualities in his work, it is necessary to point out also, however briefly, where it seems to be defective. From a purely literary point of view, the style of all these novels, outside the dialogue, is often random and inaccurate. Mr. Hardy has not trained himself, as Mr. Henry James has, on the moderation, the precision, the perfect good sense of the French school. It is, perhaps, fortunate, but he suffers in consequence from the defects of his qualities. Want of strength and precision in the use of language are only perceptible, however, when Mr. Hardy speaks in his own person; his dialogue is generally succinct, often even epigrammatic, always delightful. A more serious fault in the eyes of the novel-reader is the persistent repetition of the same situations. The critical situation is nearly always the same: a woman more or less in love with two men at the same time. And she always, at all events in the first place, accepts them both, regardless of consequences. But in situations of more detail than this grand and general one, there are often curious repetitions. For instance, it is not unusual for three men to be in love with the heroine. And we shall find that, if one of these rivals comes to make a declaration, the other two are tolerably certain to come up in succession immediately afterwards. All three may even arrive at the same time, and be shut up in different rooms awaiting their turns. This climax is attained in *The Hand of Ethelberta*. Most readers will be able to find for themselves similar mannerisms of construction.

When we turn to the moral and psychological aspect of Mr. Hardy's art, there are one or two generalizations to be made regarding the limitations there found which are striking. The most obvious is the absolute fixity with which every character, even the most apparently sinuous, presents itself to Mr. Hardy. There is no flexibility, no capacity for development. As the man is now, so he always was, so he always will be. One wonders, indeed, how the characters of these people had a genesis at all; there are no children in Mr. Hardy's novels. Elfride, and Wildeve and Somerset are equally without flexibility; they can never change; there is no growth, no adaptation. This is the source of much tragedy. Eustacia offered an admirable subject for development to an artist and psychologist. She was, we remember, 'the raw material of a divinity', but she is always the same, and Yeobright is always the same, and the end is tragedy. It is everywhere so in Mr. Hardy's novels, and the result is a certain underlying harshness. Connected with this is the isolated way in which he regards the individual. It can scarcely be said in the life Mr. Hardy describes that the family, and not the individual, is the social unit; here are only individuals. It would almost seem that in the solitary lives on these Dorset heaths we are in contact with what is really a primitive phase of society, in which the links that bind man to man have not yet come to be perceived in any save the slight and fragmentary way. At all events this seems the simplest manner of accounting for that failure to grasp at all adequately even their most obvious obligations which characterizes the men often, the women generally, in these novels. To that also we may attribute the isolated and inflexible nature of the individual which has so deeply impressed Mr. Hardy. It would appear, then, that those qualities which we have found to be distinctive of his heroines, the absence of moral feeling, the instinctiveness, had a direct relation to the wild and solitary character of their environment.

This primitive social phase is accompanied by an even more primitive phase of worship. We have spoken of this, with its constant and loving reference to the shifting aspects of earth and air, as a kind of Nature-worship. It seems scarcely fanciful even to find in it some lingering echoes of the old tree-worship. Mr. Hardy is never more reverent, more exact, than when he is speaking of forest-trees. For instance, *Under the Greenwood Tree*, opens as follows:

To dwellers in a wood, almost every species of tree has its voice as well as its feature. At the passing of the breeze, the fir-trees sob and moan no less distinctly than they rock; the holly whistles as it battles with itself; the ash hisses amid its quiverings; the beech rustles while its flat boughs rise and fall. And winter, which modifies the note of such trees as shed their leaves, does not destroy its individuality.

The fir especially is a favourite with Mr. Hardy. In *The Hand of Ethelberta*, for instance, he speaks of 'an open heath, dotted occasionally with fir-plantations, the trees of which told the tale of their species without help from outline or colour; they spoke in those melancholy moans and sobs which give to their sound a solemn sadness surpassing even that of the sea.'

Of any theology, as of any philosophy, there are few traces in Mr. Hardy's works. Every man of fine sensibility has somewhere to seek a protection against the arrows of the world, and Mr. Hardy, like Heine, finds such a shield in irony. In the society he brings before us the clergy play a very small *rôle*. Joey Chickerel's qualifications for the Church are described as of the smallest and most peculiar kind. Mr. Maybold, good and honourable as he is, has few of the characteristics of the parish priest, and even he is by no means greatly relished by his parishioners:

[quotes *Under the Greenwood Tree*, Part Second, ch. II from ' "Ay, your parson comes by fate" ' to ' "spiritual trouble" '.]

When Somerset asks Paula about her creed, she replies: 'What I really am, as far as I know, is one of that body to whom lukewarmth is not an accident but a provisional necessity, till they see a little more clearly.' And this attitude of Paula's is one which we recognize as implicit throughout Mr. Hardy's novels. Any more definite standpoint is nowhere plain. If it were possible to find traces of any philosophy, it would be of Schopenhauer's. 'Der Mensch ändert sich nie'; that is what so deeply impresses Schopenhauer, *velle non discitur*; and, as we have seen, it is that which impresses Mr. Hardy. The fragmentary ethical system of the novelist is like a pale reflection of the philosopher's, and there is the same sense of the isolation of the individual, the same feeling that there are narrow limits to what one being can be for another. In the 'Parerga', there is, indeed, a short passage of which Cytherea's cry is but a paraphrase.

The time has not yet come for forming a final estimate of Mr. Hardy's work. We may hope that it is far distant. It may be safely said, however, that he will scarcely write another novel of the peculiar power, and, it might be added, the peculiar weakness, of *Far from the Madding Crowd*. It seems more probable that he will pursue the vein of comedy which began in *The Hand of Ethelberta*, and is, perhaps, the most characteristic outcome of his genius—that subtle and unimpassioned tracing of aspects of life at once delicate and simple, which are best touched by the fine observation, the tender irony, that we have found to be the most constant elements in Mr. Hardy's work. What fresh variations are possible within these limits it would not be well to predict, but it is probable that, of stories in this manner, *A Loadicean* and *Two on a Tower* will not be the last.

THE MAYOR OF CASTERBRIDGE

May 1886

---

25. From an unsigned review, *Athenaeum*

29 May 1886, 711

The editorial file marks this review 'Graves'. Hardy's is the first
of eight 'Novels of the Week' discussed in the article.

Mr. Hardy, though in some respects probably the best of our existing
novelists, has not reached the degree of absolute merit which we once
hoped he might do. He has a wonderful knowledge of the minds of
men and women, particularly those belonging to a class which better-
educated people are often disposed to imagine has no mind, chiefly
because it cannot express itself with much fluency or 'lucidity'. Also
he knows the ways and humours of country-folk, and can depict them
vividly and in few strokes. Also he is most ingenious in devising problems, and bringing his people into situations of a complicated nature,
which, nevertheless, the reader cannot pronounce to be wholly improbable. And, most of all, he has the gift of so telling his story that it
sticks by the reader for days afterwards, mixing itself with his impressions and recollections of real scenes and people just as a very vivid
dream will sometimes do, till he is not quite sure whether it also does
not belong to them. Perhaps he has never shown these qualities better
than in his latest novel. It will not be so popular as *The Trumpet Major*,
nor does it deserve to be, recounting as it does the tragedy (if it may
be so called) of a self-willed instead of an unselfish hero. But it displays
as much as any of his books the characteristics which we have indicated
briefly, and which, combined as they are with an almost Olympian
ruthlessness towards his own creations, might under other conditions
have made of Mr. Hardy a great dramatist. At the same time it must be
said that his old faults, chiefly of style, are as prominent as ever. The

worst of these is a tendency to far-fetched and unpleasant similes and epithets, e.g., 'the sun was resting on the hill *like a drop of blood on an eyelid*', or 'the espaliers . . . had pulled their stakes out of the ground, and stood distorted and writhing *in vegetable agony, like leafy Laocoons*'. The language of the peasants again is a point on which we have an old quarrel with Mr. Hardy. It is neither one thing nor the other—neither dialect exactly reproduced nor a thorough rendering into educated English. If a man says, 'I have been working within sound o't all day', he would not say, 'The real business is done earlier than this,' but surely 'be done earlier nor this'. But this is perhaps too long a question to enter into here; only Mr. Hardy may take our word for it that his method diminishes the reader's satisfaction.

26. From an unsigned review, *Saturday Review*

29 May 1886, lxi, 757

The rather brief discussion of *The Mayor of Casterbridge* deals with it as the first of three novels reviewed in one article.

It is small dispraise of Mr. Hardy's novel *The Mayor of Casterbridge* to say that it is not equal to the author's great and most picturesque romance of rural life, *Far from the Madding Crowd*. Nevertheless, *The Mayor of Casterbridge* is a disappointment. The story, which is very slight and singularly devoid of interest, is, at the same time, too improbable. It is fiction stranger than truth; for even at the comparatively distant date—some fifty years ago—and in the remote region—which we are unable to localize—when and where the scenes are laid, it is impossible to believe that the public sale by a husband of his wife and child to a sailor, in a crowded booth at a village fair, could have attracted such slight attention from the many onlookers, that the newly-assorted couple should have been able to walk off and disappear so entirely within a few hours, and that the vendor on coming to his senses the following morning, repenting him of the evil, and perhaps thinking that £5 was too small a price for a good-looking young woman, was unable to trace them, though he appears to have attempted the task in earnest. Again, is it possible that Michael Henchard, thoroughly selfish and unprincipled when young, could have been refined by a temperance vow, and a hard-handed money-getting life, into a man of considerable delicacy, honour, and generosity? Mrs. Henchard, alias Newson, is so colourless as to be almost imperceptible. Elizabeth Jane is excellent, but rather more than a trifle dull; and unless corn-factors have hitherto been a grossly maligned race, surely Farfrae has more scruples than any corn-factor that ever lived. Are flourishing businesses established in small country towns by refusal to deal with a rival's old customers; or rather, we should say, were they *ever* thus established? No one nowadays is in the least likely to try the experiment. It is a matter for regret that the author omits to publish Donald Farfrae's secret recipe for turning 'grown' wheat into good wholesome bread stuff, 'restored quite enough to make good seconds out of it', though he frankly admits that 'to fetch it back entirely is impossible. Nature won't stand so much as that.' We are inclined to think that Nature will not.

But if Mr. Hardy's narrative is not thrilling, his descriptive powers are as great as ever. Nothing can be better than his sketches of Casterbridge, the old Roman garrison town, overgrown rather than obliterated by an English *urbs in rure*. His strongest point, however, is his capacity for portraying the average peasant, more especially the peasant who has passed middle age. The dialect of the agricultural labourers, his ways of thought, and his mode of speech are alike admirably given. The rustic dialogue, indeed, forms the most, if not the only, amusing portion of the book. One of the best specimens which, if space permitted, we should be tempted to quote at length is the conversation between Mrs. Cuxsom and Solomon Longways wherein village views on funeral rites are frankly set forth. With his keen insight into the character of the rural poor Mr. Hardy has not failed to notice that with them custom breeds, if not contempt of gifts and the giver, at any rate a lack of the courtesy of acknowledgment. Nance Mockridge, standing with her hands on her hips, 'easefully looking at the preparations on her behalf' made by her young mistress, is drawn from the life. Equally characteristic of the country mayor who has risen from the ranks is Henchard's intolerance of his stepdaughter's natural good breeding, which prompts her to go to the kitchen instead of ringing, and persistently to thank the parlour-maid for everything she does; but for a man who cannot talk English even decently his anger at Elizabeth Jane's provincialisms is not quite so intelligible.

Another proof of how thoroughly Mr. Hardy has studied the workings of the rustic mind is given in the short account of Henchard's visit to 'Fall' or 'Wide-oh', as he was called behind his back, a sort of mild professor of the black art, whose simple magic was secretly invoked by yokels of all classes, who nevertheless always comported themselves during the séance as it were under protest. Whenever they consulted him they did it 'for a fancy'. When they paid him they said, 'Just a trifle for 'Xmas or Candlemas', as the case might be. The 'skimmington' or 'skimmity' ride will, we fancy, be a novelty to most readers, though the author has doubtless witnessed, or has excellent warranty for describing, this burlesque but forcible protest against what villagers regard as unseemly pre-nuptial conduct on the part of a bride. The worst feature of the book is, that it does not contain a single character capable of arousing a passing interest in his or her welfare. Even the *dramatis personæ*, with the exception of Lucetta, who conceives so sudden and violent a passion for Farfrae, are in doubt almost up to the last moment whether they really care about anybody.

27. R. H. Hutton, *Spectator*

5 June 1886, 752–3

(See headnote to No. 8.)

Mr. Hardy has not given us any more powerful study than that of Michael Henchard. Why should he especially term his hero in his title-page a 'man of character', we do not clearly understand. Properly speaking, character is the stamp graven on a man, and character therefore, like anything which can be graven, and which, when graven, remains, is a word much more applicable to that which has fixity and permanence, than to that which is fitful and changeful, and which impresses a totally different image of itself on the wax of plastic circumstance at one time, from that which it impresses on a similarly plastic surface at another time. To keep strictly to the associations from which the word 'character' is derived, a man of character ought to suggest a man of steady and unvarying character, a man who conveys very much the same conception of his own qualities under one set of circumstances, which he conveys under another. This is true of many men, and they might be called men of character *par excellence*. But the essence of Michael Henchard is that he is a man of large nature and depth of passion, who is yet subject to the most fitful influences, who can do in one mood acts of which he will never cease to repent in almost all his other moods, whose temper of heart changes many times even during the execution of the same purpose, though the same ardour, the same pride, the same wrathful magnanimity, the same inability to carry out in cool blood the angry resolve of the mood of revenge or scorn, the same hasty unreasonableness, and the same disposition to swing back to an equally hasty reasonableness, distinguish him throughout. In one very good sense, the great deficiency of Michael Henchard might be said to be in 'character'. It might well be said that with a little *more* character, with a little more fixity of mind, with a little more power of recovering *himself* when he was losing his balance, his would have been a nature of gigantic mould; whereas, as Mr. Hardy's novel is meant to show, it was a nature which ran mostly to waste. But, of course, in the larger and wider sense of the word 'character', that sense which has less reference to the permanent definition of the stamp, and more reference to the confidence with which the varying moods may be anticipated, it is not inadmissible to call Michael Henchard a 'man of character'. Still, the words on the title-page rather mislead. One looks for the picture of a man of much more constancy of purpose, and much less tragic mobility of mood, than Michael Henchard. None the less, the picture is a very vivid one, and almost magnificent in its fullness of expression. The largeness of his nature, the unreasonable generosity and suddenness of his friendships, the depth of his self-humiliation for what was evil in him, the eagerness of his craving for sympathy, the vehemence of his impulses both for good and evil, the curious dash of stoicism in a nature so eager for sympathy, and of fortitude in one so moody and restless—all these are lineaments, which, mingled together as Mr. Hardy has mingled them, produce a curiously strong impression of reality, as well as of homely grandeur.

Our only quarrel with Mr. Hardy is that while he draws a figure which, in spite of the melancholy nature of its career and the tragic close of that career, is certainly a noble one, and one, on the whole, *more* noble in its end than in its beginning, he intersperses throughout his story hints of the fashionable pessimism, a philosophy which seems to us to have little appropriateness to the homely scenery and characters which he portrays. For example, as Mr. Hardy approaches the end of his story, he says of his hero:

Externally there was nothing to hinder his making another start on the upward slope, and by his new lights achieving higher things than his soul in its half-formed state had been able to accomplish. But the ingenious machinery contrived by the gods for reducing human possibilities of amelioration to a minimum—which arranges that wisdom to do shall come *pari passu* with the departure of zest for doing—stood in the way of all that. He had no wish to make an arena a second time of a world that had become a mere painted scene to him.

To our minds, these very pagan reflections are as much out of place as they are intrinsically false. The natural and true reflection would have been that Michael Henchard, after his tragic career of passionate sin, bitter penitence, and rude reparation, having been brought to a better and humbler mind than that which had for the most part pervaded his life, the chief end of that life had been achieved, and that it mattered little in comparison whether he should or should not turn the wisdom he had acquired to the purpose of hewing out for himself a wiser and soberer career. Those who believe that the only 'human possibilities of amelioration' of any intrinsic worth, are ameliorations of the spirit of human character, cannot for a moment admit that when that has been achieved, it can add much to such an amelioration, that it should receive the sanction of a little earthly success. If life be the school of character, and if the character, once fairly schooled into a nobler type, passes from this school to another and higher school, we have no reason to complain. What Mr. Hardy calls 'the ingenious machinery contrived by the gods for reducing human possibilities of amelioration to a minimum', appears to us to be the means taken by the moral wisdom which overrules our fate for showing us that the use of character is not to mould circumstance, but rather that it is the use of circumstance to chasten and purify character. Michael Henchard's proud and lonely death shows, indeed, that he had but half learned his lesson; but it certainly does not in any way show that the half-learned lesson had been wasted. There is a grandeur of conception about this shrewd, proud, illiterate, primitive nature, which, so far as we remember, surpasses anything which even Mr. Hardy has yet painted for us in that strong and nervous school of delineation in which he excels so much. Michael Henchard's figure should live with us as Scott's picture of Steenie Mucklebacket or David Deans lives with us. Indeed, Scott never gave to a figure of that kind so much study and such painstaking portraiture as Mr. Hardy has given to his Mayor of Casterbridge.

He has succeeded quite as well—though the figure is not so interesting—with the Mayor's step-daughter, Elizabeth Jane, a reticent and self-contained nature of singular gentleness and wisdom, cast in an altogether lower tone of vitality, though in a higher plane of self-restraint. There is much beauty and charm in the picture, though the carefully subdued tone of the character makes it seem a little tame, and we are not at all scandalised at the easy victory gained by the lively Jersey beauty over her sober-minded, un-self-asserting rival. This Jersey beauty is also admirably touched off; but as for the all-conquering Scotchman who fascinates everybody (except the reader) so easily, there must, we think, be some failure of art there. Mr. Hardy makes Farfrae vivid enough. We cannot complain of not seeing him exactly as he is represented. But we have, perhaps, a right to complain that he seems so very cold-blooded to us, so very inferior to the master whom he supplants, though to all Mr. Hardy's *dramatis personae*, Farfrae seemed so greatly the superior of Michael Henchard. Part of the reason is that Mr. Hardy paints the Scotchman from the outside, and the Southron from the inside, and that while we see the Southron as no one in the story sees him, unless it be himself, we only see the Scotchman as all the others see him. But though that explains why we like the Southron so much *better*, it hardly explains why we like the canny Scotchman, with all his imaginative sentiment, so little, though he wins so easy a victory over the hearts of the people of Casterbridge.

We will not select morsels for quotation from *The Mayor of Casterbridge*, for it is not a story which lends itself well to quotation. And though the scenery of Dorsetshire, and especially of Dorchester—which is obviously enough the original of Casterbridge—is admirably given, Mr. Hardy's art in describing the scenery of the South-West is too well known to need illustration. His impetuous and restless hero is really the centre of the story. Round him all its interest centres, and with him it ends. We cannot express too warmly our admiration for the art with which that stalwart and wayward nature has been delineated, and all the apparently self-contradictory subtleties of his moods have been portrayed.

THE WOODLANDERS
March 1887

***

28. Unsigned review, *Athenaeum*

26 March 1887, 414

In the editorial file this review is marked 'Britten'. Hardy's was the first of six 'Novels of the Week' reviewed in this article.

***

Mr. Hardy seems to have fairly settled down into what his biographers will probably call his second manner. He is less vividly 'sensational', less broadly comic, than he was in his first few novels. We no longer get scenes like the discovery of the corpse and the rest at the end of *Desperate Remedies*, or the murder of Sergeant Troy; nor anything so provocative of laughter as some parts of *Under the Greenwood Tree* nor, again, incidents quite so far removed from ordinary probabilities as in some of the earlier works. Everything—pathos and humour alike— is in a subdued key, suggested rather than displayed. Just once and again he seems to yield to the temptation involved in a novelist's omnipotence over his characters, where in real life we should be per- force content with saying, 'I wonder what would happen if—', and brings them into some situation as unlikely as that where, in the present story, the wife and the two mistresses, actual and cast-off, meet in a common anxiety, just to see, as it were, how they will be- have. In point of construction his more recent stories are excellent. *The Woodlanders* appears to us simply perfect in this respect. Every incident contributes to the development of the story; every touch helps to put the reader in the frame of mind in which the author would have him be. The various aspects of the woodland in the midst of which the story is laid, for example, are worked in with inimitable skill, and without the least appearance of straining after scenic effect. That the general drift of the story is melancholy, and its ending unsatisfactory in any but an artistic point of view, is only another evidence of its belonging to Mr. Hardy's present method. The good man suffers; the bad man not only prospers, but, what is almost worse, shows signs of amendment without having been adequately punished. The heroine is in truth a commonplace woman enough, and forgives and forgets on very slight inducement; while the really heroic woman, in her way the sweetest figure that Mr. Hardy has ever drawn, though by a kind of accident she plays a most important part in the development of events, is outside the group of personages who stand in the centre of the story, to some scarcely known, and by all unappreciated. The novel is distinctly not one for the 'young person' of whom we have lately heard, but should be read by all who can tell masterly work in fiction when they see it.

29. R. H. Hutton, *Spectator*

26 March 1887, 419–20

(See headnote to No. 8.)

This is a very powerful book, and as disagreeable as it is powerful. It is a picture of shameless falsehood, levity and infidelity, followed by no true repentance, and yet crowned at the end with perfect success; nor does Mr. Hardy seem to paint his picture in any spirit of indignation that redeems the moral drift of the book. He does not impress us as even personally disposed to resent the good-natured profligacy of his hero; and the letter which Fitzpiers sends his wife towards the close of the story—the letter which opens the way to the renewal of their married life—has in it an unashamed air, by which Grace, if she had been all that Mr. Hardy wishes us to believe her, would have been more revolted than gratified. On the whole, Mr. Hardy has painted nothing more thoroughly disagreeable than this mendacious, easy-going, conscienceless, passionate young doctor, with his fastidious selfishness and his scientific acuteness, and his aristocratic self-esteem, availing himself of the weakness of every woman for whom he feels the least fancy, and almost more attracted at the close by his mistaken belief in his wife's infidelity to him, than he was at first by her purity and innocence. Mr. Hardy's story is written with an indifference to the moral effect it conveys of which we have found distinct traces before in his books, especially in *The Hand of Ethelberta*, but which, in our opinion, lowers the art of his works quite as much as it lowers the moral tone. It is impossible to admire Giles Winterborne, and Marty South as Mr. Hardy intends us to admire them, without also feeling indignation and disgust towards Fitzpiers which Mr. Hardy not only does not express, but even renders it impossible for us to suppose that he entertains. And this affects the whole story, and makes us regard it with a sort of dislike that is most unfavourable to a work of art, the dislike which springs from the feeling that the artist has not truly estimated the significance of his own work. A more unworthy and godless creature than Fitzpiers to find favour, as he evidently does, in the mind of the artist who painted his likeness, it would not be easy to discover in our modern fiction; and though he is well drawn, he is drawn with an air of something like apology, if not sympathy, that sends a discordant vibration through the whole tale. Mr. Hardy will say that in painting Winterborne, he has given the standard by which to try Fitzpiers and find him wanting, which would be true, if only there were not a vein of positive liking for him that penetrates the tale, and annuls all the effect of Winterborne's faithfulness, manliness, and pure disinterestedness. It is evident, for instance, at the close of the tale, that Mr. Hardy spares Fitzpiers the man-trap which the vindictiveness of Tim Tangs had prepared for him, and even turns it into the means of reconciling him to his wife, from a feeling of tenderness for him which we cannot admire. We will admit that there is no case for what used to be called 'poetical justice' in novels. It is quite true that there is but little of it in real life, except the rewards and punishments which the conscience itself bestows. The man-trap, even if Fitzpiers had been caught in it, might have done him no more good, though to have been nursed by his wife in the pain and mutilation which it would have inflicted on him, would have been too good a fate for his deserts. But even putting aside the wish so commonly felt for what is called poetical justice, Mr. Hardy ought not to have allowed this sensual and selfish liar, good-natured in an easy way though he certainly was, to be received back into his wife's favour and made happy on terms so easy as are here imposed on him.

Mr. Hardy, as usual, is stronger in his pictures of genuine rural life than in any other part of his story. The account of Marty South and her hysterical father, who is killed by the nervous shock of finding that the fate he had feared for himself had become impossible, are admirably sketched, though what Mr. Hardy may mean by saying of Marty South that she behaved almost 'like a being who had rejected with indifference the attribute of sex for the loftier quality of abstract humanism', we have not the faintest idea. What is abstract humanism? And why should a woman who was breathing out a sigh of relief that the only rival she had had—indeed, the only woman for whom the man she loved had really cared— had at length forgotten that man, and that she herself could dedicate her own life to his memory without feeling that she was interfering with another woman's claims, be the representative of 'abstract humanism'? We should have thought that if she represented anything abstract at all, it would have been abstract womanhood, though the quality of abstractness appears to us wholly wanting. When Mr. Hardy becomes metaphysical, he becomes obscure.

Perhaps the best study in the book is that of the vacillating and restless old timber-merchant, Melbury, Grace's father, who makes so terrible a mess of his own and of his daughter's life, chiefly through the overweening idolatry with which he regards her. The way in which Melbury promises himself to compensate the son of his old friend for a bad turn which he had done that friend in early life, by giving his beautiful daughter to the son in marriage; the struggles he goes through to keep his word; his deep sense of the indignity it will be to Grace to give her to a man who is not her equal in education; his faithlessness the moment a chance opens of marrying her to a man who belongs to a higher social caste; the misery with which he discovers that in thus marrying her he has wronged her; the half-delirious way in which he flounders about in his eagerness to obtain a divorce, and to secure her first suitor again for her before he knows whether a divorce can or cannot be granted; the shocking way in which, in his ignorance, he compromises her, or at least would have compromised her, but for Giles Winterborne's nobility of heart; and the dumb pain with which he discovers at the close that he has once more mistaken her, and that she has thought right to forgive and return to her husband, while he, her father, was nursing his indignation against that husband—are all related with a force that brings before us the confused and morbid character of the timber-merchant's inarticulate nature in all its blurred and moody intensity, as even Mr. Hardy has seldom succeeded in bringing before us such a nature before; and this though the type is one in which he certainly delights. A more thoroughly unpleasant episode than the negotiation as to the divorce we can hardly recollect. Still, we do not deny that it is so artistically treated that its radically revolting elements are all but merged in the vivid pain with which we realize the unhappy father's disturbed and remorseful impatience with himself, and his blind eagerness, to undo the evil he has done. Perhaps the poorest part of the book is that which deals with Mrs. Charmond and her ill-regulated mind. But even that is not without force.

The pleasantest part of the story, the only really pleasant part, is the picture of the woodlands themselves. No one can rival Mr. Hardy in such descriptions of Nature as he gives us in these volumes, and his sympathies here are all perfectly wholesome as well as rich in beauty; and this we cannot say of his pictures of men and women. In the following passage the reader will be able to catch some trace of this, the purest and most fascinating element of the story:

[quotes ch. XLIV 'Grace was abased' to ' "fruits and flowers themselves." ']

There is no falling-off in power in *The Woodlanders*; but there is more that is disagreeable in it, more that disposes us to find serious fault with Mr. Hardy's moral standard, than in anything that he has published since *The Hand of Ethelberta*. If he would give us a little less 'abstract humanism' and a little more of human piety, we should find his stories not only more agreeable, but more lifelike also. There is something glaring and unmellowed in pictures of human life which even on their best side, even in such studies as those of Giles Winterborne and Marty South, leave us nothing better to admire than the fidelity of wholesome inarticulate instincts, destitute alike of faith and of hope:

> Not sobs or groans,
> The passionate tumult of a clinging hope,—
> But pale despair and cold tranquillity,
> Nature's vast frame, the web of human things,
> Birth and the grave which are not as they were.

30. Coventry Patmore, *St. James's Gazette*

2 April 1887

Coventry Patmore (1823–96), the Catholic poet and friend of
G. M. Hopkins, used *The Woodlanders* as the occasion for a short
general survey of Hardy's work. The article was reprinted in
Courage in Politics and Other Essays (1921).

The wealth of this century in prose fiction is scarcely yet appreciated.
The number of novels produced from the time of Walter Scott to the
present day which are really works of art, and which deserve and will
probably obtain a classical position in literature, is surprisingly great;
and the fact is curiously little recognized. To call a book a 'novel' is to
stamp it at once with an ephemeral character in the minds of most
readers; but it will probably be found that, while by far the larger
portion of the poetical and historical writing of the present century
which is looked upon as 'classical' will prove to be ephemeral, a
large mass of that writing which is regarded as almost by nature
transitory will take its place in the ranks of abiding fame with the
fiction of Fielding and Goldsmith. No generation has known so well
how to paint itself as our own. Indeed, no generation has ever attempted to paint itself in the same way and with the same fidelity. Hence
every past century has drawn a veil over the real life of that which went
before, and in some respects human life in the reign of Elizabeth is
almost as much a mystery as that of the time of Charlemagne or the
Ptolemies. The seventeenth and eighteenth centuries, indeed, have
made themselves comparatively visible to posterity by a number of
personal 'memoirs', like those of Mrs. Hutchinson; but, if we go
further back than that, there is scarcely any such thing as credible and
intelligible delineation of life and manners. How inestimable for times
to come such delineations are those best known who have turned from
the 'histories' of such periods to those few lifelike glimpses of the
times themselves. Now, from Miss Austen to Thomas Hardy, we have
had scores of 'fictions' which are only fictions in form; the substance
being the very reality of contemporary life, from which posterity
will be able to discern as truly what we were as a visitor to a gallery

full of Van Dyck's pictures can see how gentlemen and ladies looked in the time of Charles I. The student of 1987, if he wants to know anything really about us, will not find it in our poets or our philosophers or our parliamentary debates, but in our novelists; in many of whose works he will at once recognize the veracity of our portraits, feeling, as we do when we look at a portrait by Velasquez or Titian, that it must be like—nay, that it is—the life itself; and in presence of our 'memoirs' and novels he will feel that the 'catastrophic' period—as, for want of a better name, he may call the unintelligible preceding ages of society—is over, and that the world has become credible.

During the past very few years, death has made sad havoc among our greatest novelists of the class under consideration. Dickens did not belong to it; for though in some respects he was the greatest of the tribe of story-tellers, it is not to his works that posterity will look for our true likeness. But Thackeray, Trollope, George Eliot and Mrs. Gaskell have each produced more than one work of indisputable right to a place in this category. Among living writers there are two—one well and one at present comparatively little known—whose work in this kind can scarcely be surpassed; namely, Thomas Hardy and L. B. Walford. Mr. Hardy, though less perfect, is much the greater artist of the two: for, depending for his interest mainly on manners, he confines himself, in his best work, almost exclusively to the manners of the humblest and simplest classes; and in depicting them evokes a tenderness, reality, and force for the like of which we know not where to look in contemporary literature, unless it be in the poems of his friend William Barnes. In Hardy's *Under the Greenwood Tree*, a gamekeeper and his son, the mistress of the village National school, three or four small tradesmen, and a labourer or two, are the entire *dramatis personae*—with the exception of a young clergyman who is little more than a 'walking gentleman'—and plot there is really none. Yet out of these materials Hardy has made a prose-idyll which deserves to rank with the *Vicar of Wakefield*; though, and partly indeed because, it is as unlike Goldsmith's story as can well be, being absolutely unique in its way. In this and his other novels Hardy is in every point the reverse of the 'unnatural' school. His love of nature is so passionate and observant, that it is impossible to read him without a sense that he is in some degree wasting his powers and experience by expending them upon prose. No poet has ever discerned more acutely or expressed more forcibly, tenderly, and daintily the inexhaustible beauties of wood, heath, field, and lane; and yet he is so good an artist that nature always keeps its place in his writings as the unobtrusive background of a humanity full of the most breathing life and interest, though, for the most part, as unsophisticated as nature itself. No one, not even the authoress of *Silas Marner*, has ever interpreted rustic manners and passions so faithfully and lovingly: and the borderland between rusticity and the lower grades of 'gentility', which other novelists have made the subject of their most biting sarcasm, is treated by Hardy with a kindliness and sympathetic humour which are all his own. No other novelist, again, has so well understood the value of unity of place. The scene of his drama is scarcely ever shifted; and this constancy to it, and the extraordinary fidelity with which its features are described and kept before us—as in the case of the great heath in *The Return of the Native*, and the old Roman town in *The Mayor of Casterbridge*—give to the whole work a repose and harmony which are, in their kind, incomparable. It is in his heroines, however, that Hardy is most original and delightful. The central female figures of *Under the Greenwood Tree, A Pair of Blue Eyes, Far from the Madding Crowd, The Return of the Native, The Trumpet Major, A Laodicean, Two on a Tower, The Mayor of Casterbridge*, and *The Woodlanders*, have never made their appearance in any other story; and yet each has the charm of the simplest and most familiar womanhood, and the only character they have in common is that of having each some serious defect, which only makes us like them more. Hardy is too good an observer not to know that women are like emeralds and rubies, only those of inferior colour and price being without flaw; and he is too rich in human tenderness not to know that love never glows with its fullest ardour unless it has 'something dreadful to forgive'. The most heart-rending pathos is evoked by him, in nearly all his novels, from this source; for there is nothing so tragic as to see the pardonable frailties of amiable characters heavily punished.

Hardy, like all writers who have written so much, has not always written up to himself. *The Hand of Ethelberta* was signally below his true mark, and in *The Woodlanders*, his latest novel, he is least happy. Two of the principal characters, Fitzpiers and Mrs. Charmond, are throughout repulsive, and give an ill-flavour to the whole book; Grace Melbury, though in the main charming, never takes hold of our sympathy very strongly, and forfeits it altogether when she marries Fitzpiers; and the whole interest of the story is spoilt by our being expected to believe in that incredible event, the abiding repentance and amendment of a flippant profligate. In the secondary characters and their natural surroundings, however, Hardy is all himself. The tragic weight with which he, more than any living writer, knows how to invest the very humblest ranks of rustic life has never been more nobly depicted by him than in the by-plot of Winterborne and Marty South. The comparative dumbness of the passions and affections of persons in their class becomes, in the hands of Hardy, a deeper source of pathos than the tragic reticence of such feelings in those who are apt of speech.

Why such a master of language should, in his latest work, have repeatedly indulged in such hateful modern slang as 'emotional', and 'phenomenal' (in the sense of 'extraordinary' instead of 'apparent'), and in the equally detestable lingo of the drawing-room 'scientist', seems quite inexplicable.

31. From an unsigned review, *Saturday Review*

2 April 1887, lxiii, 484–5

The Woodlanders is the first of three novels discussed in one article.

In *The Woodlanders* Mr. Hardy returns to that region of Wessex in which his early successes were made. Without attempting too rashly to conjecture the exact scene of the story, we can plainly enough gather from indications which the author gives that it lies near the centre of the county of Dorset, not far from the hilly and orchard-covered confines of the beautiful Vale of Blackmore. This district inspired the most characteristic pieces of the late Mr. Barnes; and it is sequestered, picturesque, and individual enough to be well worthy of the devotion of a poet or a novelist. Mr. Hardy has treated other parts of his native county before, but we have not found ourselves in exactly the company we meet with in *The Woodlanders* since he published *Under the Green-wood Tree*.

The opening pages of *The Woodlanders* give a very impressive notion of the solitude that reigns over vast tracts in this region of orchards. The villages are few and far apart, and they are apt to lie just off the desolate high-road, up cosy lanes, as though to escape the notice of those who walk and drive along the highway. It is in the concentration of a wood-land village, where all persons are known to one another, and all are thrown upon the emotional resources of each other, that great dramas may be silently enacted, in the simplicity of an almost primitive form of society. Mr. Hardy, as he has so often proved, enjoys nothing so much as to observe the effect of bringing the unsophisticated elements of village life into contact with the world and outer fashion. It is his peculiarity that, while others have so freely chronicled the comic elements of the result, he has been mainly drawn to the tragic ones. The tone of his best novels, as will have been observed, is almost always what the old playwrights knew as tragi-comical, the solemn problems of life being presented in his pages tempered by the humours of what is often little else than a chorus of peasants. In *The Woodlanders* we find the natural order of development in a cider-village disturbed by two figures whose place should be rather in London or Paris than in a remote Dorsetshire community. These two personages set all the wood-land music in a discord, and what would else be comedy comes in their hands to a tragic issue.

In the tiny village of Little Hintock the principal native inhabitant is a timber merchant of the name of Melbury, whose one daughter, Grace, has been educated, as the saying runs, 'above her station'. She is absent when the story opens, but is expected home very shortly. By an old vague agreement Grace Melbury is half-betrothed to Giles Winterborne, a fine young fellow engaged in the apple trade. This man is the hero of the story. Several of the villagers, and Winterborne in particular, keep the tenure of their houses upon lifehold, and are at the mercy of the lady of the manor. This is a very eccentric personage, widow of a rich man much older than herself, who married her off the stage, and who has died, leaving her quite young. Mrs. Charmond is seldom at Hintock House, and when she appears she is not much approved of. Her manners are thus discussed by some spar-makers at work:

'My brother-in-law told me, and I have no reason to doubt it,' said Creedle, 'that she'd sit down to her dinner with a frock hardly higher than her elbows.

"Oh, you wicked woman!" he said to himself when he first saw her; "you go to your church, and sit, and kneel, as if your knee-joints were greased with very saint's anointment, and tell off your hear-us-good Lords as pat as a business man counting money; and yet you can eat your victuals such a figure as that!" Whether she's a reformed character by this time I can't say; but I don't care who the man is, that's how she went on when my brother-in-law lived there.'

The other disturbing element is a Dr. Fitzpiers, a young physician of great, though superficial, abilities and dangerous good looks, who settles at Little Hintock, to be in the midst of a country practice. Another leading character is Marty South, a taciturn, lonely girl, who lives by making spars, and who nourishes a dumb and hopeless love for Giles Winterborne. These are the principal characters which unite to form the impassioned drama of this romance.

It is in no carping spirit, but rather to ensure that justice should be done to Mr. Hardy, that we venture to encourage the reader to go carefully through the early chapters of the first volume of *The Wood-landers*. They will probably feel, with ourselves, that after the very felicitous opening scene with Marty South in her cottage, the narrative becomes not a little stiff and laboured for several chapters. We do not remember any previous book in which Mr. Hardy has been so un-fortunate as he is here in making Melbury get out of bed and walk in his garden at two o'clock in the morning in order that his wife may follow him, and may be told certain incidents in his early life in tones loud enough to be heard by Marty South, who also happens, pro-videntially, to be out in her garden at that unearthly hour. This, or we are much mistaken, is forced indeed. But Mr. Hardy soon warms to his work, throws off what may perhaps be signs of fatigue, and, by the time he is half-way through the first volume, has completely recovered his tone. The second volume is, in our opinion, one of the best that he has ever written, and the third is little inferior to it. It is a pity that the beginning of the book should have the air of being written in defiance of Minerva.

While we are finding fault, we may as well have our quarrel out with Mr. Hardy. We are not of those who call in question the wit and in-genuity of the conversation which he puts into the mouths of his countryfolk. The objection to such talk as unnatural is made by those who do not know the Wessex yeoman and journeyman, by those who, when they meet an inhabitant, talk over his head with their London jargon, or strike him into suspicious and sarcastic silence by their fashionable airs. But, although we know the Dorsetshire man too well not to be aware that Mr. Hardy holds the secret of his speech, and perfectly well understands what he is doing in reproducing his idiom, we yet think that the novelist is a little inconsistent in his standard of conversation. It appears to us that he vacillates between giving an exact facsimile of the village talk and doing what many French novelists think it proper to do—that is to say, putting pure town talk into the lips of their peasants. We will give an instance of what we conceive to be confusion in this matter from the amusing passage at the beginning of Volume II, where Grammer Oliver talks to Grace about the bargain she had made to sell her brain for dissection after death to Dr. Fitzpiers. Most of this conversation is in the broadest Dorset, with its delightful appeal to the girl to 'save a poor old woman's skellington from a heathen's chopper'; but it ends thus:

Ay, one can joke when one is well, even in old age; *but in sickness one's gaiety falters;* and that which seemed small looks large, and the grim far-off seems near.

This, surely, strikes a thoroughly false note, especially the words which we have italicized, than which nothing less in keeping with poor old Grammer's habits of mind or speech could well be conceived. Occasional lapses of this kind, and a habit of using strained and over-technical words for simple things, seem to us to be the snares against which Mr. Hardy needs to guard himself.

We are giving, however, but a poor idea of the richness and humanity of the book. Mr. Hardy has not often drawn a more sympathetic character than that of the undemonstrative, patient, and self-denying Giles Winterborne. The picture of him when Grace first compares him wittingly with the shallow and flashy Edred Fitzpiers, when she sees Giles in the sunset light, following his apple-mill, and looking like the very genius of the orchards, is in a high degree subtle and original. Not less admirable in their own way are the passages in which Grace and Mrs. Charmond lose their way in the wood; that in which Fitzpiers, dead asleep from fatigue, is carried through the moonlight upright in his saddle; or the final scene in which Giles dies in the hut in the copse. Mr. Hardy has never written a novel in which the landscape takes a more important place than it does in *The Woodlanders*; it does not intrude itself, but at every point the novelist introduces some touch which brings up a picture before our eyes, and we see the warm-coloured figures of his vivid drama moving against a background of rich orchard-country, with the light violet mist floating over it, and vaulted by a low sky, which is constellated with what are not stars, but every variety of pale green and light golden and dark red apples. We may instance the description of the sudden coming of winter as a particularly favourable instance of the sympathetic treatment of landscape, not as an outside adornment, but as an essential part of the scheme of the story. The humorous element in *The Woodlanders* is not very prominent. We have already casually mentioned the two principal comedians—the old Creedle, and Grammer Oliver, the ancient caretaker. In closing we may express a hope that Mr. Hardy, whose characters are wont to be so essentially persons of flesh and blood, will not be led astray by the desire to idealize. Giles Winterborne is perhaps, a little too consciously treated as the incarnation of a phase of village civilization, and not quite enough as an individual.

32. William Wallace, *Academy*

9 April 1887, xxxi, 251–2

William Wallace (1844–97) was a Fellow of Merton College and Whyte Professor of Moral Philosophy at Oxford from 1882 to 1897: his chief works were on Hegel and Schopenhauer.

The Woodlanders is decidedly the best and most powerful work Mr. Hardy has produced since *Far from the Madding Crowd*. With the possible exception, also, of *Two on a Tower*, it will be regarded as his most disagreeable book, not only by the ordinary clients of Mr. Mudie, who feel dissatisfied unless Virtue passes a Coercion Bill directed against Vice at the end of the third volume, but even by those of Mr. Hardy's own admirers who complain, as Mr. Morley complains of Emerson, that he is never 'shocked and driven into himself by "the immoral thoughtlessness" of men', that 'the courses of nature and the prodigious injustices of men in society, affect him with neither horror nor awe'. In recent fiction, even in recent French fiction, there has figured no more exasperating scoundrel than Edred Fitzpiers, who yet, in the third volume of *The Woodlanders* figures as the repentant, or, at all events, the returned prodigal—weakly susceptible alike to vulgar sensuality and to superficial coquetry in woman, cultured up to the verge of altruism, yet perpetually wallowing in the mire of egoism. Nine out of ten readers of *The Woodlanders* will say that the best thing in it is the thrashing that Fitzpiers's father-in-law administers to him, when he expresses his hope that his wife may die. Mentally, they will clap their hands at this exhibition of honest indignation on the part of old Melbury. Yet, by the mere act of doing so, they virtually approve of Mr. Hardy's mission in *The Woodlanders*, which is to exhibit, as he says, 'The Unfulfilled Intention which makes life what it is'. In *Far from the Madding Crowd*, when he was younger, or more of an optimist or less of an Emersonian, he exhibited the Fulfilled Intention in the death of Troy and in the marriage of Bathsheba Everdene and Gabriel Oak—the Fulfilled Intention, that is to say, of his own imagination. In *The Woodlanders*, he gives us the Unfulfilled Intention of the actual world. There is, therefore, a little of Gabriel Oak in Giles Winterborne; but not enough to round off his life with domestic happiness. There is a little of Bathsheba Everdene in Grace Melbury—enough to make her marry the man of her fancy and not of her heart. As for Edred Fitzpiers, he is but a superfine (an intellectually, not morally superfine) Sergeant Troy who escapes the gun of Captain Boldwood. But then we have an entirely new creation in Marty South, the poor girl who ascends from the ridiculous in the first chapter, in which she loses her hair, to the sublime in the last chapter, in which she loses her hero, and, standing by his tombstone, 'looks almost like a being who had rejected with indifference the attribute of sex for the loftier quality of abstract humanism'. Thus the Unfulfilled Intention has its compensating advantages in nature and in art—it gives variety to both. Men and women hang by each other in consequence of their weaknesses; they are not indissolubly united through their virtues. But Mr. Hardy not only justifies—by reproducing—the Unfulfilled Intention, he provides, in *The Woodlanders*, a strong plot, diversified rather than marred by whimsicalities of incident. Melbury, the timber merchant, and the centre of the group of woodlanders, is in his way the impersonation of the Unfulfilled Intention. Because he carried off Giles Winterborne's mother from Giles Winterborne's father, therefore he must marry his daughter Grace to Giles himself. But he also gives Grace a good—in the sense of town—education. She drifts from Giles to Fitzpiers, the doctor of her district, with his modern culture and his old blood. Then, when Fitzpiers proves unfaithful and elopes with Mrs. Charmond, the 'great lady' of the district, poor Melbury tries to get a divorce for his daughter that she may marry Winterborne, and so give effect to his intention after all. He fails tragically. Winterborne, who is of the stuff of which martyrs are made, loses his life to save the reputation of Mrs. Fitzpiers when she is fleeing from her returned husband. That is all he can do. Fitzpiers and his wife are brought together again. There is one weak character in *The Woodlanders*, and one incident in it which is not only eccentric but farcical. Mrs. Charmond is too much of a third-rate French actress. Her purchase of the locks of poor Marty South is a piece of vulgarity, not of coquetry. Then the story of the man-trap trick, which comes in at the end, and by means of which Tim Tangs seeks to revenge himself on Fitzpiers for the intrigue which he suspects him (and with reason) to have had with his Suke before his marriage is too obviously a piece of hurried stage 'business' to bring Edred and Grace together again. Creedle and Upjohn admirably sustain the reputation of Mr. Hardy as an artist in rustic originals: their talk is not too philosophical. Even *Far from the Madding Crowd* does not contain more passages worthy of quotation than *The Woodlanders*—passages in which Mr. Hardy permits his readers, though not himself, to turn from contemplating the tragedy of the Unfulfilled Intention, in order to enjoy the pensive contentment of a Coleridgean sabbath of the soul.

33. J. M. Barrie, 'Thomas Hardy: the Historian of Wessex', *Contemporary Review*

1889, lvi, 57

At this date Barrie was 29 and a rising novelist. In spite of their obvious difference of temperament, he remained a personal friend of Hardy until his death. The *Contemporary Review* had been founded in 1866 primarily as a religious periodical; at this time it was edited by Sir Percy Bunting.

Leading men in the trade have differed of late in print about what constitutes a story. The author of *The Lady of the Aroostook* has wasted his time—for he might have been writing another novel—in scorning tales with plots. There are only two sides to the controversy. All the stories are told, says the plaintiff, while the defence is that he only is a storyteller who tells a story. This has no point unless it means that the exciting plots have been exhausted, and that a storyteller must deal in sensation. All the stories will certainly never be told while there is life on the earth, and Mr. Howells is a proof of it. His books are stories because his characters reveal themselves by their words and actions as they work their way to matrimony. Mr. Wilkie Collins is not more a storyteller than Mr. Howells. They are masters in the same art, but with different methods; and rules to make them write alike would be a calamity. Each has found out the best way for himself. Thus all so-called stories are properly labelled except those that are descriptive reporting. However brilliant description of character may be it will not do by itself; a writer may plot marriage, murder, and magic, and not be a storyteller. We do not want to hear the points of the horse, but to see him running. Mr. Howells seldom goes wrong here, but Mr. James more frequently, and of English writers Mr. F. C. Philips is a staring, because clever, warning.

No living novelist keeps more in the background than Mr. Thomas Hardy, who is, therefore, a storyteller. Except that they all follow the same calling, he has little in common with Mr. Collins or the 'American school', standing midway between them, for, on the rare occasions on which he does attempt to ride sensation, it flings him, and he has not Mr. Howells's pleasure in choosing for hero the commonest man in the street. The American school, indeed, love to dwell with conventional persons, upon whom Mr. Hardy turns his back. If he had got Daisy Miller as far as Casterbridge, she would have returned home of no use to Mr. James. Mr. Hardy would have discovered queer ideas in her head, and encouraged their growth. Some would rather say that he would have given them to her, for there is a public that compares Mr. Hardy, when he is writing of young ladies, to the conjurer who brings strange things out of an empty box. He has critics whom he seems to vex, but every one, at all events, must admit that he writes with something to say, except when he loses himself, as he tends to do every time he wanders beyond Wessex.

Life has impressed him in three ways. The provincial towns and villages, and heaths and woods of Wessex, which were the world of his youth, have taken hold of him, as the scenes and persons of her early days possessed George Eliot, and their influence is still so strong that when he escapes from it he is comparatively colourless. No reader of his Wessex tales would have him shake this influence off, for it is part of his greatness as a novelist, the part that may make the historian of Wessex a personage to posterity when it has lost the names of all his contemporaries in fiction save one. Mr. Hardy's fixed ideas about young women, whatever their rank or upbringing, are so original, adhered to with such tenacity from book to book, and so cunningly illustrated as to cry for comment. Lastly, he feels deeply the tragedy of humanity. Several of his stories, not necessarily the best, end like Shakespearian tragedies. The end may have been led up to with noise and bustle, but when it comes all is quiet enough. Passion has spent itself. Here is an open grave, but in a bird's-eye view of the world it is too small to be noticed. Elfride is in it, and the two men who loved her can only look in and turn away. What fires have burned in their breasts, what days of misery and delight she has given them, how jealous they have been of each other, and this is the end. Mr. Hardy's sad philosophy rings as true as his English yeomen or his picture of Egdon Heath, and he ignores the childish repugnance to 'unhappy endings', like one who thinks that the art of storytelling may aim higher than to rest the brain of Darwins or Ruskins when they are tired of thinking. Fiction is not necessarily a substitute for marbles. In one sense Mr. Hardy may be said to have gone a stage beyond the tragic writers of the world's younger days, for he sees that in real life the comedy often has a tragic ending, and he has no higher ambition than to be true to life. Not Mr. Meredith himself has a firmer conception of the greatness and smallness of individual man. A few men and women are taken, and round their life of a moment Mr. Hardy weaves a strange tale, but he always has one eye on the mighty world in which they are such insignificant atoms. 'The more I see of life', Yeobright says, 'the more do I perceive that there is nothing particularly great in its greatest walks, and therefore nothing particularly small in mine of furze-cutting.' There is no cynicism in this, for Mr. Hardy always writes from his heart. It is only a philosophy come to him a little before its time, a grand philosophy of the future towards which the world is shaping.

This view of life is one of Mr. Hardy's links with posterity. The other is that he has written history, which cannot be rewritten into anything better. There are clever novelists in plenty to give us the sentimental aspect of country life, and others can show its crueller side. Some paint its sunsets, some never get beyond its pig-troughs or its ale-houses; many can be sarcastic about its dulness. But Mr. Hardy is the only man among them who can scour the village and miss nothing; he knows the common as Mr. Jefferies knew it; but he knows the inhabitants, as well as the common. Among English novelists of today he is the only realist to be considered, so far as life in country parts is concerned. The professional realists of these times, who wear a giant's robe and stumble in it, see only the seamy side of life, reproducing it with merciless detail, holding the mirror up to the unnatural instead of to nature, and photographing by the light of a policeman's lantern. The difference between them and the man whose name they borrow is that they only see the crack in the cup, while he sees the cup with the crack in it. There are novelists of society whose realism is as genuine as Mr. Hardy's, but they are not so fortunate in their subject. The face of society has changed but little since Thackeray reflected it, and his portraits swallow theirs. With country life it is different. The closing years of the nineteenth century see the end of many things in country parts, of the peasantry who never go beyond their own parish, of quaint manners and customs, of local modes of speech and ways of looking at existence. Railways and machinery of various sorts create new trades and professions, and kill old ones. The rustics of Warren's malthouse, who went to the Casterbridge fair with sheep-crooks in their hands and straw woven round their hats, are already to be seen tailor-made twice a year in Oxford Street. Thus, the shepherds and thatchers and farmers and villagers, who were, will soon be no more, and if their likeness is not taken now it will be lost for ever. Mr. Hardy has given much of his life to showing who these rustics were and how they lived, and his contemporaries have two reasons for believing his pictures true. One is that Billy Smallbury, Poorglass, Grandfather William, and the others are still to be met with, though their days are numbered. Posterity will not have them to measure the rustics of Mr. Hardy by, but it will have the other and lasting test. The truth lives on in literature, because it is felt to be true, and one knows that whoever reads of Dick Dewy in 1989 will feel as sure of him as we are of the Vicar of Wakefield. Frequently it is said good-naturedly of novelists that they provide material from which history can be written. One may venture to say that such good history as the courtship of Fancy Day will never be boiled down or written up into anything better. With Bathsheba's story and Henchard's, it will keep as it is, and not turn sour.

There must be many persons who find it difficult to realize that there is no town called Casterbridge in the map. Mr. Hardy has given England a town. Unfortunately, he has not limited himself to the country of which Casterbridge is the centre. Rich as English literature is by his Wessex tales, it would have been richer had he not sometimes wandered abroad and astray for his chief characters. Never a careless writer, he has thrown away skill on books that have no value and little momentary interest. He is only on firm ground in the country, and not even then when he brings Society figures into it. Some writers have created great characters representative of a class with which they had little personal acquaintance, but Mr. Hardy has no such art. London society and London professional life must be known to him, at least superficially, but they are strange to the Wessex he has by heart, and in attempting to draw them he fails absolutely. Even a man of letters is not in his ken, for Elfride's lover, Knight, who is meant to be a very admirable man, is simply the most insufferable prig in fiction. *The Hand of Ethelberta* is a 'comedy in chapters', hardly less doleful than most modern comedies in acts, and it is a disappointment of a double kind. It is not a comedy, and its London life is preposterous. *A Laodicean* and *Two on a Tower* are not comedies, but they may be classed among Society novels. They are both dull books: here and there, nasty as well, and the besom of oblivion will soon pass over them. The tranter's dance, Bob Loveday's escape from the pressgang, Henchard or Bathsheba Everdene in the market-place—any one of these scenes outweighs all Mr. Hardy's Society stories.

Silas Marner is a great novel, but when the wealth of rural life given us by Mr. Hardy is taken into account, it must be conceded that he has enriched the fiction which deals with heaths and villages much more than George Eliot. Mr. Jefferies, it is true, has done as much for the natural scenery, for the hedges and ditches, and wild and garden flowers, and woods and glades and commons, but he has not done more. Mr. Hardy's passionate love of Nature is sunk into him: he not only knows the land of Wessex with the life that grows out of it, he has not only seen it in every weather, but he has felt its moods; they have been communicated to him until he has shared Nature's joys and struggles, and become one of its poets. Only a poet could have put Egdon Heath so wonderfully into *The Return of the Native*, only a poet could have described the thunderstorm of *Far from the Madding Crowd*. Yet, being a true novelist, the scenery is with Mr. Hardy only a fine setting. Not the heath, but those who cross it, are his subjects. His first book, *Desperate Remedies*, is only a study in other people's methods. With *Under the Greenwood Tree*, which made way with the public as slowly as *Lorna Doone*, the Wessex series began, and perhaps since Goldsmith's death there has been no such idyll of country life. It is not Mr. Hardy's greatest book, but it is his most perfect; from the moment Dick Dewy appears, singing of 'daffodowndillies', till he and Fancy, newly married, listen to the nightingale, the story glides on like a Wessex stream. It is Mr. Hardy's one novel in which there is nothing to jar. A tranter and his son, a schoolmistress, a gamekeeper, and a village choir are the simple company of whom an artist's magic make us one. Here, and in *Far from the Madding Crowd*, which first awakened the public to the new novelist, the rustics are at their best. They are never again quite so fresh and natural when they meet to drink cider. In the following books one has now and again a suspicion that they are introduced as a puppet-show between the more serious acts. They took the public so well in the earlier stories that they must be offered again and again, as Mr. Sothern had to go on playing Dundreary. Characters at first, they become rather characteristics, only those eccentricities being given prominence that are calculated to raise the readiest laugh. There are times when they are only a funny chorus, playing somewhat obviously for applause. The most unlettered villager may have natural wit or humour, but 'rustics' are not usually amusing by intention, and in Mr. Hardy's earlier novels they are unconscious humorists, as where Fancy's stepmother will not have Dick Dewy eat his dinner with her second-best knives and forks lest people should think she has nothing better.

Hundreds of touches equally true to life are to be found in the rustic pictures of the early novels, and there are even many in the later ones. But there is now a tendency to spoil the rustics by putting clever sayings into their mouths. 'Why should death deprive life of four-pence?' asks a toper, taking possession of the four penny pieces set apart for keeping down the eyelids of a dead woman. A drunken hag is on trial, and, on a constable's repeating certain remarks of hers, she argues, 'I was not capable enough to hear what I said, and what's said out of my hearing isn't evidence.' The same woman would see Henchard humiliated because 'I do like to see the trimming pulled off such Christmas candles.' A pretty wife is 'an uncommon picture for a man's best parlour', a woman gets married 'by the grace of God and a ready young man'. Any one of these remarks will pass, but we get them in sheaves. Rustics do not fling such smart things about promiscuously. Sometimes, too, the author goes to the other extreme, making his rustics hardly human in their ignorance. 'Oh, and what d'ye think I found out, Mrs. Yeobright? The parson wears a suit of clothes under his surplice! I could see his black sleeve when he held up his arm.' A clever City man could evolve rustics capable of providing this sort of amusement to other City men. It is not the realism that gives Mr. Hardy's rural figures a chance of living on.

English fiction is so much wealthier in heroines than in heroes that the ladies who have immortality will survive as widows. To create an attractive young man is the hardest thing in the trade: when he is meant to be a fine fellow he is nine times in ten a prig; at the best he has only the making in him of a nice lady. Scott admitted his failures here, and Pickwick is worth all Dickens's other heroes. Mr. Hardy's heroes, how-ever, by whom is meant the men that fall in love with his Bathshebas and Anne Garlands, will accompany his young ladies into the next century, a fortunate arrangement, for these exasperating and adorable women are not for travelling alone. Somerset, Swithin, and the other men of the Society novels will be happily lost, but Gabriel Oak, Troy, Bob and John Loveday, Henchard (triumphing at last over the Scots-man, who speaks a fearsome tongue of his own) have still, one feels, a career before them. These are Mr. Hardy's greatest 'rustics', for every one of them is country born and bred. The village or farm chorus is delightful, but its quaintness is comparatively only a knack the author has. Having the manners and ways of the most homespun country folk at his finger ends, so to speak, he can play upon them as easily as Bathsheba thrummed her much-discussed piano, but it is another matter to catch a rustic young and make a man of him as Mr. Hardy does with Gabriel Oak. *Far from the Madding Crowd* is a great novel, and it gets some of its greatness from Gabriel and Troy. Oak is the hero whom novelists try to draw eternally, the good fellow with a head as well as a heart, and where nearly all are unsuccessful Mr. Hardy triumphs. John Ridd is the prominent yeoman of romance, Gabriel Oak of realistic fiction. A manlier Englishman was never drawn. Gabriel is the true growth of Wessex soil, and, with the brothers Loveday, forms one of a strong trio. John Loveday, the gallant soldier who bravely leaves his sweetheart, 'to blow his trumpet till silenced for ever upon one of the bloody battlefields of Spain', and the more fickle but not less gallant Bob, are part of England's greatness. Yet the chivalrous trumpet-major is not the soldier of whom Mr. Hardy's readers will think first. The trumpet blows to introduce gay, witty Sergeant Troy, whom Bathsheba marries because he says he must have her or another. The whole incident of Troy's wooing is incomparable. Grant that women are Bathshebas, and it is obvious that he is not to be resisted. The lady-farmer is not the only person whom he carries off her feet. His brilliant audacity casts a glamour over the readers as well, and they race after the sergeant, unable to reflect, captivated, until the knot is tied. Mr. Hardy does not introduce Troy to preach a moral. The moral is there, and an awful tragedy beats it into Bathsheba's heart, but such things are, such men are, and that is sufficient for the author, who is always an artist, here a supreme one. He does not draw a male flirt to show that the species are contemptible, but because there are male flirts; nor are the two terrible scenes, Fanny's death and Bathsheba opening the coffin, introduced to warn womenkind against the Troys. Bathsheba's mistake and its results are part of the tragedy of life which this author feels so keenly, so oppressively one might say. Never until Troy was shown at work had we learned from fiction how such a being may mesmerize a bewitching and clever woman into his arms. Many writers say their Troys do it, but Mr. Hardy shows it being done. There is the devil's fascination in the wonderful scene in the hollow where Troy goes through his sword exercise, with Bathsheba for an audience:

In an instant the atmosphere was transformed to Bathsheba's eyes. Beams of light, caught from the low sun's rays, above, around, in front of her, well-nigh shut out earth and heaven—all emitted in the marvellous evolutions of Troy's reflecting blade, which seemed everywhere at once, and yet nowhere specially. These circling gleams were accompanied by a keen rush that was almost a whistling—also springing from all sides of her at once. In short, she was enclosed in a firmament of light, and of sharp hisses, resembling a sky-full of meteors close at hand.

The ungenerous critics who are constantly bringing silly charges of plagiarism against Mr. Rider Haggard say that there is a similar scene in *Allan Quatermain*. Umslopogaas terrifies a cowardly Frenchman by whirling an axe around him much as Troy's sword encircles Bathsheba. But why compare the scenes, unless to point out that the one writer is an artist while the other is not? Sergeant Troy, whatever may come of it, has fairly earned, one feels, the lock of hair of which his sword deprives Bathsheba. He has given fiction a great scene. The Zulu's joke, on the other hand, is merely vulgar and disgusting (because men calling themselves Englishmen look on and enjoy the victim's terror), and makes *Allan Quatermain* a book that I, for one, would not put into Mr. Lang's hands.

Novels have been divided according as they are popular with men or with women, though, indeed, only the favourites of the latter go into many editions. The lady who is at Mr. Mudie's counter daily may not skip everything except the love passages, but she prefers novels that are 'sentimental', and has an aversion to complex characters. She is never sure how the Wessex persons, especially the heroines, will behave, and thus, though there is more lovemaking in the histories of Elfride and Eustacia than in the courtship of Mr. Besant's simple English girls, Mr. Hardy is disliked by lady readers, while the other novelist charms them. In an old library copy of *The Return of the Native*, I have been shown, in the handwriting of different ladies, 'What a horrid book!' 'Eustacia is a libel on noble womankind', and (should this be mentioned?) 'Oh, how I *hate* Thomas Hardy!' For this the heroines are responsible. They are usually delightful, as Mr. Besant's are in a smaller way, but they are also riddles, which Mr. Besant's are not. Mr. Hardy seems by the time he began to write to have formed a theory about young women, which every one of his books, since he adopted a method of his own, has been largely devoted to illustrating. It is very subtle and elaborate, though in some cases it leaves not quite an essence of roses behind it, and it amounts to this, that on the subject of matrimony no woman knows her own mind. This is her birthright, whatever her degree, and she makes free use of it. Mr. Hardy's maidens, 'husband-high', are persons who think marriage a terrible thing to contemplate, engagements not quite so fearful, and arrangements to get engaged presently comparatively safe. There never, however, were ladies more anxious to swim if it could be done without going into the water. They think they would like to marry, but are not sure when they arrive at the altar. They hesitate about becoming engaged lest they should then cease to love; they marry in secret, get engaged in secret, and even ask the gentleman whom they engage to get engaged to by-and-by to keep it to himself. They are seldom sure of their own love unless there is ground for believing that it is not returned, and the only tolerably safe thing to predict of them is, that first they will have two lovers and then marry a third. After marriage, we may suppose, they become more conventional, but until then they are for disturbing the peace of man. As Henchard, the grandest male figure in Mr. Hardy's novels, says: 'These cursed women —there's not an inch of straight grain in 'em!'

Let us run through the novels in a paragraph, beginning with *Far from the Madding Crowd*. Bathsheba steps out to show the way that all Mr. Hardy's future heroines are to tread. She is out when Gabriel calls to ask her hand, but she runs eagerly after him—to say that she won't have him! No wonder Gabriel mistakes her meaning, though she explains. She has panted after him to say that 'nobody has got me yet as a sweetheart, instead of my having a dozen as my aunt said: I *hate* to be thought man's property in that way, though possibly I shall be had some day.' All the complications arise, not from Bathsheba's hating to be thought man's property, but from the other fact that she also loves it. She becomes a farmer, and is admired by all the male farmers except one, to whom, therefore, she sends a valentine with the words 'Marry Me' on it. He is thereupon enamoured of her, and she promises to become engaged to him soon, only he must not make this public. A third lover, Troy, appears, and they arrange a secret marriage, which only takes place because, at the last moment, Troy seems to prefer some other body. The soldier supposed to be dead, she gets secretly engaged to the second lover again, and eventually proposes to Gabriel because his passion for her seems to be cooling. *The Hand of Ethelberta* is on the same lines; but there is a further development of the heroine in *A Pair of Blue Eyes*. Elfride gets engaged to Stephen Smith, and, after a way Mr. Hardy's heroines have, tells him that he must not kiss her. Stephen, to do him justice is the only man who disobeys. Agreeing upon a secret marriage they elope to London, where Stephen has everything ready. Arrived in London, however, Elfride changes her mind, and insists on his sending her home again, thus putting a very good young fellow in, perhaps, the most ignominious position an ardent lover ever descended to. She writes a novel, which is 'slated' in

an ill-bred manner by a critic, who subsequently treats her so con-
temptuously that she falls in love with him. This pitiful creature of a
reviewer talks henceforth mainly of kissing, and the blow it would be
to him to discover that she had been kissed by 'another'. When he does
make this discovery he rushes away as if from dynamite, and she then
marries a third man. *The Return of the Native* opens with a lady who has
gone off to be married coming home unwed. Eustacia, the other and
real heroine, who has previously loved a seaport man, makes fierce love
to the male character in this episode, but on hearing that the half-wife
no longer cares for him, she casts about for another lover, whom she
arranges to love before seeing him. The heroine of *The Trumpet Major*
almost cajoles one man to propose to her, and then marries his brother,
because she loves Bob when she does not love John. In *Two on a Tower*,
a married lady visits an astronomer stealthily, and makes open display
of her affection for him. She secretly marries him in the belief that her
husband has died in Africa. Some time afterwards she learns that her
husband did not die until after this secret ceremony, and then she
marries a bishop. *A Laodicean* opens with Paula in chapel to be baptized
and then changing her mind. She engages to get engaged to an architect
who must not kiss her. Then she engages to get engaged to a soldier.
Finally, fearing that the architect has forsaken her, she tracks him over
the Continent, runs him down, proposes, and is accepted. In *The Mayor
of Casterbridge*, a lady, who had courted a supposed widower, comes
from Jersey to keep him to his promise. At Casterbridge she meets a
Scotsman, and marries him secretly. *The Woodlanders* is in the same
vein, but omitting it and the two first stories we have (to sum up) eight
heroines with twenty-two lovers, which leads to eleven secret engagements, three secret marriages, and three elopements that come to
nothing. Nearly every one of the ladies practically proposes to at least
one man, two run after him to do so, and one of them then marries
another. Were these eight ladies to meet their twenty-two lovers in,
say, the market-place of Casterbridge, there would, one feels, be a
strange re-shuffling of the cards. If Gabriel remained faithful to Bathsheba, Eustacia would court him on the spot. Elfride might elope with
Somerset, get secretly engaged to Troy, and subsequently marry
Henchard.

Mrs. Poyser said that women were made foolish to match the men;
but Mr. Hardy's men are made irresolute to match the women. John
Loveday and all the others play into their ladies' hands. The arrangement to get engaged presently may not strike them as the best, but they

are willing to put up with it. They remonstrate feebly against secret marriages, and then depart, like valets, to make the necessary arrangements. They all want to kiss the heroine, but Troy is the only man among them who does it and has it over without first consulting her on the subject. Strange as it may appear, the only male person in these novels who seems to have given Mr. Hardy's heroines the proper study, and to know a good way of bringing them to their senses, is a rude boy in *The Trumpet Major*. Anne and John are in the fields, and both are wishing that John had the courage to propose. The rude boy cries in irritation, as perhaps some readers have done, 'Why don't he clasp her to his side, like a man?' Yet, though these lovers are apparently diffident at the wrong time, it should be allowed that the ladies they would fain wed are the most interesting in their unconventionality, the most charming in their womanliness, and the most subtly drawn (with the exception of Mr. Meredith's) that this generation of novelists has given us. Mr. Hardy's theory of maidenhood may be wrong, though no man will say lightly that it is, but it is superbly worked out. The ordinary sweet girl heroine of these days is only the prettiest face in the novel. She would be undistinguishable after she had the small-pox.

As a 'stylist' Mr. Hardy stands higher than any contemporary novelist. His writing has not always the air of distinction which sometimes catches one's breath when reading Mr. Stevenson, but it is clear, terse, without self-consciousness, and will henceforth, one may hope, be exclusively devoted to adorning the Wessex stories, of which the last, *The Woodlanders*, is a falling away, but the second last, *The Mayor of Casterbridge*, in some ways the most dramatic and powerful. A further inducement to the author to continue this memorable series, is that when treating of Wessex life he is a humorist, and that his other novels have scarcely a glimmer of humour from beginning to end. This means that he is not a great humorist, and explains the fact that for pathos (as distinguished from tragic power) his stories are not remarkable. True humour and pathos can no more exist apart than we can have a penny-piece with only one side. Fanny crawling home to die is too awful for pathos. It is tragedy.

34. Edmund Gosse, 'Thomas Hardy', *The Speaker*

13 September 1890, ii, 295

Sir Edmund Gosse (1849–1928), critic and man of letters, was a close friend of Hardy from the early eighties until his death. This article was No. 8 of a series called 'The Speaker's Gallery'. The *Speaker*, a weekly founded in 1889, gave place to the *Nation* in 1907.

Where amateurs of the novel are gathered together it is common to hear George Meredith and Thomas Hardy spoken of in the same breath. This arises from no great similarity of style in their common work, but, doubtless, from the fact that each holds somewhat the same relation towards his immediate rivals. Neither has the great novel-reading public with him, each enlists the bulk of his readers from the class of adult male persons, and each is the peculiar favourite, in his own generation, of the literary and critical minority. Mr. Meredith is beginning to be seen clearly, in the twilight of approaching posterity; Mr. Hardy is still vaguely one of 'our young writers'—a young writer of fifty—and his position is less widely perceived as yet. It is probably by no means less firmly assured. Neither the one novelist nor the other depends for his ultimate niche in literature upon the success with which he has 'killed the girls and thrilled the boys' of his own time. Each stands or falls entirely according to the success with which he may have cultivated the highest branches of serious imaginative fiction.

Mr. Hardy became suddenly famous in the middle of the month of January, 1874. The *Cornhill*, then under the genial direction of Mr. Leslie Stephen, began to publish a new novel, which was anonymous, and which bore the curious title of *Far from the Madding Crowd*. The *Spectator*, with an odd mixture of acumen and blindness, announced, as a discovery, that this unsigned novel was a new work by George Eliot, whose name was then one to conjure by. All the world discussed the matter, and everybody voted that this promised to be a great book, by whomsoever written. It proved to be the fourth novel of a Dorsetshire architect, some thirty-four years of age, whose previous books few people had noticed. As the story in the *Cornhill* progressed, it captivated all classes of society, and before it was closed, the name of Mr. Hardy was ranked with those of the first living English novelists.

Looking back over sixteen years, it is hard to say whether Mr. Hardy's genius has developed or not since the publication of what remains his most famous book. He has never surprised us so much again, but he has rarely disappointed us. His ten novels may be divided into four classes, and if looked at in that division, they will be seen to give little indication of advance or decline. His two masterpieces are, without question, *Far from the Madding Crowd*, 1874, and *The Return of the Native*, 1878; in these he has filled large canvases with complete success. A second class consists of novels sketched on the same broad and generous plan, but, for one reason or another, executed with less *bravura*, and more unequal in their evolution; these are *A Laodicean*, 1881; *The Woodlanders*, 1887; and perhaps *A Pair of Blue Eyes*, 1873. Yet another class contains books of smaller compass, but, more obviously than the last mentioned, masterpieces of their kind: *The Trumpet Major*, 1880; *Under the Greenwood Tree*, 1872; and, less perfect in its proportions than either of these, *The Mayor of Casterbridge*, 1886. Finally come two books which, although full of cleverness, and cleverness characteristic of Mr. Hardy, are yet partial failures, *The Hand of Ethelberta*, 1876, and *Two on a Tower*, 1882. If this classification be conceded, it will be seen that there has been no definite rise or fall, but a fluctuation due to temperament or choice of subject. In point of fact, the quality of Mr. Hardy's books is singularly steady, and the worst chapter in *The Hand of Ethelberta* is recognizable, in a moment, as written by the author of the best chapter in *The Return of the Native*. No novelist of the day, moreover, has produced a body of work so coherent or so little confused by extraneous matter. Mr. Hardy is almost unique in being a novelist or nothing. He is neither a poet nor a theologian, a journalist nor a politician; his reputation lives or dies on the strength of his romances alone. He has put all his clearest visions and deepest experience into this one species of art. Nor has he written to excess; ten books in eighteen years is a modest, and yet a sufficient tale of work; it shows industry without restlessness, activity without the fatal hurry to be rich.

It has been eminently fortunate for Mr. Hardy that he has identified himself with an interesting and wholly unexhausted population. If all that is not directly or indirectly inspired by the people and scenery of the county of Dorset were expunged from his books, they would lose little in bulk and less in value. He is the laureate alike of the open wastes of *The Return of the Native*, of the undulating, pastoral country of *Far from the Madding Crowd*, of the market-towns, as in *The Mayor of Casterbridge*, and of those apple-growing parishes of *The Woodlanders*, where 'the dunghills smell of pomace instead of stable refuse'. But all these various districts are part of Dorset, and the county contains other scenes, equally distinct, enough to keep the novelist occupied for the rest of his life. It will be an ill-day for us all when Mr. Hardy is persuaded to go north of Shaftesbury or south of Portland Bill for his inspiration. When his books first appeared, so little was known of the quaint bucolic life of Wessex that his admirable peasants were treated as though they were gratuitous inventions. The pleasure which the critics should have had over the scene in Warren's Malthouse—on the occasion when Shepherd Oak, although sensitive himself, was surfeited with the trepidation of Joseph Poorgrass—was spoiled for them by their bewildering doubts of its possibility. But it is generally acknowledged now—as it has been always recognized by those who knew their Wessex—that Mr. Hardy was well within the bounds of truthful observation when he reported or arranged these exquisite dialogues of rural humour. Thus, and scarcely less entertainingly, does the native Westcountryman unquestionably talk when wholly relieved from the presence of quality. These passages it has at length become the fashion to praise, but their Shakespearian richness of humour has never, perhaps, been fully appreciated, and certainly not a slyer and more discreet form of Mr. Hardy's fun, the result of a close observation of simple character. An example may be found in the passage where John Loveday, the dragoon, suddenly gushes into a confidential statement to Anne of how he learned to be a trumpeter. This humour, full-blooded, warm, and rustic as it is, is the very essence of Mr. Hardy's books, and properly balances the poignant undercurrent of their melancholy.

The unpopularity of Mr. Hardy's novels among women is a curious phenomenon. If he had no male admirers, he could almost cease to exist. It is not merely that the mass of girls who let down their back-hair to have a long cry over Edna Lyall or Miss Florence Warden do not appreciate his books, but that even educated women approach him with hesitation and prejudice. This is owing to no obvious error on the novelist's part; he has never attacked the sex, or offended its proprieties. But there is something in his conception of feminine character which is not well received. The modern English novelist has created, and has faithfully repeated, a demure, ingenuous, and practically inhuman type of heroine, which has flattered womankind, and which female readers now imperatively demand as an encouragement. Mr. Besant gives this type to them in perhaps her most unsullied and unearthly guise. But Mr. Hardy's women are moulded of the same flesh as his men; they are liable to flutterings and tremblings; they are not always constant even when they are 'quite nice'; and some of them are actually 'of a coming-on disposition'.

This feminine realism, which, whether the ladies are pleased or no, is one of the author's charms, would probably have been excused, however, if Mr. Hardy had not shown a proclivity towards placing a more unique and singular species of womanhood as the central figure of each of his books. She is dignified and capable, like Bathsheba; she is a belated pythoness, like Eustacia; she is an innocent adventuress, like Mrs. Charmond; or she is a delicate razor cutting hones, like Lucetta. But these variations are external, and all these ladies belong to the same family. All are women lifted by circumstances a little distance out of their sphere—educated too highly for it, rendered too fine for it, yet excluded from a superior status, which they are too simple to succeed in reaching. Very often they are contrasted, in their tragic failure, with their humbler and less intelligent sisters, and the novelist loves to show that their beautiful and dignified heads, lifted into solitude above their fellows, offer a special aim to the shafts of ill-fortune. In that most curious and, to the critic, most valuable and suggestive book, *Desperate Remedies*—Mr. Hardy's anonymous first attempt at a story—this ruling vision of the writer's comes out with a sort of grotesque violence in the figure of Miss Aldclyffe, and is contrasted with Cytherea, precisely in Mr. Hardy's accepted later manner.

Besides his ten great oil-pictures, Mr. Hardy has occasionally hung up in his gallery a water-colour sketch of extraordinary charm and quality. Of these studies, as they may be called, *Interlopers at the Knap* which appeared in 1884, will occur to everyone as a typical example. But Mr. Hardy has written one short story so complete, so admirable in execution, so novel and brilliant in conception, that it raises him for a moment to the level of Tourgéneff himself. If all his works but one were doomed to perish, he might safely depend for immortality on *The Three Strangers*, 1883, with its unrivalled picture of the sheep-stealer jammed into the shepherd's chimney-corner, hob-nobbing there with his own intended hangman. From the first word to the last, this amazing little composition never flags for a moment. It is not a small thing that it contains the best of the group of Mr. Hardy's peculiarly happy pictures of country parties. But its highest merit consists, of course, in the tension of its wild emotion, raising common scenes and common speakers, in the midst of their ludicrous humours, to the heights of tragedy. It is said that short stories are beginning to be appreciated in England, as they are in France and in America. If so, Mr. Hardy may be encouraged to tell us more of his admirable Wessex tales.

No sketch of Mr. Hardy is complete without a reference to his landscape. In only one book, in *The Return of the Native*, has he allowed himself to give way, without restraint, to his impassioned love for the scenery of his county. The description of Egdon Waste, however, which opens that novel, is scarcely more beautiful, though larger and more elaborate, then the vignettes which adorn his other books so frequently. No English novelist of our day approaches him in the richness and variety of the natural colour his books suggest. Most radiant and sparkling of all, in this way, is *The Trumpet Major*, whose 'Thrilling York Hussars' light up the deep green landscape throughout with their brilliant uniforms; but *The Woodlanders*, with its rosy orchards pervading the long misty valleys, comes next to it. That Mr. Hardy's talent has its limitations is obvious; in these few words it has not been necessary to dwell on that fact. A place in the first rank of the world's novelists is hardly to be claimed for him—at least, at present. But he is one of the very few living English writers who can be measured with the great masters without sinking into insignificance; and if his strongly defined, consistent, charming gift is not to be designated genius, we may as well resign that word as obsolete and not suited to our degenerate age.

35. William Minto, 'The Work of Thomas Hardy', *Bookman*

December 1891, i, 99

William Minto (1845–1903), critic and journalist, wrote for the *Daily News* and the *Pall Mall Gazette*: from 1880 to 1893 he was Professor of Logic and Literature at Aberdeen. The *Bookman*, just starting at this date, was a popular illustrated literary magazine which survived until the 1930s. Its founder, and the editor until his death in 1923, was William (later Sir William) Robertson Nicoll.

There is a tradition that *Far from the Madding Crowd* was distinguished from the throng of serial novels and made a mark for all eyes by being mistaken for the work of George Eliot. It began to appear in the *Cornhill* in January of 1874: a new novel was due from the hand of the great authoress, and the rumour ran that here she was experimenting on her reputation with an anonymous work. The *Spectator* was certain on the point: it knew the fine Roman hand, and was not to be taken in by the mere absence of a name. It is one of many instances of the danger of judging from internal evidence. And yet there was undoubtedly considerable ground for the mistake. With books, as with persons, we are often struck at first sight with resemblances which disappear upon closer acquaintance, and leave us wondering what we could have seen to identify. Now that Mr. Hardy is more completely known as the moral historian of Wessex, the exhaustive delineator of its types— milkmaid and noble dame, honest workman, visionary, and scapegrace —with his distinctive way of looking at life and exhibiting its problems and its matter for laughter and tears, we are surprised that any portion of his work should ever have been confounded with George Eliot's. He occupies his own separate place, and their common features can be picked out only by careful analysis.

But if we go back now and read the opening chapters of the story with which Mr. Hardy first caught the public ear, we can very well understand, even though we hold him to be the greater artist of the two, how this fragment might have been ascribed to the older writer, and how natural it was to suppose that here was an old favourite back on familiar ground instead of a young and vigorous rival. These opening chapters are really more like George Eliot's work than any other portion of Mr. Hardy's that could be selected. Farmer Oak, who meets us on the threshold, is not introduced in the grave spirit in which Mr. Hardy afterwards made us acquainted with the Reddleman and Giles Winterborne, to name but two of his other peasant lovers and heroes. Gabriel's fine wearing qualities become apparent by-and-by, but on his first appearance the outward man—his mouth from ear to ear, his vast roomy boots, his big turnip of a watch hauled from his fob like a bucket from a well, his elaborate toilet when he goes a-wooing—is drawn in a spirit of condescending ridicule, as by one who exhibits rustics and their clumsy, uncouth ways for the entertainment of superior persons. There is a touch or two in the portrait that reveals Mr. Hardy as we now know him, as the champion of rural character and the exponent of the noble heart that beats beneath the smock-frock, but these significant touches, significant when interpreted by the light of Mr. Hardy's subsequent writing, might easily escape observation on a first reading. The introductory sketch of Gabriel Oak as a whole is characteristic of George Eliot's treatment of peasant life as a butt for witty observation and sly humour. The portraiture of Bathsheba, too, seemed to betray her handiwork: we remember that, while the authorship of the story was still a secret, there were some who maintained that the incident of Bathsheba on the top of the waggon-load unpacking the looking-glass could have been imagined only by a woman. It might have been remarked that George Eliot never had drawn a woman as Mr. Hardy draws Bathsheba, in whole-hearted admiration, without the least scratch of disparagement, without the faintest approach to a feline amenity. But this was not so likely to occur on a first impression. The learned cast of the diction and the vein of philosophic observation pointed in the same direction. Mr. Hardy's style can now be recognized as his own, and as one of the best in English fiction—unstrained, flexible, grave without being cumbrous, and even and steady in its logical movement, while glowing with colour when the occasion demands. He can command simple English, too, of the most perfect kind, as witness Marty South's reflections at the grave of Giles Winterborne, or Mr. Melbury's touching speech to Mrs. Charmond when he goes to that grand dame to plead his daughter's cause. But Mr. Hardy has always shared with George Eliot a strong predilection for scientific precision of description, couched in the most learned scientific language. Does he not, in his very latest story, make Tess the milkmaid's lover tell her that he lies on the periphery of the interests of his relatives, and does he not remark of Tess herself that his love encompassed her like a photosphere? This learned diction is peculiarly marked, as it happens, in the opening chapters of *Far from the Madding Crowd*.

There can be no doubt that the scientific colouring of Mr. Hardy's work has told considerably against his popularity. Considering the things that are said of him by the most competent judges, who unhesitatingly and unanimously give him a place in the very front rank of living novelists, one often speculates why it is that he is not more widely popular. Mention his name experimentally in a few companies of novel-readers, and you are sure to find one or two strong admirers, probably men of a literary turn; but for one admirer you will find five or six who have only just heard of him, or who have a vague recollection of the *Madding Crowd*, or *The Hand of Ethelberta*, or *The Woodlanders*. On the great public which is stirred and thrilled by Mr. Rider Haggard or Miss Braddon, and which is susceptible to the gentler charm of Mr. William Black, he has produced a comparatively faint impression. And there can be no doubt that part of the explanation of this is the very thing that commends him to readers of the more meditative sort, his studious knowledge of 'the human document'. Mr. Hardy is a pundit in affairs of the heart. Beneath the skin of the story-teller there is a psychologist. He studies feeling and conduct, affections and passions, as a naturalist, and with a naturalist's delight in what is strange and abnormal, out of the way, or in the way but not generally observed. He always has his curious problem in man or woman's conduct to solve, and he delights in solutions which are paradoxical but true to the fixed laws of human nature. He does not find affairs of the heart the simple things that they are to the ordinary mind. Complicated and trying situations attract him, and romantically conventional solutions are too easy to satisfy his intelligence.

Any deep-rooted tendency in a writer generally becomes more marked as he proceeds, and this tendency in Mr. Hardy is most marked of all in his *Group of Noble Dames*. They are in substance a collection of strange cases in the relations between woman and man. The interest lies in the situations rather than in the characters, in the situations and in the turns that the characters take under the pressure of the strange circumstances. The Noble Dames do not form a very attractive gallery in themselves; indeed, they are rather ordinary women, and therein lies the humour of it. They extricate themselves from their difficulties by unexpected recourse to normally feminine devices. The author unfolds the story of each of them in his easy, deliberate way with abundance of quiet humour, but the observer and theorist is uppermost. Each tale is a succession of paradoxes, and it is in these paradoxes and their explanation that the chief interest lies. The novelist seems always to be deliberately challenging comparison with the strange twists and perversities of character in real life. In the *Marchioness of Stonehenge*, for example, the Lady Caroline surprises us at every turn; that the highborn, accomplished, courted, flattered, and spoilt young lady should fall in love with the son of her father's steward, that she should marry him secretly, that she should show such energy in getting rid of his inconvenient dead body and afterwards disembarrassing herself of the consequences of their union, and that she should die of a broken heart when her disowned son refuses her the smallest share in his affection—each of these incidents is a little paradox of the heart, and the interest uppermost at the end is the question whether they are within the natural possibilities of that perverse organ. The substitute widow, also, gentle Milly, the woodman's daughter, supplies food for reflection on the strange ways of affection; her joyful acceptance of the false position, and the fierce fight she makes to keep it, are described *con amore*, as by one who delights in such curious psychological facts. If the business of the story-teller is to set us thinking by the artful exhibition of paradoxes, Mr. Hardy has certainly succeeded in his stories of Noble Dames. When we say that in them the psychologist, the observer and theorist of human nature, controls the storyteller, we do not mean that he bores us with formal dissertations on the motives of his characters. Mr. Hardy is far too much of an artist for that; he merely gives the facts and a hint of the character that reconciles them. We mean only that it is a problem that the story leaves with us, rather than an impression of beauty or nobleness, or a mere feeling of amusement.

Evidently Mr. Hardy's theory is not Pope's, that 'most women have no characters at all'. His women have very complex characters. And this volume of Noble Dames suggests another point, that Mr. Hardy seems to be deeply penetrated by the truth that woman is the weaker vessel, and in her frailty often has recourse to tortuous methods of self-defence. His ladies when put in embarrassing and trying positions, whether through their own fault or through a malicious conspiracy of circumstances, sometimes extricate themselves with a desperate unscrupulousness. The heroine of *Two on a Tower* perpetrates a very cruel wrong on the Bishop to put herself right with the world, and several of her sisters in this volume of short stories, when hard pressed by the world, take refuge in deceits or evasions that may be pardonable in view of their weakness and natural dislike to martyrdom, but cannot be called praiseworthy. We cannot commend the Lady Icenway's willingness to furnish her noble husband with an heir, though Mr. Hardy enables us to see how she might have reconciled her method with her conscience, and exonerated herself from any charge of extreme wickedness. Fault has been found with him for trespassing on forbidden ground in relating some of the frailties of his noble dames. Far too much has been made of this; there is not the faintest trace of pruriency in his short stories, any more than in his long; but it must be admitted that he is at least as indelicate as the marriage service, and does insist upon the fact of maternity and the disagreeable complications to which it may give rise when the course of affairs does not run smooth, with a frankness that unfits one or two of his tales for reading in a mixed company. A more serious objection is that in these tales he occupies himself too exclusively with the weakness of the female heart. This gives the volume too much the air of a collection of monkish chronicles in disparagement of the sex. The most pleasant way in which Mr. Hardy could free himself from this imputation would be to produce a companion volume about Noble Dames, consisting solely of stories to their honour.

That Mr. Hardy can create the beautiful as well as philosophize upon the strange, he has given ample proof. He is emphatically an artist, a creator of beautiful and noble things, keenly alive to the humorous incongruities of life, but capable also of disentangling the heroic from the commonplace. Perhaps he is better at long stories than at short. His slow, elaborate method of building up a group of characters and tracing their simple interactions, articulating them to the scenery in which they move as if they were homogeneous parts of it, needs room for its satisfactory application. What he says of one of his country-bred characters, that he is slow in his motions generally, though capable at times of as mercurial a dash as the dweller in towns, who is more to the quick manner born and habituated, is true of himself. The inhabitants of Little Hintock and Egdon Heath, fully conceived and embodied in every lineament, take a better hold of our sympathies and our memories than his Noble Dames, and will probably live longer, as they deserve to do, in literature. Whether his reputation would have been wider if he had confined himself less closely to his well-known and well-loved

Wessex, is a doubtful question. He is too great a master of his craft not to know within what limits his imagination works most prosperously. But though it is true that within the range of any one district there must always be sufficient variety of character, and sufficient variety of chance and change, to furnish stuff for an infinite variety of drama, tragic and comic, for the artist whose invention is equal to its possibilities, still restriction to a limited district must always produce a certain effect of monotony. The novelist seems to repeat himself, however much he may vary his plots. There really is nobody who can be accused of repetition with less justice than Mr. Hardy. He is not the slave of any formula, either in character or in incident. And as it is with the inner life that he mainly occupies himself, his Wessex, though geographically it can be contained in a small map, is spiritually as wide as human nature. Still, when a novelist keeps to the same social *milieu*, he cannot avoid producing a certain sameness of impression. He cannot have the dazzling variety of a Kipling, who can pick and choose character and incident from two continents and a dozen nationalities. Wessex must necessarily be more limited in the outward form, at least of its types. And the novelist who works within a limited field must accept another inevitable consequence, that there are large bodies of readers to whom the very material that he works on is radically uninteresting. It may be true that in sequestered spots such as he loves to describe 'from time to time, no less than in other places, dramas of a grandeur and unity truly Sophoclean are enacted in the real, by virtue of the concentrated passions and closely knit independence of the lives therein'. Still there must necessarily be a large number of readers for whom the lives of his Oaks and Boldwoods and Wildeves and Winterbornes possess no interest, simply because they are stupid and vulgar peasants, 'and nothing more', as the primrose was but a yellow primrose to Peter Bell. With this Mr. Hardy must have reckoned in deciding to stick to Wessex. We do not ourselves complain of him for so doing. As long as he can find passions to paint and characters to draw and dramas to unfold as profoundly moving as he continues to find in Wessex, we have no desire to see him go elsewhere in search of subjects.

TESS OF THE D'URBERVILLES

November 1891

---

36. Richard le Gallienne, the *Star*

23 December 1891

From a review signed 'Logroller', the pseudonym used by Richard le Gallienne, one of the Yellow Book group of Aesthetes and a member of the Rhymers' Club, for his regular literary column in the *Star*.

Two passages of summary have been omitted.

'On an evening in the latter part of May, a middle-aged man was walking homeward from Shaston to the village of Marlott, in the adjoining vale of Blakemore, or Blackmoor. The pair of legs that carried him were rickety, and there was a bias in his gait which inclined him somewhat to the left of a straight line.'

When a novel begins so, who needs to be told that we are once more in Mr. Thomas Hardy's 'Arcady of Wessex', that villages with all kinds of quaint cider-sounding names lie about us, Bulbarrow, Nettlecombe, Tont, Dogbury, High Stoy, Bubb Down, and that here all roads do not lead to Rome, but to Casterbridge. The devoted student of Mr. Hardy would also immediately recognize him by a less pleasing token in this passage. Who else, except maybe Mr. Meredith, would describe the unsteadiness in the walk home of an aged tippler as 'a bias in his gait which inclined him somewhat to the left of a straight line'? But this is only a trifling example of a defect in Mr. Hardy's style which is continually making one grind one's teeth, like 'sand in honey'. One cannot call it euphuism, because euphuism tends to 'favour and to prettiness'. It seems rather to come from sudden moments of self-consciousness in the midst of his creative flow, as also from the imperfect digestion of certain modern science and philosophy, which is becoming somewhat too obtrusive through the apple-cheek outline of Mr. Hardy's work. For example, a little boy talks to his sister, 'rather for the pleasure of utterance than for audition'; a wooer at a certain hot moment entreats the wooed—'Will you, I ask once more, show your belief in me by letting me encircle you with my arm?' Another lover, trying to persuade Tess that his marrying her cannot hurt his family, says 'it will not affect even the periphery of their lives', and, later on, when the time has come to forgive, he asks—'How can forgiveness meet such a grotesque prestidigitation as that?' And when Mr. Hardy would tell us that Tess had forgotten that children must be expected from their union, he says that she had been 'forgetting it might result in vitalizations that would inflict upon others', etc. Mr. Hardy continually delights in those long Latin and Greek words that seem to be made of springs rather than vowels. Think how absolutely out of colour in Arcadia are such words as 'dolorifuge', 'photosphere', 'heliolatries', 'arborescence', 'concatenation', 'noctambulist'—where, indeed, are such in colour?—and Mr. Hardy further uses that horrid verb 'ecstasize'.

Don't let anyone say that these are small matters. The more beautiful the rest of the work the more jarring such defects as these. Why, one of such words is as destructive as an ounce of dynamite in any dream-world, more especially so in Mr. Hardy's 'Sicilian Vales'. If, as I, you hold it no exaggeration to describe Mr. Hardy as our modern Theocritus (of course, a Theocritus in prose), think how the flute and the pipe would stop with a shriek before words of such 'terrible aspect.' They could not more potently destroy our illusion if they were steam-whistles, and this they are constantly doing, like the 'Doctor' in the rhyme, constantly making us dance out of Wessex—yes, 'into France', among other places; for study of French authors seems to be having a strong influence on Mr. Hardy's work just lately. Realism as a theory seems in danger of possessing him at times, though happily but inter-mittently. In that part of realism which is not theory but a necessary artistic instinct, Mr. Hardy has always been strong.

However, despite those dreadful words, and despite the painful 'moral', the noble, though somewhat obtrusive 'purpose', *Tess of the D'Urbervilles* is one of Mr. Hardy's best novels—perhaps it is his very best. The beautiful simplicity of his style when, as usual, he forgets he is writing, the permeating healthy sweetness of his descriptions, the idyllic charm and yet the reality of his figures, his apple-sweet women, his old men, rich with character as old oaks, his love-making, his fields, his sympathetic atmosphere—all these, and any other of Mr. Hardy's best qualities you can think of, are to be found 'in widest commonalty spread' in *Tess*. The motive of *Tess* is one of those simple (and yet how cruelly tangled) sexual situations round which 'the whole creation moves', and in which Mr. Hardy delights to find 'the eternal meanings'. Mr. Hardy has heretofore been more inclined to champion man the faithful against woman the coquette, but in *Tess* he very definitely espouses 'the cause of woman', and devotes himself to show how often in this world—all, alas, because the best of us is so conventionalized— when men and women break a law 'the woman pays.' Of course it is a special pleading, because a novel might be as readily written to show how often a man pays, too. Indeed, was not *Middlemarch* such a novel? It is noticeable that most of these books against men are written by men, and that *Middlemarch* is the work of a woman. Such is the gallantry of sex, and such its ironical power. But I suppose I must sacrifice principle and outline the story. . . .

Tess is the most satisfying of all Mr. Hardy's heroines. She is by no means so empty-headed as they are wont to be, but, like her sisters, she is a fine Pagan, full of humanity and imagination, and, like them, though in a less degree, flawed with that lack of will, that fatal in-decision at great moments. . . . So 'the woman pays.' Thus you see the plot is the plot of Mr. H. A. Jones, but the hand is the hand of Thomas Hardy. One would venture further and breathe 'Shakespearean', con-cerning the women, but the adjective is so apt to be misunderstood.

37. Unsigned review, *Pall Mall Gazette*

31 December 1891, 3

This is a grim Christmas gift that Mr. Hardy makes us, in his last Wessex tale. The reader, intent on the seasonable pleasures of fiction, who carries home *Tess of the D'Urbervilles* for his delectation over the Christmas fire, thinking perhaps to have another *Far from the Madding*

Crowd, may well feel a little shaken as the gay pastoral comedy of the opening chapters is shifted by degrees into the sombre trappings of the tragic muse. In *Far from the Madding Crowd*, and in other of the brighter fictions of its author, there is, it is true, tragedy as well as comedy and happy endings; but the whole effect is fairly one of rustic geniality, of a residuum of happiness when all is told. Mr. Hardy here works determinedly in his most fateful vein, however—the vein of *The Return of the Native*—with an artistic result of concentrated tragedy such as is rarely to be found in the modern novel, and such as may well make Mr. Hardy's younger contemporaries, who would write great works, despair. The art of the tale-writer who can take a simple history like that of Tess Durbeyfield (alias D'Urberville), and turn it over, and shape it, and interpret it to so profound an ethical and aesthetical result —giving it all the modern significancy you please, and yet never losing sight of the permanent, in the casual, effect, and never 'writing down' to the Philistine intelligence—is not, indeed, to be easily reduced to terms of criticism. Luckily for the validity of the present review, Mr. Hardy's art is now an old story; and it is enough to say here that he has never exercised it more powerfully—never, certainly, more tragically —than in this most moving presentment of a 'pure woman'.

Tess of the D'Urbervilles, it may be explained, is the eldest daughter of 'plain Jack Durbeyfield, the haggler', who is himself the debased last result of the ancient and picturesque Wessex family, the D'Urbervilles. Quite unconscious of his distinguished descent, Tess's father might, in his dull rôle of a poor 'haggler', or small carrier, at the village of Marlott, have failed to provide her with the wider and, as it proved, most fatal opportunities that her beauty demanded, if an antiquarian parson who knew the family history had not accosted him in a spirit of whim as 'Sir John!' and so given him new ideas of social dignity. On this simple conceit of the old parson (whose prototype it is not difficult to recognize, perhaps, in a certain vicar of more than local fame, himself laid up, by this, among the antiquities of Wessex) depends the whole course of the subsequent incomparable rustic tragedy of the life of Tess. The opening scene, where Parson Tringham and John Durbeyfield meet, and the latter is inoculated with pride of race, is in Mr. Hardy's best manner, with all the humour and all the keen sense of the slow movements of the bucolic intelligence which are peculiarly his among novelists. And here, and in some subsequent chapters, the tension of the story is not yet so painfully increased as to make it impossible to stop, as one would like, to admire the masterly workmanship of the writer. The subsequent scene of the May-day 'club revel, or club walking' of the women of Marlott, a local relic of olden May-day festivities, in whose picturesque white-robed procession, carrying peeled willow wands and white flowers, Tess first appears, is again admirably well done. Here, too, enters the hero, Angel Clare, whose character (like his name—too factitious—too obviously histrionic!) is perhaps less satisfying than the simpler rustic charactry of Tess and her father and mother, and the other country-folk, who are pure Wessex. Like Ibsen, Mr. Hardy does not, it is true, set out to provide us with satisfying heroes. He is fond of showing, on the contrary, how much cruelty, how much bitter suffering, your would-be hero may inflict by sticking too consistently and religiously to his rôle. But, judged by Mr. Hardy's own standard, Angel Clare, difficult type as he is to present, is not altogether a convincing creation, especially when looked at by the side of Tess, whose verisimilitude in art and human quality is maintained throughout with a subtlety and a warm and live and breathing naturalness which one feels to be the work of a tale-teller born and not made. All the women in the book are similarly true to nature, and, what is more rare in a sense, true to art. Indeed, the book is, among great novels, peculiarly the Woman's Tragedy! It is to be only fully appreciated perhaps by a woman, in its intimate and profound interpretation of the woman's heart through the pure and beautiful and heroic Tess, doomed to many sorrows, done to death, not by slanderous tongues, but by the tyranny of man, of nature, which makes woman emotionally subject to man, and of social circumstance. Of the other and prime instrument of Tess's tragedy, the sensual Alec D'Urberville, who is not really a D'Urberville at all, but the characteristic product of a family of *nouveaux riches* who adopt the name in buying the D'Urberville estate, not much need be said. One might question his passing conversion to Christianity, if one did not know so many similar instances of emotional gymnastics on the primrose path going down to the lowest pit of the sensualist's Inferno. After reading the book, it is Tess who fills one's mind and haunts one's imagination, and in the heartrending pity of her story one is little able to pause and do justice to the bits of rustic chorus, the wonderful descriptions of Wessex scenery in the changes of the seasons, never better done by Mr. Hardy than in this book, and to all the social and natural circumstance with which her story is interwoven. Certainly he has never written anything finer than the last scenes of the book: especially the scene where Tess and Clare, flying from justice by night, pause exhausted in the hour before day-dawn amid the lonely pillars of Stonehenge, and there are presently taken in the first grey light of morning.

The last scene fitly and terribly ends the story, having read which, we could not wish for any other, dark and tragic almost beyond comparison as the ending is. Considering the whole, one hardly wonders that editors should have hesitated over presenting such strong fare to their gentle readers; but it is a singular commentary upon the open chances of English fiction that the strongest English novel of many years should have to be lopped into pieces and adapted to three different periodicals before it succeeded in finding a complete hearing.

38. Unsigned review, *Athenaeum*

9 January 1892

In the editorial file this review is marked 'Hunt'.

Prof. Huxley once compared life to a game of chess played by man against an enemy, invisible, relentless, wresting every error and every accident to his own advantage. Some such idea must have influenced Mr. Hardy in his narrative of the fortunes of Tess Durbeyfield. The accident of birth and the untowardness of circumstances conspire to lay her once and again at the mercy of a scamp, whilst her own struggles and inclinations are always towards honourable conduct. 'As Tess's own people down in these retreats are never tired of saying among each other in their fatalistic way; "It was to be". There lay the pity of it.' In dealing with 'this sorry scheme of things entire' Mr. Hardy has written a novel that is not only good, but great. Tess herself stands, a credible, sympathetic creature, in the very forefront of his women. Angel Clare, the hero, is a thought too perfect; his errors are readily condoned by himself, and the author, in accordance with his plan, does not stop to insist upon them overmuch, so that sometimes one is driven to ask whether the touch of satire suggested by the name has not prompted Mr. Hardy's representation of the character. Alec D'Urberville, 'lover and sensualist', is the most boldly designed of villains, the very embodiment of a reckless, passionate 'child of the devil'. And those who have complained of his swift conversion from virtue to vice convict themselves of ignorance in the psychology of the sensual man. 'Sir John' D'Urbeyfield stands beside Joseph Poorgrass; his wife and the milkmaids, the dairyman and Angel Clare's pious Calvinist father, are drawn with exceeding skill. Like the scenes of pleasant rural comedy, and like the pathetic incidents abounding in the book, each of them falls naturally into the picture, each by his very existence throws into relief the figure of this imperfect woman, nobly planned, who, like the *geisha* of the Japanese legend, has sinned in the body, but ever her heart was pure.

At its commencement the work seems unlikely to touch any high issues. Tess's father, plain Jack Durbeyfield, the haggler of Marlott, is on his way home when he is met by Parson Tringham, the anti-quary, who salutes him as 'Sir John'. The salutation, made in a moment of whim, is the primary cause of all the heroine's misfortunes—for Mr. Hardy here proceeds after the manner of all the great dramatists—but it also results in a scene of humour written in his best manner:

[quotes ch. I ' "Don't you really know" ' to ' "she needn't finish it." ']

On his way home Durbeyfield meets the girls of the village, Tess amongst them, at their 'club-walking' festival; Shortly afterwards, whilst the girls are dancing alone in a meadow, Angel Clare, who is on a walking tour, joins them:

[quotes ch. II, ' "This is a thousand pities" ' to 'he left the pasture.']

Upon these two pegs the story hangs. Jack Durbeyfield's deter-mination to obtain recognition from the younger branch of the family involves Tess in ruin. After she has weathered the storm, and buried the offspring of mischance—the scene of the baptism, where Tess, urged to desperation by her inability to get her infant regularly chris-tened, rouses her little brothers and sisters and names it 'Sorrow', is one of the most impressive 'moments' in recent fiction—she goes forth to commence life anew. Once more she meets Angel Clare; and ere long 'they were converging, under an irresistible law, as surely as

two streams in one vale'. Although Tess acts as one rightly and consciously under the famous Celtic curse, 'I name thee a destiny that thy
side touch not a husband', necessity controls the battle of two contrary
inclinations, and she is forced into wedlock, without being able to
declare the one thing that shamed and sullied her fair life. To the
reader it seems as if a certain moral insensibility prevented Clare from
acting promptly as a gentleman should; and the well-meant cruelty
with which he visits her, driving her out once more to be the sport of
every evil wind, appears like fatuity. Here is the one fault of construction in the novel. Mr. Hardy does not make it sufficiently clear that
Angel Clare did not know so much as he and we know; nor has he
sufficiently explained to the reader why Tess submitted completely to
D'Urberville instead of revolting from him after his act of.treachery.
So many women would have chosen (or rather flung themselves upon)
the one, that it is wonderful that Tess should take the other course. Yet
the strength of her affectionate loyalty, joined to a certain stubborn
dignity (a relic of her noble descent), retains our respect. It is impossible
not to feel for her as we feel for the most lovable of Mr. Meredith's
women.

But was it needful that Mr. Hardy should challenge criticism upon
what is after all a side issue? His business was rather to fashion (as he
has done) a being of flesh and blood than to propose the suffering
woman's view of a controversy which only the dabbler in sexual ethics
can enjoy. Why should a novelist embroil himself in moral techni-
calities? As it is, one half suspects Mr. Hardy of a desire to argue out
the justice of the comparative punishments meted to man and to woman
for sexual aberrations. To have fashioned a faultless piece of art built
upon the great tragic model were surely sufficient. And, as a matter of
fact, the 'argumentation' is confined to the preface and sub-title, which
are, to our thinking, needless and a diversion from the main interest,
which lies not in Tess, the sinner or sinned against, but in Tess the
woman. Mr. Hardy's style is here, as always, suave and supple, although his use of scientific and ecclesiastical terminology grows
excessive. Nor is it quite befitting that a novelist should. sneer at a
character with the word 'antinomianism', and employ 'determinism'
for his own purposes a page or two later. And a writer who aims so
evidently at impartiality had been well advised in restraining a slight
animosity (subtly expressed though it be) against certain conventions
which some people even yet respect. However, all things taken into
account, *Tess of the D'Urbervilles* is well in front of Mr. Hardy's

previous work, and is destined, there can be no doubt, to rank high amongst the achievements of Victorian novelists.

39. Clementina Black, *Illustrated London News*

9 January 1892, c, p. 50

Clementina Black was a novelist and publicist of the later years of the nineteenth and the earlier part of the present century; she wrote on labour problems.

Mr. Hardy's new novel is in many respects the finest work which he has yet produced, and its superiority is largely due to a profound moral earnestness which has not always been conspicuous in his writing. Yet this very earnestness, by leading him to deal with serious moral problems, will assuredly cause this book to be reprobated by numbers of well-intentioned people who have read his previous novels with complacency. The conventional reader wishes to be excited, but not to be disturbed; he likes to have new pictures presented to his imagination, but not to have new ideas presented to his mind. He detests unhappy endings, mainly because an unhappy ending nearly always involves an indirect appeal to the conscience, and the conscience, when aroused, is always demanding a reorganization of that traditional pattern of right and wrong which it is the essence of conventionality to regard as immutable. Yet more, of course, does he detest an open challenge of that traditional pattern, and *Tess of the D'Urbervilles* is precisely such a challenge.

Mr. Hardy's story, like *Diana of the Crossways*, is founded on a recognition of the ironic truth which we all know in our hearts, and are all forbidden to say aloud, that the richest kind of womanly nature, the most direct, sincere, and passionate, is the most liable to be caught in that sort of pitfall which social convention stamps as an irretrievable disgrace. It is the unsuspicious and fundamentally pure-minded girl in whom lie the noblest possibilities of womanhood, who is the easiest victim and who has to fight the hardest fight.

Mr. Hardy's heroine is simple, sincere, and passionately faithful, and as different as possible from those fickle and elusive young women who display, in some of his other tales, affections as veering as weather-cocks. After a time of terrible anguish and self-reproach for that early fault, which, justly speaking, was no fault of hers, she goes forth, a beautiful girl of twenty, to a fresh place, meets an honourable man who loves her, and loves him in return. She tries to tell him of her past; sometimes accident and sometimes lack of courage intervenes. At last she makes her confession, just after their marrige, and the revelation drives him from her. Her sincerity makes her incapable of exercising the arts by which Bathsheba and her coquettish sisters could have drawn him back, and she is left alone. Too proud to seek the help he had arranged for her, she struggles against poverty, rough usage, and the revived pursuit of her first lover. As the toils thicken round her, she writes a heartrending appeal to her husband in Brazil—the most pathetic letter, surely, in all English fiction—and it arrives only after he has started home to find her. Getting no reply, pressed by her poverty-stricken family and by her pertinacious suitor, she yields in sheer hopelessness and despair, and, after one brief gleam of comprehension and reconciliation, the story closes with her tragic death. The true country life of hard toil makes a continual background to the figure of country-born Tess; but the background is not always dark. The wholesome life of the dairy farm, and the wonderful pictures of changing aspects and seasons, the descriptions of three or four solitary walks, remain with us like bits of personal experience. Perhaps no other English writer could have given precisely these impressions. Yet these, characteristic as they are, are not the essence of the book. Its essence lies in the perception that a woman's moral worth is measurable not by any one deed, but by the whole aim and tendency of her life and nature. In regard to men the doctrine is no novelty; the writers who have had eyes to see and courage to declare the same truth about women are few indeed; and Mr. Hardy in this novel has shown himself to be one of that brave and clear-sighted minority.

40. From an unsigned review, *Saturday Review*

16 January 1892, 73-4

Tess is here dealt with as the first of a batch of four novels. The final passage to which exception is taken contains a misprint, 'road' for 'load', which has misled the reviewer. (See R. L. Purdy, *Thomas Hardy, a Bibliographical Study*, pp. 74-5.)

The sequence of lightning and thunder is not more prompt than that of cause and effect in Mr. Hardy's story. A parson riding through a country lane in the South of England meets an old haggler called Durbeyfield, and informs him that the name he bears is a corruption of D'Urberville, and that he is the 'direct lineal representative of the ancient and knightly family of the D'Urbervilles' who appear on the Battle Abbey roll. This is all news to the haggler, but he sucks it in eagerly, and listens while the parson gives—in anything but simple language—a sketch of the departed glories of his house, and he does not at all relish his informer's advice to 'do nothing'. In fact, from that very instant Durbeyfield begins 'doing' to such an extent that in the course of five years he completely *un*does, not only himself and his family, but a number of other people as well, and his own daughter Tess is the principal victim. On his way home he imparts to a boy whom he meets 'the secret that he is one of a noble race', and that 'there's not a man in the county of South Wessex that's got grander and nobler skellingtons in his family' than he has. It is wholly beneath the dignity of such a potentate to walk home, so he sends the boy for a carriage and some rum, and drives back to his wife, repeating, as a recitative, 'I've—got—a—great—family—vault—at Kingsbere—and —knighted—forefathers—in—lead—coffins—there.' Let it at once be said that there is not one single touch of nature either in John Durbeyfield or in any other character in the book. All are stagey, and some are farcical. Tess herself comes the nearest to possibility, and is an attractive figure; but even she is suggestive of the carefully-studied simplicity of the theatre, and not at all of the carelessness of the fields.

Her life is ruined by her parents' determination to send her to claim
kinship with some rich people of the name of D'Urberville, who own a
place about twenty miles away. Tess herself goes with extreme reluctance, and is not much prepossessed with the so-called relative that
she meets, a young man of bold aspect, who regales her with straw-
berries. Of course this is the serpent who is to destroy the poor young
Eve; but the story gains nothing by the reader being let into the secret
of the physical attributes which especially fascinated him in Tess.
Most people can fill in blanks for themselves, without its being necessary to put the dots on the i's so very plainly; but Mr. Hardy leaves
little unsaid. 'She had an attribute which amounted to a disadvantage
just now; and it was this that caused Alec D'Urberville's eyes to rivet
themselves upon her. It was a luxuriance of aspect; a fullness of growth,
which made her appear more of a woman than she really was. She had
inherited the feature from her mother without the quality it denoted.'
It is these side suggestions that render Mr. Hardy's story so very disagreeable, and *Tess* is full of them. The result of this interview is that
the young man induces his blind mother to offer Tess a situation as
poultry-woman, and the Durbeyfield fortunes not being equal to the
length, of their pedigree, she is induced by her parents to accept, her
mother openly declaring that she looks upon it as a chance for Tess to
settle her future. Mrs. Durbeyfield is described as a good-natured
shiftless woman, not refined in her perceptions, but who has led a
respectable life. Yet she does not hesitate to send her daughter deliberately into temptation, with as much *sangfroid* as if she had been the
vilest of her sex. 'If he don't marry her afore, he will after', she observes to her husband, and he does not contradict her. The girl's ruin
is compassed in spite of herself, and she comes home four months
after she has first left to be upbraided by her mother for her folly in
not getting D'Urberville to marry her. Tess has nothing of her mother's
coarse fibre, and shrinks away from sight, till, after her baby's birth
and death, she departs and seeks work in a great dairy farm. Mr.
Hardy is always at his best when dealing with scenes taken direct from
nature, in which his imagination has something to go upon. His
description of life in a dairy farm in summer forms an admirable foil
to his subsequent account of the terribly hard work both for males
and females in an arable farm in winter, when swede-hacking, reed-
drawing, or threshing occupied the hands from dawn to dark. It was
during her easy and pleasant summer hours that Tess met her elective
affinity Angel Clare, the farm pupil, son of a neighbouring clergyman.

Clare is a mere shadow to the reader; but, such as he is, no less than three dairymaids sigh for him openly, while Tess does so in secret. There is a want of humour in this proceeding which is, however, intended to be tragic. 'Dear he', as one of the forlorn ones calls him, proposes to Tess, and, after much hesitation on her part, and weak efforts to tell him her history, she marries him. On their wedding evening they resolve to confess their past sins to each other, with the consequence that, while Tess gives him, as he expects, instant absolution Clare emphatically declines to pardon the error of which she can hardly be said to have been guilty. She has a brief revival of hope, occasioned by Clare's walking in his sleep, and performing a feat that must have been almost unique in the history of strength, considering that he was not a Hercules, and that Tess was a tall and well-developed young woman. He lifted her out of bed, murmuring tender words over his 'dead wife', carried her out of the house, down the river across a plank bridge, through a plantation to the Abbey church, where he laid her in an open coffin, and went away. He soon went away altogether—for Brazil—giving Tess money to support her the while, and telling her that, if he could ever make up his mind to forgive her, he would come back. The end is what every one will have foreseen. Tess accidentally meets D'Urberville, who has been converted from his ways in a wholly startling manner by some warning words of Clare's father, and is now a Methodist preacher. He hangs about her, in spite of her entreaties, for many months, denies his new opinions, and offers her the marriage which is now impossible; and when, finally, Clare has decided to be magnanimous, and to claim her as his wife, he finds that it is too late, and that she is living with D'Urberville. The tragedy culminates in D'Urberville being stabbed by Tess during a quarrel, in her hiding for some days with Clare, and in her being ultimately hanged. Few people will deny the terrible dreariness of this tale, which, except during the few hours spent with cows, has not a gleam of sunshine anywhere. Mr. Hardy says in his 'explanatory note' that he has added some chapters, 'more especially addressed to adults', to 'episodic sketches' that have appeared in various papers and periodicals. This reminds us of those artists who have exhibitions of pictures open to the public, but who hang over an inner sanctum containing their choicest works a placard marked 'For gentlemen only'. It matters much less what a story is about than how that story is told, and Mr. Hardy, it must be conceded, tells an unpleasant story in a very unpleasant way. He says that it 'represents, on the whole, a true sequence of events';

but does it? The impression of most readers will be that Tess, never having cared for D'Urberville even in her early days, hating him as the cause of her ruin, and, more so, as the cause of her separation from Clare, whom she madly loved, would have died by the roadside sooner than go back and live with him and be decked out with fine clothes. Still, Mr. Hardy did well to let her pay the full penalty, and not die among the monoliths of Stonehenge, as many writers would have done. One thing more. Mr. Hardy would do well to look to his grammar. In his 'explanatory note' he begs his too gentle reader 'who cannot endure to have it said what everybody thinks and feels', to remember a sentence of St. Jerome's. To have *what* said? To what does 'it' refer? Then, he says:

The Durbeyfield waggon met many other waggons with families on the summit of a road, which was built on a well-nigh unvarying principle, as peculiar, probably, to the rural labourer as the hexagon to a bee. The groundwork of the arrangement was the family dresser.

Now, by all the rules of syntax it is the summit of the road that was built on the unvarying principle and on the family dresser, but the context shows that it is really the inside of the waggon to which he means to refer. These things ought not to be.

41. R. H. Hutton, *Spectator*

23 January 1892, 121–2

This unsigned review appears to be Hutton's last discussion of a Hardy novel, since the *Spectator* did not review *Jude*, and Hutton died in 1897. (See headnote to No. 8.)

Mr. Hardy has written one of his most powerful novels, perhaps the most powerful which he ever wrote, to illustrate his conviction that not only is there no Providence guiding individual men and women in the right way, but that, in many cases at least, there is something like a malign fate which draws them out of the right way into the wrong way. Tess of the D'Urbervilles is declared by Mr. Hardy to be 'a pure woman', and as he has presented her, we do not doubt that her instincts were all pure enough, more pure probably than those of a great number of women who never fall into her disgrace and shame. She was, of course, much more sinned against than sinning, though Mr. Hardy is too 'faithful' a portrait-painter to leave out touches which show that her instincts even as regards purity, were not of the very highest class. The coarse expression which he attributes to her in relation to her companions, when she declares that if she had known what they were like, she would not have so let herself down as to come with them, betrays perfectly well her knowledge of the dangers before her—indeed, she had had plenty of forecast of those dangers, and she was well aware that the looseness of her companions was more or less due to the profligacy of the man whom she disliked and feared, and to whom her ruin was ultimately due. Yet she deliberately forsook their company, because they were insolent and taunting, to put herself into the power of the very person who, as she knew, was responsible for their misconduct as well as for the temptations thrown in her own way. That course was not due to an instinct of purity, but to an instinct of mere timidity and disgust. But though we quite admit that in her instincts Tess was as pure as multitudes of women who never suffered what she had to suffer, we cannot at all admit that, if she be 'faithfully presented', she was at all faithful to her own sense of duty in the course of the story. Again and again, and yet again, he shows her shrinking from the obvious and imperative duty of the moment when she must have felt that the whole sincerity of her life was at stake. To accept the love of her husband without telling him that she had been the more or less innocent victim of a man to whom she had borne a child, was not certainly the act of a 'pure woman', and whatever palliation there may have been for it in her passionate love, it was the very way to ensure the steady lowering of her sense of duty, and invite the misery which was the natural consequence. But even after that and after she had confessed to her husband, which very naturally produced a great alienation, she repeatedly shrinks from the obvious and emphatic duty of the hour, which she must have felt to be the duty enjoined by her love for him, no less than the duty enjoined by the barest self-respect. She will not stay with her parents, where she would have been comparatively safe, and where her husband had assumed that she would be safe, but goes out into all the great dangers of field-life—dangers, we mean, for a character and beauty such as hers. When she comes to the end of her resources, and is aware that, under the terms of her husband's instructions, she ought to have applied to his father and mother for more means, she is deterred from doing so by the most trivial pride, which was natural enough, but which the sense of her general unprotectedness ought at once to have overruled. Still worse, when, on her return from this failure of purpose, she finds herself once more in the snares of the miserable man who had been her ruin, instead of at once taking refuge with her father and mother-in-law, who were her natural protectors, she trusts entirely to letters which had to go to Brazil and (as it proved) to return from Brazil, before her husband could get them, and never once thinks of repeating the application from which nothing but the least justifiable of motives had deterred her. We must say that had Tess been what Mr. Hardy calls her, a really pure woman, she could not possibly have hesitated to apply to her father and mother-in-law when she felt, as she did feel, that it was a question of life and death to her fidelity of purpose and her purity of heart whether she obtained their protection or not. On the whole, we deny altogether that Mr. Hardy has made out his case for Tess. She was pure enough in her instincts, considering the circumstances and the class in which she was born. But she had no deep sense of fidelity to those instincts. If she had, she would not have allowed herself time after time to be turned from the plain path of duty, by the fastidiousness of a personal pride which was quite out of proportion to the extremity of her temptations and her perils. It is no doubt true that her husband behaved with even less fidelity to her than she to him. Perhaps that was natural in such a pagan as Mr. Hardy depicts him. But we cannot for a moment admit that even on his own portraiture of the circumstances of the case, Tess acted as a pure woman should have acted under such a stress of temptation and peril. Though pure in instinct, she was not faithful to her pure instinct. We should, indeed, say that Mr. Hardy, instead of illustrating his conviction that there is no Power who guides and guards those who are faithful to their best lights, has only illustrated what every Christian would admit, that if fine natures will not faithfully adhere to such genuine instincts as they have, they may deteriorate, and will deteriorate, in consequence of that faithlessness.

While we cannot at all admire Mr. Hardy's motive in writing this very powerful novel, we must cordially admit that he has seldom or never written anything so truly tragic and so dramatic. The beauty and realism of the delineations of the life on the large dairy-farm; the sweetness and, on the whole, generosity of the various dairymaids' feelings for each other; the vivacity of the description of the cows themselves; the perfect insight into the conditions of rustic lives; the true pathos of Tess's sufferings; the perfect naturalness, and even inevitability, of all her impulses; the strange and horrible mixture of feelings with which she regards her destroyer, when, believing that all her chance of happiness is over, she sells herself ultimately for the benefit of her mother and brother and sisters; the masterful conception of the seducer as a convert to Antinomianism, and the ease with which his new faith gives way to a few recitals by Tess of her husband's ground for scepticism (with which, however, we are not favoured); the brilliant description of the flight of Clare and Tess, and of the curious equanimity with which Tess meets the consciousness of having committed murder, seeing that it has restored her for five days to her husband's heart—are all pictures of almost unrivalled power, though they evidently proceed from the pantheistic conception that impulse is the law of the universe, and that will, properly so called, is a non-existent fiction. We confess that this is a story which, in spite of its almost unrivalled power, it is very difficult to read, because in almost every page the mind rebels against the steady assumptions of the author, and shrinks from the untrue picture of a universe so blank and godless— Shelley's 'blank, grey, lampless, deep, unpeopled world'. We can hardly give a better conception of the force of the picture, than in the passage in which Tess goes to sleep under the shadow of Stonehenge, with Clare at her side, after she has gathered from her husband that for their love there is, in his belief, no resurrection, and after calmly recommending to him her sister as her successor in this world:

[quotes ch. LVIII ' "Angel, if anything happens" ' to ' they were again silent.']

For the last words of a murderess who makes not an effort of any kind to ignore or deny the murder, this picture could only have been conceived as the outcome of a pantheistic philosophy. The only fault in Mr. Hardy's style is an excess of pedantic phraseology in various parts of the book, which reminds us of George Eliot in her scientific mood.

42. Andrew Lang, *New Review*

February 1892, vi, 247–9

This was part of the monthly Chronicle of Literature and the Drama, by Andrew Lang. (See headnote to No. 11.) The *New Review*, which was published by Longmans and edited at this time by Archibald Grove, ran from 1889 to 1897.

Mr. Hardy's new novel, *Tess of the D'Urbervilles* demands more space than, in a crowd of hustling books, it is likely to receive. Indeed, the story is an excellent text for a sermon or subtly Spectatorial article on old times and new, on modern misery, on the presence among us of the spirit of Augustus Moddle. That we should be depressed is very natural, all things considered; and, indeed, I suppose we shall be no better till we have got the Revolution over, sunk to the nadir of humanity, and reached the middle barbarism again. Then, *sursum corda!* Mr. Hardy's story, though probably he does not know it, is a rural tragedy of the last century—reversed. In a little book on *The Quantocks*, by Mr. W. L. Nichols (Sampson Low), may be read the history of 'Poor Jack Walford'. Wordsworth wrote a poem on it in the Spenserian measure, but he felt that his work was a failure, and it remains unpublished. Reverse the *rôles* of the man and woman in this old and true tale, add a good deal of fantastic though not impossible matters about the D'Urbervilles, and you have the elements of *Tess*. The conclusion of *Tess* is rather improbable in this age of halfpenny newspapers and appeals to the British public. The black flag would never have been hoisted, as in the final page. But one is afraid of revealing the story to people who have not yet read it. The persistent melancholy they perhaps like, or perhaps can make up their minds to endure. The rustic heroine, in the very opening of the book, explains to her little brothers that our planet is 'a blighted star'. Her mother possesses 'the mind of a happy child', yet coolly sends her into conspicuous danger, remarking, 'If he don't marry her afore, he will after'. Poor Tess is set between the lusts of one Alec D'Urberville and the love, such as it was, of one Angel Clare. 'Now Alec was a Bounder', to quote Mr. Besant; and Angel was a prig, whereas Tess was a human being, of human passions. Here are all the ingredients of the blackest misery, and the misery darkens till 'The President of the Immortals has finished his sport with Tess'. I cannot say how much this phrase jars on one. If there be a God, who can seriously think of Him as a malicious fiend? And if there be none, the expression is meaningless. I have lately been reading the works of an old novelist, who was very active between 1814 and 1831. He is not a terse, nor an accurate, nor a philosophic, nor even a very grammatical writer, but how different, and, to my poor thinking, how much wiser, kinder, happier, and more human is his mood. It is pity, one knows, that causes this bitterness in Mr. Hardy's mood. But Homer is not less pitiful of mortal fortunes and man 'the most forlorn of all creatures that walk on earth', and Homer's faith cannot be called consolation: yet there is no bitterness in him; and probably bitterness is never a mark of the greatest art and the noblest thought.

There are moral passages of great beauty in *Tess*: for example, in that scene where the bemused villagers stagger home through the moonlight, which casts halos round the shadows of their heads no less than if they had been happy shepherds on the sides of Latmos. There are exquisite studies of the few remaining idyllic passages in rural life, like that walking of the white-clad women in May, which Mr. Hardy compares to the Cerealia. It certainly does resemble the rite of the Thesmophoria. There are touches highly picturesque and telling, as when the red spot on the ceiling, no bigger than a postage stamp, widens into a broad splash of blood. The style is pellucid, as a rule, but there are exceptions. 'Human mutuality' seems, to myself, an ill phrase. 'There, behind the blue narcotic haze, sat "the tragic mischief" of her drama, he who was to be the blood-red ray in the spectrum of her young life.' Here is an odd mixture of science and literature. A face is, or rather is not, 'furrowed with incarnated memories representing in hieroglyphic the centuries of her family's and England's history'. 'In those early days she had been much loved by others of her own sex and age, and had used to be seen about the village as one of three—all nearly of the same year—walking home from school side by side, Tess being the middle one—in a pink pinafore of a finely reticulated pattern, worn over a stuff frock that had lost its original colour for a nondescript tertiary—marching on upon long, stalky legs, in tight stockings which had little ladder-like holes at the knees, torn by kneeling in the roads and banks in search of vegetable and mineral treasures; her then earth-coloured hair hanging like pot-hooks; the arms of the two outside girls resting round the waist of Tess; her arms on the shoulders of the two supporters.' The question is, does this give the picture intended, or is it a little confusing? Why people who are drinking beer should be said to 'seek vinous bliss' is not apparent. A woman, at the public-house in the evening, finds her troubles 'sinking to minor cerebral phenomena for quiet contemplation, in place of standing as pressing concretions which chafe body and soul'. Here is the very reef on which George Eliot was wrecked. However, tastes differ so much that the blemishes, as they appear to one reader, of Mr. Hardy's works may seem beauty-spots in the eyes of another reader. He does but give us of his best, and if his best be too good for us, or good in the wrong way, if, in short, we are not *en rapport* with him, why, there are plenty of other novelists, alive and dead, and the fault may be on our side, not on his.

43. William Watson, *Academy*

6 February 1892, xli, 125-6

Sir William Watson (1858–1925), poet, and contributor to *The Yellow Book*, was thought to be in the running for the Laureateship after Tennyson. He was a personal friend of Hardy. This review was later reprinted in his *Excursions in Criticism* (1893).

In this, his greatest work, Mr. Hardy has produced a tragic masterpiece which is not flawless, any more than *Lear* or *Macbeth* is; and the easiest way of writing about it would be to concentrate one's attention upon certain blemishes of style, read the author a lecture upon their enormity, affect to be very much shocked and upset by some of his conclusions in morals, and conveniently shirk such minor critical duties as the attempt to abnegate one's prejudices, inherited or acquired; to estimate in what degree the author's undoubtedly impassioned ethical vision is steady and clear; and, while eschewing equally a dogmatic judicialism and a weak surrender of the right of private censorship, to survey the thing created, in some measure, by the light of its creator's eyes. What is called critical coolness seems, no doubt, on a cursory view, an excellent qualification in a judge of literature; but true criticism, when it approaches the work of the masters, can never be quite cool. To be cool before the *Lear* or the *Macbeth* were simply not to feel *what is there*; and it is the critic's business to feel, just as much as to see. In so tremendous a presence, the criticism which can be cool is no criticism at all. The critical, hardly less than the creative mind, must possess the faculty of being rapt and transported, or its function declines into mere connoisseurship, the pedant's office of mechanical appraisement.

One may, however, feel the greatness of Mr. Hardy's work profoundly, and yet be conscious of certain alloying qualities; but let it be said at once, such qualities are of the surface only. None the less, with respect to the over-academic phraseology which here and there crops up in this book, I myself have but one feeling—a wish that it were absent. This terminology of the schools is misplaced; I can feel nothing but regret for these nodosities upon the golden thread of an otherwise fine diction. In a certain sense they disturb a reader all the more for the very reason that they are *not*—like Mr. Meredith's singularities of speech, for example—ingrained in the very constitution of the style and, obviously, native to the author, nor are they so frequent as to become a habit, a characteristic mannerism which one might get used to; rather they are exceptional and excrescent—foreign to the total character of Mr. Hardy's English—and serve no purpose but to impair the homogeneity of his utterance. The perfect style for a novelist is surely one which never calls attention to its own existence, and there was needed only the omission or modification of a score or two of sentences in these volumes to have assimilated the style of *Tess* to such an ideal. Nothing but gain could have resulted from the elimination of such phrases as 'his former pulsating flexuous domesticity'. Possibly Mr. Hardy intends some self-reference of a defensive sort when he observes that

advanced ideas are really in great part but the latest fashion in definition—a more accurate expression, by words in *logy* and *ism*, of sensations which men and women have vaguely grasped for centuries;

touching which, one is impelled to ask—Are the words in *logy* and *ism* necessarily more accurate instruments of thought than simpler phrases? Recalling the other memorable case in which a great novelist finally allowed her passion for elaborate precision of statement to metallicize an originally pliant style, one doubts if there was any truer psychological accuracy in the delineation of Deronda than in that of Silas Marner. Mr. Herbert Spencer's diction is no doubt very accurate, but probably not more so than Lord Tennyson's.

Fortunately, however, *Tess* is a work so great that it could almost afford to have even proportionately great faults; and the faults upon which I have dwelt—perhaps unduly—are casual and small. Powerful and strange in design, splendid and terrible in execution, this story brands itself upon the mind as with the touch of incandescent iron. To speak of its gloom as absolutely unrelieved is scarcely correct. Dairyman Crick provides some genuine mirth, though not in too abundant measure; and 'Sir John', with his 'skellingtons', is a figure at once humorous and pathetic. But with these exceptions, the atmosphere from first to last is, indeed, tenebrous; and after the initial stroke of doom, Tess appears to us like Thea, in Keats's poem:

> There was a listening fear in her regard,
> As if calamity had but begun;
> As if the vanward clouds of evil days
> Had spent their malice, and the sullen rear
> Was with its storèd thunder labouring up.

The great theme of the book is the incessant penalty paid by the innocent for the wicked, the unsuspicious for the crafty, the child for its fathers; and again and again this spectacle, in its wide diffusion, provokes the novelist to a scarcely suppressed declaration of rebellion against a supramundane ordinance that can decree, or permit, the triumph of such wrong. The book may almost be said to resolve itself into a direct arraignment of the morality of this system of vicarious pain—a morality which, as he bitterly expresses it, 'may be good enough for divinities', but is 'scorned by average human nature'. Almost at the outset, this note of insurrection against an apparently inequitable scheme of things is struck, if less audaciously, upon our introduction to the Durbeyfield household.

All these young souls were passengers in the Durbeyfield ship, entirely dependent on the judgment of the two Durbeyfield adults for their pleasures, their necessities, their health; even their existence. If the heads of the Durbeyfield household chose to sail into difficulty, disaster, starvation, disease, degradation, death, thither were these half-dozen little captives under hatches compelled to sail with them—six helpless creatures, who had never been asked if they wished for life on any terms, much less if they wished for it on such hard conditions as were involved in being of the shiftless house of Durbeyfield.

In one way and another, this implicit protest against what he cannot but conceive to be the maladministration of the laws of existence, this expostulation with 'whatever gods there be' upon the ethics of their rule, is the burden of the whole strain. And a joyless strain it is, whose theme is the havoc wrought by 'those creeds which futilely attempt to check what wisdom would be content to regulate'; the warfare of 'two ardent hearts against one poor little conscience', wherein the conscience at last is calamitously victorious, the hearts rent and ruined; and, over all, like an enveloping cloud, 'the dust and ashes of things, the cruelty of lust, and the fragility of love'. Truly a stupendous argument; and in virtue of the almost intolerable power with which this argument is wrought out, *Tess* must take its place among the great tragedies, to have read which is to have permanently enlarged the boundaries of one's intellectual and emotional experience.

Perhaps the most subtly drawn, as it is in some ways the most perplexing and difficult character, is that of Angel Clare, with his half-ethereal passion for Tess—'an emotion which could jealously guard the loved one against his very self'. But one of the problems of the book, for the reader, is involved in the question how far Mr. Hardy's own moral sympathies go with Clare in the supreme crisis of his and Tess's fate. Her seducer, the spurious D'Urberville, is entirely detestable, but it often happens that one's fiercest indignation demands a nobler object than such a sorry animal as that; and there are probably many readers who, after Tess's marriage with Clare, her spontaneous disclosure to him of her soiled though guiltless past, and his consequent alienation and cruelty, will be conscious of a worse anger against this intellectual, virtuous, and unfortunate man than they could spare for the heartless and worthless libertine who had wrecked these two lives. It is at this very point, however, that the masterliness of the conception, and its imaginative validity, are most conclusively manifest, for it is here that we perceive Clare's nature to be consistently inconsistent throughout. As his delineator himself says of him: 'With all his attempted independence of judgment, this advanced man was yet the slave to custom and conventionality when surprised back into his early teachings.' He had carefully schooled himself into a democratic aversion from everything connected with the pride of aristocratic lineage; but when he is suddenly made aware that Tess is the daughter of five centuries of knightly D'Urbervilles, he unfeignedly exults in her splendid ancestry.

He had become a rationalist in morals no less than an agnostic in religion; yet no sooner does this emancipated man learn from his wife's own most loving lips the story of her sinless fall, than his affection appears to wither at the roots. 'But for the world's opinion', says Mr. Hardy, somewhat boldly, her experiences 'would have been simply a liberal education.' Yet it is these experiences which place her for a time outside the human sympathy of her husband, with all his fancied superiority to conventionalisms and independence of tradition. The reader pities Clare profoundly, yet cannot but feel a certain contempt for the shallowness of his casuistry, and a keen resentment of his harsh judgment upon the helpless woman—all the more so since it is her own meek and uncomplaining submission that aids him in his cruel punishment of her. 'Her mood of long-suffering made his way easy for him, and she herself was his best advocate.' Considering the proud ancestry whose blood was in her veins, and the high spirit and even fierce temper she exhibits on occasion, one almost wonders at her absolute passivity under such treatment as he subjects her to; but the explanation obviously lies in her own unquestioning conviction of the justice of his procedure. One of Mr. Hardy's especially poetic traits is his manner of sometimes using external Nature not simply as a background or a setting, but as a sort of superior spectator and chorus, that makes strangely unconcerned comments from the vantage-ground of a sublime aloofness upon the ludicrous tragedy of the human lot; and, in the scene of Tess's confession, a singularly imaginative effect is produced by kindred means, where Mr. Hardy makes the very furniture and appurtenances of the room undergo a subtle change of aspect and expression as the bride unfolds her past, and brings Present and Future ruining about her head:

Tess's voice throughout had hardly risen higher than its opening tone; there had been no exculpatory phrase of any kind, and she had not wept. But the complexion even of external things seemed to suffer transmutation as her announcement progressed. The fire in the grate looked impish—demoniacally funny, as if it did not care in the least about her strait. The fender grinned idly, as if it too did not care. The light from the water-bottle was merely engaged in a chromatic problem. All material objects around announced their irresponsibility with terrible iteration. And yet nothing had changed since the moments when he had been kissing her; or rather, nothing in the substance of things. But the essence of things had changed.

One detail of this scene strikes me as a crudity in art, though it may be a fact in nature. It is where she is suddenly aghast at the effect of her own confession: 'Terror was upon her white face as she saw it; her cheek was flaccid, *and her mouth had the aspect of a round little hole.*' This may be realism, but even realism is eclectic, and rejects more than it uses; and this is surely one of those non-essential touches which, drawing attention upon themselves, purchase a literal veracity at the expense of a high imaginative verisimilitude.

After this, D'Urberville's re-intrusion upon her life, and his resumed mastery of it, are matters which, in their curious air of predestination, affect us somewhat in the manner of spectral interferences with human fates; and this impression is incidentally aided by the use made, very sparingly—with that fine, suggestive parsimony which reveals the artist's hand—of the one preternatural detail, the legend of the D'Urberville coach and four. Thenceforward, as the tragedy climbs towards its last summit of desolation and doom, criticism in the ordinary sense must lie low, in the shadow of so great and terrible a conception.

There is one thing which not the dullest reader can fail to recognize— the persistency with which there alternately smoulders and flames through the book Mr. Hardy's passionate protest against the unequal justice meted by society to the man and the woman associated in an identical breach of the moral law. In his wrath, Mr. Hardy seems at times almost to forget that society is scarcely more unjust than nature. He himself proposes no remedy, suggests no escape—his business not being to deal in nostrums of social therapeutics. He is content to make his readers pause, and consider, and pity; and very likely he despairs of any satisfactory solution of the problem which he presents with such disturbing power and clothes with a vesture of such breathing and throbbing life.

44. Mrs. Oliphant, *Blackwood's Magazine*

March 1892, cli, 464-74

Margaret Oliphant (née Wilson, 1828-97) was a prolific novelist and historical writer of the last half of the nineteenth century. The review formed part of a literary feature-article, No. XXVII in a series entitled 'The Old Saloon'. Reviewed together with *Tess* was Mrs. Humphry Ward's *David Grieve*.

We confess that it is with a sense of relief that we turn from these highly instructive volumes to the bold romance provided for us by no amateur or didactic performer, but by the true professional, the practised hand of Mr. Hardy, to whom we owe already a good many sharp sensations, but none so strong and startling as that contained in the history of Tess. We acknowledge that Mr. Hardy is not one of our first favourites in fiction, and that his new book is not greatly to our taste. Taste, as everybody knows, is the one thing upon which there is no discussion. Some of us (though it is a fact unintelligible in France and perhaps in certain quarters in England) sincerely like the literature that suits the young person, and some prefer to have their novels hot, and lock them up in cupboards for their private delectation. Though we strongly object to being instructed in any illegitimate way, yet, for our own part, we prefer cleanly lives, and honest sentiment, and a world which is round and contains everything, not 'the relations between the sexes' alone. We state this as a question of private preference, to which all persons have a right; and we may add that we have never been able to get over a certain expedient of grotesque and indecent dishonesty in that exceedingly droll book of Mr. Hardy's, entitled *Two on a Tower*— so grotesque that the sense of the comic in it goes much too far to be vanquished by any disapproval. Therefore the reader will see that we bring no favouritism into our delighted sense of having come from the fictitious into the real when we step from David Grieve to Tess Durbeyfield. We have a great many objections to make to Tess. The fact that what we must call the naughty chapters have had to be printed surreptitiously, in what we presume ought to be described as elderly

Reviews, while the rest has come out in the cheerful young newspaper open to all men, is of itself a tremendous objection to our old-fashioned eyes. But with all this, what a living, breathing scene, what a scent and fragrance of the actual, what solid bodies, what real existence, in contrast with the pale fiction of the didactic romance! We feel inclined to embrace Mr. Hardy, though we are not fond of him, in pure satisfaction with the good brown soil and substantial flesh and blood, the cows, and the mangel-wurzel, and the hard labour of the fields—which he makes us smell and see. Here is the genuine article at least. Here is a workman who, though he has his lesson hidden beneath his apron, is an artist first of all, and knows how to use his colours, and throw his shadows, and make us feel the earth under our feet. Hail to the profession, the brotherhood of imagination and art! It is sad to think that he too is didactic, and has a meaning, an *arrière pensée*, a text from which he preaches; but, at all events, in his first two volumes we have many opportunities of forgetting that, and, as a matter of fact, scarcely perceive or think of it. Fortunately, so long as nature and art are predominant, there is no need to rush to the locked drawers and cupboards of the Reviews. We mean no reproach, for we are obliged to confess that we do not know which were the Reviews to which Mr. Hardy paid the equivocal compliment of supposing them closed to innocent eyes, and we do not mean to inquire. These elderly organs have not happened to come under our observation, at least when so employed.

Tess of the D'Urbervilles is the history, Mr. Hardy tells us, *par excellence*, of a pure woman, which is his flag or trumpet, so to speak, of defiance upon certain matters, to the ordinary world. It is time enough, however, to come to that after we have done justice to the real pictures which an artist cannot help giving, with qualities of life and truth which are independent of all didactic intentions. Tess is a country girl of an extraordinary elevated and noble kind. Everybody knows what Mr. Hardy's peasants in Wessex are. They are a quaint people, given to somewhat highflown language, and confused and complicated reasoning, like, it was at first supposed by hardy guessing, to George Eliot's peasants, yet not really so, except in being more dignified, more grandiose in speech than the usual article, as it comes across the ordinary senses of more common people. They are sometimes a little grotesque, but their sentiments are usually fine. John Durbeyfield, the father of Tess, is an example of this somewhat artificial personage. If he is not good Dorsetshire, he is at least good Hardy, which answers just as well;

and the book begins by a very foolish communication made to this rural 'higgler' by an old antiquarian parson of the fact that he is the lineal representative of the old race of the D'Urbervilles, whose marble tombs are to be seen in a great church near. The unfortunate weakly and silly straggler by the country roads takes the information to heart, and rears a structure of foolish hopes upon it which lead to nothing but dismay and trouble. The first scene, in which he has himself driven home in the rude fly of the village as Sir John, to the dismay yet elation of his family, all but the queenly Tess, who is the flower of it, and who is throughout ashamed of the whole business, is of a very heavy comic kind; but the family, always granted the Hardy element in it, is a vigorous and real picture. The father, too fond of beer; the mother singing at her washing-tub, rocking the cradle with her foot, strong yet slatternly, kind yet mercenary—quite ready to sell the beautiful daughter for the benefit of the family, and think no harm, yet loving and serving them all in her rude way. The background of children of all ages, and the one flower of womanhood, Tess, growing out from among them like a tall lily worthy of a better fate. It is a pardonable extravagance to make of Tess a kind of princess in this *milieu*, which is a mistake that even the most experienced make from time to time, since there is scarcely a vicaress or rectoress who has not some such favourite in the parish—some girl with all the instincts of a lady, as the kind patroness will tell you. We doubt much, however, whether having passed the Sixth Standard improves the phraseology in the manner believed by Mr. Hardy; but this is of little importance. Tess is, we are ready to allow, the exceptional creature whom we have all seen, beautiful in the bloom of first youth, capable of all things, as the imaginative spectator feels, and whom it is dreadful to think of as falling eventually into the cheerful comely slattern, with a troop of children, which her mother is. But is it not rather dreadful to the superficial eye to think of any lily-girl turning into the stout matron, which, alas! is the almost inevitable end of British beauty?

Tess is plunged at once into the abyss of evil. We need not follow a story which by this time everybody has read, through all its details. It is amusing, however, to find that such a democrat as Mr. Hardy, finding nothing worth his while in any class above that of the actual sons of the soil, should be so indignant at the trumpery person who has assumed the name of D'Urberville, having no sort of right to it. What could it matter? We are aware that the name of Norfolk Howard has been assumed in similar circumstances, which has made the world laugh, but had no more serious result. Mr. Hardy, however, takes it very gravely, though it is a godsend to him, opening the door for all that follows. The idea of sending Tess to seek her fortune by claiming kindred with the wealthy family which calls itself D'Urberville throws her at once into the hands of the young sensualist and villain of fiction, the rural Lothario with whom we are so well acquainted. Tess is spotless as a lily—that may be granted: but a girl brought up in the extraordinary freedom and free-speaking of rural life would scarcely be entirely ignorant of evil; and indeed, as a matter of fact, she has the instinct to discourage and escape as much as possible from the advances of the seducer and rustic profligate Alec D'Urberville, whose character is well known.

That she should have been taken advantage of, and dragged into degradation by mingled force and kindness, is possible; but not that, pure-minded and spotless, yet already alarmed and set on her guard as she had been, she should have trusted herself at midnight with the unscrupulous young master who was pursuing her, and whose habits she was fully informed of, in order to escape from the drunken and riotous companions who, odious as they were, were still a protection to her. The girl who escapes from her fellow-servants in their jollity by jumping up on horseback (and how about the horse? does that fine animal nowadays lend itself to such means of seduction?) behind a master of such a character, and being carried off by him in the middle of the night, naturally leaves her reputation behind her. 'At almost any other moment of her life she would have refused such proffered aid and company', Mr. Hardy says; 'but coming as this invitation did at the particular juncture, when fear and indignation at her adversaries could be transformed by a spring of the foot into a triumph over them, she abandoned herself to her impulse, put her toe on his instep, and leapt into the saddle behind him.' Thus poor Tess yields not to any impure suggestion, which is the last thing to be thought of in such a case, but to those mingled motives of vanity and excitement which have so large a share in this kind of moral downfall. The sense of triumph over others left behind, and intoxicating superiority for the moment to all rivals, has far more to do, we believe, with feminine offences of this description than any tendency towards vice. No one could doubt what was to follow: the girl, perhaps, alone might have hoped in some incomprehensible way that she should yet escape. And indeed Mr. Hardy, at the last moment, generously gives her an opportunity of running away, of which the real Tess certainly would have availed herself; but then where would the story have been, and all the defiant pleas of the author for that virtue which is proved in his estimation by the breach rather than the observance?

If Mr. Hardy had not labelled this poor girl as a specimen of exceptional and absolute purity, nothing could have been more piteous than her story. The villain, we should have said, was of an antiquated type, recalling Pamela and those days when seduction was one of the arts on which young men of pretension prided themselves. We may be wrong, but we imagine that even among the vicious this is scarcely the case now: however, Alec D'Urberville is that uneasy thing possessing the means and position without the traditions of a gentleman, which has special rules of its own. But poor little Tess, at sixteen going back to her house with her young eyes so fatally opened, has nothing but our pity, especially when, after a vague interval, she reappears in the harvest-field, among the other women at their work, with a baby dependent on her. The situation is one which is as old as poetry. Mr. Hardy seems to have a notion that he has invented it—but unfortunately it is not so. It has been treated in all the methods, and romance has invariably leant to the charitable side. If it is the woman who pays, at least it is the woman, the inevitable sufferer, who has all the sympathy. And the unfortunate child thus brought into the world is also a most powerful agent in fiction. Generally it has been supposed by the story-teller to be a means of redemption for the fallen woman. One remembers how Mrs. Browning treats it in *Aurora Leigh*, elevating and developing the being of the girl Marion, who is a still greater martyr than Tess, by the revelation of maternity and the glory of the new life. But the philosophy of enlightenment and the *fin de siècle* has nothing to do with such imaginations. Naturally a new creed must treat such a situation in a new way, especially when the principles of that creed are indignation (against whom? unhandsomely we are given to understand that it is against God—but then when there is no God?) and wrath, and have no sympathy with the everlasting reconstruction which another philosophy perceives to be going on for ever in the moral as well as in the material world. Mr. Hardy scornfully admits the possibility that the downfall of poor Tess may have been 'a retribution' —it being 'a morality good enough for divinities', though 'scorned by average human nature', to visit the sins of the fathers upon the children. 'Doubtless some of Tess D'Urberville's mailed ancestors, rollicking home from a fray, had dealt the same wrong even more ruthlessly upon peasant girls of their time': but he does not allow any return in the processes of nature. This silly cant is very unworthy of any man acquainted with the secrets of the heart, and versed were it ever so little in those great problems of humanity which it is the occupation of the poet to fathom; but it is 'the height of the fashion', and we know how in the lower walks of life fashion is exaggerated, so that perhaps Mr. Hardy, as an exponent of peasant life, feels himself justified in going a little further than the commonest of sense permits. His unfortunate young mother is compelled to look upon her poor baby in a different and original way from all previous sufferers of her kind. She holds it on her lap in the reaping-field, 'and looking into the far distance, dandled it with a gloomy indifference that was almost dislike: then all of a sudden she fell to violently kissing it some dozens of times, as if she would never leave off, the child crying at the vehemence of an onset which strangely combined passionateness with contempt'.

The moralizings which follow when the unfortunate baby dies are equally remarkable. Tess is in despair, not for the loss of her child but chiefly about its salvation. 'Like all village girls, she was well grounded in the Holy Scriptures, and she had carefully studied the histories of Aholah and Aholibah, and knew the inferences to be drawn therefrom.' Mr. Hardy, perhaps not having had Tess's advantages in this way, probably believes that these are historical personages like Ruth and Esther. We do not ourselves know Wessex, which is clearly in every way a most remarkable province, and therefore cannot affirm that village girls there do not study diligently the prophecies of Ezekiel: but we certainly have not in any other quarter of the world encountered any who did. But Tess's studies were more enlarged and remarkable still. 'She thought of the child consigned to the nethermost corner of hell, as its double doom for lack of baptism and lack of legitimacy; saw the *arch-fiend tossing it with his three-pronged fork* like the one they used for heating the oven on baking days; to which picture she added many other quaint and curious details of torment taught the young in this Christian country.' Now, so far as we are aware, except, perhaps, in some quaint piece of medieval divinity still less likely to have fallen under Tess's notice than ours, the arch-fiend with the three-pronged toasting-fork (it is well to be particular), with which she was so familiar as to think that it was like the one used for heating the oven, occurs in certain grim passages of the *Inferno*, but in no more popular reading. We have admitted that we have less faith in the Sixth Standard than Mr. Hardy, but it seems probable that we spoke in ignorance. Has it come to that, that Dante is taught and familiarly studied in our

village schools? No wonder in that case that to pass the Sixth Standard
should be a high test of a liberal education. But we cannot help fearing
that Mr. Hardy has here incautiously muddled up the views of the poet
with those of the Catechism. We have known this done with Milton,
whose scenes and conversations in Heaven have furnished many excellent persons with details unknown to Holy Scripture. However, we
don't really blame the author of *Tess* for getting confused in his
theology. He is not a religious Reformer like Mrs. Humphry Ward.
Theological teaching is not his forte; but then, heaven be praised! the
noble art of story-telling is—if he could but forget the very unlovely
cant of his time.

The next division of the story begins with something very different
from this dreary stuff. It is the picture of the great dairy to which Tess,
free of all encumbrances, her baby dead and oblivion closing over all
her trouble, goes as 'a skilful milkmaid', 'between two and three years
after her return from Trantridge'. She must now have been, therefore,
between eighteen and nineteen, and a most accomplished woman; for
not only did she know *au fond* the prophecies of Ezekiel and the *Inferno*
of Dante, but she had been at sixteen an expert poultry-woman, and
now was an exceptional milkmaid, so that her gifts in every way were
great. In addition to which she was beautiful—not ruddy and buxom
as a country girl, but with the beauty of ancient ancestry and noble
blood. The establishment into which she is received is idyllic, and
nothing can be more vivid, living, and actual than the great farm, with
its innumerable cows, its rustic patriarch at the head, the pretty maids
all a-row, the fringe of rougher men. There is, however, a serpent in
this Eden—though it is no vicious person, no deceiver or rustic profligate like poor Tess's previous master, but a gentleman of the last and
most painful degree of refinement, studying farming in preparation for
emigrating, an Agnostic, a musician, a philosopher, and every other
superfine thing that can be conceived. 'Mr. Angel Clare—he that is
learning milking, and that plays the harp'—is how one of the ordinary
milkmaids describes him. We do not know whether it is usual for an
intending farmer to learn milking, but we are sure that it is not at all
usual for a young man of the nineteenth century to carry a harp about
with him, which is an inconvenient piece of luggage. Emily did it in
the *Mysteries of Udolpho*, but she is, we think, the last person in fiction
who inconvenienced herself in this way, and, on second thoughts, we
believe it was a lute, which resembles a guitar, we believe, and is much
more handy to carry about. However, it is perhaps not less unlikely

that a parson's son in Wessex should carry a harp about with him, than that he should be called Angel Clare. He is truly worthy of the name, being the most curious thing in the shape of a man whom we think we have ever met with—at least out of a young lady's novel. We can at our ease gently deride David Grieve for being feminine, for he is the creation of a lady. But before Mr. Angel Clare we stand aghast. What is he? Had he, too, been framed by a woman, how we should have smiled and pointed out his impossibility! This is how a man looks to the guileless feminine imagination, we should have said. But before the name of Mr. Hardy we can only gasp and be silent. The thing must be male, we suppose, since a man made it, and it is certainly original as a picture of a man. Let us, however, without lingering upon this pale image, put forth one of those pictures of which Mr. Hardy has the secret when he chooses to use the hues of nature. It is needless to say that poor Tess finds her doom in the superfine pupil, and that they soon begin to fall in love with each other.

[quotes ch. XX 'Dairyman Crick's household' to 'other women of the world.']

This wonderful piece of landscape speaks for itself. That the man who can do it should waste his gifts in echoing the mean prose of fashionable philosophy fills one's soul with impatience. However, we have said enough on this subject.

Tess falls in love with Angel Clare; and he, so far as such a vision can, loves her, and asks her to marry him. We may say, however, that all the milkmaids are, as one woman, in love with the gentleman–pupil, and the spectacle of these daughters of the fields, in their fullness of flesh and blood, weeping upon each other's bosoms without jealousy, but with a passion which makes one, alas! take to drinking, and another try to drown herself, when the die is cast, is exceedingly Hardyish, and just a very little grotesque, though also touching. It is idyllic—with a twist—and pretty, yet apt at moments to be laughable. Tess is brought to a sudden pause and horror by her lover's proposal, and declares it to be impossible; but gradually is brought round, though always with the certainty that she must tell him what her antecedents have been. One knows how difficult even in real life it is to make a confession much less serious than this—and in fiction it is inevitable that all the difficulties should be increased. So that the fated days run on, and Tess does not tell. One practical difficulty arises here, which Mr. Hardy does not seem to think of. The dairy-farm is not more than a walk, though a long one, from Tess's home. Wessex is a very primitive country, we allow, and there seem to have been no railways within reach; but is it possible that, at a distance of twenty miles at the most, no whisper of such a story should have reached the large rural household with all its connections—every milkmaid and every man having her and his separate ways of hearing the country gossip? The scene of poor Tess's downfall, her home, the churchyard which contains her infant's grave, are all within easy reach—the dairyman is a connection of her mother's —and yet nobody has heard of that episode in her life. This, we think, is a little remarkable. It is like Alec D'Urberville's horse, a phenomenon in rustic life.

However, the terrible intelligence is only conveyed to Clare on the evening of the wedding-day, after he himself has made a confession of a similar description to Tess, which of course she forgives at once, and, emboldened, proceeds to tell him. Then, equally of course, the insufferable being whom Mr. Hardy has set up as a man and an Agnostic proves what stuff he is made of, and flings his bride from him. He becomes immediately a compound of ice and iron. Pity is not in him, nor understanding, nor common-sense, nor, least of all, love. He hears with his ears the piteous plea, and sees the extreme youth, the profound humiliation, the heartrending shame of the poor girl whom he has persecuted into marrying him, and whose trembling objections and terrors he has up to this moment refused to listen to. The best man would no doubt have been hard put to it to endure such a shock; but this being is supposed to know all the secrets of rural life, and the point of view of the children of the fields, yet no consideration, no tenderness nor humanity, is in him. He deserts the unhappy girl without a struggle —leaving her from that moment to herself. 'Tess', he said as gently and as civilly as he could speak, 'I cannot stay in the room with you.' Now, Mr. Hardy is strong on the injustice of the fact that 'the woman pays', but he never makes this injustice apparent to his hero. Nor does he apparently disapprove of Clare's action, or of the remorseless abandonment of his heroine, which of course is required by the exigencies of the story.

We need not follow poor Tess in her abandonment. Clare sets off for Brazil, as the farthest point possible, we suppose, and every kind of misfortune happens to lure her on to the fatal conclusion. Her father dies, and the burden of her mother's family falls upon her. She drops out of the prosperous milkmaid condition into the roughest work of the fields, giving room for more and yet more telling descriptions of rural operations. Then Alec D'Urberville comes once more across her path, the destroyer of her youth. He is a revivalist preacher when she sees him next, having been, with grotesque particularity, brought to repentance of his sins by the ministrations of Angel Clare's Low Church father; but Tess changes all that in a moment, partly by the mere sight of her, and partly by her repetition of Mr. Angel's arguments against revelation, which are so potent (Mr. Hardy wisely does not state them, but only tells us the effect, historically) that D'Urberville flings his religion to the winds, and begins a systematic pursuit of his former victim. He is ready to marry her, but that, of course, is impossible: he shows himself, however, the Providence of her family, and the matter ends as—everything we have been made to understand concerning Tess forbids us to believe that it could do. When Clare finally becomes ashamed of himself and returns home, he hunts down his wife in seaside lodgings and fine clothes with D'Urberville. She has a wild interview with him in her beautiful dressing-gown; then rushes upstairs to the room in which she has left her lover, stabs him in his bed with the carving-knife, which has been put ready to cut the cold ham for breakfast, laid out in their sitting-room, and, rushing after her husband, joins him—for a brief honeymoon of passion and mad love and enjoyment. Clare, who behaved so brutally to her when he heard of the distant sin of her youth, for which she was so little to blame, receives her out of the arms of the other without a moment's hesitation; and Tess, who, according to any natural interpretation, and of all we know of her, must have died of shame rather than meet the eyes of her husband clothed in the embroideries of the nightgown, which Mr. Hardy does not spare us—forgets every tradition of natural purity, and passes from one to another as if, which indeed she says, the murder had made all right.

We have not a word to say against the force and passion of this story. It is far finer in our opinion than anything Mr. Hardy has ever done before. The character of Tess up to her last downfall, with the curious exceptions we have pointed out, is consistent enough, and we do not object to the defiant blazon of a Pure Woman, notwithstanding the early stain. But a Pure Woman is not betrayed into fine living and fine clothes as the mistress of her seducer by any stress of poverty or misery; and Tess was a skilled labourer, for whom it is very rare that nothing can be found to do. Here the elaborate and indignant plea for Vice, that it is really Virtue, breaks down altogether. We do not for a moment believe that Tess would have done it. Her creator has forced the *rôle* upon her, as he thinks (or says) that the God whom he does not believe in, does—which ought to make him a little more humble, since he cannot, it appears, do better himself. But whatever Mr. Hardy says, we repeat that we do not believe him. The lodgings at the seaside, drawing-room floor; 'the rich cashmere dressing-gown of grey white, embroidered in half mourning tints'; 'the walking costume of a well-to-do young lady', with a veil over her black hat and feathers; her 'silk stockings' and 'ivory parasol',—are not the accessories of purity, but the trappings of vice. Tess would have flung them out of the window. She would not have stabbed Mr. Alec D'Urberville, her potential husband, with the carving-knife intended for the cold ham (which, besides, awakens all sorts of questions, as—why did Alec D'Urberville, a strong young man, allow himself to be stabbed? and how did it happen that the lodging-house carving-knife, not usually a very sharp instrument, was capable of such a blow?), but have turned him head and shoulders out of the poorest cottage in which he had insulted her with such a proposition. It is no use making men and women for us, and then forcing them to do the last thing possible to their nature. If Tess did this, then Tess, after all her developments, was at twenty a much inferior creature to the unawakened Tess at sixteen who would not live upon the wages of iniquity; and thus two volumes of analysis and experience are lost, and the end is worse than the beginning—which, after watching Tess through these two volumes, and following the progress of her thoughts much more articulately than she could have done herself, we absolutely decline to believe. Whoever that person was who went straight from the endearments of Alec D'Urberville to those of the Clare Angel or the Angel Clare, whatever the image is called, Mr. Hardy must excuse us for saying pointedly and firmly that she was not Tess; neither was she a Pure Woman. This is the portion of the book which was served up to keen appetites in the Reviews, and we rejoice to think that it was so. Let the cultivated reader keep the nastiness for which it seems he longs. We are delighted to find ourselves on the side of the honest lover of a story who requires no strong stimulation of criminality thrown in against all the possibilities of natural life.

Mr. Hardy's indignant anti-religion becomes occasionally very droll, if not amusing. Against whom is he so angry? Against 'the divinities', who are so immoral—who punish the vices of the fathers on the children? Against God?—who does not ask us whether we wish to be created; who gives us but one chance, etc. But then, if there is no God?

Why, in that case, should Mr. Hardy be angry? We know one man of fine mind whom we have always described as being angry with God for not existing. Is this perhaps Mr. Hardy's case? But then he ought not to put the blame of the evils which do exist upon this imaginary Being who does not.

45. Mowbray Morris, 'Culture and Anarchy,' *Quarterly Review*

April 1892, clxxiv, 319–26

Mowbray Morris edited *Macmillan's Magazine* from 1885 to 1907: in that capacity he had refused *Tess* for serial publication. For consideration here the book was grouped with Shorthouse's *Blanche, Lady Falaise* and Mrs. Humphry Ward's *David Grieve*. After a general introduction, *Tess* is taken first. See Introduction, p. xxx for Hardy's reactions.

As even the freshest of these books is now some three months old, it will be well perhaps to preface our explanation with a summary of their respective contents. In this busy curious time of ours, unresting like the star, but not like it unhasting, it would be unfair to presume too much on our readers' memories. Books die even faster than they are born; and we greatly doubt whether anyone who read these three on their first publication could give a clear account of them now; of two out of the three, indeed, it had been no easy matter to give a clear account within half-an-hour after turning the last page. And on this occasion we shall waive the good old rule of precedence to ladies, and give first place to Mr. Hardy. In truth, as a work of fiction, if not as a piece of literary composition, it is the only one that on its merits would be worth serious consideration at all.

We are required to read the story of Tess (or Theresa) Durbeyfield as the story of 'A pure woman faithfully presented by Thomas Hardy'. Compliance with this request entails something of a strain upon the English language. Mr. Squeers once with perfect justice observed that there was no Act of Parliament which could prevent a man from calling his house an island if it pleased him to do so. It is indisputably open to Mr. Hardy to call his heroine a pure woman; but he has no less certainly offered many inducements to his readers to refuse her the name. Told plainly and without sentiment, the story is to this effect. Tess is a pretty village-girl who is seduced by a small squire in the neighbourhood. In due course a child is born and dies, and the mother betakes herself to another part of the country where she is unknown, and where her misadventure is therefore unlikely to debar her from employment. This she finds at a large dairy-farm; but she finds there also a certain Angel Clare, the son of an Evangelical parson, a young gentleman of crude notions and an amorous temperament, who, unable to gratify his father by taking Orders so long as the Church 'refuses to liberate her mind from an untenable redemptive theolatry', takes instead to studying the habits of cows and the art of milking, and to strumming on a harp between whiles. He has already filled the hearts of the three other dairy-maids in the story with a hopeless passion, but to the charms of Tess he falls a ready victim. She refuses him more than once, conceiving herself, after that little affair on the other side of the country, no fit subject for honest wedlock; but in the end she relents and becomes his wife. She has always intended to explain to him the reasons of her refusal, but can never quite screw her courage to the sticking-place. But on the evening of her marriage-day, emboldened by the revelation of sundry little peccadilloes on his own part, she makes her confession. It has a result she did not anticipate. Angel does not recognize the parallel between their cases that seems so clear to her. This is perhaps not altogether surprising, but his mode of explanation is certainly one of the most surprising things in literature. 'Forgive me [she cries to him] as you are forgiven! *I* forgive *you*, Angel.' 'You— yes, you do.' 'But you do not forgive me?' 'Forgiveness does not apply to the case. You were one person, now you are another. How can forgiveness meet such a grotesque prestidigitation as that?' Considering all the circumstances of the scene we take this to be one of the most unconsciously comical sentences ever read in print. Mrs. Ward has with great truth (and the most surprising frankness!) observed in her book that Dissent kills the sense of humour. Mr. Hardy is not the first to prove that to other things than Dissent belongs this fatal power. But to . resume. Angel is obdurate. He provides his wife with a sum of money, and his parents' address that she may apply for more when she needs it, and departs for Brazil. On his first stage (in a dog-cart) to that remote land he encounters one of the heart-broken dairy-maids, and promptly engages her to accompany him on his travels in lieu of his discarded wife. The girl, who admits that she loves him 'down to the ground', asks for nothing better; but the mercurial Angel repents of his offer as suddenly as he has made it, adjures the disappointed victim of his charms to think of him 'as a worthless lover but a true friend', turns her out of the dog-cart, and drives off to Brazil alone. Tess for a time behaves in a manner sufficient to satisfy the most exacting husband. But her money fails, employment is hard to find and scantily paid; her appeals to her husband are unanswered, and she is too proud to apply to his parents. In her sorest need she encounters her seducer, who has now developed a fancy for itinerant preaching, but in whom the sight of Tess (his 'dear witch of Babylon' with the 'most maddening mouth since Eve') at once awakens the original and unregenerate Adam. He proposes a renewal of their former relations, to which, after some decent hesitation, Tess consents. Meanwhile in far Brazil trouble, need, sickness, and other infirmities, aided by the conversation of a casual stranger, have worked a change in Angel also. His passion revives; after all, he reminds himself, 'Was not the gleaning of the grapes of Ephraim better than the vintage of Abi-Ezer?' He returns to England, but too late. He tracks his wife to the watering-place of Sandbourne, only to find her living in luxury with the degenerate field-preacher. Husband and wife meet at last—he worn with hardship and illness to a mere yellow skeleton; she 'bewilderingly otherwise' than he had expected to find her, more beautiful than ever, in a rich cashmere dressing-gown with embroidered slippers to match, and her brown hair dishevelled, as of one newly-risen from bed—certainly in more senses than one a bewildering vision to an expectant husband. Not unnaturally he asks her, 'How do you get to be like this?'—but he asks also for her forgiveness. 'I did not think rightly of you—I did not see you as you were!' he pleads. 'I do now, dearest Tessy, mine!' But she explains that it is too late, that she is no longer his, that there are obstacles—or at least one obstacle, in bed upstairs—to a complete reunion; and she implores him to 'Go away, Angel, please, and never come any more!' He goes; but he has not gone far when he is joined by his wife, in a walking-dress of the latest fashion with an ivory-handled parasol. She has removed the obstacle by the simple expedient of stabbing it to the heart with a carving-knife as it lay in bed ('I owed it to 'ee and to myself', she observes), and is once more her own Angel's unfettered wife. They enjoy a brief but blissful honeymoon, first in an empty house in the New Forest, then amid the ruins of Stonehenge. In this last, and somewhat draughty, bridal-chamber the officers of justice surprise them. Tess is tried, found guilty, sentenced, and hanged, imploring Angel with almost her last breath to marry her sister, who is growing, she assures him, into a beautiful girl, and with whom she is quite willing to share her husband 'When we are spirits'.

It is a queer story and seems to have been published in a queer manner. The bulk of it originally made its appearance (with some slight modifications) in an illustrated weekly paper; but some chapters, which Mr. Hardy distinguishes as 'most especially addressed to adult readers' had to be relegated (as 'episodic sketches') to other periodicals whose editors presumably take a more liberal view of their duties towards their neighbours, or whose readers are more habitually adult. Finally, with the modifications made good and the episodic sketches restored to their appointed places, the whole work was issued in the orthodox three volumes. Putting the sense of the ridiculous and the sense of self-respect out of the question, one might have thought that a writer who entertains such grandiose views of the mission of the novelist would see something derogatory in this hole-and-corner form of publication. It recalls the amusing stories one used to read in the papers, before Mr. Balfour had succeeded in bringing Ireland back to some part of its senses, of the straits the Nationalist orators were put to to get rid of their speeches, letting off a few words here and a few words there wherever and whenever they could momentarily escape the vigilance of the police. However, it is not our business to object to a process in which so stern a champion of the novelist's art can see no shame, nor to talk of self-respect to a writer who has evidently no respect for others. Mr. Hardy assures us that 'The story is sent out in all sincerity of purpose, as representing on the whole a true sequence of things'. We have no wish to doubt him, but we could wish that he had made his qualifying phrase clearer by explaining where the sequence of things was not true; without this knowledge his purpose must necessarily remain somewhat doubtful. Is it in the episodic sketches, and the passages that his first editor requested him to modify, that the sequence departs from the straight road of truth? This doubt, we say, throws none on Mr. Hardy's sincerity, yet it cannot but throw some on his purpose. When Tess removes the obstacle with a carving-knife, the sincerity of her purpose is unquestionable; but that unfortunately in the existing state of the law only makes matters worse for her. For the first half of his story the reader may indeed conceive it to have been Mr. Hardy's design to show how a woman essentially honest and pure at heart will, through the adverse shocks of fate, eventually rise to higher things. But if this were his original purpose he must have forgotten it before his tale was told, or perhaps the 'true sequence of things' was too strong for him. For what are the higher things to which this poor creature eventually rises? She rises through seduction to adultery, murder, and the gallows. Higher than the gallows, indeed, this frail nature of ours is often incapable of rising while lodged in its earthly tenement. That is the humour of it! Again, it would appear from the opening scenes that the author had it in his mind to illustrate the great principle of Heredity which, as we all know, is, like a man called Habakkuk, capable of everything. His heroine's father, tipsy, ineffectual old Jack Durbeyfield the haggler, is, it seems, the lineal descendant of an ancient and knightly race of Norman warriors who once held large possessions in the West Country. This is, we suppose, designed to account for a certain superiority claimed (though not very clearly proved) for Tess over her rustic associates: it is this that despite her education and surroundings makes her essentially a 'pure woman'; and perhaps it is this also that has familiarized her with the prophecies of Ezekiel and the poetry of Dante, subjects which are unlikely to play a conspicuous part in the meditations of a village beauty of less exalted lineage. But here again the author's purpose obviously breaks down. The Tess of Mr. Hardy's inner consciousness is as much a creature of fantasy as Titania or Fenella. Some such lass may, for aught we know, have herded pigs or dug potatoes in the mystical hamlet of Auburn, but assuredly she never drew breath in any fields trod by human foot. Yet even when thus gloriously free from sense and the reality of things, Mr. Hardy cannot keep true to his own ideals; *desinit in piscem*, his maid of honour ends in a mermaid's tail. A girl unconsciously raised by the mixture of gentle blood in her veins to a higher level of thought and feeling would never have acted as Tess acted. Deserted by her husband, with all the world, as she conceived, against her, she might have joined her fortunes with some man she could love and respect; she would never have gone back at the first opportunity to her seducer, a coarse sensual brute for whom she had never professed to feel anything but dislike and contempt.

Considering the book then, with our necessarily imperfect knowledge, it seems only that Mr. Hardy has told an extremely disagreeable story in an extremely disagreeable manner, which is not rendered less so by his affectation of expounding a great moral law, or by the ridiculous character of some of the scenes into which this affectation plunges the reader. No one who remembers how Mr. Hardy used to write in his earlier and happier moods, can accuse him of having been born without the sense of humour. But his assumption of the garb of the moral teacher would appear to have destroyed his relish for this salt of life. Even then it surpasses our comprehension how any man who had once known its taste could have penned that impossible episode where the three green-sick dairy-maids, in their scant white night-gowns, sit shivering on end in their beds, 'like a row of avenging ghosts', to gaze with reproachful admiration on their successful rival. Of course, as the scene is laid in the author's favourite Wessex, the reader is pleased with many charming natural descriptions, with many clever sketches of village life and humours. Mr. Hardy's rustics have always, it is true, had a smack of caricature about them; but they have generally been extremely amusing caricatures, and founded, moreover, as Dickens's are founded, on the essential facts of humanity. While for his powers of description, only Charles Kingsley and Mr. Blackmore have rivalled, we will not even of them say surpassed, him in bringing that beautiful West Country home to us; and there are passages in these three volumes equal to the best he has yet done in that way. But it is hard to conceive what further pleasure a wholesome-minded reader will find in this book. Not long since Mr. Hardy published in one of the magazines his recipe for renewing the youth of fiction, which he conceived, and not without justice, to have grown, like Doll Tearsheet, 'sick of a calm'. The national taste and the national genius have returned, he said, to the great tragic motives so greatly handled by the dramatists of the Periclean and Elizabethan ages. But the national genius perceives also that these tragic motives 'Demand enrichment by further truths— in other words, original treatment; treatment which seeks to show Nature's unconsciousness, not of essential laws, but those laws framed merely as social expedients by humanity, without a basis in the heart of things'. Here, it will be observed, Mr. Hardy speaks only, and prudently, for himself as representing the national genius, being evidently conscious that the national taste might decline his interpretation. But was there ever such foolish talking? Mr. Hardy must have read the dramatists of the Periclean and Elizabethan ages very carelessly, or have strangely forgotten them, if he conceives that there is any analogy between their great handling of great tragic motives and this clumsy sordid tale of boorish brutality and lust. Has the common feeling of humanity against seduction, adultery, and murder no basis in the heart of things? It is the very foundation of human society. In the explanatory note from which we have already quoted, a sentence of St. Jerome's is offered as a sop to 'Any too genteel reader who cannot endure to have it said what everybody thinks and feels'. Does everybody then think and feel that seduction, adultery, and murder have their basis in the heart of things, that they are the essential laws of Nature? If Mr. Hardy's apology means anything at all, it can mean only that. His apology is, in truth, as much beside the mark as the sentence from St. Jerome with which he thinks to enforce it: 'If an offence come out of the truth, better is it that the offence come than that the truth be concealed.' Now this—and here we must be excused for plain speaking —this is pure cant, and that worst form of cant which takes its stand on a mischievous reading of the old aphorism, 'To the pure all things are pure'. St. Jerome's argument would be a good one enough to salve the conscience of a delicate-minded witness in a court of law, who in the interests of truth might be required to speak of inconvenient things. It is absolutely no argument for a novelist who, in his own interests, has gratuitously chosen to tell a coarse and disagreeable story in a coarse and disagreeable manner.

As we have found fault with Mr. Hardy's manner, equally with his subject, we must spare a few words to that. Coarse it is not, in the sense of employing coarse words; indeed he is too apt to affect a certain preciosity of phrase which has a somewhat incongruous effect in a tale of rustic life; he is too fond—and the practice has been growing on him through all his later books—of writing like a man 'who has been at a great feast of languages and stolen the scraps', or, in plain English, of making experiments in a form of language which he does not seem clearly to understand, and in a style for which he was assuredly not born. It is a pity, for Mr. Hardy had a very good style of his own once, and one moreover excellently suited to the subjects he knew and was then content to deal with. The coarseness and disagreeableness of his present manner come from within rather than from without. That they come unconsciously we most willingly believe; indeed it would be only charity to suppose that they come from an inherent failure in the instinct for good taste, and a lack of the intellectual cultivation that can sometimes avail to supply its place, added to a choice of subject which must always be fatal to an author, no matter what his other gifts may be, who has not those two safeguards. But whatever be their origin, there they are and must be apparent to the simplest reader. To borrow a familiar phrase, Mr. Hardy never fails to put the dots on all his i's, he never leaves you in doubt as to his meaning. Poor Tess's sensual qualifications for the part of heroine are paraded over and over again with a persistence like that of a horse-dealer egging on some wavering customer to a deal, or a slave-dealer appraising his wares to some full-blooded pasha. We shall not illustrate our meaning; there are more than enough chapters in the three volumes to make it only too clear. The shadow of the goddess Aselgeia broods over the whole book. It darkens the sunny landscape of the Froom valley equally with the poultry-farm and gardens of the Slopes, the silent glades of the Chase with the seaside villa at Sandbourne; for Angel Clare is as much a prey to its influence as Alec D'Urberville, and the three dairy-maids as much as Tess. From first to last his book recalls the terrible sentence passed by Wordsworth on 'Wilhelm Meister': 'It is like the crossing of flies in the air.'

46. W. P. Trent, 'The Novels of Thomas Hardy', *Sewanee Review*

November 1892, i, 1

W. P. Trent (1862–1939), historian and literary scholar, professor of English at Columbia University after 1900, was at this time a professor at the University of the South at Sewanee, Tennessee. He was one of the founders of the *Sewanee Review*, which he edited for seven years.

. . . It is time, however, as our author uses 'I' with the greatest infrequency in his writings, to pass to a consideration of his novels in detail, and of his general characteristics as a writer of fiction.

A man of letters is himself often a good critic of his own youthful work, and so Mr. Hardy fairly sums up the defects of *Desperate Remedies*, when he says of it in the 'Prefatory Note' appended to its re-issue in 1889: 'The principles observed in its composition are, no doubt, too exclusively those in which mystery, entanglement, surprise and moral obliquity are depended on for exciting interest.' In other words, Mr. Hardy means to say that he had fallen under the spell of that wonderful weaver of plots, Wilkie Collins. But Collins in his best work avoided the mistake into which his follower fell, of failing to observe a due proportion between the mystery and entanglement of his plot and the value, that is the interest, of his characters and their actions. We do not like to be perplexed or mystified about people unless we are greatly interested in them, and with the possible exception of the steward Manston, there are no very interesting characters in *Desperate Remedies*.

The plot is too intricate to be given here in detail. There are marriages that are no marriages, there is a murder, there is an illegitimate son of an aristocratic mother, there is a beautiful love-sick heroine who gets into every sort of trouble, and a love-sick hero who plays detective and gets her out. In short, we have all the materials for a story eminently suitable for the *New York Ledger*, materials put together in a very artificial way, but in a way that excites and interests the reader to his heart's content. But the question immediately occurs, if a man of thirty-one could seriously occupy himself in developing such a plot, how was it that he ever succeeded in writing a great novel? An answer is easily found. An ultra-sensational novel with a mixed-up plot and an artificial method of presentation does not necessarily mean an unpromising volume. When such a novel is written in a style which is at once recognized as individual in its simplicity, its strength, its grace; when it is found to be distinguished by passages and scenes of rare descriptive power; when its author, time and again dazzles us with a flashing simile or an exquisitely poetic epithet; when he not infrequently lets drop a pearl of wisdom which no swine save skimming readers can possibly be found to spurn; when to crown all he takes an impassive peasant and makes him talk as though nobody were near to overhear him; then we may well feel sure that our novice in authorship gropes only because he is seeking for a method and that he is not unlikely to find one.

That all the above promising traits were to be found in *Desperate Remedies* by a careful reader of 1871 will not, we think, be disputed by the careful reader of 1892. Of course such a proposition cannot be definitely established in an article like the present, but the book is easily accessible, and the accuracy of our statement can be tested. We feel inclined, however, to support ourselves by at least one quotation:

His clothes are something exterior to every man; but to a woman her dress is part of her body. Its motions are all present to her intelligence if not to her eyes; no man knows how his coat-tails swing. By the slightest hyperbole it may be said that her dress has sensation. Crease but the very Ultima Thule of fringe or flounce, and it hurts her as much as pinching her. Delicate antennæ, or feelers bristle on every outlying frill. Go to the uppermost: she is there; tread on the lowest: the fair creature is there almost before you.

Under the Greenwood Tree is a year-long rural idyl, as simple in its plot as *Desperate Remedies* is complex. The nine chapters of the first part entitled 'Winter', are taken up with a wonderfully humorous description of the old-fashioned wind-instrument choir of the parish of Mellstock trudging around on Christmas night to serenade every dweller in the parish, and with an equally humorous description of the party given by honest Reuben Dewy, the tranter, or wagoner. The other parts, named after the other seasons, commemorate the love of Dick Dewy, the tranter's son, for Fancy Day, the village schoolmistress—a love which ends in the most typical of rural weddings, in spite of the fact that the young rector himself is somewhat smitten with the fair schoolmistress who plays the first organ set up in the parish church. The despair of the old choir at the advent of this organ and their visit to the rector in expostulation are described with a humour that puts Mr. Hardy alongside of Dickens if not, as some think, above him. Obviously no quotation can do justice to the exquisite truth to nature, to the simplicity, the humour, the genial charm of this idyl which is as much above most genre sketches of the modern school as a representative poem of Wordsworth's is above the best effusion of Bryant. The fresh smell of woods and fields blows through the all but poetic pages; like Antaeus the reader rises up refreshed from a touch of mother earth. Mr. Hardy has at last learned his method. He reproduces nature, whether in flower, or tree, or cloud, or field, or man—not the man of streets and parlours—but the man of the fields, who is as much a natural object as a tree or a boulder—yet his method of reproduction is not that of the photographer, but of the painter. He is realistic, but at the same time idealistic; in other words, he is an artist, and the subtitle of his book, 'A Rural Painting of the Dutch School', does not belie its qualities.

223

We said above that Mr. Hardy is as humorous as Dickens, and we appealed to the description of the choir's visit to the rectory in proof of the assertion. As this scene takes up a whole chapter, it must remain unquoted, but who could fail to quote a few paragraphs from the chapter describing Dick Dewy's first visit to the house of his sweetheart's father, Geoffrey Day, in the depths of Yalbury wood? Geoffrey and Dick and Fancy, the sweet link between them, are seated at the noon-day meal. Mrs. Day the second is bustling about overhead preparing to make a disagreeable descent upon the party below. The conversation meanwhile has turned on matrimony.

'If we are doomed to marry, we marry; if we are doomed to remain single, we do;' replied Dick.

Geoffrey had by this time sat down again, and he now made his lips thin by severely straining them across his gums, and looked out of the fireplace window to the end of the paddock with solemn scrutiny. 'That's not the case with some folk,' he said at length, as if he read the words on a board at the farther end of the paddock.

Fancy looked interested, and Dick said 'No?'

'There's that wife o' mine. It was her doom not to be nobody's wife at all in the wide universe. But she made up her mind that she would, and did it twice over. Doom? Doom is nothing beside an elderly woman—quite a chiel in her hands.'

A Pair of Blue Eyes, Mr. Hardy's third novel, gives the heart history of a rather susceptible but very charming young lady, Miss Elfride Swancourt, who, by the way, is said to be unpopular with her own sex. It has at least one strong character, Henry Knight, the reviewer, Elfride's second lover. It contains also one very powerful scene, the rescue of Knight from the cliff through the heroism and presence of mind of Elfride. It is not only an interesting story, but a very subtle study of feminine instincts, yet although a successful novel as a whole, it can hardly be placed among our author's masterpieces. The last scene of all in which Elfride's two disappointed lovers encounter her husband at her tomb, is pathetic in the extreme.

Far from the Madding Crowd has already been described as inferior only to *Tess of the D'Urbervilles*. It combines all the charm of *Under the Greenwood Tree* with more than the power and interest of *Desperate Remedies*. It is the first work to prove that Mr. Hardy possesses the power of creating characters that live. Farmer Oak, the faithful, modest, sensible hero, is a character that no one can forget, a nobler, a longer lived character, perhaps, than even Adam Bede. Joseph Poorgrass, Mr. Hardy's masterpiece in the way of peasant characters, is a personage whom Fielding would not have disdained to create—Fielding who in the creation of characters is the Zeus of English novelists. Bathsheba Everdene, the heroine—Mr. Hardy disdains to give his heroines common names thereby linking himself to the romancers— Farmer Boldwood, Sergeant Troy, the maltster, are all excellent in their way, although inferior to the two first mentioned. But with his advance in characterization, Mr. Hardy does not fall behind, nay rather, he advances in his other qualities. Never has the life of the farm and the sheepfold been more truthfully or more charmingly described; never has the homely picturesqueness of the English peasant received so attractive a setting. The humour that welled up in *Under the Greenwood Tree*, flows here in a full stream, witness Joseph Poorgrass drunk in the public house testifying to the evils of the affliction known as 'a multiplying eye'—an affliction which had a way of always coming on when he had been in a public house a little while, as he meekly confessed to Shepherd Oak. In style, too, Mr. Hardy has improved. He has become more practised in his use of that noble instrument, the prose of his native tongue. There is less straining for effect, there is less dependence upon the aid of a flashing figure or epithet; in other words, there is more Sophoclean roundedness, and less Æschylean pointedness than in his earlier works.

But—and without this *Far from the Madding Crowd* would not be a great novel—there is a human interest about this story which lifts it above its predecessors. Human interest is a term used by some writers with reference to passion rather than to action, but we here use it inclusively. It is to be remarked, however, that for a novel or a romance to be truly inspiring, the human interest that emerges from passion or suffering should not predominate. Men and women must act their parts, in the true sense of the phrase, in a novel as well as on the stage; and unless one character acts a great part, or some of the characters combine to act a great part, the novel must often fail of truly inspiring its readers. Now Farmer Oak, though in a modest way, does live a great life and act a great part, and Bathsheba Everdene and Farmer Boldwood, if they do not live great lives, nevertheless go through fires of affliction that try their souls and lend them an inevitable interest. Hence it is that we place this novel among the few great novels of our generation—because even 'far from the madding crowd' Mr. Hardy has seen that there is something more than the life of plant, and stone, and stream, something more than the animal life of Joseph

Poorgrass and his kind—the life of men who love greatly, and endure greatly, and dare greatly like Shepherd Oak, the life of women who pass through Sloughs of Despond to reach at last the Delectable Mountains like Bathsheba Everdene.

The Hand of Ethelberta (1876) was described by its author as 'A Comedy in Chapters'. It bears out fairly well the claims of its sub-title. The heroine, Ethelberta, is a butler's daughter, who, having been educated above her station, marries a young, wealthy, and well-born husband and is soon left a fashionable widow. She now essays the difficult rôle of moving in polite society while still preserving secret relations with her family. Her sister becomes her maid, her brother her footman, and once she is actually waited on at a dinner party by her father, the butler. Naturally such a plot furnishes Mr. Hardy with much opportunity for delicate satire on fashionable society as well as for indulging in his accustomed humour. Ethelberta publishes poems, recites her own stories, loves a poor gentleman, is wooed by several eligible suitors, and finally marries a worn-out peer. If it were not that she gets the upper hand of her old husband and is enabled to lift up and support her family the end of the story would be tragic, rather than comic; but, viewed as a whole, it is an amusing comedy which deserves more popularity than it seems to have had. Certainly Mr. Hardy has drawn few more interesting characters than his 'squirrel haired' Ethelberta.

Two years later, 1878, appeared the book which some regard as our author's masterpiece, but to which we are inclined to give the third place among his works—*The Return of the Native*. Here again we have a rural setting and a powerful and moving plot. The characters, too, are striking and well drawn, and one of them, Clym Yeobright, the hero, just misses greatness. Unlike Mr. Hardy's previous works, it is predominantly a tragedy; but it is not a thoroughly artistic success, because our pleasure at the artist's triumph is overbalanced by dis-agreeable sensations caused by the repulsiveness of many of his charac-ters and of the environment in which they move. Mr. Hardy himself must have felt the effect of this repulsiveness, for his humour is almost entirely absent. A passion for excessive realism, too, has taken a greater hold upon this essentially poetic idealist, and it is only when he is in the presence of inanimate nature that his soul appears to be truly inspired. The descriptions of Egdon Heath in this novel, and of the effects of its sombre vastness upon its scattered inhabitants, are un-equalled, so far as our reading goes, in modern fiction. But if nature has taken hold of Mr. Hardy as it has done of few men since Wordsworth, it has not disturbed him 'with the joy of elevated thoughts', as Wordsworth sang; it has not proved itself to be the power 'whose secret is not joy, but peace' of Matthew Arnold; but rather it has proved itself to be the mysterious, inscrutable counterpart in the world of the senses, of that 'insoluble enigma' with which Herbert Spencer and so many modern minds have found themselves confronted in the world of thought. In other words, Mr. Hardy seems to have fallen a victim to the *malheur du siècle*, and so Clym Yeobright, and his mother, and Eustacia Vye, and Wildeve, and the other characters, love their loves and hate their hates on Egdon Heath without ever seeming to think that there is any thing beyond this present life, as pagan in heart as the old Celts that built the barrow crowning the hill that overlooked the immemorial plains. Everything about the novel is pagan from the barrow to the peasants who light a fire upon it every Guy Fawkes day; and the only truly noble character, the Reddleman, is as much pagan as Christian in his virtues. It is just here that we can lay our finger on the radical defect of this book, a defect which we shall expect to find characterizing much of Mr. Hardy's future work. The writer of a great novel must be enough of an optimist to impart a *spring* to his work. Pessimism imparts no *spring* to any thing, and pessimism is but another name for the deadly languor that accompanies the *malheur du siècle*, is, in fact, the symptom by which one is usually enabled to diagnose the disease.

We do not mean to say that Mr. Hardy is a pessimist in the sense that he is an apostle of pessimism. He does not set out with the avowed intention of making his readers fall out of love with life. He sees as well as any one that there is much in human nature that is noble and true, that there is much in life that is capable of giving pure and genuine pleasure. But, as a recent critic, Mr. William Sharp, has pointed out, there seems to be a large-eyed sadness about his face as he looks forth upon the world. He finds much that is inexplicable, much that is solemn, much that does not answer to his sense of justice in the life that surges about him, and he does not hesitate to reproduce in his novels all that he sees. As a realist he is warranted in doing this, but as a poet and idealist he ought sometimes at least to see further into the mystery we call life. If he relied more upon his poetical qualities he would avoid one of the pitfalls of realism—he has bravely escaped the others—the tendency to paint life as repulsive by stripping it of its hopefulness, its self-sufficing energy, its *spring*. Shakspere, whom Mr.

Hardy resembles in many ways, did not make this mistake. The Shakspere of *As You Like It* and *The Merry Wives of Windsor* did, it is true, pass into the Shakspere of *Hamlet* and *Othello*—the poet of a laughing, sunny world into the poet of the passions and the storms of life. But however much he was impelled to question life and fate, Shakspere never failed to leave his hearers or readers that hopefulness which is the spring of human existence. And in his last years, the years of *The Tempest* and *A Winter's Tale*, he reached a calm serenity of spirit and a clearness of vision which makes one feel that our troubled, thoughtful novelist may perhaps in time reach a similar 'coign of vantage' from which to survey the world. If, as we shall see, Mr. Hardy has written in *Tess of the D'Urbervilles* a tragedy which instinctively suggests such tragedies as the *Lear* and the *Othello*, who shall say that he may not in the years to come write a story of our modern life which shall suggest something of the wisdom, the genial charm of *The Tempest?*—even if he still finds it necessary to close with a note as solemn as

> We are such stuff
> As dreams are made on, and our little life
> Is rounded with a sleep.

The reader of Mr. Hardy's next novel, *The Trumpet Major* published in 1880, will at once ask himself, 'Is not this author making a brave struggle against the scepticism, the pessimism that have been assailing him? Will not the optimism of the poet and idealist finally conquer the pessimism of the realist?' If Mr. Hardy had died after writing *The Trumpet Major* the last question might well have been answered in the affirmative. Few more charming, spontaneous, wholesome stories than this have ever been written by an English novelist. Sweet Anne Garland may well be set by Sweet Anne Page, and her two devoted swains, fickle Bob Loveday, the sailor, and staunch John Loveday, the Trumpet Major, are worthy to live as long as the language in which their adventures are told. This is the only one of Mr. Hardy's stories that at all claims the title—the great title in spite of some modern critics—of an historical romance. The scene is laid on the southern coast of England during the exciting days of Napoleon's contemplated invasion. The historical setting is worthy of all praise—indeed, as we shall see later, Mr. Hardy shares with Thackeray the power to move as freely in the past as in the present. We consider *The Trumpet Major* to be the most charming of Mr. Hardy's stories, and if all its characters had possessed the nobility of the unselfish hero and if its action had been more tense and pitched upon a higher plane it would easily have been his greatest work. As it is, it is one of the cleanest, most interesting, most wholesome stories that can be recommended to readers old or young.

In *A Laodicean* (1881) Mr. Hardy became less spontaneous and charming, although more subtle and, perhaps, more powerful. The heroine, Paula Power, the Laodicean, neither hot nor cold, is a most interesting study in feminine psychology. The three leading male characters—Somerset, the architect, Dare, the adventurer, and Captain de Stancy, the scion of a decayed family—are well drawn; the action is sufficiently complicated to be interesting; but the story as a whole, though in Mr. Hardy's manner is not representative of him at his best. Perhaps we miss our author's humour, his interpretation of nature, his power to move our souls; perhaps we are disappointed in having to exchange Wessex peasants for middle class gentlemen and ladies whom more than one living artist could have drawn as well. But if *A Laodicean* cannot be ranked among Mr. Hardy's master-pieces, it evidently served as an inclined plane to let the author of *The Trumpet Major* down to the level of the author of *Two on a Tower* (1882).

This romance, as the author entitled it in the English edition, is in some respects a successful, and in all respects, a powerful book. It is not devoid of humour, as the delightful description of the choir practice amply proves. It is certainly a romance if a strange and almost bizarre plot can give a story a claim to that title. It does not yield to any of our author's stories as a character study, nor does it yield to any story of modern times in its absolute truth to the fundamental principles of human nature under certain given circumstances. More than any of Mr. Hardy's novels it gives one the impression of being a study undertaken on definite lines and with a definite object. That object is the endeavour to show the misery that must come to the woman who allows her passion for a man to blind her to the obstacles which difference of age, of rank, of education, of social aim, have set between them. The absorbing, the disastrous passion of Lady Constantine for her young astronomer, Swithin St. Cleve, the secret marriage, the terrible complications that arise upon her discovery that she was not a widow when she contracted this marriage, her anxiety to do no wrong to the budding genius of her boy husband, who still finds more to gaze at in the stars of heaven than in her own love-lit eyes, her open marriage to the Bishop of Melchester to save her reputation, the awakening of St.

Cleve to the fact that there are other women in the world besides his quondam wife and patroness, and finally the death scene in the tower when the heart of her that loved not wisely, but too well, has snapped beneath its weight of grief—all these particulars make up a story of intense power and interest. But it is a painful story. The Genius of Pessimism is slowly rising from the magic jar in which our author has endeavoured to imprison him. It is almost too much to ask us to sit quietly by while the beautiful and loving creature Mr. Hardy has given life to becomes involved in the meshes of a fate that knows no unloosing. It is too much to ask us to read a romance that contains not a single heroic character. Natural and true to life in many respects this story may be, but its truthfulness is not the truthfulness of great art, because repulsiveness forms no element of the truth of art.

Passing over the novelette entitled 'The Romantic Adventures of a Milkmaid' (1884) which demands no serious consideration, we come to the least attractive of all Mr. Hardy's novels, *The Mayor of Casterbridge* (1886), a work, by the way, which the booksellers find to be unpopular. In the setting of this story we recognize much of our author's old power. The quiet rural town is set as distinctly before us as Cranford is. But the people to whom Mr. Hardy introduces us upon its streets are not the people Mrs. Gaskell makes us know and love. There is to our mind not a really attractive character in the whole book. The good ones have a tendency to become commonplace, the bad ones can hardly be said to be interesting. It is true that Michael Henchard, the self-made hero, is a remarkable character study from the point of view of a psychologist or a sociologist, but that does not make him a proper hero for a novel, and we are forced to conclude that even the genius of Mr. Hardy cannot long sustain its eagle flight when, to borrow a metaphor from Shelley, its wings are cramped by the constraining folds of the serpent of pessimism.

But the darkest hour is that which immediately precedes the dawn. In *The Mayor of Casterbridge* the sun of Mr. Hardy's genius seems almost sunk from sight; in *The Woodlanders* (1886–7) it is seen rising slowly from the waves. Again we have the intimate sense of the mystery and the passion of nature; again we have the wonderful power of describing rural characters; again we have the closely knit and powerful action; we even have glimpses of the old humour. Still there is an indefinable something that separates the author of *The Woodlanders* from the author of *Far from the Madding Crowd*. Twelve years have made Mr. Hardy a more practised writer, they have given him a wider experience, but they have not made him any more in love with life. On the contrary, as has been indicated, they have frequently made him see little in life except a purposeless struggle in the coils of an implacable fate. And so Giles Winterborne in *The Woodlanders* fails in the pursuit of his love, which is his life, when Farmer Oak, in *Far from the Madding Crowd* succeeds. Honesty, loyalty, and love meet death for their reward; while a barely decent repentance on the part of a rather repulsive personage is rewarded by the love of a heroine who though scarcely noble is worthy of a better fate. It, therefore, matters little when we view *The Woodlanders* as a whole, whether the descriptions of the forests to be found in its pages are unexcelled in truth and beauty even by Mr. Hardy himself, or whether the scene which describes Marty South dressing the grave of Winterborne is the finest in the whole range of our author's novels; for the total impression produced by the book is painful because the fate that rules its characters is to Mr. Hardy, as well as to his readers, the relentless fate of alien times and peoples. And yet how powerful and original the book is, and who else among modern Englishmen could have written it!

It must not be imagined that during this long period of incessant novel writing Mr. Hardy refrained entirely from trying his hand on that popular form of literature, the short story. His novelette, 'The Romantic Adventures of a Milkmaid', has been already mentioned, but it may be recalled again to praise the character of the lime-burner Jim, and to condemn the generally improbable features of the plot. Besides this story, Mr. Hardy wrote before the year 1888 at least six stories of notable merit, five of which were in this year collected in a volume entitled *Wessex Tales, Strange, Lively, and Commonplace*. The tales thus brought together were entitled 'The Three Strangers', 'The Withered Arm', 'Fellow Townsmen', 'Interlopers at the Knap', and 'The Distracted Preacher'. An interesting story not included in this collection is 'What the Shepherd Saw'.

Mr. Hardy has done nothing more realistic in the more technical sense of that word than in these stories. By this we mean that he has kept a stricter guard over his poetic and romantic tendencies than elsewhere in his works. He allows himself to be humorous, but rarely to flash his imagination over the scene he is observing with his wide-awake eyes. In *Under the Greenwood Tree* he had proved himself to be as close an observer of animate and inanimate nature as one could well wish to have for a guide, but the closeness of his observation had not prevented him from sometimes looking at things with the eyes of a poet. It is Hardy the pure proseman who confronts us in *Wessex Tales*, and certainly we could not well afford to lose this aspect of his genius. There are few stories in all literature more perfectly worked out in every detail than the 'Three Strangers', there are few that show more keen observation and humour than 'The Interlopers at the Knap' and 'The Distracted Preacher'. But it is a dry, white light which plays over these stories, not the delicate, subtly-tinted light that plays over the exquisite idyl that describes the wooing of Richard Dewy and Fancy Day.

It is, however, a subtly-tinted light that plays over Mr. Hardy's second volume of short stories published three years later, and entitled *A Group of Noble Dames*. This Wessex *Decameron* consists of ten tales, each of which concerns itself with the fortunes of a noble dame, and each of which is a work of perfect art. Not only is Mr. Hardy able to show his wonted power of characterization within the narrow limits he has set himself—which cannot always be said of him in *Wessex Tales*—but he is also able by a few sure touches to surround his characters with environments such as he has not hitherto attempted to depict. The ability to transport himself and his readers into the past which he had shown eleven years before in *The Trumpet Major*, is shown here to a greater degree. The eighteenth century lives for us again in nearly every story as truly as it does in the poems of Austin Dobson. This is high praise, but it is deserved. A more charming book has not been given to the world for many years, and its charm and grace are ample proof that Mr. Hardy does not always live under the shadow of pessimism.

But it is a book not a year old which has made Mr. Hardy the most prominent living English novelist. *Tess of the D'Urbervilles* is possibly too fresh in our minds and the verdicts of its various critics and readers are still too jarring and confused to enable us to feel certain that we are criticizing it fairly, and not merely taking up the cudgels for or against certain very pronounced opinions of its author. For in this novel, as in *Two on a Tower*, Mr. Hardy seems to have succumbed to a popular tendency, and to have written a novel with a purpose. We say *seems*, for after all the purpose may have developed itself after the inception of the story—the opening incident of which at least was founded on fact—or it may have ceased to affect the writer the moment he became deeply interested in his characters. We confess that the power and the movement of the story are so great that it is only when we read a review of it that we are conscious that its author had any purpose save that which is common to every true writer of fiction—viz. to tell a story which shall please. But this unconsciousness of a novelist's purpose is the highest tribute that can be paid to his work.

It would be useless to enter here upon any elaborate account of the plot of a book every one is reading or has read. As we all know Tess, the milkmaid heroine, has fallen from virtue through no fault of her own. Subsequently her great passion for a second and nobler lover sweeps her into a marriage with him after she has failed to tell him of her condition, although she has attempted to do so. Her confession of her secret to her husband is one of the most powerful and painful scenes in all literature. After the weak man has deserted her, she undergoes in patience a life of unspeakable torture, but at last falls again to her former betrayer in order to keep her mother and her family from starvation. Her husband returns to her, and in her remorse she stabs her betrayer to death. After a brief period of ecstatic bliss with the now repentant man, whose desertion has brought her to such a pass, she is seized by the officers of the law and led to the scaffold. Her story ends with the husband and her young sister moving away with averted eyes from the black flag that floats above the gloomy modern jail. In the words of her Creator, ' "Justice" was done, and Time, the arch-satirist, had had his joke out with Tess.'

'How horrible, how pessimistic,' exclaims one reader. 'How absurd', says another, 'to attempt to prove that such a woman was pure', this last personage being swift to remember Mr. Hardy's sub-title, 'A Pure Woman Faithfully Presented'. 'What is the good of such stories when they only make one weep?' says a third. 'It is the greatest tragedy of modern times,' says a fourth. 'It is a dangerous book to put into the hands of the young,' says a fifth. And so on through a chorus of praise and blame which seems to us to be as a rule beside the point.

In the first place, we see little use in arguing whether or not Tess was really pure. We may see some excuse for her second fall, another may not. But what no one can fail to see is that in Tess Mr. Hardy has drawn a great character, nay, his greatest character, and we venture to say the greatest character in recent fiction. She seizes one at once and never looses her hold. What does it matter to us, from the point of view of art, whether she is pure or not, provided she does not repel us? There is here no allurement to sin, no attempt to make wrong right, no disposition to paint vice in the colours that belong to virtue. We see in her only a beautiful earth-born creature struggling against a fate too strong for her, a fate that brings her to a dishonoured grave, and yet not a fate that will cut her off from the peace and joy of another world than this. She is elemental, this peasant's daughter with the blood of a Norman noble in her veins. She has the elemental freshness, the odour of earth, that Mr. Hardy's other peasants have, but she has also an elemental strength and nobility that they have not. This elemental freshness, this elemental strength and nobility, make her a woman fit to set in the gallery of Shakspere's women—which is but to say that she is a creation of genius that time cannot devour. Her story is pure tragedy—the greatest tragedy, it seems to us, that has been written since the days of the Elizabethans—it lacks 'the accomplishment of verse', but at least it is told in the strongest and purest prose. If this be true, how vain to call it a horrible book? As well call the *Othello* horrible. Granted that it leaves a sensation of pain that lingers with a reader for hours, still it is the bitter-sweet pain that tragedy always leaves, and the pain is overbalanced by the pleasure we gain from our appreciation of the artist's triumph. Mr. Hardy may take his leave of us with a pessimistic fling, but he has succeeded malgré pessimism in producing a great work of art. He must have kept his eye fixed upon the nobleness, the pathos of his heroine's life, he must have seen a rift in the black sky above her, he must have sunk his realism in idealism, his pessimism in optimism, oftener than he was perhaps aware of.

Viewed in its details, this book impresses one as strongly as it does when viewed as a whole. Its subordinate characters are admirably drawn and all help on the action. The husband, Angel Clare, is scarcely worthy of Tess's love, but Mr. Hardy has the authority of the Greeks for setting the man's selfishness and subservience to conventionalism as a foil to the natural purity and charm of the woman. Euripides makes Admetus serve as a foil to Alkestis. Mrs. Durbeyfield, the silly mother, who is responsible for Tess's fall, is a creature seen time and again among her class. Angel Clare's evangelical father and mother are also touched off in a few strokes which have the inevitableness that a master's hand alone can give. It is perhaps needless to praise Dairyman Crick and the love-lorn milkmaids, for with such characters Mr. Hardy is always at home, and with them he never fails to be humorous, even if he does not rise to the humour that belongs of right to the creator of Joseph Poorgrass.

But this is also a novel of powerful and memorable scenes. That in which Tess christens her child of shame, giving him the name of

Sorrow, while her little brothers and sisters act as clerk and congregation, is piercing in its pathos, to borrow an expression of Matthew Arnold's. This scene was omitted from the first American edition of *Tess*, and the book was thereby greatly mutilated. No one who has read it can ever forget it or forget the lesson of charity it teaches. Very powerful also are the scenes describing Tess's confession to her husband and the consequences of that confession, although it is impossible to deny that the sleep-walking experiences of the pair are somewhat exaggerated. With the departure of Angel Clare the clouds of doom begin to mass above Tess's head and the tragedy gathers such swift intensity that it is almost vain to speak of scenes. But who will forget Tess's first day at the bleak upland farm, or her frustrated visit to her father-in-law's house, or her second meeting with her betrayer, or her sudden deed of frenzy, or her capture on Salisbury plain under the Shadow of Stonehenge? To forget these scenes would imply the power to forget the sight of Lear upon the wintry heath or of Othello in the death chamber of his 'gentle lady'.

But *Tess* has merits that lie apart from the power of characterization and of dramatic presentation which its author so constantly displays. Never has Mr. Hardy's knowledge of nature stood him in better stead than in the descriptive passages which here and there break the tense thread of the action. They have the effect that all description should have in a novel, of heightening the impression which the author is endeavouring to convey by means of his characters and their actions. We read them only to plunge once more into the narrative of Tess's adventures with a sense of the impotence of nature to avert the doom of her choicest creation. At times it seems as if this modern Englishman were really a Greek endowed with the power of personifying the trees and streams past which his heroine glides, just as he seems to be a Greek in his never-ceasing sense of the presence of an inexorable fate. In fine, the Hardy of this novel is the Hardy who has charmed and impressed us before, but also a Hardy of heightened and matured powers—a master of fiction.

But it is high time to bring this article to a close, and in doing so we shall attempt to sum up the qualities that appear to us to make Mr. Hardy a great novelist. It would be pleasant to compare him with his contemporaries and to endeavour to show why we believe him to stand both in breadth and depth of genius supreme among his living rivals. But this would require another article, and it is a kind of criticism which certain recent writers pronounce to be unscientific. We might be able to defend its usefulness in spite of the stigma which seems nowadays to attach to everything deductive, but we forbear.

Our first reason for considering Mr. Hardy great is that he possesses a great and individual style. He has the rare power of saying exactly what he wants to say in clear, strong, and charming English, even though his diction is at all times Latin rather than Teutonic, as Mr. Sharp has pointed out. He does not write rhetorical prose or, as a rule, poetic prose, but a prose that has a rhythm which does not suggest poetry, and that always fits its subject-matter as closely as a well-cut garment.

The second quality of Mr. Hardy's greatness is his wonderful power of describing and interpreting inanimate nature. We have so often referred to this power that we shall now content ourselves with observing that if meditative Wordsworth be substituted for blythe-hearted Chaucer in Landor's famous lines to Browning, they will be found not inapplicable to Mr. Hardy:

> Since Chaucer was alive and hale
> No man has walked along our roads with step
> So active, so enquiring eye, or tongue
> So varied in discourse.

A third quality of our novelist's greatness is his power as a narrator. His characters move, the action never halts. He has the threads of his plot well in hand, and although he does not attempt to manage many threads, he leaves his readers confident of his power to do so should he wish. One feels in reading Hardy that this man has found his true vocation, that he is not a social reformer like Mrs. Ward or a philosopher like George Eliot, using the novel as the best means to reach the masses, but a story-teller, a lineal descendant of the cyclic bards of Greece, of the troubadours of France, of the ballad singers and dramatic poets of merry England.

Fourth and last of Mr. Hardy's qualities that may be mentioned here is his power of characterization. His gallery of women is unique, even if he has seldom drawn one whom his average male reader would care to marry. Bathsheba Everdene, Elfride Swancourt, Ethelberta Petherwin, Eustacia Vye, Mrs. Yeobright, Anne Garland, Paula Power, Lady Constantine, Grace Melbury, Marty South, the 'ever-memorable' group, and finally, to crown all, Tess, the milkmaid—who of our modern novelists can make such a showing! There they stand, flesh and blood women, whose every action, whose most delicate sensation is thoroughly understood by their creator. We can only regret that he has not chosen to portray a larger number of them as distinctly noble, but he has given us Marty South and Tess, and the others are all admirable in their kind and degree. For his own sex Mr. Hardy has done as well, if not better. The peasants of *Under the Greenwood Tree*, Henry Knight, Farmer Oak, Joseph Poorgrass, Wildeve, Clym Yeobright, the Reddleman, Bob Loveday and his brother, the Trumpet Major, Dare, Swithin St. Cleve, Michael Henchard, Giles Winterborne, and Angel Clare, are all striking characters, five of whom are noble men, and one of whom, Joseph Poorgrass, is destined to immortality.

It is unnecessary to repeat how great a debt we owe to this novelist for making his favourite Wessex, that strange country of pagan survivals, as well known to us almost as our own birthplace. His success as a provincial novelist has made many critics and readers overlook the fact that he has claims to a higher place among writers of fiction—a place not far below the exalted station where we have put Fielding and Scott and Thackeray, and for which Bulwer and Dickens and George Eliot are yet struggling. As he is still in the prime of life, and as his last work shows such an immense stride forward in his powers of characterization and of dramatic presentation, we hesitate to affirm that he will not eventually lift himself to this high and secure position. He gives one always the impression that he has not put forth his full powers, and that there is yet more to come. If, as the years go by, he attains more and more to the philosophic mind, if he sees further into the secrets of life and nature and learns that pessimism and realism do not comprise the last words that art has in store for man; if he gives fuller scope to these poetic powers which are his by nature and which his wide observation and his deep study of the poets have strengthened, it may be that he will put a still greater distance between himself and his contemporaries—some of whom, like Mr. George Meredith, are pressing him close—and that he will yet write his name among the supreme masters of fiction—that is, among the benefactors of the human race.

47. Andrew Lang, a rejoinder,
Longman's Magazine

November 1892, xxi, 100

Lang's rejoinder to Hardy's preface to *Tess* was made in the literary gossip feature 'At the Sign of the Ship' to which Lang contributed regularly. *Longman's Magazine* had been running since 1882, when it superseded the old *Fraser's*. The preface to which Lang refers was added when the one-volume edition of *Tess* appeared at the end of September 1892. (See No. 42 and headnote to No. 11).

There is something very graceful and instructive in the modern practice of writing apologetic or critical prefaces to new editions of novels. In his first edition the author stands the fire of criticism without replying. He waits, like the British infantry of old, till he sees the colour of his opponents' eyes, and then, in the preface to a fresh edition, he lets fly at those assailants. Somehow it is commonly the author of a very successful book who thus gives us his own views of his own art and of his critics. One would rather expect the unsuccessful writer to stand on the defensive, but he, poor gentleman, has no new edition, no opportunity of retaliation. Could I write a successful novel—which is not a probable chance—I think I might contemplate the royalties with an avaricious grin, and quote

> *Criticus* me sibilat; at mihi plaudo
> Ipse domi simul ac nummos contemplor in arcâ.

Especially if most of my critics had danced triumphantly before me, beating cymbals and hailing the conqueror, while only a few 'hesitated' —or howled—'dislike', methinks I could possess my soul in peace. But this frame of mind is growing rare, and authors do what Buffon did not—they reply to their reviewers. Mr. Hardy has just answered the graceless persons—a small minority—who did not admire without qualification his tale, *Tess of the D'Urbervilles*. The following extract from his preface is culled out of the *Illustrated London News*. The last sentence, of course, is not Mr. Hardy's:

'In the introductory words to the first edition I suggested the possible advent of the genteel person who would not be able to endure the tone of these pages. That person duly appeared, mostly mixed up with the aforesaid objectors. In another of his forms he felt upset that it was not possible for him to read the book through three times, owing to my not having made that critical effort which "alone can prove the salvation of such an one." In another, he objected to such vulgar articles as the Devil's pitchfork, a lodging-house carving-knife, and a shame-bought parasol appearing in a respectable story. In another place he was a gentleman who turned Christian for half-an-hour the better to express his grief that a disrespectful phrase about the Immortals should have been used; though the same innate gentility compelled him to excuse the author in words of pity that one cannot be too thankful for: "He does but give us of his best." I can assure this great critic that to exclaim illogically against the gods, singular or plural, is not such an original sin of mine as he seems to imagine. True, it may have some local originality; though, if Shakespeare were an authority on history, which, perhaps, he is not, I could show that the sin was introduced into Wessex as early as the Heptarchy itself. Says Glo'ster to Lear, otherwise Ina, king of that country—

> As flies to wanton boys are we to the gods;
> They kill us for their sport.

Needless to say that the 'great critic' is Mr. Andrew Lang.'

Mr. Hardy's argument is logical indeed. 'I said from the first', he observes, 'that the genteel person'—meaning the Snob—'would not like my book. Some people did not like my book, therefore they are genteel persons.' Nothing can be more convincing. Then Mr. Hardy selects myself (as I signed my notice in the *New Review*), and he makes a reply which, I am sure, is only a petulant expression of annoyance, and does not seriously signify what it seems to signify. Mr. Hardy has no means of knowing what my private shade of theological dogma is. He cannot tell whether I am, as a matter of creed, a Christian or not. Nor can he really suppose that I, being, *ex hypothesi*, an unbeliever, pretended for half-an-hour to belief, in order that I might pick a hole in a phrase of his. The charge of so superfluously playing the part of Tartuffe for a critical and literary purpose is comic or melancholy according to your humour. As Mr. Hardy says, he 'exclaimed illogically against the gods' in the phrase, 'The President of the Immortals (in Æschylean phrase) had ended his sport with Tess'. This was the moral and marrow of his romance, as I supposed, and the phrase must seem equally illogical to an Atheist and a Christian, to a Buddhist and a Bonze. For nobody in his senses now believes in a wicked malignant President of the Immortals, whatever Glo'ster may have said in his haste while Ina was a monarch of the West Saxons. No; one need not be a Christian, nor pretend to be a Christian, before resenting a comment on the 'President of the Immortals' which is confessed to be illogical, and which—if Mr. Hardy does not believe in a malignant 'President'—is insincere and affected. And here I may add the expression of my regret that my quotation, 'he does but give us of his best', has annoyed Mr. Hardy. For he always does give us of his best—of his best labour and earnest endeavour—and this is a virtue not universal among artists.

As to *Tess* and my own comparative distaste for that lady and her melancholy adventures, let me be unchristian for half-an-hour and give my reasons. But, first, let me confess that I am in an insignificant minority. On all sides—not only from the essays of reviewers, but from the spoken opinions of the most various kinds of readers—one learns that *Tess* is a masterpiece. One hears the same opinion from a great classical scholar, who seldom deserts the ancients for the moderns, and from a Scot living his life out in a remote savage island, which, by the way, is *not* Samoa. There is no absolute standard of taste in literature, but such a consensus of opinion comes as near being a standard as one generation can supply. So I confess myself in the wrong, as far as an exterior test can make me in the wrong; and yet a reviewer can only give his own impression, and state his reasons, as far as he knows them, for that impression. In the *Illustrated London News* of October 1 there is not only the beginning of a new tale by Mr. Hardy, but an eloquent estimate of Mr. Hardy's genius by Mr. Frederick Greenwood. Thence one might cull texts to serve in an apology for one's own sentiments about *Tess* and some other books of Mr. Hardy's, and for a disquisition on the general relations of the faults of a work of art to our final estimate of its value. Mr. Greenwood, greatly admiring, as every one must admire, the talent of Mr. Hardy, says that one of his tales (*The Hand of Ethelberta*) is 'forbidding in conception'. Now, to my private taste—and *on n'a que soi*, even when one is a reviewer— *Tess* is also 'forbidding in conception'. I have not read *The Hand of Ethelberta*, but *Tess* is not the only one of Mr. Hardy's novels which repels me by what is, to me, the 'forbidding' character of its 'conception'. There is a tale of his about a woman who adored an effigy of a dead lover. I gladly forget the rest. Well, 'it gars me a' grue', to quote a better writer, and the *frisson*, if new, is none the better for that. There is *Two on a Tower*, where the heroine, a widow, is not infrequently described as 'warm'. Her child, by a second marriage, through some legal misadventure or mischance, is to be born without a legitimate father. So she marries a clergyman—a bishop if my memory holds good—and imposes the babe on that prelate. It may be my 'gentility', or it may be my partiality for a married clergy, but somehow I do find the 'conception' of *Two on a Tower* to be 'forbidding'. I don't like the practical joke on the clergyman; and the 'warmth' of the widow seems too conspicuously dwelt upon.

Again, I find a similar 'forbidding' quality in *Tess*, as I do, and have always done, in *Clarissa Harlowe*. Poor Tess, a most poetical, if not a very credible character, is a rural Clarissa Harlowe. She is very unlike most rural maids, but then she comes of a noble lineage. She is not avenged by the sword of Colonel Morden, but by that lodging-house carving-knife, which seems anything but a trusty stiletto. She does not die, like Clarissa, as the ermine martin dies of the stain on its snowy fur, but she goes back to the atrocious cad who betrayed her, and wears —not caring what she wears—the parasol of pomp and the pretty slippers of iniquity. To say that all this is out of character and out of keeping is only to set my theory of human nature against Mr. Hardy's knowledge of it. I never knew a Tess, as Mr. Thackeray was never personally acquainted with a convict. Her behaviour does not invariably seem to me that of 'a pure woman', but perhaps I am no judge of purity, at all events in such extraordinary disadvantageous circumstances. As to purity, people are generally about to talk nastily when they dwell on the word. The kind of 'catastrophe' spoken of by Mr. Hardy has been adequately treated of by St. Augustine, in his *De Civitate Dei*. To my own gentility it is no stumbling-block. Other girls in fiction have been seduced with more blame, and have not lost our sympathy, or ceased to be what Mr. Hardy calls 'protagonists'. The case of Effie Deans will occur to the studious reader. It is not the question of 'purity' that offends me, but that of credibility in character and language. The villain Alec and the prig Angel Clare seem to me equally unnatural, incredible, and out of the course of experience. But that may only prove one's experience to be fortunately limited. When all these persons, whose conduct and conversation are so far from plausible, combine in a tale of which the whole management is, to one's own taste, unnatural and 'forbidding', how can one pretend to believe or to admire without reserve? Of course it may be no fault in a book that it is 'forbidding'; many people even think it a merit. *Le Père Goriot* is 'forbidding'; *Madame Bovary* is 'forbidding', yet nobody in his senses denies their merit. But then, to myself, those tales are credible and real. *Tess* is not real nor credible, judged by the same personal standard. To be sure, *Tess*, unlike *Madame Bovary*, is at all events and undeniably a romance. When Angel Clare, walking in his sleep, carries the portly Tess, with all her opulent charms and 'ethereal beauty' to a very considerable distance, he does what Porthos, or Guy Livingstone, could hardly have done when wide awake. It is a romantic incident, but if an otherwise romantic writer had introduced it, the critics, one fears, would have laughed. At all events, when any reader finds that a book is beyond his belief, in character, in language, and in event, the book must, for him, lose much of its interest. Again, if he be struck by such a defect of style as the use of semi-scientific phraseology out of place, he must say so; he must point out the neighbourhood of the reef on which George Eliot was wrecking her English. An example of a fault so manifested, and of such easy remedy (for nobody need write jargon), I selected and reproduce. A rustic wife is sitting in a tavern, taking her ease at her inn. 'A sort of halo, an occidental glow, came over life then. Troubles and other realities took on themselves a metaphysical impalpability, sinking to mere cerebral phenomena for serene contemplation, and no longer stood as pressing concretions which chafed body and soul.' 'Men and hangels igsplain this', cried Jeames, on less provocation. First, one does not know whether this description of Mrs. Durbeyfield's tavern content is to be understood as her way of 'envisaging' it, or as Mr. Hardy's. It can hardly be Mrs. Durbeyfield's, because the words 'cerebral' and 'metaphysical' were probably not in her West Saxon vocabulary. So the statement must be Mr. Hardy's manner of making clear and lucid to us the mood of Mrs. Durbeyfield. It is, apparently, a mood which the philosopher may experimentally reproduce by eating as good a dinner as he can get, and drinking a fair quantity of liquor, such as his soul loves, when he is troubled and anxious. Now, if I may venture to imagine Mr. Herbert Spencer in these conditions, and analysing his own state of mind, after dinner, for *Typical Developments*, he probably would, and he legitimately might, put his results into technical language. But where a novelist, or a poet, deals with a very unscientific character, like Mrs. Durbeyfield or Sir John Falstaff, then the use of psychological terminology seems to my sense out of place. How can a trouble, say want of pence, become a metaphysical impalpability? How can it sink to a cerebral phenomenon, and how is it lightened by so sinking? Everything, all experience, is a cerebral phenomenon. How a trouble, not being a 'gathering', can be a 'pressing concretion', or wherefore a 'concretion' at all, are questions which baffle one. Intelligible or not (and I confess to being no metaphysician), the phraseology seems inappropriate. Inappropriateness, as far as I am able to judge, often marks the language of Mr. Hardy's characters. To take a specimen at random. Alec, who has been 'converted' for a moment from his profession as a rural Don Juan, meets Tess again, and says, 'Ever since you told me of that babe of ours, it is just as if my emotions, which have been flowing in a strong stream heavenward, had suddenly found a sluice open in the direction of you through which they have at once gushed.' Now 'babe' is good, is part of the patois of Zion, but the rest of the statement is so expressed as to increase one's feeling of unreality, as if one were reading a morally squalid fairy tale. And this sense of unreality is exactly what I complain of in *Tess*.

Well, for all these reasons—for its forbidding conception, for its apparent unreality, for its defects of style, so provokingly superfluous—*Tess* failed to captivate me, in spite of the poetry and beauty and economic value of its rural descriptions, in spite of the genius which is obvious and undeniable in many charming scenes. To be more sensitive to certain faults than to great merits, to let the faults spoil for you the whole, is a critical misfortune, if not a critical crime. Here, too, all is subjective and personal; all depends on the critic's taste, and how it reacts against a particular kind of error.

As Mr. Greenwood says, 'some blemish there is in *Under the Greenwood Tree*, as there is not in the Medicean Venus, and one or two other works'. Modern taste perhaps regards the whole conception and treatment of the Medicean Venus as one error and blemish, if we compare it with the works of the great age. But, of course, all work has its blemishes, or almost all work. Shakespeare is as far as possible from being impeccable, and we know what Kirchhoff and Möllendorff say about the *Odyssey*, what M. Renan said about St. John's Gospel, and M. Scherer about Molière. To some tastes faults appear which to others are unapparent. But there are faults and faults, tastes and tastes. We all admit the existence of blemishes in the works which are most dear to us; there are palpable faults in *Rob Roy*, in *Tom Jones*, in *Tartuffe* (they tell me), and, they tell me, in *Vanity Fair*. The question is, how far do these faults offend the reader, and spoil, for him, the merit of the work before him? Here, again, we deal with the subjective. A man says that *Pickwick* is 'low' and boisterous; well, my genteelness (or 'gentility') is unoffended by *Pickwick*. He says that *Rob Roy* is prolix, that Thackeray preaches too much, that the *dénouement* of *Tartuffe* is inartistic.

Perhaps—nay, very probably—these censures are just, but the faults do not spoil the merits, for me. On the other hand, I confess that what seem to me faults in *Tess*, do not exactly spoil, but leave me less patience than I could wish, to enjoy the book's many and notable merits. Yet what is all this but saying that one prefers *Far from the Madding Crowd* to *Tess* and some of Mr. Hardy's other works? Arguing about it proves nothing, especially in the face of a consensus of praise from almost everybody who is not 'genteel'. I might say that *Tess* is not only a romance, but a *tendenz* story, a story with a moral, that moral, or part of it, being, apparently, the malignant topsy-turviness of things, the malevolent constitution of the world, the misfortunes of virtue, the conspiracy of circumstances against the good and 'pure'. A lurking vein of optimism may make one distrust this conclusion (if this indeed be the conclusion), and one may be comforted by one's very power-lessness to believe; may say, like the unconsciously heterodox old woman, 'After all, perhaps it is not true'. And that is a consolation for oneself, but not good for the novel. So I have ventured to say my say, though I had not intended at any time to speak again about any work of Mr. Hardy's.

48. D. F. Hannigan, *Westminster Review*

December 1892, cxxxviii, 655–9

The article is entitled 'The Latest Development of English Fiction'. Denis F. Hannigan translated works by Balzac and Flaubert.

If the novel is to be a faithful picture of actual life, and not a mere romantic narrative intended mainly to amuse young persons in their hours of leisure, the hackneyed moralizing of such critics as Mr. Andrew

Lang must be disregarded as utterly beside the question—What is the proper sphere of fiction?

This well-known critic has thought fit to emphasize his intense dislike of both the conception and the style of Mr. Thomas Hardy's novel, *Tess of the D'Urbervilles*, in the *New Review* for February of the present year. Mr. Lang half-playfully sneered at the pessimism of *Tess*, and expressed the belief that its *dénoûment* is quite improbable 'in this age of halfpenny newspapers and appeals to the British public'. Perhaps the critic had before his mind the case of Mrs. Maybrick, but his observation has, after all, very little force. In Mrs. Maybrick's case there was a conflict of medical testimony, and, rightly or wrongly, the British public had got hold of the idea that the verdict was not warranted by the facts. But it is absurd for Mr. Lang or any other latter-day critic to maintain that a woman convicted of murder would escape death merely because she possessed some personal fascination, or because the circumstances connected with the crime were more or less romantic. It is not so long since Mrs. Pearcey met her doom, and public opinion has not yet arrived at such a stage in England as to make it at all certain that, in such a contingency as that indicated in Mr. Hardy's book the culprit would be saved by her sex from the ordeal of capital punishment. 'The black flag', says Mr. Lang, with a sickly and rather callous kind of badinage, 'would never have been hoisted as in the final page.'

Comfortable critics of this sort cannot sympathize with the temptations, the struggles, the miseries of a noble but half-darkened soul like that of poor Tess Durbeyfield. Mr. Hardy himself has vigorously dealt with the 'genteel' reviewer in the preface to the fifth edition of the novel, and most rational persons will be inclined to think that Mr. Lang cuts a very sorry figure under the lash of the novelist's just resentment. A more modest type of author than Mr. Thomas Hardy does not exist. He shrinks from 'blowing his own trumpet'. He refers to his book as an 'unequal and partial achievement', and seems to be utterly unconscious of the fact that he has written one of the greatest novels of this century. What he tries to avoid is not disparagement but misrepresentation. In the last paragraph of his novel he says: 'Justice was done, and the President of the Immortals (in Æschylean phrase) had ended his sport with Tess.' This sentence arouses the 'virtuous indignation' of Mr. Lang, who cannot give adequate expression to his horror at such a supposed insult to the Deity. Really it is no wonder that the novelist should protest against the assumed wrath of the 'gentleman who turned Christian for half an hour the better to express his grief that a disrespectful phrase about the Immortals should have been used'.

Some critics would allow a writer of fiction no freedom. He should write conventional stories to please their somewhat valetudinarian tastes. He should draw a veil over all the unpleasant facts of life. Seduction should barely be hinted at; adultery should not even be mentioned; and the existence of such an institution as the gallows should not be obtruded on the delicate-minded reader's attention.

To this school of critics Mr. Andrew Lang belongs. We trace in him the prudishness and exclusiveness of the fashionable preacher who has turned aside from religious paths to wander through the flowery meads of literature. Mr. Lang is perfectly welcome to enjoy what he is pleased to call 'Romance', and to praise the blood-curdling Zulu narratives of his friend Mr. Rider Haggard; but why does he attempt to depreciate a novel, which is obviously outside the range not only of his sympathies but of his critical powers?

In the November number of *Longman's Magazine* Mr. Lang returns to the subject, and says that he considers the book 'unreal'. He admits the theme is capable of treatment in a novel, and refers to *The Heart of Midlothian* and *Madame Bovary*. What an intellectual jumble it is to couple Scott's old-fashioned romance with Flaubert's grimly realistic work! 'It is not the question of purity', says Mr. Lang, 'that offends me, but that of credibility of language and character.'

Mark the egotism of this kind of criticism. 'Offends *me*'. Is there no criterion for Mr. Lang except the *ego*?

It is idle to say that the criticism of a work of fiction is a mere matter of personal feeling. There is a standard of judgment for a novel as well as for pictures or musical compositions. The critic who can only praise a book which does not 'offend' him is the most wretched of critics. A good critic can point out the beauties of a work, whose conception appears to him revolting. But Mr. Lang cannot do this: he is the slave of his predilections. Many readers are, no doubt, shocked by the subject dealt with so painfully in Nathaniel Hawthorne's *Scarlet Letter:* but few persons of literary judgment will refuse to acknowledge the power and intensity of that work. The coarseness of Zola's *L'Assommoir* cannot blind us to its wonderful vividness of description, its harrowing presentation of the miseries and vices of the scum of the Parisian population, its pitiless, but faithful, portraiture of life's bitter realities.

So with *Tess of the D'Urbervilles*. It is a monumental work. It marks a distinct epoch in English fiction. From beginning to end it bears the hall-mark of Truth on every page of it. It is a more impressive narrative of crushing facts than George Eliot's *Adam Bede*. It is more deep and poignant than anything that either Zola or Guy de Maupassant has written. It is a work worthy of Balzac himself. There is no coarseness in it, no nastiness of detail, and yet nothing essential is avoided. From the time when poor Tess falls a victim to the lascivious pursuit of the base D'Urberville up to her death upon the scaffold, every step in her sad history is recorded. We can follow her career as if we knew her and lived with her. We feel her sufferings; we respect her shortcomings; we lament the chain of circumstances that led to her doom; and finally, we forgive and pity her. The beautiful passages in the book are so numerous that to quote them would be only heaping up extracts and, so to speak, breaking the harmony of an exquisite novel. The descriptions of field-life are clear, forcible, and true. The knowledge of Nature shown by the author is as wonderful as it is rare. The picture of Tess, after the murder, lying down to sleep in her exhaustion beneath one of the pillars at Stonehenge is, perhaps, the most touching and splendid scene in the entire novel. A few sentences will afford an idea of the author's power:

[quotes ch. LVIII from 'In a minute or two' to ' "I am ready," she said quietly.']

It is easy to find fault with the style of even the greatest book. Victor Hugo is not free from mannerisms. George Eliot is often pedantic. Thomas Hardy, in this his latest and greatest novel, uses occasionally barbarous words, which are neither English nor Latin. He might have avoided the introduction of such verbal coinages as 'juxtapose', 'dolorifuge', and 'theolatry'. What does it matter, however, if an author here and there sins against philology? Small critics grasp at such things; let them! There are spots on the sun. The fact remains that *Tess of the D'Urbervilles* is the greatest work of fiction produced in England since George Eliot died.

It has not come as a solitary work of pronounced merit. Mr. George Meredith's novel, *One of Our Conquerors*, deserves a place beside *Tess*. It is, from the standpoint of pure narrative, much inferior; but it is a decidedly strong book. Another novel exhibiting realistic power of no mean order is Lucas Malet's *Wages of Sin*. In this work a great stride is made, and the traditional notions of 'morality' are dissipated. The result is a true picture of a real man and a real woman.

Of course the orthodox reviews expressed some alarm at the appearance of Mr. Hardy's novel. Very curiously, they coupled it with Mrs. Humphry Ward's *David Grieve*—a book as different from it as *Sandford and Merton* is from *The Mill on the Floss*.

Meanwhile, the author of *Tess* may rest on his laurels. He has revolutionized English fiction. His book is a success, and Mrs. Grundy and her numerous votaries must, for a time at least, hide their heads in shame.

Some day, perhaps, this novel will be dramatized, and then we may see on the English stage a play far better than anything supplied by Ibsen. It will, if the work is effectively done, be the noblest modern British drama.

JUDE THE OBSCURE

November 1895

49. Unsigned Review, *Athenaeum*

23 November 1895, 709

The editorial file marks this review 'B. Williams'.

To the attentive student of literature a certain field of interest might be presented by a study of the bad books of great writers as throwing a light on the genius of their authors. There are, it is true, cases where the study is useless from any point of view; Balzac's early works, for example, are not only extraordinarily bad, but so bad that they show no glimmering of the mind that could write *La Peau de Chagrin*. Generally, however, the bad work of a great writer not only indicates some of the elements of his greatness, but exaggerates one or two of them in a manner which may often render them more readily perceptible than when blended in the harmony of some more perfect work. 'A Lesson to Fathers', paradoxical as it may sound, helps to the comprehension of Wordsworth's charm and his greatness, and some of Browning's most crabbed poems write in large characters part of the power which is more coyly disclosed in 'Rabbi Ben Ezra'. A great man's bad work is like a Titan's overthrow: it calls rude attention to the strength which had been masked in the easy hitting of the mark.

Now, here we have a titanically bad book by Mr. Hardy. We have had bad books from him before; but so far his bad books have been feeble rather than anything else. In *Jude the Obscure*, however, we have Mr. Hardy running mad in right royal fashion. In all his greatest novels the tragic effect is partly gained by the sense of an inevitable doom which hangs heavy over the characters. In *Far from the Madding Crowd*, in *The Mayor of Casterbridge*, in *Tess of the D'Urbervilles*, this sense of an *ineluctabile fatum*, which sometimes turns to naught men's worthiest efforts, is a legitimate and potent element in the tragedy. But Mr. Hardy's idea of Destiny is by no means stationary, and in its latest development in this book it becomes almost grotesque. Even in *Tess of the D'Urbervilles*, though there the idea was not so pronounced as to be repellent, the notion seems shaping itself in Mr. Hardy's mind that fate is not a mere blind force that happens at times to upset men's calculations and to turn their strength into weakness, but rather a spiteful Providence, whose special delight it is to score off men, and whose proceedings make anything but absolute quietism an absurdity. In *Tess*, as we said, there are indications of this notion, but here it is predominant. The way it is done is extremely simple: you take a man with good aspirations—a weak man he must be, of course—and put down to his credit all his aspirations and the feeble attempts he makes to realize them, while all the mistakes he makes, which render his life a failure, you put down to the savage deity who lies in wait to trip him up. It reminds one a little of Victor Hugo's remark about the cause of Napoleon's defeat at Waterloo, 'Napoléon avait été dénoncé dans l'infini, et sa chute était décidée. Il gênait Dieu,' which is really a very fair burlesque of Mr. Hardy's primitive theory.

It is not meant to be implied that an impossible theory of the universe is necessarily incompatible with a good novel, although there is a considerable likelihood of this being so. But what is fatal to Mr. Hardy's art in this latest and extreme development of his theory is that it makes him so angry. It is always fatal to lose one's temper, but it is particularly so for a novelist for several reasons. In the first place a scolding tone is the worst possible form of stating views, because it irritates the reader, and instead of raising sympathy creates an unreasonable antipathy in his mind. And this book reads almost like one prolonged scolding from beginning to end: the preface; the mottoes to the different parts of the book; occasional remarks in the author's own person, such as this about an Oxford college, 'The outer walls of Sarcophagus College—silent, black, and windowless—threw their four centuries of gloom, bigotry, and decay into the little room she occupied'; and still more the actions and words of the characters, all jar by their querulous bitterness and their limited outlook on life. Another reason why this bitterness is fatal to art is that the novelist loses his sense of humour. In this self-imposed task of heaping obloquy on Fate or Providence or Destiny or what you will, he casts about for all sorts of devices for making his characters miserable. It is wonderful, for example, what a number of trains they miss and how much of their misery depends on this. Then that idiotic

son of Jude who is brought on as a sort of chorus to accentuate his and
Sue's misery, and who puts the finishing touch to their woes, seems a
quite gratuitously improbable being. Or how could an author who had
not sacrificed his very real sense of humour make a rustic, even with
Jude's unhealthy hypertrophy of culture, talk like this to the cousin he
is in love with, 'Wifedom has not yet annihilated and digested you in
its vast maw as an atom which has no further individuality', or the same
cousin say to her husband, 'She or he, "who let the world or his own
portion of it choose his plan of life for him, has no need of any other
faculty than the ape-like one of imitation." J. S. Mill's words, those are.
Why can't you act upon them? I wish to always'? No wonder the
husband 'moaned, "What do I care about J. S. Mill!"' And finally the
crowning absurdity of the double re-marriage makes the whole book
appear dangerously near to farce.

The fact is that Mr. Hardy, in his anger against Destiny and in his
desire to make Destiny and its offspring Society odious, has overreached
himself, and has entirely failed in attaining what, in his preface, he
professes to be his object—to expose 'the tragedy of unfulfilled aims'.
In truth, there is no tragedy, at any rate so far as Jude's unfulfilled aims
go, because it is impossible to understand the man and feel any sympathy with him, and without the sympathy at least of human fellow
feeling there is no tragedy possible. To take about as strong an instance
as is possible among modern novelists: there is a tragedy in Sir Wil-
loughby Patterne's fate for which one feels a sympathy; for however
odious he is made, he is always a man, and one knows enough about
him to say that he would have done exactly what he is said to do. Now
about Jude one does not feel that; he is rather a flabby atom without
any individuality, who does things because Mr. Hardy wants to point
a moral by them, or he does not do them for the same reason, and that
Mr. Hardy may rage furiously because he is made miserable thereby.
He is meant to be weak, of course, but as he is presented from one
point of view his refinement at least would have saved him, if not
from Arabella altogether, at any rate from his shameful return to her
in the middle of the book; for as she appears in these pages she is
nothing less than loathsome and repulsive in the highest degree, and
she certainly would be to a man enamoured of Sue's comparative grace
and refinement. There is another reason why the tragedy is not a real
tragedy as Mr. Hardy sees it. His whole point would seem to be that
men are made miserable by the combined efforts of Destiny and Society
when they are disobedient to Society's laws. But the fact is that Mr.

Hardy's characters have a habit of trying to combine obedience to their own private wishes with obedience to Society, or rather to get all they can out of Society and also to outrage her laws when it pleases them. Sue and Jude may have been right in their detestation and abandonment of the marriage tie—that is not the question: the point is that if they act as they did with their eyes open, it is absurd of them to repine because Society and Destiny do not accept their conduct in the same way that they do. A brave and fearless bearing might help to convert Society and Destiny to their views, and at least they would have the consolation of having done what they thought right; but there is no tragedy in the foolish weakness of their behaviour as displayed here—it is merely ludicrous.

As for the question about which Mr. Hardy chooses to exhibit his theory of the universe, one may, perhaps, be allowed to wish that it had not been that dreary question of the marriage tie and its permanence. Not that the subject is in itself out of place in fiction; Mr. Meredith has triumphantly shown that it is in place; but lately so many of the inferior writers of novels have stirred up the mud with this controversy that one would have been content if so great a writer as Mr. Hardy had not touched it, if he was not going greatly to dignify it. Of course, if a man be bent on railing at Destiny, here he has a subject ready to hand from almost the earliest dawn of literature. How far these characters were right or wrong is not a matter to be discussed here; that most of them make themselves exceedingly ridiculous is, in our opinion, much more disastrous.

It goes without saying that as this book is by Mr. Hardy, it is yet a work in some respects worthy of a great writer. The sense of a gloomy background of nature, conveyed more by little hints than by set descriptions, is still as striking as ever, and some of the minor characters that pass over the stage are decidedly telling. Phillotson, the husband of Sue, both in his strength and his weakness is a very living character; and Arabella's father, though little more than hinted at, furnishes a suggestion of a gloomy, sullen force which is undeniably real. In a way the whole book recalls those now famous shadow-plays at the Chat Noir—wonderful landscapes, strangely horrific when meant to suggest the terrible, and true by their very reticence—but the characters mere paper marionettes, well cut out, it is true, but still cut out, and the words they purport to say recited by a man, standing visibly to the audience in front of the show, to accompaniment of solemn music.

50. W. D. Howells, *Harper's Weekly*

7 December 1895

William Dean Howells (1837–1920), the American novelist, had been an admirer and friend of Hardy from the early eighties. This review is reprinted in *Criticism and Fiction and other Essays*, by W. D. Howells (1959), under the title 'Pleasure from Tragedy'.

It has never been quite decided yet, I believe, just what is the kind and what is the quality of pleasure we get from tragedy. A great many people have said what it is, but they seem not to have said this even to their own satisfaction. It is certain that we do get pleasure from tragedy, and it is commonly allowed that the pleasure we get from tragedy is nobler than the pleasure we get from comedy. An alloy of any such pleasure as we get from comedy is held to debase this finer emotion, but this seems true only as to the whole effect of tragedy. The Greek tragedy kept itself purely tragic; and English tragedy assimilated all elements of comedy and made them tragic; so that in the end Hamlet and Macbeth are as high sorrowful as Orestes and Oedipus.

I should be rather ashamed of lugging the classic and the romantic in here, if it were not for the sense I have of the return of an English writer to the Greek motive of tragedy in a book which seems to me one of the most tragical I have read. I have always felt in Mr. Thomas Hardy a charm which I have supposed to be that of the elder pagan world, but this I have found in his lighter moods, for the most part, and chiefly in his study of the eternal-womanly, surviving in certain unconscienced types and characters from a time before Christianity was, and more distinctly before Puritanism was. Now, however, in his latest work he has made me feel our unity with that world in the very essence of his art. He has given me the same pity and despair in view of the blind struggles of his modern English lower-middle-class people that I experience from the destinies of the august figures of Greek fable. I do not know how instinctively or how voluntarily he has appealed to our inherent superstition of Fate, which used to be a religion; but I am sure that in the world where his hapless people have

253

their being, there is not only no Providence, but there is Fate alone; and the environment is such that character itself cannot avail against it. We have back the old conception of an absolutely subject humanity, unguided and unfriended. The gods, careless of mankind, are again over all; only, now, they call themselves conditions.

The story is a tragedy, and tragedy almost unrelieved by the humorous touch which the poet is master of. The grotesque is there abundantly, but not the comic; and at times this ugliness heightens the pathos to almost intolerable effect. But I must say that the figure of Jude himself is, in spite of all his weakness and debasement, one of inviolable dignity. He is the sport of fate, but he is never otherwise than sublime; he suffers more for others than for himself. The wretched Sue who spoils his life and her own, helplessly, inevitably, is the kind of fool who finds the fool in the poet and prophet so often, and brings him to naught. She is not less a fool than Arabella herself; though of such exaltation in her folly that we cannot refuse her a throe of compassion, even when she is most perverse. All the characters, indeed, have the appealing quality of human creatures really doing what they must while seeming to do what they will. It is not a question of blaming them or praising them; they are in the necessity of what they do and what they suffer. One may indeed blame the author for presenting such a conception of life; one may say that it is demoralizing if not immoral; but as to his dealing with his creations in the circumstance which he has imagined, one can only praise him for his truth.

The story has to do with some things not hitherto touched in fiction, or Anglo-Saxon fiction at least; and there cannot be any doubt of the duty of criticism to warn the reader that it is not for all readers. But not to affirm the entire purity of the book in these matters would be to fail of another duty of which there can be as little doubt. I do not believe any one can get the slightest harm from any passage of it; only one would rather that innocence were not acquainted with all that virtue may know. Vice can feel nothing but self-abhorrence in the presence of its facts.

The old conventional personifications seem drolly factitious in their reference to the vital reality of this strange book. I suppose it can be called morbid, and I do not deny that it is. But I have not been able to find it untrue, while I know that the world is full of truth that contradicts it. The common experience, or perhaps I had better say the common knowledge of life contradicts it. Commonly, the boy of Jude's strong aspiration and steadfast ambition succeeds and becomes in some measure the sort of man he dreamed of being. Commonly, a girl like Sue flutters through the anguish of her harassed and doubting youth and settles into acquiescence with the ordinary life of women, if not acceptance of it. Commonly, a boy like the son of Jude, oppressed from birth with the sense of being neither loved nor wanted, hardens himself against his misery, fights for the standing denied him, and achieves it. The average Arabella has no reversion to her first love when she has freed herself from it. The average Phillotson does not give up his wife to the man she says she loves, and he does not take her back knowing her loathing for himself. I grant all these things; and yet the author makes me believe that all he says to the contrary inevitably happened.

I allow that there are many displeasing things in the book, and few pleasing. Arabella's dimple-making, the pig-killing, the boy suicide and homicide; Jude's drunken second marriage; Sue's wilful self-surrender to Phillotson: these and other incidents are revolting. They make us shiver with horror and grovel with shame, but we know that they are deeply founded in the condition, if not in the nature of humanity. There are besides these abhorrent facts certain accusations against some accepted formalities of civilization, which I suppose most readers will find hardly less shocking. But I think it is very well for us to ask from time to time the reasons of things, and to satisfy ourselves, if we can, what the reasons are. If the experience of Jude with Arabella seems to arraign marriage, and it is made to appear not only ridiculous but impious that two young, ignorant, impassioned creatures should promise lifelong fealty and constancy when they can have no real sense of what they are doing, and that then they should be held to their rash vow by all the forces of society, it is surely not the lesson of the story that any other relation than marriage is tolerable for the man and woman who live together. Rather it enforces the conviction that marriage is the sole solution of the question of sex, while it shows how atrocious and heinous marriage may sometimes be.

I find myself defending the book on the ethical side when I meant chiefly to praise it for what seems to me its artistic excellence. It has not only the solemn and lofty effect of a great tragedy; a work far faultier might impart this; but it has unity very uncommon in the novel, and especially the English novel. So far as I can recall its incidents there are none but such as seem necessary from the circumstances and the characters. Certain little tricks which the author sometimes uses to help himself out, and which give the sense of insincerity or debility, are absent here. He does not invoke the playful humour which he employs elsewhere. Such humour as there is tastes bitter, and is grim if not sardonic. This tragedy of fate suggests the classic singleness of means as well as the classic singleness of motive.

51. Mrs. Oliphant, 'The Anti-Marriage League', *Blackwood's Magazine*

January 1896, clix, 135–49

Mrs. Oliphant (see headnote to No. 44), writing in the year before her death, saw Hardy as ranging himself with Grant Allen and the propagandists for 'free love'. (Allen's *The Woman Who Did* had appeared in 1895.) The article begins with a general discussion of the moral responsibilities of fiction before dealing with individual works by Hardy and Allen.

. . . I do not know, however, for what audience Mr. Hardy intends his last work, which has been introduced, as he tells us, for the last twelve months, into a number of decent houses in England and America, with the most shameful portions suppressed. How they could be suppressed in a book whose tendency throughout is so shameful I do not understand; but it is to be hoped that the conductors and readers of *Harper's Magazine* were so protected by ignorance as not to understand what the writer meant then—though he now states it with a plainness beyond mistake. I hesitate to confess that until the publication of Mr. Hardy's last book, *Tess*, I was one of those who had not been convinced of the extent of his power, or of the amount of real genius he possessed. The difference between that book and the former books from his hand was, it appeared to me, very great. It marked the moment of his supposed emancipation from prejudices of modesty which had previously held him (more or less, and sometimes rather less than more) from full enunciation of what was in him. And certainly the result of the *débordement* was very remarkable. To demonstrate that a woman, twice fallen from the woman's code of honour and purity, was by that fact proved to be specially and aggressively pure, was a task for a Hercules, and Mr. Hardy has no more succeeded in doing this than others have done before him; but the rustic landscape, the balmy breathing of the cows, looming out of the haze in the mystery of the dawn—the rapture of the morning in the silent fields, the large figures of the men and women shaping out of the mist and dews—were things to call forth the enthusiasm of admiration with which indeed they were received. But I suppose Mr. Hardy, like so many people, deceived by a simplicity which clings to genius, even when most self-conscious, was not aware what it was which procured him this fame, and ingenuously believed it to be the worser part, the doctrine he preached, and the very hideous circumstances of guilt, unjustified even by passion, of his theme, and not these better things—which thus uplifted him suddenly to the skies.

This perhaps explains, or partially explains, the tremendous downfall of the present book, which, by following *Tess*, accentuates its own grossness, indecency, and horror. Nothing, I think, but a theory could explain the wonderful want of perception which induces a man full of perceptions to make a mistake so fundamental; but it is done—and thus unconsciously affords us the strangest illustration of what Art can come to when given over to the exposition of the unclean. The present writer does not pretend to a knowledge of the works of Zola, which perhaps she ought to have before presuming to say that nothing so coarsely indecent as the whole history of Jude in his relations with his wife Arabella has ever been put in English print—that is to say, from the hands of a Master. There may be books more disgusting, more impious as regards human nature, more foul in detail, in those dark corners where the amateurs of filth find garbage to their taste; but not, we repeat, from any Master's hand. It is vain to tell us that there are scenes in Shakespeare himself which, if they were picked out for special attention, would be offensive to modesty. There is no need for picking out in the work now referred to. Its faults do not lie in mere suggestion, or any *double entendre*, though these are bad enough. In the history of Jude, the half-educated and by no means uninteresting hero in whose early self-training there is much that is admirable—Mr. Hardy has given us a chapter in what used to be called the conflict between vice and virtue. The young man, vaguely aspiring after education, learning, and a position among the scholars and students of the land, with a piteous ignorance of the difficulties before him, yet that conviction of being able to triumph over them, which, as we know, has often in real life succeeded in doing so—is really an attractive figure at his outset. He is virtuous by temperament, meaning no evil; bent upon doing more than well, and elevating himself to the level which appears to him the highest in life. But he falls into the hands of a woman so completely animal that it is at once too little and too much to call her vicious. She is a human pig, like the beast whom in a horrible scene she and her husband kill, quite without shame or consciousness of any occasion for shame, yet not even carried away by her senses or any overpowering impulse for their gratification, so much worse than the sow, that it is entirely on a calculation of profit that she puts forth her revolting spell. After the man has been subjugated, a process through which the reader is required to follow him closely (and Jude's own views on this subject are remarkable), he is made for the rest of his life into a puppet flung about between them by two women—the fleshly animal Arabella and the fantastic Susan, the one ready to gratify him in whatever circumstances they may meet, the other holding him on the tiptoe of expectation, with a pretended reserve which is almost more indecent still. In this curious dilemma the unfortunate Jude, who is always the puppet, always acted upon by the others, never altogether loses our esteem. He is a very poor creature, but he would have liked much better to do well if they would have let him, and dies a virtuous victim of the eternal feminine, scarcely ever blameable, though always bearing both the misery and the shame.

We can with difficulty guess what is Mr. Hardy's motive in portraying such a struggle. It can scarcely be said to be one of those attacks upon the institution of Marriage, which is the undisguised inspiration of some of the other books before us. It is marriage indeed which in the beginning works Jude's woe; and it is by marriage, or rather the marrying of himself and others, that his end is brought about. We rather think the author's object must be, having glorified women by the creation of Tess, to show after all what destructive and ruinous creatures they are, in general circumstances and in every development, whether brutal or refined. Arabella, the first—the pig-dealer's daughter, whose native qualities have been ripened by the experiences of a barmaid—is the Flesh, unmitigated by any touch of human feeling except that of merciless calculation as to what will be profitable for herself. She is the native product of the fields, the rustic woman, exuberant and overflowing with health, vanity and appetite. The colloquy between her and her fellows in their disgusting work, after her first almost equally disgusting interview with Jude, is one of the most unutterable foulness—a shame to the language in which it is recorded and suggested; and the picture altogether of the country lasses at their outdoor work is more brutal in depravity than anything which the darkest slums could bring forth, as are the scenes in which their good advice is carried out. Is it possible that there are readers in England to whom this infamy can be palatable, and who, either in inadvertence or in wantonness, can *make it pay?* Mr. Hardy informs us he has taken elaborate precautions to secure the double profit of the serial writer, by subduing his colours and diminishing his effects, in the presence of the less corrupt, so as to keep the perfection of filthiness for those who love it. It would be curious to compare in this unsavoury traffic how much of the sickening essence of his story Mr. Hardy has thought his first public could stomach, and how many edifying details he has put in for the enlightenment of those who have no squeamish scruples to get over. The transaction is insulting to the public, with whom he trades the viler wares under another name, with all the suppressed passages restored, as old-book dealers say in their catalogues, recommending their ancient scandal to the amateurs of the unclean. It is not the first time Mr. Hardy has adopted this expedient. If the English public supports him in it, it will be to the shame of every individual who thus confesses himself to like and accept what the author himself acknowledges to be unfit for the eyes—not of girls and young persons only, but of the ordinary reader—the men and women who read the Magazines, the public whom we address in these pages. That the prophets should prophesy falsely is not the most important fact in national degradation: it is only when the people love to have it so that the climax is attained.

The other woman—who makes virtue vicious by keeping the physical facts of one relationship in life in constant prominence by denying, as Arabella does by satisfying them, and even more skilfully and insistently than Arabella—the fantastic *raisonneuse*, Susan, completes the circle of the unclean. She marries to save herself from trouble; then quits her husband, to live a life of perpetual temptation and resistance with her lover; then marries, or professes to marry him, when her husband amiably divorces her without the reason he supposes himself to have; and then, when a selfish conscience is tardily awakened, returns to the husband, and ends in ostentatious acceptance of the conditions of matrimony at the moment when the unfortunate Jude, who has also been recaptured by the widowed Arabella, dies of his cruel misery. This woman we are required to accept as the type of high-toned purity. It is the women who are the active agents in all this unsavoury imbroglio: the story is carried on, and life is represented as carried on, entirely by their means. The men are passive, suffering, rather good than otherwise, victims of these and of fate. Not only do they never dominate, but they are quite incapable of holding their own against these remorseless ministers of destiny, these determined opera-tors, managing all the machinery of life so as to secure their own way. This is one of the most curious developments of recent fiction. It is perhaps natural that it should be more or less the case in books written by women, to whom the mere facility of representing their own sex acts as a primary reason for giving them the chief place in the scene. But it has now still more markedly, though much less naturally, become the method with men, in the hands of many of whom women have returned to the *rôle* of the temptress given to them by the old monkish sufferers of ancient times, who fled to the desert, like Anthony, to get free of them, but even there barely escaped with their lives from the seductions of the sirens, who were so audacious as to follow them to the very scene of the macerations and miseries into which the unhappy men plunged to escape from their toils. In the books of the younger men, it is now the woman who seduces—it is no longer the man.

This, however, is a consideration by the way. I have said that it is not clear what Mr. Hardy's motive is in the history of Jude: but, on reconsideration, it becomes more clear that it is intended as an assault on the stronghold of marriage, which is now beleaguered on every side. The motto is, 'The letter killeth'; and I presume this must refer to the fact of Jude's early and unwilling union to Arabella, and that the lesson the novelist would have us learn is, that if marriage were not exacted, and people were free to form connections as the spirit moves them, none of these complications would have occurred, and all would have been well. 'There seemed to him, vaguely and dimly, something wrong in a social ritual which made necessary the cancelling of well-formed schemes involving years of thought and labour, of foregoing a man's one opportunity of showing himself superior to the lower animals, and of contributing his units of work to the general progress of his generation, because of a momentary surprise by a new and transitory instinct which had nothing in it of the nature of vice, and could be only at the most called weakness.' This is the hero's own view of the circumstances which, in obedience to the code of honour prevalent in the countryside, compelled his marriage. Suppose, however, that instead of upsetting the whole framework of society, Jude had shown himself superior to the lower animals by not yielding to that new and transitory influence, the same result could have been easily attained: and he might then have met and married Susan and lived happy ever after, without demanding a total overthrow of all existing laws and customs to prevent him from being unhappy. Had it been made possible for him to have visited Arabella as long as the new and transitory influence lasted, and then to have lived with Susan as long as she pleased to permit him to do so, which was the best that could happen were marriage abolished, how would that have altered the circumstances? When Susan changed her mind would he have been less unhappy? when Arabella claimed him again would he have been less weak?

Mr. Hardy's solution of the great insoluble question of what is to be the fate of children in such circumstances brings this nauseous tragedy suddenly and at a stroke into the regions of pure farce—which is a surprise of the first quality, only too grotesque to be amusing. There are children, as a matter of course: a weird little imp, the son of Arabella, and two babies of Susan's. What is the point of the allegory which Mr. Hardy intends us to read in the absurd little gnome, nicknamed Old Father Time, who is the offspring of the buxom country lass, is a secondary subject upon which we have no light: but it is by the means of this strange creature that the difficulty is settled. In a moment of dreadful poverty and depression, Susan informs her step-son, whom she loves and is very kind to, of the severe straits in which she is. The child —he is now fourteen—asks whether himself and the others are not a great burden upon the parents who are already so poor; and she consents that life would be easier without them. The result is that when she comes in after a short absence she can find no trace of the children, until she perceives what seems to be, at first, suits of their clothes hanging against the wall, but discovers to be the children themselves, all hanged, and swinging from the clothes-pegs: the elder boy having first hanged them and then himself to relieve the parent's hands. Does Mr. Hardy think this is really a good way of disposing of the unfortunate progeny of such connections? does he recommend it for general adoption? It is at least a clean and decisive cut of the knot, leaving no ragged ends; but then there is no natural provision in families of such a wise small child to get its progenitors out of trouble. I read, not long ago, a book in which a young lady of extreme loveliness and genius, to whom it had occurred to begin her life in an irregular manner, confessed to her lover, when fortunate fate brought him to her side after a long separation, by way of making a clean breast of all small peccadilloes before their reunion—that she had killed the baby. He thought no worse of her, and they lived happy ever after. It is no doubt startling at the first glance. But is this to be the way? Mr. Hardy knows, no doubt as everybody does, that the children are a most serious part of the question of the abolition of marriage. Is this the way in which he considers it would be resolved best? . . .

52. Edmund Gosse, *Cosmopolis*

January 1896, i, 60–9

(See headnote to No. 34.) The *Life* prints three letters to Gosse from Hardy on the subject of this review. In the third, dated 4 January 1896, Hardy speaks of having just read *Cosmopolis*, and thanks Gosse for 'the generous view you take of the book', saying that he will discuss the review in more detail when they meet. In the first, dated 10 November 1895, he says 'Your review is the most discriminating that has yet appeared'. At this date the *Cosmopolis* review had not yet appeared, so it would seem that either Gosse reviewed the book twice, or he sent Hardy an early version of his article and Hardy made a slip in speaking of its 'appearance', or the first letter was in fact written to some other reviewer and has been wrongly included in the Gosse correspondence. There is no doubt about the second letter, which has often been quoted for its amplifying remarks on Hardy's whole conception of the story. *Cosmopolis*, described as 'An International Review', was a new venture with many distinguished contributors: it was, however, to be comparatively short-lived.

Among the novelists who, with so remarkable a vitality and variety, have illustrated the latest generation of English thought and feeling, three, by general consent, have attracted the most enthusiastic attention of men of letters. Mr. George Meredith, Mr. Thomas Hardy, the late Mr. Stevenson—these are certainly the names which occur, before any others, to the historian of literature as he reaches the fourth quarter of the nineteenth century. These three have, in no small measure, already entered into their rest; if, which every reader deprecates, Mr. Meredith and Mr. Hardy should write no more, these three, at least, have become classical. Other eminent novelists of our day may have surpassed them in wide popularity, others may possess a more strenuous moral purpose, a greater fluidity of invention, a more ebullient flood of narrative, but those men and women have their reward. The Authors' Club bends, awe-stricken before the enormous volume of their 'sales'. But pure literary renown, sapped though it is by the commercial spirit, is still a commanding element. Still a great number of English novelists, and many of them with no small success, hear the voice yet speaking which said two hundred years ago:

> Travaillez pour la gloire, et qu'un sordide gain
> Ne soit jamais l'objet d'un illustre écrivain,

and among these we say Meredith, Hardy, Stevenson, as one hundred and fifty years ago we might have said Richardson, Fielding, Sterne.

When so high a position as this has been definitely secured by a living writer, it seems to me futile, if not impertinent, to continue, in speaking of his successive books, that strain of purely indulgent eulogy which is the agreeable mode in criticism when welcoming the work of a man who by meritorious production is conquering a place in literature. There is something either patronizing or obsequious, surely, in speaking of Mr. Meredith, for instance, with a less judicious freedom than we use in the consideration of Thackeray or Balzac. We do not hold it artistic to admire every excrescence on the strongly individualized work of the dead; we ought not to suppose that there is any disrespect in admitting that the psychology of Stevenson is sometimes puerile, or that the pertinacious euphuism of Mr. Meredith often painfully clouds the lucidity of his intelligence. We take our favourites as we find them, and, because they are great, we neither expect them to be, nor declare that they are, faultless. Nor is Mr. Hardy, although the author of pages and scenes indescribably felicitous, one of those monsters that the world ne'er saw, a perfect writer. In *Jude the Obscure*, he has aimed, in all probability, higher than he ever aimed before, and it is not to be maintained that he has been equally successful in every part of his design.

Before these pages find a reader, everybody will be familiar with *Jude the Obscure*, and we may well be excused, therefore, from repeating the story in detail. It will be remembered that it is a study of four lives, a rectangular problem in failures, drawn with almost mathematical rigidity. The tragedy of these four persons is constructed in a mode almost as geometrical as that in which Dr. Samuel Clarke was wont to prove the existence of the Deity. It is difficult not to believe that the author set up his four ninepins in the wilds of Wessex, and built up his theorem round them. Here is an initial difficulty. Not quite thus is theology or poetry conveniently composed; we like to conceive that the relation of the parts was more spontaneous, we like to feel that the persons of a story have been thrown up in a jet of enthusiasm, not put into a cave of theory to be slowly covered with stalactite. In this I may be doing Mr. Hardy an injustice, but a certain hardness in the initial conception of *Jude the Obscure* cannot, I believe, be denied. Mr. Hardy is certainly to be condoled with upon the fact that his novel, which has been seven years in the making, has appeared at last at a moment when a sheaf of 'purpose' stories on the 'marriage question' (as it is called) have just been irritating the nerves of the British Patron. No serious critic, however, will accuse Mr. Hardy of joining the ranks of these deciduous troublers of our peace.

We come, therefore, without prejudice to his chronicle of four unnecessary lives. There are the poor village lad, with his longing for the intellectual career; the crude village beauty, like a dahlia in a cottage-garden; the neurotic, semi-educated girl of hyper-sensitive instincts; and the dull, earthy, but not ungenerous schoolmaster. On these four failures, inextricably tied together and dragging one another down, our attention is riveted—on Jude, Arabella, Sue and Phillotson. Before, however, we discuss their characteristics, we may give a little attention to the scene in which these are laid. Mr. Hardy, as all the world knows, has dedicated his life's work to the study of the old province of Wessex. It is his as Languedoc belongs to M. Ferdinand Fabre, or the Isle of Man to Mr. Hall Caine. That he is never happy outside its borders is a commonplace; it is not quite so clearly perceived, perhaps, that he is happiest in the heart of it. When Mr. Hardy writes of South Wessex (Dorsetshire) he seldom goes wrong; this county has been the theatre for all his most splendid successes. From Abbot's

Cornal to Budmouth Regis, and wherever the wind blows freshly off
Egdon Heath, he is absolute master and king. But he is not content
with such a limited realm; he claims four other counties, and it must
be confessed that his authority weakens as he approaches their confines.

Jude the Obscure is acted in North Wessex (Berkshire) and just across
the frontier, at Christminster (Oxford), which is not in Wessex at all.
We want our novelist back among the rich orchards of the Hintocks,
and where the water-lilies impede the lingering river at Shottsford Ash.
Berkshire is an unpoetical county, 'meanly utilitarian', as Mr. Hardy
confesses; the imagination hates its concave, loamy cornfields and
dreary, hedgeless highways. The local history has been singularly
tampered with in Berkshire; it is useless to speak to us of ancient records
where the past is all obliterated, and the thatched and dormered houses
replaced by modern cottages. In choosing North Wessex as the scene
of a novel Mr. Hardy wilfully deprives himself of a great element of
his strength. Where there are no prehistoric monuments, no ancient
buildings, no mossed and immemorial woodlands, he is Samson shorn.
In Berkshire, the change which is coming over England so rapidly, the
resignation of the old dreamy elements of beauty, has proceeded further
than anywhere else in Wessex. Pastoral loveliness is to be discovered
only here and there, while in Dorsetshire it still remains the master-
element. All this combines to lessen the physical charm of *Jude the
Obscure* to those who turn from it in memory to *Far from the Madding
Crowd* and *The Return of the Native*.

But, this fortuitous absence of beauty being acknowledged, the
novelist's hand shows no falling off in the vigour and reality of his
description. It may be held, in fact, to be a lesser feat to raise before us
an enchanting vision of the valley of the Froom, than successfully to
rivet our attention on the prosaic arable land encircling the dull hamlet
of Marygreen. Most attractive Mr. Hardy's pictures of purely country
life have certainly been—there is no picture in *Jude* to approach that of
the life on the dairy farm in *Tess*—but he has never treated rural scenes
with a more prodigious mastery and knowledge. It is, in fact, in knowledge, that Mr. Hardy's work of this class is so admirable. Mere
observation will not produce this illusion of absolute truth. That it is
not enough to drive in an open carriage through the rural districts was
abundantly proved, in the face of Europe, by M. Zola's deplorable
fiasco of *La Terre*. The talent of M. Zola, long unduly exalted, now
perhaps as unduly decried, covers so wide a ground of human experience that a failure in one direction proves no want of skill in another,

but as a student of the peasant his incompetence is beyond question. Curiously enough—and doubtless by a pure accident—there are not a few passages of *Jude the Obscure* which naturally excite comparison with similar scenes in *La Terre*. The parallel is always in Mr. Hardy's favour; his vision of the peasant is invariably more distinct, and more convincing than M. Zola's. He falls into none of the pitfalls laid for the Parisian romancier, and we are never more happy than when he allows us to overhear the primitive Wessex speech. Our only quarrel with Mr. Hardy, indeed, in this respect, is that he grows now impatient of retailing to us the axiomatic humour, the crafty and narrow dignity of the villager.

To pass from the landscape to the persons, two threads of action seem to be intertwined in *Jude the Obscure*. We have, first of all, the contrast between the ideal life the young peasant of scholarly instincts wished to lead, and the squalid real life into which he was fated to sink. We have, secondly, the almost rectilinear puzzle of the sexual relations of the four principal characters. Mr. Hardy has wished to show how cruel destiny can be to the eternal dream of youth, and he has undertaken to trace the lamentable results of unions in a family exhausted by intermarriage and poverty. Some collision is apparent between these aims; the first seems to demand a poet, the second a physician. The Fawleys are a decayed and wasted race, in the last of whom, Jude, there appears, with a kind of flicker in the socket, a certain intellectual and artistic brightness. In favourable surroundings, we feel that this young man might have become fairly distinguished as a scholar, or as a sculptor. But at the supreme moment, or at each supreme moment, the conditions hurl him back into insignificance. When we examine clearly what these conditions are, we find them to be instinctive. He is just going to develop into a lad of education, when Arabella throws her hideous missile at him, and he sinks with her into a resigned inferiority.

So far, the critical court is with Mr. Hardy; these scenes and their results give a perfect impression of truth. Later on, it is not quite evident whether the claim on Jude's passions, or the inherent weakness of his inherited character, is the source of his failure. Perhaps both. But it is difficult to see what part Oxford has in his destruction, or how Mr. Hardy can excuse the rhetorical diatribes against the university which appear towards the close of the book. Does the novelist really think that it was the duty of the heads of houses to whom Jude wrote his crudely pathetic letters to offer him immediately a fellowship? We may admit to the full the pathos of Jude's position—nothing is more heart-rending than the obscurity of the half-educated—but surely, the fault did not lie with Oxford.

The scene at Commemoration (Part VI) is of a marvellous truth and vividness of presentment, but it would be stronger, and even more tragic, if Mr. Hardy did not appear in it as an advocate taking sides with his unhappy hero. In this portion of his work, it seems to me, Mr. Hardy had but to paint—as clearly and as truthfully as he could— the hopes, the struggles, the disappointments of Jude, and of these he has woven a tissue of sombre colouring, indeed, and even of harsh threads, but a tapestry worthy of a great imaginative writer. It was straightforward poet's work in invention and observation, and he has executed it well.

But in considering the quadruple fate of the four leading characters, of whom Jude is but one, we come to matter of a different order. Here the physician, the neuropathist, steps in, and takes the pen out of the poet's hand. Let us for a moment strip to its barest nomination this part of the plot. Jude, a neurotic subject in whom hereditary degeneracy takes an idealist turn, with some touch, perhaps, of what the new doctors call megalomania, has been warned by the local gossips not to marry. But he is physically powerful and attractive, and he engages the notice of Arabella, a young woman of gross instincts and fine appearance, who seduces and marries him. He falls from his scholastic dream to the level of a labourer, and is only saved by the fact that Arabella wearies of him and leaves him. He goes to Oxford, and, gradually cultivating the dream again, seems on the first rung of the ladder of success, when he comes across his own cousin Sue, and loves her. But she has promised to marry Phillotson, a weary middle-aged school-master, and marry him she will, although she loves Jude, and has forced him to compromise her. But she finds Phillotson intolerable, and leaves him to join Jude, only to find herself equally unhappy and unsatisfying, dragging Jude once more down to mediocrity. Arabella crosses Jude's life again, and jealousy forces Sue to some semblance of love for Jude. Sue becomes the mother of several children, who are killed in a fit of infantile mania by a boy, the son of Jude and Arabella, whose habitual melancholy, combined with his hereditary antecedents, has prepared us for an outbreak of suicide, if not of murder. This horrible event affects Sue by producing religious mania. She will live no longer with Jude, although both couples have got their divorce, but fatally returns to be the slave of her detested schoolmaster, while Jude, in a paroxysm of drunken abandonment, goes back to Arabella and dies.

It is a ghastly story, especially when reduced to this naked skeleton. But it does not appear to me that we have any business to call in question the right of a novelist of Mr. Hardy's extreme distinction to treat what themes he will. We may wish—and I for my part cordially wish—that more pleasing, more charming plots than this could take his fancy. But I do not feel at liberty to challenge his discretion. One thing, however, the critic of comparative literature must note. We have, in such a book as *Jude the Obscure*, traced the full circle of propriety. A hundred and fifty years ago, Fielding and Smollett brought up before us pictures, used expressions, described conduct, which appeared to their immediate successors a little more crude than general reading warranted. In Miss Burney's hands and in Miss Austen's, the morals were still further hedged about. Scott was even more daintily reserved. We came at last to Dickens, where the clamorous passions of mankind, the coarser accidents of life, were absolutely ignored, and the whole question of population seemed reduced to the theory of the gooseberry bush. This was the *ne plus ultra* of decency; Thackeray and George Eliot relaxed this intensity of prudishness; once on the turn, the tide flowed rapidly, and here is Mr. Hardy ready to say any mortal thing that Fielding said, and a good deal more too.

So much we note, but to censure it, if it calls for censure, is the duty of the moralist and not the critic. Criticism asks how the thing is done, whether the execution is fine and convincing. To tell so squalid and so abnormal a story in an interesting way is in itself a feat, and this, it must be universally admitted, Mr. Hardy has achieved. *Jude the Obscure* is an irresistible book; it is one of those novels into which we descend and are carried on by a steady impetus to the close, when we return, dazzled, to the light of common day. The two women, in particular, are surely created by a master. Every impulse, every speech, which reveals to us the coarse and animal, but not hateful Arabella, adds to the solidity of her portrait. We may dislike her, we may hold her intrusion into our consciousness a disagreeable one, but of her reality there can be no question: Arabella lives.

It is conceivable that not so generally will it be admitted that Sue Bridehead is convincing. Arabella is the excess of vulgar normality; every public bar and village fair knows Arabella, but Sue is a strange and unwelcome product of exhaustion. The *vita sexualis* of Sue is the central interest of the book, and enough is told about it to fill the specimen tables of a German specialist. Fewer testimonies will be given to her reality than to Arabella's because hers is much the rarer case. But her picture is not less admirably drawn; Mr. Hardy has, perhaps, never devoted so much care to the portrait of a woman. She is a poor, maimed 'degenerate', ignorant of herself and of the perversion of her instincts, full of febrile, amiable illusions, ready to dramatize her empty life, and play at loving though she cannot love. Her adventure with the undergraduate has not taught her what she is; she quits Phillotson still ignorant of the source of her repulsion; she lives with Jude, after a long, agonizing struggle, in a relation that she accepts with distaste, and when the tragedy comes, and her children are killed, her poor extravagant brain slips one grade further down, and she sees in this calamity the chastisement of God. What has she done to be chastised? She does not know, but supposes it must be her abandonment of Phillotson, to whom, in a spasm of self-abasement, and shuddering with repulsion, she returns without a thought for the misery of Jude. It is a terrible study in pathology, but of the splendid success of it, of the sustained intellectual force implied in the evolution of it, there cannot, I think, be two opinions.

One word must be added about the speech of the author and of the characters in *Jude the Obscure*. Is it too late to urge Mr. Hardy to struggle against the jarring note of rebellion which seems growing upon him? It sounded in *Tess*, and here it is, more roughly expressed, further acerbated. What has Providence done to Mr. Hardy that he should rise up in the arable land of Wessex and shake his fist at his Creator? He should not force his talent, should not give way to these chimerical outbursts of philosophy falsely so called. His early romances were full of calm and lovely pantheism; he seemed in them to feel the deep-hued country landscapes full of rural gods, all homely and benign. We wish he would go back to Egdon Heath and listen to the singing in the heather. And as to the conversations of his semi-educated characters, they are really terrible. Sue and Jude talk a sort of University Extension jargon that breaks the heart. 'The mediaevalism of Christminster must go, be sloughed off, or Christminster will have to go', says Sue, as she sits in a pair of Jude's trousers, while Jude dries her petticoat at his garret-fire. Hoity-toity, for a minx! the reader cries, or, rather, although he firmly believes in the existence of Sue, and in the truth of the episode, he is convinced that Mr. Hardy is mistaken in what he heard her say. She *could* not have talked like that.

A fact about the infancy of Mr. Hardy has escaped the interviewers and may be recorded here. On the day of his birth, during a brief absence of his nurse, there slipped into the room an ethereal creature, known as the Spirit of Plastic Beauty. Bending over the cradle she scattered roses on it, and as she strewed them she blessed the babe. 'He shall have an eye to see moral and material loveliness, he shall speak of richly-coloured pastoral places in the accent of Theocritus, he shall write in such a way as to cajole busy men into a sympathy with old, unhappy, far-off things.' She turned and went, but while the nurse still delayed, a withered termagant glided into the room. From her apron she dropped toads among the rose-leaves, and she whispered: 'I am the genius of False Rhetoric, and led by me he shall say things ugly and coarse, not recognizing them to be so, and shall get into a rage about matters that call for philosophic calm, and shall spoil some of his best passages with pedantry and incoherency. He shall not know what things belong to his peace, and he shall plague his most loyal admirers with the barbaric contortions of his dialogue.' So saying, she put out her snaky tongue at the unoffending babe, and ever since, his imagination, noble as it is, and attuned to the great harmonies of nature, is liable at a moment's notice to give a shriek of discord. The worst, however, which any honest critic can say of *Jude the Obscure* is that the fairy god-mother seems, for the moment, to have relaxed her guardianship a little unduly.

53. D. F. Hannigan, *Westminster Review*

January 1896, cxlv, 136–9

(See headnote to No. 48.)

Those who have satisfied themselves by observation and experience of the essentially artificial character of so-called British 'morality' will not be surprised to find that certain critics of the didactic school have condemned Mr. Thomas Hardy's latest novel, *Jude the Obscure*, on the ground of its outspokenness and its flagrant disregard of Mrs. Grundy's tender feelings. *Tess of the D'Urbervilles* offended the susceptibilities of such critics as Mr. Andrew Lang and Mr. James Payn, who worship the venerable Walter Scott, and prefer romance to realism. But *Jude the Obscure* will be *anathema maranatha* to hundreds of comparatively liberal-minded people who see no harm in such works as *Jane Eyre* or *Adam Bede*. Mr. Hardy does not write, like Sir Walter Besant, merely for the edification of 'the Young Person'. When invited to give his personal views some time since on the subject of 'Candour in Fiction', he emphatically claimed for the novelist the right to deal fearlessly with all the facts of life. His sympathies are manifestly with the French naturalistic school of fiction, though I for one cannot regard him as a writer of the same class as M. Zola or the late Guy de Maupassant. Through all that Mr. Hardy has written vibrates a passionate chivalry, to which we find no parallel in French realism. In our generation there has been no novelist capable of exhibiting the mysterious fascination of woman upon the other sex with the same art, with the same force of imagination. All his heroines are ideals, or at least idealized types, rather than portraits drawn from real life. To this extent, therefore, Mr. Hardy is not 'realistic' in the vulgar sense of the word. He has shrunk from the portrayal of commonplace women—if we except the case of Arabella in his last novel—and the charming creatures around whom the interest of *Far from the Madding Crowd*, *The Trumpet Major*, and nearly all his other works, including *Tess of the D'Urbervilles*, centres, seem like etherealized beings—fays, sirens, who disguise themselves as farmeresses, parsons' daughters, unconventional heiresses, bishops' wives, schoolmistresses, or agricultural working-girls.

To ordinary men of the world such creatures as Elfride in *A Pair of Blue Eyes* probably appear as unreal as Cinderella. Tess, no doubt, walks through dreadful realities to a tragic doom, and I can easily imagine the horror of a mere romantic trifler like Mr. Andrew Lang on finding a woman with such a record put forward as a heroine of fiction. But she, too, is the opposite of commonplace. Hers is a rich, voluptuous, daring, downright nature, such as old Babylon might have produced, in spite of her prosaic surroundings and her squalid miseries. The physiognomy of character, which defies external circumstances, has been recognized by Mr. Hardy, and he alone, amongst living English novelists, has fully realized the great truth that a Cleopatra may be found toiling on a Wessex farm, that the soul of a Mary Stuart may animate a nineteenth-century middle-class girl.

Are there such women around us as those delineated by the author of *Tess?* I am sure such beings are possible; and if we admit their possibility, let us thank Mr. Hardy for having presented to us in his pages entrancingly fascinating creatures, who, unlike the objectionable crowd of so-called 'advanced' women, are free from mammon-worship, low ambition and aggressiveness, and are essentially feminine, like Helen of Troy, Mary Magdalen, and that fair Heloïse whose name shines like a star through the monastic gloom of the Middle Ages.

How poor and artificial a heroine Diana Vernon is, in comparison with Paula Power, or even Ethelberta, notwithstanding the disappointment we naturally feel at her unorthodox conduct in marrying the wrong man! Diana Vernon is, at least in my judgment, a mere fancy-portrait, and a rather repulsive type of womanhood withal. Paula is not unreal, but an idealization of a modern girl, and what a splendid creature she is!

Mr. Hardy, then, is a worshipper of the ideal woman, and his heroines are all free from the vice of what I venture to describe as feminine masculinity (disregarding the criticism of logic-choppers)—the novelist has stripped them of materializing influences, so that, to use in a different sense the words of a popular English poet, 'all that remains of them now is pure womanly'. It has frequently amused me to hear 'good young men' abuse Mr. Hardy for having on his title-page called poor Tess 'a pure woman'. Why did these admirably moral prigs forget Tom Hood's immortal line, which fully explains the novelist's meaning?

While Mr. Hardy's heroines are types, or ideals, the *milieu* in which they are placed is as true as any pen-picture of English life and English landscape can possibly be; and the Wessex described in his novels is essentially and unmistakably English.

Jude the Obscure is a very different kind of book from *Tess of the D'Urbervilles*. In *Tess* the entire interest of the novel is attached to the life of a woman; in *Jude*, just as in *The Mayor of Casterbridge*, it gathers round the career of a man. The history of Jude's ineffectual efforts to obtain a University education is intensely pathetic. If Samuel Johnson could come back to earth and read this portion of Mr. Hardy's last novel, I venture to think that he would have found it hard to keep back his tears, stern Briton though he was; and, but for the miserable priggery of this tail-end of the nineteenth century, the first part of *Jude the Obscure* would be held up by the critics as one of the most touching records in all literature. This story of crushed aspirations can only be appreciated by those who have the power of true sympathy. Unfortunately, we live in an age when nearly all human beings are concerned only with their material success in life. The word 'failure' makes them tremble; and, no doubt, Mr. Hardy's apparent pessimism is distasteful to the innumerable throng of vulgar-minded aspirants whose only gospel is to 'get on' by hook or by crook. How could we expect the modern young man, whose thoughts are fixed solely on the Woolsack or on the results of a successful experiment on the Turf or the Stock Exchange, to enter into the feelings of a poor rustic stone-cutter who dreamed of taking out his degree and becoming a clergyman! The love-affairs of so obscure an individual may excite the attention of the unambitious middle-aged man, but not of the youthful prig of our day. The relations between Sue and her cousin will necessarily appear impure to those who see nothing but uncleanness in the relations of a married man and a woman who is not his wife. But Mr. Hardy is not to blame for the brutishness of some of his readers' minds any more than Miranda (to borrow a favourite illustration of Mr. Ruskin) is to blame for Caliban's beastly thoughts about her.

The 'plot' (hideous word!) of *Jude the Obscure* has been sketched, and, indeed, misrepresented, by so many of the smug journalistic critics of this book, that it is better to let all intelligent and honest readers find out the true history of Jude Fawley for themselves by reading the novel. It is certainly 'strong meat', but there is nothing prurient, nothing artificial in this work; it is *human* in the widest sense of that comprehensive word. The tragic chapter with which the novel closes is perhaps the finest specimen of pure narrative that Mr. Hardy has ever given us —there is nothing equal to it in *Tess of the D'Urbervilles*. The character of Sue is nearly as fascinating as that of Elfride in *A Pair of Blue Eyes*. In concentrated power the novel, as a whole, is inferior to *Tess*, and it lacks the fresh, sweet atmosphere which makes *The Woodlanders* one of the most delightful of books. In Arabella we have a faithful portrait of a foul-minded woman whom we can compare to no other female personage in Mr. Hardy's novels. Some of the language put into the mouth of Phillotson, the husband of Sue, is a little incongruous, for it is scarcely likely that a village schoolmaster would talk about 'the matriarchal system'.

But in spite of certain defects of form which are perhaps inevitable, having regard to the intricacies of a story involving matrimonial complications, *Jude the Obscure* is the best English novel which has appeared since *Tess of the D'Urbervilles*. Mr. George Meredith's epigrammatic cleverness cannot atone for his poverty of invention, his lack of incident, his fantastic system of misreading human nature, and, if the word 'novelist' means a writer of human history, Mr. Hardy is incomparably superior to his supposed rival. I would class the author of *Tess* with Fielding, Balzac, Flaubert, Turgenev, George Eliot and Dostoievsky; while Mr. Meredith is the literary brother of Bulwer Lytton, Peacock and Mérimée. The mosquito-like criticism of the day need not trouble a novelist who has already won fame. He is the greatest living English writer of fiction. In intensity, in grip of life, and, above all, in the artistic combination of the real and the ideal, he surpasses any of his French contemporaries. *Jude the Obscure* is not his greatest work; but no other living novelist could have written it.

54. Unsigned review,
Illustrated London News

11 January 1896, cviii, 50

The reader closes this book with a feeling that a huge pall has blotted out all the light of humanity. In one way, that sensation is a tribute to Mr. Hardy's mastery of his art. He has carried you from one broken hope to another, through a series of painful climaxes; and such is the spaciousness which his grasp of elemental things imparts to the story that a tragedy of three lives seems to fill the world with sorrow, and invite irony from the heavens. In *Jude*, even more than in *Tess*, Nature plays a sort of ironical chorus; the most casual circumstances fall into the dismal harmony of fate: an organ peals a hymn of gratitude at the very moment when Jude finds his children dead; and the first conversation that reaches his tortured ear from the street is between two parsons who are discussing the eastward position. The humour which glances through most of Mr. Hardy's books—a humour which is never boisterous and not always genial, but still akin to the buoyancy of life—is here subdued to an undercurrent of grim mockery. 'Weddings be funerals 'a believe nowadays', remarks the widow Edlin concerning one of the matrimonial adventures in the story. 'Fifty-four years ago, come Fall, since my man and I married. Times have changed since then.' That is amusing; but it does not kindle you to mirth. There is a child, a terrible little elf, Jude's boy by his first marriage, with 'an octogenarian's face', set in listless indifference to the surface of things which usually engages a child's attention, with a deep and brooding pessimism which seems to have grown with him out of the cradle. It is upon this gruesome fragment of humanity, and not upon his father, that the burden of life falls most heavily. 'Little Father Time', as the child is nick-named, observes the arrival of other children with disapproval and alarm. There are three in all, and when little Jude learns from Sue, the mother of two, that a fourth is expected, he breaks into reproaches, murders his two brothers, and hangs himself. Now, up to this point, woe has been heaped upon woe, and the reader has accepted it all, with some reservations, as a natural evolution of the circumstances. The tragedy of the children strains his belief to snapping point; and then comes a perfectly superfluous touch which snaps it altogether. Jude reports to the suffering mother of two of the dead little ones the opinion of the doctor, who, oddly enough, happens to be 'an advanced man'. He is so 'advanced' as to assure the father that unnatural children who murder their brothers and commit suicide are becoming common, owing to the 'universal wish not to live'. This is too much. Fortunately, it comes so near the end that the extraordinary power and even beauty of the book are not destroyed; but it is strange that Mr. Hardy did not perceive how he had imperilled the whole fabric by a stroke which passes the border of burlesque. The horror of the infant pessimist is changed in a moment to ghastly farce by this inopportune generalization of the 'advanced' doctor. We all know perfectly well that baby Schopenhauers are not coming into the world in shoals. Children whose lives, stunted by poverty or disease, have acquired a gravity beyond their years, may be found everywhere in the overcrowded centres of population; but such a portrait as little Jude Fawley, who advocates the annihilation of the species, and gives a practical example of it at a tender age, does not present itself as typical of a devouring philosophy.

The immediate effect of this error in Mr. Hardy's scheme of all-embracing tribulation is that the reader renews his 'will to live' and be moderately cheerful, and is not at all disposed to take very seriously the final permutations of the conjugal tie which has played such pranks throughout the novel. Jude begins the real business of life by marrying Arabella, a coarse young woman of his rural district. That enterprise is a speedy failure, and Arabella goes off to Australia, where she commits bigamy, while Jude yields to the enchantments of his cousin Sue. Sue, however, marries Phillotson, the schoolmaster, and finding that match insupportable, rejoins Jude with her husband's consent. Arabella returns, and then there is a general divorcing, Jude divorces his wife; the schoolmaster divorces his. Arabella re-marries the bigamist, but Jude and Sue, after various unsuccessful expeditions to the registry-office and the church, decide that marriage is a mistake. After the death of her children, Sue, hitherto a most philosophical lady, much given to quoting Mill and Humboldt, is suddenly seized by a fit of what she calls renunciation. In this frame of mind she insists on returning to Phillotson, who marries her again. The deserted Jude takes to strong liquor, in which he falls a victim to Arabella, now a widow, who re-marries him. After a last despairing interview with his Sue, he dies. The perpetual shuffling of partners hovers dangerously near the ridiculous, though, to be sure, it seems Mr. Hardy's intent to show us what a tragi-comedy is the matrimonial bond, of which 'the letter killeth', while the spirit is the sport of the whimsical humour of Nature. We may be rather staggered by the self-denial of the schoolmaster who, at the cost of his own social ruin, allows his most attractive and most perplexing wife to go her ways with her lover; but Sue, with all her pedantry, and in spite of the too evident effort to focus in her all the restless imaginings of our modern adventurous womanhood, is an intensely vivid personality. When the pedantry is sloughed off, when she no longer 'talks profound', when the blow of the children's tragic end to her nervous system plunges her into a reaction, and makes her regard her broken marriage with Phillotson as a sacramental obligation, which must be renewed at the price of even greater suffering—then, it is possible, Sue is more unreal than ever to many students of her career, and more truly feminine to many more. As for Jude, the young stone-cutter, whose soul, laden with theology, appeals vainly to the heads of colleges, while his body is doomed to manual labour, drink and Arabella, he may strike us now and then as phantasmal. But read the story how you will, it is manifestly a work of genius, moving amid ideas and emotions of so large a significance that most of our fiction is to *Jude the Obscure* as a hamlet to a hemisphere.

55. Richard le Gallienne, *Idler*

February 1896, ix, 114–15

The review is part of a feature entitled 'Wanderings in Bookland' (the next work to be discussed after *Jude* is *The Second Jungle Book*). The *Idler* was a magazine founded by Jerome K. Jerome in 1892 and edited by him, with Robert Barr, until 1898.

The other day I saw the position of a certain successful novelist referred to as being nothing short of parallel with that of 'a Hebrew prophet or a Roman *vates*'! No wonder, then, that our novelists affix grave prefaces to their stories, and generally write as men burdened with a mission. But the preacher turned novelist is a different thing from the novelist turned preacher. Not all Mr. Hardy's strenuous 'purpose' in *Jude the Obscure* can rob him of a novelist's first great gift, the power of creating living human beings. It is true that Jude and Sue have their lapses into unreality, and there are situations in the book which it takes all Mr. Hardy's dramatic power to make credible, but allowing to the full all such criticisms *Jude* remains perhaps the most powerful and moving picture of human life which Mr. Hardy has given us. No doubt the picture is dark, darker, perhaps, even than reality. Such pessimism is only half true of life as a whole. *Jude*, indeed, is a masterly piece of special pleading, much as was *Les Misérables*. But just as in optimistic novels of the old pattern, the hero is blessed with impossible good fortune from start to finish, Val Jean and Jude are cursed with almost equally bad luck. In one case everything prospers; in the other everything goes wrong. A malignant fate seems to dog their footsteps, at every turn of the way they make tragic mistakes, and their very wisdom is always for the worst. Undoubtedly there are actual lives of such unrelieved misfortune, and a novelist is quite within his right in taking such for his theme, yet he must not present them to us as typical human lives—for such, even amid the hardest conditions, they are not. Too many reviewers have treated *Jude* as a polemic against marriage. Nothing could be more unjust. It is true that the tragedy of Jude and Sue was partly brought about by the marriage laws, but their own weakness of character was mainly responsible for it; and Mr. Hardy's novel, in so far as it is an indictment, is an indictment of much older and crueller laws than those relating to marriage, the laws of the universe. It is a Promethean indictment of that power, which, in Omar's words,

> with pitfall and with gin,
> Beset the path we were to wander in,

and to conceive it merely as a criticism of marriage is to miss its far more universal tragic significance. And here in passing I must refer to a grossly unjust and exceedingly pointless and clumsy attack recently made upon Mr. Hardy by no other than Mrs. Oliphant in *Blackwood's Magazine*. No doubt Mrs. Oliphant means well, but she does exceeding ill in thus, either wilfully or involuntarily, distorting the purpose of Mr. Hardy's book. Her insinuation—to put it mildly—that Mr. Hardy has deliberately catered for unclean appetites, and that he published an expurgated edition of his story first in *Harper's*, just to whet such appetites for the complete book (when, as everyone knows, that first truncated publication was a condition of the magazine editors which caused Mr. Hardy no little pain and worry), is either very malignant or very mistaken, and should certainly be libellous. There is no need further to allude to the pitiful spleen of 'M. O. W. O.' except to warn the reader against it, and all such outbursts of grandmotherly prejudice. No doubt *Jude*

> is not meat
> For little people or for fools,

it is as Mr. Kipling said of Mowgli's marriage, 'a story for grown-ups', and it will only be the childish or second-childish among these whom it can possibly offend. It handles delicate problems and situations with infinite delicacy and tenderness, and if in depicting certain aspects of country life, Mr. Hardy's realism is a little 'coarse', well, country life *is* coarse, so what would you have?

56. Unsigned review, *Saturday Review*

8 February 1896, lxxxi, 153–4

It is doubtful, considering not only the greatness of the work but also the greatness of the author's reputation, whether for many years any book has received quite so foolish a reception as has been accorded the last and most splendid of all the books that Mr. Hardy has given the world. By an unfortunate coincidence it appears just at the culmination of a new fashion in Cant, the Cant of 'Healthiness'. It is now the better part of a year ago since the collapse of the 'New Woman' fiction began. The success of *The Woman Who Did* was perhaps the last of a series of successes attained, in spite of glaring artistic defects, and an utter want of humour or beauty, by works dealing intimately and unrestrainedly with sexual affairs. It marked a crisis. A respectable public had for a year or more read such books eagerly, and discussed hitherto unheard of topics with burning ears and an air of liberality. The reviewers had reviewed in the spirit of public servants. But such strange delights lead speedily to remorse and reaction. The pendulum bob of the public conscience swung back swiftly and forcibly. From reading books wholly and solely dependent upon sexuality for their interest, the respectable public has got now to rejecting books wholly and solely for their recognition of sexuality, however incidental that recognition may be. And the reviewers, mindful of the fact that the duty of a reviewer is to provide acceptable reading for his editor's public, have changed with the greatest dexterity from a chorus praising 'outspoken purity' to a band of public informers against indecorum. It is as if the spirit of McDougallism has fled the London County Council to take refuge in the circles called 'literary'. So active, so malignant have these sanitary inspectors of fiction become, that a period of terror, analogous to that of the New England Witch Mania, is upon us. No novelist, however respectable, can deem himself altogether safe today from a charge of morbidity and unhealthiness. They spare neither age nor sex; the beginner of yesterday and the maker of a dozen respectable novels suffer alike. They outdo one another in their alertness for anything they can by any possible measure of language contrive to call *decadent*. One scarcely dares leave a man and woman together within the same corners for fear of their scandal; one dares scarcely whisper of reality. And at the very climax of this silliness, Mr. Hardy, with an admirable calm, has put forth a book in which a secondary, but very important, interest is a frank treatment of the destructive influence of a vein of sensuality upon an ambitious working-man. There probably never was a novel dealing with the closer relations of men and women that was quite so free from lasciviousness as this. But at one point a symbolical piece of offal is flung into Jude's face. Incontinently a number of popular reviewers, almost tumbling over one another in the haste to be first, have rushed into print under such headings as 'Jude the Obscene', and denounced the book, with simply libellous violence, as a mass of filth from beginning to end.

If the reader has trusted the reviewers for his estimate of this great novel, he may even be surprised to learn that its main theme is not sexual at all; that the dominant motive of Jude's life is the fascination Christminster (Oxford) exercises upon his rustic imagination, and that the climax of its development is the pitiless irony of Jude's death-scene, within sound of the University he loved—which he loved, but which could offer no place in all its colleges for such a man as he. Only as a modifying cause does the man's sexuality come in, just as much as, and no more than, it comes into the life of any serious but healthy man. For the first time in English literature the almost intolerable difficulties that beset an ambitious man of the working class—the snares, the obstacles, the countless rejections and humiliations by which our society eludes the services of these volunteers—receive adequate treatment. And since the peculiar matrimonial difficulties of Jude's cousin Sue have been treated *ad nauseam* in the interests of purity in our contemporaries, we may perhaps give her but an incidental mention in this review, and devote ourselves to the neglected major theme of the novel.

The story opens at once upon this with the departure of the Marygreen schoolmaster to Oxford. Marygreen, by-the-bye, is apparently 'Great Fawley', in Berkshire. 'My dream', says he, 'is to be a University graduate, and then to be ordained'; and Jude, his favourite scholar, helping pack, listens open-mouthed. 'The boy is crazy for books,' explains Miss Fawley to a neighbour; and the reader sees him dreaming of them instead of scaring rooks, and as a consequence being dismissed by his indignant employer. None but those who have lived without learning until the age of thought and knowledge can tell of the strange reverence scholarship has from the unlearned. Apart from its stimulating mystery, it is to many an illiterate imagination the promise of emancipation and power. Jude, immensely depressed by his dismissal and the scolding he receives from his aunt, tramps up the long white road to the steep counterscarp of the chalk-downs, and thence, peering towards the legendary Christminster, sees as the sun sets something emerge awhile from the blue indistinctness.

[quotes part first, ch. III from 'Some way within the limits' to 'shapes of chimaeras.']

So the book opens. In that hour Christminster lays its grip upon his soul. He talks of it, questions men on the road about it, above all dreams of it and its treasury of knowledge. He revisits that spot again and again; for after dark one can see in the sky the dim reflections of the yellow lamps of the place.

'It is a city of light,' he said to himself.

'The tree of knowledge grows there,' he added a few steps further on.

'It is a place that teachers of men spring from and go to.'

'It is what you may call a castle, manned by scholarship and religion.'

Then comes the inevitable struggle for books, a begging letter to Mr. Phillotson, and 'At last a packet did indeed arrive at the village, and he saw from the ends of it that it contained two thin books. He took it away into a lonely place, and sat down on a felled elm to open it. . . . The book was an old one—thirty years old, soiled, scribbled wantonly over with a strange name in every variety of enmity to the letterpress, and marked at random with dates twenty years earlier than his own day.'

If the reader is one of those who have been educated from the beginning, it may interest him to learn that today in the second-hand bookshops old out-of-date text-books are sold by the thousand. Yet here for the first time in fiction is one of the readers of these books. Jude drives the van round the district with his aunt's loaves, and meanwhile he would 'slip the reins over his arm, ingeniously fix open, by means of a strap attached to the tilt, the volume he was reading, spread the dictionary on his knees, and plunge into the simpler passages from Caesar, Virgil, or Horace, as the case might be, in his purblind stumbling way, and with an expenditure of labour that would have made a tender-hearted pedagogue shed tears.'

Respectable but timid people naturally considered him a dangerous person, and complained to the Marygreen policeman.

That is the 'Obscene' Jude of the scandalized reviewers; and it is hard to say how many hundreds of his kind—village cobblers, bakers and so forth—are covetously seeking after knowledge. We may pass over the perfectly natural incidents of his encounter with Arabella, their marriage, and her desertion of him, to see him again, in Christminster, beating himself against the gates that are closed to him for ever. Is he not over nineteen, the age limit that practically restricts almost every Oxford and Cambridge scholarship to the middle class? He is full of the glamour of Oxford; he marches the streets of a night communing with the ghosts of her great past; the mere fact of such reverence in a stonemason's mind is surely a triumph of irony. He spouts Latin to humorous undergraduates, prowls round quadrangles, peers through gates. His pilgrimage to Christminster ends at last with a series of imploring letters to the Heads of Colleges, letters which go unanswered save by one distinguished personage:

BIBLIOLL COLLEGE.

'SIR—I have read your letter with interest, and, judging from your description of yourself as a working-man, I venture to think that you will have a much better chance of success in life by remaining in your own sphere and sticking to your trade than by adopting any other course. That, therefore, is what I advise you to do—Yours faithfully,

T. TETUPHENAY.

To Mr. J. Fawley, Stonecutter.'

An effectual quietus to his low-born ambitions. He declares upon drink:

At ten o'clock he came away, choosing a circuitous route homeward to pass the gates of the College whose Head had just sent him the note. The gates were shut, and, by an impulse, he took from his pocket the lump of chalk which as a workman he usually carried there, and wrote along the wall: '*I have understanding as well as you; I am not inferior to you; yea, who knoweth not such things as these?*'—Job xii. 3.

It is at Christminster that he, being already married to the runaway Arabella, meets and falls in love with his cousin Sue. And this development of the sexual side of the man is a necessary part of his complete presentation. He is energetic, he is deeply emotional, and the complication was inevitable. The man of the lower class who aspires to knowledge can only escape frustration by ruthlessly suppressing affections and passions; it is a choice of one tragedy or another. To have veiled the matter, to have ignored sex altogether in deference to the current fashion, would have gone far to make Jude the Obscure into a John Halifax, Gentleman. Sue, however, is no mere figure of sexual affection, as Arabella is of passion; she is the feminine counterpart of Jude's intellectual side, clearer minded, unimpassioned, an exceptional but a possible woman. She points the moral of the Christminster defeat with her acute modern-spirited comments, and participates so far in the main theme of the story, in addition to her rôle as a detracting feminine influence. But her cold-bloodedness seems, for some incomprehensible reason, to have roused the common reviewer to a pitch of malignant hatred.

It is impossible by scrappy quotations to do justice to Mr. Hardy's tremendous indictment of the system which closes our three English teaching Universities to what is, and what has always been, the noblest material in the intellectual life of this country—the untaught. Sufficient has been quoted to show how entirely false is the impression that this book relies mainly upon its treatment of sex trouble—that it is to be regarded as a mere artistic and elaborate essay upon the great 'Woman Who' theme. That is really as much criticism as is needed here just now. The present reviewer will not even pretend to taste and dubitate, to advise and reprimand, in the case of a book that alone will make 1895 a memorable year in the history of literature. Let it suffice further to quote the last scene of all, the death of Jude, one of the most grimly magnificent passages in English fiction. Arabella has decided in her own mind that Jude is sleeping peacefully, and has slipped out to see something of the festivities in Christminster.

[quotes, with some omissions, part sixth, ch. XI from 'It was a warm, cloudless, enticing day' to ' "*unto the bitter in soul.*" ']

That is the voice of the educated proletarian, speaking more distinctly than it has ever spoken before in English literature. The man is, indeed, at once an individual and a type. There is no other novelist alive with the breadth of sympathy, the knowledge, or the power for the creation of Jude. Had Mr. Hardy never written another book, this would still place him at the head of English novelists. To turn from him or from Mr. Meredith to our Wardour Street romancers and whimpering Scotch humourists is like walking from a library into a schoolroom.

57. A. J. Butler, 'Mr. Hardy as a Decadent', *National Review*

May 1896, xxvii, 384–90

A. J. Butler (1844–1910) was primarily an Italian scholar: he held the chair of Italian at University College, London, from 1898 until his death. The *National Review* had been founded in 1883; at this time L. J. Maxse was just beginning his editorship.

Mr. Thomas Hardy's position in literature is somewhat peculiar. Without having ever been restricted to an audience quite as select as that which kept Mr. Meredith's reputation alive for so many years till the general public found him out, he so far resembles that eminent writer that his fame has probably always been greater among this brethren of letters than among the mass of novel-readers; to these, at all events until controversies arose over the work which he produced a couple of years ago, his name said less than those of a dozen writers without a quarter of his ability. He has never been the subject of what is popularly called a 'boom'. We have not been used to seeing announcements of the sum 'per thousand words' which proprietors of magazines have offered for his forthcoming story, nor are publishers' advertisements of his works accompanied by a statement of the numbers subscribed for by 'the trade', or sold up to date. He has few conspicuous mannerisms; a certain tendency to over-elaborate terms of expression (as when he calls chalk downs 'cretaceous uplands'), and somewhat far-fetched similes, being the chief defects to be found in this kind; and even these, contrary to what is sometimes observed, are if anything less frequent in his later than in his earlier work. At the same time his style is sufficiently marked to have sensibly affected more than one of the ablest among our younger story-tellers.

Except for a short period early in his career, he has never been an over-rapid producer. About a dozen novels and some short stories represent the work of a quarter of a century, for almost that time has passed since his first book, *Desperate Remedies*, appeared. It was anonymous, and created no great stir in the novel-reading world; a few persons recognized, however, in spite of some awkwardness of construction, that the author had the root of the matter in him—that he possessed in no scanty measure the powers of observation, invention and expression which are the three primary requisites for the making of a novelist, together with a sense of humour, especially humorous appreciation of the rustic mind and its manifestation in speech, enough, if only the scene of the story had been laid in Scotland instead of 'Wessex', to have made half a dozen reputations. A year later, still anonymously, appeared *Under the Greenwood Tree*, a charming little 'Dutch picture' of country life. But neither this book nor its successor, *A Pair of Blue Eyes*, the first to which the author put his name, attracted any very great notice, though professional tasters of fiction were further convinced that a new and capable teller of stories had arisen.

The first book of Mr. Hardy's which got talked about in drawing-rooms was *Far from the Madding Crowd*. It had run through the *Cornhill Magazine*, and appeared in book form towards the end of 1874. Henceforward, though no one book of Mr. Hardy's can be said to have earned for him the popularity which we have seen attained in the same period by half-a-score of novelists far inferior to him in the first three qualities above indicated, and totally devoid of the fourth, his place as one of our foremost writers of fiction may be said to have been established. In the course of these twenty years, though eight or ten stories have come from his pen, his vein seems to be by no means exhausted. It is hardly too much to say that every successive book has shown not merely a development of his original qualities, but the acquirement or manifestation of new aptitudes. *The Return of the Native*, published in 1878, first revealed a capacity for 'describing a scene and colouring it with a mood' (to borrow an apt phrase from Mr. Quiller-Couch), of which former works had shown little more than indications, though looking back one can see that it was there. This faculty of catching, as it were, the essence of a particular aspect of external things, correlating it with an aspect of the human mind, and putting it into words so as to arouse the desired emotion in the reader, is one of which it is easier to feel the presence than to define the nature. It is very capriciously distributed, being quite distinct from what is called 'word-painting'. Many writers who can call up a scene with great cleverness before the reader's eye seem to be quite without it. Indeed, it is possible to be a very great writer of fiction, and yet lack this particular faculty; just as it is probably possible to be an intelligent and appreciative reader and judge of fiction, and yet be unsusceptible to its operation.

Perhaps a few instances may make the position clearer; though here again so elusive is the faculty, and so dependent for its operation on the reader's own mood, either habitual, or at the moment of reading, that it would be no surprise to find that someone or other took an exactly contrary view of all, or any of them. To the present writer, however, it seems that Chaucer has the faculty—there is the whole mood of Spring in the opening of the Prologue; while Spenser, with all his power of describing, had it little or not at all. Milton had it, but not Dryden; Cowper, but not Keats; Shelley, but not Byron, though Byron tried hard for it. These are all poets, and indeed it was probably not till the present century was well advanced, and prose fiction had become a great branch of imaginative literature, that examples of this faculty can be found in modern prose. It is not very conspicuous in Sir Walter Scott,[1] though his lesser namesake Michael had a double portion of it. Even in one who has never visited the tropics, certain passages in *Tom Cringle* and *The Cruise of the Midge*, read first in childhood, still retain undiminished their power of calling up a particular mood. Dickens had it; Thackeray far less. Charlotte Brontë had it, Emily perhaps even more (though this is from a vague and distant recollection); George Eliot had little or none of it.

Anyone who from this very sketchy attempt at definition and illustration can see what the faculty in question is, can hardly fail to recognize its presence in abundant measure in Mr. Hardy's work. As has been said, *The Return of the Native*, though not in all respects one of his best stories, was the first in which it was conspicuous. There are scenes in that book of which, even when the details are forgotten, the impression —the mood—is ready at the least touch of association to become perceptible again. The same may be said of certain parts of *Two on a Tower*, and even in a fuller degree of *The Woodlanders*. An anecdote may serve as an indication of the way in which the last mentioned book was able to tune the mood of at least some among its readers. Not long after it came out, two friends were walking through the country of coppices which lies on the border of Surrey and Sussex. *Apropos*, apparently, of nothing in particular (certainly there had been no mention of the book), one turned to the other, and said: 'Have you——.' Before he could get any further with his question, the other replied: 'Yes, I have.' 'Well that's prompt,' was the amused rejoinder. But it

---

[1] As one instance of it, however, a friend calls attention to the passage in *Rob Roy* immediately preceding the meeting with Diana Vernon, after Rob Roy's escape.

was all right. The sight of a heap of chips, the *débris* of some hurdle-making operation, had, by a sufficiently remote resemblance, been enough to call up with absolute certainty, in two minds still pervaded by the atmosphere of the book, a scene near its opening.

So much for Mr. Hardy as a craftsman. But it would seem, in these days, when so much emphasis is laid on the entire disconnection of art from everything but itself, and every suggestion of a moral or didactic aim on the part of the artist is so loudly repudiated, to be quite impossible for a novelist who claims to be anything higher than the merest romancer to abstain from delivering a thesis. Scott, it may pretty safely be said, never heard of 'art for art's sake', yet one could hardly point to a single novel that has been produced by the professors of that doctrine, or honoured with their approbation, which does not contain ten times more 'preachment' than all the Waverley Novels put together. The theme, no doubt, does not vary much, but such as it is, it is enough to convert what should be a story into what is practically a dissertation. Let it be observed that this question, whether a work of fiction should teach, is quite distinct from another one, which is often apt to be confused with it, namely, that which relates to what has been called 'the young person'; and both again are distinct from the question as to how far the artist ought—aesthetic, not ethic 'ought'—to exercise any selection in respect of the subjects upon which he employs his art; and in anything I may have to say about Mr. Hardy's recent development, I shall endeavour to keep them quite distinct.

The first question could hardly have arisen in regard to any book written by Mr. Hardy until very recently. On the contrary, he seemed to stand aloof from his personages, watching with a kind of Olympian detachment their struggles in the web of their own actions. In the slang of modern criticism the characters have been 'convincing', the events 'inevitable'. There has been a 'moral', only as there is one to everything that happens in life; and if the general impression left by such stories as *The Trumpet Major*, perhaps the most satisfactory of all his books, or *The Woodlanders*, perhaps the most powerful, is that in the lives of most people, and especially of most good people, renunciation must always play a larger part than enjoyment, this is after all only the axiom that has been enforced by all sages and saints since the world began, to say nothing of most nurses. 'You can't have everything' is a formula with which most of us have been familiar from our tenderest years; and, in truth, it lies at the base of social existence.

But to every axiom, to every formula, come periods when its

authority in some field or another ceases to be taken universally for granted; and just now one of those periods seems to have set in with regard to those above mentioned. So far as they deal with the relations of men and women to each other the axiom is questioned, the formula is denied, and the 'problem' results. Meanwhile literature, at all events that branch of literature which is now being considered, namely fiction, cannot but suffer. Fiction has no more to do with 'problems' than *Paradise Lost* with demonstrations. In the case of ladies whose views of life are based on a hasty generalization from a limited experience of one or two among the less estimable of the opposite sex, or young gentlemen who have no experience at all save what they get from the perusal of French novels, the only harm done is a certain lowering of the standard of taste. If they did not write this sort of thing they would write nothing else. But when a man possessing Mr. Hardy's power of observation and knowledge of human nature, conscious as he must be that upon the validity of the axiom, the authority of the formula, the whole fabric of society depends, when such a man gets caught by the fashion of the period, he turns upon society as if it were the creator of axiom and formula, instead of, in a sense, their creature, and rates it. And so we lose a good novel, and get instead what boys call a 'jaw.'

And, after all, extensive as Mr. Hardy's knowledge of human nature is, it is evidently incomplete, or else he has been guilty of what is surely unpardonable in a 'realistic' writer, a suppression of a whole side of the truth. Life may not be 'all beer and skittles', but neither is it all squalid, unredeemed tragedy; nor is it usually found that out of any dozen persons with whom we may fortuitously be brought into contact, there will not be one to whom can be attributed the possession of any elevated or generous feeling, together with sufficient resolution to act upon it. Yet in his latest story, *Jude the Obscure*, the reading of which has called forth these remarks, it may safely be said that Mr. Hardy has not given a hint showing any knowledge on his part that such people exist, and, indeed, except for a chance reference in one line—which readers may discover if they can—there is not a single mention in the whole book of any person for whose character one can feel either affection or respect. Surely such characters occasionally form an influence in the lives of the social class where Mr. Hardy finds his types. How, to take one conspicuous instance, can that be called other than one-sided realism which, in depicting such lives, totally ignores the parson? Strange as it may appear to the average 'literary' mind, the parson in country districts is, as Mr. Hardy can hardly fail to know, not always either the unimportant, uninterested resident in the parish such as he appears, on the rare occasions when he does appear, in Mr. Hardy's books; nor yet the dictatorial priest whom it pleases other purveyors of fiction to imagine. When any efforts towards sanitary, social, or moral reform are made, it is ten to one that the parson is the prime mover; nor is he always the less popular or less influential therefore. If Mr. Hardy had used his eyes better when he was visiting the district whose external features he has described with a sureness and truth of touch such as hardly another living writer possesses, he would have seen a country-town which, fifty years ago was a bye-word among country-towns for decay, an asylum for criminals well-known to Bow Street runners, and has now (mainly—as the present writer may be allowed to remember—through the energy of one man, a member of the body which, if Mr. Hardy's picture be complete, plays no part in rural life) become a thriving and healthy centre of various work, directed chiefly towards the intellectual, moral and social elevation of the class in which Mr. Hardy finds his Judes, his Arabellas, his Susannas. Or one might refer him to the vicar of his 'ceremonial church of St. Silas', whose devoted work has converted the suburb of 'Beersheba' from a slum which could hardly be named in polite society to a decent artizan quarter. Surely men like these, and they are not solitary instances, are real elements that should not be ignored in anything that claims to be a faithful picture of rural life and its possibilities.

As to the second question, whether a certain instinct which forms a most important factor in human life and society should be treated by the novelist as non-existent, or existent only when kept within the bounds prescribed by recognized morality, one can only say: 'Has anyone whose opinion is worth a moment's consideration ever demanded that it should, or has any writer of consequence allowed his work to be trammelled by any such demand?' Of course it is quite possible for good work to be done without the question arising.

> In Man's life
> Is room for great emotions unbegot,
> Of dalliance and embracements, unbegot
> Ev'n of the purer nuptials of the soul,

says Mr. Watson—a rebuke which if it were heeded would, it may be feared, reduce to utter silence some of those to whom one would suppose it to be specially addressed. On many accounts, too, it may be well to direct the thoughts of the 'young person' rather to those other emotions than to this particular one.

But to require the writer of fiction to confine himself within this limit, and to produce no work that had better be excluded from the schoolroom is absurd on the face of it. Such a requirement if logically enforced would put *Othello* on the Index; and if it be not a bathos to mention other works after that, would have deprived the world of *The Heart of Midlothian*, *The Cloister and the Hearth* and *Adam Bede*. Only the matter is a grave one, and should be treated with gravity and reticence, and with as little insistence on detail as possible. A writer, who if he never produced sustained work of the calibre of Mr. Hardy's, had an immeasurably surer literary judgment, has left on record his dread of being, as he calls it, 'shoved toward grossness' by a love of putting things plainly.[1] Where Stevenson saw 'peril', Mr. Hardy deliberately wades in. It is all very well to talk about writing for men and women; but there are passages in Mr. Hardy's later books which will offend men in direct proportion to their manliness, and which all women, save the utterly abandoned—and it is not among these presumably that Mr. Hardy seeks his readers—will hurry over with shuddering disgust.

This brings us to the third point. Is the artist in any way limited as to his choice of subject? Is the operation of killing a pig, to take an example from *Jude the Obscure*, with every physical detail faithfully reproduced, as legitimate a theme for artistic treatment as 'Mystic Uther's deeply-wounded son', watched by weeping queens in Avilion? This is an extreme case of a question which may be, and is, endlessly debated; and only one aspect of it need be considered here. Probably it will hardly be denied that on any showing the artist should take pleasure in the exercise of his art. The idea that he exercises it with any moral end in view is, as we have said, repudiated; nor indeed, though the Society for the Protection of Animals have reprinted the passage in their organ, can one for a moment suppose that Mr. Hardy wrote in the interests of that estimable body. It is hard to see what third motive is possible. Then, does Mr. Hardy really take pleasure in contemplating the process of pig-sticking? Or is there, after all, a third motive, not more 'artistic' indeed than the moral one, but not contrary to the facts of the human mind, though usually manifested at a less mature period of its development? Does he simply want to show that he 'doesn't care', or, as it is popularly called, 'defies Mrs. Grundy'? If so, he is surely sacrificing a good deal for a cheap amusement. Whatever sport may lie in the defiance of 'Mrs. Grundy' there can be nothing more certain in

[1] R. L. Stevenson: *Vailima Letters*, p. 174.

literature than that a tendency to dwell on foul details has never been a 'note' of any but third-rate work. The broad and not always seemly humour of Chaucer, or of Shakespeare himself, stands on another footing altogether. Humour possesses a wonderfully antiseptic property, and one cannot conceive any ordinarily healthy adult mind taking any harm from the *Reve's Tale*, or the jokes of Mercutio; though a refined mind might prefer humour of another order. But with what may be called the 'night-cart' side of nature humour has nothing to do; and one need not, perhaps, wonder that Mr. Hardy, having deliberately chosen to depict that side, has—only for the time, let us hope—undergone a total suppression of his once delightful faculty for genially depicting its humorous side. Let him take warning by the terrible fate of M. Daudet, who, as we were told the other day, can see no fun in *The Jumping Frog*. To such a pass has long contemplation of the details of lives like those of his Saphos and Astier-Réhus brought the creator of the chamois who drank mulled wine, and the faithful camel! As for the 'champion night-men', if the phrase may be permitted, the Flauberts and the Zolas, it would be impossible, by the wildest flight of imagination, to associate them with humour in any shape.

58. R. Y. Tyrrell, *Fortnightly Review*

June 1896, lxv, n.s. lix, 857–64

R. Y. Tyrrell (1844–1914) held various classical chairs at Trinity College, Dublin, from 1871 onwards. The editorship of the *Fortnightly* had at this time recently been taken over by W. L. Courtney. The reference in the second paragraph to the 'hill-top' novels picks up a phrase for which Grant Allen was originally responsible: in the preface to his book *The British Barbarians* he says 'This is a Hill-Top Novel, and a Hill-Top Novel is one which raises a protest in favour of purity.' Reviewers who did not share Grant Allen's idea of purity were glad to extend the term to cover anything that looked like propaganda for free love or 'the new morality', and it became for a time a convenient short-hand description which would be at once understood.

'Lowliness', we are told, 'is young Ambition's ladder', but in England adult Ambition, when no longer militant but triumphant, can afford not only to kick away the ladder of lowliness, but even to flout those who have raised her to the topmost rung. Thomas Hardy is at the summit of British novelists, and the British public will endure anything from him. His past brilliant triumphs in fiction have fairly raised him to this position. The *Athenaeum* was hardly guilty of exaggeration when it compared the tragic figure of Tess on Salisbury Plain to that of Oedipus at the 'Sheer Threshold' hard by Colonus, or Lear on the heath in the storm. *The Return of the Native, Far from the Madding Crowd, Two on a Tower*, and many other works equally great, had prepared the public for the crowning triumph of *Tess of the D'Urbervilles*. Hence it is but natural that the Press should be most unwilling to see in *Jude the Obscure* signs of degeneracy or deficiency. But it does seem remarkable that such a book should be received, even by many excellent critics, with such unstinted and unqualified applause. The criticism of the *Saturday Review* (8 February 1896)[1] may be taken as a sample of the heights of the eulogy to which his admirers are prepared to soar. The reviewer calls *Jude* 'the most splendid of all the works that Mr. Hardy has given the world'; proclaims it as a masterpiece 'that will alone make 1895 a memorable year in the history of literature'; and declares that 'had Mr. Hardy never written another book this would still place him at the head of English novelists'. Now, while reverently paying to Mr. Hardy the tribute of our willing acknowledgment of his splendid successes hitherto achieved, we cannot but hold that *Jude* represents a deplorable falling off not only in conception, but in execution. We cannot think that the unquestionably high authority which has praised the book even with rapture is unprejudiced by a commendable gratitude for past pleasure, or by personal admiration of the author. Neither of these feelings, natural in themselves, ought to influence the verdict of criticism. Either Mr. Hardy's powers have undergone a sad deterioration (which Heaven forbid), or he has determined to try the patience of his public and to see whether they will accept in lieu of a novel a treatise on sexual pathology, in which the data are

[1] No. 56 in this volume (editor).

drawn from imagination, and are, therefore, scientifically invalid, and in which his dramatic faculty has largely deserted him, and even his eminent descriptive powers are not conspicuously present. These are decided views, and we hasten to justify them.

If we consider broadly and without prejudice the tone and scope of the book, we cannot but class it with the fiction of Sex and New Woman, so rife of late. It differs in no wise from the 'hill-top' novels, save in the note of distinction and the power of touch which must discriminate Mr. Hardy at his worst from the Grant Allens and Iotas at their best. In method, indeed, *The Woman Who Did* is superior to *Jude*, inasmuch as it deals far more sincerely with free love as a practical institution. Mr. Hardy's work cannot but emit occasional sparks, which sometimes glow into sustained splendour; but even an enchanted palace would be vitiated by a whiff from the atmosphere of the *Pot Bouille* or *Germinal*, and the airs from the 'hill-top' would infect the Delectable Mountains themselves. Mr. Hardy is here and there as picturesque and delightful as ever, but (to parody a well-known couplet)—

> You may paint, you may perfume, the scene as you will:
> But the stench from the 'hill-top' will hang round it still.

When the *Saturday* Reviewer avers that 'the recognition of sexuality in the book is merely incidental', and that 'Mr. Hardy with an admirable calm has put forth a book in which a secondary, but very important, interest is the frank treatment of the destructive influence of a vein of sensuality upon an ambitious working man', he seems to us to have misrepresented the tone of the work as completely as he has misconceived its aim. The book is steeped in sex. The aspirations of the stone-cutter Jude towards a University career form quite a subordinate underplot. The main theme is an elaborate indictment of marriage as being necessarily the death of pure passion and even of healthy sexual desire. 'There probably never was a novel', writes the *Saturday* Reviewer, '*dealing with the closer relations of men and women* that was quite so free from lasciviousness as this.' The words which we have italicized remind us of Sir Andrew Aguecheek's boast that he is as good as any man in Illyria, whatsoever he be, under the degree of his betters; but we are quite ready to accept the reviewer's statement, only adding that the same might be said of *La Terre*, and of nearly all the novels of Zola, which disgust rather than allure. Mr. Hardy has long been creeping nearer and nearer to the fruit which has been so profitable to the French novelist, but which till quite recently his English fellow-craftsman has been forbidden to touch. *The Woodlanders, A Pair of Blue Eyes*, and above all, *Tess*, have shown Mr. Hardy's eminent skill in going as near French *lubricité* as a writer can venture without awakening the nonconformist conscience in our strangely-constituted society, in fact in hoodwinking the not very perspicacious Mr. Podsnap and Mrs. Grundy. But in *Jude* there is no approach towards lasciviousness, or even what might be called warmth of colouring. Let the reader turn to the daintily-written scene in *A Pair of Blue Eyes*, in which the heroine rescues her lover by means of a rope made of all her underclothing, and walks home with him clad only in her gown, which, drenched with rain, is glued by a head-wind to her figure, every curve of which is thus delicately outlined. Let him compare this with a similar incident in *Jude*, when Sue comes into Jude's lodging drenched from head to foot, having waded through a river in her escape from the training school. He will not find in *Jude* the subtle touches which in *A Pair of Blue Eyes* drew for us a picture so alluring and so vivid. She assumes his garments while her own are being dried at the sitting-room fire; but we acquit Mr. Hardy of the attempt which a French writer would certainly have made to render the scene suggestive. However, there flourishes in Paris side by side with the poisoned flower of *lubricité* an ugly weed called *gauloiserie*. We venture to describe as *gauloiserie* the disagreeable incident in which appears 'the characteristic part of a barrow pig', though some critics find in it a 'symbolism' which completely vindicates it.

But though we meet no such daring experiments as the scene in the pavilion in *A Laodicean*, or in the hayfield in *The Woodlanders*, or in the wood near the beginning of *Tess*, the novel is, as we have said, steeped in sex. Not long after Jude has made the acquaintance of his cousin Sue, the heroine of the tale—if tale it can be called—he says to her, 'Sue, I believe you are as innocent as you are unconventional.' The reader will perhaps be disposed to form a somewhat different judgment on learning that she has just informed him that at eighteen she had formed an acquaintance with an Oxford undergraduate, with whom she subsequently lived for fifteen months. So candid a girl could not have withheld this episode in her life from the Authorities of the Training College; but they were apparently as satisfied as Jude was with her statement: 'But I have never yielded myself to any lover, if that is what you mean; I have remained as I began.' Yet she subsequently did not by any means remain as she began. She married a schoolmaster, Richard Phillotson, old enough to be her father, jumped out of a window because he did not take the view of the relations between them which the undergraduate had accepted, and left him with his full consent to live with Jude, with whom she made several unsuccessful attempts to go through a marriage ceremony, being always repelled by its 'vulgarity', and held back by a conviction that 'it is as culpable to bind yourself to love always as to believe a creed always, and as silly as to vow always to like a particular food or drink'. Though divorced from Phillotson, she does not commit the vulgarism of marriage with Jude, but becomes the mother of two or three children by him, when she is awakened by their tragic death to a sense that she is really Phillotson's wife in the eye of Heaven, and is married to him again, at first insisting on the old condition, but finally suing humbly for the establishing of a relation which he is quite ready to forego, because she feels that she deserves a signal punishment for having secretly met and kissed Jude. To what end is all this minute registry of the fluctuations of disease in an incurably morbid organism? Why dwell on this fantastic green-sickness? Marriage laws do not suit Sue's warped and neurotic nature, but neither would free love. If marriage is no better than 'a license to be loved on the premises', as she calls it, does the absence of the license mitigate the coarseness of the connection? She has no sense of the dignity of womanhood and motherhood, and so all her relations with the other sex become impure in her morbid imagination. She is a flirt in the worst sense of the term:

The fact of the kiss would be nothing: all would depend upon the spirit of it. If given in the spirit of a cousin and friend, she saw no objection: if in the spirit of a lover she could not permit it. 'Will you swear that it will not be in that spirit?' she had said. 'No; he would not.' So they separated, but quickly ran back, and embracing most unpremeditatedly kissed each other. When they parted for good it was with flushed cheeks on her side, and a beating heart on his.

This childlike view of the import of a kiss is hardly consistent with her summing-up of her own character:

'At first I did not love you, Jude; that I own. When I first knew you I merely wanted you to love me. I did not exactly flirt with you, but that inborn craving which undermines some women's morals, almost more than unbridled passion —the craving to attract and captivate, regardless of the injury it may do the man—was in me; and when I found I had caught you I was frightened. And then—I don't know how it was—I could not bear to let you go, possibly to Arabella again—and so I got to love you, Jude.'

This, be it observed, is said on the eve of her leaving him for the last time for Phillotson, whose person she loathes.

Here, finally, is her deliberate opinion of marriage, possessing that added value which accrued to the praise of honesty in the mouth of the Scot who avowed that he had 'tried baith':

'It is foreign to a man's nature to go on loving a person when he is told that he must and shall be that person's lover. There would be a much likelier chance of his doing it if he were told not to love. If the marriage ceremony consisted in an oath and signed contract between the parties to cease loving from that day forward, in consideration of personal possession being given, and to avoid each other's society as much as possible in public, there would be more loving couples than there are now.'

Jude's case seemed to him even harder. The complete abolition of the marriage rite, and the general diffusion of Oxford degrees of D.D. among the ignorant and dissolute proletariat, would have left him still dissatisfied. He would still have smarted under a sense of 'the scorn of nature for man's finer emotions' and her 'wilfulness in not allowing issue from one parent alone', and thus depriving the lover of the pleasure he might have had in contemplating the children of his former mistress, the fruit of her marriage with another man.

That matrimony has its disadvantages as well as its advantages was recognized by a very ancient Greek poet, who complained that, as for women, we can get on neither with them nor without them. The compatriots of that poet thoroughly investigated the whole theory of communism in women as well as in property. They faced the question of the abolition of the family as a factor in society, and the most practical of them saw that such a revolution would undermine two of the most potent forces of civilization, the sense of proprietorship and the feeling of natural affection. It was chiefly this consideration that induced Aristotle to declare against the scheme of Plato, but both the Platonic theory and the Aristotelian criticism of it are serious, practical, and succinct. Mr. Hardy has devoted about five hundred pages to repeating, again and again, what Susarion said in three senarii:

> Κακὸν γυναῖκες, ἀλλ᾽ ὅμως, ὦ δημόται,
> Οὐκ ἔστιν οἰκεῖν οἰκίαν ἀνεὺ κακοῦ.
> Καὶ γὰρ τὸ γῆμαι καὶ τὸ μὴ γῆμαι κακόν.

The vagueness of the theme has infected the character-drawing. The characters are not distinctly conceived. The publican, whom Arabella hopes to ensnare into matrimony, now encourages and again rebuffs her, for no reason, but that she may be a perpetual thorn in the side of her former husband. Arabella had no motive for wheedling Jude into marriage a second time after their divorce, and the suddenness of the antipathy which followed their second union as quickly as it had followed their first, shows how baseless was her course of action. Hence the lapses from dramatic fitness which pervade the book. Jude, of whose usual conversation we may quote as an example, 'wifedom has not yet annihilated and digested you in its vast maw as an atom which has no further individuality', sometimes talks like Gibbon or Johnson, but oftener like Herbert Spencer. This is somewhat surprising in a slightly educated mechanic, however ambitious; but still more remarkable is the suddenness with which he acquires the language and manner of that class of the learned, whom some cruelly call prigs. Aged eleven, he talks like a rustic lad: 'Aunt hev got a great fuel house', and so forth. Not many days after, so far as we can judge, we find him reciting, in very literary language, a kind of antiphonic anthem or paean in praise of Christminster:

'It is a city of light. The tree of knowledge grows there. It is a place that teachers of men spring from and go to. It is what you may call a castle manned by scholarship and religion.'

Sue, who often uses a style like that of George Eliot, after she came under the blighting influence of science, sometimes, on the other hand, talks like a maid of all work. 'I shall do as I like for all him', 'I don't think of you like that means', and 'O yes, I am bad and obstinate and all sorts', sound strange in the mouth of a girl who quotes freely from J. S. Mill and Shelley's *Epipsychidion*, talks at large about Athens, Rome, Alexandria and Jerusalem, and thus describes her own education:

'I don't know Latin and Greek, though I know the grammars of those tongues. But I know most of the Greek and Latin classics through translations, and other books, too. I read Lemprière, Catullus, Martial, Juvenal, Lucian, Beaumont and Fletcher, Boccaccio, Scarron, De Brantôme, Sterne, De Foe, Smollett, Fielding, Shakespeare, the Bible and other such; and found that all interest in the unwholesome part of these books ended with its mystery.'

The subordinate characters are still more deficient dramatically. Here is the way in which a common carter delivers himself about Oxford. The sentiments are those of a man of culture, and are not rendered more dramatically suitable by clothing them in an uncultivated dialect:

'Em lives on a lofty level; there's no gainsaying it, though I myself med not think much of 'em. You need be religious or you need not, *but you can't help striking in your homely note with the rest.*'

Surely such sentiments, especially that which we have italicized, are as much outside the intellectual sphere of an ignorant carter as would be a quotation from Aeschylus or Dante.

Even in Mr. Hardy's style we miss that careful finish which has made some of his novels gems of English prose. John Stuart Mill long ago in his *Logic* pointed out as a vulgar error the confusion between *predicate* and *predict*. We have it at least twice in *Jude*: 'Her actions were always unpredicable,' writes Mr. Hardy, and 'She was beginning to be so puzzling and unpredicable.' Moreover, the use of *evince* when the writer means no more than *show*—'after evincing that she was struck by Sue's avowal'—and still more 'during a lengthened period' instead of 'for a long time', belong to that style which is unkindly called penny-a-lining or journalese, and which makes us think for a moment of Marie Corelli. The affectation of scholarship in the introduction of Greek words—wrongly transliterated, by the way, as in 'All hemin *eis* Theos ho Pater'; the coining of such an outlandish name as Tetuphenay (τετυφέναι) for the Oxford Head who gave some very good advice to the priggish young mechanic; the pedantic subdivisions and the 'architectonic' air of the whole work, as if it were a scientific treatise— all these qualities are to us at least not attractive but somewhat irritating. When Nature implants in a young man eager desires for a certain career, such as those which animated Jude, she generally gives him the powers and the resolution by which he may achieve his ambition. When he has no powers and no resolution he is simply uninteresting. Phillotson promised well, but ultimately became quite commonplace. Arabella is a mere blur. The sublime is constantly aimed at, certainly in the closing scene, which some critics admire so much, and also, we suppose, in the scene where Jude, being drunk, recites (Heaven knows why) the Nicene Creed in Latin in a public-house. The latter, at all events, we found perilously near the Ridiculous. Mr. Hardy is through-out in the thraldom of a fixed idea. But he is not really so serious or so very angry as he would wish to appear. He is like the Homeric lion, who 'lasheth his sides with his tail, and greatly stirreth himself up to fight'. He feels all the time that he has no such bitter quarrel with anyone or anything, and that neither 'the disaster which may press in the wake of the strongest passion known to humanity', nor 'the tragedy of unfulfilled aims', is a theme so new or so fruitful as to justify such very copious illustration, undiversified by any attempt to suggest a remedy or a mitigation of the evils which either the one or the other may be held to carry in its train. He is depressing because he is himself somewhat depressed.

The book is addressed by the writer expressly 'to men and women of full age', and he adds—in a tone which seems to show that he thinks the matter one of very little moment—'I am not aware that there is anything in the handling to which exception can be taken.' These are indeed *regia verba*, and justify our complaint that Mr. Hardy conceives himself to be in a position in which he may flout his readers. It seems that if his readers are of full age they are bound to accept without question his manner of handling his subject, whatever it may be. If it should seem prurient or coarse, being of full age they are bound to suppress all protest against it. This is a new and terrible penalty imposed on the elderly, a harmless though not very interesting class. Tennyson has made a person of full age cry—

> Fear not thou to loose thy tongue;
> Set thy hoary fancies free;
> What is loathsome to the young
> Savours well to thee and me.

But we should hope that Tennyson's

> Gray and gap-tooth'd man as lean as death

is not a fair sample of Mr. Hardy's readers of full age. We claim for them the right to hold and even express, on questions of what is decent in literature, opinions not less refined than the opinions of those who are still young. Nay, more, we should expect that the reader of full age would belong to just that class who would feel that the world presents other and to them more tractable difficulties than sex-problems, or marriage-problems (which, however, they would gladly see treated carefully by the Leckys and Herbert Spencers of the day), and that life is serious enough to dispose them to turn away with some impatience from a work in which there is not a practical suggestion for reform, and (what is worse) in which there is not material for a smile from the first page to the last—a dismal treatise as 'chap-fallen' as Yorick's skull in the hands of Hamlet.

59. Havelock Ellis, 'Concerning
Jude the Obscure', Savoy Magazine

October 1896, No. vi, 35–49

Havelock Ellis's review-article was reprinted in 1931 under the same title, and was included in *From Marlowe to Shaw: The Studies, 1876–1936, in English Literature of Havelock Ellis*, edited by John Gawsworth (1950). The *Savoy* belongs to the same group of nineties periodicals as *The Yellow Book*, drawing on *avant-garde* experimentalists and advanced thinkers. (See headnote to No. 24.)

The eighteenth century is the great period of the English novel. Defoe, Richardson, Fielding, Goldsmith, Sterne and Jane Austen initiated or carried towards perfection nearly every variety of fiction; they had few or no rivals throughout Europe. Scott, with his incomparable genius for romance, was left to complete the evolutionary process.

Yet it was Scott, as we too often forget, who marred everything and threw the English novel into disorganization from which it has not even today recovered. Those jerry-built, pseudo-mediaeval structures which he raised so rapidly and so easily, still retain, I hope, some of the fascination which they possessed for us when we were children; they certainly retain it for a few of those children of a larger growth whom we call men of genius. But Scott's prodigious facility and the conventional unreality of his view of life ruined the English novel. By means of his enormous reputation he was enabled to debase the intellectual and moral currency in this department of literature to the lowest possible limit. It is a curious illustration of our attitude towards these things that Scott's method of paying off his debts by feverish literary production seems only to arouse our unqualified admiration. The commercial instinct in our British breasts is so highly developed that we glory in the sight of a great man prostituting his fame to make money, especially in a good cause. If he had paid off his debts at the gaming table, or even at the stock exchange, perhaps we should have been shocked. As he only flung his own genius and art on to the table to play against a credulous public his virtue remains immaculate. But a fate works through these things, however opaque the veil of insular self-satisfaction over our eyes. Scott, the earlier Scott, was a European influence, manifested in Manzoni, down through Hendrik Conscience to the drivel of Paul Féval. Since Scott no English novelist has been a force in European literature.

This may seem too stringent a judgment of so copious a branch of literature. But it is because the literature of fiction is so copious that we need a stringent clue to guide us through its mazes. A man cannot be too keen in grasping at the things that concern himself, too relentless in flinging aside those things that for him at least have no concern. For myself, at all events, I find now little in nineteenth-century English fiction that concerns me, least of all in popular fiction. I am well content to read and ponder the novels that seem to me assuredly great. In the next century, perhaps, I shall have time to consider whether it were well to read *Robert Elsmere* or *The Heavenly Twins*, but as yet the question is scarcely pressing.

If that is the case, I may be asked, why read Thomas Hardy? And I must confess that that question occurred to me—long a devout admirer of Mr. Hardy's work—some fourteen years ago, and I found it unanswerable.[1] For while he still seemed to me a fine artist, I scarcely regarded him as a great artist in the sense in which I so regarded some English novelists of the last century, and some French and Russian novelists of this century. Moreover, Mr. Hardy was becoming a popular novelist. For it may be a foolish fancy, but I do not like drinking at those pools which are turbid from the hoofs of my fellow creatures; when I cannot get there before the others I like to wait until a considerable time after they have left. I could not read my Catullus in peace if I had an uneasy sense that thousands of my fellow creatures were writing to the newspapers to say what a nice girl Lesbia was, and how horrid a person Gellius, condescending to approve the poet's fraternal senti-ments, lamenting the unwholesome tone of his Atys. It is my felicity that the railroad that skirts the Lago di Garda still sets but few persons down for Sermione. Nor am I alone in this. The unequalled rapture of Lamb's joy in the Elizabethan dramatists was due to the immensity of the solitude in which at that moment they lay enfolded. Indeed this attitude of mind is ancient and well-rooted. The saviours of mankind, with what at first sight seems an unkindly delight, have emphasized the fact that salvation belongs to the few. Yet not only is religion a sacred mystery, but love also, and art. When the profane are no longer warned

[1] I may here mention that, in 1883, I published in the *Westminster Review* a somewhat detailed study of the whole of Mr. Hardy's work up to that date.

away from the threshold it is a reasonable suspicion that no mystery is there.—So it was that I ceased to read Mr. Hardy's novels.

But since then things have somewhat changed. The crowd thickened, indeed, especially when *Tess* appeared, for that book chanced to illustrate a fashionable sentimental moral. But last year, suddenly, on the appearance of Mr. Hardy's latest book, a great stampede was heard in the land. Noisy bands of the novelist's readers were fleeing in every direction. Although it was still clearly premature to say that peace reigned in the Warsaw of *Tess's* admirers, I detected at least an interesting matter for investigation.—Thus I returned to Mr. Hardy's work.

That work is now very considerable, remembering the brief space of twenty-five years over which it is spread. The *damnosa haereditas* of Scott still afflicts nearly all our novelists with a fatal productiveness. The bigger the burden you lay on the back of Posterity the sooner he is certain to throw it off. And the creature's instinct is right; no man, not even a Goethe, is immortally wise in fifty volumes. There are few novelists who can afford to write much. Even Balzac, the type of prolific imagination in fiction, is no exception. Content to give the merest external impression of reality, he toiled terribly in moulding the clay of his own inner consciousness to produce a vast world of half-baked images, which are immensely impressive in the mass but crumble to pieces in your fingers when you take them up. Mr. George Meredith is, perhaps, our nearest modern English counterpart to Balzac. There is a prodigious expenditure of intellectual energy in the crowd of Meredith's huge novels. To turn from, let us say, *The Hand of Ethelberta* to *Evan Harrington*, is to feel that, intellectually, Hardy is a mere child compared to Meredith. There never was a novelist so superhumanly and obstreperously clever as Mr. Meredith. One suspects that much of the admiration expended on Meredith, as on Browning, is really the reader's admiration of his own cleverness in being able to toddle along at the coat-tails of such a giant. Crude intellect is as much outside art as crude emotion or crude morals. One admires the splendid profusion of power, but the perfected achievement which alone holds our attention permanently is not to be found among these exuberantly brilliant marionettes. It is all very splendid, but I find no good reason for reading it, since already it scarcely belongs to our time, since it never possessed the virtues which are independent of time. Like Balzac, George Meredith has built to his own memory a great cairn in literature. No doubt it will be an inspiring spectacle for our race to gaze back at.

There are really only two kinds of novels which are permanently interesting to men. The first contains those few which impress us by the immortal power with which they present a great story or a great human type. Such are the *Satyricon*, *Petit Jehan de Saintré*, *Don Quixote*, *Gil Blas*, *Tom Jones*. These books are always modern, always invigorating. They stand foursquare, each on its own basis, against every assault of time. The other class of novels—holding us not less closely, though it may be less masterfully—appeal by their intimate insight into the mysteries of the heart. They are the books that whisper to us secrets we half-knew yet never quite understood. They throw open doors into the soul that were only ajar. The men who write them are not always great masters of style or of literary architectonics, but by some happy inspiration they have revealed themselves as great masters of the human heart. Such books are full of the intimate charm of something that we remember, of things that chanced to us 'a great while since, a long, long time ago', and yet they have the startling audacity of the modernest things. Among them are *Manon Lescaut*, *Adolphe*, *Le Rouge et le Noir*, some of Dostoieffsky's novels. If any of Mr. Hardy's novels may claim to be compared with the immortals it is the books of this class which we should bear in mind.

The real and permanent interest in Mr. Hardy's books is not his claim to be the exponent of Wessex—a claim which has been more than abundantly recognized—but his intense preoccupation with the mysteries of women's hearts. He is less a story-teller than an artist who has intently studied certain phases of passion, and brings us a simple and faithful report of what he has found. A certain hesitancy in the report, an occasional failure of narrative or style, only adds piquancy and a sense of veracity to the record. A mischievous troll, from time to time —more rarely in Mr. Hardy's later work—is allowed to insert all sorts of fantastic conceits and incidents. Such interpolations merely furnish additional evidence in favour of the genuine inspiration of the whole document. We realize that we are in the presence of an artist who is wholly absorbed in the effort to catch the fleeting caprices of the external world, unsuspected and incalculable, the unexpected fluctuations of the human heart.

The great novelists of the present century who have chiefly occupied themselves with the problems of passion and the movements of women's hearts—I mean Paul Heyse and George Meredith, together with Goethe, who may be called their master—have all shown a reverent faith in what we call Nature as opposed to Society; they have all regarded the impulses and the duties of love in women as independent of social regulation, which may or may not impede the free play of passion and natural morality. Mr. Hardy fully shares this characteristic. It was less obvious in his earlier novels, no doubt, although Cytherea of his first book, *Desperate Remedies*, discovered the moral problems which have puzzled her youngest sisters, and Eustacia in *The Return of the Native* sank in what she called 'the mire of marriage' long before Sue experienced her complicated matrimonial disasters. For Hardy, as for Goethe and Heyse, and usually for Meredith the problems of women's hearts are mostly independent of the routine codes of men.

The whole course of Mr. Hardy's development, from 1871 to the present, has been natural and inevitable, with lapses and irregularities it may be, but with no real break and no new departure. He seems to have been led along the path of his art by his instincts; he was never a novelist with a programme, planning his line of march at the outset, and boldly affronting public reprobation; he has moved slowly and tentatively. In his earlier books he eluded any situation involving marked collision between Nature and Society, and thus these books failed to shock the susceptibilities of readers who had been brought up in familiarity with the unreal conventionalities which rule in the novels of Hugo, Dickens, Thackeray and the rest. *Far from the Madding Crowd* first appeared in the *Cornhill*, from which a few years earlier Thackeray had excluded Mrs. Browning's poem, *Lord Walter's Wife*, as presenting an immoral situation. It was not until *Two on a Tower* appeared, in 1882, that the general public—led, if I remember rightly, by the *Spectator*—began to suspect that in reading Mr. Hardy's books it was not treading on the firm rock of convention. The reason was, not that any fundamental change was taking place in the novelist's work, but that there really is a large field in which the instincts of human love and human caprice can have free play without too obviously conflicting with established moral codes. Both in life and in art it is this large field which we first reach. It is thus in the most perfect and perhaps the most delightful of Mr. Hardy's early books, *Under the Greenwood Tree*. The free play of Fancy's vagrant heart may be followed in all its little bounds and rebounds, its fanciful ardours and repressions, because she is too young a thing to drink deep of life—and because she is not yet married. It is all very immoral, as Nature is, but it succeeds in avoiding any collision with the rigid constitution of Society. The victim finally takes the white veil and is led to the altar; then a door is closed, and the convent gate of marriage is not again opened to the intrusive novel-reader's eye. Not by any means because it is considered that the horrors beyond are too terrible to be depicted. The matter does not appear to the novelist under this metaphor. Your wholesome-minded novelist knows that the life of a pure-natured English-woman after marriage is, as Taine said, mainly that of a very broody hen, a series of merely physiological processes with which he, as a novelist, has no further concern.

But in novels, as in life, one comes at length to realize that marriage is not necessarily either a grave, or a convent gate, or a hen's nest, that though the conditions are changed the forces at work remain largely the same. It is still quite possible to watch the passions at play, though there may now be more tragedy or more pathos in the outcome of that play. This Mr. Hardy proceeded to do, first on a small scale in short stories, and then on a larger scale. *Tess* is typical of this later unconventional way of depicting the real issues of passion. Remarkable as that book no doubt is, I confess that on the whole it has made no very strong appeal to me. I was repelled at the outset by the sub-title. It so happens that I have always regarded the conception of *purity*, when used in moral discussions, as a conception sadly in need of analysis, and almost the first time I ever saw myself in print was as the author of a discussion, carried on with the usual ethical fervour of youth, of the question: 'What is Purity?' I have often seen occasion to ask the question since. It seems to me doubtful whether anyone is entitled to use the word 'pure' without first defining precisely what he means, and still more doubtful whether an artist is called upon to define it at all, even in several hundred pages. I can quite conceive that the artist should take pleasure in the fact that his own creative revelation of life poured contempt on many old prejudices. But such an effect is neither powerful nor legitimate unless it is engrained in the texture of the narrative; it cannot be stuck on by a label. To me that glaring sub-title meant nothing, and I could not see what it should mean to Mr. Hardy. It seemed an indication that he was inclined to follow after George Eliot, who—for a large 'consideration'—condescended to teach morality to the British public, selling her great abilities for a position of fame which has since proved somewhat insecure; because although English men and women are never so happy as when absorbing unorthodox sermons under the guise of art, the permanent vitality of sermons is considerably less than that of art.

Thus I was not without suspicion in approaching *Jude the Obscure*. Had Mr. Hardy discovered the pernicious truth that whereas children can only take their powders in jam, the strenuous British public cannot be induced to devour their jam unless convinced that it contains some strange and nauseous powder? Was *Jude the Obscure* a sermon on marriage from the text on the title-page: 'The letter killeth'? Putting aside the small failures always liable to occur in Mr. Hardy's work, I found little to justify the suspicion. The sermon may, possibly, be there, but the spirit of art has, at all events, not been killed. In all the great qualities of literature *Jude the Obscure* seems to me the greatest novel written in England for many years.,

It is interesting to compare *Jude* with a characteristic novel of Mr. Hardy's earlier period, with *A Pair of Blue Eyes*, or *The Return of the Native*. On going back to these, after reading *Jude*, one notes the graver and deeper tones in the later book, the more austere and restrained roads of art which Mr. Hardy has sought to follow, and the more organic and radical way in which he now grips the individuality of his creatures. The individuals themselves have not fundamentally changed. The type of womankind that Mr. Hardy chiefly loves to study, from Cytherea to Sue, has always been the same, very human, also very feminine, rarely with any marked element of virility, and so contrasting curiously with the androgynous heroines loved of Mr. Meredith. The latter, with their resolute daring and energy, are of finer calibre and more imposing; they are also very much rarer in the actual world than Mr. Hardy's women, who represent, it seems to me, a type not uncommon in the south of England, where the heavier Teutonic and Scandinavian elements are, more than elsewhere, modified by the alert and volatile elements furnished by earlier races. But if the type remains the same the grasp of it is now much more thorough. At first Mr. Hardy took these women chiefly at their more obviously charming or pathetic moments, and sought to make the most of those moments, a little careless as to the organic connection of such moments to the underlying personality. One can well understand that many readers should prefer the romantic charm of the earlier passages, but—should it be necessary to affirm?—to grapple with complexly realized persons and to dare to face them in the tragic or sordid crisis of real life is to rise to a higher plane of art. In *Jude the Obscure* there is a fine self-restraint, a complete mastery of all the elements of an exceedingly human story. There is nothing here of the distressing melodrama into which Mr. Hardy was wont to fall in his early novels. Yet in plot *Jude* might be a farce. One could imagine that Mr. Hardy had purposed to himself to take a conventional farce, in which a man

and a woman leave their respective partners to make love to one
another and then finally rejoin their original partners, in order to see
what could be made of such a story by an artist whose sensitive vision
penetrated to the tragic irony of things; just as the great novelists of old,
De la Sale, Cervantes, Fielding, took the worn-out conventional
stories of their time, and filled them with the immortal blood of life.
Thus *Jude* has a certain symmetry of plan such as is rare in the actual
world—where we do not so readily respond to our cues—but to use
such a plot to produce such an effect is an achievement of the first
order.

Only at one point, it seems to me, is there a serious lapse in the art
of the book, and that is when the door of the bedroom closet is sprung
open on us to reveal the row of childish corpses. Up to that one admires
the strength and sobriety of the narrative, its complete reliance on the
interests that lie in common humanity. We feel that here are real
human beings of the sort we all know, engaged in obscure struggles
that are latent in the life we all know. But with the opening of that
cupboard we are thrust out of the large field of common life into the
small field of the police court or the lunatic asylum, among the things
which for most of us are comparatively unreal. It seems an unnecessary
clash in the story. Whatever failure of nervous energy may be present
in the Fawley family, it is clear that Mr. Hardy was not proposing to
himself a study of gross pathological degenerescence, a study of the
hereditary evolution of criminality. If that were so, the story would
lose the wide human significance which is not merely stated explicitly
in the preface, but implicitly throughout. Nor can it be said that so
wholesale a murder was required for the constructive development of
the history; a much less serious catastrophe would surely have sufficed
to influence the impressionable Sue. However skilful Mr. Hardy may
be in the fine art of murder, it is as a master of the more tender and
human passions that he is at his best. The element of bloodshed in *Tess*
seems of dubious value. One is inclined to question altogether the
fitness of bloodshed for the novelist's purpose at the present period of
history. As a factor in human fate bloodshed today is both too near
and too remote for the purposes of art. It is too rare to be real and poignant to every heart, and in the days of well-equipped burglars and a
'spirited' foreign policy it is too vulgar to bring with it any romance of
'old unhappy far-off things'. Our great sixteenth-century dramatists
could use it securely as their commonest resource because it was then
a deeply-rooted fact both of artistic convention and of real life. In this

century bloodshed can only be made humanly interesting by a great psychologist, living on the barbarous outskirts of civilization, a Dostoieffsky to whom the secret of every abnormal impulse has been revealed. In Mr. Hardy's books bloodshed is one of the forms put on by the capricious troll whose business it is to lure him from his own work. But that cupboard contains the only skeleton in the house of *Jude the Obscure*. On the whole, it may be said that Mr. Hardy here leads us to a summit in art, where the air is perhaps too rare and austere for the more short-winded among his habitual readers, but, so far as can yet be seen, surely a summit.—So at least it seems to one who no longer cares to strain his vision in detecting mole-hills on the lower slopes of Parnassus, yet still finds pleasure in gazing back at the peaks.

But I understand that the charge brought against *Jude the Obscure* is not so much that it is bad art as that it is a book with a purpose, a moral or an immoral purpose, according to the standpoint of the critic. It would not be pleasant to admit that a book you thought bad morality is good art, but the bad morality is the main point, and this book, it is said, is immoral, and indecent as well.

So are most of our great novels. *Jane Eyre*, we know on the authority of a *Quarterly* reviewer, could not have been written by a respectable woman, while another *Quarterly* (or maybe *Edinburgh*) reviewer declared that certain scenes in *Adam Bede* are indecently suggestive. *Tom Jones* is even yet regarded as unfit to be read in an unabridged form. The echo of the horror which *Les Liaisons Dangereuses* produced more than a century ago in the cheerfully immoral society of the *ancien régime* has scarcely even today died down sufficiently to permit an impartial judgment of that powerful and saturnine book. *Madame Bovary*, which Taine regarded in later days as fit for use in Sunday schools, was thought so shocking in the austere court of Napoleon III that there was no alternative to prosecution. Zola's chief novels, which today are good enough to please Mr. Stead, the champion of British Puritanism, were yesterday bad enough to send his English publisher to prison. It seems, indeed, on a review of all the facts, that the surer a novel is of a certain immortality, the surer it is also to be regarded at first as indecent, as subversive of public morality. So that when, as in the present case, such charges are recklessly flung about in all the most influential quarters, we are simply called upon to accept them placidly as necessary incidents in the career of a great novel.

It is no fortuitous circumstance that the greatest achievements of the novelist's art seem to outrage morality. *Jude the Obscure* is a sufficiently great book to serve to illustrate a first principle. I have remarked that I cannot find any undue intrusion of morality in the art of this book. But I was careful to express myself cautiously, for without doubt the greatest issues of social morality are throughout at stake. So that the question arises: What is the function of the novelist as regards morals? The answer is simple, though it has sometimes been muddled. A few persons have incautiously asserted that the novel has nothing to do with morals. That we cannot assert; the utmost that can be asserted is that the novelist should never allow himself to be made the tool of a merely moral or immoral purpose. For the fact is that, so far as the moralist deals with life at all, morals is part of the very stuff of his art. That is to say, that his art lies in drawing the sinuous woof of human nature between the rigid warp of morals. Take away morals, and the novelist is *in vacuo*, in the region of fairy land. The more subtly and firmly he can weave these elements together the more impressive becomes the stuff of his art. The great poet may be in love with passion, but it is by heightening and strengthening the dignity of traditional moral law that he gives passion fullest play. When Wagner desired to create a typically complete picture of passion he chose the story of Tristram; no story of Paul and Virginia can ever bring out the deepest cries of human passion. Shakespeare found it impossible to picture even the pure young love of Romeo and Juliet without the aid of the violated laws of family and tradition. 'The crash of broken commandments', Mr. Hardy once wrote in a magazine article, 'is as necessary an accompaniment to the catastrophe of a tragedy as the noise of drum and cymbals to a triumphal march'; and that picturesque image fails to express how essential to the dramatist is this clash of law against passion. It is the same in life as in art, and if you think of the most pathetic stories of human passion, the profoundest utterances of human love, you probably think most readily of such things as the letters of Abélard and Héloise, or of Mlle. de Lespinasse, or of the Portuguese nun, and only with difficulty of the tamer speech of happier and more legitimate emotions. Life finds her game in playing off the irresistible energy of the individual against the equally irresistible energy of the race, and the stronger each is the finer the game. So the great artist whose brain is afire with the love of passion yet magnifies the terror and force of moral law, in his heart probably hates it.

Mr. Hardy has always been in love with Nature, with the instinctive, spontaneous, unregarded aspects of Nature, from the music of the dead heatherbells to the flutter of tremulous human hearts, all the things that are beautiful because they are uncontrolled by artificial constraint. The progress of his art has consisted in bringing this element of nature into ever closer contact with the rigid routine of life, making it more human, making it more moral or more immoral. It is an inevitable progression. That love of the spontaneous, the primitive, the unbound—which we call the love of 'Nature'—must as it becomes more searching take more and more into account those things, also natural, which bind and constrain 'Nature'. So that on the one side, as Mr. Hardy has himself expressed it, we have Nature and her unconsciousness of all but essential law, on the other the laws framed merely as social expedients without a basis in the heart of things, and merely expressing the triumph of the majority over the individual; which shows, as is indeed evident from Mr. Hardy's work, that he is not much in sympathy with Society, and also shows that, like Heyse, he recognizes a moral order in Nature. This conflict reaches its highest point around women. Truly or falsely, for good or for evil, woman has always been for man the supreme priestess, or the supreme devil, of Nature. 'A woman', said Proudhon—himself the incarnation of the revolt of Nature in the heart of man—'even the most charming and virtuous woman, always contains an element of cunning, the wild beast element. She is a tamed animal that sometimes returns to her natural instinct. This cannot be said in the same degree of man.' The loving student of the elemental in Nature so becomes the loving student of women, the sensitive historian of her conflicts with 'sin' and with 'repentance', the creations of man. Not, indeed, that any woman who has 'sinned', if her sin was indeed love, ever really 'repents'. It is probable that a true experience of the one emotional state as of the other remains a little foreign to her, 'sin' having probably been the invention of men who never really knew what love is. She may catch the phrases of the people around her when her spirit is broken, but that is all. I have never known or heard of any woman, having for one moment in her life loved and been loved, who did not count that moment as worth all other moments in life. The consciousness of the world's professed esteem can never give to unloved virtue and respectability the pride which belongs to the woman who has once 'sinned' with all her heart. One supposes that the slaves of old who never once failed in abject obedience to their master's will mostly subdued their souls to the level of their starved virtues. But the woman who has loved is like the slave who once at least in his life has risen in rebellion with the cry: 'And I, too, am a man!' Nothing that comes after can undo the fine satisfaction of that moment. It was so that a great seventeenth-century predecessor of Mr. Hardy in the knowledge of the heart, painted Annabella exultant in her sin even at the moment of discovery, for 'Nature' knows no sin.

If these things are so, it is clear how the artist who has trained himself to the finest observation of Nature cannot fail, as his art becomes more vital and profound, to paint morals. The fresher and more intimate his vision of Nature, the more startling his picture of morals. To such an extent is this the case in *Jude the Obscure*, that some people have preferred to regard the book as a study of monstrosity, of disease. Sue is neurotic, some critics say; it is fashionable to play cheerfully with terrible words you know nothing about. 'Neurotic' these good people say by way of dismissing her, innocently unaware that many a charming 'urban miss' of their own acquaintance would deserve the name at least as well. In representing Jude and Sue as belonging to a failing family stock, I take it that Mr. Hardy by no means wished to bring before us a mere monstrosity, a pathological 'case', but that rather, with an artist's true instinct—the same instinct that moved so great an artist as Shakespeare when he conceived *Hamlet*—he indicates the channels of least resistance along which the forces of life most impetuously rush. Jude and Sue are represented as crushed by a civilization to which they were not born, and though civilization may in some respects be regarded as a disease and as unnatural, in others it may be said to bring out those finer vibrations of Nature which are overlaid by rough and bucolic conditions of life. The refinement of sexual sensibility with which this book largely deals is precisely such a vibration. To treat Jude, who wavers between two women, and Sue, who finds the laws of marriage too mighty for her lightly-poised organism, as shocking monstrosities, reveals a curious attitude in the critics who have committed themselves to that view. Clearly they consider human sexual relationships to be as simple as those of the farmyard. They are as shocked as a farmer would be to find that a hen had views of her own concerning the lord of the harem. If, let us say, you decide that Indian Game and Plymouth Rock make a good cross, you put your cock and hens together, and the matter is settled; and if you decide that a man and a woman are in love with each other, you marry them and the matter is likewise settled for the whole term of their natural lives. I suppose that the farmyard view really is the view of the ordinary wholesome-minded novelist—I mean of course in England—and of his ordinary critic. Indeed in Europe generally, a distinguished German anthropologist has lately declared, sensible and experienced men still often exhibit a knowledge of sexual matters such as we might expect from a milkmaid. But assuredly the farmyard view corresponds imperfectly to the facts of human life in our time. Such things as *Jude* is made of are, in our time at all events, life, and life is still worthy of her muse.

'Yes, yes, no doubt that is so,' some critics have said in effect, 'but consider how dangerous such a book is. It may be read by the young. Consider how sad it would be if the young should come to suspect, before they are themselves married, that marriage after all may not always be a box of bonbons. Remember the Young Person.' Mr. Hardy has himself seemingly, though it may only be in seeming, admitted the justice of this objection when in the preface to his book he states that it is 'addressed by a man to men and women of full age'. Of course there is really only one thing that the true artist can or will remember, and that is his art. He is only writing for one person—himself. But it remains true that a picture of the moral facts of the world must arouse moral emotions in the beholder, and while it may not be legitimate to discuss what the artist ought to have done, it is perfectly legitimate to discuss the effect of what he has done.

I must confess that to me it seems the merest cant to say that a book has been written only to be read by elderly persons. In France, where a different tradition has been established, the statement may pass, but not in England nor in America, where the Young Person has a firm grip of the novel, which she is not likely to lose. Twenty years ago one observed that one's girl friends—the daughters of clergymen and other pillars of society—found no difficulty, when so minded, in reading *en cachette* the works of Ouida, then the standard-bearer of the Forbidden, and subsequent observation makes it probable that they are transmitting a similar aptitude to their daughters, the Young Persons of today. We may take it that a novel, especially if written in English, is open to all readers. If you wish to write exclusively for adult readers, it is difficult to say what form of literature you should adopt; even metaphysics is scarcely safe, but the novel is out of the question. Every attempt to restrict literature is open to a *reductio ad absurdum*. I well remember the tender-hearted remonstrance of an eminent physician concerning a proposal to publish in a medical journal a paper on some delicate point in morbid psychology: 'There are always the compositors.' Who knows but that some weak-kneed suggestible compositor may by Jude Fawley's example be thrust on the downward road to adultery and drink? With this high-strung anxiety lest we cause our brother to offend, no forward step could ever be taken in the world; for 'there are always the compositors'. There would be nothing better than to sit still before the book of Ecclesiastes, leaving the compositors to starve in the odour of sanctity.

But why should the Young Person not read *Jude the Obscure?* To me at least such a question admits of no answer when the book is the work of a genuine artist. One can understand that a work of art as art may not be altogether intelligible to the youthful mind, but if we are to regard it as an ensample or a warning, surely it is only for youth that it can have any sort of saving grace. *Jude* is an artistic picture of a dilemma such as the Young Person, in some form or another, may one day have to face. Surely, on moral grounds, she should understand and realize this beforehand. A book which pictures such things with fine perception and sympathy should be singularly fit reading. There is probably, however, much more foxiness than morality in the attitude of the Elderly Person in this matter. 'Don't trouble about traps, my little dears,' the Elderly Person seems to say; 'at your age you ought not to know there are such things. And really they are too painful to talk about; no well-bred Young Person does.' When the Young Person has been duly caught, and emerges perhaps without any tail, then the Elderly Person will be willing to discuss the matter on a footing of comfortable equality. But what good will it be to the Young Person then? The Elderly Person's solicitude in this matter springs, one fears, from no moral source, but has its origin in mists of barbarous iniquity which, to avoid bringing the blush of shame to his cheek, need not here be investigated. 'Move on, Auntie!' as little Sue said to the indignant relation who had caught her wading in the pond, 'this is no sight for modest eyes!'

So that if the Young Person should care to read *Jude* we ought for her own sake, at all events, to be thankful. But our thankfulness may not be needed. The Young Person has her own tastes, which are at least as organically rooted as anyone else's; if they are strong she will succeed in gratifying them; if they are not, they scarcely matter much. She ranks *A Pair of Blue Eyes* above *Jude the Obscure,* likes Dickens more than either, and infinitely prefers Marie Corelli to them all. Thus she puts her foot down on the whole discussion. In any case it ought to be unnecessary to labour this point; there is really little to add to Ruskin's eloquent vindication for young girls of a wholesome freedom to follow their own instincts in the choice of books.

To sum up, *Jude the Obscure* seems to me—in such a matter one can only give one's own impressions for what they are worth—a singularly fine piece of art, when we remember the present position of the English novel. It is the natural outcome of Mr. Hardy's development, along lines that are genuinely and completely English. It deals very subtly and sensitively with new and modern aspects of life, and if, in so doing, it may be said to represent Nature as often cruel to our social laws, we must remark that the strife of Nature and Society, the individual and the community, has ever been the artist's opportunity. 'Matrimony have growed to be that serious in these days', Widow Edlin remarks, 'that one really do feel afeard to move in it at all.' It is an affectation to pretend that the farmyard theory of life still rules unquestioned, and that there are no facts to justify Mrs. Edlin. If anyone will not hear her, let him turn to the Registrar-General. Such facts are in our civilization today. We have no right to resent the grave and serious spirit with which Mr. Hardy, in the maturity of his genius, has devoted his best art to picture some of these facts. In *Jude the Obscure* we find for the first time in our literature the reality of marriage clearly recognized as something wholly apart from the mere ceremony with which our novelists have usually identified it. Others among our novelists may have tried to deal with the reality rather than with its shadow, but assuredly not with the audacity, purity and sincerity of an artist who is akin in spirit to the great artists of our best dramatic age, to Fletcher and Heywood and Ford, rather than to the powerful though often clumsy novelists of the eighteenth century.

There is one other complaint often brought against this book, I understand, by critics usually regarded as intelligent, and with the mention of it I have done. 'Mr. Hardy finds that marriage often leads to tragedy,' they say, 'but he shows us no way out of these difficulties; he does not tell us his own plans for the improvement of marriage and the promotion of morality.' Let us try to consider this complaint with due solemnity. It is true that the artist is god in his own world; but being so he has too fine a sense of the etiquette of creation to presume to offer suggestions to the creator of the actual world, suggestions which might be resented, and would almost certainly not be adopted. An artist's private opinions concerning the things that are good and bad in the larger world are sufficiently implicit in the structure of his own smaller world; the counsel that he should make them explicit in a code of rules and regulations for humanity at large is a counsel which, as every artist knows, can only come from the Evil One. This complaint against *Jude the Obscure* could not have arisen save among a generation which has battened on moral and immoral tracts thrown into the form of fiction by ingenious novices. The only cure for it one can suggest is a course of great European novels from *Petit Jehan de Saintré* downwards. One suggestion indeed occurs for such consolation as it may yield. Has it not been left to our century to discover that the same hand which wrote the disordered philosophy of *Hamlet* puts the times into joint again in *The New Atlantis*, and may not posterity find Thomas Hardy's hand in *Looking Backward* and *The Strike of a Sex*? Thus for these critics of *Jude* there may yet be balm in Utopia.

THE WELL-BELOVED

March 1897

60. Unsigned review, *Athenaeum*

10 April 1897, 471

In the editorial file this review is marked 'Britten'.

'Problems' seem to be going out, 'temperaments' to be coming in. Of course, in one sense the two are almost inseparably associated, for it is most often upon the temperament that the existence of the problem depends. That is to say, given a particular concurrence of circumstances, the course of action to be adopted will appear to one person in the form of a problem, while another, like Col. Hay's hero, will 'see his duty . . . and go for it there and then.' 'Je trouve ça tout simple; c'est son devoir,' said a French officer to us once, in discussing some point of conduct. As a rule, it will be found that most of the 'problems' of recent fiction could have been readily solved by the application of this calculus; and nothing but reluctance to apply it has caused difficulties to arise. Mr. Hardy's line has usually been to recognize this fact, not without some suggestion of a want of finish in the constitution of things, under which temperaments have been so compounded that duty and inclination but too rarely point the same way. In his present 'Sketch of a Temperament', however, he takes a somewhat different line. There is no implied conclusion, no 'moral', as we call it, whatever. It is really a sketch or study. But temperament may be studied in two ways for the purposes of fiction. You may take a case of some abnormal, or, at any rate, unusual, mental or moral configuration, and trace the course of conduct to which in stated circumstances it will give rise. This is the easier form, and that which is most affected by less experienced writers of fiction. It is not easy to predict how abnormal temperaments will behave, so you are not so likely to be caught tripping in the development of your events as you are if you people your story with persons actuated by motives—or, in other words, governed by temperaments—of a kind well known to the average observant person. But when a familiar type of character (as we also call it, though temperament of course, strictly speaking, precedes character) is taken and allowed to display itself in conduct which the reader feels to be consistent, then perhaps the highest triumph of the novelist's art is attained.

In his present story Mr. Hardy has adopted a sort of intermediate method. He has imagined a temperament which we believe to be that of the great majority of male human beings—nay, of male beings of every species. 'We have not yet rounded Cape Turk,' says Mr. Meredith somewhere; not instinct—or temperament if you like to call it so—but hard reason, aided in certain cases by the policeman, alone can persuade the normal man to monogamy. It is all very well to talk about the pursuit of the 'Well-Beloved', to sublimate the elementary instinct into a fantasy of a 'Beloved One' who does not usually 'care to remain in one corporeal nook or shell for any great length of time, however he [the pursuer] may wish her to do so'; our forefathers were quite familiar with the idea, but they called it being off with the old love before you were on with the new. But conscious as most people must be of possibilities of this kind in themselves, 'it is', as Mr. Hardy's hero says, 'a sort of thing one doesn't like to talk of', and, indeed, it has usually exhausted itself before a man reaches the age when he finds out that after all people are for the most part built very similarly, and therefore does not mind talking of anything. The great majority of 'professionizing moral men' bring this sort of thing to an end by marriage, usually selecting their partner for life from motives of course not necessarily excluding that of her form being the temporary residence of 'the Beloved', though by no means so frequently including this claim as a social convention would have the world believe. The mediaeval people knew all about it, and laid terrible snares for the modern matter-of-fact interpreters of their writings, as a short perusal of recent Dante literature will show.

Where Mr. Hardy's hero differs from the mass of mankind is not, therefore, as he himself supposes, in the fact that his 'Beloved' has had many incarnations. His practical painter friend hits the real peculiarity when he says, 'Essentially, all men are fickle, like you; but not with such perceptiveness.' It is no use for Pierston to protest against the word, and plead that he has always been 'faithful to the elusive creature whom I have never been able to get a firm hold of'. We are all like that. It is only another version of *amare amabam, et quaerebam quod amarem*. The peculiarity of Pierston's temperament lies really in its refinement. 'You are', says his friend, 'in practice as ideal as in theory.' Of the physical side of passion, he knows as little as any man so susceptible can do. As a result, he retains his youth, and the pathos of his wooing at sixty is hardly disturbed by any such suggestion of the ludicrous as a similar spectacle would ordinarily arouse. The effect is perhaps helped by the out-of-the-world air which Mr. Hardy's skill is able to throw over the isle of Portland, in which the really critical episodes of the story take place. Whether it be really the isolated corner of the earth which the story represents we do not know, but as portrayed here it is a background which helps one not to be surprised at any of the action.

[quotes, with some comments, part second, ch. XII from ' "Then I saw a soldier" ' to ' "the worst of.it somehow." ']

On the whole, the book is a more pleasing sample of Mr. Hardy's later manner than some we could name. We would not give Geoffrey Day, or Gabriel Oak, or John Loveday for a wilderness of Pierstons, nor Fancy or Bathsheba for twenty generations of Avice Caros; but this is an agreeable book to peruse. It must be in assertion of the great principle that so much is said about the 'island custom', for though doubtless interesting from an anthropological point of view, it has really no influence on the action of the story, and need not have been even alluded to. It would appear, indeed, that *The Well Beloved* was written before some of Mr. Hardy's more recent developments. One can only hope that the fact of his now bringing it out in book form indicates a desire to renew those pleasant relations with his readers that should never have been interrupted.

WESSEX POEMS

December 1898

61. Unsigned review, *Saturday Review*

7 January 1899, lxxxvii, 19

Mr. Hardy enjoys a great reputation for his very clear, and sometimes powerful, presentation of the limited life of the country folk who live in a backwater out of the main stream of the world. Even more, his work has for some years been one of the important influences determining the estimate of life of many thoughtful, if imperfectly educated, people. We come, therefore, to anything he chooses to publish predisposed to respect. But as we read this curious and wearisome volume, these many slovenly, slipshod, uncouth verses, stilted in sentiment, poorly conceived and worse wrought, our respect lessens to vanishing-point, and we lay it down with the feeling strong upon us that Mr. Hardy has, by his own deliberate act, discredited that judgment and presentation of life on which his reputation rested. It is impossible to understand why the bulk of this volume was published at all—why he did not himself burn the verse, lest it should fall into the hands of the indiscreet literary executor, and mar his fame when he was dead.

The pieces of verse at the beginning of the volume are expressions of the feelings natural to every thoughtful young man coming to his first grips with life, and finding that his imaginings surpass its possibilities. There are the lines to the lady-love who has changed to grosser clay; there is the thought that suffering is more bitter because it falls from blind chance, and not from the flattering, if painful, action of some malignant deity; there is the lament that Nature is indifferent; that the children of a lady who has married another will not be so 'high-purposed' as they would have been had she married Mr. Hardy; and there is the revulsion from love. The feelings do not ring quite sincere; they are not strongly felt; they are, in truth, the outpourings in verse common to all the weak, undeveloped natures of intelligent young men, and it is the custom to lock them away, or burn them. Only two of them, 'The Heiress and the Architect', and 'Neutral Tones', show any forecast of Mr. Hardy's mature strength.

Then comes a very pleasant ballad 'Valenciennes', with two really good stanzas in it:

> I never hear the zummer hums
> O' bees; and don' know when the cuckoo comes;
> But night and day I hear the bombs
> We threw at Valencieën.

and

> O' wild wet nights, when all seems sad,
> My wownds come back, as though new wownds I'd had;
> But yet—at times I'm sort o' glad
> I fout at Valencieën.

There is in it a genuine realization of the pathos of the old, shell-deafened pensioner's plight, the true insight into his feelings, and naturally the right form comes.

Of four of the other ballads it can only be said that they are some of the most amazing balderdash that ever found its way into a book of verse. In 'San Sebastian' a sergeant, harrowed by remorse, tells the story of the siege of that city, and how Heaven has punished him for ravishing a young girl during the sack of it, by giving his daughter her eyes. In 'Leipzig' a Casterbridge workman tells the story of Napoleon's defeat, as it was told him by his German mother,

> When she used to sing and pirouette,
> And touse the tambourine
> To the march that yon street-fiddler plies.

In 'The Peasant's Confession' an improbable peasant tells how he led astray and killed an officer, who told him the gist of the orders he was carrying from Napoleon to Grouchy. The stories of the siege and of the battles are alike bald, mechanical and lacking in spirit; while that essential quality of the ballad, a lilting easy flow, is entirely wanting. Consider such a verse as—

> With Gordon, Canning, Blackman, Ompteda,
> L'Estrange, Delancey, Packe,
> Grose, D'Oyly, Stables, Morice, Howard, Hay,
> Von Schwerin, Watzdorf, Boek.

Even worse than these three is 'The Alarm'.

'The Dance at the Phoenix', save for the idiotic lines

> But each with charger, sword, and gun,
> Had bluffed the Biscay wave,

is far better. It is better in story, and has the real ballad ring. While 'My Cicely' is exceedingly interesting; for it is instinct with the feeling of Poe, and there sounds through it a far-away, faint echo of his peculiar music.

Mr. Hardy is hardly more fortunate with the poems which purport to be dramatic, than with his ballads of the wars of Napoleon. The situations in 'The Burghers', when the husband surprises the flying lovers, and when he gives them gold and jewels for their livelihood, afford admirable opportunities for the display of dramatic power; but such is the poorness, the clumsiness rather, of the treatment that they lose all their inherent dramatic force, and are entirely unreal, lifeless and flat. The scene too in 'Her Death and After', where the lover, for the sake of the dead wife's neglected child, blackens her name, and declares falsely to her husband that he is the child's father, is even more unreal. Consider the bald infelicity of this ending of their dialogue:

> '—Sir, I've nothing more to say,'

> 'Save that, if you'll hand me my little maid,
> I'll take her, and rear her, and spare you toil.
> Think it more than a friendly act none can;
> I'm a lonely man,
> While you've a large pot to boil.

> 'If not, and you'll put it to ball or blade—
> To-night, to-morrow night, anywhere—
> I'll meet you here ... But think of it,
> And in season fit
> Let me hear from you again.'

Mr. Hardy reaches a higher level in the verse which he calls 'personative' in conception. Such verses as 'Friends Beyond', 'Thoughts of Ph-a', 'In a Eweleaze near Weatherbury', are instinct with the intimate, penetrating charm of real feeling, completely, strongly felt; they have the value of originality of sentiment and idea; and were the form equal to the matter, they would be poetry. Last of all comes a veritable poem, 'I look into my glass'. It is an original thought realized and felt completely; and the expression is so clear and simple, that it will surely live when the rest of the book has been forgotten:

[quotes the poem.]

62. Unsigned review, *Academy*

14 January 1899, lvi, 43–4

It has become almost the fashion for prose-writers of all kinds to make at least one attempt in verse; and indeed for celebrities generally to essay some art outside that which earned them their fame. A painter or sculptor will make his bow to the public in verse—like Mr. Storey or Mr. Woolner; a distinguished draughtsman, at the close of his career, becomes a popular novelist; a parliamentary leader writes philosophy, a queen turns poetess, a Kaiser becomes everything by turns, and nothing long. Leaders of society take to the stage, leaders of the stage to society. Housemaids turn lady-novelists, lady-journalists turn amateur housemaids. Everybody seems infected with the child's spirit of make-believe: 'Let us play we are actors, or novelists, or singers,' they say, and they play it. The number of prose-writers who have made their appearance as poets is legion. Mr. George Meredith we do not count, for he has always combined the two characters; but Mr. R. D. Blackmore, Mr. Quiller-Couch, Mr. Conan Doyle, are modern instances one at once remembers, while in the elder generation were Charlotte Brontë and George Eliot. Perhaps the father of novelist versifiers was Smollett. It is a dubious experiment for a proseman to sit in the Siege Perilous of poetry, as the examples of Mr. Ruskin and Mr. Lecky remind us. To adapt Tacitus, all would have agreed Mr. Ruskin was capable of writing poetry, if he had not written it. With novelists the odds are still greater. As a rule their whole training and nature is not only un-lyrical but anti-lyrical. Their desire is to tell a story or paint a character, and to do so with detailed elaboration, with the aid of constant side-lights, rejecting nothing as common or mean which will serve that central purpose. It is a method anti-poetic even in the case of the ballad. Drama would give them more native scope. But in poetic drama the central figures must be kept on the heroic plane, and accordingly few novelists have essayed poetic drama. When even George Eliot made no unquestioned success as a poet, it needs some courage for a great novelist to come forward in later life with a volume of verse in his hand.

This is what Mr. Thomas Hardy has done. Save for what might be styled a 'character-song' in one novel, and another slight song in a recent play, he has been sternly faithful to his one remarkable talent. All his life he has been drawing the English peasant, most unpoetical of peasants, with realism faithful to his stolidity, coarseness and absence of any romance save that of destiny, which is present in all things ruled by Fate. One would expect that Mr. Hardy could scarcely have had time to master the mere *technique* of verse; that his strong, grim hand would be too heavy for poetry; that with all the forceful picturesqueness of his clean English, it was a tongue 'that in chiming numbers would not run', too unalloyedly vernacular and sturdy of limb for the supplejointed Muse. One might also surmise that, like Mr. Conan Doyle, he would rely for most of his success on the ballad. And all these things are so. But what could not have been expected is that, though ballads form the bulk of the book, it is not in these he shows at his best.

No, and the fact is surprising—is contrary to all which could be argued from his vocation as novelist. Here, where he has opportunity for dramatic and characteristic writing, is not his happiest work; but, on the contrary, it must be looked for among the lyrical and personal poems of the opening section. There we find tokens that the stuff of the poet is not lacking in Mr. Hardy, had he chosen to bestow on verse the same concentration which has made him a novelist, had he developed technique by unremitting practice. Dryden achieved his mastery of versification by constant writing, and that Shakespeare did the same there is evidence enough in his plays. Few can write even a fluent song by mere gift of nature, unless they have nothing to say in it—when it seems to come easily enough to over-many versifiers. But Mr. Hardy has something to say. And in some lyrics sheer closeness of thought and feeling seems to make violent seizure of Poetry. Such a compelling hand is laid on her in the following verses:

[Quotes 'She to him,' III.]

The image of the cankered vane is imaginative and subtle. Again, in the poem called 'Neutral Tones', the truth of feeling carries the reader over the lack of metrical finish.

[quotes the poem.]

This is concentrated and bitten in with a sparing effectiveness, reminding one of like vignettes in the novels.

But when we come to the ballads, it is different. Based on Wessex stories and memories, we can imagine how effective they would be in Mr. Hardy's prose. The misfortune is that we are reminded of this. We feel the novelist's method, the novelist's hand, and wish the narrative disembarrassed of its metre. Here, too, the technical inexpertness which we have already implied is chiefly in evidence; and the effect is intensified, somehow, by the dialect—which it always needs a crafty hand to make palatable in poetry. The itinerary in 'My Cicely' is an extreme example of the novelist's manner misleading the poet:

> Passing heaths, and the House of Long Sieging,
> I neared the thin steeple
> That tops the fair fane of Poore's olden
> Episcopal see.

And so on. In prose Mr. Hardy could have made it interesting; in poetry it fatally suggests a versified guidebook. Let us hark back to the lyrics, where a charming poem awaits us for *bonne bouche*:

[quotes the poem 'Beneath a knap where flown Nestlings play,' etc.]

That daintily perfect lyric is enough in itself to show the poet in Mr. Hardy, and to justify a book which must, besides, be interesting to all whom his art has captivated—and they are legion. With its sweetness fresh in our mouth, we can close the volume, and thank the writer.

63. E. K. Chambers, *Athenaeum*

14 January 1899, 41

E. K. Chambers (later Sir Edmund, 1866–1953), civil servant and scholar, is best known for his work on Shakespeare.

It is not often that a writer at an advanced, if not quite the eleventh, hour essays two new arts at a blow. Nevertheless, this is the case with Mr. Hardy, who has not only published a volume of poetry, but has also adorned it with thirty drawings and designs from his own pencil. These illustrations, which recall the fact that Mr. Hardy was originally apprenticed in an architect's office, are thoroughly in keeping with some of the most marked characteristics of the book itself. Primitive in execution, and frequently inspired by a somewhat grim mortuary imagination, they are still full of poetry, and show a real sense of the decorative values of architectural outline and nocturnal landscape. Even without the verses, they are a new light on Wessex.

As for the verses themselves, many of which date back to the sixties, while some are of yesterday, it is difficult to say the proper word. Much that Mr. Hardy has amused himself by collecting is quite trifling, conceived in the crude ferments of youth, and expressed with woodenness of rhythm and a needlessly inflated diction. On the other hand, there are certain things which stand out unmistakably, not from their fellows merely, but from the ruck of modern verse as a whole. Two or three of these, which take more or less of a ballad form, are vigorous studies of types of Wessex character, and are marked by the observation and saturnine humour which one would naturally expect from the writer of Mr. Hardy's novels. Such are 'The Fire at Tranter Sweatley's', one of the few pieces in the volume which have been printed before, and 'Valenciennes', in which 'Corp'l Tullidge' recalls the great fight and its disastrous results to his own hearing:

> 'We've fetched en back to quick from dead;
> But never more on earth while rose is red
> Will drum rouse Corpel!' Doctor said
> O' me at Valencieën.

'Twer true. No voice o' friend or foe
Can reach me now, or any livèn beèn;
And little have I power to know
Since then at Valencieèn!

I never hear the zummer hums
O' bees; and don' know when the cuckoo comes;
But night and day I hear the bombs
We threw at Valencieèn . . .

As for the Duke o' Yark in war,
There be some volk whose judgment o'en is meän;
But this I say—'a was not far
From great at Valencieèn.

O' wild wet nights, when all seems sad,
My wownds come back, as though new wownds I'd had;
But yet—at times I'm sort o' glad
I fout at Valencieèn.

Well: Heaven wi' its jasper halls
Is now the on'y Town I care to be in . . .
Good Lord, if Nick should bomb the walls
As we did Valencieèn.

The majority, however, of Mr. Hardy's small cluster of really remarkable poems, even though they may be dramatic in their setting, are not so in their intention. They are personal utterances, voicing a matured and deliberate judgment on life, which hàs, indeed, found expression more than once in his novels. More than anything it was this that gave offence to the narrower minds in *Tess of the D'Urbervilles*. 'The President of the Immortals had finished his sport with Tess': this is the note upon which the tragedy ends. And this is the note, too, more or less, of all the poems in which Mr. Hardy really speaks, is really convincing. The tragedy of life as the outcome of the sport of freakish destinies: this is briefly the conception which dominates his inmost thought. And the mood of melancholy, or perhaps rather melancholic irritation, to which such a conception gives rise, is the one from which his verse must well, if it is to attain anything beyond a mediocre inspiration. From this spring the sombre irony and mournful music of what is perhaps his finest single effort, 'My Cicely'. A Londoner, hearing of the death of his Wessex love, sets out to visit her grave. The description of the journey is magnificent:

[quotes from 'I mounted a steed' to 'Extinguished had he'.]

On arriving, he learns that the dead lady is but a namesake. His has married beneath her, and keeps a hostel on the very road by which he had come. He had seen her, unrecognizing, as with liquor-fired face and thick accents she had jested with the tapsters:

> I backed on the Highway: but passed not
> The hostel. Within there
> Too mocking to Love's re-expression
> Was Time's repartee!

He deludes himself with the fond belief that the dead one, 'she of the garth', was his real love, 'the true one':

> So, lest I disturb my choice vision,
> I shun the West Highway,
> Even now, when the knaps ring with rhythms
> From blackbird and bee;
>
> And feel that with slumber half-conscious
> She rests in the church-hay,
> Her spirit unsoiled as in youth-time
> When lovers were we.

Equally uncompromising in its pessimism is 'Friends Beyond', with its dream—as all these things are but dreams—of the cessation of life, the deadening of desire, in the grave. Here, again, the touch of Wessex makes the treatment singularly effective:

[quotes the poem]

We do not conceal our opinion that Mr. Hardy's success in poetry is of a very narrow range. He is entirely dependent for his inspiration upon this curiously intense and somewhat dismal vision of life, which is upon him almost as an obsession. Where he is not carried along by this, his movement is faltering, and his touch prosaic. But within such close limits his achievement seems to us to be considerable, and to be of a kind with which modern poetry can ill afford to dispense. There is no finish or artifice about it: the note struck is strenuous, austere, forcible; it is writing that should help to give backbone to a literature which certainly errs on the side of flabbiness. And this applies to diction as well as sentiment. Very little of this volume is actually in dialect, but, on the other hand, Mr. Hardy is liberal in the introduction of vigorous and unworn provincialisms. Such forms, for instance, as 'lynchet', 'church-hay' and 'knaps', to cull only from the poems quoted in this article, should do something to renew and refresh a somewhat wilted vocabulary.

POEMS OF THE PAST AND PRESENT

November 1901

64. Unsigned review, *Saturday Review*

11 January 1902, xciii, 49

Almost every poem in this book has something to say, which it says
in a slow, twisted, sometimes enigmatic manner, without obvious
charm, but with some arresting quality, not easy to define or to estimate.
It is a grey book, with its 'sad-coloured landscape', its outlook on the
race at Portland Bill, 'that engulphing, ghast, sinister place', and on
'puzzled phantoms', questioning

> What of logic or of truth appears
> In tacking 'Anno Domini' to the years.

The best poems in it are brooding, obscure, tremulous, half-inarticulate
meditations over man, nature and destiny. Nature, 'working by touch
alone', and Fate, who sees and cannot feel, talk in whispers.

> Unlightened, curious, meek
> She broods in sad surmise . . .
> —Some say they have heard her sighs
> On Alpine height or Polar peak
> When the night tempests rise.

In 'The Lacking Sense', a poem written in a kind of Mrs. Browning
metre, but with a tight grip on a difficult substance, we see Nature
working in the dark, 'wounding where she loves', because she is blind,
asking man's forgiveness and his help:

> Assist her where thy creaturely dependence
> gives thee room,
> For thou art of her womb.

In 'The Mother Mourns', a strange, dreary, ironical song of science, Nature laments that her best achievement, man, has become discontented with her in his ungrateful discontent with himself. It is like the whimpering of a huge animal, and the queer, ingenious metre, with its one rhyme set at wide but distinct and heavily recurrent intervals, beats on the ear like a knell. Blind and dumb forces speak, conjecture, half awakening out of sleep, turning back heavily to sleep again. Many poets have been sorry for man, angry with Nature on man's behalf. Here is a poet who is sorry for Nature, who feels the earth and its roots, as if he had sap in his veins instead of blood, and could get closer than any other man to the things of the earth.

Who else could have written this crabbed, subtle, strangely impressive poem?

[quotes 'An August Midnight.']

No such drama has been written in verse since Browning, and the people of the drama are condensed to an even more pregnant utterance than 'Adam, Lilith, and Eve'. It has an atmosphere not easily to be found outside this book, a mysterious, almost terrifying atmosphere, which we shall find again in the phantom love-poems, the phantom war-poems, and such reflective poems as 'A Wasted Illness', with its

> vaults of pain,
> Enribbed and wrought with groins of ghastliness,

> And hammerings,
> And quakes, and shoots, and stifling hotness, blent
> With webby waxing things and waning things,
> As on I went.

Abstract thought takes form in some given symbol, as in 'The Church Builder', with its architectural imagery, its deliberate building up of spiritual horror. Nearly the whole book shivers with winter.

> The ancient pulse of germ and birth
> Was shrunken hard and dry,
> And every spirit upon earth
> Seemed fervourless as I,

the author tells us, in a poem, 'The Darkling Thrush', which is a kind of personal parable. 'We are too old in apathy,' he says elsewhere, in a farewell to love, and, in the second of the 'De Profundis' poems, turns to himself, as to 'one born out of due time, who has no calling here':

330

Let him to whose ears the low-voiced Best seems
    stilled by the clash of the First,
Who holds that if way to the Better there be, it
    exacts a full look at the Worst,
Who feels that delight is a delicate growth cramped
    by crookedness, custom, and fear,
Get him up and be gone as one shaped awry; he
    disturbs the order here.

It is this melancholy sincerity that gives much of its quality to a book otherwise of very varying merit. Mr. Hardy has never written with flowing rhythms, either in prose or in verse, and his verse often halts, or dances in hobnails. But he has studied the technique of verse more carefully than most of his critics seem to be aware, and he has a command of very difficult metres which, if it were unvarying, would be really remarkable. But his command of his material is uncertain, and he will often spoil a fine poem by a single poor line, as the second 'De Profundis' is spoilt by this line: 'And my eyes have not the vision in them to discern demonstration so clear.'

He crowds syllables together inharmoniously, so that we find, in a single stanza, 'watch'dst', 'gleam'dst', 'brav'dst', each impossible to be spoken. He is always experimenting in metrical effects, and he has made some perfectly successful experiments of a very unusual kind; but he is too fond of long lines, in which the cadence gets lost by the way, especially when they are set side by side with short lines. He can sometimes write gaily and trippingly, as in the delightfully naughty jingle of 'The Ruined Maid', which Congreve could not have done better. And he can be gravely and severely terse in short lines, as in the first 'De Profundis'; he can be weighty and measured in a metre of his own, as in the fine, somewhat Wordsworthian address 'To an unborn Pauper Child'. Neither in verse nor in prose is Mr. Hardy a master of style. Both in prose and in verse he has intensely interesting things to say, and he can say them in an intensely personal way. He can always force words to say exactly what he wants them to say. But their subjection is never quite willing, they seem to have a spite against him because he is stronger than they. That is why they have never given up to him all their souls along with all their service. Some of their magic remains over: his verse does not sing, But so far as it is possible to be a poet without having a singing voice, Mr. Hardy is a poet, and a profoundly interesting one.

65. T. H. Warren, *Spectator*

5 April 1902, 516

T. H. (later Sir Herbert) Warren (1853–1930) was President of Magdalen College, Oxford, and Professor of Poetry from 1911–16.

This collection does not, of course, mark Mr. Hardy's first appearance in the ranks of the poets. In 1898 he put out a volume entitled *Wessex Poems, and other Verses,* of much the same size and character as that before us. It differed, however, from the present book in that it contained thirty illustrations by the author and also a preface, which stated that some of the pieces included had previously been turned into prose and printed as such. Both had their significance. The illustrations showed force, character and individuality; but they were obviously not the work of an artist working in his proper medium. Mr. Hardy's poems display, if not so conspicuously the same defect. Poetry is not his proper medium. He is not at home, he does not move easily, in it. Mr. Hardy undoubtedly has genius; he is a master of fiction. And poetry is a kind of fiction. Dante, indeed, defined it as being fiction, but 'fiction set to music', the music, that is, of language. Mr. Hardy is a master of fiction, but not a master of music.

Not that he has no music, for he has at times a haunting rhythm and a wild, eerie, melancholy *timbre* and ring all of his own. But either he is not certain of his effects, or else he deliberately chooses to be harsh and rough, uncouth and uncanny, and thinks that his style suits his theme. 'Did you ask, dulcet rhymes from me?' he would very likely say, ironically, with Walt Whitman. The reader certainly gets neither dulcet rhymes nor dulcet themes from Mr. Hardy. For in his poetry as in his prose; nay, in his poetry even more than in his prose, Mr. Hardy seems to prefer the unpleasant to the pleasant, the ugly to the fair. He is very much of what is called a realist. That is to say, he prefers the seamy to the smooth side of life, and appears to think that it is necessarily the more real, or, at any rate, the more important. Life, he holds, is a poor business at best. The one consolation is that it will not last, things will be all the same a hundred years hence, for we, at any rate, shall be dead, buried and done for. He has many fine and original

332

ideas and much sombre strength. But he has a morbid taste for the ghastly and the gruesome. This appeared in the illustrations as well as in the poems themselves in his first volume. He is specially attracted by the charnel-house. He cannot picture a wedding in a village church without laying bare the crypt and the graveyard and imagining the bride a corpse and the bridegroom a skeleton. Tennyson knew this mood. His wild song in the 'Vision of Sin', while much more artistic, leaves Mr. Hardy far behind in his own vein. He, too, could 'hob and nob with brother Death'.

> Death is king and Vivat Rex!
> Tread a measure on the stones.
> Madam—if I know your sex
> From the fashion of your bones.

So he sings. But this is not Tennyson's prevailing note. It was perhaps frequent with him in his youth. But he soon outgrew it, just as Scott outgrew the German horrors of Bürger's 'Lenore'. Shakespeare, too, of course, knew the mood, as he knew every mood, and has rendered it with surpassing force in the well-known grave-digger's scene in *Hamlet*; but with him it is one of a thousand moods, and to dwell on it overmuch he makes a sign of madness. Poor Lamb, like so many of earth's wittiest and most humorous spirits, a 'man of humorous-melancholy mark', had much to make him melancholy. But his writing is full of healthy sanity. In one of his most characteristic pieces, his lines on a young girl lately taken from the living, the sprightly Quakeress 'Hester', he says:

> A month or more hath she been dead,
> Yet can I not by force be led
> To think upon the wormy bed
> And her together.

Mr. Hardy needs no forcing, he is always thinking of the 'wormy bed'. He cannot describe a charming maid or happy wife without the 'wormy bed' rising in his mind.

But indeed, apart from this, he describes too seldom either charming maid or happy wife. 'God-Forgotten', 'The Bedridden Peasant', 'To an Unknowing God', 'The Ruined Maid', 'Tess's Lament', 'The Tree' (or an old man's story of how his love revealed to him that she had agreed with a previous lover that she would marry him if he murdered his wife, but unfortunately 'he wived the gibbet-tree'), 'The Church-Builder', who lavishes his all on building a church, and then becomes

bankrupt and hangs himself on the rood,—these are typical names and
themes of his vein. It must be admitted that the war seems to have
stirred him to a nobler spirit, to a kind of grim resolve, if not to any
enthusiasm. One of the best and most powerful pieces is that called the
'Souls of the Slain', where he imagines himself standing on Portland
Bill and seeing the ghosts of those who had died in South Africa flit
home to England to find their reward or disappointment, not in their
own fame or shame, but in the love or coldness of their nearest and
dearest.

The death of the great and good Queen, again, moves him to something like a generous flush of loyalty, though strangely expressed.
What are we to say of lines like these:

> Let one be born and throned whose mould shall constitute
> The norm of every royal-reckoned attribute?

Are they graceful poetry or odd prose? The pieces called 'A Man' and
'At the Pyramid of Cestius' are also really fine in idea. But the one
thing that really seems to lift Mr. Hardy out of himself and inspire him
is the sight of the starry heavens. One of the most touching pieces in this
book is that on the 'Comet at Yalbury, or Yellham', one of the finest
that on a 'Lunar Eclipse':

> Thy shadow, Earth, from Pole to Central Sea,
>   Now steals along upon the Moon's meek shine
>   In even monochrome and curving line
> Of imperturbable serenity.
>
> How shall I link such sun-cast symmetry
>   With the torn, troubled form I know as thine,
>   That profile, placid as a brow divine
> With continents of moil and misery?
>
> And can immense Mortality but throw
>   So small a shade, and Heaven's high human scheme
> Be hemmed within the coasts your arc implies?
>
> Is such the stellar gauge of earthly show,
>   Nation at war with nation, Brains that teem,
> Heroes, and women fairer than the skies?

That is fine; a fine thought and forcibly expressed. And yet it is barely
poetry. The fact is, as we said at the beginning, Mr. Hardy is barely a
poet. His verse has many of the qualities of poetry, such as are often

found in what Dryden called 'the other harmony of prose'. He has a wonderful, almost too great, command of vocabulary. His diction bristles with rare words, but, if far-fetched and bizarre, they will always be found to be the words of a scholar, and of good pedigree. He occasionally strikes out a really poetic phrase of his own, such as the 'mothy curfew tide'. He can describe in verse as in prose the Wessex scenery, the misty water-meadows in lush Dorsetshire vales, the crisp turf on the bare Wiltshire downs; but he does it best as a prose poet. And there is less of real poetry in this volume than in the last. There is no tale so moving as the 'Dance at the Phoenix', no country song so good as 'Friends Beyond', with its true rustic echo.

And even when Mr. Hardy is good he is liable to be coarse, and in one piece in this collection permits himself a Swiftian turn such as was pardonable, or at least not surprising, in Swift two centuries ago, but which we do not expect, and which ought not to be sprung upon us in a book by an English writer of repute in the twentieth century. At the end of the volume are some 'Imitations', as Mr. Hardy calls them, of Sappho and Catullus, Schiller and Heine and Victor Hugo. They are not very close, but are interesting as exhibiting Mr. Hardy as an accomplished scholar, and that not only in English.

THE DYNASTS, PART FIRST

January 1904

---

66. Max Beerbohm, 'Thomas Hardy as Panoramatist', *Saturday Review*

30 January 1904, xcvii, 137–8

Max Beerbohm (later Sir Max, 1872–1956), caricaturist and writer of satirical novels and essays, had been one of the original *Yellow Book* group of aesthetes. This article seems to have appeared also in *Littell's Living Age*, ccxl, 1904. A final paragraph of minor theatrical news is omitted here.

Eight years ago *Jude the Obscure* was published. Since then Mr. Hardy has given us two or three volumes of poetry, and now a volume of drama, but no other novel. One assumes that he has ceased as a novelist. Why has he ceased? The reason is generally said to be that he was disheartened by the many hostile criticisms of *Jude the Obscure*. To accept that explanation were to insult him. A puny engine of art may be derailed by such puny obstacles as the public can set in its way. So strong an engine as Mr. Hardy rushes straight on, despite them, never so little jarred by them, and stops not save for lack of inward steam. Mr. Hardy writes no more novels because he has no more novels to write.

A fascinating essay could be written on the autumnal works of great writers. Sooner or later, there comes for the great writer a time when he feels that his best work is done—that the fire in him has sunk to a glow. And then, instinctively, he shrinks from the form in which he cast the works of his youth and of his prime, and from the themes he then loved best. But he cannot be idle—the fire still glows. Other forms, other themes, occur to him and are grasped by him. In England,

during recent years, great writers in their autumn have had a rather
curious tendency: they have tended to write either about Napoleon or
about Mrs. Meynell. The late Mr. Coventry Patmore wrote about Mrs.
Meynell. Mr. Meredith has written both about Mrs. Meynell and
about Napoleon. Mr. Hardy now readjusts the balance, confining
himself to Napoleon. So far, his procedure is quite normal: a new
theme, through a new form. But I mislead you when I speak of Mr.
Hardy as 'confining himself to Napoleon'. 'Excluding Mrs. Meynell'
would be more accurate. He is so very comprehensive. Pitt, Sheridan,
Nelson, George III, and, throughout Europe everyone who played a
notable part during the First Empire—here they all are, in company
with various spirits, shades and choruses, marshalled into the scope of
six acts and thirty-five scenes. Nor has Mr. Hardy done with them yet.
This book is but a third of his scheme. The trilogy will comprise
nineteen acts and one hundred and thirty scenes. Prodigious, is it not?
And it marks its schemer as (in the stricter sense of the word) a
prodigy. Normally, the great writer, forsaking the form of his greatness, gravitates to littler forms. The theme may be great or little, but
he treats it within a little compass. Mr. Hardy's vitality would seem to
have diminished only for his own special form. At any rate, it is such
that he believes it sufficient for an attack on the illimitable and the
impossible.

Impossible his task certainly is. To do perfectly what he essays would
need a syndicate of much greater poets than ever were born into the
world, working in an age of miracles. To show us the whole world,
as seen, in a time of stress, by the world that is unseen by us! Whoever
so essays must be judged according to the degree by which his work
falls infinitely short of perfection. Mr. Hardy need not fear that test.
The Dynasts is a noble achievement, impressive, memorable.

To say that it were easy to ridicule such a work is but a tribute to the
sublimity of Mr. Hardy's intent, and to the newness and strangeness
of his means. It is easy to smile at sight of all these great historic figures
reduced to the size of marionettes. I confess that I, reading here the
scene of the death of Nelson, was irresistibly reminded of the same
scene as erst beheld by me, at Brighton, through the eyelet of a peep-
show, whose proprietor strove to make it more realistic for me by
saying in a confidential tone ''Ardy, 'Ardy, I am wounded, 'Ardy.—
Not mortially, I 'ope, my lord?—Mortially, I fear, 'Ardy.' The dialogue here is of a different and much worthier kind; yet the figures
seem hardly less tiny and unreal. How could they be life-sized and

alive, wedged into so small a compass between so remote and diverse scenes? Throughout this play the only characters who stand to human height, drawing the breath of life, are the Wessex peasants. 'When', says Mr. Hardy in his preface, '*The Trumpet Major* was printed, more than twenty years ago, I found myself in the tantalizing position of having touched the fringe of a vast international tragedy without being able, through limits of plan, knowledge, and opportunity, to enter further into its events; a restriction that prevailed for many years.' Well, that restriction has vanished. But remains the difference between a writer's power to project the particular thing which he has known lovingly in youth and his power to project the general thing which he has studied in maturity. For my own part, I wish these Wessex peasants had been kept out of *The Dynasts*. They mar the unity of an effect which is, in the circumstances, partially correct. The general effect of littleness does, without doubt, help the illusion which Mr. Hardy seeks to create. That miraculous syndicate of which I dreamed anon would have kept the figures as tiny as here they seem—as tiny, but all alive, like real men and women beheld from a great distance.

Pushing ingenuity a step further, one might even defend the likeness of these figures to automata. For Mr. Hardy's aim is to show them, not merely as they appear to certain supernal, elemental spirits, but also as blindly obedient to an Immanent Will, which

> works unconsciously, as heretofore,
> Eternal artistries in Circumstance,
> Whose patterns, wrought by rapt æsthetic rote
> Seem in themselves Its single listless aim,
> And not their consequence.

From the Overworld the Spirit of the Years watches the eternal weaving of this pattern. The Spirit Ironic watches, too, smiling. The Spirit Sinister, too, watches laughing. There is a Spirit of the Pities; but she is young, as Mr. Hardy insists, and quite helpless. Beneath them 'Europe is disclosed as a prone and emaciated figure, and the branching mountain-chains like ribs, the peninsular plateau of Spain forming a head. . . . The point of view then sinks downwards through space, and draws near to the surface of the perturbed countries, where the peoples, distressed by events which they did not cause, are seen writhing, crawling, heaving, and vibrating in their various cities and nationalities. . . . A new and penetrating light descends, enduing men and things with a seeming transparency, and exhibiting as one organism the anatomy of life and movement in all humanity.' The Spirits draw nearer still to earth. They flit over the English ground, near the open Channel. A stagecoach passes. 'See now', says one of the passengers to another, 'how the Channel and coast open out like a chart. . . . One can see half across to France up here.' The irony of this contrast between their vision and the vision just vouchsafed to us strikes the keynote of the whole drama. How ridiculous that historic debate in the House of Commons! Sheridan thundering at Pitt, and Pitt at Sheridan, and above them in the gallery, in the guise of human Strangers, those abstract Spirits, sitting till they are 'spied' by an officious Member! Anon these Spirits are in the cathedral of Milan. Napoleon, in all his trappings, places the crown of Lombardy upon his brow. Before him the Cardinal Archbishop swings a censer. The organ peals an anthem. 'What', asks the Spirit of the Pities, 'is the creed that these rich rites disclose?' And the Spirit of the Years answers

> A local thing called Christianity,
> Which the wild dramas of this wheeling sphere
> Include, with divers other such, in dim,
> Pathetical, and brief parentheses.

The Imperial procession passes out to the palace. 'The exterior of the cathedral is seen, but the point of view recedes, the whole fabric smalling into distance and becoming like a rare, delicately-carved ornament. The city itself sinks to miniature, the Alps show afar as a white corrugation . . . clouds cover the panorama', and our next sight is of the dockyard at Gibraltar. Thus we range hither and thither, with the Spirits, listening to their reflections on the infinite littleness and .helplessness and unmeaning of all things here below. We see, at last, the toy field of Austerlitz, and the toy death-bed of Pitt. Thereat the book closes, looking strangely like a duodecimo.

The book closes, and (so surely has it cast its spell on us) seems a quite fugitive and negligible little piece of work. We wonder why Mr. Hardy wrote it; or rather, one regrets that the Immanent Will put him to the trouble of writing it. 'Wot's the good of anythink? Wy, nothink' was the refrain of a popular coster-song some years ago, and Mr. Hardy has set it ringing in our ears again. But presently the mood passes. And, even as in the stage-directions of *The Dynasts* we see specks becoming mountain-tops, so do we begin to realize that we have been reading a really great book. An imperfect book, as I have said— inevitably imperfect. And less perfect than it might quite easily have been. That Mr. Hardy is a poet, in the large sense of the word, nobody will dare deny. But his poetry expresses itself much more surely and finely through the medium of prose than through the medium of rhyme and metre. I wish he had done *The Dynasts* in prose, of which he has a mastery, rather than in a form wherein he has to wrestle—sometimes quite successfully—for his effects. No one, again, will deny that Mr. Hardy is, in the large sense of the word, a dramatist. But his drama expresses itself better through narration than through dialogue and stage-directions. He writes here not for the stage; and, except an eye to the stage, there is no reason or excuse for using a form which must always (be our dramatic imagination never so vivid) hamper and harass us in the study. But, when every reservation has been made, *The Dynasts* is still a great book. It is absolutely new in that it is the first modern work of dramatic fiction in which freewill is denied to the characters. Free-will is supposed to be a thing necessary to human interest. If it were so indeed, we should get no excitement from Homer. Not that Mr. Hardy's negation resembles Homer's. Achilles and the rest were life-sized puppets, whose strings were being pulled, at near hand, by gods scarcely larger than they. Mr. Hardy's puppets are infinitesimal—mere 'electrons', shifted hither and thither, for no reason, by some impalpable agency. Yet they are exciting. Free-will is not necessary to human interest. Belief in it is, however, necessary to human life. Cries Mr. Hardy's Spirit of the Pities

> This tale of Will
> And Life's impulsion by Incognizance
> I cannot take.

Nor can I. But I can take and treasure, with all gratitude, the book in which that tale is told so finely.

67. John Buchan, *Spectator*

20 February 1904, 292

John Buchan (1875–1940) writer of biographies, historical novels
and adventure stories, was to become Lord Tweedsmuir.

Mr. Hardy has undertaken a drama on what is perhaps the most
dramatic subject which the modern world can conceive,—the ferment
of Europe under the Napoleonic Wars. He has sought to bring all the
many issues of that confused time into the focus of his art, and he therefore provides a multitude of varied characters and a frequent shifting
of scene. It is a great intention, and deserves to be judged strictly on the
definition of it which he has given us in his preface. It must necessarily
be a play rather for the study than the stage. No drama, no series of
dramas, on the ordinary model can represent all the details of the
panorama, the network of causes, and the wide variety of characters
which are essential to his scheme. Stagecraft is a convention some
distance removed from actuality, but the convention which Mr. Hardy
has chosen is many degrees further from reality than the ordinary
illusion of the stage. Again, the unities, which in an elastic form must
be present in an acting play, are wholly remote from his conception.
Time and space scarcely have their normal significance in the rarefied
world of his fancy. The drama which he seeks is not the conflict of
personalities familiar to us in ordinary life, but the clash of nations and
civilizations and cosmic forces. His intention, in a word, is epic; and it
is only for convenience, and to suit the idiosyncrasies of his own genius,
that he has used the dramatic form.

The intention is to show the events which shook the world as a kind
of puppet-show, behind which moves the force which the author
chooses to call the Immanent Will, causeless and incomprehensible.
For this purpose there come interludes when all action ceases, and the
reader is given a vision of a gaunt and skeleton Europe, seen as if from
an infinite height, with the peoples struggling like ants, and a nerve-
like network of currents, emanating from the Will, interpenetrating
both ants and skeleton. Mr. Hardy attains to a kind of gruesome

sublimity in these curious stage directions. The disease of 'grandeur', the sense of the littleness and the transience of life, seize the onlooker like a vertigo on high mountains. For a brief moment, to borrow a technical term, a philosophical creed is visualized, and the spectral grips the mind with all the strange vividness of a dream. The philosophy itself is a kind of hard Pyrrhonism, what some people will no doubt call Aeschylean, but which seems to us to be far enough removed from the noble fore-ordination of Greek tragedy. We should be hard pressed to define it. In his preface Mr. Hardy tells us that he has abandoned the masculine pronoun in allusion to the First Energy, since all thinkers have long since given up the anthropomorphic conception of it. From this we gather that Mr. Hardy's Will is something a thousandfold more distant from humanity than the Fate of other poets, since by personifying it they seem to assume that its attributes have at least a far-away cousinship with mortal nature. Other poets, too, have seen that to fail to adopt this wise conviction would be so to divorce the substance of things from their dramatic presentment, so to belittle mortal effects, that the unreality of it all would become too spectral for art. Human drama, even on Mr. Hardy's theory, demands some illusion in its philosophy as well as in its staging. Sometimes, indeed, there is a hint that Destiny is not adamant. Says the Spirit of Rumour, in appropriately awkward verse:

> There may react on things
> Some influence from these, indefinitely,
> And even on That, whose outcome we all are.

But on the whole, the philosophy is consistent in its fatalism:

> A local thing called Christianity,
> Which the wild dramas of this whirling sphere
> Include, with divers others such, in dim,
> Pathetical, and brief parentheses;
> Beyond whose reach, uninfluenced, unconcerned,
> The systems of the suns go sweeping on
> With all their many-mortaled planet train
> In mathematic roll unceasingly.

Apart from metaphysics, there must be some central mundane idea to give unity to the puppet-show. Mr. Hardy finds this in the duel between England and Napoleon, the real conflict of civilizations and temperaments. 'I want nothing on this continent,' Mack is told by the Emperor; 'The English only are my enemies.' And again:

Her rock-rimmed situation walls her off,
Like a slim, selfish mollusk in its shell,
From the wide views and fair fraternities
Which on the mainland we reciprocate.

And so, with these conceptions, mundane and supra-mundane, as a basis, the first part of the great drama down to Austerlitz and the death of Pitt is worked out on the stages of Wessex, London, Paris, Germany, with a vast number of actors, from the protagonists, Napoleon, Nelson and Pitt, down to nameless Wessex peasants and women of Paris. In one department Mr. Hardy is a master. His peasants, especially his Wessex men, have the true Shakespearian ring. Their humour is like Touchstone's, their talk is racy of the soil and human as life itself. The citizens who crowd around Pitt's coach, the lonely watchers by the beacons on the Wessex heath, the sailormen just come from Trafalgar, are as real as anything Mr. Hardy has done. And this, in the midst of so much spectral life, is the highest praise. Of the great figures, Napoleon is so far only a brooding shadow; but Pitt is alive, and the King and Nelson. The death of the English Premier and the last scene at Trafalgar are fine pieces of drama, and minor scenes, like the attack by Sheridan in the House of Commons, have considerable life and colour. All through the play, even when it sinks to its worst, we are impressed with a certain epic grandeur in the conception; it is in the execution that faults arise. We fear that Mr. Hardy's reach must be held to exceed his grasp; but let us add that the reach is a very great one. The cardinal error seems to us to lie in the philosophy, which is too cold, bloodless and formal to be adequate to the needs of human life. But even with this limitation we can imagine a great drama, in which a chorus of dignified spirits should proclaim in noble verse a lofty if heartless creed. But the group of spirits, piteous, ironic and merely didactic, who provide, in the style of a Greek chorus, a running commentary on the action, do not talk in noble numbers, but in the worst jargon of the schools. They conduct their espionage in the spirit of a very young man who has just begun to dabble in metaphysics, and is imperfectly acquainted with the terminology. The result of this constant harping on the Immanent Will in pseudo-scientific terms becomes in the end merely comic. These Personages never speak without expressing a banal thought in the worst verse.

Gloomy Villeneuve grows rash, and, darkly brave,
Leaps to meet war, storm, Nelson—even the grave,—

is the style of Recording Angel II; while,

> Plunging mid those teeth of treble line
>   In jaws of oaken wood
> Held open by the English navarchy
> With suasive breadth and artful industry,
> Would smack of purposeless foolhardihood,—

is the manner of Recording Angel I. But the low-water mark is reached by the Chorus of the Years in what the author calls 'aerial music':

> It will be called, in rhetoric and rhyme,
>   As son to sire succeeds,
> A model for the tactics of all time;
> 'The Great Campaign of Eighteen-hundred-five,'
> By millions of mankind not yet alive.

Phrases like 'an untactical torpid diplomacy' and 'the free trajection of our entities' are impossible in any music, aerial or otherwise. These sinister spirits have indeed led Mr. Hardy into strange deeps. Under their influence he is capable of the very worst lyrics and the most turgid meditations. Only when he gets back to common earth, as in the Trafalgar song of the boatmen, does he approach either true vigour or melody. But though he is at his worst among the spirits, his verse throughout is full of the gravest technical faults. He has a habit of falling into that unpleasing form of blank verse where every line is a complete sentence. As compared with the excellent prose in which his peasants talk, the metrical work is halting, turgid and singularly lacking in music. The rhythms, even in passages where the thought is admirable, tend to be weak and impoverished, and it is rarely that a single fine line breaks the tortured monotony.

And yet we should hesitate to pronounce the work a failure. The outlines of a great conception rise out of the misty philosophy and awkward rhythms. It is the work of a poet, who, lacking most of the poetic gifts, has, on the one hand, a kind of cosmic imagination, and, on the other, the clearest insight into the humour and pity of humble life. It is the work of a poet, but it is rarely poetry. We can imagine Mr. Hardy writing a drama of Wessex folk of the first quality, but it must not be in verse, for his Muse is too unskilful, and he must refrain from calling up spirits from the vasty deep, for he has no turn for transcendental poetry. Sometimes, indeed, he gets the better of himself, and writes, as if by accident, fine lines, as when Napoleon sees England ruined:—

> Till all her hulks lie sodden in their docks,
> And *her grey island eyes* in vain shall seek
> One jack of hers upon the ocean plains!

or when the chaplain on the 'Victory' says of the dead Admiral,

> He has homed to where
> There's no more sea;

or when the London citizen, with a quaintness almost Shakespearian speaks of Nelson,

> Who is now sailing shinier seas than ours.

But such lines are oases in very sandy deserts, and it is only when we turn to the Wessex scenes and familiar prose that we recognize the infallible touch of the true artist.

68. Edward Wright, 'The Novels of Thomas Hardy', *Quarterly Review*

April 1904, cxcix, 499–523

This was probably the Edward Wright who edited Bacon's Essays and Marvell's poems in the 'Little Library' series in 1903 and 1904.

On a review of the works of the earlier Greek poets Aristotle concluded that dramatists were able sooner to arrive at excellence in diction and characterization than in the construction of the fable; and English literature, modern as well as ancient, is, by its main defect in narrative art, a lamentable proof of his assertion. From Spenser to Browning and

George Eliot, the weak point with us has been the structure of the plot. Dramatic design, like sculpture, is an art not easily to be naturalized in this country. Ben Jonson was one of the first English writers to compose plays with all the incidents regularly interwoven and all the parts interdependent; and for this reason he was considered by some critics, from the Jacobean age to the Restoration period, to be a better dramatist than Shakespeare. Being, however, vastly inferior to several of his contemporaries in the creation and development of character and the genius for dramatic poetry, he failed to excite a general feeling for form and so establish it as a tradition binding upon later writers. Happily, the sense of literary form was, to some extent, popularized in England during the eighteenth century, when the art of painting was also founded in this country; and, on the rise of the novel, there was a possibility of the art of construction being acquired by the English mind, with the splendid examples set before it, first, by the author of *Clarissa Harlowe,* and then by the author of *The Bride of Lammermoor.*

Vainly, however. The loss of the sense of literary form was part of the price we had to pay for the magnificent results of the romantic movement. Coleridge, Hazlitt and other critics of the romantic school, English and German, must be said to have been collaborators in innumerable badly constructed works of the last century, in that they either exalted the superstition of Shakespeare's consummate skill as a playwright into a sort of literary religion, or brought the inferior plays of other Elizabethan dramatists into fashion by dwelling on detached passages of exceptionally poetic quality and lightly passing over structural defects which should have been treated as intolerable. Owing in no small measure to the influence of these critics, our drama, in an age when great poets were attempting to write for the stage, became, in Beddoes' phrase, 'a haunted ruin', and soon decayed utterly; while many volumes of fiction, remarkable and, at times, excellent in characterization, feeling and philosophy, remained second-rate productions in regard to proportion, compactness, correlation of parts and general design.

Thackeray, in the first portion of *Vanity Fair,* and in some later works, effected a marked improvement in the art of novel-writing in England, in construction as well as in style; but to have definitely raised the standard of workmanship in this respect is one of the fine achievements of the author of *The Return of the Native.* We think it is well to insist upon this, primarily, in attempting even a brief estimate of Mr. Hardy's work as a novelist. For although the best writers of the younger

346

generation have followed him in studying conciseness, arrangement, dramatic point and, in a few instances, purity and expressiveness of style, yet, unfortunately, the average English work remains, not only pitifully inferior to the French, but inferior also in constructive art and vividness to the average American novel of the present day. Hence, as Mr. Hardy complained some sixteen years ago, in a valuable essay on the reading of fiction, probably few general readers consider that to a masterpiece in story, no less than to a masterpiece in painting or sculpture, there appertains a beauty of shape capable of giving to the trained mind an equal pleasure.

Yet, no doubt, many persons, who did not care whether or not the English novel in Mr. Hardy's hands had become a well-knit drama instead of the string of episodes which once it was, appreciated other splendid qualities in his rustic stories. First of all, he revealed to them the true romance of country life. He painted for them the woods, downs, meads and heaths, where the Wessex labourer toiled, in a new and most impressive light. In that happy compromise between an essay in criticism and an anthology, *Landscape in Poetry*, the late Professor Palgrave remarked in the literary treatment of natural scenery a general development. There was first a simple pleasure in describing single familiar objects; scenes were next lightly drawn as a background in the representation of human actions and manners. Then, as men gathered into cities for the business of life, and repaired to the country for pleasure and refreshment, a form of literature arose in which the loveliness and the benignity of the green earth were extolled. This idea of nature as a fair, beneficent power obtained in Wordsworth's poetry its grandest and most complete expression; and, in an era of extraordinary industrial expansion, it has become one of the commonplaces of European letters.

It implies, however, a conception of the conditions of rustic existence which is not borne out by the experiences of the peasant himself. Not by residing in a thatched cottage, amid verdant fields circled by soft blue hills, does he become a poetic figure. The poetry of his mode of life consists in his having to work for his living in a dependence on the moods of sky, air and earth, almost as absolute as is the dependence on the moods of sky, air and water, of mariners in a lone sailing vessel on the high seas. Dawn and darkness, rain, wind, mist and snow, the frost in winter, the summer drought—these, for him, are personal obstructors or assistants; and every hour of the day he must study and prepare for them. He does not always see in a sunset the beauty which Turner and

Shelley have taught us to appreciate; he usually glances at it for another purpose, which Mr. Hardy illustrates in the scene in *The Woodlanders*, where the peasant girl Marty South is planting fir trees.

She looked towards the western sky, which was now aglow like some vast foundry wherein new worlds were being cast. Across it the bare boughs of a tree stretched horizontally, revealing every twig against the evening fire, and showing in dark profile every beck and movement of three pheasants that were settling themselves down on it in a row to roost.

'It will be fine to-morrow,' said Marty, observing them with the vermilion light of the sun in the pupils of her eyes, 'for they are a-croupied down nearly at the end of the bough. If it were going to be stormy they'd squeeze close to the trunk.'

This is excellent writing, inspired by knowledge and instinct with poetry; but a still finer and more complete revelation of the country-man's point of view is found in *Far from the Madding Crowd*, where the shepherd, tending his lambing ewes on a winter's night upon the downs, pauses to glance at the sky.

[quotes ch. II from 'To persons standing alone' to 'art superlatively beautiful.']

This shepherd is a type of the countryman described by Mr. Hardy with the greatest sympathy. Mr. Hardy's conception of the English peasant is somewhat partial, but most striking; and we fancy that such characters as Gabriel are depicted with the greatest sympathy because they clearly reflect a main idiosyncrasy of their author in noble con-junction with a higher quality of soul. They are supposed to unite the enervating fatalism that distinguishes Mr. Hardy with a power of silent, grand endurance in adversity that a Roman Stoic would have admired. For instance, the scene in *Far from the Madding Crowd*, from which we have just cited a passage, closes with a spectacle of disaster. The flock of ewes, representing Gabriel's savings after years of toil and thrift, and his prospect of acquiring a position of independence and comfort, are worried by a young dog into a chalk-pit, at the bottom of which he discovers them stretched all dying or dead. Misfortunes accumulate, as they often do in Mr. Hardy's novels. Gabriel finds him-self rejected by the woman he loves, poverty-stricken, and unable to obtain any sort of employment. Then, with that healthy disinclination to grieve over past sorrows, which amounts almost to temperamental cheerfulness in the generality of the English labouring classes, the shepherd goes in search of work.

He had sunk from his modest elevation as pastoral king into the very slime-pits of Siddim; but there was left to him . . . that indifference to fate which, though it often makes a villain of a man, is the basis of his sublimity when it does not.

Mr. Hardy's heroes are all drawn on the same model. Gabriel Oak in *Far from the Madding Crowd*, John Loveday in *The Trumpet-Major*, Giles Winterborne in *The Woodlanders*, are men of a similar nature. Michael Henchard in *The Mayor of Casterbridge*, though lacking their inexpressible tenderness and purity of heart, is related to them in passive fortitude; and Clym Yeobright in *The Return of the Native*, joins their family. A student and a sojourner in cities, he has, at first, a facility of expression, a radiant activity and a resilience of mind, which exclude him from the company of Mr. Hardy's heroes; but when he turns again for peace of soul to the rugged heath where he was born, he at last becomes as subdued in spirit as the strong rustic men who have been taught to go softly all their days, and to whom the sad art of renunciation is almost an instinct. Here, at least, Mr. Hardy's poetic exaggeration of nature's utter sternness, as opposed to Wordsworth's equally poetic exaggeration of her benignity, leads to the conception of a fine type of character.

The disciplinary influence of country life supplies indeed, one of those grandly constructive ideas which give to the Wessex novels their singular unity and consistency. It underlies the whole of the characterization. While Mr. Hardy's heroes are countrymen in whom the dumb passiveness of the peasantry under affliction rises into a moral grandeur of resignation, his men of the meaner sort are either townsmen or persons of urban culture. Manson, Sergeant Troy, Wildeve, Fitzpiers, D'Urberville and some characters in the shorter tales, have many traits in common; and, through not having been chastened by a life of labour under natural conditions, they strangely resemble those women in Mr. Hardy's novels who, belonging to the yeoman or better class, lead a sheltered, pleasant existence. Men and women, their characteristics can be given almost in the same words. They have somewhat of the moral poverty of children in that their reason and their propensities have no reciprocating influence; so they live on present emotions, and regard neither the past with understanding nor the future with circumspection. Though possessing as little real energy of resistance to fate as Mr. Hardy's peasants, they have a buoyancy of spirit arising from the unrestrained sensibility which is the moving force of their lives; and, stimulated by whatever pleasing object chance places in their way, they are full of dangerous activity. The effect is that the men are refined sensualists and the women light-hearted coquets, who, in a search for personal admiration or fine shades of feeling, often become the victims of an overwhelming passion. Irresponsible, fascinating creatures, these 'children of a larger growth' are sometimes transfigured into incarnations of the tragic power of love, blind, disastrous and ineluctable in its working. As wayward as fate itself, they invade, for some light whim, the settled lives of men whose calmness is but the equilibrium of great powers, and leave them terribly disordered. They are singularly apt to make the first advances; yet with all their eagerness for admiration they remain indifferent to the deep inarticulate devotion which they are at pains to excite. The tumult and not the depth of soul they approve, and thus they are won lightly by the voluble inconstant men whose failings they more innocently and weakly reflect.

If Mr. Hardy is often ungenerous, sometimes cruel, and occasionally unpleasant in his characterization of women, yet there are to be found in his works heroines nobly conceived. Marty South in *The Woodlanders*, Elizabeth-Jane in *The Mayor of Casterbridge* and Tess of the D'Urbervilles, are tenderly drawn. They are girls who have had to work in the woods and fields, instead of living comfortably indoors. Sharing the hard conditions and rough experiences of such men as Winterborne and Gabriel Oak, they, too, have learnt to suffer greatly in silence, and to regard happiness, in accordance with their author's sad philosophy, as 'but the occasional episode in a general drama of pain'. They accept misfortunes with the same fatalism, with the same passivity, rising often in moments of trial to similar stoic greatness. Of these women, Marty South is the most typical; for Elizabeth-Jane, that 'dumb, deep-feeling, great-eyed creature', is rescued from her lot by adoption and marriage, while Tess, with her beauty and her strange career, appears a queen of tragedy rather than a peasant girl. In outward seeming Marty South, dressed in her working clothes, illiterate, poor, and unlovely, is merely a pitiable figure; yet Mr. Hardy makes her one of the most exquisite and touching characters in the Wessex novels. Personally, we are moved more by her story than by that of Tess; it is related more simply and naturally, from the time when first we meet her, toiling wearily at a man's work all the day and most of the night, and selling, for her sick father's sake, the long beautiful hair that redeemed her from plainness, until at last we leave her, standing above the grave of the man whom she loved, but who had given her no word of love in return. How finely, for instance, are her feelings revealed as she talks to him, when they are planting fir trees, and he, absent in mind, is anxiously devising how to win another woman. Marty holds up the little trees while he spreads the roots towards the south-west in order, as he explains, to give them a strong holdfast against the great gales from that quarter.

'How they sigh directly we put 'em upright, though while they are lying down they don't sigh at all,' said Marty.

'Do they?' said Giles. 'I've never noticed it.'

She erected one of the young pines into its hole, and held up her finger. The soft musical breathing instantly set in, which was not to cease night or day till the grown tree should be felled—probably long after the two planters had been felled themselves.

'It seems to me,' the girl continued, 'as if they sigh because they are very sorry to begin life in earnest—just as we be.'

'Just as we be?' He looked critically at her. 'You ought not to feel like that, Marty.'

The thought is, indeed, a sad one; but Mr. Hardy is a true enough observer to depict many a charming group of rustics with that *joie de vivre* which, whatever may be said to the contrary, is still to be found in this country. Interpreting everything in the terms of his own profound melancholy, he tries to explain that the more humble classes are alone sufficiently ignorant of the real conditions of life to be persistently cheerful; but, though his philosophy is false, he is loyal to facts. The truth is that 'Merry England' is a land that still exists, though hidden for some centuries in obscurity. The English are a spirited people, sentimental and yet humorous at heart; the aristocratic *morgue* of the uppermost social strata, the puritanic rigour which still keeps many of the middle and lower-middle classes somewhat sour of mind, are alike foreign to the genius of the race. It is naturally of a light-hearted and rather improvident nature, living for the day, and trusting to its strength to provide for the morrow when the morrow comes. The fatalism which Mr. Hardy exaggerates as a trait of our rural population is simply an inveterate cheerfulness of soul, which causes them to accept a misfortune as a thing that was to be, in order to avoid constant anxiety for the future and vain regret for the past. Doubtless, this disposition to escape from worry makes at times more for serenity of mind than for strength of character; and Mr. Hardy, besides ascribing it, as we have remarked, to some of his worst personages, notices it as a weakness in Joan Durbeyfield. Yet, after all, such a disposition is not wholly bad.

There was a time, we fancy, when the Wessex peasantry infected Mr. Hardy himself with somewhat of its gaiety. Among his types of character there is one occurring so frequently as to be remarkable. Sometimes it is a rustic lad, Clym Yeobright or Edward Springrove, sometimes it is a rustic maid, Fancy Day or Grace Melbury, who returns home with urban manners and habits of thought; but in all cases these acquirements yield at last to an instinctive delight in country life, and the reversion brings with it happiness. Happiness Mr. Hardy must in some measure have attained when, leaving London, he rediscovered Wessex, and found to his hand materials of such value as no writer since Scott had possessed. Here was a land untouched by modern unrest, the land of an ancient, youthful-hearted people, where the passions were frank and simple, where the outlook on all things was natural and wholesome, and life ran still calmly in the channels of instinct and custom.

That charming pastoral, *Under the Greenwood Tree*, the earliest of the Wessex novels, must have been composed by a man who was moved to joy in escaping from the smoke and business of the city, and in discerning the true field for displaying the great powers within him. What knowledge does a town-bred child in playtime acquire like the knowledge of wild life which a rustic lad obtains almost unwittingly? On what fund of picturesque tradition can a citizen draw like the tales of courtships at maypole dances, of midsummer-eve rites and other immemorial usages, of sorcerers and witches, smugglers, press-gangs and preparations along the English shore against Napoleon's armies, which one Dorsetshire man tells us he heard, some fifty years since, from a gentle old dame born ere England went to war with her American colonies? And if few writers of the present day have gathered such material for their works, none other has cultivated so carefully gifts naturally so fine. A relish for old rustic ways and forms of speech of genuine Saxon idiom, a turn for story-telling, a rare perception of the character of a landscape as well as of a person, a quick sense of humour, and that intensity of imagination and feeling that stamps the real poet, these were the foundations of a genius which has been developed by study. One of the most dramatic of novelists—except on the rare occasions when he is melodramatic—Mr. Hardy has endued with life and colour all that a student of antiquities, history, architecture and folk-lore could discover relating to his native county; and with wonderful accuracy, lightness and charm he has revealed the poetry with which the ways of the woodman and the farmer, the neatherd, the shepherd and other rural figures, are still surrounded.

Surprising, indeed, is Mr. Hardy's achievement as a whole. In an age when, to very refined people, England appeared to be a vast manufactory, with a population that had lost the poetry of tradition without acquiring the feelings of true culture, when Spain and Italy were cherished as the sole countries of Europe untouched by the general vulgarity of material progress, he found in the daily occupations of the peasantry of a neglected agricultural province the matter for a series of idylls and tragedies which, for their qualities of romantic emotion and poetic charm, can almost be compared with the Waverley Novels. The popularity of Scott Mr. Hardy can never dream of attaining, by reason of the unwholesomeness of his view of life; but on no English novelist of modern times, except perhaps Mr. George Meredith, were the gifts necessary for greatness more abundantly bestowed.

Mr. Hardy's dramatic skill is especially displayed in *The Return of the Native* which, in construction, is his best work. The informing idea of this novel consists of a subtle study of the influence which a vast stretch of rugged heath exercises over the minds of its inhabitants. The feelings, now of passionate attachment, now of blank weariness, which it provokes in the principal characters in the story give rise to the conjuncture of events involving the catastrophe. The tale opens, therefore, with an impressive picture of Egdon Heath. So impressive is it that many a reader will forget sooner the conduct of the action itself than the scene of the action—a swarthy wilderness extending between

the distant rims of the world [like the] original of those wild regions of obscurity which are vaguely felt to be compassing us about in midnight dreams of flight and disaster.

Interest in the bleak expanse centres at last on its crowning point, a hill surmounted by a tumulus, whereon, in the twilight, is seen the figure of a stately woman standing black and solitary against the pale wintry horizon like the very genius of Egdon Heath. Thus strikingly is the heroine of the tragedy presented. She hastens away, leaving the scene clear for a company of rustics who ascend and prepare a November bonfire. While it burns, and flames answer it from the heights encircling the heath, the chorus of peasants, with slow roundabout ways of expression and a homely ignorance as delightful as the racy shrewdness and humour which it serves to enhance, discuss things generally and their neighbours in particular, and so, like the two servants in the opening scene of a modern play, introduce the chief characters and explain the action.

The heroine, Eustacia Vye, is a sombre, passionate woman, distantly related, perhaps, to Flaubert's Emma Bovary, but with a nature of a larger and more imperious cast. She is a personification of romantic revolt, not of romantic sentimentality. The native of a gay, busy seaside town, she languishes in the solitude and monotony of the great heath, where circumstances compel her to abide; and to interrupt the tediousness of life she lightly fascinates the innkeeper, Wildeve, in the absence of a man of a finer nature on whom she might exercise her power. For she holds 'that love is a doleful joy; yet she desires it as one in a desert would be thankful for brackish water'.

The hero, Clym Yeobright, is a man after Mr. Hardy's own heart. Born and bred on Egdon Heath, he leaves his home to see the cities of the world and win a competency if not a fortune; but soon, discontented with town life, he returned with an intellectual relish and affirmed affection for his native wilds such as Thoreau scarcely felt for Walden. In his views he anticipates in some measure the resurgence of Rousseauism, now associated with Tolstoy's name. The retrogression to the austerity and wholesomeness of peasant life, enforced by such culture as should help men, not to rise in the world, but to glorify a life of rustic toil with knowledge and imagination, is now his ruling idea.

Eustacia, aware of his return, and prompt for any mad prank that will disperse the tedium of existence, calls upon him disguised as one of the mummers who perform at his mother's house the old miracle-play of St. George. Yeobright penetrates her disguise, and is affected by her unconventional conduct, as perhaps she wishes him to be. In the event the lady wins the hermit, and marries him. Egdon Heath thereupon begins, like some dark spirit of tragedy working in secret behind the scene, to govern their destinies. Passion subsides into domestic love; and in Eustacia there revives the longing for the distractions of a life in town. It was partly for this purpose that she married; and she employs all her charms in order to prevail upon her husband to take her away from the dreary waste. Yeobright, however, is reluctant. Stronger almost than his affection for his wife is this idealist's hatred of the town and love of the country. He wants nothing save to live and die with her on Egdon Heath, passing his days in the delight of study, and teaching the labouring men around him to appreciate intelligently their happy state. Eustacia at first cannot but respect his sincerity and ardour; still, the weariness frets her. At length her husband, having strained his eyes by study, puts into practice his professions in the matter of rustic toil, and, dressed in peasant's clothes, cuts furze all day on the waste, returning home at evening too tired for anything but sleep. His wife is divided between revolt and despair. This antagonism of temperaments, which threatens to end in an elopement, is brought to a sadder conclusion by the suicide of Eustacia.

The two ideas in *The Return of the Native*, the disturbance created in a little sequestered community by the arrival of some educated child of the soil, and the influence exercised upon the mood of the inhabitants by the nature of their surroundings, occur in different forms in other novels of Mr. Hardy. By means of the first idea he exhibits the contrast between the older generation of country people and the younger. The second idea enables him to trace, in the course of the narrative, the gradual eradication of the new views of life and the new restlessness by the old pervasive influences, and so to bring the story, when he will, to a pleasant close, as in the first and gayest of the Wessex tales, *Under the Greenwood Tree*. This work, and the much later novel, *The Woodlanders*, are variations on the same theme, the one idyllic, the other tragical. Even the heroines resemble each other more than the generality of sisters. Both are the heiresses of countrymen of the old school, both are educated in town, the stories opening with their return to the little knot of cottages in sylvan surroundings where they were born, the typical scene of Mr. Hardy's novels, a spot

outside the gates of the world, where may usually be found more meditation than action, and more listlessness than meditation; where reasoning proceeds on narrow premisses, and results in inferences wildly imaginative; yet where, from time to time, dramas of a grandeur and unity truly Sophoclean are enacted in the real, by virtue of the concentrated passions and closely-knit interdependence of the lives therein.

Soon after their arrival, Fancy Day, in *Under the Greenwood Tree*, and Grace Melbury, in *The Woodlanders*, find awaiting them a pair of lovers, a rustic lad and a man of the higher class. Were they acquainted with the principles underlying Mr. Hardy's system of characterization, they would not, of course, hesitate in their choice. However, Fancy, a light-hearted girl, touched by the spirit of spring moving in the woods around her, chooses the villager, Dick Dewy, a sprightly son of nature; and the idyll ends with a nightingale singing their epithalamium. Grace, with a temperament more slowly and more deeply moved, allows herself to be chosen by Dr. Fitzpiers. On her marriage, misfortunes quickly follow. Their house stands in a region of woodlands and apple-orchards; and close by are the homes of Grace's rustic lover, the cider-maker Giles Winterborne, of Marty South, Giles's affectionate companion, and of Mrs. Charmond, a wealthy young widow acquainted with Fitzpiers.

Mrs. Charmond and Fitzpiers are society representatives of Eustacia Vye and Wildeve, but they look somewhat unreal in comparison when they emerge into the bright clear air of Wessex. There, owing to a common feeling of lassitude which affects those who dwell in the country without knowing an oak from a beech, they drift from coquetry into passion. The elopement which threatened in *The Return of the Native* now takes place; in the sequel the man grows weary and returns home. Mr. Hardy, however, cannot tell this sort of story half as well as some foreign writers; nor does he show his real power in any kind of society novel, of which he has written several that are, for him, rather successful essays in the art of sinking. Of course, one estimates a man by his best works; and these careful, studied, but somewhat uninspired tales serve merely to show that Mr. Hardy, like most writers, has his limits. But when, as in *The Woodlanders*, he combines a matchless story of rustic life with this inferior work, the result is irritating. It produces the effect of a Millet inserting into the foreground of a masterpiece, such as 'Les Glaneuses,' the figures of an actress and a physician, painted in some fashionable style of portraiture. The required contrast between the primitive ways of the woodlanders and the manners of the modern world might surely have been obtained by more simple means.

Indeed, this is done in the character of Grace Melbury. Her husband's desertion moved her but little. Having made love to her merely as the most striking figure in a dull landscape before Mrs. Charmond appeared, he had wooed but the artificial lady in her, touching her heart even less than she had touched his. Left to herself, a deep change comes over her; and the spirit of her native place enters her soul. The sylvan life about her rouses that in her nature which is stronger than her acquired sense of refinement; and, craving for the homely existence of her own people, even in its roughness and defects, she turns on her father crying:

'I wish you had never, never thought of educating me. I wish I worked in the woods like Marty South! I hate genteel life, and I want to be no better than she.'

'Why?' said her amazed father.

'Because cultivation has only brought me inconveniences and troubles . . . If I had stayed at home I should have married——.'

For Winterborne, whom she had forsaken just as he was reduced to poverty—Gabriel Oak was treated in the same manner—now appeared to her, as he stood by his cider-presses, clothed in the poetry of nature.

He looked and smelt like Autumn's very brother, his face being sunburnt to wheat-colour, his eyes blue as cornflowers, his sleeves and leggings dyed with fruit-stains, his hands clammy with the sweet juice of apples, his hat sprinkled with pips, and everywhere about him that atmosphere of cider which, at its first return each season, has such an indescribable fascination for those who have been born and bred among the orchards. Her heart rose from its late sadness like a released bough; her senses revelled in the sudden lapse back to nature unadorned . . . and she became the crude country girl of her latent early instincts.

After a meeting, in which, by an accident, Grace's new feelings for Giles are displayed, they determine to keep apart from one another. Winterborne, more profoundly saddened by the untoward disclosure which increases Grace's unhappiness than by his own suffering, past and present, falls ill; and the story deepens into tragedy as Grace, driven to seek his aid in a moment of trouble, unwittingly brings about his death. Her husband has returned; and, in trying to take refuge with a distant friend, she finds herself homeless on a rainy night. She resorts to Giles in her dismay; and he, rising up from a sick-bed, surrenders his house to her, and, sleeping outside under a damp shelter of hurdles, is brought back dying. The tale closes with a reconciliation between Fitzpiers and his wife, which is not very convincing. Yet Mr. Hardy more than redeems this defect by the description, on the last page, of Marty South mourning over the grave which Grace and she, in companionship of grief, used to dress every week with flowers, and which now she remains to tend alone. The girl's words have much of the music and all of the pathos of Sir Ector's lament over Launcelot in *Le Morte d'Arthur*.

[quotes ch. XLVIII from 'She entered the churchyard' to ' "and did good things." ']

Yes, Marty South and Winterborne are truly heroine and hero in *The Woodlanders*; even the situation of Grace Melbury and Fitzpiers is presented, we think, with more dramatic force in an earlier work, *Far from the Madding Crowd*. The analogous characters in this book, being nearer to the rustic life, are drawn with greater vividness. Of all the educated women in the Wessex novels who move among the peasantry with unrest and sorrow in their wake, Bathsheba Everdene, the mistress of Weatherbury farm, is the most mischievous and fascinating. With finer intellectual powers than Mr. Hardy commonly allows to women, and with a wild disposition that prevents her from obtaining the position of governess, which Fancy Day and Grace Melbury demurely fill, she is armed with an authority denied to Eustacia Vye. The disasters which must hence ensue are adumbrated on the appearance at Weatherbury farm of the brilliant Sergeant Troy, a man who, more infected with urban ideas than Bathsheba, matches her in his failings, even to a touch of masterful brutality answering to her capriciousness. Mr. Hardy's favourite crisis is then reached. It is that which occurs when Fancy Day and Maybold, Eustacia and Wildeve, Grace Melbury and Fitzpiers, encounter one another. In each case the position is worked out in an astonishingly different manner, but never with such power as in *Far from the Madding Crowd*. Like Grace Melbury and Fitzpiers, Bathsheba and Troy, with but little in common save their weaknesses, marry. Then in their path the menacing figure of Boldwood, Bathsheba's rejected wooer, and the pathetic form of Fanny Robin, Troy's old love, stand like ministers of fate. The catastrophe—Troy's desertion of his wife, and Boldwood's murder of Troy—though effected in a manner rather roundabout, is a natural consequence and a finely tragical one.

By way of contrast the story is lightened with a series of beautiful pictures representing the varied business of farming in Wessex at a period when the continuity with the past remained in all things unbroken.

Between the mother, with her fast-perishing lumber of superstitions, folk-lore, dialect, and orally transmitted ballads, and the daughter, with her trained National teachings and Standard knowledge under an infinitely Revised Code, there was a gap of two hundred years as ordinarily understood. When they were together the Jacobean and the Victorian ages were juxtaposed.

The difference between Joan Durbeyfield and her child Tess represents the difference in social atmosphere between *Far from the Madding Crowd* and *Tess of the D'Urbervilles*. There are other works of Mr. Hardy, equally fine, but upon the excellences of which we cannot, in this brief estimate, enlarge, such as *The Trumpet-Major*, *The Mayor of Casterbridge* and the *Wessex Tales*, in which the same conditions prevail as in *Far from the Madding Crowd*. They are pictures of rustic life prior to 1851, when newspapers and modern thought, railways and industrialism began to effect in the minds and the mode of living of the peasantry a change, hastened by the result of the Education Act of 1870.

Mr. Hardy seems to be divided in opinion with regard to the alteration. The poet and lover of nature contend in him with the equalitarian. The fruits of even legitimate ambition have been purchased at the price of contentment and simple pleasures. In gaining by agitation better wages and a position of greater independence, the peasants have forefeited something more than picturesqueness of appearance. In *Far from the Madding Crowd* the memorable Joseph Poorgrass and his companions had certain intimate and kindly relations with the land upon which they laboured, not possessed by their less dependent successors. Living and dying on the spot where their forefathers had lived and died, they lost the character of hirelings in that of natural guardians; and, although none of them would have been so terribly bold as the new man, Andrew Randle, who lost a place by telling the squire that his soul was his own, they acquired, by way of compensation, that sympathy with their surroundings, that sense of long local participation, which are not least among the pleasures of life.

In the period described in *Tess of the D'Urbervilles* Wessex is a different world. The revolution is not entirely the result of that superficial instruction obtained at school, which, as Mr. Hardy has shown, is often counteracted by natural influences. New economic conditions have perturbed the character of the working classes. The migrations of Tess, of Car Darch and her companions, of Marian and other milkmaids, from Trantridge to Talbothays, from Talbothays to Port Bredy and other places, and their frequent changes of occupation, denote these altered conditions. The agricultural labourers now remove almost yearly from farm to farm; and they are acquiring some of the virtues and many of the defects of a nomadic race. The women are relinquishing their modest grace for the rollicking airs of factory hands; and the men are cultivating urban vulgarities in place of that humorous simplicity which makes Mr. Hardy's rustics of the older generation so akin to Shakespeare's. Moreover, domestic stability having an immense influence on conduct, uncertainty of residence is resulting in laxer morality and more cynical views of the duties of life. The gradual erosion of local feeling and local peculiarities, the disappearance of small tradesmen like John Durbeyfield, who were the main force in village life, have now obliterated so much of the old romance of Wessex that one can partly understand how it was that Mr Hardy, in the prime of his genius, brought to a conclusion his novels of country life with *Tess of the D'Urbervilles*.

Before *Tess* was written there seemed scarcely a rustic employment which Mr. Hardy had not described. The multitude of countrymen who peopled the Wessex of his novels were distinguished from one another almost as much by their different occupations as by their characters. Happily, he had not dealt with the one pastoral scene which in a century of utilitarian change had lost little of its natural picturesqueness. It may be that for a long time Mr. Hardy delayed to depict a rural dairy in order to avoid direct comparison with the author of *Adam Bede*. Truly, no little courage was required to intrude upon a scene over which the indomitable Mrs. Poyser reigned. The creator of such a rival to that lady as Joseph Poorgrass need not, perhaps, have hesitated overmuch; but Mr. Hardy had grown too melancholy to retain in all its fullness the genius for richly humorous work which informed his earlier stories. He was now so deeply immersed in philosophy that cheerfulness was quite excluded.

When at last he elected to be measured against his predecessor in the novel of country life, it was surprising how much his tale had in common with hers, and yet how superficial were the points of resemblance. It might be thought that they had been designed merely to bring out the more profound dissimilarity in treatment. The coincidence of 'The Chase', as the spot where Tess and Hetty Sorrel, girls of about the same age, were wronged by the young squires, may not, for instance, have been unintentional; while Alec D'Urberville's combination of the parts of the seducer and the preacher appears almost to be a travesty of the characterization of the older writer. But instead of inviting us to study 'the psychology of a canary bird', as George Eliot says of Hetty Sorrel, Mr. Hardy asks us, in what may be an indignant rehandling of the theme, to follow a more harrowing tale, whose pathos is enhanced by the nobility and patience of the chief sufferer. It must be admitted that in pathetic effect *Tess* is superior to *Adam Bede*. Mr. Hardy, in his sympathy with his heroine, exhibits at times an intensity of emotion not surpassed by either of the Brontës. In concluding the tale, not by the murder of the child and the transportation of the mother, but by the death of the seducer at the hand of the wronged woman, he wrought it into a more tragic narrative, evolving the tremendous conception of fate.

On the other hand, George Eliot's story is more simple, more natural and far more probable. If her fault is want of art, Mr. Hardy's defect is artificiality. Too much machinery is employed in *Tess* to bring about the catastrophe; and, in the latter part of the tale especially, disaster follows disaster in so close and yet so disconnected a manner that all sense of verisimilitude is destroyed. There is an analogous defect in his characterization. Keeping to the general law of human nature, George Eliot traces in Hetty Sorrel and Arthur Donnithorne a common weakness of character which, without the machinations of a third person, would result in a terrible calamity. Believing, as Mr. Hardy in his earlier works appears to have been inclined to believe, that

> In tragic life, God wot,
> No villain need be! Passions spin the plot;
> We are betrayed by what is false within,

she was able to spare even Donnithorne some traits of nobility, and so to surround the miserable couple in their career of sin and crime with natures, such as Dinah Morris, Adam Bede, and Mrs. Poyser, so sweet, strong and sane that Mrs. Carlyle, who was no easy critic of humanity, said she felt herself in charity with the whole human race after reading the book. Mr. Hardy, having chosen to illustrate an exception to the law in question, and an exception so extraordinary as to be almost incredible, was unable, in creating his characters, to preserve the balance and the general truth to nature which is found in *Adam Bede*. Having conceived a strangely immaculate heroine, who, from no impulse of her own, proceeded from fornication to adultery, and ended in murder, he had first to make her life such a succession of unmerited troubles, misfortunes and disasters, as dispels the credulity of the most sympathetic reader; and next to encompass her about with so many persons of nefarious or brutal, vicious, weak, or scornful natures— Alec D'Urberville, Farmer Groby, Car Darch and her companions, the Durbeyfields and their landlord, Angel Clare's brothers and Angel Clare himself—that verisimilitude in the characterization, as well as verisimilitude in the fable, is sacrificed to pathetic effect.

Yet, with all its deficiencies, its lack of balance and its sophistical irrelevancies, *Tess of the D'Urbervilles* remains a melodramatic novel excelling in wild pathos and poetic beauty. This poetic beauty is not a little due to the fact that the work is one which reveals most completely Mr. Hardy's unrivalled genius in the description of country life and natural scenery. Possessing one of the soundest and most expressive of styles in modern prose, Mr. Hardy is singularly felicitous in purely descriptive passages. As in his diction he combines plainness and concreteness of statement with great imaginative force, so in depicting natural scenery he unites keen, fresh observation of characteristic details with a broad poetic interpretation of the general aspect. Intimate knowledge, clearness of outline, variety and novelty in points of view, are some of his secondary qualities. He has little in common with the writers of the profusely picturesque order. He prefers images which convey emotions to images which create pictures in the mind; yet he can, when he will, excel a naturalist like Richard Jefferies, and equal Ruskin in the grandeur of his thought. To illustrate this let us quote two descriptions of snowstorms in *Far from the Madding Crowd* and *Tess.*

[quotes *Far from the Madding Crowd*, ch. XI from 'Winter, in coming' to 'any intervening stratum of air at all.']

The scene of the snowstorm in *Tess* is also another Wessex upland, where the heroine worked in the winter:

[quotes ch. XLIII from 'After this season' to 'achromatic chaos of things.']

Since writing *Tess of the D'Urbervilles* Mr. Hardy has averted his eyes from the spectacle of the world, and devoted himself to the study of Schopenhauer and von Hartmann. In *The Well-beloved* the elements of idealistic philosophy, and not the facts of life, are his theme. When a man loves a woman it is not the woman herself whom he loves, but the image of her in his own mind. To Mr. Hardy this subjective notion is the veritable Well-beloved. The various women by whom his metaphysical hero is attracted are merely blank forms which the glorious ideal animates for a moment and then reduces into insignificance as she passes into another shape, carrying along with her the affections of the constant-inconstant lover. There is, of course, no probability either in characterization or plot; in the track of this hypothesis we pass into that misty region beyond space and time where, in Doudan's phrase, we hear the choir of ideas celebrating the impossible on the ruins of reality.

Jude the Obscure, that much discussed work, is another of Mr. Hardy's essays in metaphysics. It is a wild attempt to realize in narrative form some current pessimistic theories, by imagining a world where all women will have an innate aversion against marrying and bearing children; and where, even when children are born, they will resort to suicide out of an instinctive desire not to live. These ideas are embodied in Sue Bridehead, and the son of Jude. Mr. Hardy would have us

believe that Jude Fawley came from Mellstock where lived that more
amiable idiot Tommy Leaf, and the gallant Dick Dewy. As a matter of
fact, Jude is a native of that part of the Utopia of the philosophers over
which the author of *The Metaphysics of Love* dismally reigns. He is
Schopenhauer's perfidious-lover 'seeking to perpetuate all this misery
and turmoil which otherwise would come to a timely end'. Lest the
shade of the great hypochondriac should thereby be offended, Jude is
also intended to personify the more gratifying idea of the rapid extinction of the human race by degeneration. Some very unpleasant details
are introduced in order to make the account of this ghastly hallucina-
tion resemble a novel of misery, but vainly; the principal characters and
the main events, as described, are as far removed from the realities of
this world as are those in *The Well-beloved*. What is but too real and
apparent is the frame of mind of which the work is an expression. One
sees that the professed humanitarian in our day can excel Swift himself
in appalling misanthropy.

Besides revealing Mr. Hardy's impressions of his fellow-creatures and
the universe generally, *Jude the Obscure* is significant in regard to his
relation to contemporary thought. The author represents the younger
and more febrile generation who inherited the ideas of the rationalists
by whom George Eliot was disciplined in thought. The world, in their
view, was not under divine governance; men, instead of being
immortal souls, were mere animals, which would at last yield up
their place on earth to some lower type better fitted to survive in
more degrading conditions; in the meantime, they said, let us pro-
mote righteousness and do our best to make the lot of the survivors
of our race as pleasant as possible. From their peculiar standpoint they
were illogical but human; Mr. Hardy is inhuman but logical. They
denied the evidence of the religious instincts because these were something that could not be measured by the utilitarian standard of immediate pleasure and immediate pain; he applied the same test of
rationalistic enquiry to the ethical code to which George Eliot, for
example, had adhered amid all her doubts. *Jude the Obscure* is his
answer to his teachers. He replies, in effect, that since, as you say, the
travail of the whole human race, of the whole world, leads in the end
to nothing, duty, morality and life itself to me are nothing: 'What is
it all but a trouble of ants?' as Tennyson said, speculating on the same
idea only to reject it vehemently.

> Then bitter self-reproaches as I stood
> I dealt me silently,

As one perverse—misrepresenting Good,
In graceless mutiny.

So Mr. Hardy writes in one of his poems. And in this passage he shows, at least, that, despite the inordinate power which a sensibility so quick, delicate and acute as not to be entirely healthy, exerts over his imagination, he can at times perceive something else than a soul of evil in things that the rest of men account to be good. Yet we must admit that, even from the verses in question, it is evident how completely his judgment is swayed by feeling, for it was only in the aesthetic rapture of gazing at a lean black stretch of moorland, transfigured in the light of a setting sun, that he was moved to accuse himself so sternly.

It seems to be a difficult matter to avoid extravagance of statement in attempting a comparison between a modern novelist, however brilliant, and a great poetic dramatist. Jane Austen and Shakespeare—how often, since Macaulay, have these disparate names been coupled together! And now, after reading in the letters of the late Lord Acton that if Sophocles had lived in the light of our culture George Eliot might have had an equal, we really hesitate to mention a grand poet of such ancient and universal fame as Euripides in conjunction with a modern prose-writer like Mr. Hardy. Yet we think that some curious points of resemblance in temper of mind and general outlook on life might be discovered in the novels of the author of *Jude the Obscure* and the plays of the dramatist whose *Hippolytus the Veiled* was resented on moral and artistic grounds by the Athenians.

In their work an intense love of natural beauty, a dislike to town life and a warm regard for the honest home-keeping countryman, are alike observable; and in their women of strange, passionate and irresponsible temperament, they display a similar type of heroine. Each of them, one would say, was a man of vehement but partial sympathies and brooding imagination, with an intellect of a high but receptive order, given to cloudy speculation based more upon emotions than upon ideas. In happier circumstances, with their genius for expressing romantic feelings with exquisite realistic art, they might both have clothed the most commonplace truths of life with fresh beauty and significance, as Mr. Hardy, indeed, has done in his first and best novels; but, children of an age of scepticism, their religious instincts were soon sophisticated, and their works then reflected, in a want of nobility and balance, the continual inward struggle between the wild idealism of their hearts and the despondency of their minds. Yet the Greek poet

never went so far as Mr. Hardy goes in blind revolt. Like most thinking men, he found that man by logic alone cannot discover for what
end he was born, with a soul in which goodness was mingled with evil,
into a world where suffering was inseparable from joy. Instead, however, of finding in this inability of our understanding to explore the
unsearchable ways of Providence a cause for excessive disparagement of
the worth and the purpose of life, Euripides, the rationalist, in his last
and strangest drama, wrote, in a passage splendidly paraphrased by Mr.
Gilbert Murray:

> Knowledge, we are not foes!
> I seek thee diligently;
> But the world with a great wind blows,
> Shining, and not from thee;
> Blowing to beautiful things,
> On, amid dark and light,
> Till Life, through the trammellings
> Of Laws that are not the Right,
> Breaks, clean and pure, and sings,
> Glorying to God in the height!

Mr. Hardy's philosophic creed is that of a sentimental materialist; he is
a mighty yet restless and woeful spirit, a prince of modern English
literature by reason of his earlier works, but in certain of his later works
a misdirected force.

THE DYNASTS, PART THIRD

February 1908

---

69. Harold Child, *The Times Literary Supplement*

27 February 1908

Harold Child (1869–1945) was associated with Bruce Richmond in founding *The Times Literary Supplement* in 1902, and assisted A. B. Walkley in dramatic criticism. He was later to write a book on Hardy (1916).

In war time the stationers' shops or newspaper offices show in their windows large maps stuck with little flags to mark the advance or retreat of the opposing forces. As if from a great height, the passing pedestrian looks down on a vast stretch of country, and he may actually see a hand appear and move a little flag an inch forward or half an inch backward. He is probably glad or sorry, according as the change indicates success or failure for the side which has his sympathies; but his head is more engaged than his heart. Then he turns away, to buy an evening paper for the details of the little flag's movement, and as he reads it the mention of a name he knows or a snatch of descriptive writing bears in upon him with a rush the remembrance that these are not little flags at all, but bodies of men. Each little flag stands for how many hundreds or thousands of sentient men, every one of them with hands as large and as compact of flesh and blood as the hand that moved the little flag so easily. And that swift inch or half-inch forward or backward means how many days and nights of toil and terror, death and agony, awful din and more awful silence. It is some hours before he can soar again to the height from which the armies become little flags; and then he can only do it by forgetting that armies are composed of men.

Mr. Hardy at once soars and remembers. He has brought us now to the close of his great drama of the Napoleonic wars; and, soaring so high as we may above the complete work for a bird's-eye view, we see nothing more prominent in this remarkable achievement than his success in unifying what for our passing pedestrian must remain two different points of vision. He can see Napoleon's Russian army as

> A dun-piled caterpillar
> Shuffling its length in painful heaves along;

but he sees that the heaves are painful, and he remembers that the caterpillar is composed of men, 'tattered men like skeletons', men with 'icicles dangling from their hair that clink like glass-lustres as they walk', men who sob like children or burst into raving songs of madness when they learn that their Emperor has deserted them—till the frost stills them into eternal silence as they crouch exhausted round their dying fire. He sees the field of Waterloo like our map with the little flags on it; but he overhears Napoleon's thoughts as he stands in the wood of Bossu alone after all is over. Marie Louise's sobs and the Prince Regent's oaths are as loud in his ears as the cannon of Leipzig. And this unity is not achieved by sudden soarings and swoopings. In spite of the language of the stage-directions ('the point of vision changes' and so forth), we are not conscious of being snatched hither and thither, up and down; and the eye, as it were, is not wearied by sudden alterations of focus. The vision of the mind and the vision of the heart are unified. We see little flags and men at once, and the unity embraces not only the warriors but the passing pedestrian himself—all who are affected by the events.

The secret is Mr. Hardy's choice of Phantom Intelligences—Spirits of the Years, of the Pities, of Rumour and others—as his chorus, the spectators through whose senses he shall follow the story of his drama. But it is one thing to choose a point of view, another to get to it, and yet another to keep it; and first to have risen to such a point as this and then to have held to it throughout the long and crowded work appears to us an intellectual feat of rare worth and power. From these dizzy heights we see armies like caterpillars; but the supernatural sensibility with which our author endows us for the time enables us to see also the minutest workings of the brain and the heart of every man in every army. After reading the first part of the drama we hazarded a guess that the complete work would prove to be a drama, not of men, but of nations. The guess was at once too wide and too narrow. *The Dynasts* is a drama not of nations only, but of human life; it is also a drama of individual persons. And in the drama of human life, according to Mr. Hardy's philosophic theory, there is a sense in which Napoleon's valet and the rustic who came to Casterbridge to see Boney burned are as important, and as unimportant, as Napoleon himself. Each and all are the puppets of the blind, senseless, Immanent Will, the

> Will that wills above the will of each,
> Yet but the will of all conjunctively.

It matters not that of all the characters, named and nameless, in the drama Napoleon alone is conscious of being a puppet in the control of that Will. Of the rest, each one contributes his share without knowing it; and each one, therefore, by a strange perversion, as it might seem, wins dignity and being, not their opposites.

It was natural, perhaps—it was certainly pardonable—to protest, earlier in our acquaintance with *The Dynasts*, that dramatic interest, human interest, was likely to suffer from that apparently deadening notion of the blind, senseless, purposeless force ruling these men and kingdoms. It was not so clear then as it is now that this philosophic notion was to be the great bond of unity between all the myriad scenes and persons of the drama. Moreover, in this last volume, more completely than in its predecessor, Mr. Hardy has answered that objection in another way. Not only are the doings more exciting—that was only to be expected as the drama drew to a close and we came to Moscow, Leipzig, Elba and Waterloo; the pity and the horror and the humour of those doings are more concentrated and more clearly exhibited. The little scene of the French flight after Vitoria, racily droll; Napoleon at Fontainebleau after Leipzig; the Prince of Wales worried by the Princess at the opera; the women's camp near Waterloo—all are full of that firm and vivid truth of poor humanity which has long been associated with the name of Thomas Hardy. And of all the written descriptions and pictures of the retreat from Moscow is there one that contains anything so tremendous as this little passage?

ANGEL I
Harassed, it treads the trail by which it came,
To Borodino, field of bloodshot fame,
Whence stare unburied horrors beyond name!

ANGEL II
And so and thus it nears Smolensko's walls,
And, stayed its hunger, starts anew its crawls,
Till floats down one white morsel, which appals.

What has floated down from the sky upon the Army is a flake of snow.

The characterization, too, is wonderfully distinct for a drama in which the men and women speak only in snatches and are scarcely described at all. When Mr. Bernard Shaw wishes his readers to understand a character, he prints his history, his appearance and his views on life in a stage-direction. Mr. Hardy does not; yet, if we wished to pick a character in the drama whose personal flavour and ways are not absolutely clear, we could only hit on Napoleon. True, we see Napoleon taking snuff and sipping grog, Napoleon when *pituita molesta est*, Napoleon humming tunes; but not even Mr. Hardy has succeeded in seeing Napoleon without, as well as with, his destiny and catching him as a mere man. But with the others the case is different. There are, of course, thanks to the form the author has adopted, a score of people, generals, *aides* and others, who must depend upon their relation to the Immanent Will for their identity; but Wellington is no figurehead, no *portrait d'apparat*, and Picton, Marie Louise, all the persons for whom space allowed and dramatic need demanded character, even down to the nameless mother of a nameless girl who fell in love at the Duchess of Brunswick's ball, and the Vicar of Durnover who has only to speak twice and to spit twice, are as roundly human as could be. There is one unquotable remark of Wellington's after Vitoria which seems to bring the whole man before us in a flash; and what of a little touch like this?

Wellington goes in the direction of the hussars with Uxbridge. A cannon-shot hisses past.

UXBRIDGE (*starting*)
I have lost my leg, by God!
WELLINGTON
By God, and have you! I felt the wind o' the shot.

Could any two lines give us so much of Wellington and of war? These men may be the puppets of the Immanent Will, but they are men for all that, and their joys and sorrows rouse our sympathy none the less because the Will is purposeless. Mr. Hardy is justified. At the same time it is interesting to note that he makes things as easy as possible for those to whom the Immanent Will is a nightmare. He may jeer with

the Spirit Ironic; with the Spirit of the Years he may be coldly
impartial; but the Pities have the last word. Through them, all along,
we have suffered with the sufferers: with them we are encouraged—
or, at least, allowed—to hope.

> But—a stirring thrills the air
> Like the sounds of joyance there
> That the rages
> Of the ages
>
> Shall be cancelled, and deliverance offered from the darts that were,
> Consciousness the Will informing, till It fashions all things fair!

So ends *The Dynasts*: and whether the author—the Immanent Hardy—
agrees with the Pities or not, we are profoundly grateful to the dramatist who chooses that note—the only tolerable, the inevitable right note
—on which to close his great work of art.

A great work of art—the title cannot be denied to *The Dynasts*; yet
it is given under compulsion. By all the rules the enterprise should have
been a colossal failure. The dramatic form is the most difficult to read;
it is not meant to be read. And when it is used as in *The Dynasts*—
scraps of dialogue in rugged, sometimes bald, sometimes stiffly conventional blank verse interspersed with long and often complicated
descriptions in prose; the scene abruptly shifted from Salamanca to
Moscow, from Casterbridge to the Tuileries; the characters now armies
and now men, and the whole cut up by commentative songs, ballads,
odes and what not, in the kingdoms of the air—the effort to read it
ought to be as irritatingly 'jumpy' to the mind as the several kinds of
print sometimes make it to the eye. By all the rules *The Dynasts* should
be chaos, a drama impossible to act (that, indeed, it remains), a book
impossible to read. Persual of the three volumes together proves it a
great work of art, unified by its philosophic conception, its vision and
its workmanship, in which poetry constantly keeps 'breaking in'
through the businesslike directness of both verse and prose. It would be
too much to say that *The Dynasts* succeeds in spite of its form; but it is
true that the daring which chose that form is only equalled by the
skill and mental supremacy which have brought it to success. Looking
back now, it is difficult to see in what other form Mr. Hardy could have
done what he set out to do. There were so many requisites—swiftness,
spaciousness, vividness, compression, intensity, comprehensiveness,
shock, surprise—that no form of narrative, whether in prose or in
verse, could have encompassed them all. The only way, as Mr. Hardy

has convinced us, was to make a large demand upon the reader; to ask him to imagine himself a spectator, using his eyes on certain things shown him and all the knowledge and thought at his service to fill in and connect the pictures. It is a large demand—there is no denying that. *The Dynasts* is not an easy book to read; it is not a book to read at all without a previous working knowledge of the story it tells (only a very confused idea of the action of Waterloo will be gained from these packed yet vivid stage-directions), nor without a willingness on the reader's part to bring all he has to the task. If he does so, he will be rewarded. He will learn that through intellectual and emotional mastery of his subject, and especially through the commanding unification of what in the average man are two points of view, Mr. Hardy has achieved a work of art by doing violence to a form, and has sublimated a vast and infinitely various material into a single shapely whole. For a like achievement we can only go back to one thing—the historical plays of Shakespeare, where great and small are, as here, seen with a single eye, and where, as here, the common life of common humanity is made a part of the progress of history.

The thing has been done. Could it be done again? We would advise no lesser mind to try. And by which would Mr. Hardy's fame and his readers' good have won the greater increase—*The Dynasts*, or the three novels which might have taken its place? Speculation is fruitless; and at least we have got *The Dynasts*.

70. From an unsigned review *Edinburgh Review*

April 1908, ccvii, 421

Two introductory paragraphs are omitted.

Now and again genius, which is Nature, comes like a *deus ex machina* to defeat the best-laid schemes of mechanical critics. And just at the moment when they have decreed that the 'study-drama' is an impossibility, here steps down to them Mr. Hardy with his *The Dynasts*, a play in three volumes, 'nineteen acts and one hundred and thirty scenes' (to quote the title-page), which no one will pretend could by any possibility be presented. Yet *The Dynasts* is not only not a nonsense, but is perhaps the most notable literary achievement of the last quarter-century. It is certainly unlucky for our critic of the mechanical school that at the very moment when he has decided that the 'study-drama' could not exist, the most remarkable and most absolute example of such a thing which has ever been written should see the light.

It is too early yet to decide the exact place in literature which *The Dynasts* is destined to take. All the critic can say at present is that it is entirely a thing apart; there is nothing beside which it can be placed for the sake of comparison. Though in dramatic shape, it has in many regards more in common with some of the epics of the world, it is in form a poem. Yet it must be owned that what we are wont to reckon the essentials of poetry are, over large tracts, very plentifully lacking, and that the fine essence of this poem is to be extracted from its interspersed prose passages. No wonder that the reviewers have been nonplussed, that certain of them have given utterance to judgments inept enough; others have preferred the non-committal—as that *The Dynasts* is a 'notable production'; while one of the inept kind has said that it was wise of the author not to use his materials for an historical novel. Non-committal even was it to write that the subject was the greatest any author had chosen since Milton. But the critic recognized the fact that, though a drama, *The Dynasts* must be looked upon as an epic also.

Let us try—no easy task—to give what seems to us the general scope and object of the book. The subject is the Napoleonic wars. We begin with the preparations in England to meet an expected invasion from Boulogne. We end with Waterloo. Mr. Hardy professes as one of his objects that of the keeping alive in memory the part which England played in these dynastic struggles. He has many other objects: at any rate he has many other theories which force themselves to the front in the course of his work. We used the word 'dynastic' struggles: for they are that to our author, not national struggles. Oddly enough he writes throughout with complete detachment, in an apparent lack of moral or intellectual sympathy with the whole concern. Fortunately his artistic and dramatic sympathies are so great that they override the other want. Of Mr. Hardy's philosophic theories we will speak later. On his work their influence is chiefly negative, so they can be put aside for the present. What is positive, and a positive gift almost unique, is Mr. Hardy's instinct for realistic drama, or we might say for heroic drama which is touched by the spirit of the novel, and can at once, without an effort, shift the point of view from some field of public action to note the effect thereof on insignificant private persons. The skill with which Mr. Hardy shifts his point of view is without any parallel, we believe, in any literature. It is the parts of his work where he displays this gift that form its most sure title to immortality. Now we pass with him into the clouds and see armies like caterpillars slowly wending from opposite sides of Europe to meet each other, or (as in the third part) to join in the invasion of France. Even when we gaze from these ethereal heights the object of view is not necessarily a great action. It may be only the escort which is bringing the young Austrian Princess Marie-Louise to France to wed with Napoleon. Again we drop to earth and behold a field of battle: next moment (maybe) we are merely in one room of one of the thousand houses of Berlin waiting for news of the same battle—Jena; we are with passengers in a coach discussing the news of the day; we are with Napoleon and his Minister of the Navy; we are on the high seas; we are in a London drawing-room, or at a great reception at Carlton House, or upon the 'Wessex' downs. We are in a cellar with some stragglers and their doxies, and watch from thence Moore's army in its retreat; and we are in the lone cemetery at Coruña and hear the talk of the sappers who are digging the leader's grave and the hurried funeral rites. We are at the famous ball in Brussels, or in a bedroom where a girl has got up early in the morning to see her hero march out, and then throws herself weeping on the bed; and we are on the field of Waterloo. It has been said that all this is not dramatic; that it wants the juxtapositions, the dramatic moments of old heroic drama. But in the true sense it is highly dramatic, in that it gives not the deeds of isolated heroes, but a touch of the *tragédie humaine* as Mr. Hardy sees it. For all this is a tragedy to our author. He is a Schopenhauerian: all action of the Will is tragic. But every artist has a right to present life as he sees it—nay, he is bound to present life as *he* sees it, and in no other way. And though this poem is (as we have said) in its kind an absolutely new experience in literature, it is yet in line with an observable tendency in modern literature, as may easily be seen when we take account of certain essential features in the growth of modern fiction. Of these we will speak hereafter. They will be further evidence of the permanent value of *The Dynasts*—at any rate to such as understand that a writer must follow the impulses of the Time Spirit, which are not in his individual control.

By a pleasant little personal note Mr. Hardy's beloved 'Wessex' figures for a good deal in this drama. We could wish, indeed, that he had dropped that word. To make Captain Hardy and Wellington himself talk about 'Wessex' is too much like making them contribute to the apotheosis of Mr. Hardy. But as the writer explains in his preface, Dorsetshire, both by the residence of the king at Budmouth, and by the part which all the south coast took in preparations against invasion, was brought into close touch with these dynastic struggles. We know from *The Trumpet Major* and the *Wessex Poems* that Mr. Hardy's thoughts have long dwelt on this subject—the Napoleonic wars. The first scene of the first volume opens upon 'a ridge in Wessex' over which the coach is passing while the inside passengers (by a fiction which would be impossible of presentment) talk the politics of the day, the rupture of negotiations with 'Boney'. Then we are wafted to Paris with Bonaparte and Decrès his Minister of Marine; thence back to the old House of Commons, where the debaters speak in blank verse yet keep very near to the 'Parliamentary History'; in Boulogne harbour next, to see in dumb show, and from far above, the 'army of England' exercising, the English men-of-war lying on watch outside the bay; to a fashionable reception in London; then to the crowning of the Emperor in Milan, the act which made Napoleon in his own eyes 'the successor not of Louis XIV but of Charlemagne'. So ends Act I. In the second act we pass from Gibraltar and a dialogue 'twixt Nelson and Collingwood, through two French scenes—scenes we mean from the French side (Villeneuve at Ferrol and the Boulogne camp once more)—back to Wessex to listen to a Dogberry and Verges (too near, unhappily, their prototypes) who are in charge of Rainbarrows beacon. In Act III we begin at Boulogne, but pass suddenly to the Austrian frontier, and see in dumb show the preparations which are being made to strike at Bavaria, the ally of France. The next act is chiefly concerned with the great blow at Ulm and Mack's capitulation. Then in Act V we have Trafalgar in various scenes, and Nelson's death; and then pass suddenly back to London streets, and to hear Pitt's Guildhall speech—'England has saved herself by her exertions and will save Europe by her example.' Last act of all (in this part) gives us Austerlitz in many scenes of the fight, the bringing of the news to Pitt while in Somersetshire, and Pitt's death at Putney. Such is the general scheme of treatment throughout all the parts. But no enumeration like this can give any notion of their vividness, the ingenious fashion in which dialogue alternates with description, the still greater ingenuity with which world-shaking episodes are interspersed with scenes from common life. These last are intimately connected with the mighty episodes and with the whole movement of the drama.

On the excellence of all these things there cannot be two opinions. It is when he comes to consider the medium through which these effects are conveyed that the critic finds all the rules of his art and his own past experience more or less at fault. Brandes, in the second volume of his study of Shakespeare, supplies an instance to prove that, as he says, in art the form is everything. The example is from a poem by Count Sterling written earlier than *The Tempest*, and containing in very tolerable verse all the substance of the famous 'cloud-capped towers' passage in Shakespeare's last drama. Yet, though Sterling's verse is tolerable, we feel at once that it has not in it the stuff of immortality, which stuff of immortality must, it follows, lie not in the ideas of Prospero's speech but in the mould into which the ideas have been cast. The proposition seems established; yet it falls to the ground in the case of Mr. Hardy's *Dynasts*. For it must frankly be acknowledged that the versification taken as a whole is extremely bad verse. We have been already accustomed, in Browning and Mr. George Meredith, to verse which seems not to be poetry and yet is; to verse that is not melodious nor beautiful as verse, and yet somehow conveys an effect of beauty. But though these poets often adopt methods which seem outside the technique of poetry, we feel that they are masters of their own method. With Mr. Hardy in *The Dynasts* we have not as a rule this sense. It is true that his *Wessex Poems are* poems. But the most part of them are in ballad form; and the ballad is the prose of poetry.[1] Even in his novels, though his imagination overrides defects, we sometimes see a groping after the right phrase, showing that our author is not a master of English. In a considerable part of the verse of *The Dynasts* it is not easy to see what its creator would be at. The versification is of two kinds. All the human agents speak either in prose or in blank verse. There are, beside the 'humans', a series of quasi-supernatural beings (more strictly supernatural quasi-beings), who act as showmen and commentators on the scenes; their full function we will

---

[1] The initial sonnets in this volume have indeed a certain Shakespearean charm. But, like much of the dialogue of Mr. Hardy's peasants, they betray their inspiration too nakedly.

hereafter explain. These beings often utter themselves in a kind of lyrics. It might tax a critic to say from which medium, the blank verse or the lyric, melody was most usually absent. Nor do the immelodies of Mr. Hardy bear the stamp of purpose as do Browning's harshnesses when they occur.

> Let him now own me still a dab therein.

We can imagine the kind of person and the occasion that in Browning might have provoked such a line. But it would not have been Napoleon trying to impress the Austrian generals after Ulm.

Here are examples of Mr. Hardy's blank verse such as might be found anywhere throughout the three volumes:

> Strange suasive pull of personality.

>   Of her we view
> The enterprise is that of scores of men,
> The strength but half a one's.

> Why must ye echo as mechanic mimes
> These mortal minions' bootless cadencies?

> Some enemy queues my way to coffin me.

>   Beg the Emperor, my father,
> That he fulfil his duty to the realm,
> And quite subordinate thereto all thought
> Of how it personally impinge on me.

> I am no theologian, but I laugh
> That men can be so grossly logicless,
> When war defensive or aggressive either
> Is in its essence Pagan and opposed
> To the whole gist of Christianity.

> Whose emissaries knock at every door
> In rhythmic rote, and groan the great events
> The hour is pregnant with.

> Right glad we are you tongue such tidings, sire;
> To us the stars have visaged differently.

These passages are only not selected at pure hazard in that they are chosen to represent different styles of the verse in which Mr. Hardy indulges. They are adequate specimens of the blank verse through these three volumes. They seem, it must be owned, to bring us down to a very low level, more near than almost any verse in literature to that verse which lies outside literature, and which, enshrined in quarto manuscript books, represents the leisure of some country doctor or country parson who has paid a sly and shy court to the Muses. The third of these nine examples means in prose that Louise, Queen of Prussia, had enterprise of character equal to many times twenty men's, but only half a man's physical strength. The natural interpretation would be that scores of men are embarked on the same or a similar enterprise to the Queen's. Obscurity is not necessarily a fault in verse, but it must be compensated by a special fulness of meaning. Mr. Hardy has a partiality for dactylic endings in his blank verse—end words such as 'purposings', 'equanimity'—the use of which betokens an ear ill-trained to the melody of verse. The specimens we have given are enough to show that his use of alliteration (so delicate a matter) can be deplorable. In the rhymed verse we have more shocking examples:

> Behold again the Dynasts' gory gear,
> Since we regarded what has progressed here

which ones hesitates whether to liken to the Richardson theatre or the pantomime.

Finally, as regards the use or the invention of peculiar words, the ἅπαξ λεγόμενα which we may look for in every original writer of verse—not necessarily in every original writer of prose. There are a fair number of these in *The Dynasts*, and some of them are happy. 'Queues my way' for 'follows me' we have already met with. That is not good. 'Wide-waked' for having great consequences is much happier. 'Twinkle-tipt' is applied to a regiment of cavalry. 'Enghosted by the caressing snow', is used in the description of the retreat from Moscow. It is not altogether satisfying—meaning as it does only that the bodies of the soldiers are covered by a white pall. 'Prim ponderosities' is applied to the lines of Torrès Védras. Isolated the phrase is harsh enough, but in its place it is not inappropriate.

We have only after reading Mr. Hardy to take up for a moment Marlowe or Shakespeare, and note how lightly and easily their verse flows, how right are their epithets and their alliterations, the heaven of difference lying between 'the topless towers of Ilium' and the 'Dynasts' gory gear', to realize how far down stands Mr. Hardy's verse as verse.

We dwell on these defects fully and without fear, for two reasons.

First because a large number of Mr. Hardy's critics who have succumbed to the charm of this work as a whole, and have not discovered where that charm lay, the while they felt conscious of its technical short-comings, have been tempted to minimise these last by vague phrases which fall very far short of the truth, and so have (wrongly) given an air of insincerity to their judgments. One reviewer, we believe, wrote to the effect that the reader will find in Mr. Hardy's verse none of the magnificences of Milton—a judgment abundantly true, but hardly adequate. A better criticism (though this was not printed) was that the badness of the verse was designed to make us enjoy the interlarded prose. This is not quite a true account of the matter. But there is no doubt that it is almost always in the descriptions in the little bits of prose in small type, that we gain the true thrill which comes from a work of genius. Here we get a hundred instances of that poetical imagination which clothes all Mr. Hardy's prose work with a shining garment, a sort of magic light shed upon common things, as in that game of cards in *The Return of the Native* played by the light of glow-worms. Now it is the manœuvring of Napoleon's cavalry at Boulogne 'flashing in the sun like a school of mackerel'; now such a touch as this towards the end of a House of Commons debate:

The candle-snuffers go round, and Pitt rises. During the momentary pause before he speaks the House assumes an attentive attitude, in which can be heard the rustling of the trees without, a horn from an early coach, and the voice of the watch crying the hour.

Or this, which follows the wreck of Godoy's palace near Madrid:

The mob desists dubiously and goes out; the musical-box upon the floor plays . on, the candle burns to its socket, and the room becomes wrapt in the shades of night.'[1]

Or, once again, the French and Russian armies bivouacking face to face on the eve of Borodino:

The two multitudes lie down to sleep, and all is quiet save for the sputtering of the greenwood fires, which, now that the human tongues are still, seem to hold a conversation of their own.

And this at the end of the description of the burning of Moscow:

Large pieces of canvas aflare sail away in the gale like balloons. Cocks crow, thinking it sunrise, ere they are burnt to death.

---

[1] And yet in the last four words of this passage we have a shadow of Mr. Hardy's defects, even as a writer of prose.

Like the examples in blank verse, these of prose are chosen almost at hazard. It would be impossible to give the number of such passages or a just notion of their excellence.

It has been said that a great part of the effect of Mr. Hardy's work is managed by the constant change in the point of view. This is not alone a mere physical change, as when we are rapt into the clouds so as to see a great part of Europe at one *coup d'oeil*, to be brought back maybe within the four walls of a single room. It is a change also in the intellectual point of view, as when, after hearing the talk of the movers or seeming agents of all these great events, we find ourselves in the company of simple peasants, soldiers, a country parson—what not. Perhaps Balzac never wrote anything cleverer (though it occurs in a dullish story) than that chapter of his 'Médecin de Campagne' called 'Le Napoléon du Peuple', which allows us to see the true 'Napoleonic Legend' of the peasantry, the career of the great conqueror transformed into genuine folk-lore. Much of the same effect do we get by some of the rapid changes in Mr. Hardy's scene.

There is, however, a further change in point of view beyond all these. Not only do we upon occasion fly up to the clouds, but we find ourselves upon occasion (it has already been said) in the company of certain non-human personalities, if they are personalities, spirits if they are spirits; at any rate, they are called so. There is a Spirit of the Years, a Spirit of the Pities, a Spirit Ironic, a Spirit Sinister and certain Recording Angels. Such a movement outside the body with a partial annihilation of time and space is from an artistic point of view most desirable. In such a vast drama as this is, were we always merely on the plane of humanity, a certain monotony and tediousness must ensue. For of course we who look backwards through the courts of time are not in fact quite on a level with the actors in the piece. In a single historic play we might make shift to be so. But *The Dynasts* is an epic as well as a play. And though in the great epics of the world the supernaturals appear in obedience to other than artistic considerations, there can be no doubt that on the artistic side alone they fill an important place: that it is a great advantage in Homer and even in Virgil to breathe from time to time another an Olympian air. When Milton presumes 'into the heaven of heavens' 'an earthly guest' the effect is more doubtful. But the splendid passage which celebrates his return to earth would not otherwise have been written.

In Mr. Hardy's case, however, the supernatural beings (if so we call them) have to support a definite philosophic doctrine; looked at in another way, we may say they have to exist in spite of Mr. Hardy's philosophic doctrine, which puts no small strain on their vital powers. We have, in fact, to forget, so soon as we have read, that they are for their author only 'impersonated abstractions'. This, it must be owned, gives one pause. But let the author explain himself (if so he can) in the words of his preface:

It was thought proper to introduce, as supernatural spectators of the terrestrial drama, certain impersonated abstractions, or Intelligences, called Spirits. They are intended to be taken by the reader for what they may be worth as contrivances of the fancy merely. Their doctrines are but tentative, and are advanced with little eye to a systematized philosophy warranted to lift 'the burthen of the mystery' of this unintelligible world. The chief thing hoped for them is that they and their utterances may have dramatic plausibility enough to procure for them, in the words of Coleridge, 'that willing suspension of disbelief for the moment which constitutes poetic faith'.

The wide prevalence of the Monistic theory of the Universe forbade, in this twentieth century, the importation of Divine personages from any antique Mythology as ready-made sources or channels of Causation, even in verse, and excluded the celestial machinery of, say, *Paradise Lost* as peremptorily as that of the *Iliad* or the *Eddas*, And the abandonment of the masculine pronoun in allusions to the First or Fundamental Energy seemed a necessary and logical consequence of the long abandonment by thinkers of the anthropomorphic conception of the same.

A word may be said on this philosophy. It is no impeachment of a man's character, not even of his religious instincts, if in these times of distracted counsels he know not which way to look. The more sensitive, delicate, poetic a man may be, the more the difficulties of the universe and the burden of pain are likely to oppress him. The vulgar optimist is a far less venerable figure than pessimists of the type of Leopardi or Mr. Hardy. But though the attitude which our author takes up throws no reflexion on his character and is some evidence of his poetic temperament, it does at the same time indicate a sort of hysteria not consistent with perfectly sound judgment. We all know the type of woman who, by the very extent of her affection for husband or son, is driven merely on the hint of mishap (a delay in homecoming or some such matter) to insist upon a tragedy where no evidence exists for more than a trifling misfortune. Like Rachel, she refuses to be comforted, or to listen to any hint of comfort. Mr. Hardy is in such case.

He might perhaps plead that his pessimism is essentially that of

Schopenhauer, and that he is not obliged to set forth once again the elaborate ratiocination of *Die Welt als Wille und Vorstellung*. But after all, Schopenhauer does not impose himself upon us as a gospel. Mr. Hardy seems to want to bluff his philosophy. How could the 'wide prevalence' of any theory 'forbid' the importation of divine personages? And what is the meaning of

And the abandonment of the masculine pronoun in allusions to the First or Fundamental Energy seemed a necessary and logical consequence of the long abandonment by thinkers of the anthropomorphic conception of the same?

In simple language, we suppose, it means that as all thinkers have long since abandoned the idea of a deity, it was *impossible* (even for poetic purposes) to assume either a God or supernatural presences and powers. Are then Goethe, Coleridge, Carlyle, Tennyson, Browning to be rated out of the order of 'thinkers'? Or among metaphysicians was not Kant a thinker, nor Fichte, nor Lotze, to come down to our own day? Surely this is bluff, if ever bluff there were. And bluff of this sort springs out of hysteria.

In a word, it was open to Mr. Hardy as a philosopher to hold a theistic or (to use the polite term) an agnostic theory of the universe. As a poet it was open to him to use or to dispense with supernatural agents or witnesses. But it is not, in common sense, open to him to try to force his philosophy upon us, and while he introduces his Spirit of the Pities and the others speaking, to tell us beforehand that they are only 'impersonated abstractions'. A man has enough to do at one while to be a poet: let him not try to be a propagandist also. Least of all let him be the propagandist of negative ideas; for all that is negative is the necessary antithesis of *poiēsis*, the creative art. And the negative side of things (if to our author they are so) can always be left alone.

There can be no question that *The Dynasts* suffers immensely from the insistence by the author on his own philosophical creed. The 'Immanent Will' which is absolutely impersonal, which must be spoken of as 'IT', which is generally spoken of as 'unconscious', 'unthinking', this is an idea which may be graspable in the region of metaphysics, but certainly not in the sphere of creative art. And the repetition in the mouths of the 'impersonated abstractions', the Spirits, of the doctrine of the insensibility, the irresponsibility of this IT becomes unspeakably wearisome. We know beforehand what is going to happen at each pause in the human drama. The Spirit of the Pities is going to complain of the sufferings of mankind; the Spirit of the Years is going to remind her that complaints are vain, because IT can neither hear nor change. We catch ourselves counting whether it is the twenty-fourth or twenty-fifth time that this doctrine has been repeated. Naturally enough there is not the intoxication of poetry in a hogshead of this watery philosophy. Consequently the verse in italics, which is the verse spoken by the impersonated abstractions, is on the whole decidedly worse than that spoken by the human beings, where it should be far better.

The following may be taken as an average specimen of the Chorus of Pities and the doctrine of the Spirit of the Years:

SEMICHORUS I OF THE PITIES (Aerial music)
O Great Necessitator, heed us now!
If it indeed must be
That this day Austria smoke with slaughtery,
Quicken the issue as Thou knowest how;
And dull to suffering those whom it befalls
To quit their lodgment in a flesh that galls!

SEMICHORUS II
If it be in the future human story
To lift this man to yet intenser glory,
Let the exploit be done
With the least sting, or none,
To those, his kind, at whose expense such height is won!

SPIRIT OF THE YEARS
Again ye deprecate the World-Soul's way
That I so long have told? Then note anew
(Since ye forget) the ordered potencies
Nerves, sinews, trajects, eddies, ducts of IT
The Eternal Urger, pressing change on change.

At once, as earlier, a preternatural clearness possesses the atmosphere of the battle-field, in which the scene becomes anatomized and the living masses of humanity transparent. The controlling Immanent Will appears therein, as a brain-like network of currents and ejections, twitching, inter-penetrating, entangling, and thrusting hither and thither the human forms.

This presentation of Europe as a huge man and the human beings as a sort of blood-corpuscles in which the pulsing of the Immanent Will is visible has certainly originality and a touch of the gruesome poetic. But this is the third time of its appearance; and though we are only in the first volume, the doctrine of the inexorable Will has been repeated half a dozen times at least.

In spite of difficulties, however, we do succeed in believing to some extent in the Spirits Ironical, Sinister, Pitiful. And when, as now and again happens, they take human shape and appear at a reception in London or in the gallery of the House of Commons, the effect is piquant.

Moreover, to suppose the impossible, and imagine the supernatural portions of this book treated with something of the high lyrical power which shines in *Prometheus Unbound*, it is a question whether the whole work would not lose thereby. It is to suppose the impossible; for Mr. Hardy evidently lacks the 'physical' gifts of the poet, the miraculous leaping together of sound and sense which Byron and Shelley show in their best verse at their best moments. All such achievement would, indeed, be foreign to *The Dynasts*, which succeeds by its own methods and by hitherto unproved rules. The beauty is 'in the picture'.

But it is very difficult to select from the book portions which give any fair idea of its beauty as a whole. As it should do, the death of Nelson inspires Mr. Hardy; and in the part which relates thereto we find his versification at its best:

[quotes part first, act V, scene IV, from ' "Hardy, how goes the day" ' to ' "as you care for me," ' with some omissions]

Some of the verse, here, it will be seen, is decidedly good as verse. For example:

> 'Who in simplicity and sheer good faith
> Strove but to serve his country,'

And that touch of the 'grey dial'

> 'Marking unconsciously this bloody hour'

is of the higher flights of imagination.

The lyrical passage of this section shows Mr. Hardy at his best in this *genre* also. Of course the inevitable 'doctrine' has to follow:

CHORUS OF THE PITIES (Aerial music)

> *'His thread was cut too slowly! When he fell,*
> *And bade his fame farewell,*
> *He might have passed and shunned his long-drawn pain*
> *Endured in vain, in vain!'*

SPIRIT OF THE YEARS

> *'Young Spirits, be not critical of That*
> *Which was before, and shall be after you!'*

The same 'doctrine' precedes an excellent description of a part of the Battle of Vitoria in the third volume (act II. sc. ii.). For still one is more tempted to quote the prose than the verse.

[quotes from ' "*You see the scene*" ' to 'in front of the town.']

And to close all, take these two passages, connected respectively with the burning of Moscow and with the French retreat. In the first Mr. Hardy shows the excellence of his historic writing.[1]

[quotes part third, act I, sc. VI, from 'When the bulk' to end of scene.]

In the second passage we have from our author a form of verse he has used many times with great effect in other volumes—the ballad form:

[quotes part third, act I, scene XI, from 'Mad Soldier's Song' to ' "They are dead." ']

Mr. Hardy's attitude (pessimistic on the whole) toward these events is his own; and there is no reason in the nature of things why no Spirit Heroic appears alongside of the Spirit of the Pities or the Spirit Ironic. But there is, we have said, also an element which is of the Time Spirit. A certain abstraction from humanity along with the impartiality which takes in every kind of scene and every rank in life, this is of our age; this marks all that is most vital in modern fiction, a world-sense of a new order. It was shadowed forth by Balzac in his insatiable curiosity in human things: it is almost propounded as a doctrine in the title *Comédie Humaine* which Balzac selected to comprehend all his work. Dickens, Thackeray, Flaubert, Zola, Ibsen, Tolstoi, Dostoievsky and Gorky have each in their fashion laboured to develop the same idea. But that will not be the last word. And Mr. Hardy's poem also passes beyond this. Behind this 'realism' or 'naturalism' Time is labouring to bring forth another birth to which, as it has not yet taken a fully

---

[1] Some slight and quite permissible 'dealings with' historical facts for the sake of artistic effect are to be met with in these volumes. Thus in the scene (vol. ii, act iii. sc. 1) which is meant to be typical of the horrors of the Coruna retreat Napoleon is introduced. But Napoleon quitted the French army at Astorga, and the sufferings of the British had then hardly begun. Seemingly, too, Napoleon receives on this occasion Canning's reply to the joint note of the two emperors (Napoleon and Alexander), whereas in fact the reply had by this time been in his hands a month.

It is probably also for artistic reasons that Sir Harry Burrard is kept altogether off the field of Vimiera and made to put a stop to the pursuit by message.

recognizable shape, no just name has yet been given. 'Symbolism' expresses only a part of it. What it is or will be is the poetising of this drama of common life. It will show that the common-placeness of common things lies in us—in our way of regarding them—not in the things themselves. Every one of the writers we have mentioned has done something (unconsciously or almost so) toward bringing about this new birth of time. Dickens, when he spread over all his creations ('inventions' were the better word, perhaps) a weird light which is almost supernatural; Thackeray, when 'without a hero' he produced one of the most tremendous dramas that literature knows; Zola, when he turned a market-hall into a grim poem; Flaubert, when he expended the gems of his prose style on familiar scenes and objects; the Russians, who have shown a deeper, more poetic reading of human nature than had as yet been known, at any rate to prose fiction. In this stream of tendency, in this action of the Time Spirit, Mr. Hardy's *The Dynasts* will, we believe, in future times be acknowledged to take a great place. Its effect as a work of art may turn out to be the very opposite of the philosophy which Mr. Hardy preaches. For, after all, this working of thought which we have tried to indicate or foreshadow, is it not essentially Carlyle's 'Natural Supernaturalism'? Yet if one day Mr. Hardy should discover that he has 'in action' preached against his own pessimistic theories, it is to be hoped he will not be too much distressed. Even he allows us some glimmer of hope in his final chorus, though the day-star appears to him very far off.

Schopenhauer, in the third book of his greatest work, *Die Welt als Wille und Vorstellung* (*The World as Will and Idea*), explains how the man of genius alone, by the imagination of genius, at the same while that he loses his own individuality, sees things too not in their time relations and as presented only to the logic of thought, but in a kind of eternity, as a sort of Platonic existence. By such process (says our philosopher) the man of genius is for the while—his consciousness is for the while 'freed from bondage to the Will'. This joy at least, for it is within his own theories, Mr. Hardy must have confessed while he was creating a work of such undoubted genius as *The Dynasts*.

71. Henry Newbolt, 'A New Departure in English Poetry', *Quarterly Review*

January 1909, ccx, 193–209

Sir Henry Newbolt (1862–1938) is chiefly known as a writer of patriotic verse, but he also wrote critical essays on poetry. Several introductory pages are here omitted.

From the moment when the first volume of *The Dynasts* appeared, there was, to one watcher at least, no doubt that the new light was in the sky. It was barred by some small patches of mist or cloud,[1] but it was unmistakably rising; it was, in my belief, the forerunner, not of one day only, but of many great days in the poetical life of the English-speaking race. For Mr. Hardy has done something more than produce a brilliant and novel development; he has shown the line along which further developments can be successfully made. Indeed the advantages of the new road are so striking, and the mass of material lying ready to be carried along it so great, that it will not be surprising if those who come after Mr. Hardy are for some time content to follow it closely rather than strike off at once on divergent tracks of their own. He has found out a way, and it is a highway.

[1] In his anxiety to give concise expression to ideas new in English poetry, Mr. Hardy has introduced artifices which disfigure his style and obscure his meaning. Here and there he tangles his syntax with extravagant inversions and misplaced parentheses. Repeatedly he uses the prefixes un- and in- to convey the idea, not of a reversal of the action expressed by a verb, but of the mere absence of such action. Thus from the line, 'His projects they unknow, his grin unsee', he wishes us to understand that 'They know not his projects, see not his grin'. On this principle we might say that Mr. Hardy was unwriting his book for fifty years before he began writing it. His practice is the more confusing because in some passages he follows the ordinary usage: 'I have unlearnt to threaten her (England) from Boulogne.' In other ways, too, he abuses the inventor's privilege; as when he writes 'finite' in place of 'final', 'voidless' for 'unavoidable', and 'quipt' for 'equipped', making these words deny their ancestry and relations for the sake of some small temporary emergency.

To understand fully what it is that Mr. Hardy has achieved, it is necessary to consider for a moment what was the problem before him. A strong bent of patriotism, traditional, local, personal, had long interested him in 'the vast international tragedy' of Napoleon's career. 'The provokingly slight regard paid to English influence and action throughout the struggle by those continental writers who had dealt imaginatively with it, seemed to leave room for a new handling of the theme which should re-embody the features of this influence in their true proportion.' He determined accordingly to set out the story of this 'Clash of Peoples' in a poem of gigantic scale, and with the British nation for hero.

For a work of this kind there were two conventional forms available; but the fate of certain forerunners gave warning that neither could be relied upon. A play must be either for the stage or the closet; but few poetical stage plays ever come to the light or survive their birth by more than a day or two; while any publisher will give evidence that no one now buys a play which is not acted. The epic, on the other hand, is too transcendental; its tone is too unfamiliar for the expression of a modern view of life. It can give the form and pressure of an age, but it will be an age distant by something more than time; its characteristic method is to exhibit the heroic element in a man or a generation by a process of semi-deification, by making the characters at once highly typical and extremely singular, by giving them a stature and a speech that never were on land or sea. This would not suit Mr. Hardy's genius; it is in the most familiar tones of life that he is always at his best; and his idea of the heroic—the modern idea of the heroic—is no longer a vision of men who are more than men, who are abnormally gifted and perhaps inequitably tended by superhuman powers, but a story of men great among their fellowmen, because in them is more forcibly shown forth the working of the one universal power—whether it be held natural or divine—by whose operation all alike must live and move and have their being.

Of the two inadequate forms the epic was clearly the less promising for an experiment. The poet was forced back upon the drama—forced therefore to grapple with his problem hand and foot. Not only was there the initial difficulty of ensuring that the drama, when written, should command the hearing usually given only to an acted play; it was also necessary to enlarge the machinery by which it was to be presented. Scope must be found, not only for the events, characters, and motives displayed in its action, but also for a clear exposition of the writer's philosophical view of them. In other words, Mr. Hardy, having decided on a chronicle play, had to provide for it a theatre under his own management, and fit it with a running commentary at once imaginative and philosophical, complex and consistent.

His solution of both these difficulties is a simple one, so simple that it has—for those who look back upon it—the inevitableness of the greatest triumphs. For his theatre he took the reader's mind; for the commentary, his own; add some ten years' labour, and the thing is done. The full meaning and promise of these devices will be more apparent if I attempt some account of the result.[1] Let us deal first with the chronicle play or historical pageant, taken by itself. This begins with the outbreak of war between England and Spain in March 1805, and ends at midnight after Waterloo, when 'the moon sinks, and darkness blots out Napoleon and the scene'. It is presented, I have said, in the mind of the reader, as in a theatre under the absolute control of the author; and rarely has any play been so vividly seen by the outward eye as this by the inward. Mr. Hardy's success here is mainly due to his stage directions, which differ by the whole breadth of genius from any hitherto imagined. They are terse, brilliant, memorable, and in their power of suggestion almost hypnotic. What we are told to see, we see. Tract after tract of Europe lying below us like a map in relief; men and nations moving, swarming, contending like ants; armies creeping across provinces like molluscs on a leaf; ships of the line and transports floating over the sea like moths. Then, when the moment of action approaches, at the mere word of command our point of view descends nearer to earth, voices come to us as they come to those who descend a mountain in clear air, 'thin and small, as from another medium', till at last we lose the sense of distance, and hear the characters speaking in the tones of the life we share ourselves.

Once on earth, too, the necessary scene-shifting is performed with

---

[1] The purpose of this article being to draw attention to the merit and novelty of Mr. Hardy's design, I need not turn aside to criticize either the details of the work or the craftsmanship displayed. It is enough to warn the reader that in so vast a poem he will, not unnaturally, have some disappointments to suffer. Mr. Hardy's peculiar philosophy has the artistic disadvantage of forcing him to belittle all human character, and to impoverish and even falsify history by stripping it, to a considerable extent, of human motives. Unfortunately, too, the poet's command of his instrument is not by any means perfect; his verse can be grandly deep and exquisitely poignant, but it can also too often sound a scrannel note or fall into the key of prose. These blemishes do not affect my argument.

a swiftness and a power of unbroken illusion not possible upon any material stage; and when flesh and blood have played out their dramatic moments, we are taken back with equal sureness to the high aerial point of view. For instance, after the ceremony in Milan Cathedral, grandiose and ironically suggestive, where Napoleon is crowned by his own hands with the crown of Lombardy, as Emperor of the French and King of Italy, the Act ends with this direction:

The scene changes. The exterior of the Cathedral takes the place of the interior, and the point of view recedes, the whole fabric smalling into distance and becoming like a rare, delicately carved alabaster ornament. The city itself sinks to miniature, the Alps show afar as a white corrugation, the Adriatic and the Gulf of Genoa appear on this and that hand, with Italy between them, till clouds cover the panorama.

The gigantic proportions of the work may be guessed from the fact that it contains 130 scenes, introduced and closed with this same vivid intensity of setting; and that among them are numbered nearly twenty of the greatest battles in European history, all sharply distinguished from one another, all fully presented to sight and intellect at once, with their outward features and underlying significance. For test examples the English reader will probably turn to Trafalgar and Waterloo rather than to Austerlitz and Wagram, or even to the fights of the Peninsula. In neither will he be disappointed; for Mr. Hardy has not only described, condensed, and dramatized both with remarkable skill, but to the authentic history of both he has dared to add inimitable touches of his own. The plain unadorned story of Nelson's dying hours, as told by Dr. Beatty, is one of the most moving passages in our language; that any hand could give a fresh touch of beauty to it, without taking from its simplicity, would have been thought impossible before the following lines were written:

NELSON (*suddenly*)
What are you thinking, that you speak no word?

HARDY (*waking from a short reverie*)
Thoughts all confused, my lord; their needs on deck,
Your own sad state and your unrivalled past;
Mixed up with flashes of old things afar—
Old childish things at home, down Wessex way,
In the snug village under Blackdon Hill
Where I was born. The tumbling stream, the garden,
The placid look of the grey dial there,

Marking unconsciously this bloody hour,
And the red apples on my father's trees,
Just now full ripe.

If the poet can hear on board the 'Victory' words audible to no other ears, he can see on the eve of Waterloo that which was visible to no eyes but his. When the sound of the drums beating the *générale* with 'a long-drawn metallic purl of sound' echoes into the historic ball-room, and the Highlanders 'march smartly down the room and disappear', we, too, can now discern, 'stepping out in front of them, That figure— of a pale drum-major kind, Or fugleman—who wore a cold grimace'. To set off this grimace there was needed one touch of tenderness and one of humour; both are given in the little scene next morning, in which two Englishwomen, mother and daughter, stand at a window in their dressing-gowns to see the troops march out to the battle, and the younger lady is reproved by mamma for waving a tearful goodbye to a young Hussar officer, her partner of a few hours ago.

It is not in battlefields only that Mr. Hardy shows his imaginative power; he is equally characteristic, equally sure, in drawing-rooms and debates, at a birth or a burial. The old House of Commons lives again under his hand. Pitt and his fellow politicians denounce each other with the method and accent which belong to English party strife and to no other game ever played by man.

So now, to-night, in the slashing old sentences,
Hear them speak—gravely these, those with gay-heartedness—
Midst their admonishments little conceiving how
Scarlet the scroll that the years will unwind.

Then for humour we have the birth of the King of Rome; for pathos deeper than death the visit of the doctors to the mad old king; for heroism in rags, the sergeant of the rear-guard at Astorga; for rustic drollery the Wessex men on Rainbarrow's Beacon; and for sheer horror the retreat from Moscow, the white mounds of snow along the wayside, and the camp-fires burning on long after those around them are all frozen 'stiff as horn'. One scene has a solemn music unlike any other; it is that in which we hear the poignantly familiar sentences of the burial service, mingled with the boom of the enemy's guns, over the grave of Sir John Moore at Coruña; but there is a touch of the same sombre grandeur in the dirge of Albuera, in the lament for the dying army in Walcheren, and in the boatmen's wild chanty of the Trafalgar storm.

In short, the dramatist has made of us not only an audience, but the very theatre itself; his play masters both sense and feeling. There remains only the appeal to the intellect—the ordered commentary or interpretation—and it is for this that the second effort of invention was required. The material nearest to hand was, of course, the Greek chorus, but it required great modification; and it has been suggested that in his experiment Mr. Hardy has owed much to Goethe or to Shelley. Certainly he has something like a 'Prologue in Heaven'; and in such lines as the following he echoes a rhythm of 'Hellas':

SEMICHORUS I

Ere systemed suns were globed and lit
The slaughters of the race were writ;

SEMICHORUS II

And wasting wars, by land and sea,
Fixed, like all else, immutably.

But what he has done belongs, in fact, not to Goethe or Shelley, nor even to the Greeks, but entirely to himself. He has throughout inter-woven with the historical fabric of his drama the utterances of a company of 'Phantom Intelligences', bearing the names of the Ancient Spirit of the Years, the Spirit of the Pities, the Spirits Sinister and Ironic, the Spirit of Rumour, the Shade of the Earth, Spirit-messengers, and Recording Angels. They differ fundamentally from the Greek type of chorus in more ways than one. Not being persons visibly embodied in a visible play, they are not bound down by the appearance of human life; their comments are not narrowed by considerations of possibility or appropriateness; they remain poised above the scene, invisible, omnipresent, unconditioned. Further, while the Greek chorus represented in its comments 'first, the national spirit, next, the universal sympathy of human nature', and was therefore, 'in a word, the spectator idealized', the new chorus represents the author alone. The 'Intelligences' are certainly personified moods of the human mind in criticism, but they are moods of one and the same mind; taken all together they are the utterance of Mr. Hardy's philosophy, of his reasoned verdict on the life of men, and his belief as to the working of the universe and the nature of its First Cause.

It is the author himself, then, who is with us throughout, annotating, criticizing, unifying the play. The conflict of his moods works out in the main as a struggle between two opposing lines of thought—one founded on scientific experience, and expressed by the Spirit of the

Years; the other based on feeling, and uttered by the voice of the
Pities. The creed professed under the influence of the former has two
main tenets. The holder of it believes, first, in one 'Immanent Will',
the creator and director of all forms of life, the sole cause of characters,
decisions, and events; and this belief is enforced in a very original and
striking manner, once when we are shown a general view of Europe
before the play begins, and five times afterwards at supreme moments
of crisis. At each of these moments 'a new and penetrating light descends
on the spectacle, enduing men and things with a seeming transparency'.
In this preternatural clearness 'the controlling Immanent Will appears,
as a brain-like network of currents and ejections, twitching, inter-
penetrating, entangling, and thrusting hither and thither the human
forms'. The theory is emphasized, not only in these special scenes, but
throughout the drama. All living things are but clockwork, set in
motion by a mainspring beyond their knowledge or control; they do
not *act* in any true sense of the word; they merely 'click out' their
allotted parts.

Secondly, this 'Will' is at the same time both active and unconscious, intelligent and motiveless.

> It works unconsciously, as heretofore,
> Eternal artistries in Circumstance,
> Whose patterns, wrought by rapt æsthetic rote,
> Seem in themselves Its single listless aim,
> And not their consequence.

Everything in man's history goes to show

> That like a knitter drowsed,
> Whose fingers play in skilled unmindfulness,
> The Will has woven with an absent heed
> Since life first was; and ever will so weave.

Again and again, by reproach rather than rebellion, and in words of the
most pathetic beauty, the Pities are heard urging their appeal, their
protest against the injustice of an order by which suffering is laid on
men though free-will is denied them. 'Yea, yea, yea!' they exclaim,
'Why make Life debtor when it did not buy?' To this eternal question,
so often asked by human pain, the Spirit of the Years replies:

> Nay, blame not! For what judgment can ye blame? ...
> The cognisance ye mourn, Life's doom to feel,
> If I report it meetly, came unmeant,

> Emerging with blind gropes from impercipience
> By random sequence—luckless tragic Chance,
> If ye will call it so.

To this, in the After-scene which closes the whole book, the Pities reply in turn with another question:

> Thou arguest still the Inadvertent Mind.
> But, even so, shall blankness be for aye?
> Men gained cognition with the flux of time,
> And wherefore not the Force informing them,
> When far-ranged aions past all fathoming
> Shall have swung by, and stand as backward years?

The Spirit of the Years has no new answer to give; and the Pities, after a magnificent repetition of the older world's hymn to the All-powerful and All-good, ends with an outpouring of hope:

> But—a stirring thrills the air
> Like to sounds of joyance there,
> That the rages
> Of the ages
> Shall be cancelled, and deliverance offered from the darts that were,
> Consciousness the Will informing, till It fashion all things fair!

This is not the time to criticize, to ask Mr. Hardy why he has given the name of 'Will' to that which never wills, or where he finds a place for 'Chance' in his clockwork universe, or how man's evolution came to depart so far from evolutionary law as to result in the acquisition of an 'unneeded' faculty. When a man of genius formulates a system of theology in poetry, the poetry is apt to survive the theology; *Paradise Lost* is an instance in point, and *The Dynasts* is not likely to prove an exception. But I do not care to imagine a time when Englishmen will not read this poem with delight, and value it among their great possessions; nor do I believe that there will be wanting a succession of younger adventurers to set sail for the El Dorado from which Mr. Hardy has brought back so rich a treasure. It is likely enough that in the present state of this celestial commerce they will be little honoured and poorly enough paid for the cargoes which they distribute to their fellow-citizens; but they will remember that it is the distribution and not the price that is important.

A great nation cannot spiritually subsist upon its present, any more than it can materially subsist upon its past; we may be sure of its decadence from the moment when it can no longer draw nourishment from its own history. It is right then to be dissatisfied with an unmixed diet of shorter poems; it would be unhealthy to live entirely on the more instinctive emotions. The feelings of the day or the hour may be noble feelings, and find expression in a splendid lyric poetry; but for the comprehensive and invigorating survey of the past a more sustained effort and a more impressive form are needed. It is a great thing that we should have a school of historians—historians who are more than collectors of dry bones for the museums of the future—but it is not enough. All true history is ποίησις; but there are thoughts and feelings about the past which take a wider range, and call for a more penetrating and more memorable expression than prose can give them. It is for these that Mr. Hardy has planned a new departure in English poetry.

72. W. L. Phelps, from
Essays on Modern Novelists
1910

This essay originally appeared in the *Atlantic Monthly* (Boston). William Lyon Phelps (1865–1943), professor, critic and man of letters, taught at Yale University from 1892 to 1933.

The father of Thomas Hardy wished his son to enter the church, and this object was the remote goal of his early education. At just what period in the boy's mental development Christianity took on the form of a meaningless fable, we shall perhaps never know; but after a time he ceased to have even the faith of a grain of mustard seed. This absence of religious belief has proved no obstacle to many another candidate for the Christian ministry, as every habitual church-goer knows; or as any son of Belial may discover for himself by merely reading the prospectus of summer schools of theology. There has, however, always been a certain cold, mathematical precision in Mr. Hardy's way of thought that would have made him as uncomfortable in the pulpit as he would have been in an editor's chair, writing for salary persuasive articles containing the exact opposite of his individual convictions. But, although the beauty of holiness failed to impress his mind, the beauty of the sanctuary was sufficiently obvious to his sense of Art. He became an ecclesiastical architect, and for some years his delight was in the courts of the Lord. Instead of composing sermons in ink, he made sermons in stones, restoring to many a decaying edifice the outlines that the original builder had seen in his vision centuries ago. For no one has ever regarded ancient churches with more sympathy and reverence than Mr. Hardy. No man today has less respect for God and more devotion to His house.

Mr. Hardy's professional career as an architect extended over a period of about thirteen years, from the day when the seventeen-year-old boy became articled, to about 1870, when he forsook the pencil for the pen. His strict training as an architect has been of enormous service to him in the construction of his novels, for skill in constructive drawing has repeatedly proved its value in literature. Rossetti achieved positive greatness as an artist and as a poet. Stevenson's studies in engineering were not lost time, and Mr. De Morgan affords another good illustration of the same fact. Thackeray was unconsciously learning the art of the novelist while he was making caricatures, and the lesser Thackeray of a later day—George du Maurier—found the transition from one art to the other a natural progression. Hopkinson Smith and Frederic Remington, on a lower but dignified plane, bear witness to the same truth. Indeed, when one studies carefully the beginnings of the work of imaginative writers, one is surprised at the great number who have handled an artist's or a draughtsman's pencil. A prominent and successful playwright of today has said that if he were not writing plays, he should not dream of writing books; he would be building bridges.

Mr. Hardy's work as an ecclesiastical architect laid the real foundations of his success as a novelist; for it gave him an intimate familiarity with the old monuments and rural life of Wessex, and at the same time that eye for precision of form that is so noticeable in all his books. He has really never ceased to be an architect. Architecture has contributed largely to the matter and to the style of his stories. Two architects appear in his first novel. In *A Pair of Blue Eyes* Stephen Smith is a professional architect, and in coming to restore the old Western Church he was simply repeating the experience of his creator. No one of Mr. Hardy's novels contains more of the facts of his own life than *A Laodicean,* which was composed on what the author then believed to be his death-bed; it was mainly dictated, which I think partly accounts for its difference in style from the other tales. The hero, Somerset, is an architect whose first meeting with his future wife occurs through his professional curiosity concerning the castle; and a considerable portion of the early chapters is taken up with architectural detail, and of his enforced rivalry with a competitor in the scheme for restoration. Not only does Mr. Hardy's scientific profession speak through the mouths of his characters, but old and beautiful buildings adorn his pages as they do the landscape he loves. In *Two on a Tower* the ancient structure appears here and there in the story as naturally and incidentally as it would to a pedestrian in the neighbourhood; in *A Pair of Blue Eyes* the church tower plays an important part in a thrilling episode, and its fall emphasizes a Scripture text in a diabolical manner. The old church at Weatherbury is so closely associated with the life history of the men and women in *Far from the Madding Crowd* that as one stands in front of it today the people seem to gather again about its portal.

But while Mr. Hardy has drawn freely on his knowledge of architecture in furnishing animate and inanimate material for his novels, the great results of his youthful training are seen in a more subtle and profounder influence. The intellectual delight that we receive in the perusal of his books—a delight that sometimes makes us impatient with the work of feebler authors—comes largely from the architectonics of his literary structures. One never loses sight of Hardy the architect. In purely constructive skill he has surpassed all his contemporaries. His novels—with the exception of *Desperate Remedies* and *Jude the Obscure*—are as complete and as beautiful to contemplate as a sculptor's masterpiece. They are finished and noble works of art, and give the same kind of pleasure to the mind as any superbly perfect outline. Mr. Hardy himself firmly believes that the novel should first of all be a story: that it should not be a thesis, nor a collection of reminiscences or *obiter dicta.* He insists that a novel should be as much of a whole as a living organism, where all the parts—plot, dialogue, character and scenery—should be fitly framed together, giving the single impression of a completely harmonious building. One simply cannot imagine him writing in the manner of a German novelist, with absolutely no sense of proportion; nor like the mighty Tolstoi, who steadily sacrifices Art on the altar of Reality; nor like the great English school represented by

Thackeray, Dickens, Trollope and De Morgan, whose charm consists in their intimacy with the reader; they will interrupt the narrative constantly to talk it over with the merest bystander, thus gaining his affection while destroying the illusion. Mr. Hardy's work shows a sad sincerity, the noble austerity of the true artist, who feels the dignity of his art and is quite willing to let it speak for itself.

His earliest novel, *Desperate Remedies*, is more like an architect's first crude sketch than a complete and detailed drawing. Strength, originality and a thoroughly intelligent design are perfectly clear; one feels the impelling mind behind the product. But it resembles the *plan* of a good novel rather than a novel itself. The lines are hard; there is a curious rigidity about the movement of the plot which proceeds in jerks, like a machine that requires frequent winding up. The manuscript was submitted to a publishing firm, who, it is interesting to remember, handed it over to their professional reader, George Meredith. Mr. Meredith told the young author that his work was promising; and he said it in such a way that the two men became lifelong friends, there being no more jealousy between them than existed between Tennyson and Browning. Years later Mr. Meredith said that he regarded Mr. Hardy as the real leader of contemporary English novelists; and the younger man always maintained toward his literary adviser an attitude of sincere reverence, of which his poem on the octogenarian's death was a beautiful expression. There is something fine in the honest friendship and mutual admiration of two giants, who cordially recognize each other above the heads of the crowd, and who are themselves placidly unmoved by the fierce jealousy of their partisans. In this instance, despite a total unlikeness in literary style, there was genuine intellectual kinship. Mr. Meredith and Mr. Hardy were both Pagans and regarded the world and men and women from the Pagan standpoint, though the deduction in one case was optimism and in the other pessimism. Given the premises, the younger writer's conclusions seem more logical; and the processes of his mind were always more orderly than those of his brilliant and irregular senior. There is little doubt (I think) as to which of the two should rank higher in the history of English fiction, where fineness of Art surely counts for something. Mr. Hardy is a great novelist; whereas to adapt a phrase that Arnold applied to Emerson, I should say that Mr. Meredith was not a great novelist; he was a great man who wrote novels.

Immediately after the publication of *Desperate Remedies*, which seemed to teach him, as *Endymion* taught Keats, the highest mysteries of his art, Mr. Hardy entered upon a period of brilliant and splendid production. In three successive years, 1872, 1873, and 1874, he produced three masterpieces—*Under the Greenwood Tree, A Pair of Blue Eyes,* and *Far from the Madding Crowd*; followed four years later by what is, perhaps, his greatest contribution to literature, *The Return of the Native.* Even in literary careers that last a long time, there seem to be golden days when the inspiration is unbalked by obstacles. It is interesting to contemplate the lengthy row of Scott's novels, and then to remember that *The Heart of Midlothian, The Bride of Lammermoor* and *Ivanhoe* were published in three successive years; to recall that the same brief span covered in George Eliot's work the production of *Scenes of Clerical Life, Adam Bede* and *The Mill on the Floss*; and one has only to compare what Mr. Kipling accomplished in 1888, 1889 and 1890 with any other triennial, to discover when he had what the Methodists call 'liberty'. Mr. Hardy's career as a writer has covered about forty years; omitting his collections of short tales, he has written fourteen novels; from 1870 to 1880, inclusive, seven appeared; from 1881 to 1891, five; from 1892 to 1902, two; since 1897 he has published no novels at all. With that singular and unfortunate perversity which makes authors proudest of their lamest offspring, Mr. Hardy has apparently abandoned the novel for poetry and the poetic drama. I suspect that praise of his verse is sweeter to him than praise of his fiction; but, although his poems are interesting for their ideas, and although we all like the huge *Dynasts* better than we did when we first saw it, it is a great pity from the economic point of view that the one man who can write novels better than anybody else in the same language should deliberately choose to write something else in which he is at his very best only second rate. The world suffers the same kind of economic loss (less only in degree) that it suffered when Milton spent twenty years of his life in writing prose; and when Tolstoi forsook novels for theology.

It is probable that one reason why Mr. Hardy quit novel-writing was the hostile reception that greeted *Jude the Obscure.* Every great author, except Tennyson, has been able to endure adverse criticism, whether he hits back, like Pope and Byron, or whether he proceeds on his way in silence. But no one has ever enjoyed or ever will enjoy misrepresentation; and there is no doubt that the writer of *Jude* felt that he had been cruelly misunderstood. It is, I think, the worst novel he has ever written, both from the moral and from the artistic point of view; but the novelist was just as sincere in his intention as when he wrote the earlier books. The difficulty is that something of the same change had taken place in his work that is so noticeable in that of Björnson; he had ceased to be a pure artist and had become a propagandist. The fault that marred the splendid novel *Tess of the D'Urbervilles* ruined *Jude the Obscure*. When Mr. Hardy wrote on the title-page of *Tess* the words, 'A Pure Woman Faithfully Presented', he issued defiantly the name of a thesis which the story (great, in spite of this) was intended to defend. To a certain extent, his interest in the argument blinded his artistic sense; otherwise he would never have committed the error of hanging his heroine. The mere hanging of a heroine may not be in itself an artistic blunder, for Shakespeare hanged Cordelia. But Mr. Hardy executed Tess because he was bound to see his thesis through. In the prefaces to subsequent editions the author turned on his critics, calling them 'sworn discouragers of effort', a phrase that no doubt some of them deserved; and then, like many another man who believes in himself, he punished both critics and the public in the Rehoboam method by issuing *Jude the Obscure*. Instead of being a masterpiece of despair, like *The Return of the Native*, this book is a shriek of rage. Pessimism, which had been a noble ground quality of his earlier writings, is in *Jude* merely hysterical and wholly unconvincing. The author takes obvious pains to make things come out wrong; as in melodramas and childish romances, the law of causation is suspended in the interest of the hero's welfare. Animalism, which had partially disfigured *Tess*, became gross and revolting in *Jude*; and the representation of marriage and the relations between men and women, instead of being a picture of life, resembled a caricature. It is a matter of sincere regret that Mr. Hardy has stopped novel-writing, but we want no more *Judes*. Didactic pessimism is not good for the novel.

The Well-Beloved, published in 1897, but really a revision of an earlier tale, is in a way a triumph of Art. The plot is simply absurd, almost as whimsical as anything in *Alice in Wonderland*. A man proposes to a young girl and is rejected; when her daughter is grown, he proposes to the representative of the second generation, and with the same ill fortune. When *her* daughter reaches maturity, he tries the third woman in line and without success. His perseverance was equalled only by his bad luck, as so often happens in Mr. Hardy's stories. And yet, with a plot that would wreck any other novelist, the author constructed a powerful and beautifully written novel. It is as though the architect had taken a wretched plan and yet somehow contrived to erect on its false lines a handsome building. The book has naturally added nothing to his reputation, but as a *tour de force* it is hard to surpass.

It is pleasant to remember that a man's opinion of his own work has nothing to do with its final success and that his best creations cannot be injured by his worst. Tolstoi may be ashamed of having written *Anna Karenina*, and may insist that his sociological tracts are superior productions, but we know better; and rejoice in his powerlessness to efface his own masterpieces. We may honestly think that we should be ashamed to put our own names to such stuff as *Little Dorrit*, but that does not prevent us from admiring the splendid genius that produced *David Copperfield* and *Great Expectations*. Mr. Hardy may believe that *Jude the Obscure* represents his zenith as a novelist, and that his poems are still greater literature; but one reading of *Jude* suffices, while we never tire of rereading *Far from the Madding Crowd* and *The Return of the Native*. Probably no publisher's announcement in the world today would cause more pleasure to English-speaking people than the announcement that Thomas Hardy was at work on a Wessex novel with characters of the familiar kind.

For *The Dynasts*, which covers the map of Europe, transcends the sky, and deals with world-conquerors, is not nearly so great a world-drama as *A Pair of Blue Eyes*, that is circumscribed in a small corner of a small island, and treats exclusively of a little group of commonplace persons. Literature deals with a constant—human nature, which is the same in Wessex as in Vienna. As the late Mr. Clyde Fitch used to say, it is not the great writers that have great things happen to them; the great things happen to the ordinary people they portray. Mr. Hardy selected a few of the southwestern counties of England as the stage for his prose dramas; to this locality he for the first time, in *Far from the Madding Crowd*, gave the name Wessex, a name now wholly fictitious, but which his creative imagination has made so real that it is constantly and seriously spoken of as though it were English geography. In these smiling valleys and quiet rural scenes, 'while the earth keeps up her terrible composure', the farmers and milkmaids hold us spellbound as they struggle in awful passion. The author of the drama stands aloof, making no effort to guide his characters from temptation, folly and disaster, and offering no explanation to the spectators, who are thrilled with pity and fear. But one feels that he loves and hates his children as we do, and that he correctly gauges their moral value. The very narrowness of the scene increases the intensity of the play. The rustic cackle of his bourg drowns the murmur of the world.

Mr. Hardy's knowledge of and sympathy with nature is of course obvious to all readers, but it is none the less impressive as we once more open books that we have read many times. There are incidentally few novelists who repay one so richly for repeated perusals. He seems as inexhaustible as nature herself, and he grows stale no faster than the repetition of the seasons. It is perhaps rather curious that a man who finds nature so absolutely inexorable and indifferent to human suffering should love her so well. But every man must love something greater than himself, and as Mr. Hardy had no God, he has drawn close to the world of trees, plains, and rivers. His intimacy with nature is almost uncanny. Nature is not merely a background in his stories, it is often an active agent. There are striking characters in *The Return of the Native*, but the greatest character in the book is Egdon Heath. The opening chapter, which gives the famous picture of the Heath, is like an overture to a great music-drama. The *Heath-motif* is repeated again and again in the story. It has a personality of its own, and affects the fortunes and the hearts of all human beings who dwell in its proximity. If one stands today on the edge of this Heath at the twilight hour, just at the moment when Darkness is conquering Light—the moment chosen by Mr. Hardy for the first chapter—one realizes its significance and its possibilities. In *Tess of the D'Urbervilles* the intercourse between man and nature is set forth with amazing power. The different seasons act as chorus to the human tragedy. In *The Woodlanders* the trees seem like separate individualities. To me a tree has become a different thing since I first read this particular novel.

Even before he took up the study of architecture, Mr. Hardy's unconscious training as a novelist began. When he was a small boy, the Dorchester girls found him useful in a way that recalls the services of that reliable child, Samuel Richardson. These village maids, in their various love-affairs, which necessitated a large amount of private correspondence, employed young Hardy as amanuensis. He did not, like his great predecessor, compose their epistles; but he held the pen, and faithfully recorded the inspiration of Love, as it flowed warm from the lips of passionate youth. In this manner, the almost sexless boy was enabled to look clear-eyed into the very heart of palpitating young womanhood, and to express accurately its most gentle and most stormy emotions; just as the white voice of a choir-child repeats with precision the thrilling notes of religious passion. These early experiences were undoubtedly of the highest value in later years; indeed, as the boy grew a little older, it is probable that the impression deepened. Mr. Hardy is fond of depicting the vague, half-conscious longing of a boy to be near a beautiful woman; everyone will remember the contract between

Eustacia and her youthful admirer, by which he was to hold her hand for a stipulated number of minutes. Mr. Hardy's women are full of tenderness and full of caprice; and whatever feminine readers may think of them, they are usually irresistible to the masculine mind. It has been said, indeed, that he is primarily a man's novelist, as Mrs. Ward is perhaps a woman's; he does not represent his women as marvels of intellectual splendour, or in queenly domination over the society in which they move. They are more apt to be the victims of their own affectionate hearts. One female reader, exasperated at this succession of portraits, wrote on the margin of one of Mr. Hardy's novels that she took from a circulating library, 'Oh, how I *hate* Thomas Hardy!' This is an interesting gloss, even if we do not add meanly that it bears witness to the truth of the picture. Elfride, Bathsheba, Eustacia, Lady Constantine, Marty South and Tess are of varied social rank and wealth; but they are all alike in humble prostration before the man they love. Mr. Hardy takes particular pleasure in representing them as swayed by sudden and constantly changing caprices; one has only to recall the charming Bathsheba Everdene, and her various attitudes towards the three men who admire her—Troy, Boldwood and Gabriel Oak. Mr. Hardy's heroines change their minds oftener than they change their clothes; but in whatever material or mental presentment, they never lack attraction. And they all resemble their maker in one respect; at heart every one of them is a Pagan. They vary greatly in constancy and in general strength of character; but it is human passion, and not religion, that is the mainspring of their lives. He has never drawn a truly spiritual woman, like Browning's Pompilia.

His best men, from the moral point of view, are closest to the soil. Gabriel Oak, in *Far from the Madding Crowd*, and Venn, in *The Return of the Native*, are, on the whole, his noblest characters. Oak is a shepherd and Venn is a reddleman; their sincerity, charity, and fine sense of honour have never been injured by what is called polite society. And Mr. Hardy, the stingiest author towards his characters, has not entirely withheld reward from these two. Henry Knight and Angel Clare, who have whatever advantages civilization is supposed to give, are certainly not villains; they are men of the loftiest ideals; but if each had been a deliberate black-hearted villain, he could not have treated the innocent woman who loved him with more ugly cruelty. Compared with Oak and Venn, this precious pair of prigs are seen to have only the righteousness of the Scribes and Pharisees; a righteousness that is of little help in the cruel emergencies of life. Along with them must stand Clym

Yeobright, another slave to moral theory, who quite naturally ends his days as an itinerant preacher. The real villains in Mr. Hardy's novels, Sergeant Troy, young Dare, and Alec D'Urberville, seem the least natural and the most machine-made of all his characters.

Mr. Hardy's pessimism is a picturesque and splendid contribution to modern fiction. We should be as grateful for it in this field as we are to Schopenhauer in the domain of metaphysics. I am no pessimist myself, but I had rather read Schopenhauer than all the rest of the philosophers put together, Plato alone excepted. The pessimism of Mr. Hardy resembles that of Schopenhauer in being absolutely thorough and absolutely candid; it makes the world as darkly superb and as terribly interesting as a Greek drama. It is wholly worth while to get this point of view; and if in practical life one does not really believe in it, it is capable of yielding much pleasure. After finishing one of Mr. Hardy's novels, one has all the delight of waking from an impressive but horrible dream, and feeling through the dissolving vision the real friendliness of the good old earth. It is like coming home from an adequate performance of *King Lear*, which we would not have missed for anything. There are so many make-believe pessimists, so many whose pessimism is a sham and a pose, which will not stand for a moment in a real crisis, that we cannot withhold admiration for such pessimism as Mr. Hardy's, which is fundamental and sincere. To him the Christian religion and what we call the grace of God have not the slightest shade of meaning; he is as absolute a Pagan as though he had written four thousand years before Christ. This is something almost refreshing, because it is so entirely different from the hypocrisy and cant, the pretence of pessimism, so familiar to us in the works of modern writers; and so inconsistent with their daily life. Mr. Hardy's pessimism is the one deep-seated conviction of his whole intellectual process.

I once saw a print of a cartoon drawn by a contemporary Dresden artist, Herr Sascha Schneider. It was called 'The Helplessness of Man against Destiny'. We see a quite naked man, standing with his back to us; his head is bowed in hopeless resignation; heavy manacles are about his wrists, to which chains are attached, that lead to some fastening in the ground. Directly before him, with hideous hands, that now almost entirely surround the little circle where he stands in dejection, crawls flatly toward him a prodigious, shapeless monster, with his horrid narrow eyes fixed on his defenceless human prey. And the man is so conscious of his tether, that even in the very presence of the unspeakably awful object, *the chains hang loose!* He may have tried them once, but he has since given up. The monster is Destiny; and the real meaning of the picture is seen in the eyes, nose, and mouth of the loathsome beast. There is not only no sympathy and no intelligence there; there is an expression far more terrible than the evident lust to devour; there is plainly the *sense of humour* shown on this hideous face. The contrast between the limitless strength of the monster and the utter weakness of the man, flavours the stupidity of Destiny with the zest of humour.

Now this is a correct picture of life as Mr. Hardy sees it. His God is a kind of insane child, who cackles foolishly as he destroys the most precious objects. Some years ago I met a man entirely blind. He said that early in life he had lost the sight of one eye by an accident; and that years later, as he held a little child on his lap, the infant, in rare good humour, playfully poked the point of a pair of scissors into the other, thus destroying his sight for ever. So long an interval had elapsed since this second and final catastrophe, that the man spoke of it without the slightest excitement or resentment. The child with the scissors might well represent Hardy's conception of God. Destiny is whimsical, rather than definitely malicious; for Destiny has not sufficient intelligence even to be systematically bad. We smile at Caliban's natural theology, as he composes his treatise on Setebos; but his God is the same who disposes of man's proposals in the stories of our novelist.

> In which feat, if his leg snapped, brittle clay,
> And he lay stupid-like,—why, I should laugh;
> And if he, spying me, should fall to weep,
> Beseech me to be good, repair his wrong,
> Bid his poor leg smart less or grow again,—
> Well, as the chance were, this might take or else
> Not take my fancy ...
> 'Thinketh, such shows nor right nor wrong in Him,
> Nor kind, nor cruel: He is strong and Lord.

Mr. Hardy believes that, morally, men and women are immensely superior to God; for all the good qualities that we attribute to Him in prayer are human, not divine. He in his loneliness is totally devoid of the sense of right and wrong, and knows neither justice nor mercy. His poem *New Year's Eve* clearly expresses his theology.

Mr. Hardy's pessimism is not in the least personal, nor has it risen from any sorrow or disappointment in his own life. It is both philosophic and temperamental. He cannot see nature in any other way. To venture a guess, I think his pessimism is mainly caused by his deep, manly tenderness for all forms of human and animal life and by an almost abnormal sympathy. His intense love for bird and beast is well known; many a stray cat and hurt dog have found in him a protector and a refuge. He firmly believes that the sport of shooting is wicked, and he has repeatedly joined in practical measures to waken the public conscience on this subject. As a spectator of human history, he sees life as a vast tragedy, with men and women emerging from nothingness, suffering acute physical and mental sorrow, and then passing into nothingness again. To his sympathetic mind, the creed of optimism is a ribald insult to the pain of humanity and devout piety merely absurd. To hear these suffering men and women utter prayers of devotion and sing hymns of adoration to the Power whence comes all their anguish is to him a veritable abdication of reason and common sense. God simply does not deserve it, and he for one will have the courage to say so. He will not stand by and see humanity submit so tamely to so heartless a tyrant. For, although Mr. Hardy is a pessimist, he has not the least tincture of cynicism. If one analyses his novels carefully, one will see that he seldom shows scorn for his characters; his contempt is almost exclusively devoted to God. Sometimes the evil fate that his characters suffer is caused by the very composition of their mind, as is seen in *A Pair of Blue Eyes*; again it is no positive human agency, but rather an Æschylean conception of hidden forces, as in *The Return of the Native*; but in neither case is humanity to blame.

This pessimism has one curious effect that adds greatly to the reader's interest when he takes up an hitherto unread novel by our author. The majority of works of fiction end happily; indeed, many are so badly written that any ending cannot be considered unfortunate. But with most novelists we have a sense of security. We know that, no matter what difficulties the hero and heroine may encounter, the unseen hand of their maker will guide them eventually to paths of pleasantness and peace. Mr. Hardy inspires no such confidence. In reading Trollope, one smiles at a cloud of danger, knowing it will soon pass over; but after reading *A Pair of Blue Eyes*, or *Tess*, one follows the fortunes of young Somerset in *A Laodicean* with constant fluctuation of faint hope and real terror; for we know that with Mr. Hardy the worst may happen at any moment.

However dark may be his conception of life, Mr. Hardy's sense of humour is unexcelled by his contemporaries in its subtlety of feeling and charm of expression. His rustics, who have long received and deserved the epithet 'Shakespearian', arouse in every reader harmless and wholesome delight. The shadow of the tragedy lifts in these wonderful pages, for Mr. Hardy's laughter reminds one of what Carlyle said of Shakespeare's: it is like sunshine on the deep sea. The childlike sincerity of these shepherd farmers, the candour of their repartee and their appraisal of gentle-folk are as irresistible as their patience and equable temper. Everyone in the community seems to find his proper mental and moral level. And their infrequent fits of irritation are as pleasant as their more solemn moods. We can all sympathize (I hope) with the despair of Joseph Poorgrass: 'I was sitting at home looking for Ephesians and says I to myself, 'Tis nothing but Corinthians and Thessalonians in this danged Testament!'

73. F. Manning, 'Novels of Character and Environment', *Spectator*

7 September 1912, 335

Frederic Manning is best known for his novel about the First World War: *Her Privates We* (1930).

In the preface to the new edition of his works Mr. Hardy has the following passage:

Positive views on the whence and wherefore of things have never been advanced by this pen as a consistent philosophy. Nor is it likely, indeed, that imaginative writings extending over more than forty years would exhibit a coherent scientific theory of the universe, even if it had been attempted—of that universe concerning which Spencer owns to the 'paralysing thought' that possibly there exists no comprehension of it anywhere. But such objectless consistency never has been attempted, and the sentiments in the following pages have been stated truly to be mere impressions of the moment, and not convictions or arguments. That these impressions have been condemned as 'pessimistic'—as if that were a very wicked adjective—shows a curious muddle-mindedness. It must be obvious that there is a higher characteristic of philosophy than pessimism, or than meliorism, or even than the optimism of these critics—which is truth.

There is in this last sentence, and perhaps we may be forgiven if we draw attention to it, a touch of *naïveté*. Mr. Hardy probably was not blind to it himself, since he continues:

Differing natures find their tongue in the presence of differing spectacles. Some natures become vocal at tragedy, some are made vocal by comedy, and it seems to me that to whichever of these aspects of life a writer's instinct for expression the more readily responds, to that he should allow it to respond. That before a contrasting side of things he remains undemonstrative need not be assumed to mean that he remains unperceiving.

We have every sympathy with these remarks in so far as they represent a protest gainst the habit of classifying all writers under convenient heads, even though we recognize that such a scheme of classification upon proper occasions may be extremely useful. Great art is representative of life, not critical of it. The great artist has a delicacy and mobility of mind by which he is able to capture and reflect the most various and fluid moods, to seize upon the contrasting aspects of life and present each with a perfect impartiality. Such a mind is delicate in the way it realizes with an exquisite tact the essential character of every object; and mobile in its range, in the comprehensive nature of its sympathy. In our own conscious life the sensations of pain or of pleasure, emotions of hatred or of love, moods of joy or of sorrow, have no definite and objective existence for us, though we may connect them in our minds with the realities about us which have this definite existence. They flow through us; but, though they may leave some traces of their passage, they do not remain with us. To the normal mind, life, not being a solid block, but a continuous flux, is neither to be viewed from an entirely pessimistic nor from an entirely optimistic standpoint; it is an affair of compensations. Some natures, as Mr. Hardy observes, may be more responsive to the tragedy of life, and yet perceive another side, for our consciousness is always dissolving, and the aspects of life continually changing under it. On the other hand, a nature which only becomes vocal at tragedy, and which perceives another aspect of life without responding to it, is a nature in which the will has inclined the balance upon one side; and to view life almost entirely in its tragic significance is to view it incompletely. Great art, the art of Sophocles or of Shakespeare, does not leave our minds impressed by a pessimistic conception of existence. It represents the flux of all things, the cessation of pain and grief as well as of joy and pleasure. It has its compensating values. The effect of tragedy upon the mind is ultimately one of relief at the cessation of pain. We consider the quality or characteristic from which the tragic development proceeds less as an essential than as an accidental feature, a flaw in the material; and the solution of a tragic situation brings with it a sense of relief at the eradication of this flaw, the restoration to some extent of ideal conditions, and thus the recovery of balance. The significance of tragedy is not merely tragic. It leaves upon our mind the idea of compensation and readjustment; and when literature ceases to have this effect upon us it ceases to be great literature; it is no longer representative, but didactic. This, we think, is an objection which may be urged in all fairness against the art of Mr. Hardy. His nature is one which responds instinctively to tragedy, and this responsiveness to one particular aspect of life has been cultivated to the neglect of another kind of responsiveness. Truth, that higher characteristic of philosophy, to some extent, however slightly still appreciably, suffers and diminishes in proportion as a habit of thought is formed. Not only his critics, but his admirers and disciples, are apt to find in Mr. Hardy's work a didactic tendency. Well, in so far as that tendency is present in his work it is present as a flaw.

Moreover, that kind of tragedy which is based upon the idea of an ultimate compensation, and which presents life to us as a perpetual collision and readjustment of opposed forces, the effects of which are being dissolved, and from which new forces are being generated continually and in infinite variety, implies naturally a certain activity and freedom of will. Whether the notion of ourselves which we have gained from experience in practical affairs be true or false, it is at least sufficiently true to say that we regard ourselves as active agents to whom is allowed a certain freedom of choice, and upon whom ultimately falls the sole responsibility for the choice. Possibly this notion of ourselves may be an illusion, but it is an illusion which life compels us to accept. We are not concerned here with a philosophic but with an artistic conception of truth. We do not wish to be involved in the damnation of those who have attributed a consistent philosophy to Mr. Hardy. To us Mr. Hardy's nature is not a rational but an emotional nature. It is in the depth and richness of his emotional nature that he is great, and it is in *Tess of the D'Urbervilles* and *Jude the Obscure* that his nature has found its most complete expression. At the same time we do not think that, considered purely as works of art, these are Mr. Hardy's best novels. In *Tess of the D'Urbervilles* the whole of the reader's attention is focused upon a single aspect of life, and that aspect is reflected in a single person. Considered apart from Tess, Alec D'Urberville and

Angel Clare are purely superficial characters. It is only in their relation to her, only when we see them bathed in the light of her own consciousness, only in so far as she turns from one to the other of them, that they interest us. On the other hand, Tess herself is an almost entirely passive character. She interests us, not by what she does or says, but entirely by what she feels, entirely by her capacity for suffering. To understand such a nature *il faut s'abêtir*, as Pascal said; it is spontaneous, instinctive, moody; it lacks both the control of will and the control of reason. It is one of the simplest organisms, in which the nerve-centres are not localized, but spread over the whole surface of the body, and in which thought is practically identical with sensation. It is essentially feminine. The passivity of her character is so firmly insisted upon by her author, in his eagerness to retain our sympathy, as in some measure to defeat his end, for in order that our sympathy with her should be complete we must realize her own responsibility. 'Why was it that upon this beautiful feminine tissue, sensitive as gossamer and practically blank as snow as yet, there should have been traced such a coarse pattern as it was doomed to receive; why so often the coarse appropriates the finer thus the wrong man the woman, the wrong woman the man, many thousand years of analytical philosophy have failed to explain to our sense of order. One may, indeed, admit the possibility of some retribution lurking in the present catastrophe.... As Tess's own people down in those retreats are never tired of saying in their fatalistic way: "It was to be." There lay the pity of it.' This is partly ironical, no doubt; practically all Mr. Hardy's references to justice and retribution are ironical; the conflict for him resolves itself mainly into a conflict between natural instincts and social regulations. But thus to shift the responsibility for the catastrophe to God, or Nature, or Fate, or Chance, is a fault in art. The passage may be admirable as a criticism of life, or as an expression of feeling; but it destroys the illusions of an individual will and of individual activity. Sympathy is not regulated by any considerations of justice, of which it is quite independent; but we do require that the person or character with whom we are asked to sympathize should be a responsible agent. Shakespeare's Cleopatra, Euripides' Phædra, Thackeray's Becky Sharp, are all severally and in their different ways loaded with will. With the first two the question we put to ourselves is not whether their will is directed towards a proper object, but whether it is sufficiently intense. When a character is willing to sacrifice everything else in order to attain the object desired we no longer measure it by ordinary standards. The sacrifice purges the offence; and even if the object be not attained the catastrophe is the consummation of desire, the final effort of the will. Any return would be fatal to our sympathy; the will, finally immolating itself for the sake of its object, achieves some measure of triumph. It is a fault in art to substitute for this individual will the blind, impersonal forces of nature.

If, however, the tendency of Mr. Hardy's mind has been towards the expression of one particular aspect of life, the tendency is only discernible when we view the novels in their chronological order, and that is not a proper way to criticize his work. *Tess* is a great work of subjectivity, a masterpiece of its kind, but of a very special kind. No other writer, we think, of the Victorian age has shown such emotional power or so intuitive a vision. Considered, however, from another point of view, we prefer *The Return of the Native*. *Tess*, perhaps, is more complete as an expression of the peculiar qualities of Mr. Hardy's genius, but *The Return of the Native* is more complete as a representation of life. Life in it is more fluid and more various, the contrasting aspects are more impartially presented, the blind forces of nature and the tragic grandeur of humanity pitted against them are there, but implied rather by the wild expanse of Egdon Heath than expressed in any particular action. Every incident is perfectly realized: the bonfires on the heath, the stones thrown into the pond as a signal to Eustacia, the mummers, the sympathetic magic, the game of dice played by Wildeve and the reddleman by the light of glowworms, the drowning. An unreal glamour plays over the whole, and yet it is full of a human warmth; full, too, of that almost Shakespearean humour with which Mr. Hardy has endowed his clowns, a humour occasionally suffused with tears, as in that scene from *The Mayor of Casterbridge* when the village gossips talk over Mrs. Henchard's death. It is by this intuitive sympathy with humanity in all its moods that Mr. Hardy is great. His pessimism, after all, is only a habit of thought, a weariness with life that comes upon all of us sometimes, if it does not remain with us always; and that, too, springs from his sympathy with mankind, from the depth and richness of his emotional nature.

74. Charles Whibley, 'Thomas Hardy', Blackwood's Magazine

June 1913, cxciii, 823-31

Charles Whibley (1859–1930), journalist and man of letters, assisted W. E. Henley on the *National Observer* and was a regular contributor to *Blackwood's* for over twenty-five years.

It is Mr. Hardy's good fortune that he has seen set up in his lifetime the only monument which a man of letters should esteem—a complete, well-ordered edition of his works. The twenty volumes, recently published, are the eloquent testimony of a life's activity. As you see thus assembled the sum of Mr. Hardy's work, you may discern the purposes which have animated his artistic career. That he himself is conscious of a certain variety in his novels is made evident by his own wise classification, which all his readers will readily accept. Yet even where he surrendered to the spirit of his age so far as to compose 'novels of ingenuity', he is still sincere to his faith in the influence of nature, to his belief in the stern, unpitying destiny which directs the acts and impulses of mortal man.

The best of his works are ranged under the title of 'novels of character and environment'. And thus, at the word 'environment', we are carried off at once to his native Wessex. The intense feeling of locality which engrosses Mr. Hardy comes from no mere love of the picturesque, from no amiable interest in topographical exactitude. Mr. Hardy belongs by birth and temperament to the soil of England. He sees life with a clearer vision when it is lived upon the heath and in the woodlands, which he knows and loves so well. He sees sights and hears sounds in the countryside, of which others less gifted are all unconscious. A true autochthon, he discovers in the landscape of Wessex not merely what is but what has been. The roads and uplands, the streets and lanes of the country town, are haunted for him by the spirits of the past. He looks with a clairvoyant eye upon the multiform procession of strange races which have made Wessex their home since

411

the beginning of time. To the stranger Casterbridge is a busy market-town, and no more. For Mr. Hardy it is a book of history, which his discerning sight reads as other men read their newspaper. 'Caster-bridge', he writes in a vivid passage, 'announced old Rome in every street, alley, and precinct. It looked Roman, bespoke the art of Rome, concealed dead men of Rome. It was impossible to dig more than a foot or two deep about the town fields or gardens without coming upon some tall soldier or other of the Empire who had lain there in his silent unobtrusive rest for a space of fifteen hundred years.' And the memories of ancient Rome are not the only memories evoked by ancient Wessex. The country has its associations no less lively than those of the town. If a man should live with peace and understanding in a remote village, 'he must know', says Mr. Hardy,

all about those invisible ones of the days gone by, whose feet have traversed the fields which look so grey from his windows; recall whose creaking plough has turned those sods from time to time, whose hands planted the trees that form a crest to the opposite hill; whose horses and hands have torn through that under-wood; what birds affect that particular brake; what bygone domestic dramas of love, jealousy, revenge, or disappointment have been enacted in the cottages, the mansion, the street, or on the green.

That, and much more, have the villages of Wessex meant to Mr. Hardy. He sees the houses scarred with the pathos of life, like the faces of men and women, and from an inanimate present divines an animate past. He peoples the cottages with human beings of bygone days, the puppets or the ministers of an untoward fate, and he speaks to them or hears them speak with the familiarity of a complacent neighbour.

And as the men of the past keep no secrets from him, so he has learned the language of the trees and of the winds. In the opening lines of *Under the Greenwood Tree*, the first of its series, he strikes the true note of melody, which echoes through all his books. 'To dwellers in a wood', he tells us, 'almost every species of tree has its voice as well as its feature. At the passing of the breeze the fir-trees sob and moan no less distinctly than they rock; the holly whistles as it battles with itself; the ash hisses amid its quaverings; the beech rustles as its flat boughs rise and fall.' Here is lore which will always elude the town-bred man, and this lore, intimately acquired by Mr. Hardy, explains the profound emotions which he perceives in hill and vale, in the placid river or the tumbling sea. He looks upon landscape as the proper background of comedy or tragedy. The countryside is the web upon which he weaves the intricate woof of his stories. 'Fair prospects wed happily with fair times', says he; 'but, alas! if times be not fair.' So vividly conscious is he himself, so vividly conscious does he make his readers, of certain scenes, that the landscape takes its place as an actor in the drama of human life. That great masterpiece, *The Return of the Native*, is dominated by the changing strength and splendour of Egdon Heath. The opening lines, simple as they are, seem fraught with tragedy. 'A Saturday afternoon in November was approaching the time of twilight, and the vast tract of unenclosed wild known as Egdon Heath embrowned itself moment by moment. Overhead the hollow stretch of whitish cloud shutting out the sky was as a tent which had the whole heath for its floor.' So far all is silence and immobility. Then a slow change takes place. The obscurity in the air fraternises with the obscurity in the land, and Egdon Heath is turned to an animate, sentient body. 'The place became full of a watchful intentness now,' writes Mr. Hardy, 'for when other things sank brooding to sleep the heath appeared slowly to awake and listen. Every night its Titanic form seemed to await something; but it had waited thus unmoved during so many centuries, through the crises of so many things, that it could only be imagined to await one last crisis—the final overthrow.' Such was Egdon, an 'obscure, obsolete, superseded country', which Mr. Hardy looks upon in close relation with the human race. 'It was at present a place', he writes, 'perfectly accordant with man's nature—neither ghastly hateful, nor ugly: neither commonplace, unmeaning, nor tame; but, like man, slighted and enduring; and withal singularly colossal and mysterious in its swarthy monotony. As with some persons who have long lived apart, solitude seemed to look out of its countenance. It had a lonely face, suggesting tragical possibilities!' Its age, in Mr. Hardy's view, carries us much further back than the age of 'the salt, unplumbed, estranging sea'. He champions its antiquity with a sort of jealousy. 'The great inviolate place had an ancient permanence which the sea cannot claim. Who can say of a particular sea that it is old? Distilled by the sun, kneaded by the moon, it is renewed in a year, in a day, or in an hour. The sea changed, the fields changed, the rivers, the villages, and the people changed, yet Egdon remained.' And for this very reason the sinister changelessness of Egdon Heath, *The Return of the Native* should not have had what is known in the circulating libraries as a 'happy ending'. A book which begins in foreboding should end in sadness. There should have been no marriage between Thomasin and the reddleman. And to this sombre end it was that Mr. Hardy designed the book. But the necessity of 'serial publication' disposed it otherwise, and Mr. Hardy, putting the alternatives before us, leaves 'those with an austere artistic code to assume the more consistent conclusion to be the true one'.

It must not be thought that the landscape which serves as a background to Mr. Hardy's novels is bleak and silent. Rather it is the scene of manifold activities and divers superstitions. We are told that the first book put into Mr. Hardy's boyish hands was Dryden's Virgil, and it is easy to perceive Virgil's wholesome influence. Never since the *Georgics* have the industries of the countryside been turned to literary account with so fine a sense of their enduring importance as in Mr. Hardy's novels of environment. *The Woodlanders* is redolent of the scent of cider-apples. The music of the axe, laid to the trunk of the tree, accompanies the tragedy of Giles Winterborne and Marty South. In one aspect, *Far from the Madding Crowd* is one long fight against the ill-omened forces of nature. Gabriel Oak finds his enemies in fire and storm. The scenes in which Gabriel saves the ricks from burning, and thatches the stacks against the oncoming deluge, are without a rival for truth and intensity in English literature. Indeed there is scarcely an episode in the life of a farm to which Mr. Hardy has not given a just expression. Nor is he content with a mere statement of the facts. He blends with the true vision of a keen observer the sentiment of the poet. Here you find the honey-takers at work; there is a perfect picture of sheep-shearing. Now there are troubles in the fold: the ewes have broken down the fence and got into a field of young clover. Now the reaping-machine 'ticks like the love-making of a grasshopper'. Men and women assert themselves or lose themselves in their environment. 'A fieldman is a personality', writes Mr. Hardy; 'a fieldwoman is a portion of the field; she has somehow lost her own margin, imbibed the essence of her surroundings, and assimilated herself with it.' And the immutable countryside, where three or four score years are included in the present, changes neither its picture nor its frame. The perfect blending of men with inanimate things is always before Mr. Hardy's eyes. In *Far from the Madding Crowd* 'the barn is natural to the shearers, and the shearers are in harmony with the barn'. With a fine eloquence Mr. Hardy paints this shearing-barn as a symbol of human permanence:

One could say about it [he writes] what could hardly be said of the church or the castle, akin to it in age and style, that the taste which had dictated its original erection was the same with that to which it was still applied. ... The old barn embodied practices which had suffered no mutilation at the hands of time.

Here at least the spirit of the ancient builders was at one with the spirit of the modern beholder. . . . The fact that four centuries had neither proved it to be founded on a mistake, inspired any hatred of its purpose, nor given rise to any reaction that had battered it down, invested this simple grey effort of old minds with a repose, if not a grandeur, which a too curious reflection was apt to disturb in its ecclesiastical and military compeers. For once mediævalism and modernism had a common standpoint.

Thus it is that spiritually or architecturally the traditions of country life are preserved. Thus it is that the distance which separates Mr. Hardy from Virgil is no greater than the distance which separates the new Weatherbury from the old. 'The citizen's *Then* is the rustic's *Now.*' Thus it is that Mr. Hardy's rural sketches are touched with an eternal truth. 'The dairy maids and men', it is written in *Tess of the D'Urbervilles*, 'had flocked down from their cottages and out of the dairy-house with the arrival of the cows from the meads; the maids walking in pattens, not on account of the weather, but to keep their shoes above the mulch of the barton. Each girl sat down on her three-legged stool, her face sideways, her right cheek resting against the cow, and looked musingly along the animal's flank.' Here, instead, we are in a world unaffected by the thing miscalled education, inspired by the follies of politicians, a world which is and will be always what it was. The fashions of the city may shift as they will. Tess and her companions will cross the barton in pattens and sit sideways against the cow until the end of time.

And Mr. Hardy's countryside is the home not only of industry, but of those primitive beliefs now rashly dismissed as 'superstitions'. In the world of his painting the 'forecaster' still foretells the weather at a price; the quack-salver vends his cheap cures, or offers for sale the love-philtres, which seemed of efficacy in the golden age. The old wives' remedies are known and practised; nothing but the fat of adders will cure an adder's bite. The belief in witchcraft still 'lurks like a mole underneath the visible surface of manners'. Susan Nunsuch in *The Return of the Native*, models Eustacia in wax, red-ribbon, sandal-shoes, and all, until the figure would have been recognized by any inhabitants of Egdon Heath. Then she thrusts pins of the long and yellow sort into the image in all directions, and at last watches it as it wastes away over the fire, repeating meanwhile the Lord's Prayer backwards. Such incantations as this are as old as time itself, and prove again that past and present are inextricably mixed in the Wessex of Mr. Hardy's novels.

Vale and upland, farm and malt-house, are peopled by men and women old in fashion and speech as the cottages which shelter them, as the trees which give them shade. Mr. Hardy's peasants look upon the action of his dramas with the close, impartial interest of a Greek chorus. They comment upon the tragedy which unfolds itself before their eyes with a shrewdness untainted by the cunning of the town, and in a language which would have been intelligible to our fore-fathers three centuries ago. Mr. Hardy is as happy in his use of the vernacular as Scott himself. Whenever he marshals his gossiping yokels upon the scene, his style assumes a happy propriety, a noble amplitude of expression. The comments of the labourers upon Bathsheba Everdene in *Far from the Madding Crowd* are in the true vein:

'Be as 'twill, she's a fine handsome body as far's looks be concerned. But that's only the skin of the woman, and these dandy cattle be as proud as a lucifer in their insides.'

'Ay—so 'a do seem, Billy Smallbory—so 'a do seem.'

'She's a very vain feymell—so 'tis said here and there. . . .'

'Yes—she's very vain. 'Tis said that every night at going to bed she looks in the glass to put on her nightcap properly.'

'And not a married woman. Oh, the world!'

And if in one aspect the Wessex peasants resemble the Greek chorus, in another they are the true heirs of Shakespeare's age. If they met their forebears of Elizabeth's reign there would be no hesitation between them, no misunderstanding. Christian Cantle, 'a man of the mourn-fullest make', and William Worm, 'a poor wambling body', are of the true breed. Dogberry still lives in modern England. 'What can we two poor lammingers do against such a multitude!' exclaims Stubberd in *The Mayor of Casterbridge*. "Tis tempting 'un to commit *felo de se* upon us, and that would be the death of the perpetrator; and we wouldn't be the cause of a fellow-creature's death on no account, not we! . . . We didn't want the folk to notice us as law officers, being so short-handed, sir; so we pushed our Government staves up this water-pipe.' In pomp as in prudence, Stubberd falls not a whit behind his type, and the justice of the comparison proves the equal truth to nature of Shakespeare and Mr. Hardy.

We have sketched all too briefly the scene of Mr. Hardy's dramas; we have hinted at the part played by his chorus. The dramas them-selves have an elemental largeness which befits their background. They are tense and simple, like the dramas of Sophocles. If Mr. Hardy very properly claimed for himself a freedom in the choice of material which most English novelists have denied themselves, he has permitted no licence in the treatment of that material. In construction his stories are stern, even to rigidity. It is not for nothing that he passed his youth in the study and practice of architecture. His fable, as the ancient critics called it, is expounded by no more than three or four characters, whose actions are directed by the harsh necessity of fate. They are the playthings of the gods, as the Greeks would have said, or of destiny. In vain they struggle against the doom which hangs over them. 'We are but thistle-globes in Heaven's high gales', says Napoleon in *The Dynasts*, and that line might serve as a motto for the best of Mr. Hardy's works. He is conscious also to whom he owes his debt:

> A life there was
> Among these self-same frail ones—Sophocles—
> Who visioned it too clearly, even the while
> He dubbed the Will 'the gods'. Truly said he,
> 'Such gross injustice to their own creation
> Burdens the time with mournfulness for us,
> And for themselves with shame.'

There, set in another light, is his constant theme. Tess, 'poor wounded name', is driven to her destruction by a fate which she is not strong enough to control. Henchard, the Mayor of Casterbridge, is the victim of his own strength and insolent triumph. Bathsheba, with no evil intent, unseats the reason of a good man, and falls herself a victim to a fickle rascal. It was written in the book of fate that Giles Winterborne should reject the worship of Marty South, and see himself rejected by Grace Melbury. In *Jude the Obscure* instinct and intellect engage in an unequal combat. Jude fails in all the ambitions of his life because he cannot sustain upon his weak shoulders the battle of the new against the old. For this submission to fate Mr. Hardy has been called a 'pessimist'. The charge is unjust as well as irrelevant. A man is not a pessimist because he perceives the obvious truth that all is not cakes and ale in this world. A cheerful determination to look upon what is called 'the bright side of things' commonly means no more than a wilful blindness. In any case Mr. Hardy has seen life with an impartial eye, and has told us what he has discovered therein; and he does it with so fine a zest, that to charge him with pessimism is to suggest in him who brings the charge an inability to apply to a work of fiction any other test than the test of a happy ending.

If his dramas be simple in construction, Mr. Hardy spares no pains of complexity in the drawing of his characters. His women especially stand out with a clarity and personal distinction which it is not easy to match in modern literature. Eustacia, Bathsheba, Tess, Marty South, Lucetta—they are one and all alive and easily recognizable. Even in Sue Bridehead, 'the slight, pale, bachelor girl', so familiar today, was divined by the author. In the portraiture of men, Mr. Hardy is not so happy and diverse. His faithful lovers, such as Gabriel Oak and Giles Winterborne, are almost too faithful to be true; and the Troys, the Wildeves, the Fitzpiers, the men who unworthily attract beautiful women, seem now and then to be cut to a pattern. But even when we have played the devil's advocate, we can only pause in wonder before this gallery of modern portraits, seen by a visionary and drawn by a master.

Mr. Hardy did not find without a struggle the manner of his Wessex novels. In his earliest experiment he, who owes so little to his predecessors, readily submitted to the influence of his time. With perfect justice he calls *Desperate Remedies* a novel of ingenuity. So ingenious is it, with its plots and counterplots, that it reminds you of Wilkie Collins or Charles Dickens. There is a murder in it, and a sudden death, and a concealed birth, and all the apparatus of the fiction that was popular fifty years ago. Yet it contains the germ of the masterpieces, and it was presently followed, without intervention, by *Under the Greenwood Tree*, a modern and exquisite version of *Daphnis and Chloe*. And the juxtaposition of these two books is the more remarkable, because, when Mr. Hardy condescends to the romantic or the ingenious, he is sometimes beset by a sort of elfin freakishness. Surely it was a spirit of mischief which saw Viviette, in *Two on a Tower*, married to a bishop; nor must *The Well-Beloved*, who fell in love with three generations, be judged by the common standards. And Ethelberta, who, with her friends, wavers always on the borderland of comedy and farce, is a piece of whimsicality. Neigh and Ladywell, her lovers, seem to have stepped not out of life, but out of the works of the old comic writers, and the scene at Rouen, where Ethelberta hides a lover on each of three floors of the hotel, out-fantasies fantasy itself. At the same time, it may be said that even the slightest of these works is touched by the master's hand, and that two of them, *A Pair of Blue Eyes*, a piece of exquisite pathos, and *The Trumpet Major*, a light-hearted romance, alive with joyous patriotism, are worthy to rank even with the novels of character and environment.

Mr. Hardy's prose style keeps sternly in touch with the tradition of our ancient speech. He uses words with a full consciousness of their weight and meaning. His sentences are compactly knit, and have no loose edges. Moreover, his periods have a pleasant sinuous movement, which proves that he is sensitive to harmony as well as to structure. His mastery of dialect is complete, and, like all masters of dialect, he records the talk of the people with a finer freedom than he brings to the management of the cultured speech. He is not often conscious of his forerunners, and seldom echoes the cadence of another. Now and again he recalls Burton's *Anatomy of Melancholy*, but the reminiscences of the past are found rarely and at long intervals. For Mr. Hardy the English language is an instrument of precision. He will exclude no word from his vocabulary which shall clarify his meaning. He uses words of Saxon and Latin origin with impartiality. It is perhaps a defect of his style that he employs such inexpressive nouns as 'premises' or 'erection' when the dignified and simple 'house' would far better serve his turn. But it was his fortune, good or evil, to live in the days of a tyrannical science, now already 'bankrupt', and to admit into his language words of a curious shape and sound, words weighted with associations that are now half-forgotten. *Theomachist, thesmothete, nullibist, zenithal, nebulosity*—these are some of the strange words wherewith he scatters his pages. And nothing need be said against them if they had justified themselves in their places. But at times they make but a harsh discord, and appear after a brief interval as mere concessions to a scientific curiosity, that has had its day. However, these are mere blemishes upon the surface of a sober, dignified style—a style which will give Mr. Hardy a high place among writers of English prose.

There remains to say a word of Mr. Hardy's poetry. He himself sets a higher value upon it than upon his prose. 'The more individual part of my literary fruitage', he calls it. The passage of time, we think, will correct the writer's own estimate. It is not dangerous to prophesy that by the novels of environment Mr. Hardy will be esteemed in the court of posterity. Comparison, maybe, is unprofitable, and the brilliance of the prose can in no way dim the lustre of *The Dynasts*. This, in truth, is a work apart, without ancestry or descendant. It is a drama that can be played upon no stage but the stage of the imagination. It is, as its author says, 'concerned with the Great Historical Calamity, or Clash of Peoples', which rent Europe in twain a hundred years ago. And as Mr. Hardy's vast panorama unfolds itself, we are struck most keenly by the poet's amazing impartiality. He stands as far remote from the puppets of his drama as Providence itself. He is fair to Napoleon, without under-rating 'the last large words' of Pitt. With a balanced hand he leads upon the stage all the great men of the epoch, French and English, and with a rare clairvoyance he seems to see the precise relation of one event to another. And over the whole action there broods a set of 'impersonated abstractions', or Intelligences, called Spirits—Spirit of Pity, Spirit of Rumour, Spirit of the Years. The Pities, as Mr. Hardy says, approximate to Schlegel's notion of the Greek Chorus—'the Universal Sympathy of human nature—the Spectator idealized'. But whatever they be, they at once conduct and comment upon the poem; they explain and enhance the skill wherewith Mr. Hardy selects and knits up the manifold episodes of his vast drama; and they interpret with perfect lucidity the poet's doctrine of fate, the inevitable 'working of the Will'.

For the rest, it may be said of Mr. Hardy's poetry, what Dr. Johnson wrote of Bentley's, that it is 'the forcible verse of a man of strong mind, but not accustomed to write verse; for there is some uncouthness in the expression'. If we may quote a specimen, we would choose the following stanzas from 'A Trampwoman's Tragedy':

> From Wynyard's Gap the livelong day,
>   The livelong day,
> We beat afoot the northward way
>   We had travelled times before.
> The sun-blaze burning on our backs,
> Our shoulders sticking to our packs
> By fosseway, fields, and turnpike tracks
>   We skirted sad Sedge-Moor.

> Lone inns we loved, my man and I,
>   My man and I;
> 'King's Stag,' 'Windwhistle' high and dry,
>   'The Horse' on Hintock Green,
> The cozy house at Wynyard's Gap,
> 'The Hut' renowned on Bredy Knap,
> And many another wayside tap
>   Where folk might sit unseen.

Here is something of the ancient ballads, and much else beside—a haunting refrain, a noble use of place-names, and a sense of impending tragedy. But in whatever Mr. Hardy has written it is not merely the intelligence which is at work, it is an instinctive emotion; and if George Meredith be the Ben Jonson of his generation, then surely is Thomas

Hardy its Shakespeare—a Shakespeare in his keen perception of human nature, a Shakespeare, also, in the singing of his 'native wood-notes wild'.

75. Harold Williams, 'The Wessex Novels of Thomas Hardy', *North American Review*

January 1914, cxcix, 120–34

Sir Harold Williams (1880–1962), critic, scholar and bibliographer, is well known as an editor of Swift.

History has a knack of presenting us with pairs of great men of thought or action who supplement each other's work, who fill in the one-sidedness or deficiency of their contemporary in the same field of achievement. The *a priori* philosophical method of Plato is balanced by the empirical bent of his pupil Aristotle; Euripides and Sophocles exhibit a natural contrast; Goethe and Schiller are different facets of a common *tendenz*; Tennyson and Browning illustrate the trend of thought, life, and art of their day in differing ways and in differing aspects; Emerson and Hawthorne are dissimilar examples of the meeting of New England Puritanism with the spirit of art. In the central decades of the last century two great English novelists, Dickens and Thackeray, reflected separate sides of social life each in his own vein of satire, humour, and didacticism. And, later in the same century, the contrast and comparison were repeated in different terms by another pair of great novelists, Meredith and Mr. Thomas Hardy. The long life of George Meredith drew to its close, and Mr. Hardy alone remains of the great men of letters who belonged to the Victorian era of English literary story.

Mr. Hardy had not, like Meredith, to wait through long years of

comparative neglect, though it was some time before the more peculiarly technical excellence of his work received its due recognition.
When his fourth novel, *Far from the Madding Crowd*, ran its course
through the *Cornhill Magazine*, thirty-seven years ago, it commended
itself as much to the uncritical reader as to the man whose business was
with letters. But the gentle reader who escapes the obsession of trying
or trying not to see harm in the later novels has still, in many cases,
the innocent belief that Mr. Hardy is the observant painter of rural
scenes in a small corner of England, and that the narrow limitations
of his Wessex scenery preclude us from regarding him as a great
novelist. Others, of a slightly more critical capacity, look upon him
as the receptive student of French technique in the art of shaping a
narrative, and are blind to that comprehensive conviction and sympathy of outlook upon life which lie at the foundation of the greater
qualities of his work. In the latter class may be reckoned, as a pertinent
example, the late David Christie Murray, who, in unadvised moments
of leisure, strayed from hackneyed fiction to literary criticism on still
lower levels. In an unwittingly curious and amusing collection of
critical essays on his contemporaries in fiction, wherein we find him
performing the seemingly impossible feat of reviewing George Meredith and Mr. Hall Caine in a common chapter, he treats Mr. Hardy
as the craftsman who has learned a useful lesson from the French
novelists, though himself hampered by paucity of imagination and a
want of fertility in the invention of plot.

These one-sided points of view are at fault not in the direction to
which they look, but in their short-sightedness. Mr. Hardy may be the
annalist of rural life and agricultural manners; but it is surely a mistake,
at this time of the day, to breathe a sigh for another simple country-
tale like *Under the Greenwood Tree*, charming in its direct naturalness as
that book may be! And yet the sigh has been breathed in print by a
distinguished American critic of literature. If Mr. Hardy had restricted
himself to the vein of his second novel we should be safe in prophesying
that, compared with its actuality, the measure of his present fame would
have been insignificant. It is not only as the painter of village life in
remote corners of a small English county that he has sent out novels
which impress readers in his own country, and under the wholly different conditions of life in America, with their note of power and great
writing. Nor, again, has he won his outstanding position merely as a
master-craftsman.

Mr. Hardy's knowledge of country life, his powers of observation, the fine faculty he displays in putting a book together, stand him in good stead; but it is not here only that we look for that which gives him his notable place as a writer of prose fiction. If we compare secondary writers with those who take their place by right divine in the first class, we shall feel that the most marked distinction is what we may call the aura of individuality which flows from primary writers. No writer has been truly great who was not possessed by some species of egotistical conviction, an outlook on life and its problems which was for him inevitable and virtually unquestioned. This mental attitude may have been revolutionary or conventional, original or commonplace, moral or immoral according to ordinary standards, but it has always been intense. Richardson, who was wholly commonplace, created, as he claimed, 'a new species of writing', more important than Mr. Bernard Shaw, who, less distinctively conventional in outlook, is ever likely to do. Great fiction, like other forms of art, is measured ultimately by concentration of vision and emotional sincerity in the author.

That view of life which we read out of Mr. Hardy's novels is steady and whole-minded; it is as intense and thorough-going in the earlier books as in his later work. He would seem to have suffered from none of the illusions of youth. We are conscious that the young man of thirty knew with Bellario that life is 'a game that must be lost'; or in the phrase of Rabelais we could imagine him describing it as an *'insigne fable et tragique comédie'*. But though he refuses the sop which Hope holds out and most men clutch at, there is no weakness in the mental atmosphere of the novels. For, unlike many theoretical or temperamental pessimists, Mr. Hardy is imbued with the spirit of a human and a personal sympathy. Faith, hope, and love are satirized by circumstance or broken beneath the passing feet of the years which 'like great black oxen tread the world'; but, even if we have read ourselves into a mental acquiescence with the attitude of the writer, we would still wish to play our part on so great and moving a stage. The unconscious powers which rule the courses of the planets and heedlessly shape the lives of men are never lost to view. In the solitary woodland places, on Egdon Heath, in Blackmoor Vale, at the dairy-farm where Tess and Angel Clare learned to love, in the quiet cathedral town of Melchester, and in the market-place of Casterbridge we realize that the course of events in the story of obscure lives is big with the destinies of the universe. The scene is laid in a secluded agricultural county where the noise of the great industrial centres hardly comes as a distant murmur, the characters belong to the simplicity of an older and less sophisticated world than most of us are condemned to live in; but in these novels life is greater, nobler, more tragic, more fraught with tremendous issues, than in books which carry us away to the four corners of the earth or to the noisy bustle of nations and of kingdoms. Whatever may be the limitations of Mr. Hardy's insight, the similarity of the *motif* underlying his tales, or the improbability of plot in his minor books, he can claim to have invested the tragedy of the individual with a note of universal significance as only the great masters have done. It is this which lends to his novels whatever greatness they possess. Not a few among younger writers have imitated him or worked over again the hints which he has dispensed, but the peculiar note of great destiny which marks his narrative is not to be found in the copies. This is inimitable, the gift of that unfaltering steadiness of vision which belongs to genius.

It has been conjectured, and with some show of reason, that we can trace three stages in the development of human consciousness. In early and primitive man the sense of individuality is slight: the individual is sunk in the tribe. There is, secondly, the stage on which the vast majority of civilized men now stand, where the sense of the Ego, of the individual life set in opposition to the *otherness* of fellow-lives, is clearly felt. And beyond this lies a third stage, the beginnings of which we can already discern—the realization of the unity of the individual with universal life. The theory may seem a little strained; but, apart from its strict application, it is, at least, suggestive in the study of differing types of mind. The imagination of Mr. Hardy belongs distinctively to the third order; and it is as yet an uncommon type. It sees the unity of all sentient life, not as a philosophic doctrine, but as a momentous reality. Schopenhauer, watching the kitten playing in the yard, knows that it is the same as the kitten that was playing there three hundred years ago. The generations of cat-life are only a means to an end—the kitten which is always there; and only important in the light of that end. So likewise birth and death and the passing generations of men only serve to fill out the jejune chronicle of history; the important and significant fact is man who is always there. That the individual existence is 'rounded with a sleep' is less to Mr. Hardy than the knowledge that the essential elements of human life and character are not mortal; they endure unchangeably through the centuries. In the Wessex labourer of today, who ploughs the field, walks the lonely heath, sits in his village inn and talks the Old World wisdom, he sees the same man who was there a hundred, five hundred, a thousand years ago. Changes in dress, in vocabulary, in a few in-essentials of an uncomprehended religion, Christian in name but pagan in virtue, are superficialities which do not touch the real man. The temper of mind which leads Mr. Hardy to see the past in the present, to read the older generations in the face of living men and women, is only a manifestation, in lesser degree, of the tendency already noticed, which helps him to lend a mood of universality to individual life-stories. In his greater novels the ancient world is never lost to sight; in the talk, wise sayings, humour, scarcely veiled paganism, belief in witchcraft, in the houses and household utensils of the Wessex peasan-try, it still lives.

Mr. Hardy writes:

Many of the labourers about here bear corrupted Norman names; many are the descendants of the squires in the last century, and their faces even now strongly resemble the portraits in the old manor-houses. Many are, must be, the descen-dants of the Romans who lived here in great pomp and state for four hundred years. I have seen faces here that are the duplicates of those fine faces I saw at Fiesole, where also I picked up Roman coins, the counterpart of those we find here so often. They even use Latin words here, which have survived everything.

Other writers have preceded or followed Mr. Hardy in giving to their novels a local environment, sometimes even narrower than his, but no one has succeeded, by the same plan, in impressing upon us the age-old and unchanging order of life's essentials. The scene of nearly all his greater writing centres in one small county, Dorset; and he uses the unity of place to educe an artistically impressive synthesis of past and present life.

The unseen powers behind the universe are present for Mr. Hardy as an impelling force alike in the lives of men and in the realm of Nature. When he describes the fields, the copses, and the hills of Dorset, it is not as plausible and necessary background to the lives of his characters. The moods of earth and sky enter into human life, colour it, and even play their part in the story. In *The Return of the Native*, for example, Egdon Heath, a 'vast tract of uninclosed wild', broods as the genius of destiny over the lives of the men and women who pass their allotted span of time upon its slopes. The dark embrowned mass of the heath is drawn against the skyline of the narrative, and we cannot escape a consciousness of its presence even when for many pages it has not been named.

The profound influence of climatic and physical conditions upon the character of a people is admitted, but it has seldom been used by imaginative writers with conscious artistry or psychological insight. The early novels of Björnson, *Arne* and *Synnöve Solbakken*, are notable exceptions to such a statement, and there are, of course, other exceptions among English, French and Russian novels. But, however faithful the transcript of natural scenery may be in many writers, we are rarely made to feel that its connection with human life is intimate and inevitable. In Mr. Hardy's novels it is difficult to dissociate the people from their environment; and, more than this, by a fine and most distinctive gift of psychological suggestiveness, we read the colour and nature of their surroundings in their habits, speech and character. Egdon Heath pervades the lives of the peasantry in *The Return of the Native*; but Giles Winterborne and Marty South, in *The Woodlanders*, belong to the woodland places. We could not transfer characters from one book to the other without a sense of incongruity. We are conscious of an essential affinity between the atmospheric tone of natural environment and the inmost personality of characters in the tale.

Wordsworth was the first to reveal clearly a kinship between the moods of earth and sky and the moods of the human mind. But the theory he reiterates, that the simple and austere surroundings of Nature reflect themselves in the natural integrity and cheerful contentedness of country folk, is surely an extraordinary misconception, which the slightest real acquaintance with any European peasantry will immediately remove. Even Wordsworth's tramp, who lives by begging scraps from door to door, bears about

> The good which the benignant law of Heaven
> Has hung around him.

This is indeed the super-tramp! Nature is the teacher of 'moral evil and of good' to the cultured and reflective mind; but only in pastoral idyls are we justified in supposing that She is an ethical influence in the lives of those whose lot has been cast upon the soil through generations from father to son. Mr. Hardy does not labour under the illusion which Wordsworth has cultivated in the minds of town-dwellers. If, however, natural influences are not reflected ethically in the habits of a peasantry they *are* reflected in poetry of speech, in imagination, in religious beliefs, in the whole cast of temper and mind. Gabriel Oak, in *Far from the Madding Crowd*, is a man who lives in the open fields tending sheep, we read it in his whole manner; Giles Winterborne, in *The Wood-*

landers, as obviously spends his life in the shadowy silence of the woods; though Clym Yeobright, in *The Return of the Native*, has travelled, the barren features of Egdon Heath have communicated a like austerity to his view of life's meaning; and Michael Henchard (*The Mayor of Casterbridge*) is an agricultural labourer out of place in a country town. Marty South and Tess are both country girls, yet they differ, for one lives in the woods and the other in a village. Beyond this, however, it is blind circumstance and not character which separates so widely the moral issue of their lives.

The business man who rushes away, once a year, from the whirl of city life to a holiday in the country feels a joyous exhilaration in the sense of freedom and space, in the purity of the air, and the sweet scent of flowers and lush grasses. But if he protracted his holiday in a lonely district far from towns for ten or twenty years, he would find this sense of exhilaration fade into something more like melancholy. Country folk may have humour, but their ordinary habit of mind is more grave and serious than that of city people. The elemental forces of Nature, reflected in the seasons, pursue a monotonous and unchanging course. The man who watches the repeated cycle of the seasons through a long lifetime will not himself be vivacious or responsive to rapid alternations of mood. The song of birds, the sough of the wind, the music of running water, have not changed since the creation of the world. Mr. Hardy is keenly conscious of this monotony of repetition which communicates itself to the mind of country people. He describes Michael Henchard tramping the road with his wife who carries a child in her arms, and speaks of 'the atmosphere of stale familiarity which the trio carried along with them like a nimbus as they moved down the road'. This is only a reflex of the 'stale familiarity' of the sky, the fields, the hedgerows, the road with dusty grass margins, and 'the voice of a weak bird singing a trite old evening song that might doubtless have been heard on the hill at the same hour, and with the self-same trills, quavers, and breves, at any sunset of the season for centuries untold'.

The epithet commonly used to describe the more serious and less versatile nature of the countryman as compared with the man who lives in streets, is *stolid*; but the word inevitably implies staring and stockish stupidity. It may be that the countryman's ideas move more slowly than those of people from the large cities, yet not because he is stupid; his wisdom is as true, and it is more fitted to the needs of a life which has to do with the unhasting movements of Nature. The spirit of a strong and patient passivity and melancholy is written in the lives of all the more outstanding characters of Mr. Hardy's novels. His reading of peasant life is intimate and realistic, not the clever reconstruction of the young novelist who has worked up his local colour by a few weeks' stay on the spot, and writes to show us how the other half of the world lives.

There is, however, another side to the picture; and to leave Mr. Hardy's painting of peasant life at this stage would be a gross misrepresentation. Faithful adherence to the pervading atmosphere of life on the soil may have tinged his narrative with a melancholy, which to the impercipient reader seems a morbid obsession. But he is a pessimist with a deep and rich vein of humour. Melancholy lies at the base of every genuinely humorous nature. There is a strain of gravity and sadness in the character of Falstaff. Mr. Hardy's humour in characterization was never better displayed than in the first of his more distinctive novels, *Far from the Madding Crowd*. In that fine piece of critical writing, *The Art of Thomas Hardy*, Lionel Johnson points out that in the humour of these peasant characters we are made to feel that life on the English soil has not changed essentially since Shakespeare peopled his plays with country folk of his own day. 'When they speak', he writes, 'it is in a Shakespearean humour: from Shallow and Silence, to Mistress Quickly and Dull, from Lance and Lancelot, to Costard and Touchstone, we hear the old tones, taste the old wit, take the old humour, until we are ready to swear by that impressive phrase, the continuity of history.'

If we find a larger quantity of humour in the first of the greater novels, it does not fail us in that book's successors. The conversation of the bonfire-makers in *The Return of the Native* is touched with a wise humour. It is the humour of shrewd observation, untrammelled by ideas and qualifications taught in the schools; and this is the true quality of peasant humour. Its character may be instanced by Mark Clark's statement that a faculty for drinking deep is 'a talent of the Lord mercifully bestowed upon us, and we ought not to neglect it'; or by Humphrey's excuse for absenting himself from church on Sundays: ' 'Tis so terrible far to get there; and when you do get there 'tis such a mortal poor chance that you'll be chose for up above, when so many bain't, that I bide at home and don't go at all.' The play performed by the mummers in *The Return of the Native* reminds us, in its blundering ineptness, of Shakespeare's farcical sub-plots. Here are the same people —Costard, Dull, Quince, Nick Bottom, Starveling—they bear different names, but they have not changed.

The talk of these country people revolves about a few enduring subjects, the mainsprings of human life, which are always and insistently there—birth, marriage, death, religion, eating and drinking. And serious as most of these matters are, though the peasantry of these Wessex novels know them to be serious, yet there is a natural and admirable reaction of the human mind which has always prompted it to talk a little jestingly on grave subjects—even judgment and the wrath to come. It is a natural necessity, and spells profanity only to those who are shallow and superficial. The lot of the labourers whom we meet in the novels is hard, they win the right to existence by a lifelong monotony of toil as furze-cutters, farm hands, dairymaids, ploughmen, shepherds, reddlemen—it is in the moment of relief from labour, when they sit in the taproom of the village inn, or take part in a dance and supper that the kindliest of gifts bestowed on mortals lightens the interlude with odd whimsicalities of thought and turns of phrase.

The signal and final test of genius in the writer of fiction lies in the presence or absence of two faculties which can hardly be analysed or dissected apart from each other. These two are, the gift of visualizing characters who belong to the real world, who are not merely clothes-racks with names, and the power of placing them in an environment of episode and incident which would naturally arise in the clash of their postulated temperaments and natures, so that we feel them to be more than puppets controlled at the caprice of the author. If we begin to measure Mr. Hardy's novels by this standard, the necessity of uncompromising differentiation becomes apparent. He has written books in which we suspect him to be toying with his natural aptitude for inventing entanglements and hitches. Into this class fall *A Pair of Blue Eyes, A Laodicean, The Hand of Ethelberta*. The characters are unconvincing and the plot improbable. In later books, *The Well-Beloved* and *Jude the Obscure*, widely sundered as they are in intention, we begin with abstract ideas, and the story is written to clothe their metaphysical nakedness. *Jude the Obscure* is the story of a hero of tragedy commonly to be found in the philosophical writings of rationalists, and known as 'Circumstance-over-which-we-have-no-control'. Five novels, in which the author keeps himself to life on the soil of Wessex, stand in a distinctive place above Mr. Hardy's other books; they are, *Far from the Madding Crowd, The Return of the Native, The Mayor of Casterbridge, The Woodlanders* and *Tess of the D'Urbervilles*. Besides these are the volumes of short stories in which he is eminently successful, and *The*

Trumpet Major, a delightful Wessex tale, showing, however, less power than the greater novels.

Mr. Hardy is to be judged by the five novels distinctively named. The *motif* in each case, when disentangled, exhibits a strong similarity; but we are not conscious of it till we return upon our track in the mood of analysis and criticism. The type of hero chosen is the strong, patient, thoughtful and upright man belonging to the soil; he is better than the ignorant labourers and yokels about him, but neither in knowledge nor in intellectual powers does he reach to more than a very moderate standard. He is commonly brought into contact with a woman slightly his superior in culture and quickness of mind; but the type varies, and there may be more than one woman. Against the principal figures are set, on one side, country people and labourers, and, on the other, men and women of a higher social rank, whose artificiality contrasts weakly with the simpler natures of the people of the soil. But in the last point something certainly can be attributed to the author's comparative awkwardness when he gets away from his country folk. In *Tess of the D'Urbervilles* the plan is virtually reversed, and we read the tragic issue of a conflict of character between an untutored village girl and men who are her superiors in the social scale and in knowledge of the world.

The Woodlanders approximates most fully to the outlines of this sketch. Here we see two worlds of thought and feeling opposed to each other. Felice Charmond and Dr. Fitzpiers stand on one side as gentle-folk; on the other side are Marty South and Giles Winterborne as types of peasantry; and Grace Melbury, the daughter of simple country people, whose natural self has been blunted by an expensive education, links the two extremes. An able critic of Mr. Hardy's work has anim-adverted upon what he regards as the incongruous nature of this con-trast. He declares that the author achieves a positively irritating result in the combination of 'a matchless story of rustic life with this inferior work'. And he adds:

It produces the effect of a Millet inserting into the foreground of a masterpiece, such as *Les Glaneuses*, the figures of an actress and a physician, painted in some fashionable style of portraiture. The required contrast between the primitive ways of the woodlanders and the manners of the modern world might surely have been obtained by more simple means?[1]

He does not indicate the method he would prefer, and the less hypercritical reader may rest content in believing that Mr. Hardy has

[1] *Quarterly Review*, April, 1904. (No. 68 in this volume.—editor)

employed the only means possible of reaching the desired contrast—
that of bringing the two worlds into contact. And the analogy with
Millet's great picture is worse than meaningless; it is to confuse the
totally different aims of two arts. It is the business of a painter to
enshrine the visual emotion of a moment; it is the business of imaginative writing to exhibit moving incident and the clash of character.
Minor details in the plot of *The Woodlanders* may be improbable; we
do not say they are; but in its striking picture of the sundered paths of
natural men and women and the artificial world of modern civilization
the book does *not* fail.

Giles Winterborne is Mr. Hardy's true and humble man of heart for
whom circumstance is too strong. The tragedy of his life lies in his love
for Grace Melbury, the woman who has been placed out of harmony
with the rustic simplicity of her home surroundings by a high-school
education. The thin veneer of an unsuitable education blinds her to the
simple worth of the great-hearted man who loves her, and she marries
an expansive, conceited, irritating young country doctor. He is soon
faithless to her; and the marriage drifts into disaster, only to be miserably patched up again. Though Grace Melbury has passed him over,
Winterborne suffers exposure for her sake which results in his death.
Yet the memory of his self-sacrifice soon slips from her; and it is Marty
South, the hard-working, poverty-ridden cottage girl, who has loved
Winterborne hopelessly while a less worthy woman stands between,
who comes every week to lay fresh flowers on his grave. And we
realize that this girl standing there in the moonlight, 'the marks of
poverty and toil effaced by the misty hour, . . . touched sublimity at
points, and looked almost like a being who had rejected with indifference the attribute of sex for the loftier quality of abstract humanism'.
The unbefriended, toil-worn peasant girl whispers to the green sod
which covers the man she loved:

Whenever I get up I'll think of 'ee, and whenever I lie down I'll think of 'ee.
Whenever I plant the young larches I'll think that none can plant as you planted;
and whenever I split a gad, and whenever I turn the cider wring, I'll say none
could do it like you. If ever I forget your name let me forget home and heaven!
. . . But no, no, my love, I never can forget 'ee; for you was a good man, and
did good things!

She recounts his deeds—they belong to the narrow round of labouring life which they both knew—the planting of cuttings, the splitting
of gads, the turning of a cider press; for his skill in these and for himself

she loved him unutterably and forever. *The Woodlanders* closes on a great note which thrills the imagination with the poetry of an emotional truth to life. And in the gallery of noble women who adorn the pages of English fiction, from Clarissa Harlowe, Amelia and Jeanie Deans to the women of Meredith, Marty South claims her rightful place.

In differing terms the tragedy of *The Woodlanders* is the tragedy of Mr. Hardy's other novels. In the phrase Grammer Oliver borrows, we realize that 'no man's hands could help what they did, any more than the hands of a clock'. It is useless to quarrel with a writer because he is a determinist, and we may happen to hold a belief in the freedom of the will, which we justify to ourselves, either not at all, or after the manner of Locke, Bergson, or any other thinker who has given himself to the solution of a problem that can never be laid. This question, like many others, has nothing to do with our judgment of imaginative writing. If it had, there is ground enough for the battle in Shakespeare, and the question of its relation to great art may be fought out there, before it is carried further. With the vast majority of people the answer must always remain a matter of temperament and nothing more. But few writers have suffered more narrow-minded disparagement on this score than Mr. Hardy. In the region of artistic and literary criticism the whole question exists, only to be dismissed to its proper place—the philosopher's study. On the other hand, Mr. Hardy's power, which none can deny him, is not a little owing to what may appear to some readers his inability to see that, despite the harsh ironies of circumstances,

> ... thought and faith are mightier things than time
> Can wrong,
> Made splendid once by speech, or made sublime
> By song.

To say that he does not perceive this would be unjust; love and faith triumph over the wrongs of time in the concluding passage of *The Woodlanders*. But the habitual mood of his narrative tends to hide from sight the 'immarcescible crown' of life's failures. Heartless treachery betrays Fanny Robin to a miserable death in the workhouse; Michael Henchard's decline is a picture of unrelieved gloom; and the tragedy of Tess, if it seem to mortals 'a lamentation and an ancient tale of wrong', is only as sport to the Immortals.

The five prose tragedies of Wessex life reach their culmination in *Tess of the D'Urbervilles*. Few English novels written within the last forty years are better known than this: it has called forth an almost equal measure of admiration for the power and beauty of its writing and of vituperation from people who are troubled with the complaint of seeing harm in things. The clear issue of *Tess* is merely one more treatment in terms of art of a question as old as the Book of Job; it enters into Goethe's *Faust*, it underlies the narrative of *Clarissa*; and if the solution be as far from us as ever, it is improbable that the question has now been asked for the last time. The exact distribution of justice is undeniably not as apparent in the world of actual things as some would have it; and in the 'crash of broken commandments' it is not always the most guilty who suffer. The problem is not merely one of speculative interest: it has wide ethical implications. An intelligent reading of *Tess* reveals Mr. Hardy in an unexpectedly conventional light as a moralist; and the failure of the many to see this is a little difficult to understand. The conviction Angel Clare finally reaches, that 'The beauty or ugliness of a character lay not only in its achievements, but in its aims and impulses; its true history lay, not among things done, but among things willed', is surely a very moderate commonplace, even in the pulpit.

But *Tess* as a work of art is a greater thing than the same book as a criticism of ethical anomalies. Its worst faults lie in the author's obvious didacticism, which hurries him into digression and a loss of hold upon that gift of design and composition which commonly distinguishes his work. Conflict of character is dramatically conceived and dramatically executed. Tess herself must always remain an enduring figure in English fiction. The book is instinct with a fine and austere sense of poetry. In its painting of natural scenery it falls not a whit behind *The Woodlanders* and *The Return of the Native*. And there is nothing in these novels to rival the exquisite beauty of those passages in *Tess* which describe the silent loveliness of the morning and evening hours, when the shadows and lights hover and pass across the rich meadows surrounding Crick's dairy-farm. Nor can anything in Mr. Hardy's work surpass the power with which he describes Nature in her sterner aspects in the tale of Tess's toiling life on the bare chalk-lands of Flintcomb-Ash.

To return to an earlier statement—if we are to judge the place of Mr. Hardy as a writer of fiction, it is by his five greater novels. In these our imagination is intimately affined with the experience of peasant men and women; and we read in the story of their lives the inevitable event of the clash of character with character. There is a logical precision and exactitude in the treatment of character; the author is imbued with a scientific and analytic temper; but life is for him the primary art. The development of incident is not clever design; it is the unavoidable outcome of situation and character. In few novels indeed does the narrative read as an inexorable transcript. The character-study may be clever, the weaving of the plot ingenious, but very rarely are we made to feel an inherent and necessary relationship between the two. To bring the two together as the corresponding terms of a synthesis is the perfect work of the dramatist and novelist. A very general criticism of Mr. Hardy's novels is the improbability of their plot. But this is to judge him only by his secondary work—a manifest injustice.

And, once more, a town-bred criticism is sure to go astray when it walks the lanes of Wessex in a silk hat, lavender gloves, and frock-coat, and examines the lives of the people in the light of the newest fashion in ideas. Between the peasantry of Europe and the life of the cities there is a great gulf fixed. For example—in several very distinctive features the country folk have a well-understood code of morality ruling sex-relationship, which has long since been replaced by another standard in the world of modern civilization. In obedience to this older code Jude Fawley unquestioningly marries Arabella Donn. And this is only a single instance of differences of thought which extend to all the issues of life. In the standards by which conduct is judged, in the measure by which life's meaning is estimated, in the rules which guide action, the mind of the labourer on the soil has a wholly different content to that of his more sophisticated fellow in the cities. And the drift of the narrative in Mr. Hardy's Wessex novels is guided by the knowledge of an older and more primitive way of looking at things, which is often lost upon the city-bred reader.

Herein lies a secondary value of these novels. The older agricultural life dies hard; and even in England there are still large tracts of country, notably in the southwest, where large cities there are virtually none, almost untouched by the desolating influences of the great industrial centres. Yet, even here, life is not what it was to the middle of the last century. The Wessex of Mr. Hardy is 'a modern Wessex of railways, the penny post, mowing and reaping machines'. But by birth and ancestral associations he belongs to the soil and land which he describes; his writing is instinct with these associations, bred in the physical fibre and in the imagination. In the Wessex novels the older ways, the older thought, the old wisdom, speech, and humour are reflected by a master mind.

SATIRES OF CIRCUMSTANCE

November 1914

76. Lytton Strachey, *New Statesman*

19 December 1914

Giles Lytton Strachey (1880–1932) had not at this date attained his later reputation as a biographer, but had written on French literature. This review was reprinted in the posthumous *Characters and Commentaries* (1933).

Mr. Hardy's new volume of poems is a very interesting, and in some ways a baffling book, which may be recommended particularly to aesthetic theorists and to those dogmatic persons who, ever since the days of Confucius, have laid down definitions upon the function and nature of poetry. The dictum of Confucius is less well known than it ought to be. 'Read poetry, oh my children!' he said, 'for it will teach you the divine truths of filial affection, patriotism, and natural history.' Here the Chinese sage expressed, with the engaging frankness of his nation, a view of poetry implicitly held by that long succession of earnest critics for whom the real justification of any work of art lies in the edifying nature of the lessons which it instils. Such generalizations upon poetry would be more satisfactory if it were not for the poets. One can never make sure of that inconvenient and unreliable race. The remark of Confucius, for instance, which, one feels, must have been written with a prophetic eye upon the works of Wordsworth, seems absurdly inapplicable to the works of Keats. Then there is Milton's famous 'simple, sensuous, and passionate' test—a test which serves admirably for Keats, but which seems in an odd way to exclude the complicated style, the severe temper, and the remote imaginations of Milton himself. Yet another school insists upon the necessity of a certain technical accomplishment; beauty is for them, as it was—in a

435

somewhat different connection—for Herbert Spencer, a '*sine quâ non*'. Harmony of sound, mastery of rhythm, the exact and exquisite employment of words—in these things, they declare, lies the very soul of poetry, and without them the noblest thoughts and the finest feelings will never rise above the level of tolerable verse. This is the theory which Mr. Hardy's volume seems especially designed to disprove. It is full of poetry; and yet it is also full of ugly and cumbrous expressions, clumsy metres, and flat, prosaic turns of speech. To take a few random examples, in the second of the following lines cacophony is incarnate:

> Dear ghost, in the past did you ever find
> Me one whom consequence influenced much?

A curious mixture of the contorted and the jog-trot appears in such a line as:

> And adumbrates too therewith our unexpected troublous case;

while a line like:

> And the daytime talk of the Roman investigations

rails along in the manner of an undistinguished phrase in prose. Even Mr. Hardy's grammar is not impeccable. He speaks of one,

> whom, anon,
> My great deeds done,
> Will be mine alway.

And his vocabulary, though in general it is rich and apt, has occasional significant lapses, as, for instance, in the elegy on Swinburne, where, in the middle of a passage deliberately tuned to a pitch of lyrical resonance not to be found elsewhere in the volume, there occurs the horrid hybrid 'naïvely'—a neologism exactly calculated, one would suppose, to make the classic author of *Atalanta* turn in his grave.

It is important to observe such characteristics, because, in Mr. Hardy's case, they are not merely superficial and occasional blemishes; they are in reality an essential ingredient in the very essence of his work. The originality of his poetry lies in the fact that it bears everywhere upon it the impress of a master of prose fiction. Just as the great seventeenth-century writers of prose, such as Sir Thomas Browne and Jeremy Taylor, managed to fill their sentences with the splendour and passion of poetry, while still preserving the texture of an essentially prose style, so Mr. Hardy, by a contrary process, has brought the realism and sobriety of prose into the service of his poetry. The result is a product of a kind very difficult to parallel in our literature. Browning, no doubt, in his intimate and reflective moods—in *By the Fireside* or *Any Wife to Any Husband*—sometimes comes near it; but the full-blooded and romantic óptimism of Browning's temper offers a singular contrast to the repressed melancholy of Mr. Hardy's. Browning was too adventurous to be content for long with the plain facts of ordinary existence; he was far more at home with the curiosities and the excitements of life; but what gives Mr. Hardy's poems their unique flavour is precisely their utter lack of romanticism, their common, undecorated presentments of things. They are, in fact, modern as no other poems are. The author of *Jude the Obscure* speaks in them, but with the concentration, the intensity, the subtle disturbing force of poetry. And he speaks; he does not sing. Or rather, he talks—in the quiet voice of a modern man or woman, who finds it difficult, as modern men and women do, to put into words exactly what is in the mind. He is incorrect; but then how unreal and artificial a thing is correctness! He fumbles; but it is that very fumbling that brings him so near to ourselves. In that 'me one whom consequence influenced much', does not one seem to catch the very accent of hesitating and half-ironical affection? And in the drab rhythm of that 'daytime talk of the Roman investigations', does not all the dreariness of long hours of boredom lie compressed? And who does not feel the perplexity, the discomfort, and the dim agitation in that clumsy collection of vocables —'And adumbrates too therewith our unexpected troublous case'? What a relief such uncertainties and inexpressivenesses are after the delicate exactitudes of our more polished poets! And how mysterious and potent are the forces of inspiration and sincerity! All the taste, all the scholarship, all the art of the Poet Laureate seem only to end in something that is admirable, perhaps, something that is wonderful, but something that is irremediably remote and cold; while the flat, undistinguished poetry of Mr. Hardy has found out the secret of touching our marrow-bones.

It is not only in its style and feeling that this poetry reveals the novelist; it is also in its subject-matter. Many of the poems—and in particular the remarkable group of 'fifteen glimpses' which gives its title to the volume—consist of compressed dramatic narratives, of central episodes of passion and circumstance, depicted with extraordinary vividness. A flashlight is turned for a moment upon some scene or upon some character, and in that moment the tragedies of

437

whole lives and the long fatalities of human relationships seem to stand revealed:

> My stick! he says, and turns in the lane
> To the house just left, whence a vixen voice
> Comes out with the firelight through the pane,
> And he sees within that the girl of his choice
> Stands rating her mother with eyes aglare
> For something said while he was there.
>
> 'At last I behold her soul undraped!'
> Thinks the man who had loved her more than himself . . .

It is easy to imagine the scene as the turning-point in a realistic psychological novel; and, indeed, a novelist in want of plots or incidents might well be tempted to appropriate some of the marvellously pregnant suggestions with which this book is crowded. Among these sketches the longest and most elaborate is the *Conversation at Dawn*, which contains in its few pages the matter of an entire novel—a remorseless and terrible novel of modern life. Perhaps the most gruesome is *At the Draper's*, in which a dying man tells his wife how he saw her in a shop, unperceived:

> You were viewing some lovely things. '*Soon required*
> *For a widow, of latest fashion*';
> And I knew 'twould upset you to meet the man
> Who had to be cold and ashen
>
> And screwed in a box before they could dress you
> '*In the last new note of mourning*,'
> As they defined it. So, not to distress you,
> I left you to your adorning.

As these extracts indicate, the prevailing mood in this volume—as in Mr. Hardy's later novels—is not a cheerful one. And, in the more reflective and personal pieces, the melancholy is if anything yet more intense. It is the melancholy of regretful recollection, of bitter speculation, of immortal longings unsatisfied; it is the melancholy of one who has suffered, in Gibbon's poignant phrase, 'the abridgment of hope'. Mortality, and the cruelties of time, and the ironic irrevocability of things—these are the themes upon which Mr. Hardy has chosen to weave his grave and moving variations. If there is joy in these pages, it is joy that is long since dead; and if there are smiles, they are sardonical. The sentimentalist will find very little comfort among them.

438

Sometimes, perhaps, his hopes will rise a little—for the sentimentalist
is a hopeful creature; but they will soon be dashed. 'Who is digging on
my grave?' asks the dead woman, who has been forgotten by her lover
and her kinsfolk and even her enemy; since it is none of these, who can
it be?

> O it is I, my mistress dear,
> Your little dog, who still lives near,
> And much I hope my movements here
> Have not disturbed your rest.

'Ah, yes!' murmurs the ghost:

> *You* dig upon my grave . . .
> Why flashed it not on me
> That one true heart was left behind?
> What feeling do we ever find
> To equal among human kind
> A dog's fidelity?

And so, with this comforting conclusion, the poem might have ended.
But that is not Mr. Hardy's way.

'Mistress,' comes the reply:

> I dug upon your grave
> To bury a bone, in case
> I should be hungry near this spot
> When passing on my daily trot,
> I am sorry, but I quite forgot
> It was your resting-place.

That is all; the desolation is complete. And the gloom is not even
relieved by a little elegance of diction.

77. Laurence Binyon, *Bookman*

February 1915, xlvii, 143–4

Laurence Binyon (1869–1943) wrote as himself a poet of classiciz-
ing tendencies.

> What of the faith and fire within us,
> Men who march away,
> Ere the barn-cocks say,
> Night is growing grey?

We cannot but be glad that the lines, which we read in *The Times* a
month after the war began, came in time to close, as a 'postscript', Mr.
Hardy's last volume of poems. For their grave, haunting strain seems
to well from a deeper, less conscious spring in the poet's mind, and the
feeling with which they are full breathes a music into them which we
often miss in his verse.

What is it sets a poet singing? The surcharge of emotion which
issues in a lyric may spring from despair as well as joy, though with the
outflow into music a kind of joy will come. The dejection in the
thought of the lines that Shelley wrote on the sands near Naples could
not cloud the radiance of the images that gathered in his speech, or
check the melodious vehemence of his utterance; we feel that the
impulse behind the lyric was something profounder than the ostensible
stimulus. So one may perhaps wonder why Mr. Hardy, with his
ingrained bleak convictions about life and the universe, should feel
impelled to express himself in lyric form at all. What is the source of
that energy which urges him to shape stanza after stanza of careful
workmanship, marvels sometimes of concentrated effort, when the
master-thoughts within them press out at the end so bitter a drop?
Doubtless all deep sincerity has its own exuberance; its will is to
expression; and Mr. Hardy is nothing if not sincere. We could wish,
indeed, for poetry's sake, that he were less wholly consistent, that his
moods were more variable. It seems as if he could rarely surrender
himself to the moment's absorbing emotion; the steady conviction of
life's irony and pain is always there to dye the emotion with its tinge

of rueful colour. Only now and again, as in that marching song, the sense of the goodness of effort in a cause gives an unwonted kindling to the verse; or the poignant illumination of memory, bringing back hours of joy and youth and laughter, and glorifying remembered haunts and places by 'the wandering western sea', thrillingly vibrates through a cluster of little poems, deeply personal, which are intense with loss. Mr. Hardy is an artist, and has the artist's vivid sensitiveness to the inexhaustible beauties of earth and sky, in stable form and changeful colour; but he has also the artist's deeper power, the shaping instinct. And if we would understand these poems of a great artist's old age, we should perhaps refrain from asking why he seems so insistently, as with a morbid absorption in the theme, to harp on that familiar note of the implanted crookedness of things and the inbred malignity of chance. For most artists are haunted by some theme which it is their passion to express, and with the expression of which they are never satisfied. Painters are haunted by a type: and a Watteau or a Rossetti will spend themselves in drawing, over and over again, the same woman, whose last eluding charm seems ever to escape them, for all their weariless research in line and curve of neck and cheek and brow. *Life's Little Ironies, Time's Laughing-stocks, Satires of Circumstance*—the titles Mr. Hardy has chosen for tales or poems indicate the theme for which he seems to be always seeking to find the ultimate, most crystallized expression. In the group of poems which give their name to this volume he tries a severer condensation than any form yet found. Compared with the novels, they have the effect of little, deeply-bitten etchings beside large, elaborate paintings. The circumstances are various, the satire is the same. It is the satire, silent but profound, which the student of Bradshaw sometimes feels impelled to attribute to our railway-system, when planning a cross-country journey and finding the most admirable trains timed to miss the indispensable connection by just five minutes. In Mr. Hardy's world all the trains, one would think, are so timed. Or (to continue the image) it is just when the train has irrevocably started that the passenger realizes that close to him is the vision of his heart's desire, the face and the form that call to him out of all the world, the 'immer-geliebte', the 'längst-verlorene',—only she looks from the window of a carriage that is being borne away on the other line of rails, swiftly and irrevocably out of sight and reach. Yet there is nothing here of Heine's romantic sentiment with its sudden recoiling mockery; nor anything like Swift's 'saeva indignatio'; it is rather the artist impersonally striving to mould his haunting theme into this shape or to that, with the utmost suppression of irrelevance and ornament, the utmost economy of condensation. What reader of the Wessex novels has not noted their author's steady passion for the precise, the real epithet, at whatever sacrifice of superficial beauties of style? That long discipline in research of language persists in Mr. Hardy's verse. He is never seduced by sound; firm delineation, even in the shades and subtleties of feeling, is for him essential. The result is sometimes disconcerting; the mechanism of a stanza creaks and groans with the pressure of its working. There is something incongruous between the prosaic plainness of the speech and the tight structure of rather elaborate lyric form to which it is trimmed. The long 'Conversation at Dawn' is a case in point. It is interesting to all of us who are admirers of Mr. Hardy's genius to watch him at such work; but it is hard to see the gain of a metre for such matters. This is not one of the *Satires*, which are all short and pointed. And if some of this group of fifteen poems have a similar lack of inevitable form, a few are equally typical and masterly of their kind. Perhaps the most memorable is the last, 'In the Moonlight', where a lonely workman stands and stares as in a dream at a grave, as if he would raise the soul of her who lay within it.

> 'Ah—she was the one you loved, no doubt,
> Through good and evil, through rain and drought,
> And when she passed, all your sun went out.'
> 'Nay: she was the woman I did not love,
> Whom all the others were ranked above,
> Whom during her life I thought nothing of.'

It is as if Giles Winterborne had lived to gaze on the grave of Marty South. We are reminded of the novels again in the little piece, 'Seen by the Waits', where a moonlit glimpse is caught of the 'lonely manor-lady' airily dancing to the music in her room, thinking herself unseen—dancing for joy because news has come that her 'roving husband' is dead. But in this, and far more in some other pieces, we are jarred by what seems a kind of callousness. Probably we should not feel this if Mr. Hardy had more of the singing-note of a Burns, a Heine, a Poe, whose music by its victorious energy can carry the horrible and ugly from the world of fact into the world of idea. Mr. Hardy's *macabre* stories are told so evenly and bluntly that we cannot bear that he should be so calm, and feel revolted. Horror, to be tolerable, needs a strong excitement; when we are in the thrilled state, the art that has played on our pulses can make its own joy of it. Mr. Hardy is not of 'the tribe that feel in melodies', and we must take his art as it is. He will not relieve us by sheer beauty; but, oddly enough, some of these charnel pieces of which he is so fond procure us the relief of laughter. This at least is the effect of the singular little dialogue between the dead woman and the dog which scratches at her grave. Disappointed of her first fancy that it was her husband, or at least her kinsfolk, planting flowers there, she consoles her poor heart with the thought that her little dog at least was true to her; and is thus answered:

> Mistress, I dug upon your grave
> To bury a bone, in case
> I should be hungry near this spot,
> When passing on my daily trot.
> I am sorry, but I quite forgot
> It was your resting-place.

Surely the comic triumphs here over the bitter and the grim!

But we should be unjust to Mr. Hardy if we did not recognize the tenderness that is very deep in the texture of his art, though it is as little obtruded as the courage of his outlook on this so bungled planet. How typical of him is the care for the 'hurt, misrepresented names', to which history does no justice! He is haunted by the ghosts of these 'spectres that grieve'. One of the best poems in the book, a longish piece of admirable and easy narrative, 'The Abbey Mason', is inspired by the same motive; it has an unwonted mellowness of tone. But still more intimately characteristic is the 'Roman Graveyards'. The poet watches a man with a spade and basket going to dig among 'Rome's dim relics'; and he supposes him an antiquary, whose mind is filled with that Roman vastness still so towering in our imagination. But no, it is his little white cat that he is going to bury; the 'small furred life' is more to him than all the glories of the Caesars. And the mourner's mood 'has a charm' for Mr. Hardy.

78. Edmund Gosse, 'Mr. Hardy's Lyrical Poems', *Edinburgh Review*

April 1918, ccvii, 272

(See headnote to No. 34.)

When, about Christmas time in 1898, Mr. Hardy's admirers, who were expecting from him a new novel, received instead a thick volume of verse, there was mingled with their sympathy and respect a little disappointment and a great failure in apprehension. Those who were not rude enough to suggest that a cobbler should stick to his last, reminded one another that many novelists had sought relaxation by trifling with the Muses. Thackeray had published *Ballads*, and George Eliot had expatiated in a *Legend of Jubal*. No one thought the worse of *Coningsby* because its author had produced a *Revolutionary Epic*. It took some time for even intelligent criticism to see that the new *Wessex Poems* did not fall into this accidental category, and still, after twenty years, there survives a tendency to take the verse of Mr. Hardy, abundant and solid as it has become, as a mere subsidiary and ornamental appendage to his novels. It is still necessary to insist on the complete independence of his career as a poet, and to point out that if he had never published a page of prose he would deserve to rank high among the writers of his country on the score of the eight volumes of his verse. It is as a lyrical poet, and solely as a lyrical poet, that we propose to speak of him to-day.

It has been thought extraordinary that Cowper was over fifty when he published his first secular verses, but Mr. Hardy was approaching his sixtieth year when he sent *Wessex Poems* to the press. Such self-restraint —'none hath by more studious ways endeavoured, and with more unwearied spirit none shall'—has always fascinated the genuine artist, but few have practised it with so much tenacity. When the work of Mr. Hardy is completed, nothing, it is probable, will more strike posterity than its unity, its consistency. He has given proof, as scarce any other modern writer has done, of tireless constancy of resolve. His novels formed an unbroken series from the *Desperate Remedies* of 1871 to *The Well-Beloved* of 1897. In the fullness of his success, and unseduced by all temptation, he closed that chapter of his career, and has kept it closed. Since 1898 he has been, persistently and periodically, a poet and nothing else. That he determined, for reasons best left to his own judgment, to defer the exhibition of his verse until he had completed his work in prose, ought not to prejudice criticism in its analysis of the lyrics and the colossal dramatic panorama. Mr. Hardy, exclusively as a poet, demands our undivided attention.

It is legitimate to speculate on other probable causes of Mr. Hardy's delay. From such information as lies scattered before us, we gather that it was from 1865 to 1867 that he originally took poetry to be his vocation. The dated pieces in the volume of 1898 help us to form an idea of the original character of his utterance. On the whole it was very much what it remains in the pieces composed after a lapse of half a century. Already, as a very young man, Mr. Hardy possessed his extraordinary insight into the movements of human character, and his eloquence in translating what he had observed of the tragedy and pain of rustic lives. No one, for sixty years, had taken so closely to heart the admonitions of Wordsworth in his famous Preface to the 1800 edition of *Lyrical Ballads* to seek for inspiration in that condition where 'the passions of men are incorporated with the beautiful forms of nature'. But it may well be doubted whether his poems would have been received in the mid-Victorian age with favour, or even have been comprehended. Fifty years ahead of his time, Mr. Hardy was asking in 1866 for novelty of ideas, and he must have been conscious that his questioning would seem inopportune. He needed a different atmosphere, and he left the task of revolt to another, and, at first sight, a very unrelated force, that of the *Poems and Ballads* of the same year. But Swinburne succeeded in his revolution, and although he approached the art from an opposite direction, he prepared the way for an ultimate appreciation of Mr. Hardy.

We should therefore regard the latter, in spite of his silence of forty years, as a poet who laboured, like Swinburne, at a revolution against the optimism and superficial sweetness of his age. Swinburne, it is true, tended to accentuate the poetic side of poetry, while Mr. Hardy drew verse, in some verbal respects, nearer to prose. This does not affect their common attitude, and the sympathy of these great artists for one another's work has already been revealed, and will be still more clearly exposed. But they were unknown to each other in 1866, when to both of them the cheap philosophy of the moment, the glittering femininity of the 'jewelled line', the intense respect for Mrs. Grundy in her Sunday satin, appeared trumpery, hateful, and to be trampled upon. We find in Mr. Hardy's earliest verse no echo of the passionate belief in personal immortality which was professed by Ruskin and Browning. He opposed the Victorian theory of human 'progress'; the Tennysonian beatific Vision seemed to him ridiculous. He rejected the idea of the sympathy and goodness of Nature, and was in revolt against the self-centredness of the Romantics. We may conjecture that he combined a great reverence for 'The Book of Job' with a considerable contempt for *In Memoriam*.

This was not a mere rebellious fancy which passed off; it was something inherent that remained, and gives today their peculiar character to Mr. Hardy's latest lyrics. But before we examine the features of this personal mode of interpreting poetry to the world, we may collect what little light we can on the historic development of it. In the pieces dated between 1865 and 1867 we find the germ of almost everything which has since characterized the poet. In 'Amabel' the ruinous passage of years, which has continued to be an obsession with Mr. Hardy, is already crudely dealt with. The habit of taking poetical negatives of small scenes—'your face, and the God-curst sun, and a tree, and a pond edged with grayish leaves' ('Neutral Tones')—which had not existed in English verse since the days of Crabbe, reappears. There is marked already a sense of terror and resentment against the blind motions of chance—in 'Hap' the author would positively welcome a certainty of divine hatred as a relief from the strain of depending upon 'crass casualty'. Here and there in these earliest pieces an extreme difficulty of utterance is remarkable in the face of the ease which the poet attained afterwards in the expression of his most strange images and fantastic revelations. We read in 'At a Bridal':

> Should I, too, wed as slave to Mode's decree,
> And each thus found apart, of false desire
> A stolid line, whom no high aims will fire
> As had fired ours could ever have mingled we!

This, although perfectly reducible, takes time to think out, and at a hasty glance seems muffled up in obscurity beyond the darkness of Donne; moreover, it is scarcely worthy in form of the virtuoso which Mr. Hardy was presently to become. Perhaps of the poems certainly attributable to this earliest period, the little cycle of sonnets called 'She

to Him' gives clearest promise of what was coming. The sentiment is
that of Ronsard's famous 'Quand vous serez bien vieille, au soir, à la
chandelle', but turned round, as Mr. Hardy loves to do, from the man
to the woman, and embroidered with ingenuities, such as where the
latter says that as her temperament dies down the habit of loving will
remain, and she be

> Numb as a vane that cankers on its point,
> True to the wind that kissed ere canker came,

which attest a complexity of mind that Ronsard's society knew nothing
of.

On the whole, we may perhaps be safe in conjecturing that, whatever
the cause, the definite dedication to verse was now postponed. Meanwhile, the writing of novels had become the business of Mr. Hardy's
life, and ten years go by before we trace a poet in that life again. But
it is interesting to find that when the great success of *Far from the
Madding Crowd* had introduced him to a circle of the best readers, there
followed an effect which again disturbed his ambition for the moment.
Mr. Hardy was once more tempted to change the form of his work.
He wished 'to get back to verse', but was dissuaded by Leslie Stephen,
who induced him to start writing *The Return of the Native* instead. On
the 29th of March, 1875, Coventry Patmore, then a complete stranger,
wrote to express his regret that 'such almost unequalled beauty and
power as appeared in the novels should not have assured themselves
the immortality which would have been conferred upon them by the
form of verse'. This was just at the moment when we find Mr. Hardy's
conversations with 'long Leslie Stephen in the velveteen coat' obstin-
ately turning upon 'theologies decayed and defunct, the origin of
things, the constitution of matter, and the unreality of time'. To this
period belongs also the earliest conception of *The Dynasts*, an old note-
book containing, under the date 20 June 1875, the suggestion that the
author should attempt 'An Iliad of Europe from 1789 to 1815'.

To this time also seems to belong the execution of what has proved
the most attractive section of Mr. Hardy's poetry, the narratives, or
short Wessex ballads. The method in which these came into the world
is very curious. Many of these stories were jotted down to the extent
of a stanza or two when the subject first occurred to the author. For
instance, 'The Fire at Tranter Sweatley's', first published by Lionel
Johnson in 1894, had been begun as early as 1867, and was finished ten
years later. The long ballad of 'Leipzig' and the savage 'San Sebastian',

both highly characteristic, were also conceived and a few lines of each noted down long before their completion. 'Valenciennes', however, belongs to 1878, and the 'Dance at the Phoenix', of which the stanza beginning ' 'Twas Christmas' alone had been written years before, seems to have been finished about the same time. What evidence is before us goes to prove that in the 'seventies Mr. Hardy became a complete master of the art of verse, and that his poetic style was by this time fixed. He still kept poetry out of public sight, but he wrote during the next twenty years, as though in a backwater off the stream of his novels, the poems which form the greater part of the volume of 1898. If no other collection of his lyrical verse existed, we should miss a multitude of fine things, but our general conception of his genius would be little modified.

We should judge carelessly, however, if we treated the subsequent volumes as mere repetitions of the original *Wessex Poems*. They present interesting differences, which we may rapidly note before we touch on the features which characterize the whole body of Mr. Hardy's verse. *Poems of the Past and Present*, which came out in the first days of 1902, could not but be in a certain measure disappointing, in so far as it paralleled its three years' product with that of the thirty years of *Wessex Poems*. Old pieces were published in it, and it was obvious that in 1898 Mr. Hardy might be expected to have chosen from what used to be called his 'portfolio' those specimens which he thought to be most attractive. But on further inspection this did not prove to be quite the case. After pondering for twelve years on the era of Napoleon, his preoccupation began in 1887 to drive him into song:

> Must I pipe a palinody,
> Or be silent thereupon?

He decides that silence has become impossible:

> Nay; I'll sing 'The Bridge of Lodi'—
> That long-loved, romantic thing,
> Though none show by smile or nod, he
> Guesses why and what I sing!

Here is the germ of *The Dynasts*. But in the meantime the crisis of the Boer War had cut across the poet's dream of Europe a hundred years ago, and a group of records of the Dorsetshire elements of the British army at the close of 1899 showed us in Mr. Hardy's poetry what had not been suspected there—a military talent of a most remarkable kind.

Another set of pieces composed in Rome were not so interesting; Mr. Hardy always seems a little languid when he leaves the confines of his native Wessex. Another section of *Poems of the Past and Present* is severely, almost didactically, metaphysical, and expands in varied language the daring thought, so constantly present in Mr. Hardy's reverie, that God Himself has forgotten the existence of earth, this 'tiny sphere', this 'tainted ball', 'so poor a thing', and has left all human life to be the plaything of blind chance. This sad conviction is hardly ruffled by 'The Darkling Thrush', which goes as far towards optimism as Mr. Hardy can let himself be drawn, or by such reflections as those in 'On a Fine Morning':

> Whence comes Solace? Not from seeing
> What is doing, suffering, being;
> Not from noting Life's conditions,
> Not from heeding Time's monitions;
> But in cleaving to the Dream,
> And in gazing on the gleam
> Whereby gray things golden seem.

Eight years more passed, years marked by the stupendous effort of *The Dynasts*, before Mr. Hardy put forth another collection of lyrical poems. *Time's Laughingstocks* confirmed, and more than confirmed, the high promise of *Wessex Poems*. The author, in one of his modest prefaces, where he seems to whisper while we bend forward in our anxiety not to miss one thrifty sentence, expresses the hope that *Time's Laughingstocks* will, as a whole, take the 'reader forward, even if not far, rather than backward'. The book, indeed, does not take us 'far' forward, simply because the writer's style and scope were definitely exposed to us already, and yet it does take us 'forward', because the hand of the master is conspicuously firmer and his touch more daring. The *Laughingstocks* themselves are fifteen in number, tragical stories of division and isolation, of failures in passion, of the treason of physical decay. No landscape of Mr. Hardy's had been more vivid than the night-pictures in 'The Revisitation', where the old soldier in barracks creeps out on to the gaunt down, and meets (by one of Mr. Hardy's coincidences) his ancient mistress, and no picture more terrible than the revelation of each to the other in the blaze of sunrise. What a document for the future is 'Reminiscences of a Dancing Man'? If only Shakespeare could have left us such a song of the London of 1585! But the power of the poet culminates in the pathos of 'The Tramp Woman'—

perhaps the greatest of all Mr. Hardy's lyrical poems—and in the horror of 'A Sunday Morning's Tragedy'.

It is noticeable that *Time's Laughingstocks* is, in some respects, a more daring collection than its predecessors. We find the poet here entirely emancipated from convention, and guided both in religion and morals exclusively by the inner light of his reflection. His energy now interacts on his clairvoyançe with a completeness which he had never quite displayed before, and it is here that we find Mr. Hardy's utterance peculiarly a quintessence of himself. Especially in the narrative pieces—which are often Wessex novels distilled into a wine-glass, such as 'Rose-Ann' and 'The Vampirine Fair'—he allows no considerations of what the reader may think 'nice' or 'pleasant' to shackle his sincerity or his determination; and it is therefore to *Time's Laughingstocks* that the reader who wishes to become intimately acquainted with Mr. Hardy as a moralist most frequently recurs. We notice here more than elsewhere in his poems Mr. Hardy's sympathy with the local music of Wessex, and especially with its expression by the village choir, which he uses as a spiritual symbol. Quite a large section of *Time's Laughingstocks* takes us to the old-fashioned gallery of some church, where the minstrels are bowing 'New Sabbath' or 'Mount Ephraim', or to a later scene where the ghosts, in whose melancholy apparition Mr. Hardy takes such pleasure, chant their goblin melodies and strum 'the viols of the dead' in the moonlit churchyard. The very essence of Mr. Hardy's reverie at this moment of his career is to be found, for instance, in 'The Dead Quire', where the ancient phantom-minstrels revenge themselves on their gross grandsons outside the alehouse.

Almost immediately after the outbreak of the present war Mr. Hardy presented to a somewhat distraught and inattentive public another collection of his poems. It cannot be said that *Satires of Circumstance* is the most satisfactory of those volumes; it is, perhaps, that which we could with the least discomposure persuade ourselves to overlook. Such a statement refers more to the high quality of other pages than to any positive decay of power or finish here. There is no less adroitness of touch and penetration of view in this book than elsewhere, and the poet awakens once more our admiration by his skill in giving poetic value to minute conditions of life which have escaped less careful observers. But in *Satires of Circumstance* the ugliness of experience is more accentuated than it is elsewhere, and is flung in our face with less compunction. The pieces which give name to the volume are only fifteen in number, but the spirit which inspires them is very frequently repeated in other parts of the collection. That spirit is one of mocking sarcasm, and it acts in every case by presenting a beautifully draped figure of illusion, from which the poet, like a sardonic showman, twitches away the robe that he may display a skeleton beneath it.

We can with little danger assume, as we read the *Satires of Circumstance*, hard and cruel shafts of searchlight as they seem, that Mr. Hardy was passing through a mental crisis when he wrote them. This seems to be the *Troilus and Cressida* of his life's work, the book in which he is revealed most distracted by conjecture and most overwhelmed by the miscarriage of everything. The wells of human hope have been poisoned for him by some condition of which we know nothing, and even the picturesque features of Dorsetshire landscape, that have always before dispersed his melancholy, fail to win his attention:

> Bright yellowhammers
> Made mirthful clamours,
> And billed long straws with a bustling air,
> And bearing their load,
> Flew up the road
> That he followed alone, without interest there.

The strongest of the poems of disillusion which are the outcome of this mood is 'The Newcomer's Wife', with the terrible abruptness of its last stanza. It is not for criticism to find fault with the theme of a work of art, but only to comment upon its execution. Of the merit of these monotonously sinister *Satires of Circumstance* there can be no question; whether the poet's indulgence in the mood which gave birth to them does not tend to lower our moral temperature and to lessen the rebound of our energy is another matter. At all events, every one must welcome a postscript in which a blast on the bugle of war seemed to have wakened the poet from his dark brooding to the sense of a new chapter in history.

In the fourth year of the war the veteran poet has published *Moments of Vision*. These show a remarkable recovery of spirit, and an ingenuity never before excelled. With the passage of years Mr. Hardy, observing everything in the little world of Wessex, and forgetting nothing, has become almost preternaturally wise, and, if it may be said so, 'knowing,' with a sort of magic, like that of a wizard. He has learned to track the windings of the human heart with the familiarity of a gamekeeper who finds plenty of vermin in the woods, and who nails what he finds, be it stoat or squirrel, to the barn-door of his poetry. But there is also in these last-fruits of Mr. Hardy's mossed tree much that is wholly detached from the bitterness of satire, much that simply records, with an infinite delicacy of pathos, little incidents of the personal life of long ago, bestowing the immortality of art on these fugitive fancies in the spirit of the Japanese sculptor when he chisels the melting of a cloud or the flight of an insect on his sword-hilt:

> I idly cut a parsley stalk
> And blew therein towards the moon;
> I had not thought what ghosts would walk
> With shivering footsteps to my tune.
>
> I went and knelt, and scooped my hand
> As if to drink, into the brook,
> And a faint figure seemed to stand
> Above me, with the bye-gone look.
>
> I lipped rough rhymes of chance not choice,
> I thought not what my words might be;
> There came into my ear a voice
> That turned a tenderer verse for me.

We have now in brief historic survey marshalled before us the various volumes in which Mr. Hardy's lyrical poetry was originally collected. Before we examine its general character more closely, it may be well to call attention to its technical quality, which was singularly misunderstood at first, and which has never, we believe, been boldly faced. In 1898, and later, when a melodious *falsetto* was much in fashion amongst us, the reviewers found great fault with Mr. Hardy's prosody; they judged him as a versifier to be rude and incorrect. As regards the single line, it may be confessed that Mr. Hardy, in his anxiety to present his thought in an undiluted form, is not infrequently clogged and hard. Such a line as

Fused from its separateness by ecstasy

hisses at us like a snake, and crawls like a wounded one. Mr. Hardy is apt to clog his lines with consonants, and he seems indifferent to the stiffness which is the consequence of this neglect. Ben Jonson said that 'Donne, for not keeping of accent, deserved hanging'; perhaps we may go so far as to say that Mr. Hardy, for his indifference to a mellifluous run lays himself open to a mild rebuke. He is negligent of that eternal ornament of English verse, audible intricacy, probably because of

Swinburne's abuse of it. But most of what is called his harshness should rather be called bareness, and is the result of a revolt, conscious or unconscious, against Keats' prescription of 'loading the rifts with ore'.

In saying this we have said all that an enemy could in justice say in blame of his metrical peculiarities. Unquestionably he does occasionally, like Robert Browning, err in the direction of cacophony. But when we turn to the broader part of prosody we must perceive that Mr. Hardy is not only a very ingenious, but a very correct and admirable, metricist. His stanzaic invention is abundant; no other Victorian poet, not even Swinburne, has employed so many forms, mostly of his own invention, and employed them so appropriately, that is to say, in so close harmony with the subject or story enshrined in them. To take an example from his pure lyrics of reflection first, from 'The Bullfinches':

> Brother Bulleys, let us sing
> From the dawn till evening!
> For we know not that we go not
> When the day's pale visions fold
> Unto those who sang of old.

In the exquisite fineness and sadness of the stanza we seem to hear the very voices of the birds warbling faintly in the sunset. Again, the hurried, timid irresolution of a lover always too late is marvellously rendered in the form of 'Lizbie Browne':

> And Lizbie Browne,
> Who else had hair
> Bay-red as yours,
> Or flesh so fair
> Bred out of doors,
> Sweet Lizbie Browne?

On the other hand, the fierceness of 'I said to Love' is interpreted in a stanza, that suits the mood of denunciation, while 'Tess's Lament' wails in a metre which seems to rock like an ageing woman seated alone before the fire, with an infinite haunting sadness.

It is, however, in the narrative pieces, the little *Wessex Tales*, that Mr. Hardy's metrical imagination is most triumphant. No two of these are identical in form, and for each he selects, or more often invents, a wholly appropriate stanza. He makes many experiments, one of the strongest being the introduction of rhymeless lines at regular intervals. Of this, 'Cicely' is an example which repays attention:

> And still sadly onward I followed,
> That Highway the Icen
> Which trails its pale riband down Wessex
> O'er lynchet and lea.
>
> Along through the Stour-bordered Forum,
> Where legions had wayfared,
> And where the slow river up-glasses
> Its green canopy;

and one still more remarkable is the enchanting 'Friends Beyond', to which we shall presently recur. The drawling voice of a weary old campaigner is wonderfully rendered in the stanza of 'Valenciennes':

> Well: Heaven wi' its jasper halls
> Is now the on'y town I care to be in . . .
> Good Lord, if Nick should bomb the walls
> As we did Valencieën!

whereas for long Napoleonic stories like 'Leipzig' and 'The Peasant's Confession', a ballad-measure which contemporaries such as Southey or Campbell might have used, is artfully chosen. In striking contrast we have the elaborate verse-form of 'The Souls of the Slain', in which the throbbing stanza seems to dilate and withdraw like the very cloud of moth-like phantoms which it describes. It is difficult to follow out this theme without more frequent quotation than we have space for here, but the reader who pursues it carefully will not repeat the rumour that Mr. Hardy is a careless or 'incorrect' metricist. He is, on the contrary, a metrical artist of great accomplishment.

The conception of life revealed in his verses by this careful artist is one which displays very exactly the bent of his temperament. During the whole of his long career Mr. Hardy has not budged an inch from his original line of direction. He holds that, abandoned by God, treated with scorn by Nature, man lies helpless at the mercy of 'those purblind Doomsters', accident, chance, and time, from whom he had to endure injury and insult from the cradle to the grave. This is stating the Hardy doctrine in its extreme form, but it is not stating it too strongly. This has been called his 'pessimism', a phrase to which some admirers, unwilling to give things their true name, have objected. But, of course, Mr. Hardy is a pessimist, just as Browning is an optimist, just as white is not black, and day is not night. Our juggling with words in paradox is too often apt to disguise a want of decision in thought. Let us admit that Mr. Hardy's conception of the fatal forces which beleaguer human life is a 'pessimistic' one, or else words have no meaning.

Yet it is needful to define in what this pessimism consists. It is not the egotism of Byron or the morbid melancholy of Chateaubriand. It is directed towards an observation of others, not towards an analysis of self, and this gives it more philosophical importance, because although romantic peevishness is very common among modern poets, and although ennui inspires a multitude of sonnets, a deliberate and imaginative study of useless suffering in the world around us is rare indeed among the poets. It is particularly to be noted that Mr. Hardy, although one of the most profoundly tragic of all modern writers, is neither effeminate nor sickly. His melancholy could never have dictated the third stanza of Shelley's 'Lines written in Dejection in the Bay of Naples'. His pessimism is involuntary, forced from him by his experience and his constitution, and no analysis could give a better definition of what divides him from the petulant despair of a poet like Leopardi than the lines 'To Life':

> O life, with the sad scared face,
>   I weary of seeing thee,
> And thy draggled cloak, and thy hobbling pace,
>   And thy too-forced pleasantry!
>
> I know what thou would'st tell
>   Of Death, Time, Destiny—
> I have known it long, and know, too, well
>   What it all means for me.
>
> But canst thou not array
>   Thyself in rare disguise,
> And feign like truth, for one mad day,
>   That Earth is Paradise?
>
> I'll tune me to the mood,
>   And mumm with thee till eve,
> And maybe what as interlude
>   I feign, I shall believe!

But the mumming goes no deeper than it does in the exquisite poem of 'The Darkling Thrush', where the carolings of an aged bird, on a frosty evening, are so ecstatic that they waken a vague hope in the listener's mind that the thrush may possibly know of 'some blessed hope' of which the poet is 'unaware'. This is as far as Mr. Hardy ever gets on the blest Victorian pathway of satisfaction.

There are certain aspects in which it is not unnatural to see a parallel between Mr. Hardy and George Crabbe. Each is the spokesman of a district, each has a passion for the study of mankind, each has gained by long years of observation a profound knowledge of local human character, and each has plucked on the open moor, and wears in his coat, the hueless flower of disillusion. But there is a great distinction in the aim of the two poets. Crabbe, as he describes himself in *The Parish Register*, was 'the true physician' who 'walks the foulest ward'. He was utilitarian in his morality; he exposed the pathos of tragedy by dwelling on the faults which led to it, forgetful of the fatality which in more consistent moments he acknowledged. Crabbe was realistic with a moral design, even in the *Tales of the Hall*, where he made a gallant effort at last to arrive at a detachment of spirit. No such effort is needed by Mr. Hardy, who has none of the instinct of a preacher, and who considers moral improvement outside his responsibility. He admits, with his great French contemporary, that

> Tout désir est menteur, toute joie éphémère,
> Toute liqueur au fond de la coupe est amère,

but he is bent on discovering the cause of this devastation, and not disposed to waste time over its consequences. At the end he produces a panacea which neither Crabbe nor Byron dreamed of—resignation.

But the poet has not reached the end of his disillusion. He thinks to secure repose on the breast of Nature, the *alma mater* to whom Goethe and Wordsworth and Browning each in his own way turned, and were rewarded by consolation and refreshment. We should be prepared to find Mr. Hardy, with his remarkable aptitude for the perception of natural forms, easily consoled by the influences of landscape and the inanimate world. His range of vision is wide and extremely exact; he has the gift of reproducing before us scenes of various character with a vividness which is sometimes startling. But Mr. Hardy's disdain of sentimentality, and his vigorous analysis of the facts of life, render him insensible not indeed to the mystery nor to the beauty, but to the imagined sympathy, of Nature. He has no more confidence in the visible earth than in the invisible heavens, and neither here nor there is he able to persuade himself to discover a counsellor or a friend. In this connection we do well to follow the poet's train of thought in the lyric called 'In a Wood', where he enters a copse dreaming that, in that realm of 'sylvan peace', Nature would offer 'a soft release from man's unrest'. He immediately observes that the pine and the beech are struggling for existence, and trying to blight each other with dripping poison. He sees the ivy eager to strangle the elm, and the hawthorns choking the hollies. Even the poplars sulk and turn black under the shadow of a rival. In the end, filled with horror at all these crimes of Nature, the poet flees from the copse as from an accursed place, and he determines that life offers him no consolation except the company of those human beings who are as beleaguered as himself:

> Since, then, no grace I find
>   Taught me of trees,
> Turn I back to my kind
>   Worthy as these.
> There at least smiles abound,
> There discourse trills around,
> There, now and then, are found,
>   Life-loyalties.

It is absurd, he decides, to love Nature, which has either no response to give, or answers in irony. Let us even avoid, as much as we can, deep concentration of thought upon the mysteries of Nature, lest we become demoralized by contemplating her negligence, her blindness, her implacability. We find here a violent reaction against the poetry of egotistic optimism which had ruled the romantic school in England for more than a hundred years, and we recognize a branch of Mr. Hardy's originality. He has lifted the veil of Isis, and he finds beneath it, not a benevolent mother of men, but the tomb of an illusion. One short lyric, 'Yell'ham-Wood's Story', puts this, again with a sylvan setting, in its unflinching crudity:

> Coomb-Firtrees say that Life is a moan,
>   And Clyffe-hill Clump says 'Yea!'
> But Yell'ham says a thing of its own:
>   It's not, 'Gray, gray,
>   Is Life alway!'
>   That Yell'ham says,
> Nor that Life is for ends unknown.
>
> It says that Life would signify
>   A thwarted purposing:
> That we come to live, and are called to die.

> Yes, that's the thing
> In fall, in spring,
> That Yell'ham says:—
> 'Life offers—to deny!'

It is therefore almost exclusively to the obscure history of those who suffer and stumble around him, victims of the universal disillusion, men and women 'come to live but called to die', that Mr. Hardy dedicates his poetic function. 'Lizbie Browne' appeals to us as a typical instance of his rustic pathos, his direct and poignant tenderness, and if we compare it with such poems of Wordsworth's as 'Lucy Gray' or 'Alice Fell' we see that he starts by standing much closer to the level of the subject than his great predecessor does. Wordsworth is the benevolent philosopher sitting in a post-chaise or crossing the 'wide moor' in meditation. Mr. Hardy is the familiar neighbour, the shy mourner at the grave; his relation is a more intimate one: he is patient, humble, un-upbraiding. Sometimes, as in the remarkable colloquy called 'The Ruined Maid', his sympathy is so close as to offer an absolute flout in the face to the system of Victorian morality. Mr. Hardy, indeed, is not concerned with sentimental morals, but with the primitive instincts of the soul, applauding them, or at least recording them with complacency, even when they outrage ethical tradition, as they do in the lyric narrative called 'A wife and Another'. The stanzas 'To an Unborn Pauper Child' sum up what is sinister and what is genial in Mr. Hardy's attitude to the unambitious forms of life which he loves to contemplate.

His temperature is not always so low as it is in the class of poems to which we have just referred but his ultimate view is never more sanguine. He is pleased sometimes to act as the fiddler at a dance, surveying the hot-blooded couples, and urging them on by the lilt of his instrument, but he is always perfectly aware that they will have 'to pay high for their prancing' at the end of all. No instance of this is more remarkable than the poem called 'Julie-Jane', a perfect example of Mr. Hardy's metrical ingenuity and skill, which begins thus:

> Sing; how 'a would sing!
> How 'a would raise the tune
> When we rode in the waggon from harvesting
> By the light o' the moon!
>
> Dance; how 'a would dance!
> If a fiddlestring did but sound

> She would hold out her coats, give a slanting glance,
> And go round and round.

> Laugh; how 'a would laugh!
> Her peony lips would part
> As if none such a place for a lover to quaff
> At the deeps of a heart,

and which then turns to the most plaintive and the most irreparable tragedy, woven, as a black design on to a background of gold, upon this basis of temperamental joyousness.

Alphonse Daudet once said that the great gift of Edmond de Goncourt was to *'rendre l'irrendable'*. This is much more true of Mr. Hardy than it was of Goncourt, and more true than it is of any other English poet except Donne. There is absolutely no observation too minute, no flutter of reminiscence too faint, for Mr. Hardy to adopt as the subject of a metaphysical lyric, and his skill in this direction has grown upon him; it is nowhere so remarkable as in his latest volume, aptly termed *Moments of Vision*. Everything in village life is grist to his mill; he seems to make no selection, and his field is modest to humility and yet practically boundless. We have a poem on the attitude of two people with nothing to do and no book to read, waiting in the parlour of an hotel for the rain to stop, a recollection after more than forty years. That the poet once dropped a pencil into the cranny of an old church where he was sketching inspires an elaborate lyric. The disappearance of a rotted summer-house, the look of a row of silver drops of fog condensed on the bar of a gate, the effect of candlelight years and years ago on a woman's neck and hair, the vision of a giant at a fair, led by a dwarf with a red string—such are amongst the subjects which awaken in Mr. Hardy thoughts which do often lie too deep for tears, and call for interpretation in verse. The skeleton of a lady's sunshade, picked up on Swanage Cliffs, the pages of a fly-blown Testament lying in a railway waiting-room, a journeying boy in a third-class carriage, with his ticket stuck in the band of his hat—such are among the themes which awake in Mr. Hardy's imagination reveries which are always wholly serious and usually deeply tragic.

Mr. Hardy's notation of human touches hitherto excluded from the realm of poetry is one of the most notable features of his originality. It marked his work from the beginning, as in the early ballad of 'The Widow', where the sudden damping of the wooer's amatory ardour in consequence of his jealousy of the child is rendered with extraordinary refinement. The difficulty of course is to know when to stop. There is always a danger that a poet, in his search after the infinitely ingenious, may lapse into *amphigory*, into sheer absurdity and triviality, which Cowper, in spite of his elegant lightness, does not always escape. Wordsworth, more serious in his intent, fell headlong in parts of 'Peter Bell', and in such ballads as 'Betty Foy'. Mr. Hardy, whatever the poverty of his incident, commonly redeems it by the oddity of his observation; as in 'The Pedigree':

> I bent in the deep of night
> Over a pedigree the chronicler gave
> As mine; and as I bent there, half-unrobed,
> The uncurtained panes of my window-square
> Let in the watery light
> Of the moon in its old age:
> And green-rheumed clouds were hurrying past
> Where mute and cold it globed
> Like a dying dolphin's eye seen through a lapping wave.

Mr. Hardy's love of strange experiences, and of adventures founded on a balance of conscience and instinct, is constantly exemplified in those ballads and verse-anecdotes which form the section of his poetry most appreciated by the general public. Among these, extraordinarily representative of the poet's habit of mind, is 'My Cicely', a tale of the eighteenth century, where a man impetuously rides from London through Wessex to be present at the funeral of the wrong woman; as he returns, by a coincidence, he meets the right woman, whom he used to love, and is horrified at 'her liquor-fired face, her thick accents'. He determines that by an effort of will the dead woman (whom he never saw) shall remain, what she seemed during his wild ride, '*my* Cicely', and the living woman be expunged from memory. A similar deliberate electing that the dream shall hold the place of the fact is the motive of *The Well-Beloved*. The ghastly humour of 'The Curate's Kindness' is a sort of reverse action of the same mental subtlety. Misunderstanding takes a very prominent place in Mr. Hardy's irony of circumstance; as, almost too painfully, in 'The Rash Bride', a hideous tale of suicide following on the duplicity of a tender and innocent widow.

The grandmother of Mr. Hardy was born in 1772, and survived until 1857. From her lips he heard many an obscure old legend of the life of Wessex in the eighteenth century. Was it she who told him the terrible Exmoor story of 'The Sacrilege'; the early tale of 'The Two Men', which might be the skeleton-scenario for a whole elaborate

novel; or that incomparable comedy in verse, 'The Fire at Tranter
Sweatley's', with its splendid human touch at the very end? We suspect
that it was; and perhaps at the same source he acquired his dangerous
insight into the female heart, whether exquisitely feeble as in 'The
Home-coming', with its delicate and ironic surprise, or treacherous,
as in the desolating ballad of 'Rose-Ann'. No one, in prose or verse,
has expatiated more poignantly than Mr. Hardy on what our forefathers used to call 'cases of conscience'. He seems to have shared the
experiences of souls to whom life was 'a wood before your doors,
and a labyrinth within the wood, and locks and bars to every door
within that labyrinth', as Jeremy Taylor describes that of the anxious
penitents who came to him to confession. The probably very early
story of 'The Casterbridge Captains' is a delicate study in compunction, and a still more important example is 'The Alarm', where the
balance of conscience and instinct gives to what in coarser hands might
seem the most trivial of actions a momentous character of tragedy.

This is one of Mr. Hardy's studies in military history, where he is
almost always singularly happy. His portraits of the non-commissioned
officer of the old service are as excellent in verse as they are in the prose
of *The Trumpet-Major* or *The Melancholy Hussar*. The reader of the
novels will not have to be reminded that 'Valenciennes' and the other
ballads have their prose-parallel in Simon Burden's reminiscences of
Minden. Mr. Hardy, with a great curiosity about the science of war
and a close acquaintance with the mind of the common soldier, has
pondered on the philosophy of fighting. 'The Man he killed', written
in 1902, expresses the wonder of the rifleman who is called upon to
shoot his brother-in-arms, although

> Had he and I but met,
> By some old ancient inn,
> We should have set us down to wet
> Right many a nipperkin.

In this connection the 'Poems of War and Patriotism', which form an
important part of the volume of 1918, should be carefully examined
by those who meditate on the tremendous problems of the moment.

A poet so profoundly absorbed in the study of life could not fail to
speculate on the probabilities of immortality. Here Mr. Hardy presents
to us his habitual serenity in negation. He sees the beautiful human
body 'lined by tool of time', and he asks what becomes of it when its
dissolution is complete. He sees no evidence of a conscious state after

death, of what would have to be, in the case of aged or exhausted persons, a revival of spiritual force, and on the whole he is disinclined to cling to the faith in a future life. He holds that the immortality of a dead man resides in the memory of the living, his 'finer part shining within ever-faithful hearts of those bereft'. He pursues this theme in a large number of his most serious and affecting lyrics, most gravely perhaps in 'The To-be-Forgotten' and in 'The Superseded'. This sense of the forlorn condition of the dead, surviving only in the dwindling memory of the living, inspires what has some claims to be considered the loveliest of all Mr. Hardy's poems, 'Friends Beyond', which in its tenderness, its humour, and its pathos contains in a few pages every characteristic of his genius.

His speculation perceives the dead as a crowd of slowly vanishing phantoms, clustering in their ineffectual longing round the footsteps of those through whom alone they continue to exist. This conception has inspired Mr. Hardy with several wonderful visions, among which the spectacle of 'The Souls of the Slain' in the Boer War, alighting, like vast flights of moths, over Portland Bill at night, is the most remarkable. It has the sublimity and much of the character of some apocalyptic design by Blake. The volume of 1902 contains a whole group of phantasmal pieces of this kind, where there is frequent mention of spectres, who address the poet in the accents of Nature, as in the unrhymed ode called 'The Mother Mourns'. The obsession of old age, with its physical decay ('I look into my glass'), the inevitable division which leads to that isolation which the poet regards as the greatest of adversities ('The Impercipient'), the tragedies of moral indecision, the contrast between the tangible earth and the bodyless ghosts, and endless repetition of the cry, 'Why find we us here?' and of the question 'Has some Vast Imbecility framed us in jest, and left us now to hazardry', all start from the overwhelming love of physical life and acquaintance with its possibilities, which Mr. Hardy possesses to an inordinate degree.

It would be ridiculous at the close of an article to attempt any discussion of the huge dramatic panorama which many believe to be Mr. Hardy's most weighty contribution to English literature. The spacious theatre of *The Dynasts*, with its comprehensive and yet concise realizations of vast passages of human history, is a work which calls for a commentary as lengthy as itself, and yet needs no commentary at all. No work of the imagination is more its own interpreter than this sublime historic peep-show, this rolling vision of the Napoleonic chronicle drawn on the broadest lines, and yet in detail made up of intensely concentrated and vivid glimpses of reality. But the subject of our present study, the lyrical poetry of Mr. Hardy, is not largely illustrated in *The Dynasts*, except by the choral interludes of the phantom intelligences, which have great lyrical value, and by three or four admirable songs.

When we resume the effect which the poetry of Mr. Hardy makes upon the careful reader, we note, as we have indicated already, a sense of unity of direction throughout. Mr. Hardy has expressed himself in a thousand ways, but has never altered his vision. From 1867 to 1917, through half a century of imaginative creation, he has not modified the large outlines of his art in the smallest degree. To early readers of his poems, before the full meaning of them became evident, his voice sounded inharmonious, because it did not fit in with the exquisite melodies of the later Victorian age. But Mr. Hardy, with characteristic pertinacity, did not attempt to alter his utterance in the least, and now we can all perceive, if we take the trouble to do so, that what seemed harsh in his poetry was his peculiar and personal mode of interpreting his thoughts to the world. As in his novels so in his poems, he has chosen to remain local, to be the interpreter for present and future times of one rich and neglected province of the British realm. From his standpoint there he contemplates the vast aspect of life, but it seems huge and misty to him, and he broods over the tiny incidents of Wessex idiosyncrasy. His irony is audacious and even sardonic, and few poets have been less solicitous to please their weaker brethren. But no poet of modern times has been more careful to avoid the abstract and to touch upon the real.

Select Bibliography

BLUNDEN, EDMUND, *Thomas Hardy* (Macmillan, 1942): gives very full information about reviews and reception generally.

HARDY, FLORENCE EMILY, *The Life of Thomas Hardy 1840–1928* (Macmillan, 1962): this one-volume edition combines *The Early Life of Thomas Hardy, 1840–1891* (1928) and *The Later Years of Thomas Hardy, 1892–1928* (1930).

OREL, HAROLD (editor), *Thomas Hardy's Personal Writings* (1967): contains much scattered information about Hardy's reaction to criticisms.

PURDY, RICHARD LITTLE, *Thomas Hardy, A Bibliographical Study* (Oxford University Press, 1954).

RUTLAND, WILLIAM R., *Thomas Hardy, A Study of his Writings and their Background* (Blackwell, 1938): gives full accounts of most of the chief reviews of each work, with brief extracts.

WEBER, CARL J. *Hardy of Wessex—His Life and Literary Career* (Oxford University Press, 1940). *Hardy in America—A Study of Thomas Hardy and his American Readers* (1946): gives references for many reviews which appeared in the U.S.A.

Index